Essentials of
Organizational Behavior

To T.K.

For keeping it real.

SAGE was founded in 1965 by Sara Miller McCune to support the dissemination of usable knowledge by publishing innovative and high-quality research and teaching content. Today, we publish more than 850 journals, including those of more than 300 learned societies, more than 800 new books per year, and a growing range of library products including archives, data, case studies, reports, and video. SAGE remains majority-owned by our founder, and after Sara's lifetime will become owned by a charitable trust that secures our continued independence.

Los Angeles | London | New Delhi | Singapore | Washington DC

Essentials of Organizational Behavior

An Evidence-Based Approach

Terri A. Scandura

University of Miami

Los Angeles | London | New Delhi
Singapore | Washington DC

Los Angeles | London | New Delhi
Singapore | Washington DC

FOR INFORMATION:

SAGE Publications, Inc.
2455 Teller Road
Thousand Oaks, California 91320
E-mail: order@sagepub.com

SAGE Publications Ltd.
1 Oliver's Yard
55 City Road
London EC1Y 1SP
United Kingdom

SAGE Publications India Pvt. Ltd.
B 1/I 1 Mohan Cooperative Industrial Area
Mathura Road, New Delhi 110 044
India

SAGE Publications Asia-Pacific Pte. Ltd.
3 Church Street
#10-04 Samsung Hub
Singapore 049483

Copyright © 2016 by SAGE Publications, Inc.

Printed in the United States of America

ISBN 978-1-4833-4565-9

Acquisitions Editor: Maggie Stanley
Associate Editor: Abbie Rickard
Editorial Assistant: Nicole Mangona
eLearning Editor: Katie Bierach
Production Editor: Laura Barrett
Copy Editor: Megan Markanich
Typesetter: C&M Digitals (P) Ltd.
Proofreader: Theresa Kay
Indexer: Molly Hall
Cover Designer: Gail Buschman
Marketing Manager: Liz Thornton

This book is printed on acid-free paper.

SUSTAINABLE FORESTRY INITIATIVE
Certified Chain of Custody
Promoting Sustainable Forestry
www.sfiprogram.org
SFI-01268
SFI label applies to text stock

15 16 17 18 19 10 9 8 7 6 5 4 3 2 1

BRIEF CONTENTS

CONTENTS

CHAPTER 10 • Managing Conflict and Negotiation   254

CHAPTER 11 • Organizational Communication   284

PREFACE

After decades of using Organizational Behavior (OB) textbooks, I realized they were not communicating the right message for today's students. They memorized theories and dutifully wrote them down on exams, but I felt they were missing out on how to apply these theories to become a better leader. Students want take-away skills they can put into practice immediately. A new approach to teaching OB is needed and this textbook shows students how to be effective leaders and managers in organizations. With a focus on leadership and management development, students will go beyond memorizing theories and will apply the most relevant concepts to effectively motivate followers, lead their teams, and champion organizational change.

I have researched leadership for over 25 years. During five of those years, I was an acting dean at a major research university undergoing change. With this position, I put OB concepts into practice every day in my administrative position—I hired people, motivated them, set goals, and did annual performance appraisals. I helped employees, students, and faculty cope with organizational change. Based upon my research and the practical experience as an administrator with several direct reports, I began to look at my courses differently. I wanted to translate our rich evidence base into skills that managers can use every day. I also wanted to show how managers can become effective leaders through applications of course concepts. My process to achieve this was to start incorporating more skill-based assessments, role-plays, and team activities into each class meeting. Feedback from students was extremely positive and many cited these exercises as high points in their learning experience in my course evaluations. I decided to write a textbook that reviewed OB theory and distilled the most relevant concepts for the development of effective leaders in organizations. Keeping a sharp focus on what the evidence base in OB supports, I searched for and developed exercises and activities that reinforce the key takeaways from each area I taught.

This "essentials" book is not a condensed version of a larger OB textbook. It was written with an eye toward the fundamentals every managerial leader needs to know and how to apply them. I used an evidence-based approach, making prescriptions based on research. Theories are reviewed critically and students are encouraged to think critically about what they read. End-of-chapter assessments and activities make the linkage from theory to practice for students. For example, Chapter 8 includes an activity in which students role-play giving a performance appraisal. Based on my practical experience, performance appraisal is one of the most challenging scenarios a new manager faces. The activity is realistic and encourages students to practice the skill set of how to provide feedback in an effective way. This textbook fills another need by adopting an integrative OB textbook approach with a framework of leadership and management development throughout. References are made to other chapters in multiple places so students can see the connections across topics in OB. For example, Chapter 7 discusses core concepts in motivation and refers to the chapter immediately following, which focuses on the role of rewards in motivating followers. As a set, these two chapters compose a learning module entitled "leaders as motivators." Chapter 1 contains a figure that is a "map" of the field of OB that allows instructor to create integrated learning modules that can be used in courses of varying lengths (for example, six-week courses and 15-week courses).

The cases at the end of each chapter cover a wide range of organizational situations including small business, hospitals, large corporations, and many other types of organizations. My colleagues and I have tested the cases and exercises with students and they resonate with both MBAs and undergraduates. Regardless of the career paths students choose, they will find these assessments and activities valuable as they develop leadership and management skills.

TARGET AUDIENCES

I have written this book to be appropriate for MBA and Executive MBA core courses in OB as well as for upper-level undergraduate courses. Case studies and exercises will prepare students at all levels for today's workplace. The content and activities have been carefully written so students can respond to discussion questions and assessments. For undergraduates, the role-plays and team activities at the end of the chapters are particularly valuable. This experiential approach to learning supports the application of OB fundamentals and the activities are interesting and fun. Textbook reviews have also indicated that this textbook will work very well in Industrial/Organizational Psychology courses as well as courses in Higher Education Leadership. In writing the textbook, I kept in mind that some OB courses are being offered in hybrid or online formats. The features of this textbook support these formats (for example, all boxed inserts and case studies have discussion questions that can be answered by students and submitted as assignments).

APPROACH

I always wanted a concise OB textbook that did certain things for my students. This textbook was written with three guiding principles:

1. An *evidence-based management approach* to the field of OB so practice recommendations are grounded in research.
2. Emphasis on *critical thinking* in Chapter 1 and throughout the textbook so students can evaluate the strengths and weaknesses of research before they move to practice applications.
3. A focus on *leadership development* for managers so rather than just memorizing theories, students apply them to cases and a variety of activities organized in toolkits at the end of each chapter.

Evidence-Based Management

Hundreds of references to classic and current OB research are used in this textbook to build a new way of looking at the research as the foundation for leadership development. The Evidence-Based Management approach is described in detail in Chapter 1. The coverage of research is comprehensive with a focus on the most important topics managers need to become effective leaders. These are the topics I have selected to teach for over 25 years to undergraduate, MBA, and Executive MBA students. This textbook offers a research-based approach that translates theory to practice, focusing on the contemporary approaches rather than the historical/classical approaches. Most students are less interested in historical development of theory and more interested in theories they can apply to be more effective leaders. There is far less emphasis on theories that don't have solid research support than other textbooks that I have used and read. In fairness, certain topics are noted for their contribution to broad-based understanding of OB, followed by a critical assessment of the research support.

Critical Thinking

Over the years, I have heard colleagues lament, "our students don't think critically." One day while teaching, it occurred to me that I had never actually included a lecture on critical thinking—what it is and why it is important. It wasn't in my OB textbook. I researched critical thinking and started to lecture on it in my class lectures. I began to see a difference in how my students approached the material in my courses. The quality of classroom discussion improved and students began to really discuss strengths and weaknesses of theory and develop relevant examples as applications. Their answers on essay questions went beyond memorization to demonstration of understanding concepts, plus providing examples to show they could apply them as managers.

It just makes sense that we teach our students about critical thinking, and this is a major theme of this textbook. Critical thinking is defined and discussed in detail in Chapter 1 so students will understand what it is and why it is important for a managerial leader to think critically.

Leadership Development

I have an extensive background studying the importance of leadership within organizations, in addition to holding positions of leadership at several points in my career. For this reason, leadership is a major theme that flows throughout the textbook. Leadership core concepts are covered early in the textbook in Chapter 2; while I believe this is foundational to a leadership and management development approach to OB, this chapter might be assigned later as many OB instructors do (this book is written to have such flexibility). In addition to a full chapter on leadership, each chapter includes a section discussing "leadership implications" in the context of the topic being discussed, as well as end-of-chapter activities and self-assessments designed to enhance students' understanding of leadership and their own leadership styles and tendencies.

Trends in Organizational Behavior

Along with the three guiding principles of evidence-based management, critical thinking, and leadership development, this textbook also touches upon emerging topics in OB. Throughout the chapters there is an emphasis on globalization and cross-cultural OB. For example, cross-cultural differences in stress are compared in Chapter 13.

A number of the chapters include discussions on ethics as well. An example of this theme is found in Chapter 11: Organizational Communication, where the Enron case is discussed as a grapevine effect that led to uncovering major ethical violations. Finally, in a number of places, positive psychology is integrated into the presentation of OB topics. For example, mindfulness is discussed as a coaching strategy for understanding diverse employees in Chapter 3.

FEATURES

Learning Objectives

The learning objectives included at the beginning of each chapter highlight the key topics covered in the chapter, and note the skills students will develop after reading. These learning objectives are directly tied to main headers within the chapter and can be used to measure and assess students' understanding of chapter material.

Chapter-Opening Vignette

Each chapter begins with a research-based challenge facing managers based upon empirical data, often from national polls or consulting firms. For example, Chapter 8 discusses "the meaning of money." These highlights are intended to get the students' attention so they immediately see the relevance of the material in the chapter that follows.

Best Practices and Research in Action Boxes

Within each chapter, there are two types of boxed inserts to enhance the application of the material to the student's development as a leader—"Best Practices" and "Research in Action." Best Practices highlight current applications of OB research in real organizations or consulting examples. One of my favorites is a best practices box that teaches students step-by-step how to use perceptual tools to remember people's names. Research in Action vignettes demonstrate how OB research translates to leadership practice. An example is a short discussion of current research on the rise of workplace incivility that asks the question of whether we need to "send in Miss Manners." Included in each of these boxed features, there are discussion questions to stimulate the student's thinking on the application and can be used for in-class discussion. These discussion questions may be assigned prior to class to encourage students to read and apply the highlighted practice and research in these inserts. These boxed inserts can be integrated into class discussions to show how practice and research use OB theories.

Critical Thinking Questions

To support critical thinking throughout the course, critical thinking questions are integrated within the textbook. These questions encourage students to pause, think about, and then apply the material just covered to an organizational challenge for leaders. For instructors teaching online courses, these questions can be assigned to check the student comprehension of assigned textbook readings.

Key Terms

Key terms featured in each chapter have been set in bold throughout the text. Students will be able to quickly search for and locate these key terms.

The Toolkit

Each chapter contains a "Toolkit" in which the student will apply the concepts covered within that chapter. Each chapter's Toolkit contains the following features:

- **Key terms** highlighted within the chapter.
- A short **case study** illustrating one or more concepts from the chapter. These cases are followed by discussion questions that can be assigned prior to in-class case discussion.
- At least one **self-assessment**, including personality tests or leadership assessments. Students learn something about themselves and others, making the concepts relevant to their personal lives and development as a leader.
- The **toolkit activities** are team exercises, or role-plays, in which the students interact with other students to apply the material. I have used these exercises in my classes and I am pleased to provide them all in one package so you don't have to search for them, and copy them for class.
- Years ago, one of my MBA students asked me if I could compile a list of 10 books that every manager should read. I have included **Suggestions for Further Reading** to encourage further reading on classic and current books on OB topics. These books are referenced in the chapters and students may want to read them to learn more.

SAGE EDGE

Visit **edge.sagepub.com/scandura**

The edge every student needs

SAGE edge for instructors supports teaching by making it easy to integrate quality content and create a rich learning environment for students.

- **Test banks** provide a diverse range of pre-written options as well as the opportunity to edit any question and/or insert personalized questions to effectively assess students' progress and understanding
- **Sample course syllabi** for semester and quarter courses provide suggested models for structuring one's course
- Editable, chapter-specific **PowerPoint® slides** offer complete flexibility for creating a multimedia presentation for the course
- **Lecture outlines** summarize key concepts by chapter to ease preparation for lectures and class discussions
- Sample **answers to in-text questions** ease preparation for lectures and class discussions

- Suggested **course projects** are designed to promote students' in-depth engagement with course material.
- Lively and stimulating ideas for **class activities** that can be used in class to reinforce active learning. The activities apply to individual or group projects.
- **Teaching notes for cases** are designed for instructors to expand questions to students, or initiate class discussion.
- EXCLUSIVE! Access to full-text **SAGE journal articles** that have been carefully selected to support and expand on the concepts presented in each chapter to encourage students to think critically
- **Multimedia content** appeals to students with different learning styles
- **A course cartridge** provides easy LMS integration

SAGE edge for students provides a personalized approach to help students accomplish their coursework goals in an easy-to-use learning environment.

- Mobile-friendly **eFlashcards** strengthen understanding of key terms and concepts
- Mobile-friendly practice **quizzes** allow for independent assessment by students of their mastery of course material
- A customized online **action plan** allows students to track their progress and enhance their learning experience
- **Chapter summaries** with **learning objectives** reinforce the most important material`
- EXCLUSIVE! Access to full-text **SAGE journal articles** that have been carefully selected to support and expand on the concepts presented in each chapter
- **Multimedia content** appeals to students with different learning styles

ACKNOWLEDGMENTS

My love of teaching began as a Ph.D. student with the first course I taught. I am excited to bring my perspective on the field of OB as an integrated and evidence-based foundation for the development of leaders to more students. This has truly been a labor of love. I have reflected on the field of OB and realized that we have so very much to offer our students because of the research we have done. I am in awe of my OB colleagues around the world for their theoretical insights and their rigorous research. It is with gratitude and humility that I am offering this book to instructors and their students.

I would like to thank my students Monica Sharif and Ronnie Grant for their assistance with various parts of this project. I am indebted to Stephanie Maynard-Patrick for writing case studies and working with me on the ancillary materials. I cannot express my gratitude enough for all of the authors and publishers that graciously allowed me to reprint their material in this book. I thank my principal mentors George Graen and Belle Rose Ragins for their support and insights throughout my career. I offer thanks to all of my colleagues in OB (too numerous to mention) who provide me with feedback and support on everything I do. My OB colleagues at the University of Miami read drafts of the tables of contents and chapters and offered suggestions for the toolkits (and allowed me to test them in their courses): Cecily Cooper, Marie Dasborough, Linda Neider, Chet Schriesheim, and Gergana Todorova. My family and friends suffered through my periods of me being a hermit and patiently listened to me talk about this book. I thank my family Laura Scandura Rea, Sandi Kennedy, Deanne Julifs, and Tommy Scandura for always believing in me—and not just with respect to this textbook. I would also like to thank Cindy Riesman for her practical down-to-earth advice and for making me laugh at just the right times. Last, but in no way least, I thank the team at SAGE. Nicole Mangona kept track of permissions and numerous other details. I greatly appreciate all of the retweets from Lori Hart. I am also grateful to Maggie Stanley and Abbie Rickard for their support throughout the project. They encouraged me to "hear" reviewer feedback but always respected my vison for the book. Special thanks to Cynthia Nalevanko at SAGE for encouraging me to write a textbook and getting me in touch with the right people to discuss this project. Thanks also to Katie Bierach, Liz Thornton, Amy Lammers, Erica DeLuca, Gail Buschman, and Laura Barrett at SAGE for their excellent work on this project. Without all of these people in their various ways of supporting me, this book would not have been possible.

I am grateful to the reviewers of this textbook who applied their own critical perspectives to the chapters. They made this textbook better in every way and I learned from their insightful comments and suggestions for additional research evidence to include. Thanks to the following reviewers for their participation in all stages of this book's development:

Carrie S. Hurst,
Tennessee State University

Lisa V. Williams, Niagara University

Jody A. Worley, University of Oklahoma

Nancy Sutton Bell, University of Montevallo

Barbara A. Wech, University of Alabama at Birmingham

Chulguen (Charlie) Yang, Southern Connecticut State University

Carol Saunders, University of Central Florida

Mary Lynn Engel, Saint Joseph's College

Eric Chen, University of Saint Joseph

Bruce Gilstrap, University of Southern Mississippi

Chan Hellman, University of Oklahoma

Marie Hansen, Husson University

Michael Buckley, University of Oklahoma

DeNisha McCollum, John Brown University

Hannah Rothstein, Baruch College

Mary Ann Gall, Franklin Pierce University

Roberta Michel, Oakland University

Minerva Cruz, Kentucky State University

Jim Byran, Fresno Pacific University

Ivan Muslin, Marshall University

Katherine Sliter, Indiana University—Purdue University

Carrie Bulger, Quinnipiac University

Cecily Cooper, University of Miami

Kim Lukaszewski, New Paltz SUNY

Jay Jacobson, Marquette University

James W. Bishop, New Mexico State University

David McCalman, University of Central Arkansas

Adam Payne, Bentley University–Northeastern University

Robert Toronto, University of Michigan–Dearborn

Nicholas Capozzoli, Indiana University Kokomo

Joel Baldomir, Marist College

Daniel E. Hallock, University of North Alabama

John Rowe, Florida Gateway College

C. Douglas Johnson, Georgia Gwinnett College

Leon Fraser, Rutgers University

Charles Kramer, University of La Verne

Roger Dean, Washington & Lee University

Barbara Stuart, University of Denver

Heather Wherry, Bellevue University

Kimberly Hunley, Northern Arizona University

Roselynn S. Dow, Empire State College

Nell Hartley, Robert Morris University

Mim Plavin-Masterman, Worcester State University

Charlena Patterson, Catholic University of America

Eric Chen, University of Saint Joseph

Becky J. Timmons, University of Arkansas–Fort Smith

Douglas Threet, Foothill College

Herb Wong, John F. Kennedy University

Carol Harvey, Suffolk University

Lissa Whyte-Morazan, Brookline College

Geni D. Cowan, California State University, Sacramento

Robert Whitcomb, Western Nevada College

Issam Ghazzawi, University of La Verne

Mehmet Sincar, University of Gaziantep

Jeff Paul, University of Tulsa

Terri A. Scandura is currently a Professor of Management in the School of Business Administration at the University of Miami. From 2007 to 2012, she served as Dean of the Graduate School of the University. Her fields of interest include leadership, mentorship, and applied research methods. She has been a visiting scholar in Japan, Australia, Hong Kong, China, and the United Arab Emirates.

Dr. Scandura has authored or co-authored over two hundred presentations, articles, and book chapters. Her research has been published in the *Academy of Management Journal*, the *Journal of Applied Psychology*, the *Journal of International Business Studies*, the *Journal of Vocational Behavior*, the *Journal of Organizational Behavior*, *Educational and Psychological Measurement*, *Industrial Relations*, *Research in Organizational Behavior*, and *Research in Personnel and Human Resource Management* and others.

She has presented Executive Education programs on Leadership, Mentoring, Leading Change, and High Performance Teams to numerous organizations such as VISA International, Royal Caribbean Cruise Lines, the Young Presidents Organization, Hewlett-Packard, and Baptist Health Systems.

Dr. Scandura is a Fellow of the Society for Industrial & Organizational Psychology (Division 14 of the American Psychological Association), and the Southern Management Association. She is a member of the Society of Organizational Behavior (SOB) and the Academy of Management. She is a past-associate editor for *Group & Organization Management*, the *Journal of International Business* Studies, *Journal of Management*, and *Organizational Research Methods*. She currently serves on Editorial Boards for major journals including the *Academy of Management Journal*.

SECTION I

ORGANIZATIONAL BEHAVIOR AND LEADERSHIP

Chapter 1 • What Is Organizational Behavior?

Chapter 2 • Leadership: Core Concepts

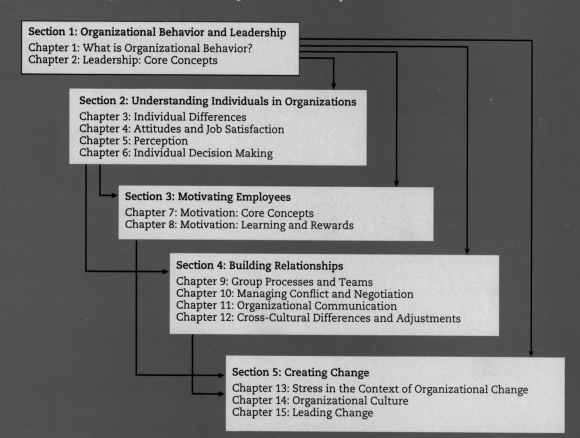

Section 1: Organizational Behavior and Leadership

Chapter 1: What is Organizational Behavior?
Chapter 2: Leadership: Core Concepts

Section 2: Understanding Individuals in Organizations

Chapter 3: Individual Differences
Chapter 4: Attitudes and Job Satisfaction
Chapter 5: Perception
Chapter 6: Individual Decision Making

Section 3: Motivating Employees

Chapter 7: Motivation: Core Concepts
Chapter 8: Motivation: Learning and Rewards

Section 4: Building Relationships

Chapter 9: Group Processes and Teams
Chapter 10: Managing Conflict and Negotiation
Chapter 11: Organizational Communication
Chapter 12: Cross-Cultural Differences and Adjustments

Section 5: Creating Change

Chapter 13: Stress in the Context of Organizational Change
Chapter 14: Organizational Culture
Chapter 15: Leading Change

1

WHAT IS ORGANIZATIONAL BEHAVIOR?

A CRISIS OF LEADERSHIP?

Recent polls conducted by the Gallup organization show that about 70% of people who hold full-time jobs in the United States either hate their jobs or have "mentally checked out."[1] This is a large impact considering that an estimated 100 million people work full-time in the United States. Workers who hate their jobs cost their organizations millions of dollars in low productivity. Even worse, many of the Gallup survey respondents reported actively engaging in destructive behavior by spreading their dissatisfaction throughout their organizations. One of the most important things the Gallup study found is that the source of dissatisfaction is not pay or the number of hours worked, however.

Most employees in Gallup's study reported that the reason for their disengagement from work was their boss. And this is not new. This study was a follow-up of an earlier study conducted from 2008 to 2010, which showed similar discontent with work and leaders. Why? Isn't there something that can be done to improve the well-being, motivation, and productivity of people at work? Is anyone working on addressing the concerns of the workforce? The answer is yes. There is a field of study called **organizational behavior** (or sometimes called OB for short) that studies the challenges leaders face in the workforce. Unfortunately, much of the knowledge that could help leaders improve the experience of work is tucked away in scientific journals that few managers have the time to read.

The goal of this book is to help you become an effective leader—not the kind of leader described in the Gallup poll that produces discontented workers. You can choose to be a leader who understands the fundamentals of OB—how to motivate followers, resolve conflicts, lead teams, and even help them manage stress during change. For example, effective communication is essential for leadership, and this is covered in Chapter 11. After reading this textbook, your approach to leading others will be grounded in the most important and current research conducted on organizations.

Learning Objectives

After studying this chapter, you should be able to do the following:

1.1. Define the concept of organizational behavior (OB).

1.2. List and give examples of the four sources of information used in evidence-based management (EBM).

1.3. Define critical thinking, and explain the critical thinking skills leaders need.

1.4. Describe the scientific method used in OB research.

1.5. Discuss four types of outcome variables studied in OB.

1.6. Compare the levels of analysis in OB research.

1.7. Develop plans for using OB research to improve employee job performance.

Get the edge on your studies at edge.sagepub.com/scandura
- Take the chapter quiz
- Review key terms with eFlashcards
- Explore multimedia resources, SAGE readings, and more!

$SAGE edge™

WHAT IS ORGANIZATIONAL BEHAVIOR?

Learning Objective 1.1: Define the concept of organizational behavior (OB).

OB is defined as the study of individuals and their behaviors at work. It is an interdisciplinary and multilevel research area that draws from applied psychology, cultural anthropology, communication, and sociology. This textbook draws upon all of these areas with a focus on applied social psychology. Social psychologists study the behavior of individuals in groups, so it makes sense that the study of how leaders influence people and their OB is grounded in this field of psychology.

OB is a relatively young field in comparison to areas in the field of medicine—and even psychology from which it draws. There were management practices in place since the early 1900s with Frederick Taylor's approach to "scientific management," which was the study of how work could be designed to make production work (particularly assembly lines) more efficient.[2] Most scholars agree, however, that OB (in contrast to management) started with the Hawthorne studies (conducted between 1927 and 1932), which led to a focus on the role of human behavior in organizations. The Hawthorne studies were two studies conducted by Australian-born psychologist Elton Mayo at the Western Electric Company near Chicago.[3]

Mayo spent most of his career at Harvard University and was interested in how to increase productivity in assembly lines. The first study was designed to examine the effects of lighting in the plants on worker productivity. However, the research team had a surprise. Productivity *increased* rather than decreased even though the lights were being dimmed. Perplexed by this finding, the research team interviewed the workers and learned that the workers appreciated the attention of the research team and felt that they were receiving special treatment. And then productivity *declined* after the researchers left the plant. This has been called the Hawthorne effect and refers to positive responses in attitudes and performance when researchers pay attention to a particular group of workers.

The second Hawthorne study was designed to investigate a new incentive system. However, instead of the incentive system increasing workers' production, the social pressure from peers took over and had more impact on worker productivity. Workers formed into small groups and set informal standards for production, requiring coworkers to reduce their production so pay was more equal among the group members.

The Hawthorne researchers concluded that the human element in organizations was more important than previously thought, and they learned that workers want attention. This is still relevant today. For example, recent work demonstrates that when employers provide gifts to employees (termed *empathy wages*), it elicits feelings of gratitude from them.[4] The "human relations" movement followed the Hawthorne studies, and OB emerged as a distinct field of study in the 1950s. Today, OB researchers have PhDs from psychology departments (in the area of industrial and organizational psychology) and business schools. They teach from the research base on OB and conduct research that addresses important challenges facing organizational leaders today.

Applied Social Psychology

Applied social psychology is the study of how people interact in groups and addresses significant challenges facing leaders today. Trends such as the need to compete in a global marketplace, organizational restructuring, and rapid changes in technology have resulted in the need to lead through change. OB is an applied field of study aimed at problem solving for organizational leaders. For example, OB researchers study how stress affects employee well-being. Another example is how a leader's vision affects follower motivation and performance toward goals. A third example is how frustrations with one's boss might lead to an employee quitting the organization (this is called turnover). Low productivity and turnover cost organizations millions of dollars. Beyond the impact on costs, employee well-being is a major concern for forward-thinking organizations today. OB researchers develop guidelines that directly address such challenges. Based on research, leaders can make better decisions to make their organization more effective and better places to work. In sum, the goal of OB as a field is to improve the functioning of the organization and how employees experience their work.

From Theory to Practice

OB is an applied science, so first it is necessary to briefly review what science is all about. The goals of science—any science—are as follows:

1. **Description:** What does the process look like?
2. **Prediction:** Will the process occur again? And when?
3. **Explanation:** Why is this happening?
4. **Control:** Can we change whether or not this happens?

For example, the forecasting of toy sales during the holiday season is an important process for the planning of manufacturing runs. Marketers have an understanding of why children want a particular toy (in other words, a theory) and can describe the colors and features of the toy. This theory is also fairly high on explanation since scientists have some understanding of why children want a particular toy. Prediction is important since marketers need to project with some accuracy what the demand will be for their products. However, sales forecasts are not always accurate, resulting in stock shortages (remember Tickle Me Elmo?) or the production of too many toys that must be sold at discounts. In this example, the science is moderate for prediction. For control, one could say that the science is low because there are many reasons why a toy may not sell that are outside of the organization's control (e.g., a better product from a competitor suddenly appearing on the market). This example illustrates why theories are so important to science. The better the initial understanding of why children want a toy, the better the marketing research department should be able to predict the demand for it. Theories are also important to OB as a science since theory is translated into leadership practice and this will be discussed next.

The phrase "there is nothing as practical as a good theory" has been attributed to social psychologist Kurt Lewin. Theories build upon prior research and extend into new areas of importance to leaders. A researcher generates hypotheses about human behavior in organizations and then gathers data to test it. Research eliminates the guesswork about what will work (or not work), and this helps leaders solve the problems they face every day. The ability to translate research to practice has been termed **evidence-based management (EBM)**.

Leader's "Fatal Flaws"

A recent survey of 545 senior managers was conducted to understand the most common areas of weakness of senior managers. The managers were given 360 assessments to determine their skill across 16 different attributes essential to leadership effectiveness. The results highlighted some of the most common weaknesses among poorly rated senior managers (the 96 managers with the lowest performance ratings), as illustrated in the chart below. OB addresses many of the flaws identified in this survey. For example, research on mentoring and coaching addresses the number 1 flaw that leaders don't develop others effectively. In Chapter 10 of this textbook, you will learn how to resolve conflict collaboratively in teams (the second fatal flaw). In the next chapter on leadership (Chapter 2), you will learn about theories of leadership that inspire and motivate others, as well as on how to build effective leader–member relationships. This textbook will review theory and research in OB that addresses these fatal flaws, which are mostly related to interpersonal skills rather than technical ones.

Senior Managers' Fatal Flaws

Percentage of Leaders With This Fatal Flaw

Source: http://www.georgeambler.com/the-leadership-flaws-of-senior-managers.

Discussion Questions:

1. Why do you think "develops others" is the number 1 area of weakness for senior managers? What can be done to address this?

2. Over 30% of the leaders in this study had "practices self-development" as a fatal flaw. What can you do to develop your own leadership skills?

EVIDENCE-BASED MANAGEMENT

Learning Objective 1.2: List and give examples of the four sources of information used in evidence-based management (EBM).

Proving Management Matters

The term *evidence-based* was originally employed in the field of medicine to guide how doctors make decisions regarding patient care. EBM improves a leader's decisions by disciplined application of the most relevant and current scientific evidence. Although many definitions of EBM are available, this is the most frequently quoted and widely used:[5] EBM means making decisions about the management of employees, teams, or organizations through the conscientious, explicit, and judicious use of four sources of information:

1. The best available scientific evidence—for example, research published on OB
2. The best available organizational evidence—for example, interviews or surveys completed by people in an organization
3. The best available experiential evidence—for example, the intuition of the leader and his or her expert opinions
4. Organizational values and stakeholders' concerns—for example, stock price or groups that focus on whether the organization employs environmentally friendly practices

How can a leader use these sources of evidence to make better decisions? The following standards may be applied by leaders using EBM to ask questions and challenge their thinking about their organizations:[6]

1. **Stop treating old ideas as if they were brand new.** This has resulted in a cynical workforce that may view innovations from leaders as short-term fads (e.g., positive changes such as total quality management, teams, and engagement). Progress cannot be made by treating old ideas as new ones; cynicism could be reduced by presenting ideas that have been able to "stand the test of time" as best practices rather than new ideas.
2. **Be suspicious of "breakthrough" studies and ideas.** Question whether some new ideas in management are really breakthroughs, and be wary of claims about new management principles that may be either overstated or understated.[7]
3. **Develop and celebrate collective brilliance.**[8] In theory, a diverse collection of independent decision makers (although not expert) makes better predictions on the average compared to an expert decision maker. In a sense, this is how a Google search operates. Each click on a link serves as a "vote" for the agreement of the search term with the link. While Google guards its algorithm for how they do this specifically, the number of click-throughs determines the order in which you see a website in your search results. Google is thus gathering the collective brilliance of Internet users. See the following box for another method that may be used to develop collective brilliance: the Delphi decision-making method.

Using the Delphi Method to Harness Collective Brilliance

The Delphi method is a systematic decision-making technique that employs a panel of independent experts. It was developed by the RAND Corporation in the 1950s for the U.S. Department of Defense as a decision-making tool. Here's how it works. Experts are given a proposal and complete an assessment of it over several rounds. These experts can be co-located, or they can be dispersed geographically and submit their ideas from anywhere in the world electronically. After each round, a facilitator provides an anonymous summary of the experts' predictions or problem solutions from the previous round as well as the rationale each expert provided. Participants are encouraged to revise their earlier solutions in light of the replies of other members of the group. Over time, the expert panel converges on the best solution or prediction. This technique allows a leader to gather information from a wide range of expert sources to make better decisions, thereby utilizing the wisdom of many (or collective brilliance).

Discussion Questions:

1. How should experts used in a Delphi decision-making process be selected? Would paying experts influence their participation in the process and/or the outcome?
2. To harness collective brilliance using Delphi, how many decision makers do you think should be invited to participate? In other words, is there a minimum number to gain a broad enough perspective? How many is too many?
3. Do you feel that this process is worth the time and effort to improve a decision? Why or why not?

Sources: Dalkey, N., & Helmer, O. (1963). An experimental application of the Delphi method to the use of experts. *Management Science, 9*(3), 458–467; Delbecq, A. L., Van de Ven, A. H., & Gustafson, D. H. (1975). *Group techniques for program planning: A guide to nominal group and Delphi processes.* Glenview, IL: Scott, Foresman; Hsu, C. C., & Sandford, B. A. (2007). The Delphi technique: Making sense of consensus. *Practical Assessment, Research & Evaluation, 12*(10), 1–8.

4. **Emphasize drawbacks as well as virtues.** An interesting example of this is the marketing of an energy drink called Cocaine. Cocaine contains three and a half times the amount of caffeine as Red Bull. It was pulled from U.S. shelves in 2007, after the FDA declared that its producers, Redux Beverages, were marketing their drink as an alternative to street drugs, and this was determined to be illegal. The FDA pointed to the drink's labeling and advertising, which included the statements "Speed in a Can" and "Cocaine—Instant Rush." Despite the controversy, Redux Beverages continued to produce and market the beverage in limited markets and online.[9]

5. **Use success (and failure) stories to illustrate sound practices but not in place of a valid research method.** For example, Circuit City went bankrupt in 2009 but was a "great company" in the now-classic book *Good to Great*. What happened to Circuit City? Alan Wurtzel, the former CEO and the son of the founder, saw the threats coming from Best Buy and Amazon in the early 2000s, and he knew the company was headed for decline. "After I left, my successors became very focused

Data and
Critical
Thinking

on the bottom line—the profit margin," Wurtzel told a group at the University of Richmond. "They were too focused on Wall Street. That was the beginning of the end," said the former CEO as he recalled the rise and fall of the great company.[10] The lesson here is that no matter how great a company is, care must be taken not to simply copy what they do in today's changing business environment. There is no substitute for a careful analysis and diagnosis before embarking on a search for solutions.

6. **Adopt a neutral stance toward ideologies and theories.** An example of this is that most management "gurus" are from North America (e.g., Peter Drucker, Tom Peters, Ken Blanchard). This is not to say that their ideology isn't useful. However, in a global world, EBM demands that we question whether ideology developed in North America applies abroad. EBM would also suggest that we search for theories developed overseas to locate experts from other countries with important ideas.

In making important organizational decisions, the leader may include information gathered from one or all the four sources described previously in the definition of EBM. This can result in a lot of information. So how can a leader sort through it all and determine what is most relevant to the problem at hand? The answer lies in **critical thinking,** a process that has been developed for over 2,500 years, beginning with the ancient Greeks and the Socratic Method, which is the process of learning by questioning everything. Critical thinking skills are applied to sort through all of the information gathered and then prioritize it (and even discard evidence that appears to be invalid or irrelevant to the problem).

WHAT IS CRITICAL THINKING?

Learning Objective 1.3: Define critical thinking, and explain the critical thinking skills leaders need.

Critical thinking can be defined as follows: "Critical thinking calls for persistent effort to examine any belief or supposed form of knowledge in the light of evidence that supports it and the further conclusions to which it tends."[11] Critical thinking involves using justification; recognizing relationships; evaluating the credibility of sources; looking at reasons or evidence; drawing inferences; identifying alternatives, logical deductions, sequences, and order; and defending an idea. Critical thinking requires the decision maker in an organization to apply a complex skill set to solve the problem at hand. A set of guidelines for critical thinking is shown in Table 1.1.[12] Critical thinking is, in short, self-directed, self-disciplined, self-monitored, and self-corrective thinking. It requires rigorous standards of problem solving and a commitment to overcome the inclination to think that we have all of the answers.[13]

When it comes to asking questions, some of the best ideas come from a book by Ian Mitroff called *Smart Thinking for Crazy Times: The Art of Solving the Right Problems.*[14] Mitroff warns us about solving the wrong problems even though leaders solve them with great precision in organizations because they don't ask the right questions. He provides the following list of the basic questions facing all organizations (and ones we should be

Table 1.1   Critical Thinking Skills

Bloom's Taxonomy

No one always acts purely objectively and rationally. We connive for selfish interests. We gossip, boast, exaggerate, and equivocate. It is "only human" to wish to validate our prior knowledge, to vindicate our prior decisions, or to sustain our earlier beliefs. In the process of satisfying our ego, however, we can often deny ourselves intellectual growth and opportunity. We may not always want to apply critical thinking skills, but we should have those skills available to be employed when needed.

Critical thinking includes a complex combination of skills. Among the main characteristics are the following:

Skills	We are thinking critically when we do the following:
Rationality	• Rely on reason rather than emotion • Require evidence, ignore no known evidence, and follow evidence where it leads • Are concerned more with finding the best explanation than being right, analyzing apparent confusion, and asking questions
Self-Awareness	• Weigh the influences of motives and bias • Recognize our own assumptions, prejudices, biases, or point of view
Honesty	• Recognize emotional impulses, selfish motives, nefarious purposes, or other modes of self-deception
Open-Mindedness	• Evaluate all reasonable inferences • Consider a variety of possible viewpoints or perspectives • Remain open to alternative interpretations • Accept a new explanation, model, or paradigm because it explains the evidence better, is simpler, or has fewer inconsistencies or covers more data • Accept new priorities in response to a reevaluation of the evidence or reassessment of our real interests • Do not reject unpopular views out of hand
Discipline	• Are precise, meticulous, comprehensive, and exhaustive • Resist manipulation and irrational appeals • Avoid snap judgments
Judgment	• Recognize the relevance and/or merit of alternative assumptions and perspectives • Recognize the extent and weight of evidence
In sum:	• Critical thinkers are by nature skeptical. They approach texts with the same skepticism and suspicion as they approach spoken remarks. • Critical thinkers are active, not passive. They ask questions and analyze. They consciously apply tactics and strategies to uncover meaning or assure their understanding. • Critical thinkers do not take an egotistical view of the world. They are open to new ideas and perspectives. They are willing to challenge their beliefs and investigate competing evidence.

Critical thinking enables us to recognize a wide range of subjective analyses of otherwise objective data and to evaluate how well each analysis might meet our needs. Facts may be facts, but how we interpret them may vary.

By contrast, passive, noncritical thinkers take a simplistic view of the world. They see things in black and white, as either-or, rather than recognizing a variety of possible understanding. They see questions as yes or no with no subtleties, they fail to see linkages and complexities, and they fail to recognize related elements.

Source: Kurland (2000). Critical thinking skills (retrieved from: www.criticalreading.com).

asking frequently if we expect to gain buy-in from employees for the implementation of their solutions):

- What businesses are we in?
- What businesses should we be in?
- What is our mission?
- What should our mission be?
- Who are our prime customers?
- Who should our customers be?
- How should we react to a major crisis, especially if we are, or are perceived to be, at fault?
- How will the outside world perceive our actions?
- Will others perceive the situation as we do?
- Are our products and services ethical?

Critical Thinking Questions: Why does asking these questions improve employee buy-in for the implementation of plans? Are there other questions you feel are important to ask?

In OB, there is a systematic method to answer questions. As the field was developing, scholars adopted much of their methodological approach from the physical sciences to address problems and opportunities faced by organizational leaders.

THE SCIENTIFIC METHOD

Learning Objective 1.4: Describe the scientific method used in OB research.

How do OB researchers know what they know? As discussed earlier, it begins with a problem to solve. For example, a problem might be a leader's concern that only about 50% of their employees are satisfied with their work. First, the leader reviews the available knowledge on job satisfaction (i.e., the scientific evidence from EBM) and learns that the way that supervisors treat followers may improve job satisfaction.

Based on theory, the leader forms hypotheses, or predictions, regarding what might improve job satisfaction. An example of a hypothesis is "A leader's appreciation of workers' efforts will lead to increased job satisfaction." The next step is to collect observations from the organization. This might be, for example, through interviews with employees or surveys completed by employees. Once data are collected, the hypothesis is tested with statistical techniques.

The basic research process described previously is depicted in Figure 1.1. As noted in the introduction to this chapter, OB is an applied field, and this is underscored by the typical outcome variables that are studied. Researchers focus on outcomes that are of interest to leaders in organizations such as employee job satisfaction and productivity. Next, the types of outcomes typically studied in OB research will be reviewed.

Figure 1.1 The Scientific Method for Organizational Behavior

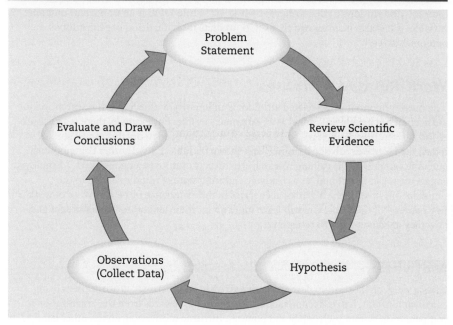

Source: Ashford, S. J., Blatt, R., & Vandewalle, D. (2003). Reflections on the looking glass: A review of research on feedback-seeking behavior in organizations. *Journal of Management, 29*(6), 773–779. p. 775.

OUTCOME VARIABLES IN ORGANIZATIONAL BEHAVIOR

Learning Objective 1.5: Discuss four types of outcome variables studied in OB.

In the preceding example, leader appreciation of workers is the independent variable. Worker engagement is the dependent variable (i.e., it *depends* on the independent variable: leader appreciation). Since OB is an applied science, the outcome variables studied are typically variables that leaders are interested in improving. There are four broad groups of outcome variables studied: performance, work-related attitudes, motivation, and employee withdrawal.

Performance

Productivity (or **job performance**) is one of the most important outcomes in OB. Performance can be actual performance as collected in organizational records (e.g., the number of forms correctly processed in an insurance company) or it may be rated

Hawthorne
Studies on
Employee
Performance

by supervisors and/or peers (e.g., the supervisor rates the follower's work quality on a scale of 1 to 7, with 1 being poor and 7 being outstanding). Organizational citizenship behavior (OCB) is the worker's willingness to go above and beyond what is required in their job descriptions to help others at work.[15,16] While OCB is an important outcome variable, it has also been shown that OCB predicts individual and organizational outcomes as well.[17]

Work-Related Attitudes

The measurement of work-related attitudes is an important aspect of OB research and job satisfaction has long been studied as an outcome variable. For example, there is a measure of job satisfaction dating back to 1935 that is still employed in organizational studies today: the Hoppock Job Satisfaction Blank shown in Table 1.2.[18] Another contemporary outcome variable that is gaining research attention is employee engagement.[19] Employee engagement can be defined "as a relatively enduring state of mind referring to the simultaneous investment of personal energies in the experience or performance of work".[20] In Chapter 4 of this book, you will learn more about these and other work attitudes and how they are studied in OB research.

Motivation

Classic views on motivation describe both extrinsic and intrinsic motivation as being equally important. Extrinsic motivation is based on the rewards from the organization's compensation system such as pay and bonuses. Intrinsic motivation, on the other hand, is related to the value of the work itself.[21] As with attitudes, motivation has been studied as an outcome variable but also as an independent variable that predicts productivity. Prosocial motivation is a new concept of motivation[22] that assesses the degree to which employees behave in a way that benefits society as a whole. You will learn more about motivation and rewards in Chapters 7 and 8 of this book.

Employee Withdrawal

As noted earlier, an employee quitting the organization is costly in terms of the money and time spent to recruit, hire, and train replacements. There is much research in OB on the reasons why employees think about quitting (turnover intentions) and actual turnover.[23] The availability of outside employment opportunities is a factor, but thoughts of quitting may be related to other outcomes such as lower job satisfaction and engagement. And if the economy improves and the job market improves with it, workers may eventually leave for other opportunities. Another costly form of employee withdrawal is absenteeism, since workers may not come to work when they are dissatisfied and there are few alternative jobs available.

Critical Thinking Questions: Is employee productivity the most important outcome variable? If not, what outcome(s) do you think is/are more important?

Table 1.2 A Measure of Job Satisfaction: The Hoppock Job Satisfaction Blank

A. Which one of the following shows **how much of the time** you feel satisfied with your job?

  1. Never.
  2. Seldom.
  3. Occasionally.
  4. About half of the time.
  5. A good deal of the time.
  6. Most of the time.
  7. All the time.

B. Choose **one** of the following statements that best tells how well you like your job.

  1. I hate it.
  2. I dislike it.
  3. I don't like it.
  4. I am indifferent to it.
  5. I like it.
  6. I am enthusiastic about it.
  7. I love it.

C. Which **one** of the following best tells how you feel about changing your job?

  1. I would quit this job at once if I could.
  2. I would take almost any other job in which I could earn as much as I am earning now.
  3. I would like to change both my job and my occupation.
  4. I would like to exchange my present job for another one.
  5. I am not eager to change my job, but I would do so if I could get a better job.
  6. I cannot think of any jobs for which I would exchange.
  7. I would not exchange my job for any other.

D. Which **one** of the following shows how you think you compare with other people?

  1. No one dislikes his job more than I dislike mine.
  2. I dislike my job much more than most people dislike theirs.
  3. I dislike my job more than most people dislike theirs.
  4. I like my job about as well as most people like theirs.
  5. I like my job better than most people like theirs.
  6. I like my job much better than most people like theirs.
  7. No one likes his job better than I like mine.

Sources: **Hoppock (1935); McNichols, Stahl, and Manley (1978).**

Job Crafting

LEVELS OF ANALYSIS IN ORGANIZATIONAL BEHAVIOR

Learning Objective 1.6: Compare the levels of analysis in OB research.

Individual behavior in an organization may be influenced by processes at different levels in the organization.[24] The most basic level is the individual level. For example, an individual's personality and experiences would explain much of their behavior, and differences in these variables among people would help explain why people behave differently. Other differences between people's behavior occur at the dyad (or two-party) level. An example would be a mentor and a protégé. Still, other sources include group and team level influences on individual behavior. An example would be a team that has high-performance norms that encourage a team member to perform at their best. Additional influences on individual behavior may come from the **organizational level.** For example, in organizations with strong cultures, the cultural characteristics can have a profound influence on an individual member's behavior. To illustrate this, one needs to look no further than the U.S. Marine Corps. The Marine Corps has a strong culture that includes pride and this inspires Marines to excel (this is evident in their recruiting ads: "The few, the proud, the Marines") (you will learn more about organizational culture in Chapter 14 of this book). There is also the **industry level** of analysis where comparisons are made across different industries (this is more typical for research in strategic management than OB). However, this level is included here to provide a complete listing of levels of analysis in organizational research. All levels may influence employee performance in organizations and this is discussed in the next section.

HOW ORGANIZATIONAL BEHAVIOR CAN INCREASE EMPLOYEE PERFORMANCE

Learning Objective 1.7: Develop plans for using OB research to improve employee job performance.

The chapters in this book will address all of the levels that may influence individual behavior and show how processes at one level may affect processes at another level. For example, a positive organizational culture may increase the commitment of individuals to their work and, in turn, their performance. Table 1.3 provides examples of hypotheses at the different levels of analysis discussed previously. This table illustrates how OB research at all levels may help leaders improve employee performance.

 Critical Thinking Question: Which level(s) do you think have the most influence on individual behavior in organizations and why?

Table 1.3	Examples of Levels of Analysis in Organizational Behavior Research	
Level	**Example Organizational Behavior Hypothesis**
Individual	The personality characteristic of conscientiousness is positively related to employee performance.
Dyad	High-quality relationships with bosses lead to higher employee performance.
Group and team	Team conflict is negatively related to employee performance.
Organizational	A strong, positive organizational culture is positively related to employee performance.
Industry	Employee performance is higher in the financial services industry compared with government organizations.

TOWARD MORE EFFECTIVE ORGANIZATIONAL LEADERS: PLAN FOR THIS TEXTBOOK

There are numerous challenges facing leaders of organizations today. Most organizations are experiencing rates of change unlike anything we have seen in the past. External pressures have been created from mergers, downsizing, restructuring, and layoffs as organizations strive to remain competitive or even survive. Other external forces are global competition, product obsolescence, new technology, government mandates, and demographic changes in the workforce itself. Internally, leaders must effectively communicate to followers, peers, and bosses. Managing poor performance is one of the most challenging tasks a manager must do. As noted at the beginning of this chapter, addressing the pervasive problem of worker disengagement will be a challenge for leaders in the years ahead. The changes organizations have undergone have resulted in followers who are filled with cynicism and doubt about their leaders. And the ethics scandals in business have fueled the perception that leaders have lost the credibility to lead their organizations in a principled way.

By now, you have realized that OB is a problem-focused discipline aimed at making organizations more effective. Your ability as a leader will be enhanced through knowledge of the theory and applications from OB research. Each chapter will review the essential and most current theory and research and relate it to how you can develop your leadership skills. At the end of each chapter, there are tools for your "toolkit," where you will directly apply the theories through cases, self-assessments, and exercises. At the end of this chapter, the Toolkit Activity is a personal leadership development plan, where you can apply the concepts and research covered in the textbook to your own development as a leader by setting goals and specific behavior strategies to meet them. For example, a student who set a specific goal to improve their coaching of other students that they tutor in accounting would formulate specific coaching behaviors and commit to engaging in them once per week. To gain feedback, the student would have the tutored students rate their coaching behavior by providing a yes or no answer to the following statement after each tutoring session: My tutor provides specific knowledge that has improved my accounting performance. Since leaders are expected to be coaches, this process should help the student improve their coaching skills for the future.

Figure 1.2 shows an overview of the entire book and how the material is tied to the themes of leadership development. This chapter has provided an overview of EBM and critical thinking that should be applied to all of the following chapters. The next

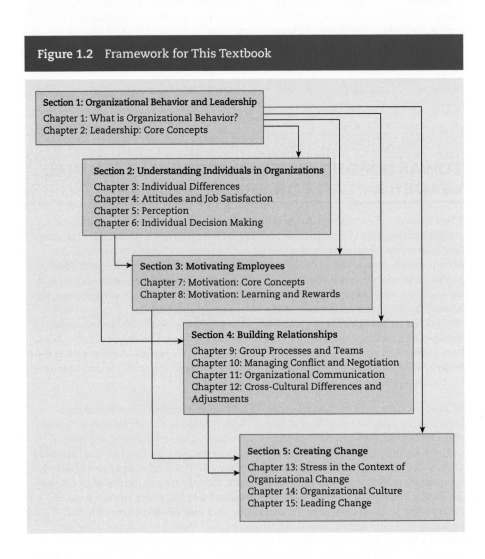

Figure 1.2 Framework for This Textbook

Section 1: Organizational Behavior and Leadership

Chapter 1: What is Organizational Behavior?
Chapter 2: Leadership: Core Concepts

Section 2: Understanding Individuals in Organizations

Chapter 3: Individual Differences
Chapter 4: Attitudes and Job Satisfaction
Chapter 5: Perception
Chapter 6: Individual Decision Making

Section 3: Motivating Employees

Chapter 7: Motivation: Core Concepts
Chapter 8: Motivation: Learning and Rewards

Section 4: Building Relationships

Chapter 9: Group Processes and Teams
Chapter 10: Managing Conflict and Negotiation
Chapter 11: Organizational Communication
Chapter 12: Cross-Cultural Differences and Adjustments

Section 5: Creating Change

Chapter 13: Stress in the Context of Organizational Change
Chapter 14: Organizational Culture
Chapter 15: Leading Change

chapter (Chapter 2) will discuss the fundamental leadership theories that will guide you for the remainder of the book. Next, the importance of understanding individuals in organizations is covered in Chapters 3 through 6 including individual differences, job attitudes, perception, and decision making. The role of leaders as motivators is covered next in Chapters 7 and 8, motivating and rewarding followers. Following this, the role of leaders as relationship builders is covered in Chapters 9 through 12, covering the topics of teams, conflict, organizational communication, and leading across cultures. Finally, the role of leaders as change agents is discussed in Chapters 13, 14, and 15, which cover managing stress during change, organizational culture, and leading change. As you read this book, refer back to this figure as a map of how to organize the vast amount of theory and research on OB that has been generated for decades. It won't seem so overwhelming if you can place the material in the five broad groupings as shown in the figure. This first chapter and the next one will comprise Section I, which is an overview of OB and core concepts in leadership.

LEADERSHIP IMPLICATIONS: THINKING CRITICALLY

The goal of this book and your OB course is for you to become a more effective leader in organizations. Critical thinking has already been applied to the OB literature since this book includes the most relevant and evidence-based theory and research. You are encouraged to apply your own critical thinking based upon your own experiences with behavior in organizations and your study of this book. To aid in this process, you will find Critical Thinking Questions to challenge you to think critically about the material throughout the book. You may choose to read further from the Suggestions for Further Reading or conduct your own research on topics you find particularly interesting. Complete the assessments and exercises in the Toolkit Activity sections to apply the material to your own leadership development. The Case Study encourages you to apply organizational science to a real-world problem. The Self-Assessment will allow you to test your experiential evidence—what you already know about OB. By studying the chapters and completing the activities, this book should serve as a point of departure for your growth as you become an effective organizational leader with a broad understanding of behavior in organizations.

KEY TERMS

absenteeism, 12
applied social psychology, 4
critical thinking, 8
employee engagement, 12
evidence-based management
  (EBM), 4

extrinsic motivation, 12
Hawthorne effect, 3
industry level, 14
intrinsic motivation, 12
job performance, 11
job satisfaction, 12

organizational behavior (OB), 2
organizational level, 14
prosocial motivation, 12
turnover intentions, 12
turnover, 12

SUGGESTIONS FOR FURTHER READING

Gill, J., & Johnson, P. (2010). *Research methods for managers* (4th ed.). Thousand Oaks, CA: Sage.

Mitroff, I. (1998). *Smart thinking for crazy times: The art of solving the right problems*. San Francisco, CA: Berrett-Koehler.

Surowiecki, J. (2004). *The wisdom of crowds*. New York, NY: Random House.

TOOLKIT ACTIVITY 1.1

Personal Leadership Development Plan

As you study the evidence-based research in this textbook, use the following development plan to tie the concepts to specific action plans and measurable outcomes for each chapter.

Name: _____

Date: _____

Leadership Development Plan

Goal	Connection to Course	Behavior Strategies and Frequency (fill in below)	Measurable Outcome
1	1A	1B	✓ 1C.1
		2B	✓ 1C.2
2	2A	2B	✓ 2C.1
		2B	✓ 2C.2

Goal	Connection to Course	Behavior Strategies and Frequency (fill in below)	Measurable Outcome
3	3A	3B	✓ 3C.1
			✓ 3C.2
		3B	

PLAN DETAIL

Complete the following for each of the goals listed previously.

1. **Goals**—This section is where you enter your development objectives. These objectives should be written so they read as goals you desire to achieve—for example, "I want to improve my team communication skills."

   A. **Connection to course material**—This section is where you tie each of your development objectives into the material you learned in this course. This will reinforce course material and help translate it into practice. For example, you would write a few paragraphs relating the exercises or material on communication to why you find your listening skills to need development. Be specific (e.g., cite exercises, articles, material from text or lecture). Fill out this chart: 1A to 3A.

   B. **Behavior strategies and frequency**—This section is the "how" portion. How will you achieve your goals? How often will you perform these tasks? This is the heart of your development plan. You should create specific strategies that will push you toward the completion of your goals—for example, "Practice active listening once a day." Fill out this chart for each goal: 1B to 3B.

GOAL: 1B

Timeframe	Behavior Strategy to Practice	Time Required
All the time	❑	
Weekly	❑	
Biweekly	❑	
Monthly	❑	

GOAL: 2B

Timeframe	Behavior Strategy to Practice	Time Required
All the time	❑	
Weekly	❑	
Biweekly	❑	
Monthly	❑	

GOAL: 3B

Timeframe	Behavior Strategy to Practice	Time Required
All the time	❑	
Weekly	❑	
Biweekly	❑	
Monthly	❑	

C. **Measurable outcome**—This section helps you measure your success toward each goal. If you are achieving your goal, how would you notice the change in your leadership? Specifically what will improve? How will you measure it? Develop or find a metric—for example, "I will have the person who I listen to fill out an evaluation of my listening skills, rating them on a 1 (poor) to 5 (excellent) scale" (1C to 3C).

Note: You can have more than three goals in your plan. Just be sure to complete all sections.

CASE STUDY 1.1

Organizational Science in the Real World

The skills and techniques of research are valuable to an organization's leaders. The following case study illustrates how research can be used to solve a challenge facing a government organization.

In 2012, the state of Florida implemented the federal government's decree that individuals applying for or renewing their driver's license must provide a number of documents to verify their identity. Resulting from the REAL ID Act of 2005, these measures were set forth by the federal government to help develop a national identity database through the Department of Motor Vehicles (DMV; or Bureau of Motor Vehicles [BMV] depending on the state) to not only prevent identity theft but also prevent terrorists and illegal immigrants from accessing identities. Phase 1 of the act had to be completed by 2014, with the target completion of all the phases by 2017.

But that was not the only change Florida was making to its driver license processes. The state of Florida merged the state's DMV with each county's tax collector in 2011. County tax collectors are often small organizations with 100 employees or fewer working at a handful of offices in each county to serve its patrons. Previously, tax collectors' offices handled vehicle registration, license plates, property taxes, and hunting and fishing licenses. The DMV handled only driver's licenses and identification cards. The purposes of this merger were to save money for the state, save time for citizens, and make the entire process easier. Thus, most DMV employees were not retained when the organizations were merged. Therefore, tax collector employees had to be trained on a host of new processes and procedures within a short period of time.

After these initiatives were rolled out statewide, the general manager of one county's tax collector offices noticed a number of changes. Turnover skyrocketed. Large numbers of employees began to exit where previously they worked for the organization until they retired. Similarly, only 1 of 6 new hires was retained for greater than 6 months prior to the changes.

Customer service declined. Before the merger, customers typically handled their transactions within half an hour or less. However, driver's licenses take significantly longer. Because the REAL ID Act requires documentation to be scanned into state and nationwide databases, it takes about an hour to apply for or renew licenses if there are no problems or delays. This has resulted in excessive wait times for customers. The tax collector tried to address this issue with requiring appointments for those seeking driver's licenses. However, not all patrons made appointments; instead, they continued to just show up, creating delays for those with appointments. While these patrons were denied and offered to schedule an appointment, they often became belligerent and sometimes verbally abusive to the staff.

Customers were often upset and irritated not only by the excessive wait time but also by the amount of documentation they had to produce. They were also upset by having to renew driver's licenses in person whereas previously they could renew by mail or the Internet. Tax collector employees were still friendly and polite with customers, but there was definitely some underlying tension and more complicated transactions. The camaraderie and morale among employees deteriorated.

Now it is your turn. Imagine that you are the office manager and are trying to solve the organization's problems. You simply can't revert the business back the way it was before the state's mandated changes, and you're not sure what needs to be fixed and where to go in the future.

Discussion Questions

1. How could research help this small organization? What would you hope to gain as the manager?
2. What dependent variables should you, as the manager, consider researching? Why?
3. Think about the research designs discussed in the Appendix on Research Designs used in OB at the end of the book. Which one(s) do you think would be appropriate for the manager to use? Would there be any benefit to using multiple methods, and if so, in what order would you conduct the research studies?

SELF-ASSESSMENT 1.1

Assessing Your Experiential Evidence

Some students think organizational behavior (OB) is common sense. Are the following statements true or false? The answers follow.

	True	False
1. A happy worker is a productive worker.	____	____
2. Larger teams perform better because there are more people to do the work.	____	____
3. Performance appraisals have high accuracy.	____	____
4. People perform better when asked to do their best.	____	____
5. When trust is broken with your leader, it is best to take the blame and apologize.	____	____
6. Money is the best motivator.	____	____
7. Leaders should treat everyone the same in their work group.	____	____
8. A work group can be "moody."	____	____
9. Group spirit improves team decisions.	____	____
10. Conflict in organizations should be minimized.	____	____
11. Models developed in the United States will work anywhere.	____	____
12. It's best to commit to a course of action and follow through no matter what.	____	____

Answers

	True	False
1. A happy worker is a productive worker.	__X__	____

What is important is what the worker is happy about. But generally, happier people are more productive. You'll learn why in Chapter 4.

	True	False
2. Larger teams perform better because there are more people to do the work.	____	_X_

No. In fact, larger teams underperform due to increased conflict, free-riding, and other group dysfunctions. Research shows that there is an optimal group size for high performance, and you will learn what it is in Chapter 9.

	True	False
3. Performance appraisals have high accuracy.	____	_X_

No. There are a number of perceptual biases that can affect how a leader evaluates followers. You need to be aware of them so you can guard against these errors, and you will know about them after reading Chapter 5.

	True	False
4. People perform better when asked to do their best.	____	_X_

While this seems intuitive, people actually achieve higher performance when the leader gives them a specific goal rather than a "do your best goal." You will read more on the motivating properties of goals in Chapter 7.

	True	False
5. When trust is broken with your leader, it is best to take the blame and apologize.	____	_X_

No. Research on trust repair shows that admitting guilt may not be the best strategy. You will learn what the research shows you should do in Chapter 2.

	True	False
6. Money is the best motivator.	____	_X_

While this may surprise you, pay may actually decrease intrinsic motivation. You will learn about how to best reward employees in Chapter 8.

	True	False
7. Leaders should treat everyone the same in their work group.	____	_X_

Research on the leader–member exchange (LMX) model of leadership shows that effective leaders treat each follower differently based upon their skills, motivation, and need for development on the job. You will read more about this in Chapter 2.

	True	False
8. A work group can be "moody."	_X_	____

What? Yes, it can. Multilevel research has shown that negative affect (a "blue" mood) can be aggregated to the group level—and it affects group functioning. You will learn more about this in Chapter 3.

	True	False
9. Group spirit improves team decisions.	____	_X_

While cohesion can be a positive force in teams, it does not always result in the best decisions. Too much group spirit can result in groupthink and impair a group's decision making. You will read about this and other group dysfunctions in Chapter 9.

	True	False
10. Conflict in organizations should be minimized.	____	_X_

Actually, research shows that some conflict can be healthy since it can generate interest and challenge for followers. In Chapter 10, you will learn more about how to harness conflict and channel it toward increased motivation.

	True	False
11. Models developed in the United States will work anywhere.	____	_X_

Research on cultural differences indicates that we need to consider cultural values before we generalize research findings from one country to another. You will learn about cross-cultural differences in Chapter 12.

	True	False
12. It's best to commit to a course of action and follow through no matter what.	____	_X_

While it is important to commit to goals, research shows that escalation of commitment to a failing course of action is a decision trap. Learn how to avoid this and other traps in Chapter 6.

How did you do? Did you feel that you had to guess at some of these? OB research takes the guesswork out of being an effective leader! So keep reading!

LEADERSHIP
CORE CONCEPTS

HAVE LEADERS LOST THEIR FOLLOWERS' TRUST?

Each year, Richard Edelman conducts a global survey on which people and institutions we trust and how much we trust them.[1] Edelman is the president and CEO of the world's largest public relations company. In 2014, they surveyed over 33,000 respondents in 27 markets around the world and measured their trust in institutions, industries, and leaders. This year, only 50% of survey respondents reported that they trust business. While half of the respondents generally trust "business," they don't trust "business in general." The loss of trust in organizational leaders appears to be a global concern. For example, South Koreans are the least likely to say that they generally trust business leaders (only 36% reported having trust in business). However, the results indicate that respondents from the United Arab Emirates (UAE) were the most likely to trust business (85%). In the United States, 60% of respondents reported trusting business, a slight increase from last year's trust barometer (58%). Given these findings, it is no surprise that trust has emerged as a major concern globally and for research in organizational behavior (OB). The role of trust and how to repair it when it is broken will be covered later in this chapter.

As mentioned in Chapter 1, the objective of this textbook is to develop leadership skills. In this chapter, we will review the essential theories of leadership—both classic and contemporary—that you will use to guide your thinking about OB. It is important that you grasp these core leadership concepts because the textbook refers back to them in future chapters. This chapter will not cover all theories of leadership, but it focuses on the ones that have the strongest research base and/or best applicability to OB today. For a more comprehensive treatment of leadership theories, you can read a textbook by Northouse.[2]

Learning Objectives

2.1: Define *leadership*, and explain the difference between being a manager and being a leader.

2.2: Compare the elements of transactional and transformational leadership.

2.3: Illustrate the leader–member exchange (LMX) model with an example.

2.4: Explain why trust is important and how to repair it.

2.5: Compare and contrast power and influence, and provide an example of each.

2.6: Explain why political skill is important for a leader to be effective.

2.7: Describe ethical leadership, and explain its importance.

2.8: Compare and contrast authentic and servant leadership.

Get the edge on your studies at
edge.sagepub.com/scandura
- Take the chapter quiz
- Review key terms with eFlashcards
- Explore multimedia resources, SAGE readings, and more!

$SAGE edge™

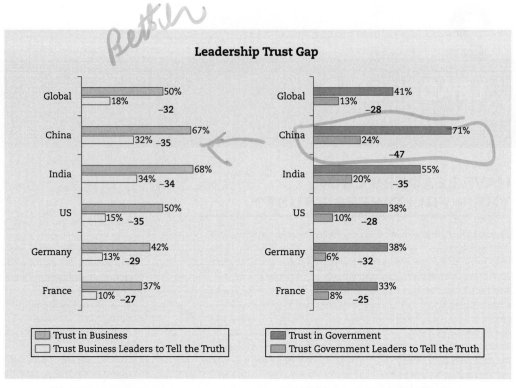

Leadership Trust Gap

	Trust in Business	Trust Business Leaders to Tell the Truth			Trust in Government	Trust Government Leaders to Tell the Truth
Global	50%	18% −32		Global	41%	13% −28
China	67%	32% −35		China	71%	24% −47
India	68%	34% −34		India	55%	20% −35
US	50%	15% −35		US	38%	10% −28
Germany	42%	13% −29		Germany	38%	6% −32
France	37%	10% −27		France	33%	8% −25

Source: Edelman, R. (2015). 2015 Trust Barometer Executive Summary. http://www.edelman.com/insights/intellectual-property/2015-edelman-trust-barometer/

WHAT IS LEADERSHIP?

Learning Objective 2.1: Define *leadership,* and explain the difference between being a manager and being a leader.

Transformational Leadership

Yukl[3] reviewed various definitions of leadership over the past 50 years and offered the following synthesis:

> Leadership is the process of influencing others to understand and agree about what needs to be done and how to do it, and the process of facilitating individual and collective efforts to accomplish shared objectives. (p. 7)

This definition captures the essence of leadership as an influence process (I will discuss power and influence later in this chapter). It also has the notion that leadership involves directing individuals and groups toward organizational goals. Yukl noted that there has been confusion in the literature about the difference between other terms like *management*—so a distinction regarding whether or not management is the same as leadership is needed.

Differentiating Management and Leadership

Managerial
Leadership

In his classic book *On Becoming a Leader*, Warren Bennis composed a list of the differences between being a manager and being a leader:[4]

- The manager administers; the leader innovates.
- The manager is a copy; the leader is an original.
- The manager maintains; the leader develops.
- The manager focuses on systems and structure; the leader focuses on people.
- The manager relies on control; the leader inspires trust.
- The manager has a short-range view; the leader has a long-range perspective.
- The manager asks how and when; the leader asks what and why.
- The manager has his or her eye always on the bottom line; the leader's eye is on the horizon.
- The manager imitates; the leader originates.
- The manager accepts the status quo; the leader challenges it.
- The manager is the classic good soldier; the leader is his or her own person.
- The manager does things right; the leader does the right thing.

Zalesnick also posed the question, "Leaders and managers: Are they different?"[5] He made an important point that both managers and leaders are needed for an organization to function optimally. The manager is a day-to-day problem solver, and the leader is focused on developing new approaches and options for the future. To some extent, leaders must engage in some problem-solving activities, and in reality, the two overlap (see Figure 2.1). As shown in the figure, leadership is about inspiring others to follow their vision for the

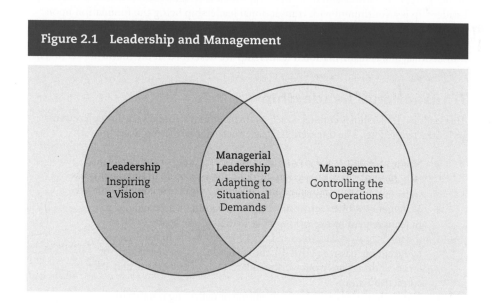

Figure 2.1 Leadership and Management

Leadership
Inspiring a Vision

Managerial Leadership
Adapting to Situational Demands

Management
Controlling the Operations

organization. Managers, on the other hand, are concerned with controlling the operations of the organization so things run efficiently. Both are needed, and some managers have the adaptability to do both and switch between the roles of leader and manager as the situation demands. These are managerial leaders as shown in the figure where the two roles overlap. It is this adaptability that has been shown to be effective in contingency or situational theories of leadership. For example, the situational leadership theory considers the "readiness" of followers in terms of their ability, motivation, and confidence to perform a task.[6] The leader adapts their style based upon how able and willing a follower is to perform a specific task.

If you are interested in becoming a leader, you will tend to be interested in research on transformational and visionary leadership. You may view yourself as charismatic. However, for those of you who view yourselves as managers who sometimes take the leadership role, you will also benefit from knowledge about leadership. Leadership is a "full-range" of behaviors, and the next section discusses both management (i.e., transactional behaviors) and leadership (i.e., transformational behaviors).

FULL-RANGE LEADERSHIP DEVELOPMENT

Learning Objective 2.2: Compare the elements of transactional and transformational leadership.

The full-range leadership development model is based upon over 25 years of research on **transformational leadership**.[7,8,9] People are more engaged when their leaders behave in certain ways at the highest end of the full-range model. The full-range model starts at the lower end of leadership, which is termed **transactional leadership**. Leadership is a continuum with transactional leadership being the foundation upon which transformational leadership is built. These behaviors range from passive to active and ineffective to effective as depicted in Figure 2.2. The specific elements of transactional and transformational leadership are described in the following sections.

Transactional Leadership

Transactional leadership is defined as behaviors that motivate followers through rewards and corrective actions. The transactional leader behaviors are (from worst to best):

- **Nonleadership/laissez-faire leadership.** This is the "near-avoidance of leadership,"[10] the least active and least effective of all of the leadership styles in the full-range model.
- **Management by exception.** This has two forms: active and passive. In management by exception, active (MBE-A), the leader looks for the follower to make errors and then corrects them. In management by exception, passive (MBE-P), the leader does not actively look for errors or deviations from work standards, but when noticed, they take corrective action.
- **Contingent reward.** This is promising or delivering rewards to followers contingent on their performance.

Figure 2.2   The Full Range of Leadership Model

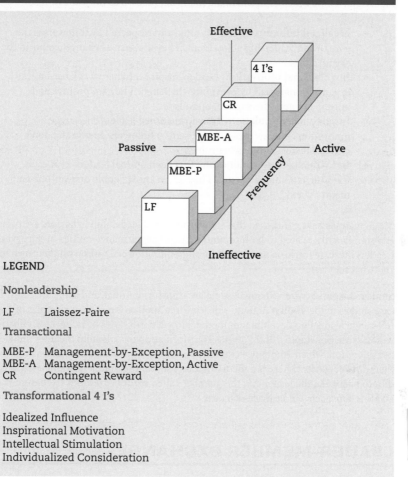

LEGEND

Nonleadership

LF   Laissez-Faire

Transactional

MBE-P   Management-by-Exception, Passive
MBE-A   Management-by-Exception, Active
CR   Contingent Reward

Transformational 4 I's

Idealized Influence
Inspirational Motivation
Intellectual Stimulation
Individualized Consideration

Source: Bass & Avolio, 1994, *Improving Organizational Effectiveness Through Transformational Leadership.* SAGE Publications, Inc.

There are times when a manager must use the transactional approach. For example, if they have a low-performing employee, a leader may need to employ the management-by-exception approaches. At the next level in the full-range model are the transformational leadership behaviors.

Transformational Leadership

Transformational leadership is defined as behaviors that mobilize extra effort from followers through emphasis on change through articulating a new vision for the organization. As noted earlier, it is this set of behaviors that is most related to positive attitudes, commitment, and performance of followers. Leadership is active, and this leads to effectiveness as shown in Figure 2.2. These behaviors include the following (known as the *four I's*):

- **Idealized influence.** Being admired and respected by followers is the core of this leadership component. They are seen as change agents in the organization.
- **Inspirational motivation.** Leaders inspire others to work hard toward organizational goals by providing challenge. They are positive and upbeat and get others to feel optimistic.
- **Intellectual stimulation.** Transformational leaders encourage innovation and new ideas. They listen to followers openly and don't criticize novel solutions to problems.
- **Individualized consideration.** Transformational leaders treat each follower as a unique person. They get to know people one-on-one and mentor them.

Meta-analyses have confirmed that transformational leadership behaviors are positively and significantly related to both productivity and performance ratings by supervisors.[11,12] Leaders increase intrinsic motivation by aligning followers' tasks with their own interests and what they value most.

Some managers are transactional, some are transformational, and some are both. The case studies in the Toolkit Activity will reinforce application of the principles of the full-range leadership development model. However, all styles must develop effective working relationships with followers. Transformational leadership includes individualized consideration, which emphasizes that the leader develops a unique relationship with each of their direct reports. There is a theory that focuses on the unique working relationships that develop between the leader and the member called **leader–member exchange (LMX)**, and this approach will be discussed next.

LEADER–MEMBER EXCHANGE

Learning Objective 2.3: Illustrate the leader–member exchange (LMX) model with an example.

Should a boss treat everyone alike? Leaders treat subordinates differently based upon their unique abilities and contributions to the work group and organization. LMX is defined as the quality of the working relationship that is developed with each follower.[13] In a relatively short period of time, leaders decide on their **in-group members** and **out-group members.** Out-group members perform to the specifications in their job descriptions, but they don't go above and beyond and don't take on extra work. In-group members do. A diagram of what in-groups and out-groups might look like in a seven-person work group is shown in Figure 2.3.

Critical Thinking Questions: Is the LMX process fair? Should managers treat all followers alike? Why or why not?

Note that there is a poor performer in the work group (labeled P7). This is a different type of relationship where the supervisor is monitoring performance and attempting to get the minimally accepted level of performance. The first goal would be to move this person to the out-group where they are performing to the basic expectations of the job. If performance does not improve, in time, they may be transferred to another work group (where they get a second chance) or dismissed from the organization altogether.

The other important thing the diagram shows is that norms of fairness must pervade this entire process.[14,15,16,17] Table 2.1 contains the short seven-item measures for both the member perceptions of LMX (LMX7) and the supervisor perceptions of LMX (SLMX7).

 Critical Thinking Questions: Develop an example by having someone you know and their boss complete the LMX and SLMX questionnaires in Table 2.1. What do you see when you compare leader and member ratings? Ask one leader to complete the SLMX measure about three followers. Do you see differences in the quality of the relationships?

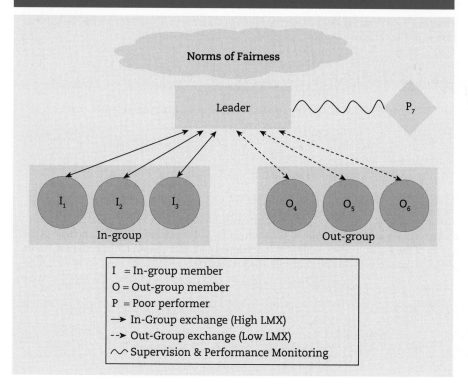

Figure 2.3 Leader–Member Exchange in a Work Group With Seven Direct Reports

Table 2.1 Leader–Member Exchange and Supervisor Leader–Member Exchange Measures

Leader–Member Exchange

The following questions ask about **your relationship with your immediate boss**—that is, **the person you report to.** Circle your answers.

Do you know where you stand with him or her? Do you usually know how satisfied he or she is with what you do?

1	2	3	4	5
Rarely	Occasionally	Sometimes	Fairly often	Very often

How well does he or she understand your job problems and needs?

1	2	3	4	5
Not a bit	A little	A fair amount	Quite a bit	A great deal

How well does he or she recognize your potential?

1	2	3	4	5
Not at all	A little	Moderately	Mostly	Fully

Regardless of how much formal authority he or she has built into his or her position, what are the chances that he or she would use his or her power to help you solve problems in your work?

1	2	3	4	5
None	Small	Moderate	High	Very high

Again, regardless of the amount of formal authority he or she has, what are the chances that he or she would "bail you out," at his or her expense?

1	2	3	4	5
None	Small	Moderate	High	Very high

I have enough confidence in him or her that I would defend and justify his or her decision if he or she were not present to do so.

1	2	3	4	5
Strongly disagree	Disagree	Neutral	Agree	Strongly agree

How would you characterize your working relationship with him or her?

1	2	3	4	5
Extremely ineffective	Worse than average	Average	Better than average	Extremely effective

Statement	Staff	Strongly disagree	Disagree	Neutral	Agree	Strongly agree
Supervisor Leader–Member Exchange						

Think about **your relationship with the following member(s) of your staff.** Enter the names of your staff members. If more than three, add names to the form. Then indicate the extent to which you disagree or agree with each statement using the 1–5 scales below with respect to each of the staff listed. Circle your answers.

Statement	Staff	Strongly disagree	Disagree	Neutral	Agree	Strongly agree
1. Regardless of how much power I have built into my position, I solve problems in his or her work.	1.	1	2	3	4	5
	2.	1	2	3	4	5
	3.	1	2	3	4	5
2. I would be willing to "bail out" him or her—even at my own expense—if he or she really needed it.	1.	1	2	3	4	5
	2.	1	2	3	4	5
	3.	1	2	3	4	5
3. I think that I recognize his or her potential.	1.	1	2	3	4	5
	2.	1	2	3	4	5
	3.	1	2	3	4	5
4. I have enough confidence in him or her that I would defend and justify his or her decisions if he or she were not present to do so.	1.	1	2	3	4	5
	2.	1	2	3	4	5
	3.	1	2	3	4	5
5. I think that I understand his or her problems and needs.	1.	1	2	3	4	5
	2.	1	2	3	4	5
	3.	1	2	3	4	5
6. I usually let him or her know where he or she stands with me.	1.	1	2	3	4	5
	2.	1	2	3	4	5
	3.	1	2	3	4	5
7. I would characterize my working relationship with him or her as effective.	1.	1	2	3	4	5
	2.	1	2	3	4	5
	3.	1	2	3	4	5

Source: Scandura, T. A., & Graen, G. B. (1984). The moderating effects of initial leader-member exchange status on the effects of a leadership intervention. *Journal of Applied Psychology, 69,* 428–436.

Leader–Member Exchange Development

So how do effective LMX relationships develop? There are three steps in the process: role-taking, role-making, and role-routinization.[18] In role-taking, the boss tests the commitment of the follower by offering extra work. Through this testing and responses, the boss forms an overall assessment of whether the follower is in-group or out-group. It is important to pay attention to the boss' signals when a person takes a new job or has a new boss. If a person wants the benefits of more challenging work, promotion potential, or higher salary, they need to respond in a way that the boss views positively. During the process of role-making, mutual expectations of the working relationship are established and the follower's role is clearer. The final step is role-routinization. Once roles are made, they become stable since the leader and follower both know what to expect. For example, relationships develop best when the leader is able to delegate tasks to the member.[19] Therefore, everyone who reports to a boss (and that's most of us) should be concerned with managing the relationship and developing a relationship by being dependable. The next sections will focus on how to manage your boss and develop a high-quality relationship.

Managing Your Boss

Research on the LMX model of leadership has demonstrated that an effective working relationship with your boss predicts all of the outcomes of OB that we discussed in Chapter 1 (performance, job satisfaction, organizational commitment, motivation, and lower turnover). Outcomes of interest to many students are career progress and LMX predicts promotions and salary increases. A classic *Harvard Business Review* article[20] termed the upward exchange process "managing your boss" and described how to develop an effective working relationship with the boss: understanding your boss, understanding yourself through self-assessment, and developing a compatible working relationship. Jean Kelley[21] offers the following guidelines for effectively managing the boss.

1. **Find out from your boss what "good" looks like and who is involved in measuring good.** Make sure you are meeting everyone's expectations.
2. **Ask your boss what kind of follow-up he or she wants for his or her comfort level.** Take the initiative to set expectations for every project you are assigned.
3. **Examine your boss's style and adjust to that style.** Is your boss a reader or a listener? Does your boss want data before you talk (a reader)? Or does your boss want to talk through the project and gather the data later (a listener)?
4. **Muster up the courage to tell your boss when you feel you haven't been fully heard.** It's your responsibility to speak up when you feel you are not being heard. Use *I* instead of *you*—for example, "I was really upset by you not hearing me" rather than "You don't listen to me."
5. **Become aware of other managers' styles, especially when they have a stake in the outcome of a project.** Do you have more than one boss or person who evaluates your work? Ask each one what is most important so that you can focus your efforts.
6. **Manage up.** No matter how poorly you may have managed your relationship with your boss in the past, the good news is that you can start over with a new project. It's about understanding your boss and teaching your boss how to work with you.

Some people may have a negative reaction to this process, feeling that it is manipulative. It is important to point out that this is not about flattering the boss or becoming a "pet" employee. Rather, this is a process of developing an effective working relationship based upon mutual expectations. Focus on your strong points—what you can offer your boss to make them more effective. This is where relationship compatibility comes in. For example, if your boss is quiet and reserved and you are more outgoing, you could be his go-to person for making public contacts and networking.

Terri Scandura on Mentoring

Critical Thinking Questions: Do you feel that the process of "managing your boss" is manipulative or just being a smart and dependable employee? Explain your position.

Follower Reactions to Authority

Part of being able to adjust to your boss' style is your understanding how you feel about authority. Some people resent authority and being told what to do (**counterdependent**). Others are compliant and give in all of the time (**overdependent**). According to Gabarro and Kotter, the best approach is to avoid these two extremes and recognize that most followers are dependent on their boss to some extent. Ideally, you will be able to create a working relationship where you feel **interdependent** (you depend on one another to get things done in the group and organization). In developing an effective working relationship, you should be dependable and honest above all, keeping your boss informed (but also using their time wisely).

Research has shown that effective working relationships with the boss can permeate the entire organization. Leaders with great boss relationships have more resources to exchange with their own followers and therefore develop more effective working relationships with them.[22] Thus, the leader in the middle is viewed as a "linking pin" between upper management and followers below, sharing important information about the organization's vision and goals with followers. These linking-pin leaders become valuable members of the organization, and they gain power and influence due to their position in organizational networks (we will discuss power in more detail later in this chapter). But first, we turn to how you can develop these important working relationships with your boss even more into a mentoring relationship, which has also been shown to relate to performance and positive career outcomes for the junior person, or mentee.

The Mentor Connection

Mentoring is defined as follows:[23]

> Mentoring is an intense developmental relationship whereby advice, counseling, and developmental opportunities are provided to a protégé by a mentor, which, in turn, shapes the protégé's career experiences.

One of the best things that can happen is when the boss becomes a mentor. Career mentoring from a boss contributes to performance, promotions, and salary increases above and beyond a high-quality LMX relationship.[24] Research on mentoring in organizations shows that having a mentor can have a powerful impact on your career, and the boss is an important place to begin.

The Value of Mentoring

You want to show him or her that you want to be a trusted member of the in-group and that you are willing to take on more responsibility. Hopefully, he or she will then view you as a mentee—someone worth the investment of the time and energy to develop. There are many cases where a boss gets promoted and a trusted in-group member is promoted along with him. So you want to be sure to do an inventory of what you have to offer your boss in exchange for career investment. For example, you might offer to take on a challenging problem that the boss has been working on (particularly if it fits your strengths). Or you might lead the team meeting while your boss is out of town (and be sure to keep them informed with a summary of how the meeting went).

Mentors provide two general types of support to protégés: (1) career support and (2) social support.[25] In addition, mentors may serve as role models to mentees. Cultivating a mentoring relationship enhances your job satisfaction and performance.[26]

Mentoring has now been conceptualized as a network of developmental relationships,[27] including peers, managers other than your boss, and people outside of the organization. However, keep in mind that research has demonstrated that the boss is a key node of your mentoring network since supervisory mentoring has been associated with higher potential, productivity, and organizational commitment.[28] A mentor expects a mentee to be trustworthy and dependable. In fact, trust is at the heart of all effective working relationships. Next, we discuss research on trust, which is essential for a leader to understand to be effective and address the "trust gap" highlighted at the beginning of this chapter.

RESEARCH IN ACTION

Getting Your Boss to Invest in You: Be Proactive!

How can you proactively adapt to a new organization? Research by Susan Ashford and Stewart Black identified the following proactive socialization tactics for organizational newcomers:

- **Seek information.** Regularly ask for information regarding the formal and informal organizational system, policies and procedures, politics, and organizational culture: How do things really get done in the organization?
- **Seek feedback.** Ask for honest feedback about your performance during and after assignments from your boss(es) and others. Don't wait for your annual performance appraisal to learn how you are doing on the job.
- **Manage your boss.** Learn as much as you can about him or her. Ask them to lunch to discuss your plans (i.e., develop an effective working relationship).

- **Negotiate more job challenge.** Ask for changes to your job, and craft it so you can be most effective, playing to your strengths but at the same time meeting organizational goals.
- **Be positive.** View every problem as an opportunity, and try to see others in your group and organization in positive ways. Be optimistic unless someone proves you wrong.

Discussion Questions

1. How important is it to be proactive during your first six months in a new job? How often should you meet with your new boss?
2. Develop some examples of how you can ask for more challenging work assignments. Draft an outline of talking points for how you would present these requests to your boss (or future boss).

Source: Adapted from Ashford, S. J., & Black, J. S. (1996). Proactivity during organizational entry: The role of desire for control. *Journal of Applied Psychology, 81,* 199–214.

THE IMPORTANCE OF TRUST

Learning Objective 2.4: Explain why trust is important and how to repair it.

The following definition of trust is often-cited: "the willingness to be vulnerable."[29] In a meta-analytic study, trust was found to be related to important outcomes—risk-taking and job performance.[30] A review of the various definitions of trust offers the following summary:[31] Trust is a psychological state comprising the intention to accept vulnerability based upon positive expectations of the intentions or behavior of another.

 **Trust Enhances Leadership**

Dirks and Ferrin[32] found that trust is related to LMX as well as job satisfaction and performance in a meta-analytic review of the literature. Several other theories of leadership mention trust (e.g., **servant leadership**, which will be discussed later in this chapter). Trust is fundamental to the development of effective working relationships with bosses (and others).

There are some helpful frameworks to organize your thinking about how trust operates in organizations. A three-part view of trust is a useful way to think about trust development with another person: calculus-based, knowledge-based, and identification-based.[33] Each of these forms will be explained in detail in the following sections.

Calculus-Based Trust

Calculus-based trust (CBT) is a form of trust based upon keeping records of what another person does for you and what you do for them. It is an "arm's length" form of trust in which neither party really becomes that vulnerable to the behavior of the other person. The expectations are like contracts, and the consequences of violating trust are punishment or the severing of the relationship. An example of CBT (sometimes called deterrence-based trust) in an organization is a leader telling a follower to perform a task because it is in their job description and reminding them that they are paid to do it (in other words, "Do it or you are fired!"). Many relationships in organizations (and in our daily lives) operate on this level. For example, this is the type of relationship most people have with the person who they hire to cut their grass. It is a straightforward transaction. If the person shows up, cuts the grass, and it looks good, you pay them. If not, you don't.

Knowledge-Based Trust

In this framework, the second level of trust is called **knowledge-based trust (KBT)**. This level of trust is grounded in how predictable the other person is. Over time, through interactions where benefits are exchanged between two parties, people come to expect the other person to come through for them. It is based upon information gathered about the other person in a variety of circumstances. An example of this form of trust in an organization would be a follower becoming the go-to person for the boss in terms of creating her PowerPoint decks for important presentations. The boss can jot down a list of bullet points in a document and send them to the follower. Within a day, the boss receives a professional-looking presentation deck to review and edit. The boss does not have to remind the person that it is in their job description (and it may or may not be). They just make the request, and it happens because the follower's behavior is predictable.

Trust

Identification-Based Trust

Finally, the highest degree of trust in this model is called identification-based trust
(IBT). This form of trust is characterized by the leader and follower sharing the same goals
and objectives. In other words, the follower identifies with the leader's vision. There is no
need for record keeping, and the predictability of the follower's behavior is assumed. The
follower sees the work group and organization in the same way that the leader does and will
perform the right tasks without being asked. For example, a trusted follower would step
in and resolve a conflict with another work group member for the leader. IBT becomes
a highly efficient form for the leader since followers take care of details while the leader
focuses on the strategic vision or negotiating resources for the group with her boss (i.e.,
working the "linking pin," as suggested by the LMX model).

Lewicki and Bunker built upon Shapiro et al.'s work and described the process through
which trust develops over time.[34] As shown in Figure 2.4, trust may transform over time
and develop different "faces" as it matures. In other words, the types of trust build upon
one another over time based on the nature of the working relationship. CBT develops
to a point (J1), and the trust level becomes KBT as the behavior of the parties becomes
predictable. As noted in the figure, most relationships in organizations fall into the KBT
range of trust. Once stable, a few relationships will reach the next point (J2) and will become
stable IBT relationships. At this point, both parties fully understand what the other party
cares about, and there is a level of empathy that emerges (i.e., the ability to put oneself in
the bosses' place and see the organization the way they do.). As noted previously, at this
level, the follower becomes able to act effectively for the boss. There is a sense of harmony

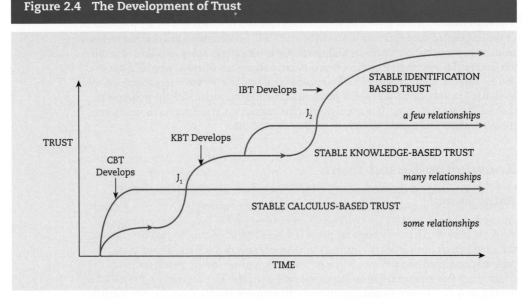

Figure 2.4 The Development of Trust

Source: Lewicki, R. J., & Bunker, B. B. (1996). Developing and maintaining trust in work relationships. In: Kramer, R. M., & Tyler, T. R.
(Eds.), *Trust in organizations: Frontiers of theory and research.* Thousand Oaks, CA: SAGE Publications.

in thoughts, emotions, and behavior. Activities that strengthen IBT are the creation of joint projects, shared goals, and shared work values.

 Gaining Trust

The development of trust is viewed as "tactical climbing" in which there are increasing levels of risk and vulnerability over time. But at any point, trust is vulnerable. Even in high-quality leader–follower relationships, IBT can revert to the CBT stage, so followers and bosses must be careful about maintaining relationships.[35] According to Lewicki and Bunker, movements between the stages of trust can be smooth and incremental or they can be dramatic and transformational. Remember that the development of trust takes time and that trust does require testing to see how durable it is.

From the examples provided, you can see the critical role that trust plays in the development of working relationships with bosses (and others including peers) in the organization. It's hard to imagine an organization that could function without trust. So it's important to understand what you need to do should you damage trust with your boss (of course, the best strategy is to never damage trust but it can happen). Research on trust repair has examined what strategies work to get the relationship back on track.

 Critical Thinking Questions: Explain how calculus-based trust explains how people view their jobs. How can a leader move a person to the two higher levels of trust?

Repairing Broken Trust

There are three important questions to ask after a trust violation has occurred (the trustee is the person who is the target of the trustor's trust):[36]

1. Is the trustee innocent or guilty of committing the transgression?
2. If the trustee is guilty of the transgression, should this be attributed to the situation or to the person?
3. If the transgression is attributed at least in part to the person, is the personal shortcoming fixable or is it an enduring characteristic of the trustee?

These questions are important because they offer guidance for repairing trust. Regarding question 1, if a trustee is actually innocent, they should emphasize lack of guilt through denial and offer any available exonerating information.[37] Not addressing the issue—remaining reticent (e.g., saying "no comment")—can be risky because people usually assume the worst.[38]

Regarding question 2, if the trustee is guilty, an apology may be an effective way to repair trust, because the expressions of remorse and repentance, which are part of an apology, can alleviate some of the trustor's concerns. However, the way the apology is given also matters. Research shows that if extenuating factors also played a role, there is benefit to mentioning these circumstances when the apology is offered.[39] Keep in mind that though explanations and excuses can restore trust, they have to be seen as adequate; incomplete explanations don't work.[40]

Excuses might be effective, depending on the characteristics of the person violating the trust and the relationship quality, but adding reparations (i.e., attempts to "make it right") increase the effectiveness of explanations.[41,42] However, further research suggests that it depends on other contingencies, and these are described next.

Finally, question 3 represents one of the most important—but least obvious—contingencies for trust repair. Will the trustor see the cause of the transgression as stemming from an enduring flaw in the trustee or something the trustee can, in fact, address? If the transgression stems from an honest mistake or lack of knowledge (i.e., a competence-related issue), people are more likely to give the benefit of the doubt and trust again. However, if the act is seen as demonstrating a lack of integrity, trust is much more difficult (if not impossible) to repair. For example, promises may restore trust but not if the trust is broken because the person has initially lied. Lying is one of the most damaging behaviors.[43] If someone is deceived, trust may not be not restored even if apologies, promises, and repeated trustworthy actions follow the deception. Even more "substantive" (rather than verbal) responses such as offering reparation or paying a personal cost are limited in their effectiveness when questions of integrity are at the center of the issue.[44]

 Critical Thinking Question: Think of a time when you tried to restore trust after it was broken. Based on this section, what would you do differently?

POWER AND INFLUENCE

Learning Objective 2.5: Compare and contrast power and influence, and provide an example of each.

It can be said that **power** is the other side of the leadership coin. Nearly all definitions of leadership include the idea of influencing others, and power is the source of **influence**. A useful distinction between power and influence follows:[45]

> Power is the *potential* of one person (or group) to influence another person or group. Some people have a lot of power but they don't need to actually exercise it. For example, a police officer sitting on the side of the interstate affects your behavior (and those ahead of you!). You remove your foot from the accelerator and slow down. It is the officer's potential to write you a ticket and not the actual behavior of writing it that changes behaviors. This is important to keep in mind. You don't always have to demonstrate your power—if you attain a managerial position and have others who report to you, it is unspoken. Often, power is best executed when it is done so in a subtle manner. Influence, in turn, is the exercise of power to change the behavior, attitudes, and/or values of that individual or group.

Influence can, therefore, be thought of as *power in use*. We will first discuss where power comes from followed by how power is effectively used in organizations.

Critical Thinking Question: What is the difference between power and influence? Provide an example of each.

Bases of Power

Five bases of power in organizations have been described.[46] Some forms of power come with a person's position in the hierarchy: **position power**. Other power may come from the personal characteristics of the person and may have no relationship to their position in the organization: **personal power.** Position power includes the following:

- **Coercive** power—the authority to punish
- **Reward** power—the authority to provide incentives or other things valued
- **Legitimate** power—the authority to make a request and get a response due to the nature of the roles between two people (e.g., boss and direct report)

While coercive power is on the list of bases of power, most leaders in organizations say that they rarely, if ever, use it. French and Raven warned that the use of coercion may result in employee resistance and other forms of dysfunctional behavior on the part of the follower. Another example of dysfunctional behavior is when followers talk badly about the boss behind their back. The personal sources of power are not tied to position but can be generated by anyone in the organization. They help explain why many people in organizations have a great deal of power although they don't have important-sounding titles and are not high in the organizational hierarchy. These personal power sources are as follows:

- **Expert power**—the ability to influence others due to knowledge or a special skill set
- **Referent power**—the ability to influence based upon others' identification with the individual and followers' desire to emulate them

As noted previously with respect to coercion, these power bases may result in different reactions from followers. Three possible outcomes of an influence attempt can be distinguished between the following:[47]

- **Commitment**—a strong effort made and enthusiastically carries out the request
- **Compliance**—willing to complete the request but does so in an apathetic manner giving minimal effort
- **Resistance**—opposed to the request and refuses to do it. They may explain why they can't complete it, try to change it, get superiors to change it, delay it or even sabotage the task by doing it wrong.

Figure 2.5 summarizes the bases of power and shows the likely responses from followers. Coercive power may be met with resistance, but referent power, in contrast, may result in commitment to the leader's vision. Compliance can be expected from legitimate power and the ability of the leader to reward followers for their work. Expertise may also result in compliance, but it is higher than legitimate power since some may admire expertise and it may have some impact on commitment. The figure also depicts another important concept with respect to power: the **zone of indifference**.[48]

> There exists a "zone of indifference" in each individual within which orders are acceptable without conscious questioning of their authority. . . . The zone of indifference will be wider or narrower depending upon the degree to which the inducements exceed the burdens and sacrifices which determine the individual's adhesion to the organization. It follows that the range of orders that will be accepted will be very limited among those who are barely induced to contribute to the system.

As shown in Figure 2.5, the zone of indifference falls between reward power and expert power and is centered on legitimate power. In most cases, followers will comply with directions from leaders because they fall within the zone in which they are indifferent. Followers become dissatisfied and resist when coercive tactics are employed. However, working within the zone does not produce high levels of commitment or engagement, which are now needed for organizations to function most effectively. To gain high levels of engagement and commitment, the leader should develop and use expert power at a minimum and try to develop referent power through being a positive role model and getting followers to respond in an emotionally positive way to his or her influence.

Organizational Sources of Power

Rosabeth Moss Kanter described power as a property of organizational systems rather than individuals.[49] She presented the following **three "lines" of power** for leaders in organizations to tap into to gain productive power:

1. **Lines of supply.** Leaders bring in the things that their group needs such as materials, money, and resources such as rewards and even prestige.
2. **Lines of information.** Leaders need to know what is happening in the organization that may affect their group's goals. Having access to information from all areas of the organization is an important source of power. Also, knowing who to share information with (and not share it with) is an essential skill that leaders need to develop.
3. **Lines of support.** A leader needs to be able to innovate to have an impact on the organization. She needs support that allows for risk-taking beyond typical organizational routines. Leaders also often need the backing of other influential managers in the organization to get things done.

As the previous discussion of power as a potential for influencing others suggests, it is important to generate one's sources of power, including supply, information, and support. However, power is simply a stored-up ability to create positive change in the organization.

Figure 2.5 Bases of Power and Follower Responses

Follower Engagment Level	Power Base Used (Follower Response)	Follower Reaction to Directives
Commitment	Referent "I admire you"	High motivation and performance
	Expert "I need your help"	
Compliance	Legitimate "It's my job"	"Zone of Indifference"
	Reward "I'm in it for the money"	
Resistance	Coercive "I resent being treated this way"	Low performance and sabotage

Sources: French, J. R. P., & Raven, B. (1960). The bases of social power. In: D. Cartwright & A. Zander (Eds.), *Group dynamics*, 2nd ed. (pp. 607–623). New York: Harper and Row.

Barnard, C. (1938). *Functions of the executive.* Cambridge, MA: Harvard University Press.

Research on influence strategies in organizations has shown how leaders effectively use power to meet their objectives.

 Influence Tactics

Influence Strategies

Next, we turn to how power is used in organizations and the specific strategies and tactics that have been shown to work (and those that don't). Yukl presented a typology of **proactive influence tactics** based upon his research. While other typologies exist,[50] Yukl's typology is comprehensive and has been researched employing a wide variety of research methods including "critical incidents, diaries, questionnaires, experiments, and scenarios."[51] He and his colleagues developed an assessment for use in research called the Influence Behavior Questionnaire (IBQ). These tactics may be used alone or in combinations, and some are more effective than others. In all cases, a careful diagnosis of the person you are trying to influence and the situation is necessary. These tactics are shown in Table 2.2.

Which Influence Strategies Are the Most Effective?

So what does research show with respect to which tactics work and with whom? As noted earlier, followers may respond to an influence attempt with commitment, compliance, or resistance. OB research has demonstrated that the different influence strategies used have different reactions from followers.

Table 2.2   Proactive Influence Tactics

Tactic	Definition
Rational persuasion	The agent uses logical arguments and factual evidence to show a proposal or request is feasible and relevant for attaining important task objectives.
Apprising	The agent explains how carrying out a request or supporting a proposal will benefit the target personally or help advance the target person's career.
Inspirational appeals	The agent makes an appeal to values and ideals or seeks to arouse the target person's emotions to gain commitment for a request or proposal.
Consultation	The agent offers to provide relevant resources and assistance if the target will carry out a request or approves a proposed change.
Collaboration	The agent offers to provide relevant resources and assistance if the target will carry out a request or approve a proposed change.
Ingratiation	The agent uses praise and flattery before or during an influence attempt or expresses confidence in the target's ability to carry out a difficult request.
Personal appeals	The agent asks the target to carry out a request or support a proposal out of friendship or asks for a personal favor before saying what it is.
Exchange	The agent offers an incentive, suggests an exchange of favors, or indicates willingness to reciprocate at a later time if the target will do what the agent requests.
Coalition tactics	The agent seeks the aid of others to persuade the target to do something or uses the support of others as a reason for the target to agree.
Legitimating tactics	The agent seeks to establish the legitimacy of a request or to verify authority to make it by referring to rules, policies, contracts, or precedent.
Pressure	The agent uses demands, threats, frequent checking, or persistent reminders to influence the target to carry out a request.

Source: Yukl, G. (2013). *Leadership in organizations* (6th ed., p. 202). Boston, MA: Pearson.

Rational persuasion is a tactic commonly employed by leaders, and it is very effective— particularly if the leader is viewed as an expert. **Apprising** involves persuading the target of influence that complying will advance his career. It is more likely to be used with peers or followers than with the boss. **Inspirational appeals** try to arouse followers' emotions and can work with all targets of influence. It may be particularly useful during times of organizational change. **Consultation** invites the person to be involved with a proposed idea and may be used in any direction as well. It may be particularly effective with peers in cross-functional teams, for example. Exchange is based on the quid pro quo in organizational life. It may be direct or indirect, but it will involve the idea that the exchange of favors will occur between the parties. This tactic has been shown to be more effective with peers than with bosses. **Collaboration** is an offer to provide assistance or resources to the person being asked to do something. It is used least with superiors in the organization but can be very effective with peers and followers.

Ingratiation is compliment-giving or acting deferential. This tactic must be used with caution, because if it is overdone or comes across as insincere it can fail entirely. **Personal appeals** are based on friendship or loyalty and may be more appropriate with a peer or someone outside the organization than with bosses or subordinates. Asking someone to do something based on a personal friendship may be a risky strategy. Legitimating tactics remind the target of their role in the organization in relation to the person making the request—for example, "I am asking you to do this because it is your job." This works with followers better than other targets. Pressure tactics are threats and relate to coercion. For this reason, pressure tactics should be used sparingly—even with followers where they are most commonly found. Finally, **coalition** tactics involve gaining the support of others. They are more likely to be used with peers or bosses, but the idea is that there is "strength in numbers" and should be used carefully especially with supervisors or those higher in the organization.

Most of the influence tactics discussed to this point involve the leader having some degree of authority. But what if you are trying to influence someone in the organization that you have no official authority or influence over? A model of *influence without authority* can be used in wide variety of situations.[52] The model is based upon the **law of reciprocity** first articulated by Gouldner: the nearly universal belief that if someone does something for you, they should be paid back.[53] In their model, Cohen and Bradford discuss the "currencies of exchange" such as sharing the vision, gaining additional resources, providing visibility, giving personal support, and showing gratitude. The influence without authority process is depicted in Figure 2.6. It begins with assuming the other person is your ally and wants to exchange with you. You need to be clear about what your goals are and then understand the other person's situation (showing empathy). Then you identify what you have to exchange (i.e., the currencies) and what you need from them. Examples of currencies are support, loyalty, and extra effort on the job. It is important to assess the quality of the relationship (if it is a supervisor, you can use the LMX7 measure in Table 2.1 in this chapter to assess relationship quality). Finally, influence the person and emphasize the give-and-take as shown in the figure.

Critical Thinking Questions: Do you think the "influence without authority" approach contains risks? If not, why not? If so, what are they?

Figure 2.6   Influence Without Authority

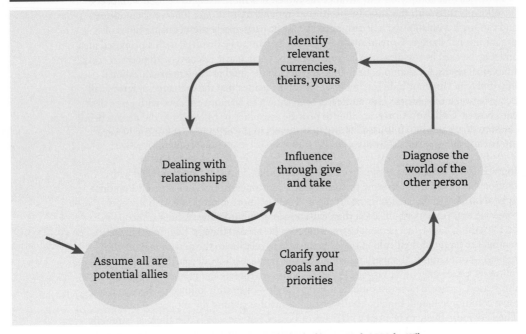

Source: Cohen, A. R., & Bradford, D. L. (2005). *Influence without authority* (2nd ed.). New York, NY: John Wiley.

Organizational
Politics

This discussion suggests that exercising power and influence effectively requires both planning and skill. OB research has identified three important political skills: Leaders need to understand the **perceptions of organizational politics, have political skill,** and must use power ethically. The next section will describe organizational political skills and how you can develop your leadership through political acumen.

ORGANIZATIONAL POLITICS AND POLITICAL SKILL

Learning Objective 2.6: Explain why political skill is important for a leader to be effective.

The power bases and influence tactics described in this chapter may be viewed by others in an organization as political. Perceptions of organizational politics have been associated with decreased job satisfaction, increased anxiety and stress, increased turnover, and reduced performance.[54] To mitigate the negative outcomes associated with perceptions of political behavior, there are two main approaches. The first is to develop political skill, and the second is to consider the ethical implications of organizational politics. Political skill has been defined as follows:

 Leader Corruption

> the ability to effectively understand others at work, and to use such knowledge to influence others to act in ways that enhance one's personal and/or organizational objectives.[55]

Political skill is essential for making all of the tactics and reciprocities described in this chapter work. The Toolkit Activity at the end of this chapter contains a self-assessment that you can complete to assess your political acumen.

The second approach to mitigate the negative impact of perceptions of politics is to ask whether the use of power, influence, and/or political skill in an organization to obtain outcomes that you prefer is ethical. The answer is that it depends on the goals and objectives being pursued in part. The ethical use of power and influence as well as **ethical leadership** have become important research agendas in OB. Next, we discuss how to apply ethics to the use of power and influence, followed by new theories of leadership that emphasize ethics, service to followers, and being authentic.

 Critical Thinking Question: In addition to the goals and objectives of an influence attempt, what are other ethical concerns regarding the use of political skills in organizations?

ETHICAL LEADERSHIP

Learning Objective 2.7: Describe ethical leadership, and explain its importance.

Leadership and ethics are intertwined, and the exercise of power and influence is an area where the tests described in the boxed insert must be applied. Ethical decision making is important to the practice of leadership and contemporary theories of leadership address morality. Research on ethical leadership has found four components:

- Moral sensitivity involves recognizing that our behavior *impacts* others.
- Moral judgment involves determining the right decision.
- Moral motivation is having the need to do the right thing.
- Moral action.[56]

Ethical leadership has been found to be negatively related to work group–level ethical behavior and relationship conflict among coworkers.[57] If leaders at the top of the organization were viewed as ethical by their followers then ethics had a cascading effect throughout the organization; lower-level employees also view their manager as ethical.[58] Thus, ethical leadership at the top of an organization has a trickle-down effect to lower organizational levels. The moral component is emerging as a key aspect of contemporary leadership theories. Next, we will discuss two other recent approaches to leadership that directly incorporate aspects of morality: servant and authentic leadership.

SERVANT AND AUTHENTIC LEADERSHIP

Learning Objective 2.8: Compare and contrast authentic and servant leadership.

As indicated previously, there is a "new wave" of leadership research that emphasizes morality. In addition to ethical leadership, two other theories have emerged: servant leadership[59] and authentic leadership.[60,61] While research on these theories is relatively new, findings indicate that followers respond positively to these leader behaviors. Servant leadership dates back to the 1970s when Robert Greenleaf was inspired about leadership while reading Herman Hesse's *Journey to the East*. In this novel, a group of men undertake a long journey. A servant named Leo sings to them and inspires them while doing his tasks. Leo disappears along the way, and the group falls into chaos and cannot complete their

BEST PRACTICES

Power and Ethics: Making Tough Choices

Perhaps the most important point about the use of influence in organizations is the ethical use of power and politics for leaders. We only need to think of the scandal where a Manhattan jury found Dennis Kozlowski and Mark Swartz guilty of stealing more than $150 million from Tyco through fraud in the sale of company shares and falsification of company records. Leaders must apply ethical tests to every action they take in the organization using the tactics in this chapter. *How Good People Make Tough Choices* provides a nine-step checklist you may use to determine if they are being ethical in their dealings with others:[62]

1. Recognize that there is a moral issue.
2. Determine the actor (and the players) in the issue.
3. Gather the facts.
4. Test for right vs. wrong: four tests.

   o Is it legal?
   o Does it feel right at the gut level?

   o Would you want to see this on the front page?
   o What would your mother/family think?

5. Test for right vs. right (when both options seem moral): e.g., truth vs. loyalty (hard decisions).
6. Apply the appropriate ethical principles (e.g., utilitarian, rights, justice).
7. Is there a third way through the dilemma?
8. Make the decision.
9. Revisit and reflect.

Discussion Questions:

1. Provide an example of the utilitarian approach in organizations (think of a decision that does the most good for the most people).
2. How does the utilitarian approach in your example differ from focusing on individual rights? What would you do differently if focusing on individual rights?
3. What approach do you think most leaders use in practice?

Source: Kidder, R. M. (2003). *How good people make tough choices: Resolving the dilemmas of ethical living.* New York: HarperCollins.

journey. The basic idea is that followers are first rather than leaders. Greenleaf's definition of the servant leader is as follows:

> The servant-leader *is* servant first. . . . It begins with the natural feeling that one wants to serve, to serve *first*. Then conscious choice brings one to aspire to lead. That person is sharply different from one who is *leader* first, perhaps because of the need to assuage an unusual power drive or to acquire material possessions.[63]

Researchers have recently developed measures of servant leadership, and it has been shown to relate to positive attitudes and performance of followers.[64] Seven servant leadership dimensions have been identified: emotional healing, creating value for the community, conceptual skills, empowering, helping subordinates grow and succeed, putting subordinates first, and behaving ethically.[65,66] Servant leaders facilitate team confidence, affirming the strengths and potential of the team and providing developmental support.[67] This developmental support is also characteristic of **humble leadership** where a leader's humility allows them to show followers how to grow as a result of work. This leads followers to believe that their own developmental journeys are legitimate in the workplace.[68]

Authentic leadership involves knowing oneself and behaving in a way that is consistent with what is intuitively right.[69] Authentic leadership has four dimensions:[70]

- **Self-awareness**—for example, seeks feedback to improve interactions with others
- **Relational transparency**—for example, says exactly what he or she means
- **Internalized moral perspective**—for example, demonstrates beliefs that are consistent with actions
- **Balanced processing**—for example, solicits views that challenge his or her deeply held positions.

These leadership theories seem to sound alike, but they also have some differences so it is important to compare and contrast them. Table 2.3 shows a comparison of transformational leadership (which we discussed earlier in this chapter under full-range leadership development), ethical leadership, authentic leadership, and servant leadership. As you can see from the table, there are some similarities among these approaches to leadership, but there are also some key differences. Transformational leadership is probably the most unique but does share some aspects of servant leadership.

 Critical Thinking Questions: Compare and contrast ethical, servant, and authentic leadership. What do they have in common, and what are the key differences?

Table 2.3 Comparison of Authentic, Transformational, Ethical, and Servant Leadership Theories

Theoretical Components	Authentic Leadership	Ethical Leadership	Transformational Leadership	Servant Leadership
Leader self-awareness	✓			✓
Relationship transparency	✓		*	
Internalized moral perspective	✓	✓	✓	
Balanced processing	✓		*	
Moral person	✓	✓	✓	✓
Moral manager	*	✓	*	✓
Idealized influence	*	✓	✓	
Inspirational motivation			✓	
Intellectual stimulation			✓	
Individualized consideration		*	✓	
Emotional healing				✓
Value for community				✓
Conceptual skills	*		✓	✓
Empowering			*	✓
Helping subordinates grow and succeed			✓	✓
Putting subordinates first			✓	✓
Behaving ethically		✓		✓
Relationships	✓		✓	✓
Servanthood				✓

✓ = focal component, * = minor or implicit component

Source: Adapted from Walumbwa, F., Avolio, B., Gardner, W., Wernsing, T. and Peterson, S. (2008). Authentic leadership: Development and validation of a theory-based measure. *Journal of Management, 34,* 89–126.

LEADERSHIP IMPLICATIONS: DEVELOPING RELATIONSHIPS AND LEADING ETHICALLY

This chapter covered the essential core leadership theories that will be referenced throughout the remainder of this textbook. For example, to motivate effectively, leaders need to build trust and establish high-quality relationships with their followers (Chapters 7 and 8). Leadership matters in teams (Chapter 9) as well. Leaders play an important role in the implementation of organizational change through transformational leadership and helping employees cope with change (Chapter 15).

At the heart of leadership is the relationship that emerges between a leader and a follower. This chapter reviewed theories that relate to the development of high-quality relationships that are based upon trust. If you are in the role of follower, guidelines for managing your boss were provided. Leadership is a two-way influence process, and this chapter also covered power and influence. Some proactive influence tactics are positive and some are negative. Thus, the use of influence must be guided by the leader's sense of what is right and ethical. Leadership ethics is another important theme throughout this textbook, and several chapters discuss the ethical implications of OB approaches.

There has been an increase in attention to ethics and morality in the study of leadership in the past 10 years. Following the scandals of Enron, Tyco, and others, researchers in OB responded by working on new theories that incorporate a moral component and placing followers first. These theories discuss the ethical leadership role and how leaders today must be authentic and serve followers rather than their own goals exclusively. These emerging theories are a good example of how OB research responds to current challenges organizations face and how researchers generate new knowledge to guide leaders. The study of ethics and morality in leadership will continue to be of interest to OB researchers as they continue to demonstrate relationships of ethical leadership with employee well-being and performance. Development of these new approaches now appears in textbooks for students and in corporate training programs to sensitize the next generation of managers to ethical aspects of leadership and improve leadership practice.

KEY TERMS

apprising, 43

authentic leadership, 46

calculus-based trust (CBT), 35

coalition, 43

collaboration, 43

consultation, 43

counterdependent, 33

ethical leadership, 45

humble leadership, 47

identification-based trust (IBT), 36

influence, 38

TOOLKIT

inspirational appeals, 43
interdependent, 33
knowledge-based
    trust (KBT), 35
law of reciprocity, 43
leader–member exchange
    (LMX), 28
mentoring, 33

out-group members, 28
overdependent, 33
perceptions of organizational
    politics, 44
personal appeals, 43
personal power, 39
political skill, 44
position power, 39
power, 38

proactive influence tactics, 41
rational persuasion, 43
servant leadership, 35
three "lines" of power, 40
transactional leadership, 26
transformational leadership, 26
zone of indifference, 40

SUGGESTIONS FOR FURTHER READING

Avolio, B. J. (2011). *Full range leadership development* (2nd ed.). Thousand Oaks, CA: Sage.

Barnard, C. (1938). *Functions of the executive.* Cambridge, MA: Harvard University Press.

Bennis, W. G. (2009). *On becoming a leader.* New York, NY: Basic Books.

Blanchard, K., Olmstead, C., & Lawrence, M. (2013). *Trust works! Four keys to building lasting relationships.* New York, NY: HarperCollins.

Cohen, A. R., & Bradford, D. L. (2005). *Influence without authority* (2nd ed.). New York, NY: Wiley.

Kidder, R. M. (2003). *How good people make tough choices: Resolving the dilemmas of ethical living.* New York, NY: HarperCollins.

Kouzes, J. M., & Posner, B. Z. (2007). *The leadership challenge* (4th ed). San Francisco, CA: Jossey-Bass.

TOOLKIT ACTIVITY 2.1

Applying the Full-Range Leadership Development Model

These short cases provide an opportunity to practice applying the full-range leadership development model. For each case, select the leadership approach you would take and explain why.

Case 1

Because of organizational restructuring directives from your boss, your department must reassign team members to new project teams. You are thinking of asking a highly capable and experienced member of your work group to handle these reassignments. This person has always been dependable and a high performer. She also has positive working relationships with other team members. She is very willing to help with the reassignments. What would you do? Circle it.

A. Do nothing and hope the problem takes care of itself.

B. Allow your follower to complete the reassignments, and tell her she may have the afternoon off when it is completed.

C. Allow your follower to complete the reassignments and only intervene if you notice a problem.

D. Allow your follower to complete the reassignments, and watch to see if she makes mistakes and then intervene to correct them.

E. Mentor your follower one on one, and discuss how doing this task will help her learn new skills. Remind her of how important the restructuring is to the overall vision and strategy of the organization, and be a positive role model.

Identify the approach from the full-range leadership development model (e.g., transactional/management by exception, passive [MBEP], or transformational four I's):

Explain why you would use this approach, citing the full-range leadership development model:

Case 2

You have noticed that one of your team members is not following through on the part of a project assigned to her. She is very motivated and has told you she wants a promotion; however, her recent actions are contradictory to her goal. The current staffing situation does not allow you to reassign the project to someone else in your work group. What would you do? Circle it.

A. Do nothing and hope the problem takes care of itself.

B. Tell her that if she wants the promotion she will need to finish the project in 1 week.

C. Allow your follower to complete the task and only intervene if you notice a problem.

D. Allow your follower to complete the task and watch to see if they make mistakes and then intervene to correct them.

E. Mentor your follower one on one, and discuss how doing this task will help them learn new skills. Remind them of how important the project is to the overall vision and strategy of the organization, and be a positive role model.

Identify the approach from the full-range leadership development model (e.g., transactional/MBEP or transformational four I's):

Explain why you would use this approach, citing the full-range leadership development model:

Source: Cases adapted from Hersey, P. & Blanchard, K. H. (1988). *Management of organizational behavior: Utilizing human resources*, Englewood Cliffs, NJ: Prentice-Hall.

CASE STUDY 2.1

Which Boss Would You Rather Work For?

Ting works for an export company in China. Last year, Ting encountered a financial difficulty because her bank required her to have a large deposit in order to buy a house. Ting approached the owner of the company and requested to receive her salary for the next half year in advance. The owner listened to her situation and convened a meeting with other high-level managers. After discussion, the company decided not only to pay for her salary in advance but also to assign a team of people to help her move into her new house. Afterward, Ting became even more dedicated to her job and the organization. She was already a good performer, but she became one of the best employees in the company. She proactively advocated and protected the reputation of the company outside the organization. For example, an unsatisfied customer once complained about the service of the bank during a dinner party Ting was attending. Noticing the customer's dissatisfaction, she interrupted the customer and promised that she would take him to lunch where they would talk and solve his problem.

Lisa had recently graduated from college with a bachelor's degree in accounting and landed her dream job as an accountant/analyst at a financial services company. Lisa was excited about the new opportunity to showcase her skills and contribute to the company. On her first day, Lisa arrived early to make a good impression. Her new boss, Samantha, didn't give Lisa a tour of the department. To make matters worse, no one in the office acknowledged her presence or introduced themselves to her. Samantha quickly put Lisa to work, however. Her first task was to prepare a bank reconciliation. She had completed similar tasks in class, but this was more complex. Lisa began working on it but got stuck. She went to Samantha for help, but Samantha told her to figure it out by herself. Lisa was shocked at Samantha's response and felt overwhelmed by her new job. She returned to her desk and continued to work on the reconciliation, which took her 3 days to complete. Although she was proud of herself for completing it, she was still hurt that her boss wouldn't help her and worried that she was not capable of handling her new position. Over the next year that Lisa worked for the company, Samantha never provided Lisa feedback on her work or provided any training beyond the videos on harassment and discrimination required by corporate headquarters. As a result, Lisa spent most of her days in her office alone. After a year, she took a job at another company.

Discussion Questions

1. Compare the experiences of the two employees (Ting and Lisa). Which boss would you rather work for? Why?
2. Think about the leadership theories that were covered in this chapter, and determine which leadership styles are exemplified in the two scenarios. Which ones should have been used?
3. What steps could Lisa have taken to develop a higher-quality LMX relationship or "manage her boss" more effectively? Do you think this would work in this case?
4. What were the outcomes for each of the employees and companies in these two scenarios? Thinking about these outcomes, why is it important for organizations to have effective leaders?

SELF-ASSESSMENT 2.1

What's Your Level of Political Acumen?

This self-assessment exercise identifies your level of political acumen in four areas determined by research. There is no "one best" approach; all approaches have strengths and weaknesses, and the goal is for you to learn about your political skill and think of ways to improve it. There are no right or wrong answers, and this is not a test. You don't have to share your results with the others unless you wish to do so. We will discuss the interpretations of this assessment in class.

Part I. Taking the Assessment

Instructions: Circle the response that best describes your behavior.

As an example, the answer to a statement could look like this:

I like a lot of variety at work.

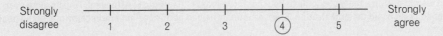

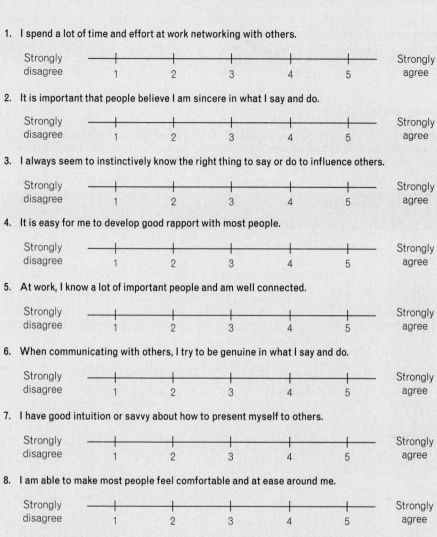

1. I spend a lot of time and effort at work networking with others.

    Strongly
    disagree   1   2   3   4   5   Strongly
    agree

2. It is important that people believe I am sincere in what I say and do.

    Strongly
    disagree   1   2   3   4   5   Strongly
    agree

3. I always seem to instinctively know the right thing to say or do to influence others.

    Strongly
    disagree   1   2   3   4   5   Strongly
    agree

4. It is easy for me to develop good rapport with most people.

    Strongly
    disagree   1   2   3   4   5   Strongly
    agree

5. At work, I know a lot of important people and am well connected.

    Strongly
    disagree   1   2   3   4   5   Strongly
    agree

6. When communicating with others, I try to be genuine in what I say and do.

    Strongly
    disagree   1   2   3   4   5   Strongly
    agree

7. I have good intuition or savvy about how to present myself to others.

    Strongly
    disagree   1   2   3   4   5   Strongly
    agree

8. I am able to make most people feel comfortable and at ease around me.

    Strongly
    disagree   1   2   3   4   5   Strongly
    agree

9. I am good at using my connections and networks to make things happen at work.

    Strongly
    disagree   1   2   3   4   5   Strongly
    agree

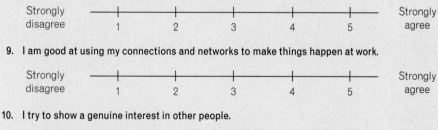

10. I try to show a genuine interest in other people.

    Strongly
    disagree   1   2   3   4   5   Strongly
    agree

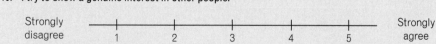

11. I am particularly good at sensing the motivations and hidden agendas of others.

    Strongly
    disagree   1   2   3   4   5   Strongly
    agree

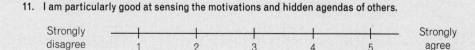

TOOLKIT

12. I am able to communicate easily and effectively with others.

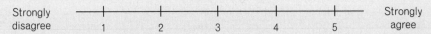

Strongly disagree   1   2   3   4   5   Strongly agree

Part II. Scoring Instructions

In Part I, you rated yourself on 12 questions. Add the numbers you circled in each of the columns to derive your score for the four political skills. During class, we will discuss each approach, its strengths and weaknesses, and how you can develop your political acumen.

Networking Ability	Apparent Sincerity	Social Astuteness	Interpersonal Influence
1. _____	2. _____	3. _____	4. _____
5. _____	6. _____	7. _____	8. _____
9. _____	10. _____	11. _____	12. _____
Total _____	_____	_____	_____

Source: Adapted from Ferris et al. (2005). Development and validation of the political skill inventory. *Journal of Management, 31,* 126–152.

SECTION II

UNDERSTANDING INDIVIDUALS IN ORGANIZATIONS

Chapter 3 • Individual Differences

Chapter 4 • Attitudes and Job Satisfaction

Chapter 5 • Perception

Chapter 6 • Individual Decision Making

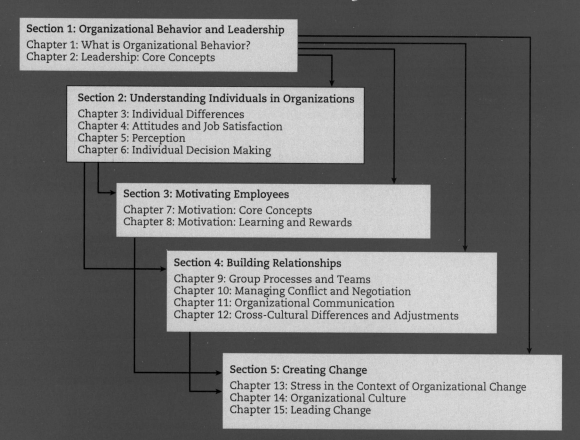

Section 1: Organizational Behavior and Leadership

Chapter 1: What is Organizational Behavior?
Chapter 2: Leadership: Core Concepts

Section 2: Understanding Individuals in Organizations

Chapter 3: Individual Differences
Chapter 4: Attitudes and Job Satisfaction
Chapter 5: Perception
Chapter 6: Individual Decision Making

Section 3: Motivating Employees

Chapter 7: Motivation: Core Concepts
Chapter 8: Motivation: Learning and Rewards

Section 4: Building Relationships

Chapter 9: Group Processes and Teams
Chapter 10: Managing Conflict and Negotiation
Chapter 11: Organizational Communication
Chapter 12: Cross-Cultural Differences and Adjustments

Section 5: Creating Change

Chapter 13: Stress in the Context of Organizational Change
Chapter 14: Organizational Culture
Chapter 15: Leading Change

3

INDIVIDUAL DIFFERENCES

THE RIGHT STUFF AT THE WRONG TIME?

On July 1, 2013, Mark Pincus, the founder and CEO of Zynga, resigned as CEO of the Internet gaming company and announced that he had "fired himself." The Internet gaming company was a rising star but experienced difficulties maintaining market share following its IPO in December 2011. Pincus hired Don Mattick, former head of Microsoft's Xbox division, to replace him.[1] While Pincus remained at Zynga as chairman and chief product officer, the organization needed a different type of leadership style to address the persistent company problems of a company culture that was widely viewed as toxic and employees quitting in droves. Markowitz cited the research of Noam Wasserman who studied founder–CEO succession and concluded that founders often find it difficult to remain as CEO as the company grows and the organization adds employees.[2] A different leadership skill set is needed to manage others, and 80% of the time the founder is not able to make the adjustment to leader of a larger and more complex organization. For example, they may keep the original management team on board and be reluctant to make changes to ensure long-term market success and continued growth. The technical guru with the brilliant idea for an Internet start-up might not have the right personality for the demands of leading a large organization, which include leadership and political skill. However, in 2015, Pincus returned to Zynga after two years of lackluster stock performance under Mattick. To survive against competitors like King (Candy Crush), Zynga will have to become innovative again. The question is whether Pincus' leadership style will change.[3] From this example, it is clear that understanding individual differences is essential for being an effective leader.

Learning Objectives

After studying this chapter, you should be able to do the following:

3.1: Define *personality*, and discuss the role of heredity.

3.2: Summarize the elements of psychological capital.

3.3: Illustrate, with an example, why moods matter at the workplace.

3.4: Explain the implications of organizational neuroscience including ethics.

3.5: Compare and contrast surface-level and deep-level diversity.

3.6: Name the characteristics of four generations at work, and describe how millennials will affect organizations.

3.7: Explain the guidelines for leading diverse workers.

3.8: Develop an example of a leader practicing mindful coaching with a follower.

Get the edge on your studies at edge.sagepub.com/scandura

- Take the chapter quiz
- Review key terms with eFlashcards
- Explore multimedia resources, SAGE readings, and more!

$SAGE edge™

WHAT IS PERSONALITY?

Learning Objective 3.1: Define *personality*, and discuss the role of heredity.

Understanding your own **personality**—and the personalities of others—is critical. This is because personality and other individual differences are relatively stable over the life course. For example, personality has been generally defined as "regularities in feeling, thought and action that are characteristic of an individual."[4] Also, personality matters because it is linked to social behavior in organizations. Personality may affect our work habits and how we interact with our coworkers. However, personality and most individual differences aren't like other areas of organizational behavior (OB) where the manager can influence the outcomes by intervention. Individual differences are aspects of OB that must be *understood*, and leaders must often work with them rather than try to change people. This is why we often hear people speak about two people who just don't get along as a "personality clash." As the example of Marc Pincus suggests, a real question for Zynga is whether he will be able to adapt and change his leadership style or whether it is related to personality traits that remain constant. Next, we will discuss research that addresses whether personality can change.

The Role of Heredity

Can a brilliant engineer who is introverted change his personality and become an extraverted visionary leader? In other words, are personality traits inborn or learned? This question has been addressed by the famous **Minnesota twin studies**. To conduct this research, twins born in Minnesota from 1936 through 1955 were asked to join a registry.[5] Identical twins (monozygotic and dizygotic reared apart, MZAs and DZAs, respectively) were confirmed through birth records, and 80% of the surviving, intact pairs were located and recruited for participation in various psychological studies. Some twins were reared apart for various reasons (e.g., adoption). These twins tell us a great deal about the contribution of heredity compared to the child rearing environment. A study showed that 50% of the variation in occupational choice (whether a person is a dentist or a soldier, for example) is due to heredity.[6] Most people are surprised to learn this. Another study of MZA and DZA twins showed that 40% of the variance in values related to work motivation could be attributed to heredity whereas 60% was due to the environment (and measurement error).[7] The implications for a leader are that while personality might change, most psychologists believe that it is a relatively stable individual difference. Instead of trying to change a coworker's personality, it is perhaps better to learn about personality differences, understand how different personalities operate at work, and then learn to work effectively with different types. Psychologists have developed inventories (personality tests) to assess personality differences. These tests are useful in training programs on conflict resolution and team building.

Myers-Briggs Type Indicator

The Myers-Briggs Type Indicator (MBTI) is the most often administered personality test to nonpsychiatric populations (i.e., the "well population").[8] The publishers of the MBTI, Consulting Psychologists Press, report that over 2 million people take the MBTI every year.

Because it was developed and normed on "well people," it has been a popular approach with organizations and is used by Hallmark, GE, and many other large organizations in their leadership training and development programs. The MBTI was developed by a mother and daughter team, Katherine Briggs and Isabel Myers-Briggs, following World War II and is based upon the personality theories of Carl Jung.[9] The MBTI is based upon four general personality preferences:

- Introversion (I) vs. extraversion (E): Extraverts tend to be outgoing; introverts tend to be shy.
- Sensing (S) vs. intuition (N): Sensing types tend to be practical; intuitive people tend to be "idea people."
- Thinking (T) vs. feeling (F): Thinking types tend to use logic; feeling types tend to use emotion.
- Judging (J) vs. perceiving (P): Judging types tend to make quick decisions; perceiving types tend to be more flexible.

People who take the MBTI are then grouped into 16 personality "types" based on these characteristics. For example, an ENTP would be extraverted, intuitive, thinking, and perceiving. This person might be attracted to starting their own business, for example. In contrast, an INTJ is introverted, intuitive, thinking, and judging and may be attracted to a scientific career. ISTJs are detail-oriented and practical, where ESTJs are organizers and may be comfortable in managerial roles.

Limitations of the Myers-Briggs Type Indicator

There has been limited research support for the reliability and validity of the MBTI. If you take the test again, you may not receive the same score, and the matter of whether people are actually classifiable into the 16 categories is questionable.[10,11] However, the MBTI remains the most popular personality test in use for organizations. Also, it is important to note that the MBTI has not been validated for selection; in other words, its publisher makes it clear that you should not use the MBTI to hire people for particular jobs in an organization.[12]

 Critical Thinking Questions: Given the limited research support for the MBTI, what are the concerns regarding organizations continuing to use it?

How the Myers-Briggs Type Indicator Is Used in Organizations

The best uses for the MBTI appears to be for conflict resolution and team building, and this is where it is most often used in management training programs and classrooms. The value of the MBTI is to enable people in organizations to discuss personality differences in their approach to work in a nonjudgmental way. All of the labels in the MBTI are neutral; it is not better or worse to be judging or perceiving, for example. Briggs and Myers-Briggs titled their book *Gifts Differing*, and this captures the essence of this approach to understanding personality. At the workplace, everyone has something to offer, and it takes all types of people for teams and organizations to be effective. For a leader, this underscores the importance of understanding individual differences because to build effective teams, everyone needs to feel valued to be engaged. The MBTI is, of course, not the only personality assessment available; next, we will discuss another personality theory that has had more research support (although it is currently not as well-known as the MBTI to most practicing managers and the general population). This personality assessment is known as the "Big Five" personality theory.

The Big 5 Personality Traits

"The Big Five"

After much research examining personality inventories, the developers of the Big Five theory of personality concluded that personality could be summarized using five factors: **openness, conscientiousness, extraversion, agreeableness,** and **neuroticism**.[13] These factors and their definitions are summarized in Table 3.1. Note that the table is organized such that the first letters of these personality traits are an acronym that spells *OCEAN*, and this will help you to remember them.

Openness is a person's willingness to embrace new ideas and new situations. Conscientiousness represents the characteristic of being a person who follows through and gets things done. Extraversion is a trait of a person who is outgoing, talkative, and sociable as well as enjoys social situations. Agreeableness is being a nice person in general. Finally, neuroticism represents a tendency to be anxious or moody (this trait is often referred to by its opposite: emotional stability). There has been a good deal of research on whether these five traits predict job performance, and results indicate that the conscientiousness dimension best predicts performance on the job (it makes sense that people who are achievement-oriented and dependable would be better employees and also better leaders).[14] This translates into success; conscientiousness is related to job satisfaction, income, and higher occupational status (e.g., being an executive, business owner, or professional).[15] While conscientiousness is the big one in terms of job performance, extraversion also has a moderate but significant relationship to performance, particularly in sales.[16]

Table 3.1 The Big Five Personality Characteristics	
Trait	Description
Openness	Being curious, original, intellectual, creative, and open to new ideas
Conscientiousness	Being organized, systematic, punctual, achievement oriented, and dependable
Extraversion	Being outgoing, talkative, sociable, and enjoying social situations
Agreeableness	Being affable, tolerant, sensitive, trusting, kind, and warm
Neuroticism	Being anxious, irritable, temperamental, and moody

Source: Barrick, M. R., & Mount, M. K. (2005). Yes, personality matters: Moving on to more important matters. *Human Performance, 18,* 359–372.

Other Big Five traits relate to other positive work outcomes. Research has also shown that emotional stability relates to the ability to cope with stress, and those with higher openness adjust better to organizational change.[17] Given the strong research support for the relationships of the Big Five personality variables and relevant performance and career outcomes, leaders need to know that instruments such as the Big Five inventories successfully predict performance and can be used as one component in making hiring decisions. For this reason, personality research has a great deal of practical utility for organizations. You can learn what your scores are on the Big Five personality dimensions by taking Self-Assessment 3.1 at the end of this chapter.

 Critical Thinking Question: What are the fairness issues involved in using personality tests for selection of new employees?

Personality Traits and Health Research

We have heard the phrase "stress kills," but is there any truth to this? Some years ago, cardiologists showed a link between a personality trait called **Type A behavior** and cardiovascular heart disease.[18] Their theory was based on observing patients in their waiting room; some sat patiently reading a magazine, for example. Others sat on the edge of their seats and got up frequently (they literally wore out the edges of the chairs and armrests!)[19] Friedman and Rosen conducted a study over a long period of time and asked questions such as the following:

- Do you feel guilty if you use spare time to relax?
- Do you need to win in order to derive enjoyment from games and sports?
- Do you generally move, walk, and eat rapidly?
- Do you often try to do more than one thing at a time?

Study respondents were then classified into one of three groups: Type A (competitive, aggressive), **Type B** (relaxed, easygoing), or **Type C** (nice, hardworking, people who try to appease others). By the end of this long-term study, 70% of the men who were classified has Type A had coronary heart disease. This study had several limitations including that it was only conducted on men who were middle-aged, and the researchers didn't take into account other factors such as the dietary habits of the study participants. However, this study generated media interest and led to additional research. A review of this research indicated that there is an association between Type A behavior (particularly hostility) and heart disease.[20] Examples of hostility-related questions are "Do you get irritated easily?" and "Are you bossy and domineering?"[21] And research has shown that the Type A behavior pattern (i.e., "stress energized") is exhibited in samples of women also.[22]

More recently, researchers have discussed an additional personality type and its relationship to health risks: the **Type D** personality. The Type D, also called the distressed personality, is a combination of negative affect ("I feel unhappy") and social inhibition ("I am unable to express myself"). Research indicated that the rates of recovery were lower for coronary heart disease patients with Type D personality.[23] A review of 10 studies of Type D personality concluded that "Type D patients are also at increased risk for psychological distress, psychosocial risk factors, impaired quality of life, and seem to benefit less from medical and

Leaders: Are They Born or Made?

With the research on the twins reared apart and evidence from the Big Five personality theory relating personality traits to leader emergence in groups, one question that arises is whether leaders are born to greatness or if leadership can be acquired by anyone. There are arguments on both sides of this issue among scholars of OB. Research suggests genetic factors contribute as much as 40% to the explanation of transformational leadership.[24] On the other hand, many people believe that transformational leadership can be learned, and experimental research has shown that leaders can be trained to exhibit charismatic behaviors and followers.[25] An integrative perspective suggests that leaders have certain inborn traits that predispose them to self-select into leadership positions.[26] Once hired into a leadership role, these people may respond to leadership training more than those who are not as interested in becoming leaders. The

best thinking on this at present is that leadership is most likely a combination of inborn and learned behavior. The implications for organizations are to carefully select those hired into leadership and then provide the training needed to enhance leader effectiveness. Those with innate leadership skills have an advantage, but an individual may be able to enhance his or her leadership capabilities.

Discussion Questions:

1. In your opinion, is leadership born (hereditary) or learned (through training, for example)? Support your position.
2. If leadership is both born and made as some researchers believe, what do you think is the best way to identify leadership potential?
3. What type of leadership training would you recommend to complement the selection process?

Sources: Arvey, R. D., Rotundo, M., Johnson, W., Zhang, Z., & McGue, M. (2006). The determinants of leadership role occupancy: Genetic and personality factors. *The Leadership Quarterly, 17,* 1–20; Howell, J., & Frost, P. (1989). A laboratory study of charismatic leadership. *Organizational Behavior and Human Decision Processes, 43,* 243–269; Judge, T. A., & Long, D. M. (2012). Individual differences in leadership. In D. V. Day & J. Antonakis (Eds.), *The nature of leadership* (pp. 179–217). Thousand Oaks, CA: Sage.

invasive treatment".[27] Thus, while research on personality and health risk continues, there seems to be a clear association between certain personality traits and higher risk of disease, suppressed immune system functioning, and slower recovery from illnesses.

Figure 3.1 summarizes the four personality types, and you can reflect on the checklist to get a sense of whether you fall into Type A, B, C, or D. This may be scary news if you think you may have Type A or D personality characteristics. However, there is some good news. Being able to express your emotions may also reflect a "healthy" Type A pattern.[28] Second, having a "hardy" personality (e.g., letting stress roll off of your back rather than ruminating on your problems) has been shown to reduce the potential for personality type to affect health.[29,30] Also, social support from family, friends, and coworkers can alleviate some of the detrimental effects of personality traits on health.[31]

 Critical Thinking Question: How might knowledge of whether you have the Type A personality affect your decision about taking a job in a high-stress environment?

Figure 3.1 Personality Types A, B, C, and D

TYPE A	TYPE B
_____ Thrives on change and fears routine	_____ Loves to have a good time
_____ Has an entrepreneurial streak	_____ Likes being the center of attention
_____ Enjoys taking risks and is driven to succeed	_____ Needs to be liked by others
_____ Is competitive and aggressive	_____ Tends to be talkative and outgoing
_____ Is impatient and is not a good listener	_____ Is relaxed and laid back
_____ Is persistent in getting what he/she wants	_____ Is not competitive and aggressive

TYPE C	TYPE D
_____ Takes everything seriously	_____ Doesn't like to take charge
_____ Thrives on details and accuracy	_____ Prefers a set of guidelines that he/she can follow
_____ Is predictable and dependable	_____ Is supportive of others
_____ Is loyal and patient	_____ Is punctual and consistent
_____ Is thoughtful and sensitive	_____ Is content and happy with life and himself/herself
_____ Likes facts	_____ Doesn't mind doing repetitive tasks

Given the discussion about the Type A behavior pattern previously, you may be wondering if there is any theory or research in OB that suggests that personality traits can change. Some scholars believe that certain personality characteristics are **state-like** instead of **trait-like** (such as Type A and the Big Five personality characteristics). By state-like, we mean that the characteristics are relatively changeable and that a person can develop them through either awareness and/or training. New research suggests that **psychological capital (PsyCap)** characteristics are more than fleeting states of mind but they are open to change. This is an emerging area of study within the movement called positive psychology, and research is showing promising results.

PSYCHOLOGICAL CAPITAL

Learning Objective 3.2: Summarize the elements of psychological capital.

Fred Luthans and his colleagues have articulated a four-part concept of PsyCap. Just like we have financial capital, these state-like qualities represent the *value of individual differences* at the workplace. In other words, PsyCap is more than "what you know" or "who you know." It is focused on "who you are" and "who you are becoming" (p. 388).[32] These four characteristics are as follows:

- **Efficacy**—a person's belief that they have the ability to execute a specific task in a given context
- **Optimism**—a positive outcome outlook or attribution of events, which includes positive emotions and motivation
- **Hope**—the *will* to succeed and the ability to identify and pursue the *path* to success
- **Resiliency**—coping in the face of risk or adversity; the ability to "bounce back" after a setback[33]

While research on PsyCap is relatively new as an area of study for individual differences, initial results show that the four elements predict job performance and satisfaction[34] and that training interventions may increase PsyCap.[35] Thus, PsyCap is important for human development, but it is also related to an organization's competitive advantage due to its impact on job performance.[36] Figure 3.2 summarizes the relationships of the four PsyCap elements and organizational outcomes that relate to the competitive advantage of organizations.

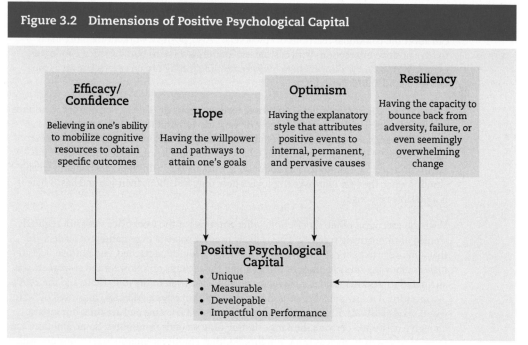

Figure 3.2 Dimensions of Positive Psychological Capital

Efficacy/ Confidence
Believing in one's ability to mobilize cognitive resources to obtain specific outcomes

Hope
Having the willpower and pathways to attain one's goals

Optimism
Having the explanatory style that attributes positive events to internal, permanent, and pervasive causes

Resiliency
Having the capacity to bounce back from adversity, failure, or even seemingly overwhelming change

Positive Psychological Capital
- Unique
- Measurable
- Developable
- Impactful on Performance

Source: Adapted from Luthans, F., & Youssef, C. M. (2004). Investing in People for Competitive Advantage. *Organizational Dynamics, 33*(2), p. 152.

Emotional
Contagion

PsyCap variables are relatively stable but can change. However, there is research in OB on states or things that change frequently—over the course of a day or even hours. These are known as **emotions and moods,** and research demonstrates that they also significantly impact OB. For example, a study of PsyCap and organizational change showed that efficacy, hope, optimism, and resiliency were related to positive emotions at work, which in turn affected the acceptance of organizational change.[37] Experiencing positive emotions enhanced the role of PsyCap in explaining *why* employees were less cynical and showed more citizenship during the change. Thus, emotions and moods play an important role in OB in explaining how personality traits translate into improved attitudes and performance.

EMOTIONS AND MOODS AT WORK

Learning Objective 3.3: Illustrate, with an example, why moods matter at the workplace.

Unfortunately, we have all had the experience of being treated rudely either in person or on the phone by a customer service representative when trying to inquire about a billing error. We wonder, "Why is this person such a crab?" Research on emotions at work seeks to address this question. Positive emotion such as pride in one's work can transform organizations and the people in them.[38] This is because positive emotions open peoples' minds, and they begin to build personal and social resources, which enable them to work more effectively. Positive emotions can be contagious: A person's positive outlook at work can affect the emotional reactions of coworkers.[39] Also, positive workers are more likely to have positive interactions with customers. Emotions serve to both broaden employee experiences and then allow them to build better functioning organizations known as the broaden-and-build model.[40]

Despite the clear implications of employee feelings about the experience of work, emotions and moods were largely ignored in most of the early OB literature. This was largely because it was expected that leaders (and their followers) behave in a rational manner at the workplace. However, as you saw in Chapter 1, Hoppock published a measure of job satisfaction or how employees feel about their work in 1935 (this measure contains strong emotion since the first item asks employees how they feel about their job and has "I hate it" is a possible response).

With the exception of job satisfaction, other emotions at the workplace were not regularly studied until relatively recently. This is likely because societal expectations of leaders are that—in order to be most effective—they should be logical, detached, and rational decision makers. Showing one's feelings or caring about the feelings of followers and coworkers was attributed to weakness and not sound leadership. However, in the mid-1980s and the 1990s, organizational researchers began studying the effects of affect. Affect is comprised of both emotions and moods. Emotions are triggered by specific events and are brief but intense enough to disrupt a person's thinking—lasting only seconds or minutes. Some emotions are internal to a person, such as pride and love.[41] Other emotions emerge in relationships with others such as shame and guilt.[42] Moods, on the other hand, are general feeling states that are not related to a something that happens to a person, but they are not intense enough to interrupt regular thought patterns or work.[43]

Moods are generally more enduring than emotions. **Positive and negative affect** are the most often-studied moods at the workplace (i.e., being happy or sad). Research has shown that happier people perform better and have higher incomes.[44,45,46] Mood at the start of the workday (i.e., "waking up on the wrong side of the bed") related to perceptions of customer emotions in a call center, and this affected the employees' mood after the calls.[47] Positive affect was, in turn, related to performance quality whereas negative affect was negatively related to productivity. The results of this research study are summarized in Figure 3.3. The start-of-workday mood affected their perceptions of customers' moods, which in turn affected their own moods. These moods were related to performance quality and quantity. So if you get up on the wrong side of the bed in the morning, pay attention to your mood. You just might be less productive that day.

Even groups can exhibit a bad mood. **Aggregating** (adding up) responses to a measure of mood from individuals in groups has found that mood can be defined for a group and it is consistent within work groups; thus, groups can be characterized as having a negative mood.[48] Also, the "group mood" appears to affect the moods of individuals in the group according to George. In other words, if a group is positive, then members of the group typically experience positive mood states as well.

Figure 3.3 The Effects of Mood, Work Events, and Employee Affect on Performance

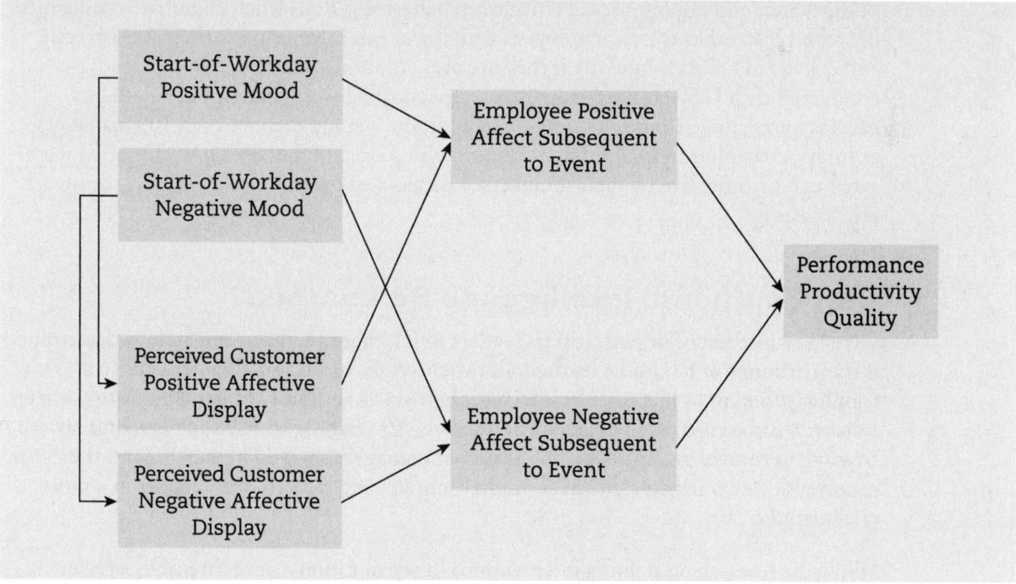

Source: Rothbard, N. P., & Wilks, S. L. (2011). Waking up on the right or wrong side of the bed: Start-of-workday mood, work events, employee affect, and performance. *Academy of Management Journal, 54*(5), 959–980. p. 963.

Critical Thinking Question: Do you think a leader should suppress his emotions and moods to be effective? Why or why not?

Hopefully, this review of current research has convinced you that emotions and feelings during the workday do matter. Some leaders are more adept than others at reading the emotions and/or moods of coworkers or customers. There has been a great deal of research and practitioner interest in recent years on understanding the individual difference called **emotional intelligence (EI)**, and next we will review the EI research.

Emotional Intelligence

Research from the field of psychology shows emotional regulation may be a form of intelligence.[49,50] Organizational leaders and human resource professionals find this concept, EI, relevant to the workplace. EI may be more important for long-term success than IQ. EI is considered to have three aspects:[51]

1. **Self-awareness**—recognizing your emotions when you experience them
2. **Other awareness**—being aware of emotions experienced by others
3. **Emotion regulation**—being able to recover from experienced emotions rapidly

EI is related to job performance.[52] For example, EI becomes a stronger predictor of performance and organizational citizenship behavior (OCB) when cognitive intelligence decreases.[53] In other words, employees with lower intelligence perform tasks correctly and engage in OCBs frequently if they are also emotionally intelligent. In a study conducted with U.S. Air Force recruiters, aspects of EI were found to be related to success in meeting recruiting quotas.[54] In addition, a study of more than 300 managers at Johnson & Johnson found that managers who scored higher on a measure of EI were rated as more effective by their followers.[55] EI has also been shown to predict teamwork effectiveness.[56]

Can Emotional Intelligence Be Learned?

Given the interest of organizational leaders in EI, there has been research to determine if the attributes of EI can be learned. In other words, can we send employees to a training program to increase their EI and improve their ability to get along with others? Research has compared managers who received EI training to a group receiving no training (a control group). After the training, managers showed higher EI, and they also reported lower work-related stress, higher morale, and treated one another in a more civil manner.[57,58]

While the research on training interventions in organizations is not extensive, a review of training interventions from diverse fields including OB, education, mental health, and sports and concluded that "it is possible to increase emotional intelligence and that such training has the potential to lead to other positive outcomes."[59]

The process through which people increase their EI (and sustain it) follows five stages of discovery:[60]

 Intelligence and Performance

1. The first discovery: Who do I want to be?
2. The second discovery: Who am I? What are my strengths and gaps?
3. The third discovery: How can I build on strengths and reduce the gaps?
4. The fourth discovery: Trying new behaviors, thoughts, and feelings
5. The fifth discovery: Developing trusting relationships that enable change

Limitations of Emotional Intelligence

EI has supporters. However, there have also been criticisms that the concept is too vague and can't be measured.[61,62,63] A critical review of the literature on EI in the workplace concluded initial claims of predictive value of EI may have been overstated.[64] A meta-analysis review of 69 studies reported a modest but significant correlation between EI and performance.[65]

How Emotional Intelligence Is Used in Organizations

Despite its critics, the EI concept has definitely impacted the workplace through EI training programs, specialized EI consultants, and articles in the business press and popular press.[66,67] The following summarizes what we can safely conclude about EI:[68]

1. EI is distinct from but positively related to other intelligences (such as IQ).
2. EI is an individual difference, where some people are more endowed and others are less so.
3. EI develops over a person's life span and can be enhanced through training.
4. EI involves, at least in part, individual's abilities to effectively identify and perceive emotion (in themselves and others), as well as possession of the skills to understand and manage those emotions successfully.

 Critical Thinking Question: What are the limits on the degree to which a person with low EI can change?

From the preceding discussion, it seems clear that emotions play an important role in the workplace. To this point, much of our discussion has been focused on relationships among coworkers. However, how leaders and employees interact with those outside the organization (including customers) is also important to organizational success. This is the focus of another area where there has been significant research: the study of **emotional labor.**

Emotional Labor: "Fake It Until You Make It"

As noted early, employees feel a range of emotions and moods during the course of the workday. However, they don't always show it. For example, if you have ever had a service job such as a waiter or waitress, you knew that you had to smile and be pleasant regardless of your emotions ("I am disgusted by your table manners!") or moods ("It's raining outside and I just feel blah"). Jobs that require employees to suppress affect (emotions and moods) are said to require emotional labor. Emotional labor is related to the effort required to effectively manage emotions to be successful on the job. All jobs have this requirement to some extent, but some have higher requirements than others (e.g., flight attendants, salespeople, customer service representatives, and nurses). The concept of emotional labor was introduced by Hochschild,[69] who investigated flight attendants and demonstrated that a significant part of their job was attending to the emotions of passengers. Emotional labor has also been studied with convenience store clerks, and customers and clerks had differing expectations of their roles and that clerks followed scripts (like actors in a role) to control customer service interactions.[70] Such acting may come with costs, however. Emotional labor (acting out service roles) has been related to emotional exhaustion and burnout.[71,72] So emotional labor while essential for high performance in certain jobs may also result in stress and strain on employees who must suppress their own emotions and moods (consider whether the magical people at Walt Disney World always feel magical, for example). Such strain may lead to coworkers to complain to one another rather than direct their negative emotions toward customers. When this happens, an **emotional contagion** effect may occur—the negative mood of one employee spreads to others in their group (like a virus, employees "catch" the negative moods of others).[73] But keep in mind that positive moods are also infectious—when an employee smiles at a customer or coworker their positive mood may spread.[74,75]

Affective Events Theory: An Organizing Framework

A proposal called affective events theory provides a useful summary of the material we have covered in this chapter thus far (see Figure 3.4).[76] This framework integrates personality, emotions, and moods and considers the impact of the work environment and events that may trigger emotional reactions (positive and negative affect). Areas in the work environment that leaders should pay close attention to are the characteristics of the job (e.g., Is it boring or interesting?), the job demands (e.g., Is the job just too difficult for the person to handle?), and the requirements for emotional labor (e.g., Does the person have to interact with the public and be courteous to irate customers?). Notice that in Figure 3.4, these work environment factors lead to work events such as daily hassles and uplifts (uplifts are moments when everything is going just great). Personality and moods play a role in how people react to hassles and uplifts. For example, a person low on emotional stability may have a stronger reaction to a daily hassle. Taken together, the work environment, events, personality, and moods combine to form an overall feeling of affect about work—positive or negative. This, in turn, leads to job satisfaction and performance. While research on affective events theory is new, it serves as a very useful way to summarize what we have covered in this chapter. This theory really puts it all together for us.

Another new development in the field of individual differences is the idea that we might be able to understand personality, emotions, and moods (for example) by studying the ways that our brains function biologically. Next, we will discuss an emerging field—brain science (or neuroscience)—which may help us understand OB in new ways.

NEUROSCIENCE

Learning Objective 3.4: Explain the implications of organizational neuroscience including ethics.

In addition to the potential of genetics to explain individual differences and personality, another emerging topic is **organizational neuroscience.** Neuroscience research is already impacting marketing and economics. The field of organizational neuroscience examines the potential of neuroscience to enhance prediction of OB. There is not a great deal of research in this area yet. Understanding how networks of brain systems operate may finally allow researchers to enter the "black box" to understand what happens in the brain when attitudes such as job satisfaction are experienced by people in organizations—for example, "mirror neurons" (brain processes that regulate a person's ability to imitate another person, either consciously or unconsciously) may increase understanding of role modeling, and learning through watching others at work.[77] Some attitudes may be embedded in a deeper part of the brain, making them implicit rather than explicit. For example, negative attitudes toward organizational change may be rooted in an older and deeper part of our brains making us react automatically rather than logically to change. Research on traits in leadership concludes that "research at the nexus of biology and psychology should yield interesting and high-impact research: It is likely that leadership researchers will start venturing further into this very fertile research landscape."[78]

Figure 3.4   Affective Events Theory (AET)

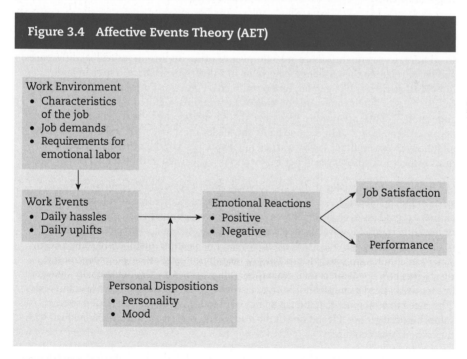

Source: Ashkanasy, N. M., & Daus, C. S. (2002). Emotion in the workplace: The new challenge for managers. *Academy of Management Executive, 16*(1), p. 77.

Ethical Issues in Neuroscience

Debates have already begun regarding the ethics of applying brain science to OB, and there are clearly issues that will need to be addressed.[79] One can imagine that knowledge of a person's brain chemistry may be employed to justify their promotion. On the other hand, this same knowledge might be employed to fire them. Would it be an invasion of privacy to be asked to submit to a brain scan in order to be hired for a position? Organizational neuroscience represents a potentially exciting field that would integrate OB theories with biology. However, the ethical concerns clearly need attention before this field moves from prediction to control and applications in organizational settings.

Neuroscience represents perhaps the deepest level of diversity since it underlies both surface characteristics and values. Other biological factors may be related to demographic characteristics such as sex and race. There is a great deal of research on diversity in organizational settings, and leaders can leverage it for competitive advantage.

Critical Thinking Question: Should there be governmental regulations on the applications of neuroscience in OB? Why or why not?

DIVERSITY

Learning Objective 3.5: Compare and contrast surface-level and deep-level diversity.

In addition to personality, there are a number of other important individual differences, and many relate to the challenges and value of a diverse workforce. These include individual attributes like gender, race or ethnicity, age, sexual orientation, and disability status: "Leadership is impossible outside of a community defined by shared values and vision."[80] Thus, we need to recognize that diversity poses a real challenge for organizational leaders. On the one hand, the leader must articulate a shared vision that all followers can embrace (as we learned in Chapter 2). On the other hand, the leader must respect the differences of her followers (as we learned in this chapter).

We first must acknowledge the powerful North American culture largely rooted in a sense of independence. Leaders need to create a shared culture that all followers can embrace regardless of such attributes as gender, race or ethnicity, age, sexual orientation, or disability status. However, leaders must also show discretion when balancing the needs of the organization with the needs of employees. For example, members of some Latin American cultures are somewhat casual with respect to being on time. Leaders must ask themselves how it will affect their team if they allow some workers to habitually show up late for work. Leaders must enforce organizational policies but do so in a respectful way. They need to remember that human beings want to belong and have a shared sense of values in social groups. Hence, one of the leader's top goals is to integrate individuals with the organization's culture.

Organizational cultures can be powerful forces (you will learn more about this in Chapter 14), but for now, note that strong cultures can bind individuals together—even those with diverse backgrounds. Leaders may be able to build consensus among diverse followers by relating to values held in common by the majority of people in the world (e.g., justice or personal happiness). It has become part of the leader's job to help diverse employees (particularly recent immigrants) adjust to the job and the organization's culture. Leading diverse followers is thus a process of adjustment, taking into account demographic differences as well as values and reactions to work.

The Multigenerational Workforce

Surface-Level and Deep-Level Diversity

The demographic attributes we typically think of when we think of "diversity" are called surface-level diversity because they are visible to observers. Surface-level diversity is defined as "differences among group members in overt, biological characteristics that are typically reflected in physical features."[81] A review of the research on surface-level diversity concluded that relationships of sex, race, and age had mixed results in the prediction of job performance and work attitude—that is, sometimes these demographic variables were related to performance and sometimes they were not. To fully understand diversity, we need to also consider deep-level diversity, which is defined as "differences among members' attitudes, beliefs, and values."[82] Research shows that prior studies that had predicted poor outcomes when groups were diverse should be interpreted with caution. This is because when deep-level diversity is considered, diversity may actually contribute positively to work group functioning and effectiveness. The values and attitudes of organizational members may matter more than surface characteristics. Another interesting diversity attribute is age; different generations have been shown by research to have different underlying mind-sets, and this may be a source of conflict at the workplace.

GENERATIONS AT THE WORKPLACE

Learning Objective 3.6: Name the characteristics of four generations at work, and describe how millennials will affect organizations.

Age is a demographic or surface-level diversity variable, but there are clear values and attitudes that have been shown to be related to what generation an employee belongs to. Much has been written about generations interacting at the workplace, and this poses some challenges for the leader. Table 3.2 shows the four generations now at the workplace, their characteristics, career goals, and work–life balance attitudes. The traditionalists were born between 1900 and 1945 and are retiring or passed on. However, trends indicate that people are retiring later than 65, so it can be expected that many will remain in the workforce for some time since retirement plans were dented by the great recession of 2007 to 2009. The boomers were born between 1946 and 1964 and are called this due to the baby boom that occurred after World War II (also called the "me" generation or yuppies for young upwardly mobile professionals). They had significant influence throughout their lives and brought about the social changes experienced in the 1960s. The generation Xers, or gen Xers, were born between 1965 and 1980 and are sometimes referred to as the "baby busters" or "latchkey kids" because many of them had to let themselves into their homes after school because their parents were both at work. Now the millennials are entering the workforce and having a clear impact on organizations (and they are the largest group in the general population). They were born between 1981 and 1999 and look for flexibility and choice.

Table 3.2 Four Generations at the Workplace

Generation	Traditionalists	Boomers	Gen Xers	Millennials
Birth Years	1900–1945	1946–1964	1965–1980	1981–1999
Current Ages	70+	51–69	35–50	16–34
Also known as…	Veterans WW II Generation The Silent Generation	Baby boomers 77 million	Xers 44 million Baby busters Post-boomers	Nexters Generation Y Nintendo Generation
On the Job	"Build a legacy" A lifetime career with one company	"Build a stellar career" Excel in career	"Build a portable career" A repertoire of skill, experience	"Build parallel careers" Several jobs simultaneously
Career Goals	Security and fair rewards Part-time schedule	Monetary gains and career progression Flexibility	Immediate rewards and career portability	Parallel careers and choice
Work/Life	Support me in maintaining balance.	Help me balance everyone else and find myself.	Give me balance now, not when I'm 65.	Work isn't everything. I need flexibility to balance all my activities.

Source: Adapted from Zemke, R., Raines, C., & Filipczak, B. (2000). *Generations at work: Managing the clash of Veterans, Boomers, Xers, and Nexters in your workplace.* New York, NY: American Management Association.

As shown in Table 3.2, the four generations have different attitudes about work and the balance between work and home life. Gen X employees want portable skills that they can take with them to their next job. The boomers strive for monetary gain and mobility whereas the millennial generation doesn't view work as the be-all and end-all of their existence. They are children of the boomers and most grew up more affluently than other generations. This generation is more interested in career options and choice rather than employment with one organization long term.

The Millennials

A survey conducted recently revealed managers are sometimes surprised at the work habits of millennials. For example, during interviews millennials asked questions like "Do I have to show up every day for work?" "Do you drug test—*often?*" and "Can my *mom* call you about the benefits package?" (p. 1).[83] Despite the discomfort with these questions that may reflect underlying attitudes toward work, other generations can't simply avoid millennials; there are an estimated 40 million in the workforce today. The consulting firm that conducted this survey offers the following advice:

Generational
Differences

- **Make training and mentoring a priority.** Millennials respond to one-on-one attention.
- **Set clear objectives—from the start—with the different generations and diversity at the workplace.** Don't assume that millennials understand the ground rules.
- **Consider the medium.** Millennials grew up on the Internet and respond to YouTube, TED Talks, and blogs. They are used to accessing information in different ways though Google searches and Wikis, for example.
- **Provide feedback early and often.** Build it into the job for millennials. Feedback is important to all generations, but millennials grew up experiencing more from parents and online learning platforms.
- **Pause before reacting.** Think through your response to what might appear to be inappropriate workplace behavior, and choose your response carefully.

Building relationships to enhance effectiveness is a two-way street. If you are a millennial, organizational consultant Jeanne Meister offers the following advice:

- **Don't "friend" your boss on Facebook or other social media platforms.**
- **Remember that social media is forever.** Don't criticize your boss or employer on social media.
- **Keep your need to text in check.** You are used to sending as many as 1,500 text messages a month, but prior generations are not.
- **Become an expert on your generation.** Your perspective is valued, so offer your ideas on how to design a product or service to fit the needs of millennials.
- **View your manager as a role model.** Ask him or her to explain the corporate culture and what is (and is not) appropriate.

LEADING DIVERSE FOLLOWERS

Learning Objective 3.7: Explain the guidelines for leading diverse workers.

A convincing example of the power of diversity is from a study of NFL draft picks for 12 players by well-known sports analysts from *NFL Countdown, Sporting News, Sports Illustrated, CBS Sportsline,* About.com, and Fanball.com. Since their reputations depend on being right, the analysts care about whether or not they make the right predictions in the NFL draft. Researchers found that the average of all analysts was a better predictor of any individual analyst. Prediction diversity matters, and this example demonstrates that diverse points of view can enhance organizational functioning through better decisions: "*Diversity matters just as much as individual ability.* That is not a feel-good statement. It's a mathematical fact."[85] Thus, the field of OB recognizes that diversity is not something that must be "managed," but rather, it is something that must be embraced because it is a business imperative. Many organizations today reflect diversity in mission statements. For example, ESPN has won

Understanding Millennials

An article with a provocative title appeared in *Time* magazine in May 2013.[86] According to research cited by Stein and conducted by the National Institutes of Health (NIH) there may be more to this than an older generation stereotyping a younger one: 58% more college students scored higher on a personality measure of narcissism in 2009 than in 1982. The study also indicated that 40% of millennials think "they should be promoted every two years, regardless of performance" (p. 28). Clearly, their personality characteristics and expectations will challenge leaders in the years ahead. But Stein also cited other research that shows some positive characteristics of this generation. He stated that they tend to be optimistic and crave new experiences (which may be more important than material things). And they are "pro-business" (p. 34), which should be a good thing for organizations. They have endured years of cynicism from baby boomers and gen Xers, who are both burnt out from overwork. Gen Xers were disengaged from work after the ethics scandals of the 1980s and 1990s. So before reacting negatively to something a millennial says, it may be best to remember that (like all prior generations before them) they have a complex mix of values and attitudes (both positive and negative), and they are worth taking the time to understand.

Discussion Questions:

1. What are some limits to using categorizations of generations such as millennials to understand behavior in organizations?
2. Can you think of people of this age group that don't fit the descriptions (i.e., they were born between 1981 and 1999)? What are they like, and why do you think they are different than how millennials are often described?
3. What is useful about these attempts to understand different generations at the workplace?

Source: Stein, J. (2013, May). The me me me generation: Millennials are lazy, entitled narcissists who still live with their parents. Why they'll save us all. *Time*, 28–34.

several awards for diversity, and their mission statement reflects the importance of valuing diversity to their profitability:

> ESPN will embrace diversity to better serve our fans and customers. We strive to attract and retain talented and diverse people, and to create an inclusive environment where all employees can contribute to their fullest potential. In a changing world in which we endeavor to grow our business, it is imperative that ESPN's workforce reflects the diversity of cultures, thinking and perspectives of its current and prospective fans and customers. Tapping the skills, ideas and perspectives of a diverse workforce will make us a better and more profitable company, and is key to sustaining our continued growth. (Diversity at ESPN, 2013, http://espncareers.com/working-here/diversity.aspx)

This seems like a great vision statement, but what can organizations do specifically to develop an inclusive and diverse work environment? One thing is to apply critical thinking by asking key questions about diversity. Leading a diverse workforce does have some challenges such as shifting power dynamics in the organization or employees not being willing to participate in diversity initiatives. A study of human resource managers revealed several questions that every leader should be asking themselves and others in their organization to promote open discussions about diversity:[87]

- Are there challenging or pressing issues in managing a diverse workforce? If so, which do you find to be most challenging?
- What are specific things you have done personally to ease those challenges?
- In regards to diversity, are there things you wish had been done differently? If so, what? And how would you have handled those things differently?
- What are specific things your company has done to ease those challenges?
- What are your (or your company's) future plans for diversity? Do you have specific plans that will be implemented in the near future? If so, what?

Asking such questions (and thinking thoughtfully about the answers) should help a leader identify what challenges the organization faces and what is (or is not) being done to address them. For example, pairing employees with different backgrounds in terms of age, gender, and race or ethnicity in a one-on-one coaching program might be something an organization could implement.

 Critical Thinking Question: What do you think is the biggest challenge in leading a diverse workforce? How can a leader address this challenge?

A case study of a multicultural organization found that the organization implemented several key managerial actions:[88]

- CEO support of diversity initiatives
- Managerial accountability
- Fundamental change in human resource practices
- Employee involvement and buy-in
- Overarching corporate philosophy regarding diversity
- Ongoing monitoring and improvement of diversity climate
- Multiple measures of success

In terms of managerial accountability, 25% of the managers' salary increase was linked to interaction with diverse individuals as an example in the multicultural organization studied. These authors concluded that is important to have a plan for diversity and inclusion initiatives and to link them to hard organizational outcomes such as revenue.

Workplace
Mindfulness

In addition to reviewing how the organization is addressing diversity, a leader can also focus on one-on-one relationships with diverse followers. Next, we will discuss a coaching technique based on research on mindfulness that may help leaders to understand the individual differences, personality, emotions, and moods of the people they work with.

MINDFULNESS

Learning Objective 3.8: Develop an example of a leader practicing mindful coaching with a follower.

Mindfulness is a new area of research in psychology, and it is being applied to the workplace also. It is a state of open attention on what is happening in the present without thinking about the past or worrying about the future. When a person is in a mindful state, they look at their feelings without labeling them as bad or good. On the other hand, much behavior in organizations may be "mindless." To assess *mindlessness*, some of the following questions are asked:[89]

- I forget a person's name almost as soon as I've been told it for the first time.
- I find myself listening to another person with one ear and doing something else at the same time.
- I find myself preoccupied with the future or the past.

Being mindful is significantly related to well-being. Are you mindful or mindless in how you go about your study, work, or life in general? Being mindful is related to the EI aspect of being self-aware (recognizing emotions when you experience them), but it is more than this. By focusing on the present, we can learn about the individual differences of followers and also be attentive to their emotions and moods. Here are mindfulness guidelines from the Mayo Clinic that may help a leader understand followers who are diverse in terms of personality and other characteristics. The first three steps help prepare for a coaching session with a follower:

1. **Make the familiar new again.** Even if you have worked with someone for a long time, learn one new thing about them. As you become more aware of this person, you will be able to identify what their personality type might be. Are they a Type A person? Are they conscientious?
2. **Focus on your breathing when you are preparing to listen to another person.** Sit in a quiet place and pay attention to your nostrils as the air moves in and out. Notice how your abdomen expands and contracts with each breath. Remember that you are not trying to accomplish anything. You are just becoming aware of your breathing and mentally preparing yourself to hear the other person's words.
3. **Prepare to pay attention.** Get in the habit of delaying judgment and/or the urge to "categorize" them (e.g., don't be too quick to put them in the in-group or the out-group). Plan to focus on the person and what they have to say—their words and the meaning of their words.

Don't forget to also be ready to pay attention to emotions or moods that may get expressed since we have learned that they matter as well.

 Developing Mindfulness

Reprinted with permission, courtesy of Mayo Clinic.

Next, begin the coaching session by following steps from the Center for Creative Leadership for mindful leadership coaching:[90]

1. **Based on your preparation, start with an empty mind.** Try not to judge or think about what the person *should* have done in the past or *should* do in the future.
2. **Be nonreactive.** Remember that during this coaching session "no reaction is required, regardless of the provocation." Create a safe, emotional space for the person to express himself or herself.
3. **Practice permissive attention.** Try to draw the person into moments of connection where distractions disappear (cell phones, street noise, or anything else that might impair their ability to focus). Try to stay focused for more than a moment on one serious line of thought, perception, judgment, or action that you might observe. Draw the person's attention to what is important (but not in a coercive way).

With a bit of practice, leaders should be able to create a coaching environment where they attend with a focus on the person being developed. Athletes refer to this as being "in the zone" where you are focused and behavior seems effortless.[91] A great coach can evoke this state from a follower and maintain it so that the person can hear their feedback without becoming defensive. Thus, mindful coaching is about preparation and execution of a few steps in each phase. Research has shown that people can be trained to experience mindfulness and that this state is related to increased attention (alerting, orienting, and conflict monitoring).[92] Like any skill, with practice, a leader can become more mindful and then use this skill to understand the entire range of individual differences we have learned about in this chapter (personality, emotions, moods, and diversity). It is important for a leader to develop the ability to understand others and then react in an appropriate way to enhance their well-being at work.

 Critical Thinking Question: Provide an example of a leader practicing mindful coaching with an employee who has missed a project deadline. This situation may be due to demands on the employee's time from arranging care for his elderly parents in recent months. Be specific regarding what the leader should say and do.

LEADERSHIP IMPLICATIONS: EMBRACING DIVERSITY

Embracing diversity is a competitive advantage, and organizations should include the following in their planning: cost, attraction of human resources, marketing success, creativity and innovation, problem-solving quality, and organizational flexibility.[93] These six dimensions of business performance are directly impacted by the management of cultural diversity. Research evidence supports the argument that diversity increases performance and organizations that embrace diversity build more inclusive work environments. In fact, ignoring individual differences may result in an apathetic or even resistant workforce. Also, by not allowing individuals to express their differences, creativity may be suppressed.

To summarize, diversity takes many forms, including all of the individual differences reviewed in this chapter: personality, emotions, and surface- and deep-level diversity. Embracing diversity relates to organizational effectiveness. A study of Standard & Poor's firms over a 15-year period showed that having women in top management teams improves firm performance for firms whose strategy is focused on innovation.[94] The study authors, Dezso and Ross, concluded that in a context of innovation "the informational and social benefits of gender diversity and the behaviors associated with women in management are likely to be especially important for managerial task performance" (p. 1072).[95] It is imperative that leaders embrace all forms of diversity to enhance the engagement of a diverse workforce and harness their productive and creative work to meet organizational goals.

$SAGE edge™

edge.sagepub.com/scandura

Want a better grade? Go to **edge.sagepub.com/scandura** for the tools you need to sharpen your study skills.

KEY TERMS

affect, 64
aggregating, 65
agreeableness, 59
boomers, 71
broaden-and-build model, 64
conscientiousness, 59
deep-level diversity, 71
emotional contagion, 68
emotional intelligence (EI), 65
emotional labor, 67
emotions, 64
extraversion, 59

generation Xers, or gen Xers, 71
millennials, 71
Minnesota twin studies, 57
moods, 64
neuroticism, 59
openness, 59
organizational neuroscience, 69
personality, 57
positive and negative affect, 65

psychological capital (PsyCap), 62
state-like, 62
surface-level diversity, 71
traditionalists, 71
trait-like, 62
Type A behavior, 60
Type B behavior, 60
Type C behavior, 60
Type D behavior, 60

SUGGESTIONS FOR FURTHER READING

Goleman, D., Boyatzis, R., & McKee, A. (2013). *Primal leadership: Unleashing the power of emotional intelligence*. Cambridge, MA: Harvard Business Review Press.

Kiersey, D. (1998). *Please understand me II: Temperament, character, intelligence.* Del Mar, CA: Prometheus Nemesis Book Company.

Luthans, F., Youssef, C. M., & Avolio, B. J. (1996). *Psychological capital: Developing the human competitive edge*. Oxford, UK: Oxford University Press.

Strauss, W., & Howe, N. (1991). *Generations: The history of America's future 1584 to 2069.* New York, NY: Morrow.

TOOLKIT ACTIVITY 3.1

Generations at Work

Based on Table 3.2, identify which generation you are in: _____

What is your current age? _____

Answer the following questions. Then, join a group of four to five classmates, and discuss how your answers are similar or different. Do they agree with the characterizations of your generation?

1. What is your preferred length of workday and the number of days worked per week?

   _____

2. Are you interested in flexible working hours? Working from home? Why or why not?

   _____

   _____

3. Do you multitask (do more than one thing at once)?

   _____

4. What frequency and form of team meetings do you prefer?

   _____

   _____

5. What style of leadership do you prefer? Why?

   _____

   _____

6. What organizational rewards are meaningful to you? Why?

_____

_____

7. How important is a balance between work and personal life to you? Explain.

_____

CASE STUDY 3.1

Managing Diversity at IBM Netherlands

A Vision on Managing Diversity

The multinational IT company IBM is convinced that it can only keep its current competitive edge by reflecting marketplace diversity in the workforce and by offering a safe work environment for all employees. The company considers workforce diversity as "the bridge between the workplace and the marketplace."

Ambition: An Inclusive Work Environment

In 1953, the CEO at that time published IBM's first equal opportunity policy letter. This letter stated simply that IBM will hire people based on their ability "regardless of race, color or creed." IBM's subsequent CEOs reinforced that policy throughout the years. Since then, equal opportunity at IBM has been an evolutionary journey that underscores the company's commitment to an inclusive work environment where people's ideas and contributions are welcome—regardless of where they come from, what they look like, or what personal beliefs they hold.

Diversity in Leadership

To stress the importance of workforce diversity, IBM has a vice president of Global Workforce Diversity who formulates global policies on managing diversity. At regional headquarters, diversity managers translate the global policies on managing diversity into regional initiatives. Next, the executive management teams of every branch office formulate local actions in order to increase and to make full use of workforce diversity in that specific IBM establishment. An example of a local action is the adjustment of human resources policies and processes in each country's offices. Due to the differences in national legislation on employment and discrimination, IBM thinks it's best to do this at a country level.

Active Input From Managers and Employees

IBM's leadership underscores its commitment to an inclusive work environment through eight executive task forces, established in 1995:

- Asian
- Black
- Gay/Lesbian/Bisexual/Transgender
- Hispanic
- Men
- Native American

- People with disabilities
- Women

The mission of each task force is to increase the success of IBM in the marketplace by focusing on the various constituencies as customers. The task forces are chaired and staffed by executives and employees from that particular constituency. Each was formed to look at IBM through the lens of their group and answer these questions:

- What is required for your group to feel welcomed and valued at IBM?
- What can IBM, in partnership with your group, do to maximize your productivity?
- What courses of action can IBM take to influence the buying decisions of your group?

There are also global diversity networks where people from various underrepresented groups can meet each other and colleagues from other backgrounds. Many subsidiaries have local chapters of these networks. IBM Netherlands has local chapters of the global diversity network groups for women (called Women in Blue) and for gays, lesbians, bisexuals, and transgenders (called EAGLE). In both cases, the initiative for the foundation of a local chapter was taken by employees.

The networks organize meetings, lectures, workshops, and social events for employees belonging to the specific underrepresented group or for those interested in managing diversity and learning more about the other. All network activities are aimed at enhancing people's personal strength. Another employee collects and distributes information via the intranet about people with disabilities. The company stimulates initiatives like this by allocating time, resources, and budget. The human resources department plays a supportive role: It organizes meetings for the initiators to exchange knowledge and ideas. It also gives them advice on how to use the intranet to draw attention for their subject and gives them information about (international) conferences on managing diversity.

Toward Inclusive Leadership

Throughout the years, global and local diversity network groups were founded for almost any of the traditionally underrepresented groups at IBM. Lately, a turn of opinion has evolved. The company now believes that the key to managing diversity is inclusive leadership. Inclusive leadership implies creating a corporate culture where people feel respected and rewarded, with all their differences and similarities. International training has been developed that focuses on this broad concept of managing diversity. Several senior managers and their advisers have already participated in the training program. Among them were some executives from the Dutch subsidiary and their local diversity coordinator. According to these participants, the training made them aware of the fact that you must focus on diversity management by including all employees.

One exercise showed that everybody sometimes feels excluded from a group and that almost everybody experiences exclusion negatively. Because of the training, they now understand that diversity concerns all employees and not just the ones belonging to a minority. IBM strongly believes that this greater understanding is the basis for realizing inclusive leadership.

Discussion Questions

1. What are the most important aspects of IBM Netherland's vision for diversity?
2. This case study is set in the Netherlands. Do you think that the diversity initiatives could work anywhere? Why or why not?
3. The executive task forces for diverse groups focus on three questions: (1) What is required for your group to feel valued? (2) What is required to maximize productivity? (3) How do you influence the buying decisions of the group? What other questions should be asked?
4. What is "inclusive leadership" at IBM? How can diversity training increase this type of leadership?

Source: Diversity@Work (http://www.diversityatwork.net/EN/en_case_004.htm). Used with permission from Richard Wynne.

SELF-ASSESSMENT 3.1

The Big Five Personality Test

Introduction

This is a personality test; it will help you understand why you act the way that you do and how your personality may be structured. Please follow the instructions below. The scoring and interpretation follow the questions. There are no "right or "wrong" answers. You don't have to share your results with others if you do not wish to do so.

Instructions

In the following table, for each statement 1 through 25, rate each with the following scale of 1 through 5: 1 = disagree, 2 = slightly disagree, 3 = neutral, 4 = slightly agree, and 5 = agree, in the box to the left of it.

Rating	Personality Statement
5	1. I feel comfortable around people.
4	2. I have a good word for everyone.
5	3. I am always prepared.
4	4. I often feel blue.
4	5. I believe in the importance of art.
3	6. I make friends easily.
5	7. I believe others have good intentions.
5	8. I pay attention to details.
1	9. I dislike myself.
4	10. I have a vivid imagination.
4	11. I am skilled in handling social situations.
4	12. I respect others.
4	13. I get chores done right away.
1	14. I am often down in the dumps.
5	15. I enjoy hearing new ideas.
1	16. I am the life of the party.
5	17. I accept people as they are.

Rating	Personality Statement
5	18. I carry out my plans.
3	19. I have frequent mood swings.
4	20. I am interested in abstract ideas.
1	21. I know how to captivate people.
4	22. I make people feel at ease.
3	23. I make plans and stick to them.
1	24. I panic easily.
4	25. I have excellent ideas.

The question numbers are shown in parentheses below. Write your score (1 to 5) on the blank following the question. For example, if you answered question (1) with a score of 2, write 2 on the blank.

E = (1) 5 + (6) 3 + (11) 4 + (16) 1 + (21) 1 = 14 (Extraversion)

A = (2) 4 + (7) 5 + (12) 4 + (17) 5 + (22) 4 = 22 (Agreeableness)

C = (3) 5 + (8) 5 + (13) 4 + (18) 5 + (23) 3 = 22 (Conscientiousness)

N = (4) 4 + (9) 1 + (14) 1 + (19) 3 + (24) 1 = 10 (Neuroticism)

O = (5) 4 + (10) 4 + (15) 5 + (20) 4 + (25) 4 = 21 (Openness to Experience)

The scores you calculate for each personality characteristic should be between 5 and 25. Scores from 5 to 10 can be considered lower and scores above 10 can be considered higher.

Following is a description of each trait.

> **Extraversion (E)** is the personality trait of seeking fulfillment from sources outside the self or in community. High scorers tend to be very social while low scorers prefer to work on their projects alone.
> **Agreeableness (A)** reflects that many individuals adjust their behavior to suit others. High scorers are typically polite and like people. Low scorers tend to "tell it like it is."
> **Conscientiousness (C)** is the personality trait of being honest and hardworking. High scorers tend to follow rules and prefer clean homes. Low scorers may be messy and cheat others.
> **Neuroticism (N)** is the personality trait of being emotional.
> **Openness to Experience (O)** is the personality trait of seeking new experience and intellectual pursuits. High scorers may daydream a lot. Low scorers may be very down to earth.

SELF-ASSESSMENT 3.2

Type A Behavior Pattern

This assessment measures the extent to which you are a Type A or Type B personality. There are no right or wrong answers, and this is not a test. You don't have to share your results with other classmates unless you wish to do so.

Part I. Taking the Assessment

As an example, the answer to a question could look like this:

I am a busy person.

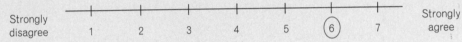

Strongly disagree   1   2   3   4   5   ⑥   7   Strongly agree

This response indicates that you are busy most of the time.

Now, answer the following questions about yourself:

1. Having work to complete "stirs me into action" more than other people.

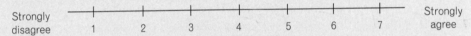

Strongly disagree   1   2   3   4   5   6   7   Strongly agree

2. When a person is talking and takes too long to come to the point, I frequently feel like hurrying the person along.

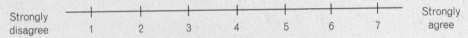

Strongly disagree   1   2   3   4   5   6   7   Strongly agree

3. Nowadays, I consider myself to be relaxed and easygoing (reversed).

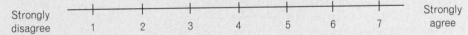

Strongly disagree   1   2   3   4   5   6   7   Strongly agree

4. Typically, I get irritated extremely easily.

Strongly disagree   1   2   3   4   5   6   7   Strongly agree

5. My best friends would rate my general activity level as very high.

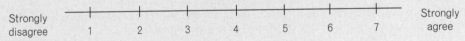

Strongly disagree   1   2   3   4   5   6   7   Strongly agree

6. I definitely tend to do most things in a hurry.

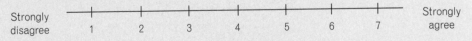

Strongly disagree   1   2   3   4   5   6   7   Strongly agree

7. I take my work much more seriously than most.

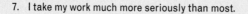

Strongly disagree ─┼───┼───┼───┼───┼───┼───┼─ Strongly agree
      1   2   3   4   5   6   7

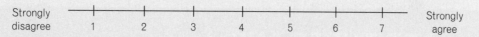

8. I seldom get angry (reversed).

Strongly disagree ─┼───┼───┼───┼───┼───┼───┼─ Strongly agree
      1   2   3   4   5   6   7

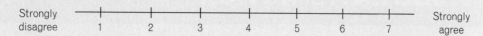

9. I often set deadlines for myself workwise.

Strongly disagree ─┼───┼───┼───┼───┼───┼───┼─ Strongly agree
      1   2   3   4   5   6   7

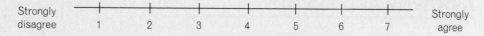

10. I feel very impatient when I have to wait in line.

Strongly disagree ─┼───┼───┼───┼───┼───┼───┼─ Strongly agree
      1   2   3   4   5   6   7

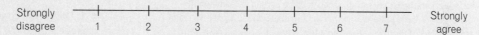

11. I put much more effort into my work than other people do.

Strongly disagree ─┼───┼───┼───┼───┼───┼───┼─ Strongly agree
      1   2   3   4   5   6   7

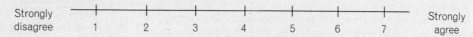

12. Compared with others, I approach life much less seriously (reversed).

Strongly disagree ─┼───┼───┼───┼───┼───┼───┼─ Strongly agree
      1   2   3   4   5   6   7

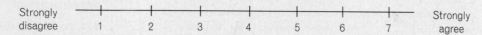

Part II. Scoring and Interpretation

Subtract your answers to questions 3, 8, and 12 (marked *reversed*) from 8, with the difference being your new score for those questions. For example, if your original answer for question 12 was 3, your new answer is 5 (8 − 3). Then add up your answers for the 12 questions. Compare your answer to the following scale:

53 or above	Type A	You may perceive higher stress in your life and be susceptible to health problems due to stress.
52 or below	Type B	You experience less stress in your life, and you are less sensitive to stress you do experience.

Source: Jenkins, C. D., Zyzanski, S. J., & Rosenman, R. H. (1971). Progress toward validation of a computer-scored test for the Type A coronary-prone behavior pattern. *Psychosomatic Medicine, 22,* 193–202. Reprinted with permission of Lippincott, Williams and Wilkins.

4

ATTITUDES AND JOB SATISFACTION

JOB SATISFACTION: A DOWNWARD TREND

The Society of Human Resource Management (SHRM) conducts a survey each year of employee attitudes toward their work. The trends for job satisfaction over time show an interesting pattern. Overall job satisfaction (the global rating of how much a person is "somewhat satisfied" or "very satisfied" with their job) experienced a positive trend from 2002 to 2009. However, the past few years have seen a downward trend, with only 83% of respondents indicating high job satisfaction compared to a peak of 86% in 2009. The survey also found that older workers are more satisfied than younger workers, and those who work for smaller organizations are more satisfied than those who work for larger organizations. The survey did not find any significant differences with respect to gender, race, industry, or job tenure. The survey also looked at the reasons why people are satisfied with their jobs. In a recovering economy, it is perhaps not surprising that job security was the most important reason for being satisfied (63% of the respondents reported this aspect as most important). However, the ability to use skills and abilities at work was a close second (62%). Consistent with research on leadership (reviewed in Chapter 2 of this textbook), having a positive relationship with the boss and the organization's financial stability were tied for third (55%).

 Critical Thinking Questions: Why do you think older workers are more satisfied than younger workers? Why would people working for small businesses be more satisfied than people working for large firms?

Job satisfaction is the most-often studied work attitude. In this chapter, we will review research on job satisfaction and other important work attitudes. First, the concept of attitude is defined followed by a discussion of why attitudes matter for both individuals and the organizations they work for.

Learning Objectives

After studying this chapter, you should be able to do the following:

4.1: Define the concept of an attitude, and know its three components.

4.2: Understand why the measurement of attitudes is important for the workplace.

4.3: Define *job satisfaction*, and know what the consequences of dissatisfaction are.

4.4: Explain the role of job attitudes and core self-evaluation in the job search process.

4.5: Discuss the concept of organizational commitment and its three components.

4.6: Define *perceived organizational support* (POS), and explain its relationship to fairness at the workplace.

4.7: Explain psychological empowerment and its relationship to job performance.

Get the edge on your studies at edge.sagepub.com/scandura

- Take the chapter quiz
- Review key terms with eFlashcards
- Explore multimedia resources, SAGE readings, and more!

$SAGE edge™

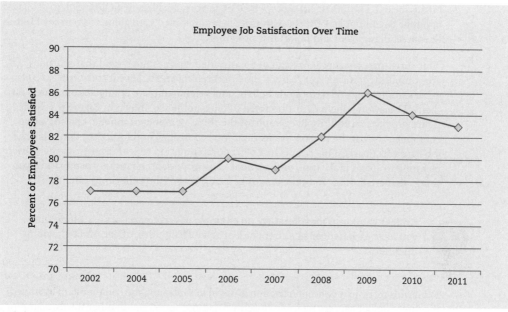

Employee Job Satisfaction Over Time

Note: Figure represents those employees who answered "somewhat satisfied" or "very satisfied."

Source: 2011 Employee Job Satisfaction and Engagement: A Research Report by SHRM.

WHAT IS AN ATTITUDE?

Learning Objective 4.1: Define the concept of an attitude, and know its three components.

Captain Jack Sparrow in *Pirates of the Caribbean* utters "the problem is not the problem; the problem is your *attitude* about the problem. Do you understand?" Most people have an idea of what an attitude is from such statements in films and Dilbert cartoons that parody concepts such as empowerment. Attitudes have been researched in psychology for many years and are one of the earliest concepts studied. From the outset, researchers maintained that it is possible to measure attitudes but also recognized that attitudes are complex.[1] It has been noted that the concept of attitude was indispensable to the study of social psychology.[2] An attitude has been defined as "a psychological tendency that is expressed by evaluating a particular entity with some degree of favor or disfavor" (p. 1).[3] Attitudes are, thus, a person's evaluation of something else. These evaluations have three components: cognitive, affective, and behavioral.[4] The existence of this three component structure has generally been supported by research.[5,6] The **cognitive** component of an attitude is a statement of belief about something—for example, "My boss is a mean person" reflects a person's statement that they believe to be factual. The **affective** component of an attitude is the emotional part. As we learned in Chapter 3, emotions often play a powerful effect on employee motivation and work behaviors—for example, an affective statement related to the previously stated cognitive component might be, "I am angry because my

Engagement

boss is mean." The behavioral component of an attitude refers to an intention to act based upon the cognitions and affect experienced—for example, "I am going to go to the Human Resources department and report my mean boss."

This three-part conceptualization of an attitude helps us understand that attitudes are complicated; it isn't just that we think something and believe it to be true. We also experience feelings related to our beliefs, and we contemplate taking actions based on them. These components are all related to one another, as shown in Figure 4.1. This figure provides an additional example of the three-component model. The cognitive component is that the person thinks their job is boring. Therefore, they don't like the job (the affect part). This results in a behavioral intention to withdraw from the work by planning to spend more time on Facebook during work hours rather than working on things that are boring, and they don't like being bored (the behavioral intention).

 Critical Thinking Question: Give an example of three parts of an attitude that you have experienced at either work or school (cognitive, affect, and behavioral intention).

While this three-part conceptualization is useful in explaining the complexity of attitudes, the three components are typically closely related and converge.[7] In other words, cognitions

Figure 4.1 Three Components of an Attitude

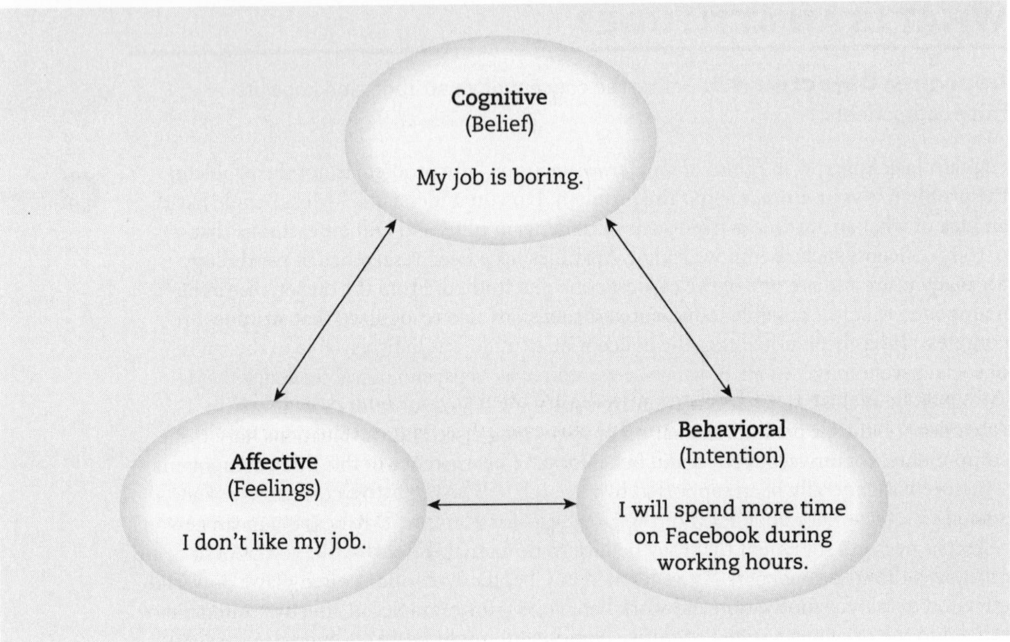

Cognitive
(Belief)

My job is boring.

Affective
(Feelings)

I don't like my job.

Behavioral
(Intention)

I will spend more time on Facebook during working hours.

may not cause affect or vice versa; these components move in the same direction. This is actually useful for a leader to recognize since research has shown that behavior does not always follow an attitude. In fact, thoughts and feelings can be changed by changing behaviors first. For example, having followers state their perceptions of the mission of the organization during a team meeting may have the effect of changing their belief that the mission is worthwhile, and they may also change the way they feel about the mission. Another example would be to have students read the honor code statement to change their thoughts ("cheating is not okay") and feelings ("I would be embarrassed if I was caught cheating"). This is because when behaviors don't line up with thoughts and feelings, cognitive dissonance may occur.

Cognitive
Dissonance

Cognitive Dissonance

Cognitive dissonance is the incompatibility between two or more attitudes or between attitudes and behavior.[8] This creates stress for an individual, and the person will be motivated to resolve the stress by making a change in one or both of the other components. Very few people can completely avoid dissonance in their lives. For example, you may be reminded of this when a child corrects you for swearing because you have told them not to do this in the past. Festinger proposed that the degree to which people are motivated to resolve dissonance is related to the importance of what creates it and how much influence the person has over it. The final motivating element is rewards. So, one of the best ways to learn to stop swearing is to have your children remind you because it is important to you, and you do have influence over what you say. The reward from swearing isn't all that much, so you are probably willing to change it to be a positive role model for your child, which is more rewarding.

Critical Thinking Question: How can the theory of cognitive dissonance be used to change the attitude of the employee depicted in Figure 4.1? In other words, how can a leader reduce the time an employee spends on Facebook during work hours?

DO ATTITUDES MATTER?

Learning Objective 4.2: Understand why the measurement of attitudes is important for the workplace.

As noted in Chapter 1, work-related attitudes are often key outcome variables in organizational behavior (OB) research. In some cases, these same attitudes are employed as predictors. As in social psychology, attitudes have become indispensable to the understanding of people's reactions to their work and leaders. Attitudes are, thus, important in and of themselves. Knowing how satisfied people are with their work or how engaged they are is important because this contributes to their well-being and life satisfaction. Also, OB research has shown that attitudes are related to behaviors that organizations care about such as job performance and turnover. A meta-analysis and additional research were conducted to examine the link between attitudes and behaviors that relate to productivity.[9]

Attitude and the Job Environment

The findings strongly suggest that job satisfaction and organizational commitment are significantly related to job performance and turnover. The authors conclude that job attitudes are one of the most important things for a leader to know about their followers.

Attitudes make a difference in employee behaviors such as job performance. However, there are contingency factors that have been found to influence the relationship between attitudes and behavior.[10] The importance of an attitude and the correspondence between the attitude and the behavior increases the prediction of behavior.[11] In other words, more specific attitudes predict more specific behaviors. For example, it is better to ask an employee how much they trust the boss rather than how much they trust all of the leaders in the organizations to predict job performance. **Social pressure** from others may also strengthen the relationship of an attitude toward behavior. A meta-analysis of research examining the link between attitudes and behavior found that how accessible an attitude is matters as well as how stable the attitude is over time.[12] For example, having direct experience with an attitude such as having a job you love increases the relationship to performance. Also, being asked frequently about an attitude increases the link to behavior (stability). For example, having yearly employee attitude surveys may increase the awareness of favorable aspects of the work and decrease turnover.

The following sections will discuss how specific attitudes significantly and positively affect outcomes for organizations such as higher job performance and lower turnover.

JOB SATISFACTION

Learning Objective 4.3: Define *job satisfaction,* and know what the consequences of dissatisfaction are.

As suggested in the research by SHRM at the beginning of this chapter, most people are satisfied with their jobs, but this has been declining somewhat in recent years. Job satisfaction is defined as "a pleasurable or positive emotional state resulting from the appraisal of one's job or job experience" (p. 1300).[13] Job satisfaction is viewed as one part of a person's reactions to their life resulting in happiness and life satisfaction.[14] Current perspectives on positive OB suggest that it is important for organizations to care about the happiness and health of their employees even if this is unrelated to performance and other outcomes.[15] Thus, job satisfaction is important because it shows how positive an employee is regarding their work. Job satisfaction can be measured as an overall (or global) concept as shown in Chapter 1, Table 1.2; the Hoppock Job Satisfaction measure is one of the oldest measures from OB research.

Job satisfaction has been examined across cultures. Typically, studies seek to understand whether U.S.-based models of job satisfaction hold in other cultures. For example, a study of over 70,000 employees in four cultural regions (Asia, Europe, North America, and Latin America) found employees' sense of achievement from work was related to job satisfaction in all regions.[16]

A review of cross-cultural research on job satisfaction concluded that the relationship of job satisfaction to performance in a number of other cultures was similar to that in the United States with an average correlation of .20 (the review included studies from India,

RESEARCH IN ACTION

The Curious Case of Post 9-11 Job Satisfaction

Can a public event change how satisfied government workers are with their jobs? Job satisfaction in the public sector may not only depend on facets such as pay, coworkers, and supervisor satisfaction but may also depend also on larger national events or crises.[17] Van Ryzin proposed that the image of public service in times of crisis may become more positive since citizens look to government institutions for security, leadership, and a sense of national purpose. This increase in the positive image of the public sector may boost the everyday morale of government workers. Also, government workers may find renewed meaning and purpose in their work since the government responds to a crisis and therefore increase their job satisfaction. The researcher compared job satisfaction data from the General Social Survey (GSS) for a sample of government workers compared to private sector

workers from the years 2000 to 2010. The findings indicate that 9-11 may have boosted government workers' job satisfaction 5 to 10 percentage points, representing 1 to 2 million additional satisfied government workers in the United States. These results suggest that people may find meaning in their work since national crises may influence government job satisfaction.

Discussion Questions:

1. This study was conducted for government employees. Do you think that the results would be different for employees in the business sector? Why or why not?
2. Do you think the economy affects job satisfaction?
3. List and discuss two other factors outside of the job that may affect job satisfaction.

Source: Van Ryzin, G. G. (2014). The curious case of the post 9-11 boost in government job satisfaction. *American Review of Public Administration*, 44(1), 59–74.

Poland, Australia, Canada, Israel, and South Africa).[18] However, international research was more likely to focus on non-work attitudes such as adaptive behaviors. In addition, job satisfaction was found to be related to life satisfaction and withdrawal behaviors (lateness and absenteeism) in other cultures.

Job Satisfaction Facets

It is recognized that it is possible for a person to be satisfied with one aspect of their work but dissatisfied with others. In other words, an employee might love the work they do but dislike their gossiping coworkers. Thus, measures of facet job satisfaction have been developed. One of the most widely known measures of facet satisfaction is the Job Descriptive Index (JDI).[19] This measure includes different scales that measure various aspects of the work experience: pay, promotions, supervision, coworkers, and the work itself. Examples of items from the JDI are shown in Table 4.1. Research has suggested the strongest relationship of these facets to overall job satisfaction is the work itself, followed by supervision and coworker satisfaction. While it may be surprising, satisfaction with pay has the lowest relationship to overall job satisfaction.[20,21] You will learn more about the role of extrinsic rewards such as pay on motivation in Chapter 8.

Table 4.1 Sample Items from the Job Descriptive Index

Think of the work you do at present. How well does each of the following words or phrases describe your work? In the blank beside each word or phrase, write the following:

- Y for "Yes" if it describes your work
- N for "No" if it does NOT describe it
- ? for "?" if you cannot decide

Pay Satisfaction

___Well-paid
___Bad
___Barely live on income

Promotion Satisfaction

___ Regular promotions
___ Promotion on ability
___ Opportunities somewhat limited

Supervision Satisfaction

___ Knows job well
___ Around when needed
___ Doesn't supervise enough

Coworker Satisfaction

___ Stimulating
___ Smart
___ Unpleasant

Satisfaction with the Work Itself

___ Fascinating
___ Pleasant
___ Can see my results

Source: The Job Descriptive Index, © Bowling Green State University (1975, 1985, 1997).

If work is the most important component of job satisfaction, then you may be wondering what the relationship is between pay and job satisfaction. In a review study including over 90 samples, researchers found that pay was only weakly related to job satisfaction. In fact, employees who were highly paid were just as satisfied as those who made less. The results of their study are summarized in Figure 4.2. Once a person reaches an income level where they can live comfortably (around $40,000 in the United States), the relationship between income and job satisfaction goes away.

 Critical Thinking Question: Why do you think that the most important aspect of job satisfaction is the work itself?

Job satisfaction matters because progressive organizations care about the well-being of their workforce. It is also important because it is related to other work attitudes, which we will review next in this chapter (such as organizational commitment and organizational citizenship behavior [OCB]). Job satisfaction may increase performance on the job. A meta-analysis including over 300 samples showed that job satisfaction is significantly and positively related to performance.[22]

Dissatisfaction with work produces responses that are summarized in Figure 4.3. As shown in this figure, responses can either be active or passive.[23] Thus, the employee can actually do something about it or choose not to respond in an active way. The second dimension is

Figure 4.2   The Relationship Between Average Pay in a Job and Job Satisfaction

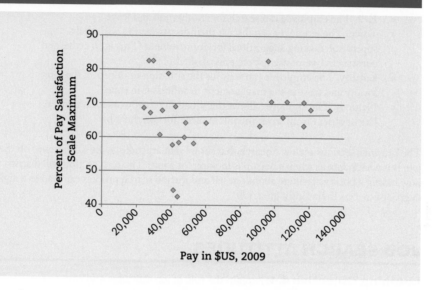

Source: Judge, T. A., Piccolo, R. F., Podsakoff, N. P., Shaw, J. C., & Rich, B. L. (2010). The relationship between pay and job satisfaction: A meta-analysis of the literature. *Journal of Vocational Behavior, 77*(2), 157–167.

Figure 4.3   Responses to Job Dissatisfaction

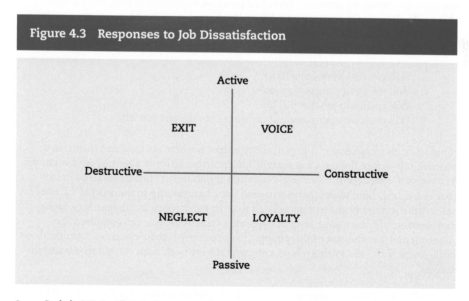

Source: Rusbult, C. E., Farrell, D., Rogers, G., & Mainous III, A. G. (1988). Impact of exchange variables on exit, voice, loyalty, and neglect: An integrative model of responses to declining job satisfaction. *Academy of Management Journal, 31*(3), 599–627.

Meaningful Work

whether the response is **constructive** or **destructive.** The employee who is dissatisfied can respond by trying to do something positive or negative about the situation. There are four responses shown in Figure 4.3, and their definitions follow.

- **Exit.** The employee can search for another job and leave.
- **Voice.** The employee can discuss their dissatisfaction with their supervisor, making suggestions for improvement. This is an active and constructive response to being dissatisfied.
- **Loyalty.** The employee can wait for the situation to improve, showing loyalty and trust in the management to address it in time.
- **Neglect.** The employee allows the situation to get worse and may be late or absent from work and put in less effort on the job.

The previous sections review research that shows that attitudes make a difference on the job. But what happens when a person is looking for a job? The next section will discuss how having a positive attitude about oneself and the job search process can lead to a higher degree of success in finding a great job.

JOB SEARCH ATTITUDES

Learning Objective 4.4: Explain the role of job attitudes and core self-evaluation in the job search process.

OB research has shown that the job search is like a "roller coaster," with ups and downs in the attitudes during the process.[24] Perceived progress, experienced affect, and the belief that a job will be found may vary on a day-to-day basis during the job search process. In this research, individuals were asked about how confident they were that they would find another job. The researchers asked questions such as the following:

1. Will you find a job if you look?
2. Will you get a good paying job?
3. Will you find a job that you like?
4. Will you land a job as good as or better than the one you left?

This research found that it is important to keep a positive attitude and maintain a positive self-image during a job search. This positive attitude about oneself is known as **core self-evaluation.** Core self-evaluation is defined as "fundamental premises that individuals hold about themselves and their functioning in the world."[25] Core self-evaluation has been strongly related to both persistence in job search behavior and success.[26] To learn your level of core self-evaluations, you can complete Self-Assessment 4.1 at the end of this chapter. To summarize, keep a positive attitude about both yourself and the job search process, which have both been related to job search success.

Core self-evaluations have also been related to job performance in a meta-analysis of 81 studies, including thousands of employees.[27] In addition to core self-evaluation, work-related attitudes are important because they reflect an employee's reactions to work and serve as an important barometer of how well the organization is attending to employee

Your Attitude May Derail Your Job Search

Those seeking employment need to pay attention to their attitudes. Your attitudes may manifest themselves in how you conduct yourself during the process. Bob McIntosh, a career trainer who leads job search workshops and an authority on the job search process, offers the following advice.

1. Don't be arrogant. People don't appreciate being looked down upon.
2. "Dress for success." Make sure you are well groomed and presentable when you might be in contact with a potential employer or someone who could help you.
3. Your countenance matters. Try not to look down at the floor or frown. Be positive and upbeat.
4. Be outgoing (or at least fake it). Use every opportunity you can to network. Don't view networking as only formal, arranged events.
5. Mind your manners. Remember to say thank you as well as something such as, "It was great seeing you."
6. Don't appear desperate and despondent. People will want to help you, but don't look like

you are giving up. If you doubt yourself, it will show, and then others will begin to doubt you.
7. Hide your anger. Keep your composure at all times. If you are angry about how you were treated unfairly in your last job, don't show this in an interview. Also, if you are frustrated with the job search, try to focus on the positive things that are happening.

Here is some sound advice from McIntosh:

Simply put, your job search is ongoing. You are being judged wherever you go. Those you try to help you take into account the aforementioned aspects of your overall attitude. Be mindful at all times how you appear to others.

Discussion Questions:

1. How many people could you let know that you are searching for a job? List their names and how you know them (e.g., your internship mentor or a former boss).
2. How would you ask them to help you in a positive and upbeat way? Write a brief speech or e-mail with your job search request.

Source: McIntosh, B. (2013). 7 things you need to consider about your attitude when looking for work. Retrieved on February 10, 2014, from http://thingscareerrelated.com/2013/12/23/6-things-you-need-to-consider-about-your-attitude-when-looking-for-work

needs. The next section will discuss job satisfaction, which is one of the most often-studied work-related attitudes.

 Critical Thinking Questions: What limitations do you see on the effect of being positive on the job search process? What is the right balance between optimism and being realistic?

ORGANIZATIONAL COMMITMENT

Learning Objective 4.5: Discuss the concept of organizational commitment and its three components.

Organizational commitment is another work-related attitude that has proven to be important in OB. Reviews (including several meta-analyses) have shown that organizational commitment relates to turnover.[28,29,30] OB research has also shown that people who are not committed to their jobs are absent more often, less motivated, as well as perform at lower levels.[31] Organizational commitment is a psychological state that describes an employee's relationship with their organization and a propensity to continue the relationship with the organization.[32] A three-component model of organizational commitment captures different aspects of this work attitude.[33] First, affective commitment refers to an employee's emotional attachment to an organization (they stay because they care about the organization and are loyal to it). Second, continuance commitment is the degree to which an employee is aware of the costs of leaving the organization (they stay because they are not able to leave). Third, normative commitment is the moral obligation to stay with the organization (they stay because it is the right thing to do).

 Critical Thinking Question: Which component of organizational commitment do you feel is most related to turnover (and why)?

Job involvement is how much an employee identifies with his or her job and views his or her performance at work as an essential part of his or her self-esteem. Job involvement has been related to employee turnover,[34] organizational citizenship, and job performance.[35]

Job Involvement

By combining organizational commitment and job involvement, we can better understand the relationship of these variables to employee withdrawal behaviors (absenteeism and turnover).[36] This relationship is shown in Figure 4.4. As this figure shows, when organizational commitment and job involvement are both high, employees can be viewed as institutionalized "stars" because their efforts are focused on both the task and the group they belong to. The other extreme case is when both organizational commitment and job involvement are low. In this case, employees are "Apathetics" because they don't put forth much effort on the task and are not concerned about the maintenance of group norms of goals. The other two quadrants represent interesting scenarios in which "Lone Wolves" are involved with their jobs to a high degree and have a task focus but they are not concerned about the maintenance of the group. They prefer to "go it alone" and are more likely to leave the organization than the final group, "Corporate Citizens." Corporate Citizens are not focused on the task, but they do attend to the maintenance of the group. They may not be star performers, but they are loyal to the organization and the group. The figure also indicates suggestions for what aspects of satisfaction are important for each type of employee. For example, the Corporate Citizen is most concerned with coworker satisfaction to maintain their organizational commitment. In contrast, if the leader has a Lone Wolf in their group, they should focus more on the satisfaction with the work itself, working condition, and pay to avoid absenteeism and turnover.

Employee engagement has emerged as an important concept due to research conducted by both OB professors and consultants. Engagement appears to be distinct from job involvement and adds to our understanding of the relationships of attitudes such as job satisfaction.

Figure 4.4 The Relationship of Organizational Commitment and Job Involvement to Employee Turnover

Organizational Commitment

	High	Low
High (Job Involvement)	**Institutional "Stars"** • Least likely to be absent or leave • Focus on work itself and future with the organization, satisfaction with pay, coworkers and supervision	**Corporate Citizens** • Less likely to leave voluntarily than lone wolves • Focus on satisfaction with coworkers
Low (Job Involvement)	**"Lone Wolves"** • More likely to leave voluntarily than corporate citizens • Focus on work itself, satisfaction with working conditions and pay	**Apathetics** • Most likely to leave voluntarily • Focus on satisfaction with rewards

Source: Blau, G. J., & Boal, K. B. (1987). Conceptualizing how job involvement and organizational commitment affect turnover and absenteeism. *Academy of Management Review,* 12(2), 288–300. Adapted from p. 293.

Employee Engagement

Employee engagement is related to job involvement and enthusiasm for the work performed.[37] Engagement has been defined as "the investments of an individual's complete self into a role" (p. 617). A study of 245 firefighters and their supervisors found that engagement plays a key role in the relationship between **perceived organizational support (POS;** discussed in the next section) and job performance. This study included job involvement, but engagement explained additional variance in performance. A large-scale study of 7,939 business units in 36 companies found that engagement was related to customer satisfaction, productivity, profit, employee turnover, and safety (fewer accidents).[38] Improving employee engagement may increase business-unit outcomes, including profit.

A survey conducted by Gallup in 2012 indicates that "52% of workers are not engaged, and worse, another 18% are actively disengaged in their work. Gallup estimates that these actively disengaged employees cost the U.S. between $450 billion to $550 billion each year in lost productivity."[39] In 2012, Gallup also conducted its eighth meta-analysis on their engagement measure (the Q12) using 263 research studies including 49,928 business and work units, with almost 1.4 million employees. Gallup researchers

Perceived Organizational Commitment

statistically analyzed business and work unit level relationships between employee engagement and performance outcomes. The findings of this large-scale meta-analysis are shown in Figure 4.5 and further confirm the well-established connection between employee engagement and nine performance outcomes including job performance and turnover.

Engaged employees feel valued by their organization. A longitudinal panel study found employee perceptions of how much they were valued by the organization was related to changes in affective commitment.[40] Also, the resources employees feel that they have on their job positively relates to engagement. A study found that three job resources relate to engagement: performance feedback, social support from colleagues, and supervisory coaching.[41] A second study found that resources of supervisor support, innovativeness, appreciation, and organizational climate mattered even more when the demands of a job were high.[42] Thus, employees respond positively to the work environment when they feel the organization supports them. This attitude—POS—will be discussed next.

 Critical Thinking Question: Do you see a significant difference between the concepts of job involvement and employee engagement? If so, what is this difference?

Figure 4.5   Employee Engagement and Work Outcomes

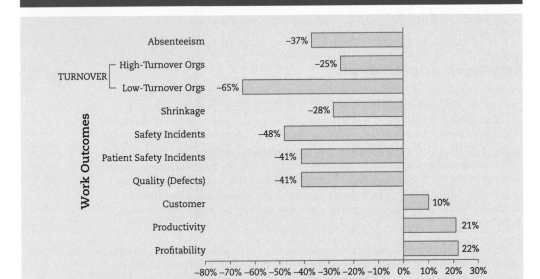

Source: Gallup (2013). State of the American Workforce: Employee engagement insights for U.S. business leaders (retrieved on January 8, 2014 from http://www.gallup.com/strategicconsulting/163007/state-american-workplace.aspx).

PERCEIVED ORGANIZATIONAL SUPPORT

Learning Objective 4.6: Define *perceived organizational support* (POS), and explain its relationship to fairness at the workplace.

An emerging line of research suggests employees pay attention to whether the organization values their contributions and cares about their well-being: POS.[43] Organizational justice and fair rewards are important to the perception of organizational support.[44] A review of over 70 studies of POS indicated that there are three major categories of beneficial treatment: fairness, supervisor support, and organizational rewards along with favorable job conditions.[45] The supervisor also plays an important role in the perception of POS, and it is important for employees to feel that they have a voice in decisions.[46] Employees with higher POS engage in more citizenship behavior and are less likely to show up late for work.[47] A meta-analysis of studies found strong, positive effects of POS on job satisfaction and organizational commitment; a moderate, positive effect on employee performance; and a strong, negative effect on intention to leave.[48] More than 20 years of research suggests that POS appears to be distinct from other attitudes and adds to understanding why some employees perform at higher levels than others.

Empowerment and Impact

Research on POS indicates that employees respond positively when they feel the organization values them. Such employees want to have a voice in decisions that affect them. Feeling a sense of power to have an impact at work is another work attitude that has been researched in recent years with results indicating strong relationships to other work attitudes and organizational effectiveness. The next section will discuss the research findings for **psychological empowerment**.

PSYCHOLOGICAL EMPOWERMENT

Learning Objective 4.7: Explain psychological empowerment and its relationship to job performance.

Psychological empowerment refers to "intrinsic task motivation manifested in a set of four cognitions reflecting an individual's orientation to his or her work role: competence, impact, meaning, and self-determination."[49] These four cognitions are defined as follows.

- **Meaning**—how much work goals align with your personal standards (i.e., how well the work "fits" your values)
- **Competence** (or self-efficacy)—your belief in your capabilities to show mastery in your work role
- **Self-Determination**—the degree to which you feel that you have a choice in your work and autonomy to carry it out according to your own preferences.
- **Impact**—refers to how much you believe that you can influence important work outcomes (e.g., administrative policies at work)

Research has shown that psychological empowerment is positively related to managerial effectiveness, innovation,[50] and organizational commitment.[51,52] Empowerment is related to lower stress as well.[53] Meaning is the driver of psychological empowerment; however,

Helping Followers Achieve Greatness

all four components make unique contributions to outcomes. For example, competence is most related to ratings of managerial effectiveness. It is important for leaders to allow their followers to experience meaning in their work but also feel that they have an impact. Also, leaders should coach followers to develop their sense of competence and allow them discretion in how they do their work.

? Critical Thinking Question: Researchers suggest that meaning is the driver of psychological empowerment. Why do you think this is the case?

As noted previously, leaders can develop their followers' feelings of empowerment. They may also create positive attitudes through developing a **sense of meaning** with respect to the work performed. By creating a sense of meaning, leaders may be able to activate other positive attitudes about work and improve employee motivation.

LEADERSHIP IMPLICATIONS: CREATING MEANING AT WORK

Research on attitudes and job satisfaction shows that attitudes relate to important workplace outcomes such as improved job performance and lower turnover. Leaders must recognize that attitudes can change and that the behaviors of leaders affect attitudes. OB research has demonstrated relationships between transformational leadership and work attitudes.[54] Followers with a transformational leader are more committed because they experience psychological empowerment at work.[55] Charismatic leaders increase their followers' commitment by (1) promoting higher levels of intrinsic motivation through goal accomplishment, (2) emphasizing the linkages between follower effort and goal achievement, and (3) creating a higher level of personal commitment by leader and followers to a common vision, mission, and organizational goals.[56] In sum, feeling part of the larger mission of the organization increases organizational commitment. Research on leader–member exchange (LMX) similarly shows that developing high-quality working relationships with followers relates to higher levels of job satisfaction, organizational commitment, and empowerment.[57]

Certain leadership styles influence the degree to which work is perceived as meaningful.[58,59] A review of the literature on finding meaning in work concluded "leaders can imbue work with meaningfulness by prompting employees to transcend their personal needs or goals in favor of those tied to a broader mission or purpose."[60] The questions used to measure the meaning of work are shown in Table 4.2.[61] Leaders should think about how they can increase followers' responses to these questions. In sum, leaders play a powerful role in creating meaning for their followers by developing high-quality relationships and then sharing the organization's overall mission with followers. This provides followers with a sense of meaning in their work, which has been shown to relate to job satisfaction.[62] In turn, employees respond with high levels of engagement and job performance.

Table 4.2 The Work as Meaning Inventory (WAMI)

Positive meaning

☐ I have found a meaningful career.

☐ I understand how my work contributes to my life's meaning.

☐ I have a good sense of what makes my job meaningful.

☐ I have discovered work that has a satisfying purpose.

Meaning making through work

☐ I view my work as contributing to my personal growth.

☐ My work helps me better understand myself.

☐ My work helps me make sense of the world around me.

Greater good motivations

☐ My work really makes no difference to the world (reversed).

☐ I know my work makes a positive difference in the world.

☐ The work I do serves a greater purpose.

Source: Steger, M. F., Dik, B. J., & Duffy, R. D. (2012). Measuring meaningful work: The work and meaning inventory (WAMI). *Journal of Career Assessment,* 1–16.

$SAGE edge™

edge.sagepub.com/scandura

Want a better grade? Go to **edge.sagepub.com/scandura** for the tools you need to sharpen your study skills.

KEY TERMS

active, 92
affective, 87
affective commitment, 96
behavioral, 88
cognitive, 87
cognitive
    dissonance, 89
constructive, 94

continuance commitment, 96
core self-evaluation, 94
destructive, 94
employee engagement, 96
job involvement, 96
normative commitment, 96
organizational commitment, 90
passive, 92

perceived organizational support
    (POS), 97
psychological
    empowerment, 99
sense of meaning, 100
social pressure, 90

SUGGESTIONS FOR FURTHER READING

Dik, B., Byrne, Z., & Steger, M. (2013). (Eds.) *Purpose and meaning in the workplace.* Washington, DC: APA Books.

Meyer, J. P., & Allen, N. J. (1997). *Commitment in the workplace: Theory, research, and application.* Thousand Oaks, CA: Sage.

Spector, P. E. (1997). *Job satisfaction: Application, assessment, causes and consequences.* Thousand Oaks, CA: Sage.

Spreitzer, G. M., & Quinn, R. E. (2001). *A company of leaders: Five disciplines for unleashing the power in your workforce.* San Francisco, CA: Jossey-Bass.

TOOLKIT ACTIVITY 4.1

What Do Workers Want From Their Jobs?

Objective: To identify what satisfies people at work.

Instructions: Rank each item under the column titled "Individual Factors" from 1 to 10, with 1 being the most important and 10 being the least important.

Individual Factors	Group Factors	What Do People Want From Their Jobs?
_____	_____	Promotion in the company
_____	_____	Tactful discipline
_____	_____	Job security
_____	_____	Help with personal problems
_____	_____	Personal loyalty of supervisor
_____	_____	High wages
_____	_____	Full appreciation of work being done
_____	_____	Good working conditions
_____	_____	Feeling of being in on things
_____	_____	Interesting work

When you have completed the ranking, meet with a group of four to five classmates, and calculate the average individual weights within their group. Rank the 10 items under the column titled "Group Factors." Discuss your answers with your group before reading further.

This same scale has been given to thousands of workers across the country. Supervisors ranked the items in this order:

1. High wages
2. Job security
3. Promotion in the company
4. Good working conditions
5. Interesting work
6. Personal loyalty of supervisor
7. Tactful discipline

8. Full appreciation of work being done
9. Help with personal problems
10. Feeling of being in on things

However, when employees were given the same exercise, their rankings tended to follow this pattern:

1. Full appreciation of work being done
2. Feeling of being in on things
3. Help with personal problems
4. Job security
5. High wages
6. Interesting work
7. Promotion in the company
8. Personal loyalty of supervisor
9. Good working conditions
10. Tactful discipline

Discussion Questions

1. In comparing the different ratings, what might account for the different opinions between you and your group?
2. What might be the cause of the supervisor's rankings being so different from the employees?
3. Do you think the results of this survey would change over time?

Source: Kovach, K. A. (1987). What motivates employees? Workers and supervisors give different answers. *Business Horizons, 30*(5), 58–65. Retrieved on March 27, 2014, from http://www.nwlink.com/~donclark/leader/want_job.html#sthash.86o3taW7.dpuf

CASE STUDY 4.1

A Crisis in Nursing

Los Rayos del Sol Medical Center is a hospital and surgery center located in Florida. A facility with 500 beds, it has recently partnered with the Mayo Clinic. Los Rayos is experiencing high turnover. The nurse average turnover rate is 14% for hospitals,[63] while Los Rayos has a turnover rate of 21%. New graduate nurses turnover at a rate of 27% within their first year, with an additional 37% of those new nurses wanting to leave.[64] At Los Rayos, new nurse turnover is 40%. The hospital spends an average of 13 weeks[65] to fill a vacant position and thousands of dollars per hire.[66] Turnover often leaves units understaffed and having poor morale and lower quality of patient care.

Why are the nurses leaving? Los Rayos strives to provide the highest quality patient care, but it also has to manage costs to comply with government regulations. Thus, over the past 10 years, Los Rayos has made a number of changes.

Ten years ago, Los Rayos changed the staffing model. All units had two licensed nurses and a housekeeper. Housekeepers were minimum wage staff that helped nurses do things like washing linens and stocking the nurses' station with basics. These tasks can take a lot of time away from nurses' normal job duties of doing rounds, charting, administering doctor's orders, and helping patients. Los Rayos promoted the housekeepers to health techs, who were supposed to do more patient care tasks, but most were not equipped with the skills. At the same time, Los Rayos reduced the number of nurses by one. This raised staffing ratios from 12 patients to one nurse to 22 patients to one nurse. Other changes included the following:

- Eight years ago, Los Rayos cut the annual employee picnic and Christmas party in order to save costs.
- Five years ago, Los Rayos expanded nurses' jobs to engage in activities like cost cutting and quality control. It required nurses to provide three to five cost-saving ideas per year or they would be negatively evaluated on their performance appraisals.

- Two years ago, Los Rayos began using tablets for patients' charts and dispensing medicine. To prevent drug theft, medicine carts were equipped with a new security system that requires nurses to scan the patient's hospital bracelet with the tablet, select the medication, and confirm the order before the tablet sent the information to the cart and unlocked the needed medicine. While it prevents theft, the process caused frustration to both the nurse and the patient.
- A year ago, Los Rayos began requiring all its nurses to take turns developing, planning, and presenting continuing education courses. Nurses are required to complete 60 hours of continuing education annually for license renewal.
- Six months ago, Los Rayos changed from 8-hour to 12-hour shifts to reduce costs and allow patients to be closer to their caretakers. However, patients from the maternity and geriatric wards have complained about only seeing nurses at the start and end of shift. Some employees like 12-hour shifts; however, most agree that these shifts are exhausting, and the nurses often state they don't have the time and energy to "go the extra mile" for colleagues and patients.

Discussion Questions

1. How might the changes Los Rayos made affect nurses' attitudes? What problems to the hospital outcomes might poor nurse attitudes cause?
2. Which of the job attitudes from the chapter do you feel is the biggest contributor to nurse turnover? The smallest contributor? Why do you think so?
3. How might leadership and the personality of nurse managers and administrators be affecting the situation?
4. If you were the director of a hospital and going to do a survey of employee attitudes, which attitudes would you include on the survey? Why?

SELF-ASSESSMENT 4.1

Core Self-Evaluations Assessment

This self-assessment exercise identifies your core self-evaluations. There are no right or wrong answers, and this is not a test. You don't have to share your results with the class unless you wish to do so.

Part I. Taking the Assessment

You will be presented with some questions representing how you might see yourself.

As an example, the answer to a situation could look like this:

I am optimistic about my future.

Not like me at all	Not much like me	Somewhat like me	Mostly like me	Very much like me

This response indicates that being optimistic about your future mostly describes you.

1. I am confident I will get the success I deserve in life.

Not like me at all	Not much like me	Somewhat like me	Mostly like me	Very much like me

2. Sometimes I feel depressed.

Not like me at all	Not much like me	Somewhat like me	Mostly like me	Very much like me

3. When I try, I generally succeed.

Not like   Not much   Somewhat   Mostly   Very much
me at all   like me   like me   like me   like me

4. Sometimes when I fail I feel worthless.

Not like   Not much   Somewhat   Mostly   Very much
me at all   like me   like me   like me   like me

5. I complete tasks successfully.

Not like   Not much   Somewhat   Mostly   Very much
me at all   like me   like me   like me   like me

6. Sometimes, I do not feel in control of my work.

Not like   Not much   Somewhat   Mostly   Very much
me at all   like me   like me   like me   like me

7. Overall, I am satisfied with myself.

Not like   Not much   Somewhat   Mostly   Very much
me at all   like me   like me   like me   like me

8. I am filled with doubts about my competence.

Not like   Not much   Somewhat   Mostly   Very much
me at all   like me   like me   like me   like me

9. I determine what will happen in my life.

Not like   Not much   Somewhat   Mostly   Very much
me at all   like me   like me   like me   like me

10. I do not feel in control of my success in my career.

Not like   Not much   Somewhat   Mostly   Very much
me at all   like me   like me   like me   like me

11. I am capable of coping with most of my problems.

Not like   Not much   Somewhat   Mostly   Very much
me at all   like me   like me   like me   like me

12. There are times when things look pretty bleak and hopeless to me.

Not like   Not much   Somewhat   Mostly   Very much
me at all   like me   like me   like me   like me

Part II. Scoring Instructions

1. For questions 1, 3, 5, 7, 9, and 11 assign the following points:

   5 = Very much like me
   4 = Mostly like me
   3 = Somewhat like me
   2 = Not much like me
   1 = Not like me at all

2. For questions 2, 4, 6, 8, 10, and 12, assign the following points:

   1 = Very much like me
   2 = Mostly like me
   3 = Somewhat like me
   4 = Not much like me
   5 = Not like me at all

In Step 1, you rated yourself on 12 questions. Add the numbers you circled in each of the columns to derive your score for your core self-evaluations.

Part 1	Part 2
1. _____	2. _____
3. _____	4. _____
5. _____	6. _____
7. _____	8. _____
9. _____	10. _____
11. _____	12. _____

Part 1 Total _____ + Part 2 Total _____ = Your Score _____

Interpretation

Your scores can range from 12 to 60. In general, scores from 12 to 24 can be considered low core self-evaluation and scores above 25 can be considered high core self-evaluation.

Source: Adapted from: Judge, T. A., Erez, A., & Bono, C. J. (2003). The core self-evaluations scale: Development of a measure. *Personnel Psychology, 56*(2), 303–331.

SELF-ASSESSMENT 4.2

Do You Experience Empowerment?

This self-assessment exercise provides feedback on how empowered you feel at work. If you don't have work experience, consider how you feel working on team projects for your classes. There are no right or wrong answers and this is not a test. You don't have to share your results with others unless you wish to do so.

Part I. Taking the Assessment

You will be presented with some questions representing how you feel about your work.

As an example, the answer to a question could look like this:

I am the type of person who is energetic in the morning.

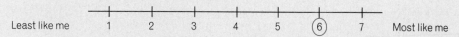

Least like me   1   2   3   4   5   ⑥   7   Most like me

This response indicates that you are energetic in the morning—for the most part.

1. The work I do is very important to me.

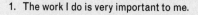
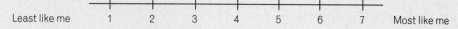

Least like me   1   2   3   4   5   6   7   Most like me

2. I am confident about my ability to do my job.

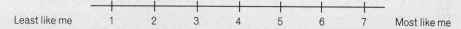

Least like me   1   2   3   4   5   6   7   Most like me

3. I have significant autonomy in determining how I do my job.

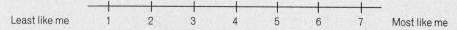

Least like me   1   2   3   4   5   6   7   Most like me

4. I have a large impact on what happens in my department.

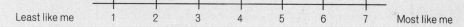

Least like me   1   2   3   4   5   6   7   Most like me

5. My job activities are personally meaningful to me.

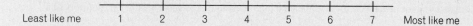

Least like me   1   2   3   4   5   6   7   Most like me

6. I am self-assured about my capabilities to perform my work activities.

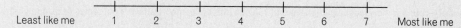

Least like me   1   2   3   4   5   6   7   Most like me

7. I can decide on my own how to go about doing my work.

Least like me   1   2   3   4   5   6   7   Most like me

8. I have a great deal of control over what happens in my department.

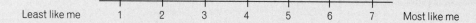

Least like me   1   2   3   4   5   6   7   Most like me

9. The work I do is meaningful to me.

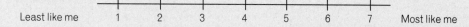

Least like me   1   2   3   4   5   6   7   Most like me

10. I have mastered the skills necessary for my job.

Least like me   1   2   3   4   5   6   7   Most like me

11. I have considerable opportunity for independence and freedom in how I do my job.

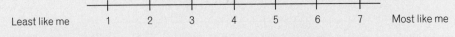

Least like me   1   2   3   4   5   6   7   Most like me

12. I have significant influence over what happens in my department.

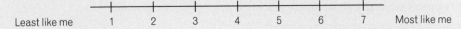

Least like me   1   2   3   4   5   6   7   Most like me

Part II. Scoring Instructions

In Step I, you rated yourself on 12 questions. Add the numbers you circled in each of the columns to derive your score for empowerment.

Meaning	Competence	Self-Determination	Impact
1. _____	2. _____	3. _____	4. _____
5. _____	6. _____	7. _____	8. _____
9. _____	10. _____	11. _____	12. _____
Total _____	_____	_____	_____

Meaning—how much work goals align with your personal standards (i.e., how well the work "fits" your values)

Competence (or self-efficacy)—your belief in your capabilities to show mastery in your work role

Self-Determination—the degree to which you feel that you have a choice in your work and autonomy to carry it out according to your own preferences.

Impact—refers to how much you believe that you can influence important work outcomes (e.g., administrative policies at work)

More information on the empowerment profiles for different contexts and norm data for the empowerment dimensions can be found in Spreitzer and Quinn (2001).

Sources: Spreitzer, G. M. (1995). Psychological empowerment in the workplace: Dimensions, measurement, and validation. *Academy of Management Journal, 38*(5), 1442–1465; Spreitzer, G. M. (1996). Social structural characteristics of psychological empowerment. *Academy of Management Journal, 39*(2), 483–504; Spreitzer, G. M., & Quinn, R. E. (2001). *A company of leaders: Five disciplines for unleashing the power in your workforce.* San Francisco, CA: Jossey-Bass.

5

PERCEPTION

WOULD YOU BE HAPPIER IF YOU WERE RICHER?

This question was investigated in a survey of working women asking them to estimate the amount of time they were in a bad mood the previous day.[1] Respondents were then asked to estimate the percentage of time people were in a bad mood with pairs of high- and low-income situations. These estimates were compared to the *actual* reports of mood provided by high- and low-income participants. The researchers learned that the women in the study exaggerated the bad moods of other people with low-income levels. The average person estimated that people with incomes below $20,000 per year spend 58% of their time in a bad mood, compared with 26% for those with incomes above $100,000 per year. However, the actual percentages were 32% and 20%, respectively. This perception bias can be explained as the *focusing illusion*, which is the tendency to overestimate the effect of a single factor on one's life satisfaction (in this example, the factor tested was income). Income actually has less effect on a person's moments of pleasurable experience than on their response to questions about their overall well-being. Why? The authors cite research suggesting that material goods are not all that strongly related to general well-being. Also, income is seen as relative (as others in a society get richer, people shift their reference point with respect to life satisfaction and income). Finally, research shows that with higher income, people spend more time working and commuting to and from work (often reported as the low points of the day) rather than spending time with family or doing other pleasurable activities. They also report higher levels of stress. So, the focusing illusion explains why people in general are not more satisfied if they are richer. If people focus only on income and ignore other factors related to well-being, they feel less satisfied with their lives.

Learning Objectives

After studying this chapter, you should be able to do the following:

5.1: Explain how perceptions can change.

5.2: Illustrate common perceptual biases with examples.

5.3: Compare the influences of internal and external attributions on judgment.

5.4: Discuss the "romance of leadership" perspective and why this halo effect is important to consider when leading others.

5.5: Explain how self-fulfilling prophecies affect job performance.

5.6: Compare and contrast the aspects of employability as seen by prospective employers.

5.7: Provide an example of how perceptions affect leader–member relationships.

Get the edge on your studies at
edge.sagepub.com/scandura
- Take the chapter quiz
- Review key terms with eFlashcards
- Explore multimedia resources, SAGE readings, and more!

$SAGE edge™

Critical Thinking Question: How can leaders employ the focusing illusion to improve follower satisfaction with pay and benefits?

Visual Illusions

As the previous example shows, **perception** plays a large role in how people view their work, their coworkers, their boss, and the overall organization they work for. Unlike individual differences, such as personality traits and cross-cultural differences, research shows that perceptions can change. Given the example and now that you understand the focusing illusion, will you look at your income differently? In this chapter, other perceptual biases will be covered, as well as the power of **attributions** at the workplace. Understanding why people perceive situations differently is essential for a leader to be effective.

WHAT IS PERCEPTION?

Learning Objective 5.1: Explain how perceptions can change.

Perception is the process through which people organize and interpret their sensory information (what they hear and see, for example) to give meaning to their world. Look at the image shown in Figure 5.1. What do you see? Write down what you see before you look at Figure 5.2.

Most people see a lot of different images but don't see the cow in the picture. Now that you have seen the cow outlined in Figure 5.2, look back at Figure 5.1. It's almost impossible not to see the cow in your mind once you have been shown that it is there. This exercise illustrates two important things about perception that leaders need to know. First, people

Figure 5.1　What Is It?

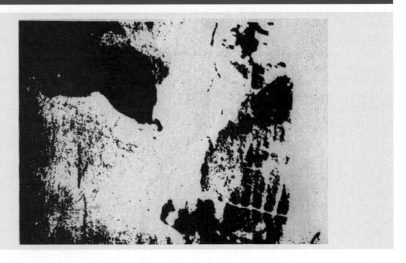

Figure 5.2   Did You See It?

Zimbardo's
Prison
Experiment

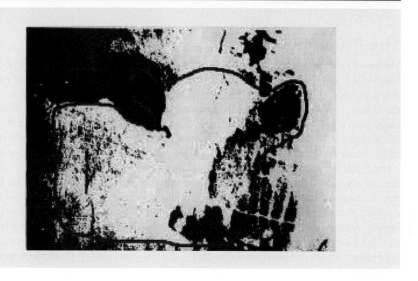

in organizations see things differently. One person might have seen a duck in Figure 5.1. Another person might have seen a turtle. A leader must understand that each person's perception is their reality, and this is how they will interpret the leader's actions and everything else that happens at the workplace. Second, perceptions (unlike personality traits which we have already discussed in Chapter 3) can change. A leader can persuade followers to see things differently as you learned when you looked at Figure 5.2 (and suddenly saw the cow). These are important fundamental ideas to keep in mind as this chapter explores the role of perceptions at the workplace.

UNDERSTANDING WHY PEOPLE DON'T SEE EYE TO EYE

Learning Objective 5.2: Illustrate common perceptual biases with examples.

One of the reasons why people see things differently in organizations is that research has shown they make perceptual errors. Perceptual errors are defined as flaws in perception due to mental shortcuts people make to simplify informed that is processed. These errors matter for a number of reasons. First, they affect interpretations of leaders' and coworkers' behavior. Second, perceptual errors (or biases) affect how job applicants are seen in interviews. Third, they affect performance appraisals. Thus, leaders need to know about these perceptual biases and guard against them. Examples of important decisions leaders make that may be affected by perceptual errors are hiring the best person for a job and being fair in performance assessment of followers. This chapter covers perceptual

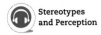
Stereotypes
and Perception

biases that have been most studied in workplace settings and are most relevant to effective leadership. These biases can be remembered with the acronym PRACH for *primacy, recency, availability, contrast,* and *halo.*

The Primacy Effect

We have heard the statement, "you never get a second chance to make a good first impression." But do first impressions really matter? There is a significant body of research that suggests they do, and this is the **primacy effect** or "belief perseverance."[2] For example, if a person smells like smoke when met by an interviewer who doesn't smoke, this impression may last and influence whether they get the job. Once a person has formed an initial impression, they maintain it even when presented with concrete evidence that it is false. Classic experimental research in psychology has demonstrated this affects problem solving[3] and the persistence of **stereotypes.**[4] Specifically, order effects research confirms that information presented early in a sequence affects judgments made later.[5] This may be due to fatigue or not paying attention. People discount information presented later due to the need to confirm their first impressions. They seek only consistent information and rule out alternatives that conflict with their initial impression.[6] More recently, experimental research has shown that the primacy effect persists due to **belief updating,** where initial information affects the conclusion one draws, and this conclusion then impacts later judgments.[7]

How quickly do we form a first impression? It may be much faster than you might think. In experimental research, subjects were shown a photograph of a person's face for only a tenth of a second.[8] Based on this "flash" photo of a face, people gave ratings of the person's attractiveness, likeability, trustworthiness, competence, and aggressiveness. Moreover, when the exposure time was increased, there was no change in the assessments. The authors concluded increased exposure time only seems to bolster a person's initial first impressions.

What can be done to address the primacy effect? Accountability influenced a person's vigilance and improved processing of all information presented in an experimental study where subjects were asked to role-play being a jury member in a murder case.[9] When people are asked to justify their decisions to others, they are more likely to process all of the information available. So a leader should keep this in mind when making important decisions. Imagine that you would have to justify this decision to your boss or in public (you never know—you might end up having to do so). Second, based upon research on belief updating, the leader should be willing to "hit the reset button" and look at a situation as if they had no prior exposure to it. From this review, it seems clear that primacy is important and first impressions do matter.

Critical Thinking Question: If you make a bad first impression in an interview, what would you try to do to change it?

The Recency Effect

Not only do people remember what they experience first but also remember the most recently presented items or experiences. This perceptual bias is called the recency effect. For example, if you are given a long list of names to remember, you will probably remember the ones you heard last and forget the ones in the middle. Actually, in terms of free recall on tasks, there is a U-shaped pattern in which the primacy effect results in the first words that are mentioned being remembered, followed by a decline in the middle words presented, then a steep increase and then leveling off (an S-shaped curve) for the words presented most recently.[10] For example, after a job interview, it is important to end on a positive note by showing the interviewer appreciation for their time.

The recency effect is pervasive.[11] Recency may affect performance appraisals (the manager remembers their direct reports' most recent behavior rather than behavior in the middle of the evaluation period). In experimental studies involving role-plays of performance appraisal sessions, recency effects were present regardless of whether the appraisal was made at the end of each task or at the end of the entire rating process.[12] However, people can improve their short-term memory by employing control processes that affect how information is stored and retrieved.[13] So how can a leader guard against the recency effect?

First, rehearsal, or repetition of information, has been shown to improve recall (think about how you might repeat a phone number you hear over and over in your mind several times to remember it until you can write it down). Coding is another technique in which you link the information you need to remember to something familiar and easily retrievable (e.g., you remember passwords by creating combinations of your pet's name with other alphanumeric characters and symbols). Another example is mnemonic coding in which you create acronyms to remember information (such as PRACH to remember these perceptual biases: primacy, recency, availability, contrast, and halo). Another technique to improve recall is called imaging, in which verbal information is linked to visual images. For example, a person would visualize an image that is associated with a word that sounds like the person's name, so someone named D. J. who is a finance professor could be remembered as Dow Jones. These types of memory techniques have been shown to improve short-term memory of long lists of information significantly.[14] By now, you have probably realized research on recency and memory improvement has implications for how you can improve your study habits and performance on exams!

The Availability Bias

Sometimes, a person's judgments are based upon what most readily comes into a person's mind. In the most frequently cited study of the availability bias, subjects were read two lists of names, one presenting 19 famous men and 20 less famous women and the other presenting 19 famous women and 20 less famous men.[15] When asked, subjects reported that there were more men than women in the first list but more women than men in the second list, even though the opposite was true (by a difference of one). Presumably, the famous names were easier to recall than the non-famous ones, resulting in an overestimate. In fact, subjects were able to recall about 50% more of the famous than of the non-famous names. Another study conducted by the same researchers found that people tend to overestimate the number of words that began with the letter r but to underestimate the number of words that had r as the third letter.[16] The first letter likely prompts people to remember more words; however, there are actually more words in the English language that have r as the third letter.

Remember Every Name Every Time

According to Benjamin Levy, who has trained thousands of executives to improve their memory, there is nothing as pleasant to another person as hearing their own name spoken. For leaders to really connect with a large constellation of different people, they need to be able to remember their names. Research on perception has indicated there are some tricks you can employ to remember peoples' names. Levy suggests the FACE method for remembering names: FACE stands for "Focus, Ask, Comment and Employ."[17]

Focus: Lock in on the person's face. Lean forward and turn your head slightly to one side. You should give the other person your ear (literally).

Ask: Inquire about his name (Is it Robert or Bob? What is the origin of your last name?). Ask or clarify that you heard the name correctly. Genuinely pay attention, and show that you really care.

Comment: Say something about the name, and cross-reference it in your head ("My best friend in high school's name was Bob"). Or relate the name to a famous movie star; for example, if the person's name is Benjamin, ask if they like to be called "Ben" like Ben Affleck.

Employ: Put the name to use right away: "Great to meet you, Bob!" A great aid to memory is to teach material to someone else. You can introduce the person to another person in the room to further fix the name in your mind. At the end of the conversation, use the name again: "It's a pleasure to meet you, Ben."

Once you master the FACE technique, you can learn the NAME technique. NAME stands for "nominate, articulate, morph, and entwine."

Nominate: Pick a feature of the person's face, and then nominate it as the feature you will use to link the name to the face. Try to focus on the eyes, nose, lips, ears, chin, or eyebrows.

Articulate: Silently make a note to yourself of what is unique about the feature you have nominated. For example, Ben's eyes are green.

Morph: Change the name into another work you can remember, but it retains an element of the original name. For example, Ben becomes a Lens.

Entwine: You nominated a physical characteristic of a person you just met. Then you articulated a mental description of the person. Third, you morphed the name into a sound-alike word. Try to create as vivid an image as you can. For example, think of Ben wearing large, funny glasses with green lenses (LENS = BEN, a person with GREEN EYES).

These tips are only the basics of how to learn to remember names every time. More detail can be found in his book *Remember Every Name, Every Time.* Does it work? Benjamin Levy stuns corporate training audiences by remembering the names of 100 to 150 people! With practice, you can learn his techniques to enhance your ability to connect with others—an essential leadership skill.

Discussion Questions:

1. Explain how the primacy effect helps you remember people's names during the focus phase of the FACE technique.
2. Practice remembering names by developing memory aids using the NAME technique for the following names: Laura Ray and Kevin Rankin.

Source: Levy, B. (2002). *Remember every name, every time: Corporate America's memory master reveals his secrets.* New York, NY: Fireside Books.

Both the ease and difficulty of recall of information affects how well people remember information.[18] In addition to information that is readily available, information that is more difficult to recall is more likely forgotten. There is evidence that shows events are judged to be more common when instances more *easily* come to mind, even when a smaller absolute *number* of instances are generated. For example, a lot of people have a fear of flying because incidents of plane crashes make headlines and high-profile news reports. However, the probability that one will die in a plane crash is much lower than in a car crash (a chance of 1 in 108 for a car accident compared to 1 in 7,229 for a plane crash based on data reported for 2013 by the National Safety Council). This is a demonstration of the availability heuristic.

Seeing Differently

How can a leader guard against making the availability bias mistake? First, they can make the things that are desired for decision making (perhaps at a later date) vivid and very easy to bring to mind (e.g., with repetition and visualization). They can also try to minimize things that influence decisions by making them more difficult to recall by using vague, abstract, complex, or uncomfortable language to describe them. Increasing the number of counter explanations reduces the persistence of the availability bias (Anderson, 1982; Slusher & Anderson, 1996).[19,20] **Elaborative interrogation** increases the willingness to let go of preconceived notions and learn material that challenges beliefs. Elaborative interrogation requires people to generate their own explanations of factual statements that are presented to them.[21] For example, a leader can write out a statement challenging their decision and then generate arguments for why this statement is false to check their thinking and perhaps avoid the availability bias effect.

When making important decisions, pause and think why you are making the decision. Is it because of information you see frequently? What is the source of the information? What motivated the person to provide it? It's important to keep in mind that we rely on what is familiar and most readily available, but taking shortcuts when making important decisions can have serious negative consequences. Another shortcut happens when we make comparisons based upon what has happened just before we make a decision or judgment: the **contrast effect.** Contrast effects are among the most significant decision biases for a leader to guard against.

Critical Thinking Question: How can elaborative interrogation be used to change perceptions of a follower who does not like to work on a team?

Contrast Effects

Figure 5.3 shows the Ebbinghaus illusion as an example of a perceptual contrast effect. The center circle is exactly the same size in Groups 1 through 3, but it looks larger in Group 1 than in Group 2 because the circles that surround it are small in Group 1 and large in Group 2. Contrast effects also happen in organizational decision making. For example, a leader's performance evaluation of a person is affected by comparisons with other people recently encountered who rank higher or lower on the same characteristics.

Experimental research on contrast effects on employee performance evaluations indicates when a leader has followers who are poor performers (who did not respond to requests to perform work) give very high ratings to average performing subordinates. On the other hand, when all subordinates responded favorably to supervisory requests, fewer rewards and lower performance ratings were given—even to outstanding performers.[22,23] The contrast effect has been found in real organizational settings as well. The greater the proportion of engineers who had low performance ratings (unsatisfactory), the more likely supervisors were to assign favorable ratings and provide rewards to just average performance

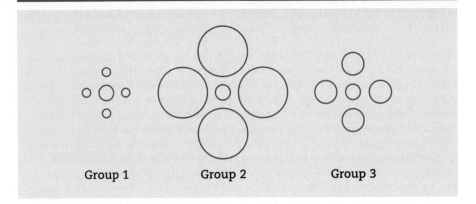

Figure 5.3 The Ebbinghaus Illusion

Group 1   Group 2   Group 3

engineers.[24] Thus, the poor performance of other engineers generated a contrast effect in which a satisfactory performer stood out even though they were not actually stellar. Leaders need to focus on individual performance and avoid comparisons that may result in the contrast effect.

Another potential challenge is in the interviewing process. An applicant for a position may be rated more favorably if they follow a sequence of poor applicants although they may not be the best person for the job. Training managers to eliminate biases including the contrast effect results in improved evaluations.[25] There is some indication that becoming aware of the contrast effect may help a leader reduce the bias when making hiring decisions and performance appraisals. In addition, using a structured interview process may reduce the contrast effect.[26] A structured interview should have the following elements:

1. Use standard and numerical score sheets.
2. Use behavioral and situational questions.
3. Ask the same questions in the same order for each applicant.
4. Avoid questions that are unrelated to the position you are interviewing for.

Training and the use of structured interviews may also reduce another pervasive decision error that may affect managerial judgments of all types including performance appraisals and hiring decisions: the **halo error** effect.

Halo Error

Halo error (or its opposite **horns error**) occurs when the rater's overall positive (or negative in the case of horns) impression or evaluation strongly influence ratings of specific attributes.[27] For example, wearing a fraternity or sorority pin to an interview may invoke a positive impression if the interviewer is a member who assumes membership in the organization translates to high performance. Research on halo errors in rating can be traced back to early organizational behavior (OB) research,[28] and there has been steady interest in its study over time.[29,30] Some researchers consider halo error to be "ubiquitous" in organizations and perhaps the most serious of rating errors that are made by managers.[31] A meta-analytic review of research on halo in ratings of job performance and concluded that halo error "substantially" increased both supervisory and peer ratings of performance.[32] Halo error results in an overall positive impression of a follower that clouds evaluation of actual performance because it is assumed that if a follower is good at one aspect of the job, they are good at everything.

 Attribution

Halo effects in OB may occur for many reasons. A manager might form a general impression after having seen a few successful task accomplishments, and subsequent judgments may be heavily influenced by this first impression (i.e., the primacy effect + halo error resulting in a strong influence on perception). Some managers may be too busy and stop paying attention to a follower's performance. Another manager may strive to make later ratings consistent with earlier ratings to prove they are right. Halo effects may also be compounded by the contrast effect in which a previously rated person interviewed influences the ratings of those interviewed later (halo + contrast). As noted earlier for contrast effects, training and the use of structured interviews may be effective in reducing halo error.

The research reviewed in the previous sections has shown that perceptual biases may result in inaccurate performance appraisals and poor decision making by leaders. Another theory addressing the effect of perceptions on performance is attribution theory—what the leader believes are the *causes* of good or bad performance of their followers.

ATTRIBUTION THEORY

Learning Objective 5.3: Compare the influences of internal and external attributions on judgment.

There is a great deal of perception research that shows that the attributions of what causes behavior in organizations matter. Attributions represent a person's attempt to assign a cause to a behavior or event they observe. Attribution theory proposes that the attributions people make about events and behavior can be either internal or external.[33] In organizational settings, attributions are particularly important when events are important, novel, unexpected, and negative.[34] In the case of an **internal attribution,** people infer that an event or a person's behavior is due to his or her own character traits or abilities. If a person makes an **external attribution,** they believe that a person's behavior is due to situational factors. For example, Damon is late to class. If the professor believes the tardiness happened because of Damon's lack of motivation to attend class, he is making an internal attribution. On the other hand, if the professor believes Damon is late because he could not find a parking space in overcrowded university lots, he is making an external attribution.

Research on attribution theory has demonstrated attributions can bias how we process information and make decisions. The first way this occurs is called the **fundamental attribution error.** This is the tendency to attribute other people's behavior to internal factors such as character traits or abilities, but when explaining one's own behavior, people tend to attribute the cause to the situation.[35] The second way attributions may cloud judgment is the **self-serving bias** that occurs when a person attributes successes to internal factors and failures to situational factors. And the further an event is in the past, the more likely the cause of a failure will be attributed to the situation. For example, Mindy gets a poor grade on a quiz and attributes her failure to unfair test questions rather than not studying for the quiz. The third way attributions may affect judgment is the **just world hypothesis,** which is the need to believe that the world is fair and that people get what they deserve. This gives people a sense of security, particularly when they encounter a challenging situation. For example, Joe gets laid off at work due to downsizing, and his coworkers attribute the layoff to Joe being an argumentative person rather than the business situation or a bad economy.

 Critical Thinking Questions: Why do you think the just world hypothesis is so pervasive? Why do you think employees demand that organizations be fair?

How can we avoid attribution bias? When we ascribe a cause to behavior, we should gather additional information. By paying attention to overall patterns of behavior, we make more accurate conclusions by considering the following:

1. **Consensus information**—information about how other people would behave if they were in the same situation. High consensus means others would behave the same way. Low consensus means other people would behave differently.
2. **Distinctiveness information**—information about how the individual behaves the same way in different situations. Low in distinctiveness means the individual behaves the same way to different situations. High in distinctiveness means the individual behaves a particular way toward a particular situation only.
3. **Consistency information**—information about how the individual behaves toward a certain stimuli across time and circumstances. High in consistency means the individual behaves the same way almost every time they are in a particular situation.

Based on this perspective, if a leader wants to improve judgments and avoid the attribution error, they should consider how well other people would do in the same situation. For example, do all employees make the same mistake when filling out forms for customers? If so, maybe the form needs to be revised. Second, how distinctive is the behavior? For example, does the employee behave rudely to all coworkers or just one in particular? Finally, how consistent is the behavior? For example, over time, the leader observes that an employee does not pay close attention to their work every Friday afternoon, and this is a consistent pattern. Attending to these three possibilities alerts the leader to investigate and gather additional information before making a definitive conclusion about the cause of behavior. Attributions play a role in how leader–member relationships develop as well.

Attributions and the
Development of Leader–Member Relationships

Attributions play a clear role in the development of high-quality relationships between leaders and followers.[36,37] A dyadic (two-party) relational approach to attribution theory is shown in Figure 5.4.[38] As shown in the figure, an internal or an external attribution might be made as we have previously discussed—for example, "I did not get a positive performance review" could be attributed to "I did not put in enough effort" (internal) or "The Human Resources department is incompetent" (external). A relational attribution offers a third and potentially powerful explanation: "My boss and I don't have a positive

Figure 5.4   Relational Attributions in Response to Negative Achievement-Related Events

	Internal attribution	Relational attribution	External attribution
	Self	Self in relation to other	Other person/ situation
"I did not get a positive performance review, because…	… I did not put in enough effort over the past few weeks."	… my boss and I don't have a positive relationship."	… my boss is incompetent."
"I was not chosen as the team leader, because…	… I have poor communication skills."	… my boss and I do not communicate well with each other."	… it was my coworker's turn— people are selected based on a policy of rotating responsibility."
"I did not meet the project's, deadline, because…	… I did not ask for additional help soon enough."	… my coworker and I did not give each other frequent enough updates."	… I had to redo all the work my coworker turned in."

Source: Eberly, M. B., Holley, E. C., Johnson, M. D., & Mitchell, T. R. (2011). Beyond internal and external: A dyadic theory of relational attributions. *Academy of Management Review, 36*(4), 731–753.

relationship." The actions a person might take to remedy the situation will vary depending upon the attribution. In the case of an external attribution (the most likely according to the fundamental attribution error), the person may feel helpless to change it except for finding another job. However, if a relational attribution is made, the person might try to improve the working relationship with the boss. Thus, relational attribution theory offers another way a person might improve their work situation by changing what they attribute the causes of an event to. If it is the relationship (and not internal or external), actions can be taken to improve the working relationship.

Attributions may affect how we process information and lead to errors in judgment. Also, they affect how we develop leader–member relationships with followers and others at work. Attributions may also affect the way that we view leaders in general. Research has found that people make significant attributions about the power of leaders, which is called the "romance of leadership." In other words, leaders are not powerful because of their expertise or behaviors but their power is derived from follower attributions of their influence over events.

THE ROMANCE OF LEADERSHIP

Learning Objective 5.4: Discuss the "romance of leadership" perspective and why this halo effect is important to consider when leading others.

The romance of leadership approach articulates why people recognize and give credit to leaders for their influence to change organizations and even societies.[39] This approach highlights the fact that leaders are often the most favored explanation for both positive and negative outcomes in organizations. There is a halo effect for leadership: People value performance results more highly when those results are attributed to leadership. Moreover, if an individual is perceived to be an effective leader, his or her personal shortcomings and even poor organizational performance may be ignored. Thus, the romance of leadership perspective challenges the public's apparent fascination with leaders and leadership in which leaders are portrayed as heroes and heroines even when there is no real evidence to support this level of admiration. Leadership is viewed as an attribution by the followers rather than a trait or behavior of the leader. This perspective is not "anti-leadership," but it places an emphasis on the follower and the situation. This helps explain why some leaders exercise so much power in organizations. The next section will focus on other ways that the perceptions affect leadership.

Critical Thinking Question: What are your perceptions of leaders? Provide an example of a situation where leaders are believed to have the power to make major changes in society.

To this point, we have been discussing perceptual shortcuts that may result in suboptimal performance of leaders and followers. Can perception have positive influences on OB processes? The answer is yes, and there is much research on the **Pygmalion effect,** which shows that perceptions of performance expectations may play a significant role in improving follower performance.

THE PYGMALION EFFECT

Learning Objective 5.5: Explain how self-fulfilling prophecies affect job performance.

Perceptions sometimes result in the self-fulfilling prophecy, or Pygmalion effect, in which the high expectations of performance by leaders actually create conditions in which followers succeed. Named after a George Bernard Shaw play, effect was first studied by Robert Rosenthal in an elementary classroom setting.[40] In his experiments, he told teachers that some of their students had the capability to be leading performers—or as he called them "intellectual bloomers."[41] The teachers, unknowingly, gave these students more learning opportunities and more positive feedback. These students had actually been chosen randomly, but the result was that they did end up performing better. As a leader, you may challenge your employees or empower them to confront a difficult situation by persuading them into positive thoughts. Having positive expectations may cause a leader to provide more attention and feedback to followers and, in turn, result in them performing at a higher level.

Research on the Pygmalion effect suggests managers can boost performance by raising their expectations of followers.[42] This occurs through higher goals being set and followers being more engaged and striving to learn more on the job.[43] A meta-analysis concluded the Pygmalion effect is fairly strong in organizations, but the work context of the research was limited since many early studies were conducted in military settings with men.[44,45] However, later research demonstrated the Pygmalion effect in nonmilitary settings and with women as well.[46,47] Leaders in organizations can communicate high expectations to followers in the following four ways:[48]

1. Create a warmer emotional climate.
2. Teach more and increasingly challenging.
3. Invite followers to ask questions of clarification.
4. Provide feedback on performance.

What about a person's expectations of himself or herself? The **Galatea effect** is present when and individual sets high expectations for himself or herself and then performs to these expectations. Such a follower already has high self-esteem and believes in his or her ability to succeed. The Galatea effect was examined by conducting an experiment where subjects' self-esteem was boosted by a series of positive feedback messages.[49] This intervention resulted in improved self-esteem, motivation, and an impact on performance. Thus, leaders need to provide ongoing feedback and provide challenging assignments to increase follower expectations. The Galatea effect suggests followers may even exceed the leader's expectations when they have confidence in their ability to succeed.

Critical Thinking Question: Based on what you have learned about the Galatea effect, how can you use the concept to improve your grades?

As might be expected, expectations may also work in the opposite direction where lower expectations lead to lower performance and this is called the **Golem effect.** Golem comes from the Hebrew slang for *dumbbell*. Bosses can "kill" followers' motivation by having low expectations. A 2-year study was conducted of 50 boss–subordinate pairings; the managers were asked to differentiate high performers from low performers. Within 5 minutes of meeting and working with new employees, managers could easily evaluate their future performance. They unanimously stated that the low performers were passive, less motivated, less proactive, and so on. Some followers were classified as not having potential; therefore, the managers spent less time providing them with instructions on how to do their jobs. The managers viewed the low performers as weak and, thus, did not assign challenging tasks to them where they could learn new skills. When the "weak" performers began to notice the bosses' treatment, they became disengaged, and their performance deteriorated and ended up matching the boss' expectations. In effect, these bosses set the followers up to fail.[50] It is possible, through training, to reverse the Golem effect ("de-Golemization") in which supervisors can change their expectations of low performance to higher performance, and followers respond positively with more effort.[51,52] Based upon the long stream of research on Pygmalion effect in organizations, it is clear that perceptions play a role in enhancing job performance.

The evidence reviewed above demonstrates that perceptions play a role in how leaders view their followers' performance. But do perceptions play a role during the application process for a job? The research described in the boxed insert suggests that how potential employers perceive you matters.

EMPLOYABILITY: HOW POTENTIAL EMPLOYERS PERCEIVE YOU

Learning Objective 5.6: Compare and contrast the aspects of employability as seen by prospective employers.

Recent research on **employability** suggests the degree to which you are perceived as employable may determine whether or not you are hired for a position. The ability to gain a job in a formal organization is an emerging area in OB research.[53] Employability is defined as "an attribution employers make about the probability that job candidates will make positive contributions to their organizations."[54] An important question, then, is what determines employer's perceptions of whether or not a job applicant has this potential and is employable by their organization. There are three important aspects to an applicant's profile that affect employers' perceptions and subsequent attributions about employability as shown in Figure 5.5. What matters to employers is proposed to be the candidate's social or interpersonal compatibility, which leads to the perception that the candidate will have positive interactions with others on a daily basis. Next, abilities, expertise, and know-how lead to the perception that the candidate is able to do the job. Finally, ambition, work ethic, and drive lead to the perception that the candidate is willing to work hard. These factors combine to form the employer's attribution of employability and therefore relates to whether or not the applicant gets a job offer.

Research examined individual differences believed to be related to employability such as openness to change at work and optimism. The next question you may be wondering is "How do I know if I am employable as perceived by employers?"[55] To see your ratings on

Do Stereotypes Play a Role in Hiring?

In an experimental study, managers of retail shops and restaurants were asked if a woman wearing a traditional religious garment (a head scarf called a *hijab*) could apply for a job (the woman was a person who was trained to play the role of the job applicant by the research team).[56] The same woman approached managers without wearing the hijab. The women confederates represented a variety of races, but in the hijab condition, all wore the traditional Muslim scarf covering the head, neck, and shoulders (all other attire was the same). Upon entering the stores, confederate applicants asked to speak to the manager, or the person in charge, and asked three standard questions: (1) "Do you have a job position open for a _____ (sales representative/ waitress)?" (2) "Could I fill out a job application?" and (3) "What sort of things would I be doing if I worked here?" Results of this experiment suggested evidence for formal discrimination (job callbacks, permission to complete application), interpersonal discrimination (perceived negativity, lack of perceived interest), and low expectations to receive job offers in the workplace for women wearing the hijab. Further, the women wearing the hijab were less likely to receive callbacks when there was low employee diversity in the store or restaurant compared to when there was high employee diversity. These findings corroborate previous research that indicates negative attitudes and behaviors toward Muslims, and they may face challenges to employment that reflect a lack of acceptance of their religious identity.[57]

The results of this study suggest we need to be careful about our schemas particularly when they may lead to discrimination based on stereotypes. A stereotype is a type of schema or prototype and is defined as "beliefs about the characteristics, attributes, and behaviors of members of certain groups."[58] An outstanding job applicant might be missed due to implicit assumptions about certain groups of people, and the study described previously sensitizes us to the role perceptions of others play in organizational decision making. It is also noteworthy that this was less likely to occur in organizations that already had a diverse workforce. This is a positive finding, underscoring the importance of attracting and maintaining a diverse workforce.

Discussion Questions:

1. Give examples of other groups that might be affected by stereotypes in the hiring process.
2. In addition to a positive diversity climate, what else can leaders do to eliminate stereotype bias in hiring?
3. Provide an example of when a stereotype of another person has a positive effect.

Source: Ghumann, S., & Ryan, A. M. (2013). Not welcome here: Discrimination towards women who wear the Muslim headscarf. *Human Relations, 66*(5), 671–698; Hilton, J. L., & Von Hippel, W. (1996). Stereotypes. *Annual Review of Psychology, 47*(1), 237–271; King, E. B., & Ahmad, A. S. (2010). An experimental field study of discrimination against Muslim job applicants. *Personnel Psychology, 63*(4), 881–906.

the dimensions of employability, you can complete Self-Assessment 5.1 at the end of this chapter. While research on employability is relatively new, it is a very important concept that offers practical advice for students preparing for their job search. Applicants for positions need to pay attention to how they present their qualifications so employers make the attribution that they are employable and will become a significant contributor to the organization's success.

Figure 5.5. Determinants of Employability

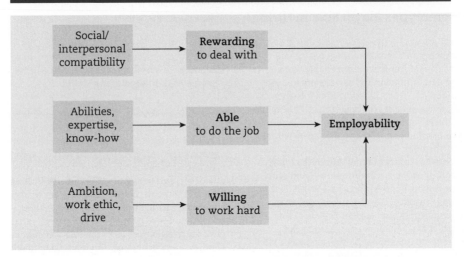

Source: Hogan, R., Chamorro-Premuzic, T. & Kaiser, R. B. (2013). Employability and career success: Bridging the gap between theory and reality. *Industrial and Organizational Psychology,* 6(1), 3–16.

Critical Thinking Questions: How can you use the knowledge of employability to improve your chances of getting hired? What dimensions of employability will you focus on?

Given that perceptions play a role in whether or not a person is employable, can they be changed? Research on **impression management** addresses this question, and the next sections will address how a leader can manage impressions of followers.

Impression Management

Social psychologists have researched self-presentation and the motivations that people have to present themselves in a positive way to others. Impression management is a set of behaviors that people use to protect their self-image or change the way they are seen by others (or both).[59,60] Impression management has been shown to affect interviews, performance appraisals, and career success.[61] A wide range of impression management tactics have been studied, and there are two different goals for using them. One goal is to use them defensively to avoid blame for poor performance or ask for forgiveness ("minimizing bad"), and the other goal is to generate respect and liking from other people ("maximizing good").[62] For example, making excuses for a failure to perform well on a team project is an example of trying to minimize teammates' perceptions of incompetence. An example of "maximizing good" is exemplification in which a person stays late at work so that others know they are a hardworking employee. Impression management strategies have been found to be either job-focused (i.e., exemplification), supervisor-focused (i.e., ingratiation), or self-focused (i.e., self-promotion).[63] Table 5.1 shows examples of impression management strategies that have been discovered by OB researchers. The strategies most relevant for leaders are the ones that maximize good intentions: exemplification, ingratiation, and self-promotion.[64] In the Self-Assessment 5.2 at the end of this chapter, you will find an assessment you can complete to determine the degree to which you would use these strategies.

 Critical Thinking Question: Do you think that impression management is consistent with being an authentic leader? Why or why not?

Body Language

Recent research by Amy Cuddy and her colleagues has indicated a person's body language is also an important aspect of impression management. For example, holding an expansive posture releases hormones that make a person feel more confident and, in turn, influences how they are perceived by others.[65] For example, think about the stance of Wonder Woman with her arms on her hips and legs planted firmly apart. In the research, "power poses" were not superhero stances but were expansive—either sitting with one's arms behind the head and legs up on a table or leaning forward on a table with arms spread apart. Another example of powerful body language is extending one's hand with the palm down for a handshake. This communicates dominance. The researchers conducted experiments in which subjects were asked to hold a power pose for 2 minutes. Saliva samples were taken before and after the power pose. Following the power pose, a hormone associated with

Table 5.1 Examples of Impression Management Strategies

Goal	Strategy	Example
Minimizing bad	Apologies	Saying you are sorry when you violate a coworker's trust
	Excuses	Not taking responsibility for your failures
	Justifications	Blaming poor performance on another department's failure to respond
Maximizing good	Exemplification	Trying to appear busy, even when things are slower at work
	Ingratiation	Using flattery to make your coworkers like you more
	Self-Promotion	Hanging your diplomas on your office wall so that people are aware of your accomplishments

Sources: Adapted from Bolino, M. C., & Turnley, W. H. (1999). Measuring impression management in organizations: A scale development based on the Jones and Pittman taxonomy. *Organizational Research Methods, 2*(2), 187–206; Bolino, M. C., Kacmar, K. M, Turnley, W. H., & Gilstrap, J. B. (2008). A multi-level review of impression management motives and behaviors. *Journal of Management, 34*(6), 1080–1109.

power (testosterone) was increased and a hormone associated with stress (cortisol) was decreased. Also, subjects self-rated themselves higher on how powerful they felt (compared to subjects that held low-power poses) and were more likely to take risks in a gambling task.[66] According to Cuddy, "poses are powerful… it's about becoming so comfortable and feeling you have so much control over how you present yourself that you become more your authentic self."[67]

LEADERSHIP IMPLICATIONS: LEADING FOLLOWERS WITH DIFFERING PERCEPTIONS

Learning Objective 5.7: Provide an example of how perceptions affect leader–member relationships.

Attribution theory provides a great deal of insight into how to lead followers that have different perceptions of reality. First, attribution theory addresses how followers see who *they* are. Second, it also addresses how followers see who *you* are as the leader. The next two paragraphs discuss each of these perceptual effects that leaders must attend to since both affect the working relationship between the leader and follower.

Social identity was introduced as a way to explain how people view their own place in society through membership in various groups.[68] Social identity is "the individual's knowledge that he belongs to certain social groups together with some emotional and value significance to him of this group membership."[69] People belong to different groups (e.g., a student can also be a coworker, a friend, and a member of a church), and these categorizations comprise their social identity.[70] Also, these groups exist in relation to other groups so people derive meaning by relating their membership in a group by comparison to other groups. Think about the team spirit we feel when our football team defeats one of its longtime rivals. We feel a sense of belonging to our university and purchase a new shirt with our team's logo to show the world we are members of that university. Leaders should increase the sense of group cohesion, or solidarity, to stay in power and motivate followers to high performance.[71] Social identity binds people to a group—especially if the group has higher status or is distinctive and motivates people to behave in a manner that is consistent with the norms of the group.[72] Thus, the self-attributions of who a person believes themselves to be (i.e., the social identity) are an important consideration for leaders.

Attributions about leadership also affect follower perceptions of who you are in the role of leader. Research has shown people have **implicit leadership schemas** (or models) in their minds about what constitutes an effective leader.[73] These models are traits and characteristics that a person thinks are being linked to a leader. For example, a person might believe all leaders are tall and highly intelligent. Followers find such models of leaders to be an effective way to categorize leaders and interpret their behavior.[74] For example, followers can accurately recall neutral leadership behaviors, but they exaggerate or distort either positive or negative leadership behaviors.[75] Such implicit assumptions about what an effective leader is serve as a benchmark for how the leader's behavior is interpreted.[76] The models then affect how followers respond to the leader and the way that the relationship develops.[77] To apply this idea, assume that you thought all leaders should be supportive of followers. But you have a leader who is not supportive, which results in a discrepancy, and you don't respond positively to the leader's request for extra effort on a task. This may affect your job performance and evaluation in the future. Changing your assumptions and responding to a task-oriented leader may be difficult to do since this approach assumes leadership is in the "eye of the beholder"—the followers.

As we have shown throughout this chapter, perceptions are malleable (recall the "cow" illusion from the beginning of the chapter). For example, a leader can change a follower's perceptions of their coworkers by ensuring that the the follower isn't making perceptual errors, such as horns error. Also, a leader's expectations of follower abilities may influence the direction and feedback provided, and this will enhance job performance through the Pygmalion effect. Stereotyping is convenient, but stereotypes are often wrong. In fact, discriminating against possible or current employees based upon stereotypes may even result in litigation. Stereotypes are based on perceptions, and you can change them. Finally, through impression management and body language, a leader can change the perceptions of others regarding their effectiveness. Knowing about perceptions and how to change them is a powerful tool for a leader as they lead organizations through uncertain times and change. For example, employees may fear change, but the leader must remember that this is a perception—and it can change through effective communication.

$SAGE edge™

edge.sagepub.com/scandura

Want a better grade? Go to **edge.sagepub.com/scandura** for the tools you need to sharpen your study skills.

KEY TERMS

attributions, 110
availability bias, 113
belief updating, 112
coding, 113
contrast effect, 115
elaborative interrogation, 115
employability, 122
external attribution, 117
fundamental attribution
  error, 117

Galatea effect, 121
Golem effect, 121
halo error, 116
horns error, 116
imaging, 113
implicit leadership
  schemas, 126
impression management, 124
internal attribution, 117
just world hypothesis, 118

perception, 110
primacy effect, 112
Pygmalion effect, 120
recency effect, 113
rehearsal, 113
self-serving bias, 118
social identity, 126
stereotypes, 112

SUGGESTIONS FOR FURTHER READING

Eden, D. (1990). *Pygmalion in management: Productivity as a self-fulfilling prophecy*. Lexington, MA: Lexington Books.

Levy, B. (2002). *Remember every name, every time: Corporate America's memory master reveals his secrets*. New York, NY: Fireside Books.

Rosenzweig, P. (2007). *The halo effect*. New York, NY: Free Press.

TOOLKIT ACTIVITY 5.1

Understanding the Pygmalion Effect

It is a scientific fact that people perform, to a large degree, according to the expectations others have for them. If deep down a manager believes his or her subordinates are incompetent and irresponsible, the chances are good that the employees will act that way. Conversely, if a manager treats employees as competent and responsible, the employees will generally live up to those expectations.

This exercise provides an opportunity to explore various scenarios that might occur within a work environment. Each scenario involves a manager and one or more employees. Divide into groups of two or three. Each group will be assigned one of the scenarios and explore the following issues relative to each one.

1. Is the manager communicating high or low expectations to the employee by his or her behavior?
2. How do you think the employee(s) will react to the manager's behavior? Choose several adjectives that you believe describe this reaction (e.g., angry, motivated).
3. If low expectations are being communicated by the manager in the scenario, answer this question: If you were the manager in this scenario and wanted your employee(s) to respond in a positive manner, what would you have done differently?
4. If high expectations are being communicated by the manager in the scenario, discuss what benefits might result. For the sake of contrast, pretend the manager in the scenario held low expectations for the employee(s). What might that low expectation manager have done in these scenarios, and what would the result be?

Scenario 1

Jim is the production floor manager at Acme Cabinets. He supervises over 100 assemblers who work on the company's day shift assembling audiovisual cabinets. He has noted a recent decline in productivity and an increase in error rate. In order to improve performance, Jim has posted a chart in the lunchroom. This chart contains the names of all the employees as well as their daily performance (by number of cabinets assembled) and their error rate (by number of mistakes).

Scenario 2

Lynn is the director of a nonprofit organization that works with local children and teachers to build their arts education programs. She has recently hired several individuals who previously worked as classroom teacher aides. Her intent was to have them do clerical tasks for her professional staff. However, one of the aides has shown an exceptional talent for painting and sculpture. Lynn has asked this aide to design a program that would introduce preschool children to art and, in order to help train the aide, has enrolled her in a child development class at a local college.

Scenario 3

Gina is the newly appointed manager of marketing communications for a large corporation. She is responsible for the activities of seven employees—all of whom have been with the company for several years and are experienced, creative, and competent at their jobs. In an effort to appear strong and managerial, Gina has "laid down the law" in her new department. She has asked everyone to account for their time by project and to submit a weekly report of their activities. In addition, she has installed a sign in/sign out board to keep track of employee breaks and lunch hours.

Scenario 4

Jill recently returned to her job as executive assistant after two months of maternity leave. Her boss, Susan, is thrilled to have Jill back because the temp assigned to cover for Jill left a lot to be desired. However, in the past week, Susan has noticed that Jill is very tired and is spending a lot of time on personal calls. While Jill's work is getting done and the quality hasn't suffered, Susan voices her concerns. Jill confesses that her babysitter isn't working out and that the baby is keeping her up at night. Susan explains that while she is sympathetic, it is important that Jill reduce the number of personal calls she is making and be more alert on the job. She also asks Jill to take on the added responsibility of a special research project because "no one else in the company is capable of finishing it on time."

Source: CRM. (2009). Pygmalion effect training activity. Retrieved on February 2, 2015, from http://www.crmlearning .com/blog/index.php/2009/08/pygmalion-effect-training-activity

CASE STUDY 5.1

Lombardi's Packers: From Last in the League to the Best Legs in the League

Vince Lombardi is one of the best coaches football has ever seen, and the Super Bowl trophy bears his name. Lombardi's ability to teach, motivate, and inspire players made him a leader on and off the field. He demonstrated these skills in his first head coaching position with the Green Bay Packers in 1959. In 1958, the Packers won one and tied 1 out of *12* games. Lombardi knew he had to make changes and spent the spring of 1959 reviewing plays and developing new strategies and tactics that would turn the Packers around.

His first step was to change the rules and policies. Veterans were required to attend practices once they arrived at training camp. Everyone had to make curfew and to be on time to meals, meetings, and practices. Violations of the rules were fined up to $25. The reason, Lombardi explained, was "a man who is late for a meeting or the bus will be sloppy. He won't run pass routes right." The biggest fine ($150) was reserved for being caught standing at a bar, because Lombardi felt "standing at a bar did not look good." It was important to manage the town of Green Bay's perceptions of the team, as some thought the players cared less about winning than having a good time. Changing the perception of the players to townsfolk was important to Lombardi because the Packers are owned by shareholders made up of the residents of Green Bay.

Lombardi told players, "You will be a professional." He felt they needed to start acting like major league players who expected to win. Rather than traveling on bumpy planes, eating crummy food, and staying in cheap hotels, Lombardi got Packers management to pay for better accommodations, food, and transportation.

Further, Lombardi required the players to dress in jackets and ties while traveling and helped pay for them to do so.

In his first meeting with all the players, he said the following:

> Gentlemen, we're going to have a football team here, and we're going to win some games. Do you know why? You are going to have confidence in me and my system. By being alert, you are going to make fewer mistakes than your opponents. By working harder, you are going to out-execute, out-block, and out-tackle every team that comes your way. I have never been a losing coach and don't intend to start here.

From watching previous games, Lombardi saw the Packers lacked the stamina to play four hard quarters. Rather than running light practices that "rested" players' legs like the previous coach, Lombardi developed grueling twice-a-day practices that he intensified each week. These practices consisted of calisthenics, running plays until they were implemented to perfection, and punishments for those not giving it their all. Lombardi's goal for the Packers players was for them to "have the best legs in the league," thus making the players stronger and able to prevent the excessive second half scoring by their opponents suffered in the previous season. Jim Ringo, who played center, said to one of the other players in camp that year, "We've never had practices like this. This guy means business. The conditioning is brutal." Those who could or would not keep up were cut or traded—even the "stars" and veterans.

Lombardi's changes seemed to have worked. In 1959, the Packers finished the season with seven wins and five losses. By the next year, Lombardi's hard-edged style turned the Packers into the most envied and successful franchise in the NFL. During the 1960s, Lombardi took the Packers on to win five NFL Championships and also victories in Super Bowls I and II.

Discussion Questions

1. How did Lombardi's actions help change the players' perceptions of themselves and their abilities? How did it create success for the Packers?
2. The Packer culture was tolerant of losing before Lombardi took over. How might this culture have created a Golem effect?
3. How did Lombardi's changes to the team's professionalism and physical ability help change the identity the Packers had created for themselves and their team?
4. Lombardi instituted a rule that players could not drink standing at a bar. While not all players would drink alcohol or visit bars, the actions of those who did would be attributed to the entire team. What kind of effect is this? Why is it important to manage perceptions held not only by oneself but also by others?

Source: Adapted from Eisenberg, J. (2009). *That first season.* New York, NY: Houghton Mifflin Harcourt.

SELF-ASSESSMENT 5.1

Employability—Perceptions of Prospective Employers

This self-assessment exercise suggests your level of employability as measured by OB researchers. There are no right or wrong answers, and this is not a test. You don't have to share your results with others unless you wish to do so.

Part I. Taking the Assessment

You will be presented with some questions representing different approaches to work. If you are not currently employed, answer the questions as you would if you were employed. There is no "one best" approach. All approaches have strengths and weaknesses, and the goal is for you to be adaptable to different change situations.

As an example, the answer regarding your approach to work could look like this:

I like to do variety of different things at work.

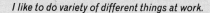

Least like me   1   2   3   ④   5   6   7   Most like me

1. I am optimistic about my future career opportunities.

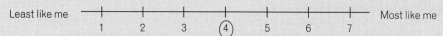

Least like me   1   2   3   4   5   6   7   Most like me

2. I feel changes at work generally have positive implications.

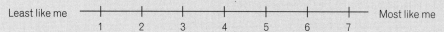

Least like me   1   2   3   4   5   6   7   Most like me

3. I stay abreast of developments in my company.

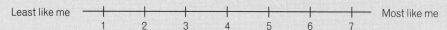

Least like me   1   2   3   4   5   6   7   Most like me

4. I have participated in training or schooling that will help me reach my career goals.

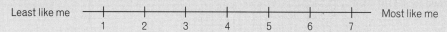

Least like me   1   2   3   4   5   6   7   Most like me

5. I define myself by the work that I do.

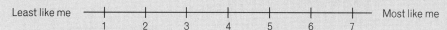

Least like me   1   2   3   4   5   6   7   Most like me

6. I feel that I am a valuable employee at work.

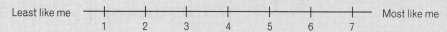

Least like me   1   2   3   4   5   6   7   Most like me

7. I feel that I am generally accepting of changes at work.

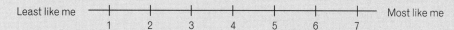

Least like me   1   2   3   4   5   6   7   Most like me

8. I stay abreast of developments in my industry.

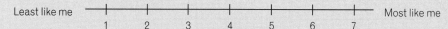

Least like me   1   2   3   4   5   6   7   Most like me

9. I have a specific plan for achieving my career goals.

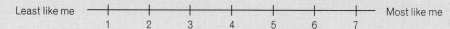

Least like me   1   2   3   4   5   6   7   Most like me

TOOLKIT

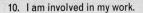

10. I am involved in my work.

Least like me ├──┼──┼──┼──┼──┼──┼──┤ Most like me
       1   2   3   4   5   6   7

11. I have control over my career opportunities.

Least like me ├──┼──┼──┼──┼──┼──┼──┤ Most like me
       1   2   3   4   5   6   7

12. I would consider myself open to changes at work.

Least like me ├──┼──┼──┼──┼──┼──┼──┤ Most like me
       1   2   3   4   5   6   7

13. I stay abreast of developments relating to my type of job.

Least like me ├──┼──┼──┼──┼──┼──┼──┤ Most like me
       1   2   3   4   5   6   7

14. I have sought job assignments that will help me obtain my career goals.

Least like me ├──┼──┼──┼──┼──┼──┼──┤ Most like me
       1   2   3   4   5   6   7

15. It is important to me that others think highly of my job.

Least like me ├──┼──┼──┼──┼──┼──┼──┤ Most like me
       1   2   3   4   5   6   7

16. My past career experiences have been generally positive.

Least like me ├──┼──┼──┼──┼──┼──┼──┤ Most like me
       1   2   3   4   5   6   7

17. I can handle job and organizational changes effectively.

Least like me ├──┼──┼──┼──┼──┼──┼──┤ Most like me
       1   2   3   4   5   6   7

18. It is important to me that I am successful in my job.

Least like me ├──┼──┼──┼──┼──┼──┼──┤ Most like me
       1   2   3   4   5   6   7

19. I take a positive attitude toward my work.

Least like me ├──┼──┼──┼──┼──┼──┼──┤ Most like me
       1   2   3   4   5   6   7

20. I am able to adapt to changing circumstances at work.

Least like me ├──┼──┼──┼──┼──┼──┼──┤ Most like me
       1   2   3   4   5   6   7

21. The type of work I do is important to me.

Least like me ├──┼──┼──┼──┼──┼──┼──┤ Most like me
       1   2   3   4   5   6   7

22. In uncertain times at work, I usually expect the best.

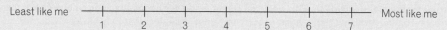

Least like me — 1   2   3   4   5   6   7 — Most like me

23. It is important to me that I am acknowledged for my successes in the job.

Least like me — 1   2   3   4   5   6   7 — Most like me

24. I always look on the bright side of things at work.

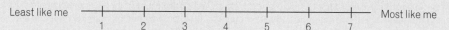

Least like me — 1   2   3   4   5   6   7 — Most like me

25. I am a believer that "every cloud has a silver lining" at work.

Least like me — 1   2   3   4   5   6   7 — Most like me

Part II. Scoring Instructions

In Part I, you rated your approaches to work on 25 questions. Add the numbers you circled in each of the columns to derive your score for the five different aspects of employability. During our session, we will discuss each approach—its strengths and weaknesses—and how you can develop employer perceptions of your employability based on this research.

Work and Career Resilience	Openness to Changes at Work	Work and Career Proactivity	Career Motivation	Work Identity
1. _____	2. _____	3. _____	4. _____	5. _____
6. _____	7. _____	8. _____	9. _____	10. _____
11. _____	12. _____	13. _____	14. _____	15. _____
16. _____	17. _____			18. _____
19. _____	20. _____			21. _____
22. _____				23. _____
24. _____				
25. _____				
Total _____	_____	_____	_____	_____

Employability Approaches

Work and career resilience—Individuals with work and career resilience possess some combination of the following attributes: optimistic about their career opportunities and work, feel that they have control over the destiny of their careers, and/or feel that they are able to make genuinely valuable contributions at work. Scores can range from 8 to 56. In general, a lower score is from 8 to 24; a higher score is above 25.

Openness to changes at work—Individuals who are open to changes at work are receptive and willing to change and/or feel that the changes are generally positive once they occur. Scores can range from 5 to 35. In general, a lower score is from 5 to 14; a higher score is above 15.

Work and career proactivity—A proactive career orientation reflects people's tendencies and actions to gain information potentially affecting their jobs and career opportunities, both within and outside their current employer. Scores can range from 3 to 21. In general, a lower score is from 3 to 11; a higher score is above 12.

Career motivation—Individuals with career motivation tend to make specific career plans and strategies. People in this category are inclined to take control of their own career management and set work or career-related goals. Scores can range from 3 to 21. In general, a lower score is from 3 to 11; a higher score is above 12.

Work identity—Work identity reflects the degree to which individuals define themselves in terms of a particular organization, job, profession, or industry. Work identity is characterized by a genuine interest in what one does, how well it is done, and the impression of others. Scores can range from 6 to 42. In general, a lower score is from 6 to 18; a higher score is above 19.

To determine your overall level of employability, add together your scores for the five dimensions above. This total employability score can range from 25 to 175. In general, a lower score is from 25 to 75; a higher score is above 76.

Source: Adapted from Fugate, M., & Kinicki, A. J. (2008). A dispositional approach to employability: Development of a measure and test of implications for employee reactions to organizational change. *Journal of Occupational and Organizational Psychology,* 81(3), 503–527.

SELF-ASSESSMENT 5.2

Your Impression Management Strategies

This self-assessment exercise identifies your impression management strategies for maximizing good impressions. There are no right or wrong answers, and this is not a test. You don't have to share your results with others unless you wish to do so.

Part I. Taking the Assessment

You will be presented with some questions representing different strategies. If you don't currently have a job or boss, then answer the questions with respect to what you would likely do.

As an example, the answer to a situation could look like this:

I tell others that I was the top person in my high school class.

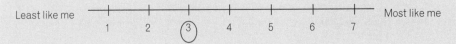

1. Talk proudly about your experience or education.

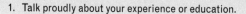

Least like me   1   2   3   4   5   6   7   Most like me

2. Compliment your colleagues so they will see you as likeable.

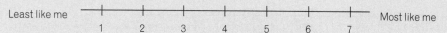

Least like me   1   2   3   4   5   6   7   Most like me

3. Try to appear like a hardworking dedicated employee.

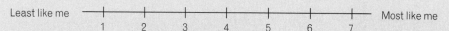

Least like me   1   2   3   4   5   6   7   Most like me

4. Make people aware of your talents or qualifications.

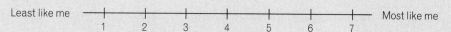

Least like me   1   2   3   4   5   6   7   Most like me

5. Take an interest in your colleagues' personal lives to show them that you are friendly.

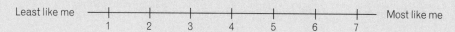

Least like me   1   2   3   4   5   6   7   Most like me

6. Stay at work late so people will know you are hard working.

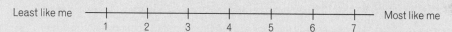

Least like me   1   2   3   4   5   6   7   Most like me

7. Let others know that you are valuable to the organization.

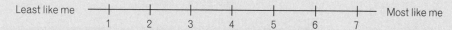

Least like me   1   2   3   4   5   6   7   Most like me

8. Praise your colleagues for their accomplishments so they will consider you a nice person.

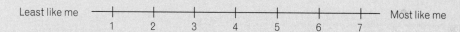

Least like me   1   2   3   4   5   6   7   Most like me

9. Try to appear busy, even at times when things are slower.

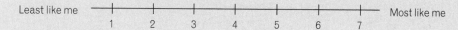

Least like me   1   2   3   4   5   6   7   Most like me

10. Let others know that you have a reputation for being competent in a particular area.

Least like me   1   2   3   4   5   6   7   Most like me

11. Use flattery and favors to make your colleagues like you more.

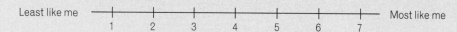

Least like me   1   2   3   4   5   6   7   Most like me

12. Arrive at work early in order to look dedicated.

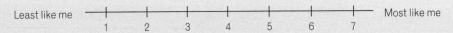

Least like me   1   2   3   4   5   6   7   Most like me

13. Make people aware of your accomplishments.

Least like me   1   2   3   4   5   6   7   Most like me

14. Do personal favors for your colleagues to show them that you are friendly.

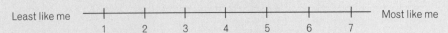

Least like me   1   2   3   4   5   6   7   Most like me

15. Come to the office at night or on weekends to show that you are dedicated.

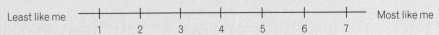

Least like me   1   2   3   4   5   6   7   Most like me

Part II. Scoring Instructions

In Part I, you rated yourself on 15 questions. Add the numbers you circled in each of the columns to derive your score for your impression management strategies. We will discuss each approach—its strengths and weaknesses—and how you can improve impressions others have of you. Scores on each dimension below can range from 5 to 35. In general, a lower score is from 5 to 14; a higher score is above 15.

Self-Promotion	Ingratiation	Exemplification
1. _____	2. _____	3. _____
4. _____	5. _____	6. _____
7. _____	8. _____	9. _____
10. _____	11. _____	12. _____
13. _____	14. _____	15. _____
Total _____	_____	_____

Source: Adapted from Bolino, M. C., & Turnley, W. H. (1999). Measuring impression management in organizations: A scale development based on the Jones and Pittman taxonomy. *Organizational Research Methods, 2*(2), 187–206.

6

THE IMPORTANCE OF DECISIONS

Business leaders make decisions every day, but are there some decisions that have a defining impact on the future of an organization? This question is addressed in the book *The Greatest Business Decisions of All Time.*[1] Based on the author's analysis, the greatest business decisions follow:

1. Henry Ford's decision to double the salaries of Ford's workforce to attract top talent and increase income so that people could afford his cars
2. The Apple board's decision to bring back Steve Jobs after he had been fired 10 years earlier, leading to innovations that have created the most valuable brand in the world
3. Sam Walton's decision to hold Saturday morning all-employee meetings for Walmart to create a culture of information sharing and rapid decision making, creating one of the largest retailers in the world
4. Samsung's decision to create a sabbatical program that allows their top performers to travel all over the world, which continues to be one of the secrets to their global brand success
5. Jack Welch's decision to create Crotonville, a training and development center that produced hundreds of great leaders who practice the "GE Way"

From these examples, it's clear that making the right decisions plays a large role in leader effectiveness. This chapter will cover both classic and contemporary research on decision making that every leader must know to make the right decisions—at the right time.

Learning Objectives

After studying this chapter, you should be able to do the following:

6.1: Describe why decision making is important to leader effectiveness.

6.2: Explain the rational decision-making model and bounded rationality.

6.3: Demonstrate understanding of prospect theory and the impact of framing on decisions with an example.

6.4: Describe the role of intuition in decision making.

6.5: List and explain major decision traps and how to avoid them: hindsight, hubris, and escalation of commitment.

6.6: Discuss the elements in Amabile's three-component model of creativity.

6.7: Illustrate the role of leadership in supporting innovation of followers.

Get the edge on your studies at
edge.sagepub.com/scandura
- Take the chapter quiz
- Review key terms with eFlashcards
- Explore multimedia resources, SAGE readings, and more!

⑤SAGE edge™

Critical Thinking Questions: What is it about each of these decisions that caused them to be listed as the most important business decisions? Propose a recent business decision that is a candidate for this list.

Behavioral Decisions

DECISION PROCESSES AND ORGANIZATIONAL PERFORMANCE

Learning Objective 6.1: Describe why decision making is important to leader effectiveness.

The greatest business decisions discussed previously suggest that decision making affects firm performance. For example, decision rationality is related to the success of strategic decisions ranging from restructuring to the introduction of new products or processes. Managers who collect information and use analytical techniques make decisions that are more effective and profitable. Political behavior on the part of managers is negatively related to decision effectiveness. For example, the use of power or hidden agendas hinders sound decisions. The bottom line is that good information and analysis are more important than politics for effective decision making.[2]

Decision making is central in Mintzberg's classic analysis of the nature of managerial work.[3] He found that managers have four decisional roles, including **entrepreneur** (looking for new ideas and opportunities), **disturbance handler** (resolving conflicts and choosing strategic alternatives), **resource allocator** (deciding how to prioritize the direction of resources), and **negotiator** (protecting the interests of the business by interacting within teams, departments, and the organization). Decision making is a fundamental part of a leader's job, and followers expect leaders to make the right decisions.[4] As a manager, you will likely be promoted on the basis of your track record for making decisions that positively impact the organization (enhancing profitability, for example).

Why Some People Can't Make Decisions

Indecisiveness is when a person cannot prioritize activities in order of importance. The book *Why Quitters Win* reports that effective leaders weigh both sides of an issue, decide quickly, and then work to gain support from those on both sides for effective execution.[5] The author, Nick Tasler, believes that it is possible to improve decisiveness through training by encouraging decisive action. People need a clearly defined starting and ending point so that they feel empowered to move forward. Also, providing incentives for decision making may boost the speed of decisions made by leaders. Tasler cites the case of the CEO of Agilent Technologies CEO who created a "speed to opportunity" metric in which leaders in the organization are regularly rated by their followers on decisiveness. This approach makes leaders aware that decisions are valued by the organization.

Why are some people more indecisive than others? Personality traits play a role. Less emotionally stable leaders who fear upsetting others allow debates to drag on for too long and make compromise decisions that are not optimal.[6] Feeling out of control and pessimism also leads to indecisiveness. Low self-esteem predicts indecisiveness, as well as attributing events to external causes and irrational beliefs.[7]

Indecisiveness may also affect students faced with the decision of which job offer to take. **Career indecision** "refers to the difficulties preventing individuals from making a career decision."[8] Career indecision is related to personality characteristics of neuroticism and agreeableness but lower extroversion and openness to experience (the Big Five personality theory was discussed in Chapter 3). Also, students' tendencies toward perfectionism are Five related to career indecision.

Constraints on Individual Decision Making

Indecisiveness may also be due to the complex nature of situations leaders face in today's rapidly changing environment. Three situational factors may hinder decision making: lack of information, unclear or conflicting goals, and the uncertainty of outcomes.[9] There may be constraints on decisions due to time, rewards, and regulations. Also, stakeholders within and outside of the organization are invested in a leader's decisions. These stakeholders may have conflicting interests that must be balanced. Decision making is arguably at the core of leadership, but it is not always easy. Leaders must often make decisions under pressure and with incomplete information.

Employees as well as leaders may suffer from indecisiveness, which may be a source of frustration for a leader. Some employees are able to support their decisions with facts and evidence. However, others rely on historical precedents, or personal experiences. In addition, employees are confronted by an overload of information that is nearly impossible to sort through and often under time constraints. The results are often poorly researched and supported decisions that waste company resources and possibly risk the effectiveness of the organization.

Effective decision making can make or break an organization, and we have all heard the saying "the buck stops here," which means that leaders must own the decisions they make. This chapter will summarize research on decision making in organizational contexts, including the decision traps leaders should avoid. First, the classic approaches to decision making will be discussed; these are decision-making essentials that every leader must know.

THE RATIONAL DECISION-MAKING MODEL

Learning Objective 6.2: Explain the rational decision-making model and bounded rationality.

One prevalent model of decision making presents a series of logical steps decision makers follow to determine the optimal choice.[10,11] For example, optimization involves maximizing the value and/or minimizing cost. The six-step process for rational decision making is shown in Figure 6.1.[12] In this model, the problem (or opportunity) is defined, and then information is gathered and analyzed. Based on this information, a broad set of alternatives or possible courses of action are identified. Next, these alternatives are analyzed in terms of the feasibility, costs, and benefits. A decision is based upon the analysis of the alternative courses of action (i.e., the decision with the lowest costs and greatest benefit). The final step is to develop a specific set of action steps for the implementation of the decision. This model includes a number of assumptions. Decision makers must have complete information, be able to develop an exhaustive list of

Rational
Decision Making

alternatives, weight them, and then choose a decision with the highest value and/or lowest cost to the organization. As you may have noticed, this rational model is often emphasized in business schools through the case study method to learn the decision-making process.

Critical Thinking Questions: In your opinion, do leaders follow the rational decision-making model in practice? Give an example of when the process is followed and an example when it is not followed. Compare and contrast the outcomes of these decisions.

Limitations of the Rational Model

Managers sometimes fail to identify the problem correctly at the start of the decision-making process.[13] Also, some only consider a few alternatives rather than a broad set of possible options. They may only consider the most obvious alternatives and not brainstorm creative solutions (creative problem solving will be discussed later in this chapter). Managers sometimes suboptimize rather than choose an optimal alternative resulting in lose-lose decisions.[14, 15] Finally, decisions are sometimes made without complete information due to the lack of availability of information relevant to the problem or time pressure. Decision makers have limits on their ability to assimilate large amounts of information, and this is known as **bounded rationality.**

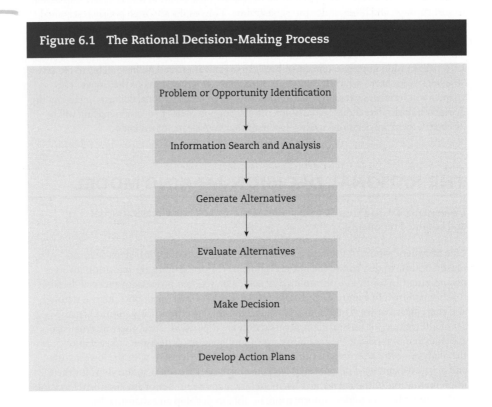

Figure 6.1   The Rational Decision-Making Process

Problem or Opportunity Identification

Information Search and Analysis

Generate Alternatives

Evaluate Alternatives

Make Decision

Develop Action Plans

Bounded Rationality

Herbert A. Simon

Human beings have a limited capacity to process large amounts of information in the context of decision making to make optimal decisions. In many instances, people satisfice—in other words, they make a decision that is satisfactory but perhaps not optimal. Decision makers operate within bounded rationality rather than perfect rationality.[16] What this means is that decision makers simplify complex problems to limit the amount of information processing needed. Within the boundaries of this simplified model, they behave rationally.[17] In addition to limiting the information analyzed, they also limit the number of alternatives considered. They accept the first acceptable alternative they encounter rather than continue their information search, analysis, and alternative generation until they find an optimal one.

Decision making is susceptible to the perceptual errors discussed in Chapter 5: Primacy, recency, availability, contrast, and halo errors may all affect how information is presented to decision makers and processed.[18] In sum, bounded rationality in decision making is the result of organizational factors (e.g., political behavior around a decision), individual limits on the ability to process information (e.g., limiting the information search), and perceptions (e.g., perceptual errors related to the limited availability of information to make a decision).

Bounded rationality is also the result of two guesses the decision maker must address: (1) a guess about uncertain future consequences and (2) a guess about uncertain future preferences.[19] In other words, the decision maker at the time of the decision can't know the future, nor can they know what they would like to see happen in the future. So the decision-making process may be influenced by other organizational processes such as the situation, interpersonal gaming, and the need to justify prior decisions. This perspective highlights the importance of uncertainty and risk to the decision-making process. The next sections will explain **prospect theory**, which is one of the most important frameworks for decision making under risk and uncertainty.

PROSPECT THEORY

Learning Objective 6.3: Demonstrate understanding of prospect theory and the impact of framing on decisions with an example.

Daniel Kahneman won the Nobel Prize in Economics in 2002, in part for his work with Amos Tversky work on the prospect theory of decision making. Their work focused on the risk perceptions in decisions people make. The authors conducted studies in which subjects were asked to make decisions when given two monetary options that involved prospective losses and gains. Consider the following options used in their studies:[20]

1. You have $1,000, and you must pick one of the following choices:

    Choice A: You have a 50% chance of gaining $1,000 and a 50% chance of gaining $0.
    Choice B: You have a 100% chance of gaining $500.

2. You have $2,000, and you must pick one of the following choices:

    Choice A: You have a 50% chance of losing $1,000 and a 50% chance of losing $0.
    Choice B: You have a 100% chance of losing $500.

Framing

Choosing B indicates that the person is more risk averse than someone choosing A. If you chose B for question 1 and A for question 2, you are like the majority of people who are presented with these decision scenarios. If people made decisions according to rational decision-making norms, they would pick either A or B in both situations (i.e., they should be indifferent because the expected value of both outcomes is the same). However, the results of this study showed that an overwhelming majority of people chose B for question 1 and A for question 2. Why? People are willing to settle for a reasonable gain (even if they have a reasonable chance of earning more) but are willing to engage in risk-seeking behaviors where they can limit their losses. In other words, losses weigh more heavily emotionally in decision making than an equivalent gain.

The Importance of How Decisions Are Framed

Prospect theory explains why decisions are sometimes irrational. People put more emphasis on gains rather than losses; they make decisions that increase their gains and avoid loss. According to the theory, people treat the two types of risk (gain versus loss) in a completely different way to maximize their perceived outcome. However, this may result in irrational decisions that are not based on a correct calculation of expected utility.

Framing refers to whether questions are presented as gains or losses. Leaders must pay attention to how decisions are framed when they are presented. As the examples of monetary choices under losses and gains illustrated, decisions may be affected by how options are presented (people are more risk averse when decisions are framed in terms of loss). Table 6.1 shows real-world examples to illustrate the role of framing in decision making and highlights the importance of considering both the probability of an outcome and the associated gain or loss from the decision.[21] For example, in scenario A, as a manager you might take a risk on an idea that is outside of the box. There is a low probability that it would pan out, but the gains would be huge. In scenario B, a business owner sells off a business that is doing well to avoid potential losses from new entrants into the market. For scenario C, there is a high probability of gain, so a business in expansion mode sells delayed invoices to a financial institution for 70% to 80% of their value just to get cash needed to grow the business. In scenario D, there is a high probability of loss, so an entrepreneur in a failing business ignores advice to divest the business and increases efforts to succeed. So it is important for managers to recognize risk as a part of business decision making that is essential for innovation. Jarrehult states the following:

> Doing what is rational is usually good, but if we only would be rational, we would miss out on many of the "Black Swans." The trick is to strike the appropriate balance between the few expensive rational decisions we need to take and the inexpensive, but plentiful, irrational decisions that we take more on a gut feeling.[21]

Note: A "black swan" is a highly consequential but unlikely event that is easily explainable, but only in retrospect.[22]

It is important to consider how information regarding risk and uncertainty is presented. Decision makers expect uncertainty and can effectively use information on uncertainty to make better decisions. In one study, college students made daily decisions about whether or not to order roads to be salted to prevent ice on roads during several winter months.

Table 6.1	Risk Behavior Regarding Gains and Losses at High and Low Probability	
	Gains	**Losses**
High Probability	**C.** Big chance to win a lot Fear of getting disappointed RISK AVERSE Accepting unfavorable settlement *Example: Court case*	**D.** Big risk to lose a lot Hoping to avoid loss RISK SEEKING Rejecting favorable settlement *Example: Casino evening*
Low Probability	**A.** Small chance to win a lot Hoping for a great gain RISK SEEKING Rejecting favorable settlement *Example: Lottery*	**B.** Small risk to lose a lot Fear of large loss RISK AVERSE Accepting unfavorable settlement *Example: Insurance*

Source: Jarrehult, B. (2013). The importance of stupid, irrational decisions. *Innovation Management*. Retrieved on September 23, 2013, from www.innovationmanagement.se/2013/09/06/the-importance-of-stupid-irrational-decisions.

Decisions were based on actual archived forecasts of the nighttime low temperature. In one condition, participants used the nighttime low temperature alone (i.e., the conventional deterministic forecast). In the other condition, students were also provided with the probability of freezing. Participants were given a budget of $30,000. The salt treatment cost $1,000 per application, but if they didn't decide to salt the roads and the temperature dropped below freezing, they were penalized $6,000. Participants were informed of the outcome each day (the temperature). At the end of the experiment, participants were paid based upon their remaining budget (about $10), so they had an incentive to make good decisions. Results of these experiments indicated that people can make good use of probability information in making decisions if they are provided with it during the decision process and if it is presented in a way that they can use. The authors concluded: "Our view is that not only do people need explicit uncertainty information to make better, more individualized decisions, but also they can understand it as long as some care is taken in how it is presented."[23]

The book *Thinking Fast and Slow* examines two modes of thinking that psychology has labeled System 1 and System 2 Thinking.[24] System 1 Thinking represents automatic and effortless decision making that is often involuntary. System 2 Thinking is complex thinking that demands mental effort, including complex calculations. System 2 Thinking is what is most often taught in business schools to prepare students to be effective decision makers.

 **Intuition Versus Data**

Yet, System 1 Thinking represents intuition, which has received research attention as well as a great deal of interest in the popular press.

Critical Thinking Questions: How can you use knowledge of prospect theory to improve your chances of getting a good deal during a negotiation? What role do you think framing of options as gains or losses plays in negotiations?

INTUITION

Learning Objective 6.4: Describe the role of intuition in decision making.

Blink: The Power of Thinking Without Thinking popularized the idea that intuition may play an important role in decision making.[25] Author Malcolm Gladwell noted that people learn by their experiences; they may not know why they know things, but they are certain they know them. He acknowledges the influences of the unconscious mind on decisions and put forth the premise that there can be value in a decision made in the "blink of an eye" rather than months of analysis. Gladwell introduced the idea of "thin-slicing" in which the unconscious mind finds patterns in situations and behaviors based upon very narrow experiences. However, he cautioned there may be errors made when thin-slicing is used to make decisions. Such quick decisions may be affected by perceptual errors discussed in Chapter 5 or by stereotypes about people, and leaders need to be aware of these biases.

Intuition has been described as follows: "the essence of intuition or intuitive responses is that they are reached with little apparent effort, and typically without conscious awareness. They involve little or no conscious deliberation."[26] Four characteristics comprise intuition: "a (1) nonconscious process (2) involving holistic associations (3) that are produced rapidly which (4) result in affectively charged judgments."[27] Intuition may be a potential means of helping managers make both fast and accurate decisions. While research on such unconscious thought processes is new, available evidence supports the idea that intuitive processes should be considered part of a leader's decision making.

Intuition is not the same thing as common sense. Intuition is perception without conscious thinking and can seem like common sense. However, intuition varies greatly from basic gut feelings to complicated judgments like a physician's quick diagnosis. According to Simon, "intuition and judgment—at least good judgment—are simply analyses frozen into habit and into the capacity for rapid response through recognition" (p. 63).[28] In other words, intuition is the unconscious operation in the brain formed by freezing sensing and judgment. By contrast, common sense is not typically repetitive; it is a more simplified thought process. Another major difference is intuition is individual and common sense is often social (i.e., what the majority of people think as a consensus).[29]

Benefits of Intuition

Leaders often rely on their gut feelings or instincts in making important decisions, particularly related to innovation.[30] In-depth interviews with 60 professionals across a

The Pepsi Challenge

An example of the costs of not following intuition is the "Pepsi Challenge," which is Coca-Cola's biggest decision-making blunder. By the mid-1970s, Coca-Cola was becoming stagnant, and Pepsi was gaining market share; the Pepsi Challenge was a successful advertising campaign that proved that taste testers preferred Pepsi over Coke. When Robert Goizueta took the helm as chairman of Coca-Cola in 1980, he announced ambitious plans to reinvent the company. Since marketing research clearly indicated that taste testers preferred Pepsi, decision makers thought that they needed to change the flavor of Coke. Coca-Cola addressed the Pepsi Challenge and spent $4 million and 2 years doing marketing research on new Coke flavors. By September 1984, they produced a sweeter Coke with a sticky taste—and it outperformed Pepsi in taste tests. When the new Coke was implemented, consumers protested. In the first four hours, the company received over 650 calls. By mid-May, calls were coming in at a rate of 5,000 per day, in addition to angry letters. People were speaking of Coke as an American symbol and an old friend they had lost. Company executives, worried about a consumer boycott, reintroduced Coca-Cola under the name "Coca-Cola Classic" and keep the "new Coke" on the shelves. Old Coke's comeback drove the share price up to the highest level in 12 years. In retrospect, the new Coke decision was unsuccessful. What happened?

The market research was flawed. First, participants were not told that by choosing the new Coke they would lose the classic Coke they loved. This seems intuitive in retrospect, but it was not tested. Second, preferences for sweeter tastes diminish after the first test. In the testing, participants in the research based their rating of the Coke flavor on just a sip and not an entire glass. This also should have been intuitive, since consumers typically drink more than one sip. Finally, the symbolic value of Coke's image to consumers was not taken into account. Coke is a strong brand, and this should have been considered. What the executives learned was that intuition may be more valuable even when it conflicts with research. Changing an existing product may not be the right decision—even if a company spends billions on market research and advertising.

Discussion Questions:

1. In retrospect, the intuitive nature of the Coke blunder appears obvious. What perceptual biases may have influenced the decision to introduce the new Coke?
2. Provide another example of a business mistake that illustrates the lack of attention to intuition.
3. What can be done to prevent bias and lack of attention to intuition from preventing decision-making failures?

Sources: Gladwell, M. (2007). *Blink: The power of thinking without thinking.* New York, NY: Little, Brown; Hartley, R. F. (2011). *Management mistakes and successes* (10th ed.). New York, NY: John Wiley.

variety of industries and occupations revealed the role that intuition plays in decision making.[31] Professionals often rely on their intuition and report the following benefits:

- **Expedited decision making**—quicker decisions that get the job done; adapting to a changing environment
- **Improvement of the decision in some way**—provides a check and balance; allows for fairness; avoids having to rework the decision; causes one to pay more attention

- Facilitation of personal development—gives one more power; develops instincts; helps to apply one's experiences; allows for positive risk taking
- Promotion of decisions compatible with company culture—helps make decisions in accord with the organization's values.[31]

Intuition in decision making has a bad reputation, but most managers acknowledge that it plays a role in their decisions.

 Critical Thinking Questions: What are the risks of relying on intuition to make decisions? What can a leader do to address these risks and gain the benefits from intuition?

Next, the types of organizational problems will be discussed with an emphasis on complex and changing decision scenarios that our leaders are facing with more frequency. Such problems have been termed **wicked organizational problems**.

RESEARCH IN ACTION

Women's Intuition: Myth or Reality?

The role of gender and emotions as antecedents to intuitive decision making was studied using a web-based experimental study with 570 undergraduate students.[32] Findings indicate the use of intuition is influenced independently by emotions as well as moods. Gender was related to decision making: Women were significantly more likely to use intuition. Female decision makers appear to rely more heavily on intuition because they access it more easily through a heightened awareness of emotions. This awareness is much stronger in female decision makers—possibly for neurobiological and social reasons.[33,34] Male decision makers, on the other hand, tend to prefer analysis. It is possible, however, that male professionals with a heightened emotional

awareness may have similar decision-making preferences as females, and this was stated as an important direction for future research. There does, however, appear to be an association between emotions and decision making, and this is important for leaders to bear in mind when making important decisions.[35]

Discussion Questions:

1. This research shows emotions are related to decision making. Describe how emotions may enhance decisions.
2. Describe the impact of the gender composition of a team on the decision-making process (consider a team that has three women and two men).

Sources: Andrade, E. B., & Ariely, D. (2009). The enduring impact of transient emotions on decision making. *Organizational Behavior and Human Decision Processes*, 109(1), 1–8; Sinclair, M., Ashkanasy, N., & Chattopadhyay, P. (2010). Affective antecedents of affective decision making. *Journal of Management & Organization*, 16(3), 382–398; Graham, T., & Ickes, W. (1997). When women's intuition isn't greater than men's. In W. Ickes (Ed.), *Empathic accuracy* (pp. 1170–1143). New York, NY: Guilford Press; Maio G. R., & Esses, V. M. (2001). The need for affect: Individual differences in the motivation to approach or avoid emotions. *Journal of Personality*, 69(1), 583–615.

Wicked Organizational Problems

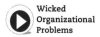
Wicked Organizational Problems

It is important for managers to know when to "think" (i.e., rely on analysis), "blink" (i.e., rely on intuition), or "smink" (employ heuristics and algorithms). An example of a **heuristic** is the way credit scores are computed and used to determine interest rates.[36] An important consideration is the complexity of the task. For example, if the task is simple, rely on analysis. As problems become more complex, intuition may have an advantage, but it is important to consider the nature of the problem. Some problems have learning environments that are "kind" in that they can be structured so analysis or heuristics can be applied. Other problems are "wicked" because they are complex, dynamic, and constrained so there are limits to whether analysis or heuristics can be applied. First, we will discuss structured problems and heuristics, followed by wicked organizational problems and decision traps leaders may fall into if they are not careful.

Heuristics

As noted previously, heuristics are used to make decisions ("sminking"). The use of heuristics, or decision rules, is an effective way to manage information and make improved decisions. Heuristics rely on one or more of the following methods to reduce effort:[37]

1. **Examining fewer cues**—for example, limiting information to only what's important
2. **Reducing the difficulty associated with retrieving and storing cue values**—for example, using less than, equal, or greater than instead of actual values
3. **Simplifying the weighting principles for cues**—for example, weighing each piece of information equally
4. **Integrating less information**—for example, selecting threshold values and accepting what is "good enough"
5. **Examining fewer alternatives**—for example, using pairwise comparisons and selecting one alternative from each set.

Heuristics underlie both intuitive and deliberate decision making.[38] The selection of decision rules is a two-step process in which (1) the task and (2) the individual's memory constrain the set of applicable rules. The individual's ability to process information and their perception of what is rational guide the final decision. Deliberate judgments are not more accurate than intuitive judgments. In both cases, accuracy depends on the match between rule employed and the characteristics of the situation. For example, the use of a financial criterion to decide whether to enter an international market may miss opportunities that can only be seen if the national culture is considered. Table 6.2 shows 10 heuristics with their definitions. For example, the recognition heuristic is commonly used in business decisions in which one of two alternatives is selected because one has the higher value on a given criterion (such as return on investment, or ROI). Another possible heuristic is the fluency heuristic, in which the one that is faster is selected (e.g., when there is a pressing need to bring a new product to market before competition enters). The equality heuristic prescribes that resources are allocated equally (e.g., allocated budgets for entertainment expenses across sales units). Imitating the majority involves doing what most people do (e.g., creating a social media account because most others in your industry have one). Imitating the successful is what is commonly referred to as "best practices," in which successful practices are imitated such as Jack Welch's workout program wherein teams present ideas to top management.[39] Whether decisions are based on intuition or analysis, using one of these 10 heuristics should reduce the effort expended in making decisions by simplifying them.

Heuristics are useful because they aid in simplifying wicked problems so that they can be solved. However, there is a danger in simplification in that it may lead to biases and decision traps. Leaders need to be aware of these traps and know how to avoid them. The next sections review common decision errors leaders make when they are faced with wicked organizational problems.

 Critical Thinking Question: Give an example of a wicked organizational problem (one that is complex, dynamic, and constrained with limited ability to use analysis or heuristics).

Table 6.2   Ten Heuristics for the Toolbox for Leaders

Heuristic	Definition
Recognition heuristic	If one of two alternatives is recognized, infer that it has the higher value on the criterion.
Fluency heuristic	If both alternatives are recognized but one is recognized faster, infer that it has the higher value on the criterion.
Take-the-best	To infer which of two alternatives has the higher value, (a) search through cues in order of validity, (b) stop the search as soon as a cue discriminates, and (c) choose the alternative this cue favors.
Tallying: Unit-weight linear model	To estimate a criterion, do not estimate weights but simply count the number of positive cues.
Satisficing	Search through alternatives, and choose the one that exceeds your aspiration level.
1/N; Equality heuristic	Allocate resources equally to each of N alternatives.
Default heuristic	If there is a default, do nothing.
Tit for tat	Cooperate first and then imitate your partner's last behavior.
Imitate the majority	Consider the majority of people in your peer group, and imitate their behavior.
Imitate the successful behavior	Consider the most successful person, and imitate his or her behavior.

Source: Adapted from Kruglanski, A. W., & Gigerenzer, G. (2011). Intuitive and deliberate judgments are based on common principles. *Psychological Review, 118*(1), 97–109.

DECISION TRAPS

Learning Objective 6.5: List and explain three major decision traps and how to avoid them: hindsight, hubris, and escalation of commitment.

Overconfidence Bias

Hindsight Bias

Some wicked problems leaders face are due to inherent biases and limitations that result in decision-making traps. **Hindsight bias**, also commonly referred to as the **I-knew-it-all-along effect,**[40] is well established and has been shown to have far-reaching effects. Hindsight bias is defined as "the tendency for individuals with outcome knowledge (hindsight) to claim they would have estimated a probability of occurrence for the reported outcome that is higher than they would have estimated in foresight (without the outcome information)."[41] Four processes underlie this belief. First, the person recalls the old event and responds consistently with the memory of it. Second, the person focuses on the outcome and adjusts their belief, pretending that they didn't know the outcome. Third, the belief is reconstructed based upon what the judgment would have been prior to the outcome. Research shows people do this by first sampling evidence related to the judgment from their long-term memories and the external world. Once an outcome is known, people seek out and retain evidence that fits the outcome rather than evidence that contradicts it. The fourth process is based upon a person's motivation to present themself favorably to others. People want to be seen as accurate, and they claim when something happens that they "knew it all along." A meta-analysis of 90 studies of hindsight bias showed moderate support for the effect.[42]

Hindsight bias is a process that may influence how outcomes of decisions are interpreted after the fact and lead to poor decision making since a leader may ignore important information in the present and then reconstruct the past as if they had the knowledge. Thus, a leader's ability to learn from past mistakes is compromised by hindsight bias. This may be compounded if the leader is also overconfident in their decision-making ability, and this is another decision trap.

Overconfidence

British Petroleum (BP) executives were confident that there were no serious risks with their Deepwater Horizon oil well in the Gulf of Mexico. They repeatedly assured government regulators that an accident was almost impossible. Several months later, one of their oil rigs exploded. Eleven people were killed, and 17 were injured. The leak spread to over a mile, resulting in one of the worst disasters in recent history with damage to the natural environment and the wildlife that relies on the Gulf for survival (over 8,000 animals were reported dead 6 months after the spill). Top decision makers had engaged in a long-standing practice of inattention to safety precautions. Investigations reveal that this accident could have been prevented with more attention to mitigation and preparation for oil spills of this nature.[43] How could decision makers fail to accurately assess the risks involved with operating these oil rigs? One reason is **overconfidence bias** (sometimes referred to as hubris). Overconfidence bias is an inflated confidence in how accurate a person's knowledge or estimates are.[44]

As we have seen with the rational decision-making model and bounded rationality, the ability to estimate probable outcomes is critical to a leader's ability to make sound

 Overconfidence

decisions in organizations. For example, accurate forecasting is significantly related to a leader's ability to create an effective vision for their organization.[45] However, leaders with more power are more likely to exhibit the overconfidence bias.[46] Those higher in the organizational hierarchy feel more empowered and overestimate their ability to accurately forecast the future. Hiring experts to assist with making decisions may not be the answer either since experts sometimes fail to make accurate predictions.[47] For example, in one study, experts in information technology (IT) were as likely to make errors due to overconfidence as novices (people with little expertise in IT) on IT-related issues.[48]

How can leaders avoid the overconfidence bias? Leaders may keep the overconfidence bias in check by assigning a trusted follower to critique the decisions (i.e., play the "devil's advocate" role), by being open to different opinions, and by placing limits on their power by having someone else approve decisions (a peer, for example). Reminding oneself of past decision-making errors might be an effective way to keep the power effect on overconfidence in check.[49]

Overconfidence can result in poor decision making and can even result in serious disasters as in the BP oil spill case. It is estimated that the oil spill cost BP over $100 billion and Tony Hayward, the CEO, was moved to a role in the company with much less power. Overconfidence, over time, may result in another decision trap that is called the **escalation of commitment** effect.

 Critical Thinking Questions: Why do you think leaders suffer from overconfidence? What can be done to limit this decision error?

Escalation of Commitment

Escalation of commitment occurs when individuals continue a failing course of action after receiving feedback that shows it isn't working. In effect, they try to turn the situation around by investing more after a setback.[50] People continue to invest in failing courses of action to recoup their losses to show they had made the right decision all along. One experiment found that decision makers continued to invest in research and development (R & D) of a failing company when they had personal responsibility for the negative outcomes.[51] This occurs because of self-justification, or the need to demonstrate that one's actions are rational. In addition to self-justification, escalation may be caused by risk perceptions (prospect theory), group decision-making dysfunctions, and an organization's tendency to avoid change.[52] This is sometimes called the **sunk costs fallacy** because the continued commitment is because a person has already invested in this course of action and does not recognize what they invested initially is sunk (or gone). Lunenburg provides the following example:

> Denver's International Airport set out to add a state-of-the-art automated baggage handling system to its airport construction. The project was never completed, which caused a delay in the opening of the airport by nearly two years and $2 billion over budget.[53]

Figure 6.2 shows the reasons why leaders may engage in escalation of commitment. Instead of viewing the money already spent as sunk costs, decision makers focus on how much they

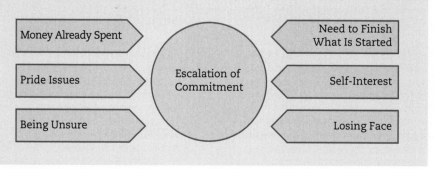

Figure 6.2 Reasons for the Escalation of Commitment Effect

Money Already Spent

Pride Issues

Being Unsure

Escalation of Commitment

Need to Finish What Is Started

Self-Interest

Losing Face

Source: Adapted from: Staw, B.M. (1981). The escalation of commitment to a course of action. *Academy of Management Review, 6,* 577–587.

have already spent.[54] Also, leaders want a sense of completion; they have the need to finish what they have started and this may also contribute to escalation.[55] Leaders may also let their ego get in the way, and the feeling of pride in their own decision-making ability (or the need to avoid "losing face") may lead to increased investment in poor decisions. Finally, being unsure of oneself may increase the need to "prove" to others they were right.

There are other examples of poor decisions due to escalation. Venture capitalists sometimes continue to invest in start-up companies even after results indicate the ideas are not panning out in the marketplace.[56] Supervisors of clerical workers in a large public-sector organization provided positively biased performance evaluations for the workers they originally supported hiring or promoting.[57] Senior bank managers escalated commitment to loans they initiated by retaining them even after the loans were not being paid on time.[58] Finally, a study of Wall Street analysts found that radical stock picks were followed with more extreme earnings projections after a company's yearly earnings reports showed their initial forecasts were wrong.[59] These examples illustrate that escalation, or "throwing good money after bad," is a serious decision trap leaders may fall into because they want to avoid regret.[60] What can a leader to do avoid escalation?

The following four antidotes to escalation have been proposed:[61]

1. **Separate the initial decision maker from the decision evaluator.** In other words, remove the ego of the decision maker from the evaluation of it.
2. **Create accountability for decision processes only, not outcomes.** Ask employees to explain or justify their decision processes (i.e., how they made the decision in the first place).
3. **Shift attention away from the self.** Make a balanced assessment by considering the impact of the decision on other people.
4. **Be careful about compliments.** Try not to inflate the decision maker's ego. Research has shown positive feedback increases the risk of becoming overconfident about one's decisions.

Avoiding Derailment Through Planning

The book *Sidetracked: Why Our Decisions Get Derailed, and How We Can Stick to the Plan* describes how decision makers often don't reach their goals due to their own decision-making traps, relationships with other people, and aspects of the situation.[62] The author's analysis suggests that things that may seem unimportant or even irrelevant to the decision may have a significant influence on sidetracking the decision maker into following a different course of action than intended. Acknowledgement of the decision biases may not be enough to avoid being sidetracked into making the wrong decision. The remedy is to start with a plan. In so doing, the leader is more prepared and better able to track progress toward goals. In the preparation of the plan, the following nine principles should be followed:

1. **Raise your awareness.** Become aware of your biases, and keep them in check.
2. **Take your emotional temperature.** Examine how your emotions may cloud your decisions.
3. **Zoom out.** Keep the "big picture" in mind and other people's roles in your plan.
4. **Take the other party's point of view.** Analyze the decision from another person's viewpoint.
5. **Question your bonds.** Reflect on ties to the others and how they may affect your plan.
6. **Check your reference points.** Uncover the real motives behind your decisions and whether you are trying to impress others.
7. **Consider the source.** Carefully examine the information, and consider the motives of the source as well as the situation.
8. **Investigate and question the frame.** Frame aspects of the decision in various ways—check whether you are too optimistic or pessimistic.
9. **Make your standards shine.** Reference your moral compass in making plans to be sure you don't get off course. (pp. 227–228)

Discussion Questions:

1. Develop a plan for progression toward your graduation using the previously given guidelines.
2. One of the ways to avoid getting derailed is to keep your moral compass in mind. Give an example of leaders who have been derailed by not following ethical principles in their decision making.

Source: Gino, F. (2013). *Sidetracked: Why our decisions get derailed, and how we can stick to the plan.* Boston, MA: Harvard University Press.

Ethical Decision Making

Guidelines for effective planning include referencing your moral compass (see the boxed insert). Three fundamental ethical philosophies guide ethical decisions in organizations.[63] First, **utilitarianism** is the consideration of decisions that do the most good for the most people. Second, **individual rights** protect individuals, such as the right to appeal a decision that affects them. Third, **justice** emphasizes social justice and the right to pursue happiness. Most individuals follow one of these philosophies in making decisions; however, the utilitarian approach is the most common among business leaders.[64] Despite the best of intentions, however, leaders do succumb to external forces such as economic conditions, scarce resources, and competition and make decisions that are unethical.[65]

Some unethical decisions may be unintended. Leaders may have **bounded ethicality:** an unconscious psychological process that hinders the quality of decision making. In other words, ethicality is limited in ways that are not visible. Similar to bounded rationality discussed earlier in this chapter, bounded ethicality refers to systematic and predictable ethical errors due to the limited capacity to process information.[66] For example, a leader may not be able to articulate the ethical challenge in a decision to rate followers' performance lower because there is a limited salary pool. People may even lie to get more money while feeling honest about it.[67] Under conditions of bounded ethicality, people make unethical decisions that they are unaware of and then engage in self-justification to explain their behavior.

In many cases, the ability to avoid decision traps and bounded ethicality involves keeping one's mind open and being able to view a problem from a variety of perspectives. Thus, the ability to think creatively may help avoid making decision errors. Creative problem solving also has a number of other benefits to leaders and their organizations, and this topic will be covered next.

CREATIVE PROBLEM SOLVING

Learning Objective 6.6: Discuss the three elements in Amabile's three-component model of creativity.

Albert Einstein wrote the following famous quote on creativity:

> Imagination is more important than knowledge. For knowledge is limited to all we now know and understand, while imagination embraces the entire world, and all there ever will be to know and understand.

Albert Szent-Gyorgyi, the Hungarian chemist who won the Nobel Prize for Medicine in 1937, defined **creativity** as follows: "Discovery consists of seeing what everybody has seen and thinking what nobody has thought." A contemporary definition of creativity is "the tendency to generate or recognize ideas, alternatives, or possibilities that may be useful in solving problems, communicating with others, and entertaining ourselves and others."[68] In the organizational context, applied creativity is a process "occurring in a real-world, industrial, organizational, or social context; pertaining to the finding or solving of complex problems; and having an actual behavioral creative product (or plan) as the final result."[69] There is a growing consensus that creativity can be defined as "production of a novel and appropriate response, product, or solution to an open-ended task."[70] Given the challenges of organizational change and the need to remain competitive, leaders desire more creative problem solving in all aspects of the work followers perform.[71] You will have the opportunity to test your creative problem solving skills and assess your creativity in the Toolkit at the end of this chapter.

Certain personality traits are related to creativity—particularly openness to experience.[72] Also, intelligence (general ability mental ability, known as "g") relates to creativity. In a meta-analysis, creativity was compared for both academic and work performance. Ratings of creativity were a faculty member's or work supervisor's evaluation of a person's creativity or potential for creative work. The implications of this study are that selecting students or

 Decision Making

workers on the basis of their intelligence may also result in scholars and employees who are creative and have high potential.[73]

 Critical Thinking Questions: Do you believe that creativity is an in-born trait that only a few people have? If so, why? If not, how would you encourage creativity in your followers?

Going With the "Flow"

Creative experiences are linked to emotional states called flow—when a person experiences a challenging opportunity aligned with their skills.[74] In other words, when both challenges and skills are high, a person may learn more during the experience. A study of 78 individuals' flow states during both work and leisure found most flow experiences are reported when working, not during peoples' leisure time.[75] Moreover, individuals that were more motivated during flow reported more positive experiences at work. Csikszentmihalyi believes that creativity results from the interaction of a supportive culture for innovation.[76] For example, an employee brings a novel idea for product packaging to their work and a group of marketing experts validates the idea as a worthwhile innovation.

Despite some evidence personality traits and intelligence relate to creativity, many experts believe most people can learn to be more creative with training.[77,78] There are a number of misconceptions about creativity in the book *The Myths of Creativity: The Truth About How Innovative Companies and People Generate Ideas*, which challenges commonly held "myths" about creative people and innovation processes.[79] This book addresses 10 common misunderstandings about how innovative organizations actually encourage creativity. These myths and the reality based on research evidence are summarized in Table 6.3. For example, rather than the lone genius working alone in a laboratory all night, creative ideas are more likely to come from teams that work on problems—especially teams that have a leader who provides a supportive climate for innovation to flourish.

Three-Component Model of Creativity

One of the most important models of creativity in organizations is the three-component model of creativity developed by Teresa Amabile from Harvard University.[80] As shown in Figure 6.3, creativity is a function of three intersecting components: expertise, creative thinking skills, and motivation. Expertise refers to knowledge (technical, processes, and academic). Creative thinking skills are how adaptable and imaginative individuals in the organization are. Finally, motivation refers to the intrinsic form of motivation—the urgent need to solve the problem faced and not the monetary rewards expected. Given the person has the expertise related to the problem, their creative thinking skills can be enhanced through training. In addition, leaders can create the right processes and workplace climates to enhance creativity. For example, leaders can give followers challenging problems to work on and allow them the freedom to innovate. Support from the organization also matters—for creativity to thrive, people need resources, a positive work group climate, and encouragement.

Table 6.3 The Myths of Creativity

	Myth	Reality (Evidence-Based Research Findings)
Eureka Myth	New ideas are a flash of insight	New ideas are the result of hard work on a problem over time, the solution may come quickly after working on it
Breed Myth	Creativity is genetic; some people are born more creative than others	Creative potential is in everyone; confidence and hard work leads to creative solutions
Originality Myth	A new idea is one person's "intellectual property"	New ideas are actually combinations of old ideas; sharing ideas leads to more innovation
Expert Myth	An expert or small team of experts comes up with creative ideas in a company	An outsider may be better able to innovate because they are not limited by considering why something won't work
Incentive Myth	Monetary incentives increase creativity and innovation	Incentives may help but may do more harm than good
Lone Creator Myth	Creative works come from one person working alone	Creativity is often a team effort, leadership makes a difference
Brainstorming Myth	Generating "crazy" ideas produces creative ones	Just "throwing ideas around" alone does not result in innovation; there's a larger process
Cohesive Myth	Everyone working on a problem should have fun together and like one another	The most creative organizations build constructive controversy and conflict into their innovation process
Constraints Myth	Limitations hinder the process	Creativity thrives under constraints
Mousetrap Myth	Once a new idea emerges, the creative process is finished	Great ideas are often rejected at first; finding the right marketing and finding the right customers is essential – new ideas must be communicated

Source: Burkus, D. (2013). *The myths of creativity: The truth about how innovative companies and people generate great ideas.* San Francisco, CA: Jossey-Bass.

Can Multicultural Experiences Enhance Creativity?

Many universities have study abroad programs where students spend a significant amount of time immersed in a culture other than their own. Research has indicated that in addition to broadening a person's global outlook, multicultural experiences also increase creativity. Exposure to multiple cultures has been related to both creative performance (e.g., learning from insights) and creativity-supporting cognitive processes (e.g., creative idea expansion).

The effects of multicultural exposure on creativity happen through a variety of experiences including living abroad, extensiveness of interactions with foreign cultures, immigration history, bilingualism, and interactions with people from different national or ethnic backgrounds. Moreover, the research evidence suggests the link between multicultural experience and creativity is strongest when the person has been totally immersed in another culture by living there. By exposure to different cultures, a person learns to access seemingly

discrepant ideas from each culture and then integrate those ideas in new ways.[81]

Individual differences also matter—particularly openness to experience in terms of the degree to which living abroad enhances creative performance and thought processes. So, in addition to enhancing your cultural intelligence (CQ) and global mind-set (you will learn more about these in Chapter 12), living in another country may also increase your creative problem-solving skills.

Discussion Questions:

1. Explain whether it is possible that more creative people seek multicultural experiences. In other words, does creativity cause multicultural interest and not the other way around?
2. Provide an example from your own experience with a person from another culture (either while abroad or someone in your country) where you had to think creatively to understand them.

Sources: Chiu, C.-Y., & Hong, Y. (2005). Cultural competence: Dynamic processes. In A. Elliot & C. S. Dweck (Eds.), *Handbook of motivation and competence* (pp. 489–505). New York, NY: Guilford Press; Leung, A. K., Maddux, W. W., Galinsky, A. D., & Chiu, C.-Y. (2008). Multicultural experience enhances creativity: The when and how. *The American Psychologist, 63*(3), 169–218.

Creative Leadership

Basadur states:

> The most effective leaders of the 21st century will help individuals and teams to coordinate and integrate their differing styles to drive change through a process of applied creativity that includes continuously discovering and defining new problems, solving those problems, and implementing the new solutions.[82]

He has conducted numerous field experiments over many years and demonstrated that training in creative problem-solving skills, attitudes, and behaviors improves creative performance.[83,84] Leaders can create the right conditions for creativity to occur in organizational settings.[85]

Figure 6.3 Three Component Model of Creativity

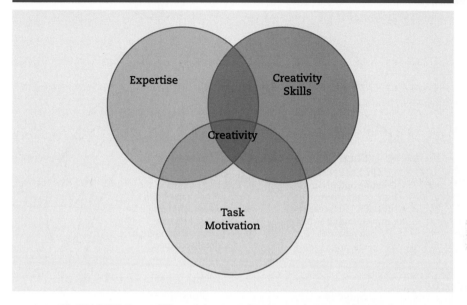

Source: Amabile, T.M. (1998). How to kill creativity. *Harvard Business Review,* September-October, 77–87.

Basadur's model of leading people to think creatively in organizations involves three creative activities: problem finding (which has two separate phases), problem solving, and **solution implementation.** He pointed out the first step is to use creative problem-solving skills to articulate the problem correctly. Next, engage in problem solving, and creativity must also apply to the implementation of solutions. The problem-finding phase is split into two phases: problem generating (creating new possibilities) and problem conceptualizing (defining the problem). Next, alternative solutions to the problem are generated in the optimizing phase. Basadur also suggested that creative problem-solving attitudes, skills, and behaviors must be applied during implementation to generate options for how the solution will be implemented and for how the needed support in the organization will be obtained. Basadur's four-phase model is shown in Figure 6.4. This model is a comprehensive model of problem solving and how leaders can influence all four steps of the process by modeling the desired behaviors and provided necessary support and encouragement to followers. Research in organizational behavior (OB) that has directly addressed the role of leadership in the innovation process will be reviewed next.

Critical Thinking Question: What phase of the creative leadership model do you think is the most important and why? If you think they are all important, rank them and explain your ranking.

Figure 6.4 The Creative Leadership Model

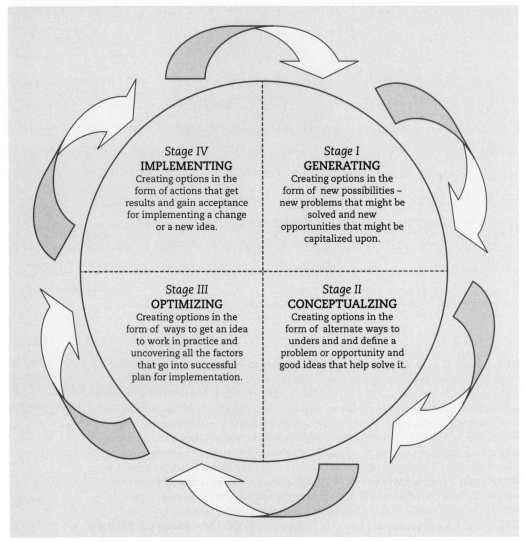

Stage IV
IMPLEMENTING
Creating options in the
form of actions that get
results and gain acceptance
for implementing a change
or a new idea.

Stage I
GENERATING
Creating options in the
form of new possibilities –
new problems that might be
solved and new
opportunities that might be
capitalized upon.

Stage III
OPTIMIZING
Creating options in the
form of ways to get an idea
to work in practice and
uncovering all the factors
that go into successful
plan for implementation.

Stage II
CONCEPTUALZING
Creating options in the
form of alternate ways to
unders and and define a
problem or opportunity and
good ideas that help solve it.

Source: Basadur, M.S. (1995). *The Power of Innovation: How to make innovation a way of life and put creative solutions to work.* Pitman Professional Publishing, available at: www.basadur.com

LEADERSHIP IMPLICATIONS: HOW LEADERS SUPPORT CREATIVITY

Learning Objective 6.7: Illustrate the role of leadership in supporting creativity of followers.

Leadership plays a role in enhancing creative problem solving. Employee innovative styles and intrinsic motivation combine with high-quality leader–member exchange (LMX; discussed in Chapter 2) to produce more creative performance and inventions from R&D personnel in a large chemical company.[86] Creative problem solving and motivation matter, and leaders play an important role in encouraging their followers to be creative. High expectations for creative performance by a leader relates to employee capacity for creativity. Leader support also increases the degree of confidence employees have in their ability to be creative.[87] A study conducted in a high-technology firm revealed a positive association between leadership and creative work involvement.[88] Also, the relationship was even stronger when employees experienced greater job autonomy. Thus, both the leader–member relationship and job design contribute to increasing employees' creative work. In sum, there are personal, work context, and leadership factors that combine to influence the creation of new ideas.[89]

 Managing for Creativity

Decision making is an essential skill that leaders must have to be effective and to move up in the organization. This chapter reviewed decision theory and provided tools that have proven to increase decision effectiveness. Also, the traps that leaders may fall into were identified, including hindsight, overconfidence, and escalation of commitment. To avoid decision traps and solve problems effectively, creative problem solving is needed. The chapter concluded with discussion of the role of leadership in enhancing creativity.

$SAGE edge™

edge.sagepub.com/scandura

Want a better grade? Go to **edge.sagepub.com/scandura** for the tools you need to sharpen your study skills.

KEY TERMS

bounded ethicality, 152
bounded rationality, 140
career indecision, 139
creativity, 153
disturbance handler, 138
entrepreneur, 138
escalation of
   commitment, 150
flow, 154

framing, 142
heuristic, 147
hindsight bias, or I-knew-
   it-all-along effect, 149
individual rights, 152
justice, 152
negotiator, 138
overconfidence
   bias, 149

prospect theory, 141
resource allocator, 138
satisfice, 141
solution implementation, 157
sunk costs fallacy, 150
utilitarianism, 152
wicked organizational
   problems, 146

SUGGESTIONS FOR FURTHER READING

Burkus, D. (2013). *The myths of creativity: The truth about how innovative companies and people generate great ideas*. San Francisco, CA: Jossey-Bass.

Gino, F. (2013). *Sidetracked: Why our decisions get derailed, and how we can stick to the plan*. Boston, MA: Harvard University Press.

Harnish, V. (2012). *The greatest business decisions of all time: How Apple, Ford, IBM, Zappos, and others made radical choices that changed the course of business*. New York, NY: Fortune.

Kahneman, D. (2011). *Thinking fast and slow*. New York, NY: Farmer, Straus & Giroux.

Tasler, N. (2013). *Why quitters win*. Henderson, NV: Motivational Press. Retrieved from http://www.nicktasler.com/author

TOOLKIT ACTIVITY 6.1

Creative Problem-Solving Exercises

The solutions are at the end of the Toolkit. Don't look ahead!

1. Remove seven matches to leave nine.

2. Move one match to make a square.

CASE STUDY 6.1

Do You Have to Spend Money to Make Money?

That is the question SABMiller, the world's second-largest brewing company that controls about 90% of the South African market, is asking itself. Looking for ways to gain greater sales and increase market share, SABMiller is trying to generate more sales by attracting women in South Africa to drink its beers. The company makes Brutal Fruit Mango-Goji Fusion beer and Flying Fish Premium Flavored Beer, which are sweeter and generally preferred by female customers.

The problem is that most women in South Africa don't frequent bars and pubs—and with good reason. For many years, the country's major religions, Christianity and Islam, kept most South African women out of bars as drinking did not fit in with the religious principles. These days, religion has little impact on a woman's decision to visit bars, but the attractiveness, cleanliness, and safety of the establishments certainly do. Leftover from the days of apartheid, illegal shebeens (informal bars often with just a few plastic chairs set up in the proprietor's front room) have transitioned to licensed bars but have yet to lose their grungy look. Most former shebeens would be considered dives in the United States, with no toilets and ramshackle conditions. Thus, going out to a bar to drink doesn't appeal to "respectable" women.

SABMiller sees women as a way to generate more money in a market with increasing competition from Heineken and Diageo. There are 17 million women of legal drinking age in South Africa. But how can the company get them to frequent bars, SABMiller's preferred sales avenue, and spend money? SABMiller's managing director in Johannesburg, Mauricio Leyva, thinks the answer can be found by working with the 6,000 bar and tavern keepers to make their establishments more attractive to women. Leyva wants to finance a $5 million in bar renovations that include adding or updating bathrooms, painting, and redesigning the establishments' seating arrangements. The company is also considering buying bar supplies, such as beer glasses, because focus groups have revealed that many women don't like drinking from bottles.

You're the director of African and Asian sales and Leyva's boss. It's your decision to approve or deny Leyva's idea of helping establishments refurbish themselves.

Discussion Questions

1. What are the key issues regarding the decision? What information are you going to want to find out before you decide on this investment?
2. Recall from the chapter the four key decision-making approaches (rational decision-making model, intuition, wicked organizational problems, and creative problem solving). Try to come to a decision for the organization using the tenants of each of these styles.
3. What differences in the results do you see?
4. What personal biases might have influenced you?
5. What elements of the situation might have made the decision easier or harder to make?
6. How do you think making a decision with others would have influenced the decisions and decision-making process? How might have other's perspectives, pressure, and persuasion influenced you?

Source: Developed from Kew, J., & Fletcher, C. (2014, May 29). SABMiller cleans up South Africa's bars to attract women. Businessweek. Retrieved from http://www.businessweek.com/articles/2014-05-29/sabmiller-cleans-up-south-africas-bars-to-attract-women.

SELF-ASSESSMENT 6.1

How Would You Rate Your Creativity?

Creative people have a lot in common. This self-assessment tool identifies the characteristics of creative people. Check it out for yourself to see how you rate. Just by completing it, you will get some ideas for improving your creativity.

Please indicate your level of agreement or disagreement with each of the following statements using a scale from 1 to 5 where 1 means strongly disagree and 5 means strongly agree. There are no "right" or "wrong" answers. Just choose the one that best represents your view of yourself. You don't have to share your results with others unless you wish to do so.

1—Strongly disagree
2—Somewhat disagree
3—Neutral
4—Somewhat agree
5—Strongly agree

	Characteristic	Score 1	2	3	4	5
1.	I go beyond the obvious to the new, different, and unusual.					
2.	I generate many ideas and come up with several possible solutions to a problem.					
3.	I can expand and work out details for an idea or a solution.					
4.	I can hold conflicting ideas and values without undue tension.					
5.	I can go beyond commonly accepted ideas to the unusual.					
6.	I can see the "whole picture"; I hold a wide range of interests.					
7.	I am aware of my own inner feelings and the feelings and thoughts of others.					
8.	I have the capacity for play, the desire to know, and openness to new ideas and experiences.					
9.	I can think for myself and make decisions; I am self-reliant.					
10.	I can put ideas into action and help shape that with which I am involved.					
11.	I can work consistently with deep concentration; I get lost in a problem.					
12.	I proceed with determination when I take on a task or project and do not give up easily.					
13.	I am able to work intensively on a project for many hours.					
14.	I am not afraid to try something new; I like adventure.					
15.	I have a keen sense of humor. I often see humor in situations that may not be seen as humorous to others.					
16.	I believe in my ability to be creative in a given situation.					
17.	Insightful and intuitive, I am able to see relationships and make mental leaps.					
18.	I am open to the ideas of others.					

Characteristic	Score				
	1	2	3	4	5
19. I can produce new products or formulas; I bring about change in procedures and organization.					
20. I am highly confident in my abilities.					
21. I enjoy challenging tasks; I have a dislike for doing things in a prescribed way.					
22. I do not depend on others to maintain my interest level; I am a self-starter.					
23. I am artistic.					
24. I am sensitive to beauty; I attend to aesthetic characteristics of things.					
25. I am involved in the arts, theater, music, dance, and/or design.					
Calculate Results (add the columns)					
Total Score (add the column totals)					

Significance of This Assessment

We are all creative but in varying degrees depending upon many factors and experiences in our lives. Perhaps the most important aspect of who has creative capabilities is dependent on the encouragement or discouragement of the use of these capabilities by others and the motivation and efforts exerted by the individuals themselves. Dozens of research studies, combined with informed opinions, point to one conclusion about creative people: Creative people may be nonconformist, but they certainly have a lot in common.

The purpose of this assessment is to evaluate creative predispositions in adults. The statements of characteristics are based on research found to be common and recurrent among creatively productive people. The statements are inclusive of behaviors, traits, interests, values, motivation, and attributes of creative people.

Completion of this assessment will help you determine which of the characteristics you already possess and which you may want to develop further if you would like to be a more creative person. Research has shown that creativity can be learned, developed, and nurtured.

Use this assessment to determine actions to improve your lowest scores. Examine the underlying reasons for the results. Discuss your results with someone who knows you well and who can act as a coach or buddy in helping you further develop these areas.

Your Results

If your raw score is over 90: Congratulations! By your own assessment, you possess the characteristics of highly creative people. It is important that you continue to look for opportunities to tap into your creativity and create an environment for yourself where your creativity can continue to flourish. The bad news is that creative people can have habits or dispositions that can upset others. Researchers have narrowed these down into seven categories: egotistical, impulsive, argumentative, childish, absentminded, neurotic, and hyperactive. In business or a professional setting, the highly creative person will need to maintain patience and understanding of others if they want to be successful.

If your raw score is between 75 and 90: By your assessment, you are a fairly creative person. It is important, at this point, that you continue to nurture these creative characteristics and further develop the ones where you had a lower score. Take a look at the end of this section to see a further breakdown of the test and identify the characteristics you want to develop further.

If your raw score is between 50 and 75: It is important to celebrate the fact that you possess some of the characteristics of a creative person; however, additional development of the characteristics—where you are not so strong—would go a long way. Take a look at the end of this section to see a further breakdown of the test and identify the characteristics you want to develop further. There are many books and courses to help develop your creativity.

If your score is below 50: Don't fret. Perhaps you have not been in an environment that nurtured your creativity or you were told as a child that you were not creative and have held that belief ever since. The truth is that creative attitudes and personality traits can be strengthened. Take a look at the end of this section to see a further breakdown of the test and identify the characteristics you want to develop further. There are many books and courses to help develop your creativity.

Further Breakdown of the Test

1. Recurrent Characteristics of Creative People Found in the Literature

Question(s) From the Test:	Creative Characteristic
16	Awareness of creativeness
5	Original
9, 20, 22	Independent
14	Risktaker/adventurous
10, 12, 19	Highly energetic
13	Thorough: must finish
6, 8	Curiosity
15	Sense of humor
4, 21	Attracted to complexity, ambiguity
23, 24	Artistic, aesthetic interests
18	Open minded
17	Perceptive: intuitive
7	Emotional: sensitivity, empathy
25	Capacity for fantasy
11, 13	Need for some privacy; alone time

2. Cognitive Abilities Important to Creative Thinking

Question From Test:	Creative Ability
1	Flexibility
2	Fluency
3	Elaboration
5	Originality
11	Concentration

Source: Davis, G. A. (1998). *Creativity is forever.* Dubuque, IA: Kendall/Hunt.

SOLUTIONS TO TOOLKIT ACTIVITY 6.1

1. **Visual logic:** Spell *nine* instead of counting the matchsticks.

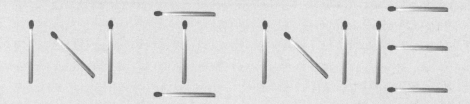

2. **Logical intelligence:** You make a square in the center of the matchsticks by pulling out the matchstick to the right slightly.

Source: Challenge your creativity: 77 problem solving exercises. Retrieved October 30, 2013, from http://dudye.com/challenge-your-creativity-77-problem-solving-exercises.

SECTION III

MOTIVATING EMPLOYEES

Chapter 7 • Motivation: Core Concepts

Chapter 8 • Motivation: Learning and Rewards

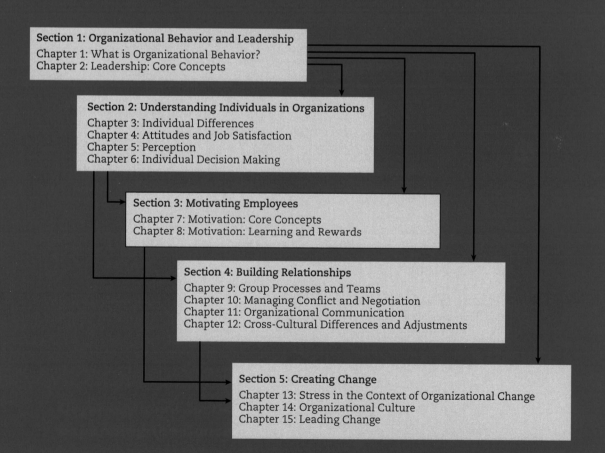

Section 1: Organizational Behavior and Leadership

Chapter 1: What is Organizational Behavior?
Chapter 2: Leadership: Core Concepts

Section 2: Understanding Individuals in Organizations

Chapter 3: Individual Differences
Chapter 4: Attitudes and Job Satisfaction
Chapter 5: Perception
Chapter 6: Individual Decision Making

Section 3: Motivating Employees

Chapter 7: Motivation: Core Concepts
Chapter 8: Motivation: Learning and Rewards

Section 4: Building Relationships

Chapter 9: Group Processes and Teams
Chapter 10: Managing Conflict and Negotiation
Chapter 11: Organizational Communication
Chapter 12: Cross-Cultural Differences and Adjustments

Section 5: Creating Change

Chapter 13: Stress in the Context of Organizational Change
Chapter 14: Organizational Culture
Chapter 15: Leading Change

MOTIVATION
CORE CONCEPTS

DO YOU HAVE GRIT?

Do you think that perseverance is as important as intelligence (IQ)? This is the question that Angela Duckworth, professor of psychology, has been investigating. She calls a high level of effort and persistence "grit" and defines it as "perseverance and passion for long-term goals."[1] Grit is the ability to stick to a goal and not give up even in the face of adversity. Research has shown that grit may be as important as intelligence. There are a lot of smart people who don't achieve, and Duckworth's research found students who had more grit but were not as intelligent as their peers worked harder and had higher GPAs. Another study Duckworth conducted was at West Point, and cadets who had the highest levels on the "grit scale" were the most likely to succeed in the rigorous summer training program known as "Beast Barracks." Grit mattered more than intelligence, leadership ability, or physical fitness. In a third study, she found that participants in the National Spelling Bee contest who had higher levels of grit ended up being ranked higher. This study revealed that success was, in part, due to participants with more grit spending more hours practicing for the contest. In Duckworth's research, grit was not related to IQ, but it was related to the Big Five personality trait conscientiousness. Her advice for people with a desire to achieve is: "If it's important for you to become one of the best people in your field, you are going to have to stick with it when it's hard. Grit may be as essential as talent to high accomplishment."[2] Meta-analytic findings support the idea that perseverance pays off since conscientiousness has been significantly and positively related to motivation in numerous studies.[3] If you would like to learn how much perseverance you have, you can take the perseverance assessment found in the Self-Assessment 7.1 activity at the end of this chapter.

Critical Thinking Question: What do you think is more important: IQ or perseverance? Explain why.

Learning Objectives

After studying this chapter, you should be able to do the following:

7.1: Identify and discuss the three parts of the motivation process.

7.2: Compare and contrast Maslow's hierarchy with McClelland's need theory.

7.3: Produce an example of a SMART goal.

7.4: Describe the job characteristics theory (JCT) and why growth needs matter.

7.5: Explain why fairness is a necessary condition for leadership using equity theory and the four types of organizational justice.

7.6: Explain how the expectancy theory of motivation predicts effort.

7.7: Demonstrate the role of leaders in the motivation process, using path–goal theory (PGT).

Get the edge on your studies at **edge.sagepub.com/scandura**
- Take the chapter quiz
- Review key terms with eFlashcards
- Explore multimedia resources, SAGE readings, and more!

$SAGE edge™

As suggested by the research on grit, motivation is important for leaders to understand; thus, there is a large evidence base on motivation in organizational behavior (OB). The next two chapters focus on the role of the leader as motivator. This chapter reviews theories of motivation that have received research support and provide evidence-based guidance for practice. The next chapter (Chapter 8) reviews research on rewards in organizations and discusses how to design reward systems that motivate.

Maslow's Theory

WHAT IS MOTIVATION?

Learning Objective 7.1: Identify and discuss the three parts of the motivation process.

The word *motivation* comes from the Latin word for *movement* (*movere*).[4] Motivation has been defined as "what a person does (direction), how hard a person works (intensity), and how long a person works (persistence)."[5] An overview of the motivation process is shown in Figure 7.1. Motivation is the process of energizing behavior by activating people's needs and drives. Once energized, it is important to direct the behavior toward goals that are important to the organization. In this chapter, we will explore models of motivation that activate and direct behavior. The third step in the figure is sustaining behavior. Research shows that goal-setting systems and reward systems are necessary to sustain behavior over the long term, and the next chapter will address rewards as motivation in practice. Finally, for motivation to be effective, feedback is needed so that the processes of energizing and directing behavior stay on track.

NEED THEORIES

Learning Objective 7.2: Compare and contrast Maslow's hierarchy with McClelland's need theory.

Early theories of motivation address the first part of Figure 7.1 by focusing on what needs or drives motivate people. The most well-known theory of need motivation is the Maslow hierarchy of needs.[6] The theory was the first to point out that there are individual differences in motivation. The first level in the hierarchy of needs is physiological needs (e.g., hunger, sex, and other bodily needs). The next level is safety needs (e.g., the need for protection from physical harm). At the third level of the hierarchy are a person's **social** needs (e.g., belongingness and friendship). The fourth level is esteem needs (e.g., status and recognition from others). Finally, at the top of the hierarchy is what Maslow termed **self-actualization,** which is the drive to meet our fullest capacity (e.g., growth and feeling fulfilled as a person). Physiological and safety needs are lower-order needs and social, esteem, and self-actualization are higher-order needs, according to the theory. When a need is not satisfied, it becomes dominant. For example, if a person's safety is threatened, then they focus on finding a place where there is no threat of physical harm.

Despite the popularity of Maslow's hierarchy due to its simplicity and intuitive appeal, it has not been supported by research evidence.[7] Needs are not arranged in this particular hierarchy, and there is no evidence that unsatisfied needs become dominant and induce

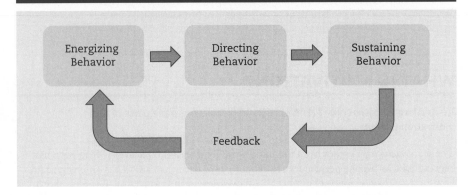

Figure 7.1 The Motivation Process

motivation. However, this theory remains a commonly mentioned theory by many practicing managers, so it is important to be aware of it.

Another need theory considers three fundamental needs:[8]

- **Need for achievement (nAch)**—the drive to succeed at high levels
- **Need for power (nPow)**—the need to influence others to do what you want
- **Need for affiliation (nAff)**—the need for close personal relationships

Most of McClelland's research was on nAch. There is some research support for the idea that people who have a higher need to achieve do perform at higher levels and people with a higher nAch may be more successful entrepreneurs.[9] However, a high need to achieve is not necessarily related to being an effective leader since those with higher nAch may be more interested in their own attainment rather than coaching others to succeed. McClelland's theory has received more research support than other need theories; however, the application of the theory to motivate followers is limited because these needs are believed to be learned at a young age (in other words, it may not be possible to increase an adult's nAch).

The **two-factor theory** relates lower- and higher-order needs and relates them to Job Satisfaction (which was discussed in Chapter 4).[10] This is also called the **motivator–hygiene theory** and sought to answer the question of what people really want from their work. When people think about what makes them dissatisfied with work, they think of things like supervision, pay, company policies, and the working conditions, which are called **hygienes.** On the other hand, when people think of what *satisfies* them, they are more likely to think of things like advancement, recognition, and achievement, called **motivators.** Hygiene factors can only bring a person's satisfaction to the level of "no dissatisfaction" (in other words, they stop complaining about their pay). To motivate people, leaders need to focus on the motivators such as providing people with a sense of achievement.

As with Maslow's theory, Herzberg's two-factor theory is widely cited, but it has not received much research support.[11] For example, the methods used in this research have been criticized because it was all self-reported data based on limited samples. Also, the relationship of satisfaction to job performance was assumed in his research but never tested.

 SMART Goals

This brief review of research on need theories is a cautionary tale. Overall, research on need theories has not provided strong research evidence for how to motivate people. In the following sections, theories aimed at understanding what directs a person's behavior toward outcomes such as high job performance will be discussed. Recalling the research on grit in the introduction to this chapter, we know that persistence plays a role in understanding how individuals attain high levels of performance. Once people set a goal, perseverance (grit) measures their ability to stick to it until it is attained. There has been a great deal of research on goal setting in OB and some of the most practical and well-substantiated guidelines for motivating followers are provided by this research.

 Critical Thinking Questions: Explain the relationship between high self-actualization (Maslow) and nAch. Next, explain the relationship between high self-actualization and motivators.[12]

GOAL SETTING

Learning Objective 7.3: Produce an example of a SMART goal.

OB research has investigated the properties of motivating goals in numerous laboratory and field experiments.[13,14] For goals to motivate employees, they must have certain properties.[15] These goal-setting principles can be remembered with the acronym *SMART* for specific, measurable, actionable, relevant, and time-based goals.

"SMART" Goals

1. **Specific:** A specific goal has been shown to be more motivating than a "do your best" goal. Answer these questions: Who is involved? What do I want to accomplish? Where will this need to occur? When will it happen? Why am I or we doing this?
2. **Measurable:** Set concrete criteria for measuring progress toward the attainment of each goal. Measuring progress provides feedback and keeps people on track. Answer these questions: How much? How many? How will I know this goal is attained?
3. **Attainable:** Goals need to be challenging, but they also need to be seen as attainable by the person setting them. When people identify goals that matter to them, it energizes them and motivates a search for ways to perform. This may require new skills or resources. Answer these questions: Is this goal realistic? Do I have the skills and abilities to achieve it? Do I have the resources needed to achieve it? Have I attained something similar in the past?

4. **Relevant:** The goal you set needs to matter—to the individual setting it and/or the organization. Goals that are relevant are more likely to gain the support and the resources needed. Relevant goals (when met) drive the team, department, and organization forward. A goal that supports or is in alignment with other goals would be considered a relevant goal. Answer these questions: Does this matter? Is this the right time to do this? How does this fit in with the broader mission of the organization?
5. **Time Based:** To be motivating, goals should have a specific time frame. This creates a sense of urgency and encourages benchmarking toward the attainment of the goal. Ask yourself these questions: When do I need to attain this goal? Are there mini-goals or benchmarks I can set to monitor progress toward the goal?

For example, a not-so-smart goal would be the following: "Improve your punctuality." In comparison, an example of a SMART goal would be as follows: "Be at work by 8:30 a.m. every day this month because everyone being at work on time contributes to our team's productivity." Toolkit Activity 7.1 contains a goal-setting exercise where you write a letter to your "future me" and can apply SMART goal setting to your own life and career.

In practice, SMART goal setting has been applied using **management by objectives (MBO)**. MBO is a performance appraisal program where leaders meet with their direct reports and set specific performance objectives jointly. Progress toward objectives is periodically reviewed and rewards are allocated on the basis of that progress.[16] Performance appraisal will be discussed in more detail in Chapter 8.

The degree to which a person is committed to a goal influences their willingness to persist and attain it. Also, motivation is higher when an employee is more committed to challenging goals compared with easy goals.[17] It is not clear whether allowing a person to participate in setting their own goals makes a difference; research findings are mixed.[18] However, if the goal is set by the leader, it is important for the leader to focus on the relevance of the goal to the person and the organization.

 Critical Thinking Question: Why would allowing followers to participate in setting their own goals make a difference? Provide an example.

The Role of Leaders in Goal Setting

An example of successful implementation of goal setting is how they do it at Microsoft.[19] Goal commitment is so important that they changed the name of the process from "goal setting" to "goal commitment." Also, the leaders are actively involved in the process of developing commitments from followers. Each leader is expected to do the following:

1. Discuss and document the commitments of all employees.
2. Revisit and refresh commitments over time.
3. Agree to success metrics for each commitment, including the "how" behind execution (e.g., the plans to be used to attain the commitments), not just the "what."

4. Align commitments across the company by cascading commitments, beginning with Microsoft's commitments and connecting to organizational, team, and ultimately individual commitments.

5. Drive management team calibration discussions so interdependencies and metrics are vetted across individuals (pp. 140–141).[20]

Job Quality and Organization

This case example shows that leaders play an important role in negotiating mutual goals one-on-one with each of their direct reports. This process assures alignment with the organization's goals, commitment, and accountability for results.

Research on goal setting has also demonstrated that employees who receive **feedback** on their progress achieve higher levels of performance than those who don't.[21] Feedback on goals guides performance and allows the person to correct behaviors that may not be working or try different performance strategies. Further, research has indicated that if employees are allowed to generate their own feedback, it may be more motivating than feedback from an outside source such as their supervisor.[22]

Goal setting has been criticized due to the fact that goal setting may undermine creativity and the flexibility of employees to adapt to changing situations. For example, focusing on only one criterion for success may preclude looking at other opportunities to improve.[23] However, despite this concern, proponents of the theory maintain that the benefits of goal setting outweigh the limitations.[24]

A SMART goals worksheet that can be used to set goals for yourself or for your followers is provided in Toolkit Activity 7.2 at the end of this chapter. As we have seen, feedback is essential to the process of motivation. In addition to setting SMART goals and learning feedback on performance, an employee may gain feedback from the work itself. Another major theory of motivation is the job characteristics theory (JCT), which looks at the motivating properties of work. We will turn to this core theory of motivation next.

JOB CHARACTERISTICS THEORY

Learning Objective 7.4: Describe the job characteristics theory (JCT) and why growth needs matter.

The work itself may have characteristics that have the potential to motivate people to higher levels of performance.[25] Also, people are more satisfied when their work is interesting, and they may be less likely to quit. JCT is shown in Figure 7.2. In this theory of motivation, jobs can be designed so that people are more motivated, satisfied, as well as perform better.

The Motivating Potential of Work

First, the JCT specifies five core job dimensions. These dimensions combine to produce the critical psychological states that enhance motivation:

1. **Skill variety**—the extent to which people use different skills and abilities at work. The employee is not doing the same repetitive tasks over and over.

Work Design and Attitude

2. **Task identity**—the task is one that people experience from beginning to end. In other words, they identify with an entire work product.
3. **Task significance**—the degree to which the job is seen as having an impact on others. The work does something good for society.
4. **Autonomy**—the employee has the freedom to plan and perform his or her own work. The employees have discretion about their work and are not intensely supervised.
5. **Feedback**—the job provides information on how effective the employee's work is. Just doing the work itself provides performance feedback.

Skill variety, task identity, and task significance combine in the job characteristics model to produce a sense of meaningfulness of the work. For example, autonomy increases a person's responsibility for the work they perform. As in goal setting, feedback provides knowledge of the actual results of a person's work. These states experienced from the nature of the work performed translate into high work motivation, work performance, satisfaction, and lower absenteeism and turnover.

As Figure 7.2 shows, the growth needs of employees affect the degree to which a person experiences meaningfulness, responsibility, and knowledge of results from their work. **Growth need strength** refers to a person's need to learn new things, grow, and develop from working. People vary in this need; some people have a high desire to grow as a result of their work and others do not. This need also affects performance. In other words, if a person's job is interesting, he or she may not have higher motivation and performance if he or she doesn't really need to grow from the work. Employees who prefer challenging work experience have less stress after their work is redesigned.[26]

Critical Thinking Questions: How do growth needs relate to higher-order needs as described in the need theories earlier in this chapter? How can a leader identify growth needs in followers?

Designing Work to Be Motivational

Based on the research on the job characteristics model, organizations have implemented **work redesign** to enhance the motivating potential of work.[27] The basic idea is to load jobs with more of the core job characteristics that have been shown to motivate. This job loading may be **horizontal** (e.g., adding different tasks at the same level) or **vertical** (e.g., adding decision-making responsibility). Recall that it is important to consider the growth needs of employees when redesigning work since these employees will respond more positively to the redesign of their work. These strategies have been referred to as **job enrichment,** and some examples follow.[28]

Job rotation involves cross-training or allowing workers to do different jobs. This increases the skill variety, task identity, and possibly the task significance. For example, a person who works on an assembly line is rotated to a clerical position in which he or she learns the purchasing process for supplies needed on the line 1 day a week. This provides variety and also allows the worker to see more of the "big picture" of what is needed to perform the work. In addition to job rotation, work may be designed to create natural work units by **combining tasks.** For example, a worker who drills holes for a door handle of a car

Figure 7.2 The Job Characteristics Model

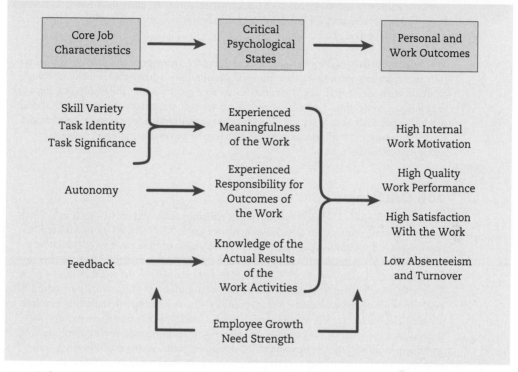

Source: Hackman, J. R., & Oldham, G. R. (1980). *Work redesign.* Reading, MA: Addison-Wesley.

would also learn to install the handle. Job rotation and combining tasks must be supported by adequate training and coaching for employees as they learn new skills on the job. Job rotation and combining tasks are examples of horizontal job loading.

Jobs may also be loaded vertically by allowing employees to establish client relationships in which workers can interact directly with clients to increase the meaningfulness of work. For example, the human resources manager for the Applied Systems Group at Spar Applied Systems redesigned the work into teams so that most workers interacted with customers to increase the focus on customer needs.[29] Another example is a study of callers requesting donations which found the callers were more persistent and motivated when they were in contact with undergraduate students funded by their efforts.[30] Thus, organizations might increase employee motivation by designing interactions with those who benefit from the employee's efforts. The authors of this study conclude:

> Consider the back room accountant who never meets the clients who benefit from her work. Merely introducing her to these clients may allow her to perceive her impact on them and feel affectively committed to them and thereby enable her to maintain her motivation.[31]

Job Crafting

This form of motivation is based on how people may be motivated by helping others—**prosocial motivation**, which has emerged as an important outcome variable in OB as described in Chapter 1.[32,33] A meta-analytic review found that the prosocial aspects of work contribute to the explanation of performance, turnover, and job satisfaction beyond that of job characteristic.[34] Thus, it appears that both the work itself and social aspects are important to motivation.

Work may be redesigned so that employees have more **autonomy** and discretion in how they perform their work to increase the level of autonomy experienced. Finally, opening feedback channels so that employees can learn more quickly about the results of their work may increase motivation (as we have seen, feedback is an important aspect of motivation in other theories such as goal setting). Research has supported the job characteristics model by demonstrating that job enrichment does reduce turnover and increases employee motivation and satisfaction.[35,36,37,38,39,40]

Job Crafting

Recent work on job design has examined **job crafting**, or the extent to which individuals can demonstrate initiative in designing their own work. The term *job crafting* is used "to capture the actions employees take to shape, mold, and redefine their jobs."[41] Jobs vary in the degree of discretion that they offer, but in many cases, employees may be able to design aspects of their own work. Outcomes include changes to the work itself as well as interactions with others that may enhance the meaningfulness of the work performed.[42] An example of job crafting would be a team member who is working on marketing research project designing a set of team-building activities and implementing them to improve the way that the team works together on the project. Additional examples of job crafting are shown in Table 7.1. A review of the job design literature states the following: "Job crafting is an exciting area of research."[43] However, the authors caution that there may be dysfunctional consequences from employees designing their own work that need research. For example, an employee might redesign their work to include extraneous meetings with other department members that causes them to be away from the office resulting in work disruptions to coworkers.

Critical Thinking Questions: What limitations (if any) would you put on allowing followers to craft their own work? What are the risks of not putting any limitations on job crafting?

There has been much research on motivation that has provided specific guidelines for leaders to follow: setting SMART goals and designing work to be motivational are key takeaway concepts. Despite effective goals and challenging work, however, motivation may be lower if employees have strong negative reactions based on how rewards are distributed or how they are treated. To effectively motivate followers and avoid costly absenteeism and turnover, leaders must follow principles of **organizational justice.**

The next sections will address this concern.

Table 7.1 Forms of Job Crafting

Form	Example	Effect on Meaning of Work
Changing the number, scope, and type of job tasks	Design engineers engaging in relational tasks that move a project to completion	Work is completed in a more timely fashion; engineers change the meaning of their jobs to be guardians or movers of projects
Changing the quality and/amount of interaction with others encountered in job	Hospital cleaners actively caring for patients and their families integrating themselves into the workflow of their floor units	Cleaners change the meaning of their jobs to be helpers of the sick; see the work of the floor as an integrated whole of which they are a vital part
Changing cognitive task boundaries	Nurses take responsibility for all information and "insignificant" tasks that may help them to care more appropriately for a patient	Nurses change the way they see the work to be more about patient advocacy, as high-quality technical care

Source: Wrzesniewski, A., & Dutton, J. E. (2001). Crafting a job: Revisioning employees as active crafters of their work. *Academy of Management Review, 26,* 179–201. p. 185.

THE IMPORTANCE OF FAIRNESS

Learning Objective 7.5: Explain why fairness is a necessary condition for leadership using equity theory and the four types of organizational justice.

Despite our parents telling us that "life is not fair," employees expect the workplace to be fair. This is, in part, due to the "just world hypothesis" (this was discussed in Chapter 5). There are situations in which employees experience anger when then don't receive what they believe they deserve on a performance evaluation and subsequent pay raise. It has been proposed that the need for fairness is a universal motive.[44] For example, an employee may feel that he should have been promoted to a higher position instead of a coworker. Employees may react to even lesser outcomes, such as who gets an office that has a window in the work group. As these examples illustrate, concerns for fairness permeate the workplace, and effective leaders need to be aware of how followers might react to their decisions.

Equity Theory

Equity theory focuses on **distributive justice** (what people receive as a result of their knowledge, skills, and effort on the job).[45] As shown in Figure 7.3, equity theory suggests that people may become demotivated or put forth less effort when they feel that what they give and what they get is not in balance. According to the theory, a person (the focal person, or FP) compares himself to the coworker (or CO). Next, he compares his inputs (skills,

Figure 7.3 Equity Theory

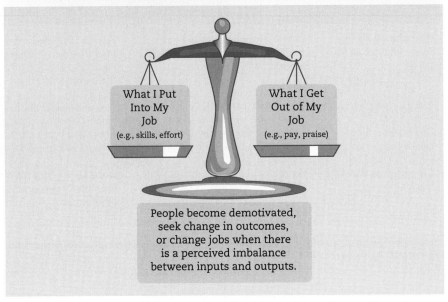

What I Put
Into My
Job
(e.g., skills, effort)

What I Get
Out of My
Job
(e.g., pay, praise)

People become demotivated,
seek change in outcomes,
or change jobs when there
is a perceived imbalance
between inputs and outputs.

Source: Adapted from: Adams, J. S. (1965). Inequity in social exchange. In L. Berkowitz (Ed.), *Advances in experimental social psychology, 2* (pp. 267–299). New York: Academic Press.

abilities, effort on the job) to his outcomes (e.g., a merit raise). Three situations can occur in this comparison:

1. **The inputs and outcomes for the FP equal the inputs and outcomes for the other (CO).** What this means is that the FP puts in effort and receives a certain pay raise. This is compared with a CO who puts in more effort and receives a higher pay raise. There is balance because the FP recognizes that the CO works harder and gets a higher raise.

2. **The input and outcomes for the FP are *lower* than the inputs and outcomes for the CO.** For example, the FP views the ratio of his inputs and outcomes as less than the CO. The FP realizes that they are "underpaid," and this causes dissonance or stress for the FP. In this situation, the FP may become demotivated (reduce inputs or efforts) to bring the ratios back to balance. If the situation persists, they may leave the situation entirely (find another job that pays better). This is referred to as **underpayment inequity.**

3. **The input and outcomes for the FP are *higher* than the inputs and outcomes for the CO.** For example, the FP makes the comparison of inputs to outcomes and views their ratio of inputs to outcomes as higher than his CO. The FP realizes that he is being "overpaid" for his contributions compared to his CO. This situation is interesting because

while we might expect the FP to work harder, this typically does not happen. People are more likely to distort the perceptions of inputs and/or outcomes to justify or rationalize their relative **overpayment inequity.** For example, they may point to their degree being from a better business school or adjust their view of their CO's input downward.

Distributive
Justice Effect

Inequitable comparisons affect employee attitudes, such as job satisfaction.[46] For example, employees in underpayment conditions engage in behavior to adjust or compensate for the inequity (theft, for example).[47] Also, employees who experience unfair situations don't help their coworkers out (organizational citizenship).[48,49] There is strong research support that indicates that perceptions of fairness affect motivation. Given the limited resources a leader has to distribute (particularly monetary compensation), leaders need to work at being perceived as fair. Research on equity (or distributive justice) was expanded to include other forms of justice that help explain how employees come to view their leader as fair.

Organizational Justice: Expanding the Concept of Fairness

The concept of equity was expanded to consider broad concerns for organizational justice at the workplace.[50] Organizational justice is the "members' sense of the moral propriety of how they are treated."[51] When people feel an event is unfair, they may even experience **moral outrage,** which is a severe reaction to the perceived injustice (including strong emotions such as anger and resentment).[52] One study found that followers even engaged in sabotage when they perceived situations to be unfair.[53] Given that OB researchers have documented the importance of fairness perceptions (particularly underpayment inequity) on demotivation, researchers became interested in how other forms of justice might somehow address fairness concerns. When leaders follow fair procedures, followers are more willing to accept distributive outcomes and their formal authority—even if they receive less.[54] Research on organizational justice turned to the development of additional forms of fairness broadening the concept into the overall umbrella term: *organizational justice.*

Organizational justice is now considered to have four components: distributive (equity), procedural, interactional, and informational.[55] As noted earlier, distributive justice refers to the fairness of decisions made as perceived by followers as described above.[56] **Procedural justice** is the perception of how fair the process was in making decisions that affect employees. There are certain rules of fair process that are expected by employees.[57,58] For example, employees want to have a voice in decisions that affect them. They also want some form of an appeal process or way to correct something they see as unfair. Third, they want procedures to be consistent across people and over time. They also want the process to be unbiased and to represent the concerns of everyone affected by the decision. Finally, procedures need to be based on accurate information. Procedural justice has been shown to be more important than distributive justice in how followers respond to the decisions of their leaders in two meta-analytic studies that included a variety of organizational and occupational samples.[59,60]

Who Cares About Fairness?

Equity sensitivity is an individual difference which affects how different people react to inequity.[61] Individuals can be thought of as being along a continuum as either benevolents (tolerant of underpayment), equity sensitives (adhere to equity norms), or entitleds (tolerant of overpayment). Benevolents don't get stressed when they experience underpayment or overpayment, but people who are equity sensitive do. Equity sensitivity may also affect the types of rewards that people prefer: Entitled employees prefer monetary rewards, whereas benevolents prefer intrinsic rewards such as the ability to learn something new on the job.[62] Equity sensitivity has also been associated with motivation: Benevolence is related to job performance and organizational citizenship.[63,64] Intriguing experimental research found benevolent individuals report the highest pay satisfaction, pay fairness, and lowest turnover intentions.[65] However, entitled individuals did *not* report lower overall pay satisfaction, perceived pay fairness, or higher turnover intentions than benevolents. The overrewarded condition was also very interesting: All three equity sensitivity groups preferred being overrewarded to being fairly rewarded and were distressed when underrewarded. These findings support equity theory for underpayment. Yet, overpayment is enjoyed by everyone, regardless of whether they are sensitive to equity or not. So whether we care about equity may depend on whether we are being overpaid or underpaid.

Discussion Questions:

1. Given the descriptions just given, do you consider yourself to be equity sensitive? In other words, do you believe that employees should be rewarded relative to their contributions?
2. Explain why overpayment satisfies employees regardless of whether they are equity sensitive or not.
3. Why is it important for a manager to consider the equity sensitivity of their followers?

Sources: Bing, M. N., & Burroughs, S. M. (2001). The predictive and interactive effects of equity sensitivity in teamwork-oriented organizations. *Journal of Organizational Behavior, 22*(3), 271–290; Blakely, G. L., Andrews, M. C., & Moorman, R. H. (2005). The moderating effects of equity sensitivity on the relationship between organizational justice and organizational citizenship behaviors. *Journal of Business & Psychology, 20*(2), 259–273; Huseman, R. C., Hatfield, J. D., & Miles, E. W. (1987). A new perspective on equity theory: The equity sensitivity construct. *Academy of Management Review, 12*(2), 222–234; Miles, E. W., Hatfield, J. D., & Huseman, R. C. (1994). Equity sensitivity and outcome importance. *Journal of Organizational Behavior, 15*(7), 585–596; Shore, T. H. (2004). Equity sensitivity theory: Do we all want more than we deserve? *Journal of Managerial Psychology, 19*(7), 722–728.

Interpersonal justice refers to how employees are treated by their leaders including respect and propriety (which refers to whether the leader refrains from offending the follower with comments that are inappropriate).[66,67] The final form of justice is **informational justice,** which refers to the perceived fairness of the communications made by leaders during a process. Informational justice includes full explanations of processes and the perception that the leader is being truthful.[68,69] For example, during the great recession of 2008, many organizations had zero pay raises. When this happened, leaders provided explanations for why raises were zero for hardworking employees because of the economic situation. Figure 7.4 summarizes the four components of organization justice and provides a sample item from an organizational justice measure to illustrate each aspect of justice.

Figure 7.4   Components of Organizational Justice

Distributive Justice
"Is your outcome justified, given your performance?"

Procedural Justice
"Have you been able to express your views and feelings during the process?"

Organizational Justice

Interpersonal Justice
"Has your leader treated you with respect?"

Informational Justice
"Has your leader explained the procedures thoroughly?"

Source: Colquitt, J. A. (2001). On the dimensionality of organizational justice: A construct validation of a measure. *Journal of Applied Psychology,* 86(3), 386–400.

 Critical Thinking Questions: Do you believe that other forms of justice can compensate for distributive justice (what people get)? Provide an example of when this happens.

Given the central role of fairness in motivation, OB theory and research has described how a leader can change the perceptions of their followers that they are being fair. Research has shown a clear relationship between fairness and effective leadership. This research is described in the following section as well as the process through which a leader can develop a reputation in the organization for being fair.

Developing a Fair Reputation

Fairness is a necessary (but not sufficient) condition for effective leadership.[70] The ability to develop high-quality relationships depends upon following norms of procedural justice and ensuring that outcomes are fairly distributed. Interpersonal and informational justice are both important in support of this; leaders must respect followers and provide truthful explanations of how they make decisions. Fairness is pivotal to relationships between leadership and

Expectancy
Theory

employee work attitudes, relationships with coworkers, and employee turnover.[71] Also, employees with good relationships with their boss also engage in more organizational citizenship when they perceive a fair climate in the work group.[72] Fairness issues emerge at the group level when followers compare their relationships with their boss (in-group or out-group) and the outcomes they receive. Thus, the procedural justice climate that a leader creates is essential to being effective in motivating followers and avoiding costly turnover.

Leaders can develop followers' perceptions that they are being fair—a fair identity.[73] When a follower presents the boss with an unfair situation, it is a predicament for the boss. For example, a coworker gets assigned to a more lucrative client; however, another direct report feels they deserved the assignment. What should the leader do to resolve this? First, the leader should have empathy and see the situation from the follower's perspective. The leader then has options to respond to the follower, but these should be carefully thought through because they have consequences for the continued trust and development of the relationship.

One set of options are verbal; the leader can deny the unfairness, show regret, or admit that it was not fair to the follower. These actions may damage the trust in the working relationship. Other options are to provide explanations to justify the action by making excuses or apologies. While these verbal responses represent better options for the maintenance of the working relationship, the follower may still not be satisfied. Finally, the leader can take actions to address the concern, such as restoring the benefit (in the example just given, the leader could assign the follower to join the coworker in working with the lucrative client). Another action would be to provide alternative recompense; assign the follower an equally valuable client to work with. A fair identity and reputation for being fair is thus negotiated and must be monitored carefully.

The example above shows that leaders play a large role in follower perceptions of fairness, which may avoid demotivation and withdrawal behaviors such as absenteeism and turnover. Leaders also help employees understand how they will be rewarded in the future. The next section will discuss theory and research on expectancy theory and how leaders motivate by articulating the pathways to goals.

EXPECTANCY THEORY

Learning Objective 7.6: Describe how the expectancy theory of motivation predicts effort.

The expectancy theory of motivation has received mixed research support but does provide insight into the process of motivation.[74] A review of research on expectancy theory noted the following: "Expectancy theory has become a standard in motivation, as reflected by its incorporation as a general framework for a wide variety of research."[75] The theory has three basic principles:[76]

1. **Employees decide to put forth effort when they believe that their effort will lead to good performance.** This is called the effort → performance relationship, which is the probability that a person believes that their effort will lead to performance (designated as the E → P expectancy).

The Importance of Leader Attention for Employee Motivation

A survey conducted by *McKinsey Quarterly* asked 1,047 executives, managers, and employees from a range of industries what practices were the most effective motivators. While most people expect financial incentives such as cash bonuses and increases in base pay to be biggest motivators, the research indicated that this was not the case. Despite the survey findings that financial incentives are frequently used (e.g., 68% of those surveyed indicated that their organization used cash bonuses), they are not the most effective.

Praise and commendation from leaders was cited as the most effective motivator with 67% reporting that this was effective, followed by attention from leaders at 63%. In addition, opportunities to lead projects or task forces were reported effective (62%). According to Dewhurst,

"these themes recur constantly in most studies on ways to motivate and engage employees."[77] With many organizations cutting back on financial incentives, now may be the best time to begin to work on more effective leadership as a motivational tool for effective motivation.

Discussion Questions:

1. Explain why praise from the immediate supervisor was the most effective motivator using the principle of feedback discussed in this chapter.
2. Use the motivator–hygiene theory to explain why financial incentives were less related to effective motivation than nonfinancial incentives such as praise, leader attention, and opportunities to lead projects.

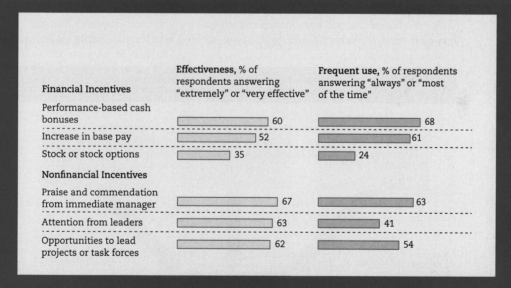

Source: Dewhurst, M. (2009). Motivating people: Getting beyond money [Commentary]. *McKinsey Quarterly.* Retrieved on January 2, 2014, from http://www.mckinsey.com/insights/organization/motivating_people_getting_beyond_money.

2. **The employee's performance will be evaluated accurately and will lead to rewards (e.g., pay raises, bonuses).** This is the follower's estimated probability that if they perform well, they will actually receive the reward from the organization (designated as the P → O instrumentality).

3. **The employees value the rewards offered by the organization.** One level of performance may have multiple outcomes (such as a salary increase *and* a bonus) (designated as the list of **valences,** Vs, which can be either positive or negative). For example, a negative outcome associated with high performance might be having to stay late at work to accomplish a task and the employee misses his daughter's violin solo at a school concert. So, receiving a salary increase and a bonus has a positive (+) valence. At the same time, having to work late has a negative (–) valence.

In the original formulation of expectancy theory, these components were multiplied to predict effort.[78] Later, these three aspects of motivation were shown to each directly predict effort (rather than needing to be multiplied together).[79,80] For example, a person's belief that he or she can perform affects performance ("I can do the task"). The person's belief in the organizational reward system also affects his or her performance ("My leader will provide me with a bonus if I perform well"). Finally, the degree to which rewards are valued also affects performance ("I really want that bonus!"). A summary of the expectancy theory of motivation is shown in Figure 7.5. Expectancy theory highlights the role that a leader plays in motivating followers by strengthening their perception that they can perform a task—their **self-efficacy** (you will learn more about self-efficacy in the next chapter).[81] Also, the leader can reassure followers that if they perform, they will be rewarded. Finally, the leader

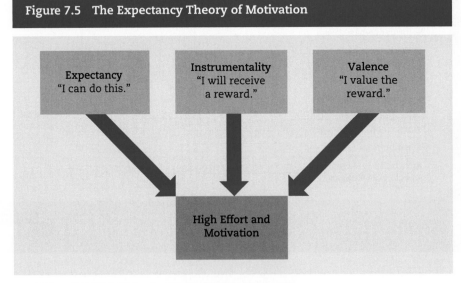

Figure 7.5   The Expectancy Theory of Motivation

Source: Vroom, V. H. (1964). *Work and motivation.* New York, NY: John Wiley.

can engage in candid conversations with followers regarding what rewards they value most (and therefore, most motivating).

Adapting Leadership to the Situation

Critical Thinking Question: Apply expectancy theory to explain whether a talented junior football player should go to the professional football league or stay and finish his college degree.

Leader transformational behavior is related to the degree to which followers set goals that are related to authentic values.[82] This goal setting translates into job performance, initiative, self-direction, and innovation on the job. Leaders influence follower motivation and performance. The path–goal theory (PGT) of leadership incorporates expectancy theory principles to provide leaders with guidelines to follow to motivate their followers.

PATH–GOAL THEORY

Learning Objective 7.7: Demonstrate the role of leaders in the motivation process, using path–goal theory (PGT).

Leaders motivate followers to accomplish goals by establishing the *paths* to the *goals*.[83] Specifically, leaders increase the quality and number of payoffs from reaching goals and then make the path to the goals clear by removing obstacles.[84]

PGT specifies four different motivating leadership behaviors:

1. **Directive leadership**—giving followers specific instructions about their tasks, providing deadlines, setting standards for performance, and explaining rules
2. **Supportive leadership**—showing consideration, being friendly and approachable, and paying attention to the well-being of followers
3. **Participative leadership**—allowing followers to have a voice in decisions that affect them, sharing information, inviting followers' ideas and opinions
4. **Achievement-oriented leadership**—challenging followers to perform at high levels, setting standards for excellence, showing confidence in followers' ability to reach goals

Adapting to the Situation

The leader should be flexible and adapt their leadership behavior to followers and the situation. The PGT incorporates a number of considerations, but it is useful because this model reflects key aspects of followers and the situation that leaders need to consider to increase motivation. The PGT model is shown in Figure 7.6. Leader behavior affects follower expectancies and instrumentalities and assures the leader offers rewards that are valued. The leader can learn of obstacles that the follower faces and help by removing them. For example, a follower may need market data from the research department in the organization to complete a report. The leader can help by calling the department and asking them to expedite the requested report. The removal of barriers and strengthening of expectancies and instrumentalities results in follower satisfaction, effort, and performance.

A key aspect of the follower that the leader needs to consider is ability—the leader must adjust expectations in relation to a person's ability to complete a task. As we learned in Chapter 3, individual differences matter including personality. For example, some followers have a higher need to socialize with others at work, which is nAff (discussed earlier in this chapter). Other followers may have a higher need for control or a preference for more structure in their work. The PGT framework also considers aspects of the situation including the job design; if the task is not clear, the leader must explain what needs to be done. In highly repetitive tasks, leaders can show concern for followers' well-being (supportive leadership). The formal authority system is another situation characteristic to consider. In other words, if the formal authority system is strong, the leader can enforce rules. Finally, the norms of the work group may influence individual motivation, and the leader can build cohesion to support the followers' expectancies (the effects of work group norms on performance will be discussed further in Chapter 9).

Figure 7.6   The Path–Goal Theory

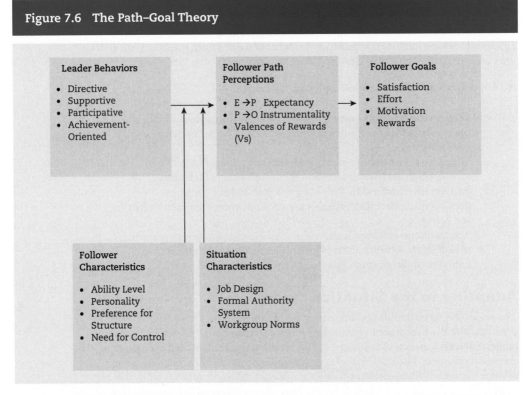

Sources: House, R. J. (1971). A path-goal theory of leadership effectiveness. *Administrative Science Quarterly, 16*, 321–328; House, R. J., & Mitchell, T. R. (1974). Path-goal theory of leadership. *Journal of Contemporary Business, 3*, 81–97.

Research on PGT has shown support for propositions of the model.[85,86] However, its strength lies in the application of motivation theory (expectancy theory, in particular) to leadership. No other leadership theory makes such a direct linkage to motivation. The framework informs leaders about what aspects of followers and the situation to consider when setting up pathways to their goals. The model is practical in that it helps leaders to clarify the motivational aspects of their expectations of goals and performance. It is also important that PGT stresses the removal of barriers to effective performance.

 Critical Thinking Question: Explain how a leader can intervene if a follower is having difficulty getting help from the purchasing department to get the supplies he needs to do his job using PGT.

LEADERSHIP IMPLICATIONS: LEADERS AS MOTIVATORS

Leaders play a major role in how motivated their followers are to perform at high levels. First, leaders must assure that followers understand their goals and are committed to them—just as they do at Microsoft. Second, leaders can design more motivating work or allow followers some discretion to craft their own work (aligned with work unit and organizational objectives). Leaders can negotiate a fair identity with their followers so that followers don't become unmotivated by perceptions of inequity. Finally, as PGT illustrates, leaders strengthen followers' expectations that they can perform at a high level (expectancy) and that they will receive rewards they value for performing (instrumentality). Leaders need to talk to their followers' to understand what rewards they value. The next step is to provide those rewards. The next chapter will discuss the motivating properties of rewards and reward systems in organizations.

$SAGE edge™

edge.sagepub.com/scandura

Want a better grade? Go to **edge.sagepub.com/scandura** for the tools you need to sharpen your study skills.

KEY TERMS ▶

autonomy, 176
combining tasks, 174
distributive justice, 177
equity theory, 177

feedback, 173
growth need strength, 174
horizontal, 174
hygienes, 170

informational justice, 180
interpersonal justice, 180
job crafting, 176
job enrichment, 174

SUGGESTIONS FOR FURTHER READING

Hackman, J. R., & Oldham, G. R. (1980). *Work redesign.* Reading, MA: Addison-Wesley.

Kanfer, R., Chen, G., & Pritchard, R. D. (Eds.). (2008). *Work motivation: Past, present, future.* Society for Industrial and Organizational Psychology Frontiers Series. New York, NY: Routledge.

Locke, E. A., & Latham, G. P. (2013). *New developments in goal setting and task performance.* New York, NY: Routledge.

Porter, L. W., Bigley, G., & Steers, R. M. (Eds.) (2002). *Motivation and work behavior* (7th ed.). New York, NY: McGraw-Hill/Irwin.

TOOLKIT ACTIVITY 7.1

Future Me Letter

Gary Wood has developed a motivational technique called "Future Me." You write a letter to yourself in the future. You give yourself thoughtful advice and encouragement like you would to a good friend. We learned about self-fulfilling prophecies in Chapter 5—the *Galatea effect* in which a person sets high expectations for themselves and then their performance meets these expectations. In a sense, writing a letter to your future me is creating a self-fulfilling prophecy.

Here are the steps:

1. **Start by outlining some ideas of how you want things to be in your life in 6 months.** According to Wood, 6 months should allow you to focus on medium-term goals and goals that are not so ambitious that they can't be attained in a reasonable amount of time.
2. **Recall the properties of SMART goals.** Write out specific, measurable, actionable, realistic, and time-based statements (for the 6-month time frame).
3. **Write the letter to yourself.** Be realistic, and give yourself sound advice and encouragement on how great it is that you reached your goals. For example, this can be tangible like landing a new job if you are 6 months from graduation. Your goals might also be more intangible such as increasing your emotional intelligence (EQ).
4. **Print the letter.** Place the letter in an envelope and seal it. Write your name on the envelope and the date 6 months from when you wrote it. Put it in a safe place. You may want to put a reminder in your calendar to open the letter.
5. **When you open the letter, reflect on your achievements, personal learning, and growth over the 6 months.** If you reached any of your goals, give yourself positive feedback and add a reward (a nice dinner out or a trip to the mall to get that jacket you have been wanting). For things you may not have attained, reflect on why and set new goals. If this is important to you, remember the concept of "grit." Stick with it!

Source: Adapted from Wood, G. (2013). Future me—Write yourself a letter from the you in six months time. Retrieved on October 31, 2013, from http://psycentral.wordpress.com/2013/08/09/future-self-letter-goals-dr-gary-wood-life-coach-birmingham.

TOOLKIT ACTIVITY 7.2

SMART Goals Template

SMART goals help improve achievement and success. A SMART goal clarifies exactly what is expected and the measures used to determine if the goal is achieved and successfully completed.

A SMART goal is as follows:

- **Specific (and strategic):** It is linked to job description, departmental goals/mission, and/or overall company goals and strategic plans. It answers these questions: Who? What?
- **Measurable:** The success toward meeting the goal can be measured. It answers this question: How?
- **Attainable:** Goals are realistic and can be achieved in a specific amount of time and are reasonable. It answers this question: Is this reasonable?
- **Relevant (results oriented):** The goals are aligned with current tasks and projects and focus in one area; it includes the expected result. It answers this question: Why?
- **Time based:** Goals have a clearly defined time frame, including a target or deadline date. It answers this question: When?

Examples:

This is not a SMART goal:

- Employee will improve their writing skills.

This does not identify a measurement or time frame, nor identify why the improvement is needed or how it will be used.

This is a SMART goal:

- The department has identified a goal to improve communications with administrative staff by implementing an online newsletter. Jane will complete a business writing course by January 2015 and will publish the first monthly newsletter by March 2015. She will gather information and articles from others in the department and draft the newsletter for supervisor review. After approval by supervisor, Jane will create an e-mail distribution list and send the newsletter to staff by the 15th of each month.

SMART Goal Planning Form

Specific—WHO? WHAT?
Measurement/Assessment—HOW?
Attainable/Achievable—IS THIS REASONABLE?
Relevant—WHY?
Time (Due Date)—WHEN?

CASE STUDY 7.1

Building Motivation

Construction Products Inc. sells construction products to various retail and wholesale markets across the United States. Its only office is in Illinois, and so it sends sales representatives on the road to different territories to obtain orders and develop relationships with retailers. You are the newest sales representative and have been assigned to the Southeast territory. A typical work day for a sales rep involves stopping at numerous stores and talking with general managers while visiting retail stores. On these visits, sales reps push for wholesale orders and fill out market reports. Most territories are responsible for about 50 retail stores and a dozen wholesale accounts. Sales reps are expected to spend a lot of time in the stores, focusing on optimizing product location within the store, training employees, and educating customers. For example, a sales rep typically tries to get larger space in the store for plywood so that more can be sold. Employees and customers need to be educated on the different grades of plywood and how to match them with building projects.

After 6 months on the job, your boss has tasked you with increasing sales in your territory by 20%. You begin by explaining the benefits of your product and why it should be the product of choice. During store visits, you socialize with store employees but realize quickly that getting everyone on the same page is not going to be as easy as anticipated. The employees don't really care if the customer gets the best material for their project. They get their paycheck regardless. Among the 50 retail stores that you are assigned to, there are 7 that agree to help you.

The next month you try a different approach in your other 43 stores. In those stores, you spend time teaching employees about various building products so they can educate their customers. They seem to grasp an understanding of the benefits your product could bring to the customers compared to competitors' products, and they understand the applications. But when you ask them to teach customers what you had shown them, you were met with looks of confusion and aggravation. Although a bit reluctant, they agreed to give it a try.

Checking the weekly sales figures over the next month, you notice that there had been little improvement in the sales of your product at these stores. Next, you follow your boss' advice and speak with the manager of one of the retail stores. You show him a printout of the sales numbers and how much income your products bring to the store as well as ask for his help getting employees on board with promoting the products. Since the store manager's main concern is revenue for the store, he quickly agreed and offered his full support.

The store manager called a meeting where he, the store employees, and you discussed techniques for presentation and how employees could effectively pitch the product to customers. You left feeling confident that the employees would be effective. However, on the next review not only had there been no improvement in sales but the employees attitudes toward you had drastically declined. They either avoided you or were unfriendly.

You realize you must come up with a completely different plan of attack to be successful and spend the next Monday morning considering your courses of action.

Discussion Questions

1. Relate the motivation techniques described in the case to those covered in this chapter. What have you tried already? What do you think should still be tried?
2. How is it different trying to motivate people who work directly for you compared to those who work for someone else (as in the situation with the store employees in the case)?
3. Explain the role that leadership plays in motivating these retail employees.
4. As a follow-up to this case, the sales representative started offering financial incentives (bonuses) to employees that met the desired sales increase. Discuss the pros and cons of using incentives.

SELF-ASSESSMENT 7.1

How Much Perseverance Do You Have?

This self-assessment exercise identifies your degree of perseverance. There are no right or wrong answers, and this is not a test. The purpose of this assessment is for you to learn about yourself. You don't have to share your results with other classmates unless you wish to do so.

Part I. Taking the Assessment

Directions for taking the perseverance scale: Please respond to the following eight items. Be honest. There are no right or wrong answers!

You will be presented with some questions representing different characteristics that may or may not describe what kind of person you are.

As an example, the answer to a question could look like this:

I enjoy solving complex puzzles.

Not like me at all	Not much like me	(Somewhat like me)	Mostly like me	Very much like me

1. I don't quit a task before it is finished.

Not like me at all	Not much like me	Somewhat like me	Mostly like me	Very much like me

2. I am a goal-oriented person.

Not like me at all	Not much like me	Somewhat like me	Mostly like me	Very much like me

3. I finish things despite obstacles in the way.

Not like me at all	Not much like me	Somewhat like me	Mostly like me	Very much like me

4. I am a hard worker.

Not like me at all	Not much like me	Somewhat like me	Mostly like me	Very much like me

5. I don't get sidetracked when I work.

Not like me at all	Not much like me	Somewhat like me	Mostly like me	Very much like me

6. I don't finish what I start.

| Not like me
at all | Not much
like me | Somewhat
like me | Mostly
like me | Very much
like me |

7. I give up easily.

| Not like me
at all | Not much
like me | Somewhat
like me | Mostly
like me | Very much
like me |

8. I do not tend to stick to what I decide to do.

| Not like me
at all | Not much
like me | Somewhat
like me | Mostly
like me | Very much
like me |

Part II. Scoring Instructions

1. For questions 1, 2, 3, 4, and 5, assign the following points:

    5 = Very much like me

    4 = Mostly like me

    3 = Somewhat like me

    2 = Not much like me

    1 = Not like me at all

2. For questions 6, 7, and 8, assign the following points:

    1 = Very much like me

    2 = Mostly like me

    3 = Somewhat like me

    4 = Not much like me

    5 = Not like me at all

Add up all the points. The maximum score on this scale is 40 (extreme perseverance), and the lowest score on this scale is 8 (not much perseverance).

Part 1	Part 2
1. _____	6. _____
2. _____	7. _____
3. _____	8. _____
4. _____	
5. _____	
Part 1 Total _____	Part 2 Total _____ = Total Score _____

Source: Adapted from the Perseverance-Persistence scale at http://ipip.ori.org/newVIAKey.htm#Industry_Perseverance_Persistence. Finholt, T. A., & Olson, G. M. (1997). From laboratories to collaboratories: A new organizational form for scientific collaboration. *Psychological Science, 8*(1), 28–36.

Interpreting your scores

Total Score	Interpretation
8–15	Low perseverance: You may be giving up too often or letting obstacles get in the way. You get sidetracked from tasks by other things.
16–23	Fair perseverance: You might sometimes give up, but you do work hard and try to remove obstacles. You may get sidetracked.
24–32	High perseverance: You don't quit very often, and you finish things despite the obstacles. You tend to stick with a task and finish most of the time. You don't get sidetracked very often.
33–40	Very high perseverance: You are not a quitter. You stay with tasks to the finish and overcome obstacles. You stay focused and don't get sidetracked.

TOOLKIT

8

MOTIVATION
LEARNING AND REWARDS

THE MEANING OF MONEY

We all have logo-imprinted gifts from universities, employers, or customer gifts. But do people value such tchotchkes more than money? Why doesn't your organization just give you cash instead of an engraved set of glasses with the company logo? Nobel laureate George Akerlof, a pioneer in the field of behavioral economics, found the answers by studying gift exchange at the workplace. Gifts are viewed as acts of kindness by an employer, which carries more meaning than cash. But will people work harder for gifts?

This premise was studied in a German university that needed to catalog books in their library.[1] Students were employed to catalog books, and some were told they would receive a bonus of 20% more than base pay. Another group was told they would receive a gift-wrapped water bottle. A third group didn't receive any bonus at all to establish the baseline for productivity. The results are shown in the following chart. The cash bonus had no effect on the speed or accuracy of cataloging the books. But those receiving the water bottle increased their data entry rate by 25% (a productivity increase that more than offset the 7 euro cost of the water bottle). It was the thought that seemed to matter; we know from research on engagement (discussed in Chapter 4) that most employees are searching for meaning in their work. This was reinforced by a second study done by the authors. Money was delivered as a bonus but either as cash or a cute origami folded shirt with a two-euro coin that had a smiley face painted on it. The origami money gift resulted in the highest increase in productivity of all (even more than the wrapped water bottle). The implications of these studies illustrate an important point for leaders. Even a slight gesture of appreciation may increase motivation. Gifts probably work best when they are personalized to the employee.

So what does money really mean? Money has symbolic meaning for employees, and it represents nonmonetary aspects of life such as achievement, success, competence, autonomy, security, and power.[2] Some people feel that money may even bring many friends. As shown in Chapter 7, perceived pay inequity will motivate employees to take action, and compensation is often the focus of employee concerns regarding fairness (and even lawsuits as the Goodyear case in Case Study 8.1 illustrates). In this chapter, the essentials of reward systems and how they are administered will be discussed in this chapter. First, the fundamentals that underlie the philosophy of reward systems as they are used in organizations will be reviewed.

Learning Objectives

After studying this chapter, you should be able to do the following:

8.1: Summarize the principles of reinforcement theory.

8.2: Describe the four steps in the modeling process articulated in social learning theory.

8.3: Compare and contrast intrinsic and extrinsic rewards.

8.4: Discuss the guidelines for using monetary rewards effectively.

8.5: Illustrate the methods for performance management with examples.

8.6: Critique the performance review process.

8.7: Understand feedback seeking by employees and how it relates to more accurate perceptions of performance.

Get the edge on your studies at edge.sagepub.com/scandura
- Take the chapter quiz
- Review key terms with eFlashcards
- Explore multimedia resources, SAGE readings, and more!

$SAGE edge™

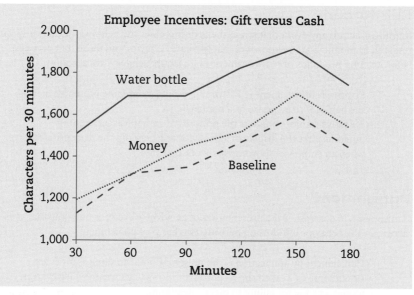

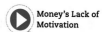
Money's Lack of Motivation

Employee Incentives: Gift versus Cash

Source: Kube, Marechal, and Puppe: "The Currency of Reciprocity," *American Economic Review,* 2012. Retrieved from HBR.org.

Critical Thinking Questions: The research on gifts described previously was conducted in Germany. Do you think that this would work in the United States or the culture you are from? Explain why or why not. Can you think of any potential limitations to the motivating potential of gifts?

REINFORCEMENT THEORY

Learning Objective 8.1: Summarize the principles of reinforcement theory.

Reinforcement theory is based upon the **law of effect,** which states that past actions that led to positive outcomes tend to be repeated, whereas past actions that led to negative outcomes will diminish.[3] The law of effect led to the development of **operant conditioning** (sometimes referred to as **reinforcement theory**).[4] In this approach to motivation, individual personality, thoughts, and attitudes don't motivate behavior. Instead, the emphasis in operant condition is on the environment. The goal of reinforcement theory is to best explain learned behavior. B. F. Skinner is the psychologist most associated with this approach, and he conducted experiments with animals the psychologist to understand how behavior could be shaped by setting up systems of rewards and punishments. These rewards (or punishments) were contingent on the response of the animals he studied (probably the most well-recognized studies are those of rats who were taught to run mazes through the shaping of their behavior with pellets of food as rewards).

Reinforcers

Reinforcement is any event that strengthens or increases the behavior it follows. Skinner's research found there are **reinforcers** that increase behavior and those that decrease behavior. The two kinds of reinforcement that *increase* behavior are as follows:

1. Positive reinforcement is a favorable event or outcome presented after the behavior (e.g., praise or a bonus).
2. Negative reinforcement is the removal of an unpleasant event or outcome after the display of a behavior (e.g., ending the daily criticism when an employee shows up for work on time).

Punishment

Punishment, in contrast, is the presentation of an adverse event or outcome that causes a *decrease* in the behavior it follows. There are two kinds of punishment:

1. Punishment by application is the presentation of an unpleasant event or outcome to weaken the response it follows (e.g., writing a letter to an employee's file for failing to meet a deadline).
2. Punishment by removal (also called extinction) is when a pleasant event or outcome is removed after a behavior occurs (e.g., withholding praise when an employee does not perform well).

 Critical Thinking Questions: Explain why punishment may not be the most effective way to encourage learning. What would you do to encourage learning instead?

A summary table of these contingencies of reinforcement is shown in Figure 8.1; it is important to consider whether the reward is applied or withheld and whether the event is pleasant or unpleasant. Figure 8.1 and the previously given definitions and examples refer to the type of reward or punishment that is applied or removed.

Schedules of Reinforcement

Skinner's research also found how often a reward (or punishment) is applied also predicts learning and motivation. He referred to this as the **schedules of reinforcement.**[5] The first schedule is continuous—a specified behavior is rewarded or punished every time it occurs. This is not seen often in organizations; however, it is useful during the learning process (e.g., when an employee is learning to use a new computer program). In this example, the employee would be allowed to leave work one half hour early (a positive event) each time he completes a module of a computer training program successfully. Once the employee has attained an acceptable level of mastery, they are moved to a partial reinforcement schedule. For example, the employee is no longer rewarded or punished every time, but they are rewarded (punished) on a more random basis as described next.

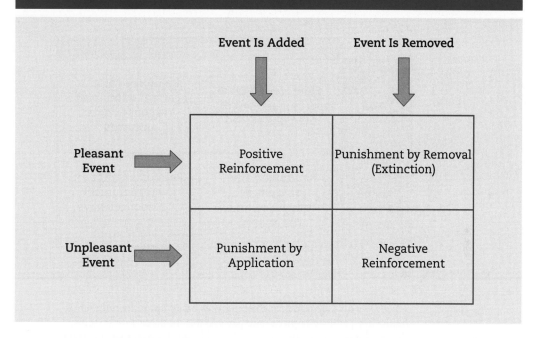

Figure 8.1 Contingencies of Reinforcement

	Event Is Added	Event Is Removed
Pleasant Event	Positive Reinforcement	Punishment by Removal (Extinction)
Unpleasant Event	Punishment by Application	Negative Reinforcement

As illustrated in Figure 8.2, the schedules of partial reinforcement are based on time (**interval**) or the number of times the response is given by the employee (**ratio**). Also, the schedule can be **fixed** or **variable** (random). These two dimensions result in four possible schedules of partial reinforcement as shown in Figure 8.2:

1. **Fixed-interval schedules are those where the first response is rewarded only after a specified amount of time has elapsed.** This schedule causes high amounts of responding near the end of the interval. An example of this in a work setting is the way pay is typically disbursed—every 2 weeks or every month, for example. After a fixed amount of time, the employee receives a paycheck.
2. **Variable-interval schedules occur when a response is rewarded after an unpredictable amount of time has passed.** This schedule produces a slow, steady rate of response. An example of this would be bringing in bagels for breakfast once a week for employees but varying which day they are brought in (e.g., sometimes on Monday and sometimes Wednesday). The employees never know when they will be treated to bagels, so the element of surprise is motivating and they may come to work on time regularly so they don't miss out.
3. **Fixed-ratio schedules are those where a response is reinforced only after a specific number of responses.** This schedule produces a high, steady rate of responding. An example of a fixed-ratio

Figure 8.2 Schedules of Partial Reinforcement

	Interval	Ratio
Fixed	Reinforced after a certain amount of time has passed	Reinforced after a certain number of responses have occurred
Variable (Random)	Reinforced after an average amount of time has passed	Reinforced after an average number of responses have occurred

schedule would be payment to employees based upon the number of items they produce (a piece-rate pay system). In piece-rate systems, the employee is paid for each article produced; for example, a worker sewing zippers into jeans is paid for each zipper correctly sewn in.

4. **Variable-ratio schedules occur when a response is reinforced after an unpredictable number of responses.** This schedule creates a high steady rate of responding. Gambling and lottery games are good examples of a reward based on a variable ratio schedule. This is why gambling results in such long-term and persistent behavior (it's the element of chance that motivates the behavior). In a work setting, this might be offering praise to an employee for good performance after one time and then again after four times and then another time after two times.

 Critical Thinking Questions: Discuss why the biweekly paycheck form of payment is not the most motivating schedule based upon the principles of reinforcement. Provide an example of a method of payment that would be more motivating.

Partial schedules are more motivating than continuous reinforcement (e.g., the employee may become accustomed to praise from the leader so it loses its motivating power on behavior). Of the partial reinforcement schedules, research has demonstrated that the variable-ratio schedule of partial reinforcement produces the most persistent, long-term effects on behavior.[6] Receiving rewards in a random fashion tends to increase effort until the reward is received.

As the previously given examples indicate, reinforcement is used in organizations in a variety of ways to increase employee motivation and performance. It is also used to extinguish undesirable behaviors. Given the strong research base supporting the principles of reinforcement theory, it represents a powerful tool most leaders use to motivate performance.[7] The application of reinforcement theory in organizational behavior (OB) is known as **organizational behavior modification (OB mod)**.

Organizational Behavior Modification

OB mod has been employed to increase performance and reduce absenteeism. Figure 8.3 shows how to apply OB mod using the principles of reinforcement theory. As shown in the figure, the first step is to pinpoint the specific behavior that needs to be changed. For example, coming to work on time every day is an example of a behavior that needs intervention if an employee is not doing it. Second, measure the baseline:

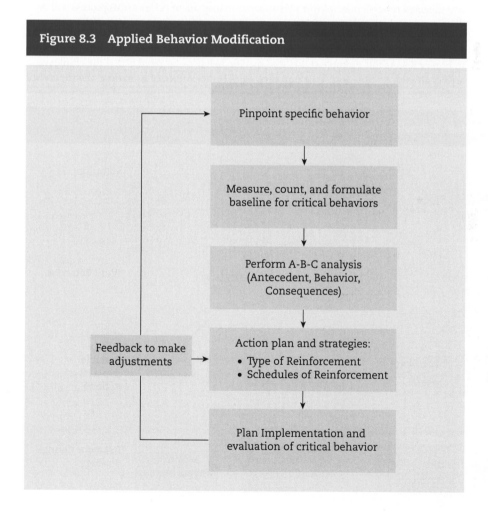

Figure 8.3 Applied Behavior Modification

How many days per month is the employee on time? Third, perform an **A-B-C analysis.** This stands for antecedents, behavior, and consequences:

- **Antecedents:** What is causing the behavior? Consider both internal and external factors.
- **Behavior:** What is the current behavior? What is the desired behavior?
- **Consequences:** What is currently reinforcing the behavior? What needs to be changed?

Fourth, develop an action plan based on reinforcement theory strategies to apply (using the contingencies of reinforcement and the schedules). Implement the plan and then evaluate the plan comparing the behavior to the baseline (after compared to before). This will provide feedback, and the plan may need to be changed or another behavior targeted for the future. If you have been a manager, this process may look familiar to you since many organizations encourage managers to meet with followers to discuss desired behaviors and expected rewards in employee performance management reviews (this process will be discussed later in this chapter).

An example of applied OB mod for an employee who is late to work frequently is shown in Figure 8.4. As this example shows, the specific behavior targeted is that the employee arrives at work on time (say, 8:30 a.m. each day). If the employee is on time, the supervisor

Figure 8.4   Applied Behavior Modification Example

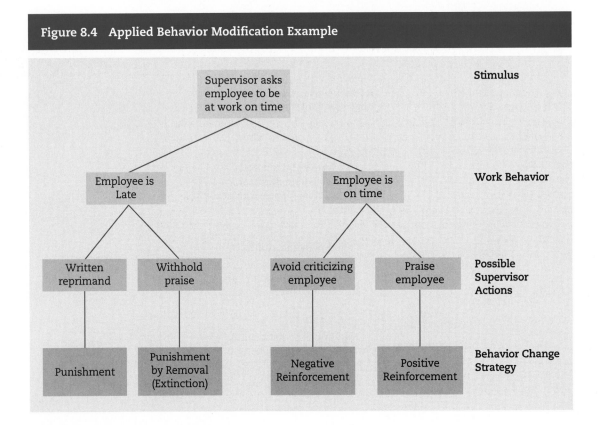

can praise them (positive reinforcement) or withhold criticism (this only works if the supervisor has consistently criticized the employee's tardiness prior to the day they arrives on time, of course). If the employee is late, the objective is to decrease the behavior so the supervisor can withhold praise to produce extinction of the behavior (punishment by removal), or write a reprimand and put it in the employee's file, which is unpleasant (punishment). Of course, the supervisor can use more than one behavior change strategy and should eventually move the employee to a variable interval or ratio schedule (i.e., apply or remove the reinforcers more randomly) once the employee is coming to work consistently on time.

 Seeking Feedback

Proponents of behavior modification argue it has a strong research base and applies to all employees regardless of individual difference and national culture.[8] A meta-analysis found that OB mod increased task performance by 17%; however, results of interventions using OB mod were stronger in manufacturing than service organizations.[9] Critics of operant conditioning and OB mod have argued that the results can be explained using theories that involve cognitions (thoughts) of employees.[10] Also, some people may react negatively to the use of operant conditioning to control the behavior of employees, feeling that it is manipulative. In response to criticisms, subsequent research incorporated thought processes into reinforcement theory. **Social learning theory** extends operant conditioning to consider the fact that people can learn from watching other people succeed or fail.

SOCIAL LEARNING THEORY

Learning Objective 8.2: Describe the four steps in the modeling process articulated in social learning theory.

Albert Bandura presented social learning theory, and it is perhaps the most influential theory of learning today.[11] Bandura believed that operant conditioning (reinforcement) did not explain all of the ways a person can learn. Social learning theory introduced the social element into how people acquire new skills and described the ways that people learn by watching other people. Known as **observational learning** (or modeling), this form of learning explains much behavior in organizations. Second, external reinforcements are not the only factors that influence motivation. Intrinsic reinforcement is related to pride, satisfaction, and a sense of accomplishment in learning something new. Social learning theory considers people's thoughts as well as their perceptions of others (a social cognitive theory). While reinforcement theorists maintained external rewards create permanent behavioral changes, social learning theory proposes that people can learn things but not necessarily change their behavior.

The Modeling Process

The modeling process has four steps:

1. **Attention.** To learn, a person has to be paying attention to another's behavior. People pay attention to things that are either interesting or new.
2. **Retention.** The information must be stored for access in the future. This is important to observational learning since a person must remember what they have observed.

3. **Reproduction.** Once information is noted and retained, the next step is that the person imitates (i.e., performs) the behavior that they recall. Repeating the behavior (i.e., practicing) leads to improved performance.

4. **Motivation.** For observational learning to work, the person needs motivation to imitate. Thus, social learning theory discusses the roles of reinforcement and punishment. For example, if you see another student rewarded with extra credit points for participating in class every day, you might begin to do the same.

As noted previously, not all reinforcement comes from external rewards such as pay. OB researchers became interested in the motivational power of both external (extrinsic) as well as internal (intrinsic) reinforcement on motivation at work. The next section will discuss these two forms of motivational rewards and what the research has shown regarding their effectiveness.

INTRINSIC VS. EXTRINSIC REWARDS

Learning Objective 8.3: Compare and contrast intrinsic and extrinsic rewards.

Expectancy theory (covered in Chapter 7) includes both intrinsic and extrinsic work motivation.[12,13] **Intrinsic motivation** is when someone works on a task because they find it interesting and gain satisfaction from the task itself. **Extrinsic motivation** involves the performance → outcome instrumentality between the task and a tangible reward. Satisfaction does not come from the task itself but rather from the extrinsic outcome to which the activity leads (e.g., working extra hours to earn a bonus). Work should be set up in a manner so effective performance leads to both intrinsic and extrinsic rewards to produce job satisfaction.[14] There are other sources of motivation in addition to intrinsic and extrinsic such as the enhancement of self-concept and the degree to which a person internalizes the goals of the organization.[15]

Rewards should be administered so that they are contingent upon effective performance. However, research on the impact of paying someone to do something that they enjoy showed surprising findings. While it appears counterintuitive, pay may not motivate people to perform at the highest levels. Also, extrinsic motivation plus intrinsic motivation (for example, pay plus challenging work) may not always combine to produce the highest motivation.

 Critical Thinking Question: Explain why paying someone to do something they like doing reduces their intrinsic motivation.

Does paying someone to do a job reduce their intrinsic motivation? Intrinsic motivation refers to their internal reasons for doing something such as enjoying the task or being interested in it. For example, are you reading this because you want to get a good grade (extrinsic), or are you interested in learning more about motivation (intrinsic)? The answer

Why the "Carrot and Stick" May Not Always Work

Daniel Pink (2009) in his book *Drive: The Surprising Truth About What Motivates Us* discusses three forms of motivation as "operating systems." Motivation 1.0 was humankind's inherent need to survive. The next operating system, Motivation 2.0, was the carrot-and-stick approach (or the rewards and punishments we discussed in reinforcement theory research). Pink is critical of the carrot-and-stick approach, pointing out the carrot and the stick can produce results that are the opposite of what leaders are looking for because rewards can transform an interesting task into drudgery; they can turn play into work. Traditional "if-then" rewards (if you do this, then you will get that) cannot produce high levels of motivation for seven reasons, according to Pink:

- It extinguishes intrinsic motivation.
- It diminishes performance.
- It crushes creativity.
- It crowds out good behavior.
- It encourages cheating and unethical behavior.
- It becomes addictive.
- It fosters short-term thinking.

Pink considered these to be bugs in human beings' current operating systems. For those driven by intrinsic motivation, the drive to do something because it is interesting and challenging is essential for high creativity and motivation. Goals that people set for themselves for mastering a skill are healthy. But goals imposed by others such as sales targets, quarterly returns, and standardized test scores can sometimes have the seven dangerous side effects listed previously. Pink presented what he believes is the next operating system for human motivation—Motivation 3.0, which goes beyond the carrot-and-stick approach and centers on intrinsic motivation. He believes there are three important aspects to this new operating system based on psychological empowerment: autonomy, mastery, and purpose. Pink highlighted autonomy as one of the most important motivating factors at work. He said that people want control over the task (what they do), time (when they do it), team (who they do it with), and technique (how they do it).[16] These three new elements of motivation are fueled by intrinsic and not extrinsic rewards.

Discussion Questions:

1. Discuss Pink's premise in light of what you have learned about the effectiveness of positive reinforcement. Why are these criticisms valid (or not)?
2. Do you agree that intrinsic motivation is a preferable way to influence performance? Why or why not? Why is autonomy so important to intrinsic motivation?

Source: Pink, D. H. (2009). *Drive: The surprising truth about what motivates us.* New York, NY: Penguin Books.

can be both, but OB researchers designed experiments to see what would happen if people were paid for doing something they enjoy.

Extrinsic rewards can lead to reduction in intrinsic motivation. For example, money was found to undermine college students' intrinsic motivation to perform a task.[17] These experiments were replicated in work organizations.[18] A meta-analysis of 128 studies found contingent rewards significantly reduced intrinsic motivation. These findings may be surprising since most people think that money matters more than other rewards. In fact, paying people money for doing something they enjoy may actually *reduce* their motivation.[19] Edward Deci and his colleagues developed the theory of **self-determination** to explain why this happens.

Self-Determination Theory

Intrinsic motivation is a function of a person's needs for autonomy and competence in the theory of self-determination (also known as **cognitive evaluation theory**).[20] The effects of a reward depend on how the person views the reward's effect on their autonomy and competence. Rewards that diminish these perceptions tend to decrease intrinsic motivation. The issue with extrinsic rewards like money is that such rewards might be interpreted by employees as controlling by the boss rather than indicators of their competence. If the reward is seen as controlling, then the individual's need for autonomy is challenged, and this undermines intrinsic motivation. If a reward is seen as useful feedback and informational, then it increases motivation. For example, setting limits for employees could be seen as either informational or controlling depending on the relationship with the boss.[21] Managers can create a climate of trust that alters whether a person views their rewards as controlling or good feedback.[22] For example, a leader can communicate a pay raise without compromising motivation by emphasizing the informational aspect of the raise as valuable feedback rather than just money.

Relationship Between Intrinsic and Extrinsic Rewards

There can be synergistic effects between intrinsic and extrinsic motivation, and there are two psychological mechanisms that illustrate this. First,[23] **"extrinsics in service of intrinsics"** refers to how extrinsic rewards may support an employee's sense of competence if they don't undermine autonomy (self-determination). For example, a reward can be more time to work on creativity projects. This has been implemented at Google, where engineers and project managers are given 20% of their work time to work on something that they are passionate about. In other words, one day per week they can work on anything they like, even if it falls outside of the scope of their job or is unrelated to the mission of the company.[24] A second mechanism is the **motivation–work cycle match**. This is the understanding that innovation occurs in phases and intrinsic motivation may be more important during the idea generation phase. However, when the project is being implemented, extrinsic rewards may be needed to ensure that deliverables are produced on time and within the budget. A longitudinal study found support for this idea in study of project teams.[25] Team members reported higher levels of radical creativity in early phases of a project compared to incremental creativity at later phases. Thus, one type of motivation may not suit all types of project work. So it's important to keep in mind that extrinsic rewards can motivate but they also have limitations. The next section will discuss what money can and cannot do in terms of motivation.

Critical Thinking Questions: Use reinforcement theory to explain why extrinsic rewards may not produce long-term effects on motivation. What should a leader do instead t o motivate workers based on the relationship between intrinsic and extrinsic motivation?

WHAT MONEY CAN AND CANNOT DO

Learning Objective 8.4: Discuss the guidelines for using monetary rewards effectively.

There are pros and cons of using money as a motivational tool.[26] On the one hand, organizations that appropriately tie pay to performance and pay more have higher rates of return.[27] For example, a study of hospitals showed that pay level practices and pay structures combined to affect resource efficiency, patient care outcomes, and financial performance. On the other hand, tying pay directly to performance can have dysfunctional or even unethical consequences.[28] For example, Green Giant, a producer of frozen and canned vegetables, implemented a pay system that rewarded employees for removing insects from vegetables. It was later discovered that employees were bringing insects from home and putting them into the vegetables to receive the monetary rewards.[29]

 Ambition Gap

Pay Dispersion

Another caveat regarding money as a motivational tool is that care must be taken when implementing systems in which employees receive different levels of rewards for individual efforts. This results in **pay dispersion,** which can cause jealously among employees or harm team performance. If pay dispersion creates **pay inequity** due to discrimination, it may result in litigation under the Equal Pay Act of 1963 (see the Case Study 8.1 for an update on legislation related to equal pay at the workplace).

To summarize, there are five evidence-based guidelines for money as a motivator: (1) define and measure performance accurately, (2) make rewards contingent on performance, (3) reward employees in a timely manner, (4) maintain justice in the reward system, and (5) use monetary and nonmonetary rewards.[30] These evidence-based guidelines are summarized in Table 8.1.

As the previous review of monetary and nonmonetary rewards shows, the ability to assess employee performance is essential to the successful implementation of any reward system. Most organizations today employ pay for performance incentive systems, which include individual merit pay.[31] A review of this research concludes with this: "Job performance is perhaps the most central construct in work psychology."[32] The approaches to performance evaluation and guidelines for effective practice will be covered next.

PERFORMANCE MANAGEMENT

Learning Objective 8.5: Illustrate the methods of performance management with examples.

As noted previously, performance management is essential for the determination of compensation and other outcomes such as promotions. But there are other objectives that are equally important. The performance management session is an opportunity

Table 8.1	Research-Based Recommendations on How to Use Monetary Rewards Effectively
Principles	**Implementation Guidelines**
1. Define and measure performance accurately.	• Specify what employees are expected to do, as well as what they should refrain from doing. • Align employees' performance with the strategic goals of the organization. • Measure both behaviors and results. But the greater the control over the achievement of desired outcomes, the greater the emphasis should be on measuring results.
2. Make rewards contingent on performance.	• Ensure pay levels vary significantly based on performance levels. • Explicitly communicate that differences in pay levels are due to different levels of performance and not because of other reasons. • Take cultural norms into account. For example, consider individualism–collectivism when deciding how much emphasis to place on rewarding individual versus team performance.
3. Reward employees in a timely manner.	• Distribute fake currencies or reward points that can later be traded for cash, goods, or services. • Switch from a performance appraisal system to a performance management system, which encourages timely rewards through ongoing and regular evaluations, feedback, and developmental opportunities. • Provide a specific and accurate explanation regarding why the employee received the particular reward.
4. Maintain justice in the reward system.	• Only promise rewards that are available. • When increasing monetary rewards, increase employees' variable pay levels instead of their base pay. • Make all employees eligible to earn rewards from incentive plan. • Communicate reasons for failure to provide promised rewards, changes in the payouts, or changes in the reward system.
5. Use monetary and nonmonetary rewards.	• Do not limit the provision of nonmonetary rewards to noneconomic rewards. Rather, use not only praise and recognition but also noncash awards consisting of various goods and services. • Provide nonmonetary rewards that are needs-satisfying for the recipient. • Use monetary rewards to encourage voluntary participation in nonmonetary reward programs that are more directly beneficial to employee or organizational performance.

Source: Adapted from Aguinis, H., Joo, H., & Gottfredson, R. K. (2013). What monetary rewards can and cannot do: How to show employees the money. *Business Horizons, 56*(2), 241–259.

 CEO Compensation

to regularly discuss an employee's performance and results. The leader can identify the follower's strengths, weaknesses, and areas for improvement. The process supports pay equity in which followers are paid according to their inputs and results, and it supports a climate of organizational justice. Performance management, thus, provides essential feedback for followers. Importantly, it can recognize exceptional performance and document weak performance. Also, it can lead to effective goal setting for future performance and identify training that may be needed to improve skills. Most organizations use the performance management process for compensation decisions, and performance improvement as well as to provide feedback to employees.[33] Next, we will discuss the sources and methods used by organizations to evaluate employee performance—who rates performance and how it is managed.

 360-Degree Ratings

Sources of Performance Management Ratings

In most organizations, the immediate supervisor is involved in the performance appraisal and often is the only person conducting the review. This appraisal is often reviewed by the human resources department. In some cases, the process is reviewed by a manager one level above the supervisor. However, recent trends have included ratings from higher management, peers (coworkers), the employee's followers, and customers. Performance appraisal may also include self-ratings in which the employee rates his own performance, and this becomes a part of the file. However, self-ratings are typically used for development purposes and not for compensation or promotion decisions because they suffer from self-interest bias, and they don't agree well with supervisor ratings.[34] In a **360 degree performance appraisal,** the input from a number of these sources is included to provide a more comprehensive view of an employee's performance. The research evidence on 360 degree suggests it increases the perspectives that provide input into the review process.[35,36] The challenge with 360 degree reviews is that organizations don't often provide necessary training for peers to provide constructive feedback. Peers, for example, tend to be more lenient than supervisors in rating their coworkers.[37,38] Despite these challenges, 360-degree feedback has been implemented successfully in numerous organizations.

An example of a successful implementation is Starwood Hotels and Resorts Worldwide. The executive team wanted to provide their managers with valuable feedback on their strengths and areas for development. They used the viaPeople 360 degree feedback system along with a proprietary, internally developed, and validated competency model, and this process produced the following individual and organizational benefits:[39]

Individual Benefits:

- A simple, easy-to-use 360 degree feedback tool
- A "self-paced" 360 degree feedback report complete with targeted questions to guide the leader through the process of uncovering strengths and development areas
- Specific interpretive tables and graphs in the feedback report that helped leaders analyze their data
- A downloadable discussion guide for report recipients and their managers—what to focus on, how to lead and focus the discussion, and how to deal with emotions/defensiveness

Organizational Benefits:

- Competency/skill strengths and development areas across division and employee level
- Better understanding the skill mix across the organization, Starwood was able to more effectively leverage the leadership strengths and refocus efforts where developmental opportunities may exist

Performance Management

- Data specific for each division provided (by viaPeople)—allowed Starwood to target local training efforts thereby saving precious resources
- Each divisional leader received analysis of their division's results so they can take specific actions on the data and have a better understanding of the team strengths/development areas.

Performance Management Methods

It is best to avoid rating traits such as having a positive attitude since they may not relate to actual performance.[40] Most organizations use a standard form to evaluate employee performance. There may be an overall global rating for performance, but there are also specific dimensions that are rated. These ratings are typically on a graphic rating scale having multiple points along a continuum. Here is an example:

Outstanding	Performance is consistently superior.
Exceeds expectations	Performance is routinely above job requirements.
Meets expectations	Performance is regularly competent and dependable.
Below expectations	Performance fails to meet job requirements on a frequent basis.
Unsatisfactory	Performance is consistently unacceptable.

An example of a graphic rating scale is shown in the Toolkit Activity 8.2 at the end of this chapter. You will have the opportunity to practice using this commonly used performance management tool.

Another approach is to use **behaviorally anchored rating scales (BARS)** in which a vertical scale is presented with specific examples of performance provided. For example, for an executive assistant, a BARS might look like this:

Performance Dimension: Knowledge of Company Policies	
Outstanding	Knows details of all policies and procedures from memory, recommends updates, and communicates policies to all employees in the office
Exceeds expectations	Maintains organized files and can look up policies; maintains updates and communications to all employees in the office
Meets expectations	Has familiarity with policies and can locate them on the organization's website, including updates; communicates policies to most employees in the office.
Below expectations	Is not familiar with policies or updates and does not communicate policies to employees in the office.
Unsatisfactory	Makes errors in locating or interpreting policies or updates; communicates incorrect information to employees in the office.

As this example shows, the creation and updating of BARS can be time consuming, but they can be more effective because they focus on specific behaviors rather than general statements such as "knowledge of work."

Some organizations use a forced-ranking method in which all employees in the work group are ranked relative to one another. This approach was made famous by Jack Welch at GE, where he committed to firing the bottom 10% of the workforce each year.[41] Even if the bottom 10% is not fired, such forced ranking systems may make managers uncomfortable and create a culture of competition. Recently, such forced-ranking systems have come under scrutiny by large corporations. Microsoft, for example, has done away with their long-standing practice of forced rankings. According to research conducted by the Institute for Corporate Productivity, only 145 of companies surveyed in 2011 reported that their appraisal process included forced rankings—down from 49% in 2009.[42] See the boxed insert for an update on why many organizations are doing away with forced rankings due to their limitations.

Performance
Reviews

Critical Thinking Questions: Do you agree that forced rankings should be eliminated in evaluating performance? Why or why not? Discuss the positive side of having competition in the organization.

PROBLEMS WITH PERFORMANCE REVIEWS

Learning Objective 8.6: Critique the performance review process.

There are issues related to performance appraisals that a leader needs to know about. Some employees view the appraisal process as unfair and showing favoritism. Others may fear the appraisal process and view it as punitive.[43] There are perceptual biases that may affect the rater's ability to accurately rate follower performance (from Chapter 5, major perceptual errors are primacy, recency, availability, contrast, and halo). These errors have been shown by research to affect the performance rating process. In addition, there may be a tendency for a rater to be too lenient (or too strict) in their ratings.[44] They might have a **central tendency error** in which they rate all dimensions of performance as average (e.g., rating every dimension as 3 on a 5-point scale). Cultural values such as power distance and collectivism may influence how a rater assesses the performance of another person.[45] Performance appraisals should be supported by training for those making the ratings to avoid these errors and increase sensitivity to the perspectives of employees from different cultural backgrounds.

These perceptual biases may be avoided by rewarding for results rather than behaviors. For example, in **profit-sharing plans,** employee bonuses are based upon reaching a financial target such as return on assets or net income. **Stock options** are a variation of profit sharing where employees are given stock options as part of their compensation package. **Gain-sharing plans** are another alternative, in which compensation is tied to unit-level performance (e.g., the employees receive a percentage of the sales increase or cost savings for efficiency improvements). These plans tend to increase performance.[46] However, the pay may be too variable for employees to rely solely on these plans for their total compensation. Also, the focus on results may encourage unethical behaviors to reach the targets.[47]

Some managers feel that performance appraisals offer little benefit relative to the time involved. Some are not comfortable with face-to-face confrontation over difficult performance issues. Finally, there is an inherent conflict in the role of the supervisor as evaluator and at the same time performance coach. Despite this discomfort on the part of

Rethinking the Review: For Whom the Bell Curve Tolls

The logic behind forced ranking systems is that employee performance falls on a bell-shaped curve—the normal distribution as you learned in your statistics courses. Thus, only a small percentage of employees fall into the outstanding category, and an approximately equal number fall into the unsatisfactory category. Most employees are considered average in terms of their performance and need further coaching and/or training to improve. Large organizations have recently been questioning whether such systems work. Concerns have been raised that forced rankings are demotivating and harm cooperation and teamwork. Some companies including Microsoft and Adobe Systems have even removed numerical ratings from their evaluation systems after learning that employees stop listening after they get their number and don't hear the essential feedback they need to improve their performance. Shelly Carlin, senior vice president of Human Resources at Motorola Solutions agrees: "In a traditional review, the employee listens until he hears the rating and then tunes out because he's doing the calculation in his head about how that will affect his bonus."[48] At Adobe Systems, Donna Morris, the senior vice president of Human Resources, noticed that turnover increased each year after the performance review process. There has also been a trend toward more frequent reviews—quarterly or monthly—rather than the traditional 1-year review.[49] Morris stated the following:

We came to a fairly quick decision that we would abolish the performance review, which meant we would no longer have one-time-of-the-year formal written review. What's more, we would abolish performance rankings and levels in order to move away from people feeling like they were labeled.[50]

The company changed to a process where check-in conversations that focus on ongoing feedback were instituted instead of numerical ratings each year.[51] In addition to reducing turnover, increasing regular feedback, and improving teamwork, many organizations feel that the performance review process must change because organizations themselves have changed. According to the founder and principal at Bersin by Deloitte, a research-based provider of human resource systems, "Organization structures have changed and companies need to be more agile. We have a shortage of key talent and the keys to success now focus on regular alignment, coaching, creating passion and engagement, and continuous employee development."[52]

Discussion Questions:

1. List the pros and cons of performance appraisals. Provide an example of when a performance appraisal has a positive benefit.
2. Based on motivation theory, we know that employees need feedback to perform well. Describe an alternative to performance appraisal that provides necessary feedback.

Sources: Bersin, J. (2013). Is it time to scrap performance appraisals? Forbes. Retrieved on December 2, 2013, from http://www.forbes.com/sites/joshbersin/2013/05/06/time-to-scrap-performance-appraisals; McGregor, J. (2013). For whom the bell curve tolls. *The Washington Post.* Retrieved on November 20, 2013, from http://www.washingtonpost.com/blogs/on-leadership/wp/2013/11/20/for-whom-the-bell-curve=tolls; Morris, D. (2013). Forget reviews, let's look forward. *Executive Perspectives.* Retrieved on November 20, 2013, from http://blogs.adobe.com/conversations/tag/donna-morris; Ramirez, J. C. (2013). Rethinking the review: After 50 years of debate, has the time come to chuck the performance review? Retrieved on November 20, 2013, from www.hronline.com/HRE/view/story.jhtmal?id=534355695&.

supervisors, research has shown employees are satisfied with their performance evaluation when the process combines development with administrative reward purposes.[53] Moreover, employees reported higher intentions to use developmental feedback when rewards were also discussed. One study found that all employees are unhappy with receiving negative feedback—even those with a strong learning orientation.[54] It appears that negative feedback does not help employees learn more from their jobs. What should a leader do instead? A leader should focus on what is important to the employee and what they learned from mistakes. Toolkit Activity 8.1, at the end of this chapter, provides some additional tips for conducting an effective performance appraisal.

Another criticism that has been leveled at the performance management process is that by focusing on individual achievement, effective teamwork is discouraged.[55,56] While the critics of individual performance management have made important points, team-based reward systems also have drawbacks. Most employees prefer that their pay be based on individual merit rather than group output.[57] This preference is strongest among the most productive and achievement-oriented employees.[58] Thus, if pay is based on group performance, an organization's best performers may become frustrated and seek other jobs. It's best to offer mixed or aggregate compensation systems, which include individual merit pay, group incentives, and gain sharing to offset the advantages and disadvantages of the different approaches.

 Critical Thinking Questions: Explain how the management of individual performance may harm team performance. How can this be addressed?

As noted previously, one of the primary goals of the performance evaluation process is to provide feedback to employees on their performance. Research has shown that some employees seek feedback from their supervisors to enhance their performance that does not depend on the formal performance management process. Thus, the formal appraisal review process is not always enough to provide followers with the feedback they need to perform well. Research on feedback seeking by followers has demonstrated that accuracy of follower perceptions of their performance is improved by more frequent feedback from leaders.

FEEDBACK SEEKING

Learning Objective 8.7: Understand feedback seeking by employees and how it relates to more accurate perceptions of performance.

As noted previously, performance management systems have been criticized for emphasis on categorizing employees and failure to address the followers need for feedback on their work on a day-to-day basis.[60] As shown in Figure 8.5, the situation affects the person's motives for **feedback seeking.** People may either want to defend their self-perception or image (ego or image defense). Alternatively, their goal may be to enhance their self-perception (or image) in the eyes of others (by asking for feedback on something they knew they did a good job on, for example). There are five patterns of feedback seeking that matter: (1) how frequently people seek feedback, (2) how they seek it (observing, comparing, or asking for it), (3) the timing, (4) who they ask for feedback from (i.e., the target), and (5) what they ask for feedback about (e.g., success on an task assignment).[61] Outcomes from feedback seeking are a more accurate perception of one's own performance and progress on goal attainment by gaining feedback when needed. Also, one's self-perception and image may be enhanced through the five strategies of feedback

Figure 8.5 Antecedents and Consequences of Feedback Seeking

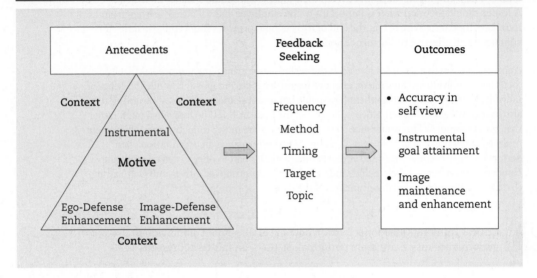

Source: Ashford, S. J., Blatt, R., & Vandewalle, D. (2003). Reflections on the looking glass: A review of research on feedback-seeking behavior in organizations. *Journal of Management, 29*(6), 773–779. p. 775.

seeking. Research on feedback seeking suggests seeking negative feedback does improve an employee's image (unless the feedback seeker is a poor performer). However, seeking positive feedback can be detrimental to a *leader's* image as seen by subordinates.

 Critical Thinking Questions: Can you explain why it isn't a good idea for a leader to seek feedback from followers? Do you agree or disagree? Why or why not?

LEADERSHIP IMPLICATIONS: MOTIVATING WITH REWARDS

As this chapter has shown, there is much research on how leaders can motivate followers using rewards. Knowing reinforcement and social learning basics is essential to understanding how reward systems operate in organizations. It is also important to become thoroughly familiar with the performance management in your organization so that it can be used effectively to provide the necessary feedback to motivate employees to high levels of performance. Also, keep in mind that feedback seeking research has demonstrated that employees need feedback far more often than yearly performance management reviews. Leaders should encourage their followers to seek feedback so they can stay on track toward reaching their goals.

⑤SAGE edge™

edge.sagepub.com/scandura

Want a better grade? Go to **edge.sagepub.com/scandura** for the tools you need to sharpen your study skills.

KEY TERMS

360 degree performance appraisal, 207

A-B-C analysis, 200

behaviorally anchored rating scales (**BARS**), 208

central tendency error, 209

cognitive evaluation theory, 204

competence, 204

extrinsic motivation, 202

"extrinsics in service of intrinsics", 204

feedback seeking, 211

fixed, 197

gain-sharing plans, 209

interval, 197

intrinsic motivation, 202

law of effect, 195

motivation–work cycle match, 204

observational learning, 201

operant conditioning, 195

organizational behavior modification (**OB mod**), 199

pay dispersion, 205

pay inequity, 205

profit-sharing plans, 209

ratio, 197

reinforcement theory, 195

reinforcers, 196

schedules of reinforcement, 196

self-determination, 203

social learning theory, 201

stock options, 209

variable, 197

SUGGESTIONS FOR FURTHER READING

Aguinis, H. (2013). *Performance management* (3rd ed.). Upper Saddle River, NJ: Pearson Prentice Hall.

Kerr, S. (2009). *Reward systems: Does yours measure up?* Cambridge, MA: Harvard Business School Press.

Ledbetter, L. (with Isom, L. S.) (2012). *Grace and grit: My fight for equal pay and fairness at Goodyear and beyond.* New York, NY: Crown Archetype.

Pink, D. H. (2009). *Drive: The surprising truth about what motivates us.* New York, NY: Penguin Books.

TOOLKIT ACTIVITY 8.1

Performance Appraisal Dos and Don'ts

Refer to these guidelines the next time you have to conduct performance appraisals.

Dos

- Reassure your staff member by building on strengths; give him or her confidence. Set the stage for a two-way conversation. Relieve tension and facilitate dialogue by communicating upfront your review process agenda. Let the employee know they have input.
- Use a "we" approach when discussing problems. Talk about their strengths and challenge areas. Deliver the negative (avoid sugarcoating), but make sure the employee knows what he or she can do about it.

- Be specific when discussing performance appraisal. Identify what success looks like for the coming year, given the organization's objectives. Create an employee development plan with specific goals and tasks.
- Keep the interview on track. Start the process by letting employees assess themselves. What are they most proud of, and what do they consider areas for development?
- Draw him or her out by asking thought-provoking questions (not the yes or no type); then listen. Restate or reflect the follower's statements. Listen with warmth, frankness, and real interest.
- Talk about job results, not activities. Seize the opportunity to acknowledge what you like and appreciate about how the employee performs.
- Function as a coach, not as inspector. Counsel—don't advise. Focus on the employee. Be truly present. Listen and make a genuine attempt to understand concerns and any feedback.
- Close properly, summarize, and plan for improvements and changes. Write down the results.

Don'ts

- Don't use negative words or too many negative criticisms. Everyone has room for improvement. Even the most talented individuals want to know how they can reach the next level. Refusing to identify issues, challenges for improvement, or not holding the individual accountable does not foster growth. When you avoid giving tough, direct feedback, you are not doing them (or you) any favors.
- Don't hammer on negatives. Don't shred personal self-esteem by telling them every negative thing you've ever noticed. Reinforce that it is behaviors and actions you want changed and that you have confidence in the person.
- Don't give insincere or excessive praise.
- Don't use generalities that cannot be backed up by examples.
- Don't dominate the conversation. Don't offer challenging feedback in general terms. Many people are told during performance appraisals that they need to improve "communication." Most people have no idea what this means. Identify how you and the follower will know that he or she met your expectations for improvement.
- Don't place emphasis on personality traits. Don't make it personal. Stick to behavior specifics.
- Don't be fussy, picky, or hurried. Don't make assumptions about how the employee is receiving the feedback. Emotionally charged situations often foster misunderstanding. Probe for understanding reactions, including confirmation of the critical points of the review.
- Don't rush or talk too much. Reviews should be interactive. Don't let whatever "form" you use dictate your process; it's not about the form. If you are doing all the talking, you've probably lost them.

Source: Basking, K. (2013). Performance appraisal do's and don'ts. Retrieved from www.evaluationforms.org/tips/performance-appraisal-dos-and-donts.

TOOLKIT ACTIVITY 8.2

Performance Management Role-Play

In this exercise, you will role-play a performance management session with another student in the class. One of you will play the role of the leader, and the other will play the role of the follower. On the next pages, you will find the leader role and the follower role. You and your partner should select a role and take 10 minutes to study the information and review the performance appraisal form. It is Monocle's practice to have the follower provide a self-assessment, so both of you should complete the form. After you have completed the form, you will conduct the performance appraisal session for 30 minutes. It is important that you both sign the performance appraisal document.

Refer back to the Toolkit Activity 8.1 on the dos and don'ts for conducting a performance appraisal, and try to follow these guidelines during the session.

Leader Role: You have an MBA from a prestigious university and have worked for Monocle Software for 20 years. Monocle conducts enterprise resource planning (ERP), which is the process of examining business functions and installing software that allows an organization to use a system of integrated software applications to manage the business and automate functions. ERP software integrates all facets of an operation, including product planning, development, manufacturing processes, sales, and marketing. ERP software typically consists of a variety of modules that are individually purchased, based on what best meets the specific needs and technical capabilities of your clients. Each ERP module is focused on one area of business process, such as human resources or project management. You are conducting an appraisal with one of your team leaders. He or she has been responsible for the accounting application. There have been a number of complaints from the client regarding the software taking too long to customize and some functions that do not work. The employees in the client company are frustrated, and they have commented that the new software doesn't work as well as what they had before. The members of this follower's team have complained that the client did not know what they wanted and has unrealistic expectations about what the software would be able to do. They have told you that they were not involved as a team in the early stages and did not have input into what was promised to the client. You observed your follower's behavior in the initial meeting and felt that he or she may not have fully understood the threats to the employees' sense of security and potential resistance to change during an ERP implementation. This contract is several million dollars, and you are concerned that the complaints are spreading throughout the client organization, and other software applications are being questioned recently. Unfortunately, you are finding out about these problems from the client and your follower's team members. He or she has not been communicating with you regularly regarding the situation. You hope to provide feedback that will turn the situation around.

Follower Role: You have a master's degree in computer science from a top regional university. You have worked for Monocle Consulting for 10 years and have worked your way up from a software developer; you were promoted 6 months ago to project team leader. You took over a project that was nearing completion at the time of your promotion and saw it through to a successful implementation. Your current assignment is your first full implementation from beginning to end. You met with the clients in the accounting area and conducted the needs assessment following Monocle's protocols. Your supervisor asked you if you needed assistance or if you wanted another team leader with more experience to sit in on some of the early meetings with the client, but you assured your boss that you were ready to handle the client on your own. There have been some difficulties with the project, and some of the programmers on your team have complained that the client did not know what they wanted and has requested numerous changes to the applications. The project is not on schedule for successful completion with the other modules, and you have had to request overtime payments for your team to complete the modules on time. Your supervisor has been reluctant to approve the overtime payments due to concerns about the overall budget for the implementation and complaints about too much weekend work by your team. You realize that there have been some client complaints, but you have tried to address their concerns by convincing them that the overall structure of the software is sound and has worked in many other companies. You have added additional features that they only learned they wanted after they had experienced the new software. Members of your team have been complaining about the clients' demands and blaming one another for the failure to complete the necessary changes during normal working hours. They are tired of being asked to work on weekends and trying to shift responsibility to one another. Despite the challenges, you remain confident that with 2 additional weeks and overtime budget approval you will complete the project on time.

Monocle Software Job Performance Management Form

Supervisor Name: _____

Employee   Name: _____

Evaluation Period: _____

Title: _____   Date: _____

Performance Planning and Results

Performance Review

- Rate the person's level of performance, using the definitions that follow.
- Review with employee each performance factor used to evaluate his or her work performance.
- Give an overall rating in the space provided, using the following definitions as a guide.

Performance Rating Definitions

The following ratings must be used to ensure commonality of language and consistency on overall ratings. There should be supporting comments to justify ratings of "outstanding," "below expectations," and "unsatisfactory."

Outstanding	Performance is consistently superior.
Exceeds expectations	Performance is routinely above job requirements.
Meets expectations	Performance is regularly competent and dependable.
Below expectations	Performance fails to meet job requirements on a frequent basis.
Unsatisfactory	Performance is consistently unacceptable.

Rate the employee's behavior on the dimensions on the following form. There is space on the form to add comments that are specific to each dimension of performance. Also, complete the sections on strengths, areas for improvement, and plans for improved performance.

A. Performance Factors

Administration—Measures effectiveness in planning, organizing, and efficiently handling activities and eliminating unnecessary activities	Outstanding ☐
	Exceeds expectations ☐
	Meets expectations ☐
	Below expectations ☐
	Unsatisfactory ☐
	N/A ☐
Knowledge of work—Consider employee's skill level, knowledge, and understanding of all phases of the job and those requiring improved skills and experience	Outstanding ☐
	Exceeds expectations ☐
	Meets expectations ☐
	Below expectations ☐
	Unsatisfactory ☐
	N/A ☐
Communication—Measures effectiveness in listening to others, expressing ideas—both orally and in writing—and providing relevant and timely information to management, coworkers, subordinates, and customers	Outstanding ☐
	Exceeds expectations ☐
	Meets expectations ☐
	Below expectations ☐
	Unsatisfactory ☐
	N/A ☐
Teamwork—Measures how well this individual gets along with fellow employees, respects the rights of other employees, and shows a cooperative spirit	Outstanding ☐
	Exceeds expectations ☐
	Meets expectations ☐
	Below expectations ☐
	Unsatisfactory ☐
	N/A ☐

Decision making/problem solving—Measures effectiveness in understanding problems and making timely, practical decisions	Outstanding	☐
	Exceeds expectations	☐
	Meets expectations	☐
	Below expectations	☐
	Unsatisfactory	☐
	N/A	☐
Expense management—Measures effectiveness in establishing appropriate reporting and control procedures; operating efficiently at lowest cost; staying within established budgets	Outstanding	☐
	Exceeds expectations	☐
	Meets expectations	☐
	Below expectations	☐
	Unsatisfactory	☐
	N/A	☐
Independent action—Measures effectiveness in time management; initiative and independent action within prescribed limits	Outstanding	☐
	Exceeds expectations	☐
	Meets expectations	☐
	Below expectations	☐
	Unsatisfactory	☐
	N/A	☐
Job knowledge—Measures effectiveness in keeping knowledgeable methods, techniques, and skills required in own job and related functions; remaining current on new developments and work activities	Outstanding	
	Exceeds expectations	☐
	Meets expectations	☐
	Below expectations	☐
	Unsatisfactory	☐
	N/A	☐
Leadership—Measures effectiveness in accomplishing work assignments through subordinates; establishing challenging goals; delegating and coordinating effectively; promoting innovation and team effort	Outstanding	☐
	Exceeds expectations	☐
	Meets expectations	☐
	Below expectations	☐
	Unsatisfactory	☐
	N/A	☐
Managing change and improvement—Measures effectiveness in initiating changes, adapting to necessary changes from old methods when they are no longer practical, identifying new methods, and generating improvement in performance	Outstanding	☐
	Exceeds expectations	☐
	Meets expectations	☐
	Below expectations	☐
	Unsatisfactory	☐
	N/A	☐

(Continued)

TOOLKIT

Customer responsiveness—Measures responsiveness and courtesy in dealing with internal staff, external customers, and vendors; employee projects a courteous manner	Outstanding	☐
	Exceeds expectations	☐
	Meets expectations	☐
	Below expectations	☐
	Unsatisfactory	☐
	N/A	☐
Employee's responsiveness—Measures responsiveness in completing job tasks in a timely manner	Outstanding	☐
	Exceeds expectations	☐
	Meets expectations	☐
	Below expectations	☐
	Unsatisfactory	☐
	N/A	☐

B. Employee Strengths and Accomplishments
Include those that are relevant during this evaluation period. This should be related to performance or behavioral aspects you appreciated in their performance.

C. Performance Areas That Need Improvement:

D. Plan of Action Toward Improved Performance:

E. Employee Comments:

F. Signatures:

Employee _____ Date _____

(Signature does not necessarily denote agreement with official review and means only that the employee was given the opportunity to discuss the official review with the supervisor.)

Evaluated by _____ Date _____

Reviewed by _____ Date _____

CASE STUDY 8.1

Pay Inequity at Goodyear Tire and Rubber

One evening when she came to work to start the night shift, Lilly Ledbetter found an anonymous note in her mailbox at the Goodyear Tire & Rubber plant in Gadsden, Alabama. She had worked for Goodyear for 19 years as a manager and was shocked at what she read. On the note, her monthly pay ($3,727) was written along with the pay (which ranged from $4,286 to $5,236) of three of her male colleagues who started working for Goodyear the same year that she did and did the same job. Ledbetter (2012) stated, "My heart jerked as if an electric jolt had coursed through my body." She filed a gender pay discrimination lawsuit under the 1964 Civil Rights Amendment and was awarded $3 million in back pay and other benefits she lost due to pay discrimination (e.g., contributions to her retirement).

The case was appealed to the U.S. Supreme Court, which ruled against Ledbetter. In the case of *Ledbetter v. Goodyear Tire & Rubber Co., 550 U.S. 618 (2007)*, the U.S. Supreme Court decided that the statute of limitations for presenting an equal-pay lawsuit begins on the date that the employer makes the initial discriminatory wage decision, not at the date of the most recent paycheck. This court decision ultimately led to the *Lilly Ledbetter Fair Pay Act of 2009* (Pub.L. 111–2, S. 181), which states the 180-day statute of limitations for filing an equal-pay lawsuit resets with each new paycheck affected by discrimination. The act is a federal statute and was the first bill signed into law by President Barack Obama in 2009. Lilly's website states the following:

> For 10 years, Lilly Ledbetter fought to close the gap between women's and men's wages, sparring with the Supreme Court, lobbying Capitol Hill in a historic discrimination case against Goodyear Tire and Rubber Company. . . . Ledbetter will never receive restitution from Goodyear, but she said, "I'll be happy if the last thing they say about me after I die is that I made a difference." (www.lillyledbetter.com)

The Lilly Ledbetter case shows that employees care a great deal about the rewards they receive from an organization, and these rewards must be fair. They pay attention to rewards—particularly what they are paid. Pay inequity may cause employees to feel undervalued by the organization and raises concerns regarding organizational justice.

Discussion Questions:

1. What are the implications of the Ledbetter case for the performance management system?
2. Explain Lilly Ledbetter's reaction to learning she was being paid less than her coworkers based upon pay dispersion.
3. How do you feel about Ledbetter never receiving compensation from Goodyear for her lower wages for 10 years?
4. Referring back to Chapter 7, relate this case to what you learned about organizational justice. What type(s) of justice does the case illustrate?

Source: Ledbetter, L. (with Isom, L. S.). (2012). *Grace and grit: My fight for equal pay and fairness at Goodyear and beyond.* New York, NY: Crown Archetype.

SELF-ASSESSMENT 8.1

Work Values Checklist

Every day, we make choices—some without careful consideration. Whether we realize it or not, often our career choice is based on values rather than the work. Values are the beliefs, attitudes, and judgments we prize. Are you aware of your values? Do you act on them?

Use this checklist to get a better idea of what's important to you. It's divided into three categories related to intrinsic, extrinsic, and lifestyle values.

Intrinsic Values

These are the intangible rewards—those related to motivation and satisfaction at work on a daily basis. They provide the inner satisfaction and motivation that make people say, "I love getting up and going to work!"

How important (on a scale of 1 to 5 with 5 being most important) are these intrinsic values to you?

1. _____ Have variety and change at work
2. _____ Be an expert
3. _____ Work on the frontiers of knowledge
4. _____ Help others
5. _____ Help society
6. _____ Experience adventure and excitement
7. _____ Take risks or have physical challenges
8. _____ Feel respected for your work
9. _____ Compete with others
10. _____ Have lots of public contact
11. _____ Influence others
12. _____ Engage in precision work
13. _____ Gain a sense of achievement
14. _____ Have opportunities to express your creativity
15. _____ Work for a good cause

Extrinsic Values

These are the tangible rewards or conditions you find at work, including the physical setting, job titles, benefits, and earnings or earning potential. Extrinsic values often trap people into staying at jobs they don't like, saying, "I just can't give up my paycheck!" They are commonly called "golden handcuffs."

How important (on a scale of 1 to 5 with 5 being most important) are these golden handcuffs to you?

1. _____ Have control, power, or authority
2. _____ Travel often
3. _____ Be rewarded monetarily
4. _____ Be an entrepreneur
5. _____ Work as a team
6. _____ Work in a fast-paced environment
7. _____ Have regular work hours
8. _____ Set your own hours/have flexibility
9. _____ Be wealthy
10. _____ Have prestige or social status
11. _____ Have intellectual status
12. _____ Have recognition through awards, honors, or bonuses
13. _____ Wear a uniform
14. _____ Work in an aesthetically pleasing environment
15. _____ Work on the edge, in a high-risk environment

Lifestyle Values

These are the personal values associated with how and where you want to live, how you choose to spend your leisure time, and how you feel about money.

How important (on a scale of 1 to 5 with 5 being most important) are these lifestyle values to you?

1. _____ Save money
2. _____ Vacation at expensive resorts
3. _____ Have access to educational/cultural opportunities
4. _____ Live close to sports or recreational facilities
5. _____ Be active in your community
6. _____ Entertain at home
7. _____ Be involved in politics
8. _____ Live simply
9. _____ Spend time with family
10. _____ Live in a big city
11. _____ Live abroad
12. _____ Have time for spirituality or personal growth
13. _____ Be a homeowner
14. _____ Live in a rural setting
15. _____ Have fun in your life and at work

Once you have completed all three checklists, write down all the values you rated as 5s. If you have less than five, add the values you rated as 4s to the list. If your list of 4s and 5s has more than 20 values, you need to stop and prioritize your list. To prioritize, select no more than four or five values from each category.

Next, analyze which of the three categories is most important to you. Consider how each is reflected in the work you currently do or in the position you would like to find. Look for overlap or values that seem to go together, such as "be wealthy" from Extrinsic Values and "save money" from Lifestyle Values. If there is no overlap or compatibility between categories, or if everything is important to you, then reprioritize your list by selecting your top 10 values. Then narrow that list down to the five values you absolutely need both on and off the job. Finally, write two or three sentences describing or summarizing how your values will translate into your ideal job. Knowing what's important will help you prepare for your next interview or help you find increased satisfaction with the job you have.

As you follow the process, if you notice that what motivates you is actually a reward or already part of your lifestyle, it means you're living your values.

Source: Boer, P. (n.d.). Work values checklist SS. Retrieved on February 5, 2015, from http://career-advice.monster.com/job-search/career-assessment/work-values-check-list/article.aspx.

TOOLKIT

SECTION IV

BUILDING RELATIONSHIPS

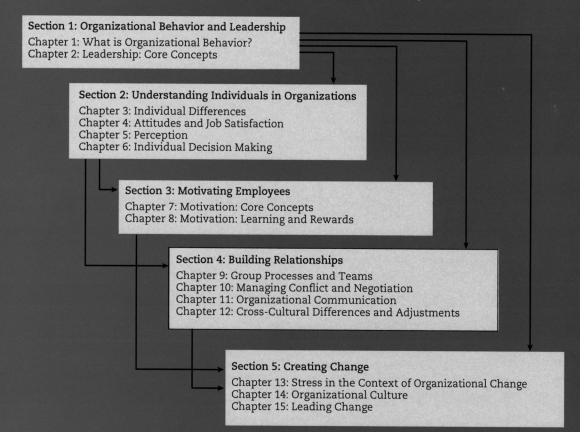

Section 1: Organizational Behavior and Leadership
Chapter 1: What is Organizational Behavior?
Chapter 2: Leadership: Core Concepts

Section 2: Understanding Individuals in Organizations
Chapter 3: Individual Differences
Chapter 4: Attitudes and Job Satisfaction
Chapter 5: Perception
Chapter 6: Individual Decision Making

Section 3: Motivating Employees
Chapter 7: Motivation: Core Concepts
Chapter 8: Motivation: Learning and Rewards

Section 4: Building Relationships
Chapter 9: Group Processes and Teams
Chapter 10: Managing Conflict and Negotiation
Chapter 11: Organizational Communication
Chapter 12: Cross-Cultural Differences and Adjustments

Section 5: Creating Change
Chapter 13: Stress in the Context of Organizational Change
Chapter 14: Organizational Culture
Chapter 15: Leading Change

9

GROUP PROCESSES AND TEAMS

WHY TEAMS MATTER: THE "ORANGE REVOLUTION"

The Orange Revolution: How One Great Team Can Transform an Entire Organization explains why teams matter and how one high-performing team creates energy that spreads throughout the organization; they use the color orange because it is often associated with high levels of positive energy.[1] The authors based their book on a study of 350,000 employees working in teams at Zappos.com, Pepsi, New York's Madison Square Garden, American Express, and Nokia. They found that working in successful teams enhanced employee engagement. As discussed in Chapter 4, employee engagement is an important work attitude that relates to numerous positive work outcomes including higher job performance. The theme of the orange revolution is that successful teams feel engaged at work when people feel invested in their team. This engagement relates strongly to what leaders do, which they characterize as the "Basic 4 + Recognition." The basic four include setting goals, having good communication, developing trust, and being accountable. Recognition is the "plus" factor, which is having leaders who appreciate the strengths of others.

Beginning in the 1960s, organizations experimented with teams in the workplace, and there was an explosion in interest in team-based organizations in the 1980s. Some employees were skeptical and viewed teamwork as a "fad" that would go away. However, it is now clear that teamwork is here to stay, and most organizations employ teams to make significant decisions and develop new ideas. After the downsizings of the 1980s and 1990s, leaders needed a way to get more done with fewer people. Teams turned out to be one answer to this challenge. Teams allow for more creative solutions and build commitment to the implementation of innovative ideas. Whether it is orange or some other color, teamwork revolutionized the world of work. It is thus essential for a leader to understand team basics and how to lead teams effectively.

This chapter reviews the essential research on small groups from social psychology and discusses current approaches to **work teams.** The emphasis will be on leading teams, since this is a core competence, given that most organizations now use work teams to maximize organizational performance. As we will learn in this chapter, teams are also one of the best forums for learning, since employees share their skills and expertise with one another. Teams are now often charged with making important decisions, and a variety of techniques for team decision making will be discussed.

Learning Objectives

After studying this chapter, you should be able to do the following:

9.1: Explain the difference between a working group and a team.

9.2: Illustrate the relationship between team purpose and performance by using a team charter.

9.3: Compare and contrast two models of team development.

9.4: Describe the three main aspects of team effectiveness.

9.5: Demonstrate how to assess the cohesion of your team.

9.6: Explain how team norms influence team behaviors.

9.7: Explain why team-shared mental models are important.

9.8: Compare the leader options for participative decision making using the normative model.

9.9: List and explain five team decision-making methods.

Get the edge on your studies at **edge.sagepub.com/scandura**
- Take the chapter quiz
- Review key terms with eFlashcards
- Explore multimedia resources, SAGE readings, and more!

$SAGE edge™

WHAT IS A TEAM?

Learning Objective 9.1: Explain the difference between a working group and a team.

Numerous definitions of teams appear in the literature; however, the one offered in *The Wisdom of Teams* captures the essence of most definitions: "A team is a small number of people with complementary skills who are committed to a common purpose, performance goals, and approach for which they hold themselves mutually accountable."[2]

This definition reflects evidence-based research that has shown that teams are more effective when the number of people on the team is relatively small (e.g., 4 to 6 members for a project team). Also, research has shown that commitment to a common goal and performance strategies enhances performance. Finally, team members must accept team goals and make a commitment to being accountable for them.

A question often asked is whether all work should be done by teams. The answer to the question is no. In many cases, teams become dysfunctional when there is actually no need for the task to be performed by a team at all. The team may flounder as it searches for a meaningful goal that everyone on the team can commit to. Teams should not be used when an individual can perform the task as well as a team (e.g., the leader could delegate the ordering of supplies to one person rather than having a team discussion about it). Also, if a performance goal can be met by adding up individual contributions (known as an **additive task**) then members of the work unit can work independently and their efforts can be combined later. The right time to use teams is when a performance goal requires **collective effect** and a work project that reflects the contributions of everyone on the team. To accomplish a team goal, different skill sets, perspectives, or experiences are often needed.[3] There is a useful distinction between a work group and a team, and this will be discussed next.

 Critical Thinking Question: In addition to the type of task, provide some other situations in which teams should not be used.

Work Group Versus Team

Some of the literature on groups and teams is confusing because the terms *group* and *team* are used interchangeably. To clarify this, the distinction between the group and team has been articulated.[4] A work group interacts primarily to share information with other members (e.g., members of a work group attend a monthly staff meeting and share what they are working on). They are not responsible for a collective work product, or their individual contributions can be added up to create something. An example of a work group is the service department of an automobile dealership, which consists of a service manager and 12 service advisers who report to the manager. Each service adviser meets with their own customers independently, and the contributions are summed for an overall customer rating of the dealership's service department. If conflicts arise in work groups, the group typically looks to the leader to resolve them.

A work team, in contrast to a work group, depends on one another, and they must interact to create something that no one person on the team could create. There is

Team
Development

synergy on the team that means that the team can produce something beyond the sum of individual member contributions. An example of a work team is a task force assembled to brainstorm ideas for improving patient safety in a hospital. The team depends highly on the participation of all members for success since each member contributes a unique perspective that influences the quality of the suggestions for patient safety. If conflicts emerge within a work team, the members manage it internally since there is often no designated leader. This is a **self-managed work team (SMWT),** which will be discussed later in this chapter. Some work groups can become teams, and a strong purpose or performance challenge sets a work group on the path to becoming a real team.

TEAM PURPOSE

Learning Objective 9.2: Illustrate the relationship between team purpose and performance by using a team charter.

Setting goals for teams is just as important as it is for individuals. As discussed in Chapter 7, goal setting increases to motivation and performance. It's important to keep in mind that team goals should also be SMART (specific, measurable, actionable, relevant, and time based). Effective teams have a sense of shared purpose, and it is one of the components of the definition of a team. Specific team goals predict specific team performance (e.g., setting challenging goals for quantity results in higher team output).[5] Also, feedback on performance affects the allocation of resources when individuals strive to accomplish both individual and team goals. Resource allocation is an example of a team regulatory process, which will increase team performance. Also, feedback on team performance is essential for teams to make the correct allocation of resources for future team performance. Team members who receive no team-level feedback can't effectively set team goals and, as a result, set completely unrealistic goals.[6]

Team purpose is typically discussed in the early stages of a team's development. Teams follow predictable patterns over their life cycles, and team development will be discussed in the following section.

TEAM DEVELOPMENT

Learning Objective 9.3: Compare and contrast two models of team development.

Teams don't emerge just by putting individuals together. Teams go through a process of development over time, and success is not guaranteed. Research on teams recognizes the role of time in the development of the team. Next, two important models of team development are discussed: the five-stage model and the **team performance curve.**

Five-Stage Model

A classic model of team development is the five-stage model, which includes five stages: **forming, storming, norming, performing,** and **adjourning.**[7,8] During the forming stage, team members may experience stress due to the uncertainty of not knowing the other team members and understanding their role on the team. Initial interactions may be tentative as team members "test" one another to determine what the expectations will be. The team leader should clarify the team purpose and set up ground rules through a **team charter** (discussed later in this chapter and in Toolkit Activity 9.1 at the end of this chapter). As the team interacts on project work, conflicts emerge regarding the goals and contributions of team members, and the group enters the storming stage. There may be challenges to the leader of the group (either a formally assigned leader or an informal one). The team leader should openly address conflict and maintain a focus on the team purpose and ground rules established in the charter. At the end of this stage, the leadership question is typically resolved, and it is clear who will lead the group. Also, a status hierarchy, or pecking order, may be established. If the storming phase does not destroy the team and result in abandonment of the process by all members, the team moves to the next stage of development, which is called norming. In this stage, the members of the team form a cohesive unit and close relationships among team members develop. The group establishes further "unwritten rules," or norms, for what is acceptable behavior (beyond that specified in the team charter). For example, if the team allows members to show up late for meetings without sanctions, then lateness may be considered acceptable by team members, and they show up late frequently. During the norming phase, the leader should remind the followers of the ground rules and address deviations constructively. Once norms are established, the team should be performing by producing collective work products. The group shifts from relationship development and norm articulation to the work itself and goal attainment. For a work group or a task force that is permanent, the performing stage is the last stage. In this phase, the team leaders should celebrate success along the way to achieving the team goal. However, in some cases, teams are temporary and have a specific goal to accomplish. When this is the case, the team finalizes their work in the adjourning stage and disbands. The team leader should arrange a celebration activity such as a party or dinner to reward the members for achieving the team purpose.

While the model proposes that teams move through the phases smoothly, in actuality the team may regress to a previous stage or runs the risk of adjourning at any stage. For example, the level of conflict during the storming stage may result in team members deciding it's just easier to work alone. Even after the norming stage, the group is at risk of adjournment if the performance norms are repeatedly violated and the team determines that members aren't really committed.

In many student project teams—and also at work—teams are temporary and have a clear deadline. Teams don't follow the typical stages of development in such teams. In fact, there is a transition between an early phase of inactivity followed by a second phase of significant acceleration toward task completion. This process is called **punctuated equilibrium**.[9] There is an initial meeting in which the group's goals are discussed. Following this meeting, not much gets done until about halfway to the deadline. This midpoint transition occurs regardless of the total time allowed for the project. In other words, it doesn't matter whether the total time for the project is 1 hour or 6 months. At about halfway toward the completion of a project, team members begin to revisit goals and discuss how to get the group moving toward finishing the task. Following this midpoint discussion, there is a burst of new activity as team members scramble to reach their goals in time.

You may be able to relate to this by recalling times when you and your team pulled an "all-nighter"—a meeting that lasts hours and is intense right before your team project is due for a

Team
Training and
Performance

class. It is important to recognize that this doesn't apply to all types of teams; the punctuated equilibrium effect appears to be most prevalent in temporary teams with a fixed deadline.[10] The takeaway message from this research is clear: Try not to procrastinate when a team project is assigned. The team leader should keep the momentum going by setting early benchmarks to avoid having to rush at the end of the project.

Not all team development follows an upward pattern of productivity. A second model of team development addresses the potential performance losses that may occur during the initial storming or procrastination phases. This model is known as the team performance curve.

 Critical Thinking Question: How else can you keep a team from procrastinating on the start of a project? Describe what you would do specifically.

Team Performance Curve

Like the punctuated equilibrium model, the team performance curve recognizes that team performance over the course of the life of the team is not always linear and performance does not always increase over time.[11] Figure 9.1 combines the five-stage model with the team performance curve and shows there may be a performance decrease as the team goes through the storming phase. A working group is a collection of people without a common sense of purpose. As the figure shows, this produces a certain level of performance, and some tasks are appropriate for a working group because they are additive. The team leader may attempt to transform his or her group into a team by introducing a common goal—particularly a challenging one. As team members organize to attain the goal, storming occurs and the team

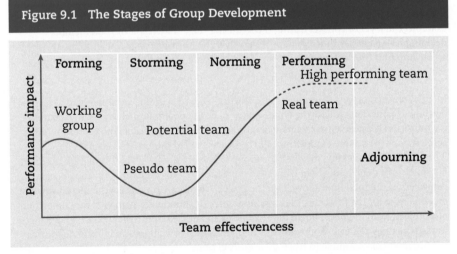

Figure 9.1 The Stages of Group Development

Sources: Adapted from: Katzenbach, J. R., & Smith, D. K. (1993). *The wisdom of teams: Creating the high-performance organization.* New York: Harper Business; Tuckman, B. (1965) Developmental Sequence in Small Groups. *Psychological Bulletin, 63,* 384–399; Tuckman, B., & Jensen, M. (1977) Stages of Small Group Development. *Group and Organizational Studies, 2,* 419–427.

performance may actually *decline* for a period of time. Some working groups remain at this point as a pseudo team because they are not on the path toward becoming a high-performance team. If the team gets past the storming and establishes productive norms, they reach a point where they can be considered a potential team. At this stage, the team has the potential to become a real team, which exhibits the characteristics of the team definition (i.e., they are committed to a common purpose, performance goals, and approach for which they hold themselves mutually accountable). A small number of teams become high-performance teams, which have all of the characteristics of real teams plus team members are deeply committed to the growth and development of the other team members. For example, a team member would teach another member how to use new presentation software. Thus, in high-performance teams, team interests become more important than individual interests, and high-performance teams are rare. Given high-performance teams are rare yet essential for organizations, the next sections will discuss team effectiveness and how it is defined and measured.

Team Performance

Critical Thinking Question: How can the use of a team charter help a team get through the storming phase? How does it help establish team norms and lead to high performance?

TEAM EFFECTIVENESS

Learning Objective 9.4: Describe the three main aspects of team effectiveness.

The question of how to know if a team is effective is an important one. Team effectiveness has a number of dimensions. The input-process-output model defines the different aspects of team effectiveness.[12] First, input refers to the individual characteristics of team members (e.g., skills and abilities) and the resources they have at their disposal. Inputs may also refer to knowledge and personality. For example, a study of 51 teams found both general mental ability (IQ) and personality (particularly conscientiousness, agreeableness, extroversion, and emotional stability) increased team performance.[13]

Process is the second aspect of team effectiveness and refers to how the team interacts. Examples of process include team development and patterns of participation. Also, trust, cross-training, and coordination relate to team effectiveness.[14,15] Third, the most obvious measure of team effectiveness is team output—the collective work product generated from the team (team performance). Output has three components: (1) performance as rated by those outside of the team, (2) how well team member individual needs are met, and (3) the willingness of team members to stay on the team.[16]

Team effectiveness reflects three broad categories: performance, behaviors, and attitudes as shown in Figure 9.2.[17] The figure indicates important inputs to team processes such as the organization environment and design of the task. On the output side, performance is the team's productivity, quality, or innovation as examples (i.e., the collective work product). Behaviors are what people do such as being absent from team meetings.

An important team process that has received much research attention is team conflict, which will be covered in Chapter 10. Attitudes are team members' reports on their

Figure 9.2   Model of Team Effectiveness

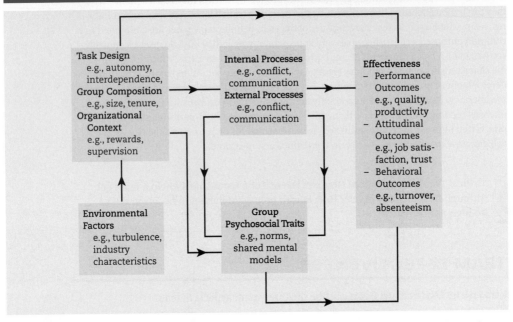

Source: Cohen, S. G., & Bailey, D. E. 1997. What makes teams work: Group effectiveness research from the shop floor to the executive suite. *Journal of Management*, 23, 239–290.

Team Effectiveness

experience in the team such as team satisfaction. These attitudes and behaviors matter because organizational behavior (OB) research has demonstrated that team behaviors relate to team outcomes such as job performance and satisfaction. For example, motivating and confidence building are teamwork processes that develop and maintain members' motivation and confidence that the team will accomplish its goals.[18] A review of the research on team effectiveness concluded that team performance is the most commonly studied outcome; however, more recent studies have included **team affect** (the team atmosphere) and **team viability** (a collective sense of belonging similar to team cohesion).[19] **Cohesion** is one of the most important team processes and is the "team spirit" experienced in high-performing teams. Cohesion will be discussed later in this chapter.

In addition to team affect and viability, team learning and creativity are also indicators of team effectiveness. Learning and creativity have been shown to enhance team satisfaction and performance. These team effectiveness outcomes are emerging as important aspects of teamwork and will be covered in the following sections.

Team Learning

Individual development of team members is an important metric for teams and defines a high-performance team. Team learning is now considered essential and has received a considerable amount of research. Viewing teams as a forum for learning began with the publication of the influential book *The Fifth Discipline: The Art and Practice of the Learning Organization*.[20] Author Peter Senge views teamwork as one of the key experiences that leads to employee learning:

 **Team Learning**

> When you ask people about what it is like being part of a great team, what is most striking is the meaningfulness of the experience. People talk about being part of something larger than themselves, of being connected, of being generative. It becomes quite clear that, for many, their experiences as part of truly great teams stands out as singular periods of life lived to the fullest. Some spend the rest of their lives looking for ways to recapture that spirit. (p. 13)

Team learning is an ongoing process through which teams acquire, combine, and apply knowledge.[21] For example, asking questions, seeking feedback, improvising, discussing errors, challenging underlying assumptions, and reflecting on specific results or unexpected outcomes increases a team member's knowledge.[22] Team learning originates in individual intuitions, is amplified through interpretation, and emerges at the team level as collective thoughts and actions. Moreover, team learning significantly affects team performance.[23]

 Critical Thinking Question: Describe a situation in which you learned something from interacting with others on a team (this can be related to task, process, or your individual development).

In addition to learning, research has also shown that teams enhance creativity and innovation. Creativity as a result of teamwork is recognized as essential to make high-quality decisions that relate to organizational effectiveness.[24] The next section will discuss research on team creativity.

Team Creativity

In Chapter 6, you learned that individual creativity is a key aspect of the decision-making process. Research has shown that creativity in teams matters as well. Due to synergy, team creativity is not just the additive sum of individual team member creativity. Team creativity involves both processes and outcomes of developing new ideas for innovation. Team creativity is a collective phenomenon that encompasses what team members do behaviorally, cognitively, and emotionally as they define problems, generate ideas, and attempt new ways of doing their work.[25] Communication of new ideas and sharing information with diverse others leads to higher creativity.[26] Also, shared team goals result in higher creativity. In a study of project teams, more creative teams recognized that there was a need to be creative to be successful, and they valued participation by all team members. Interestingly, more creative teams also spent more time socializing with each other, both inside and outside of work.[27]

Diversity may enhance team creativity, and this is considered one of the benefits of having a diverse workforce. Diversity in teams can increase flexibility, creativity, and problem solving.[28] A meta-analysis of team diversity and team performance found

 Team-Building

having members with diverse skill sets and backgrounds does appear to enhance team creativity and innovation.[29] Specifically, differences in functional expertise, education, and organizational tenure were most related to team performance. A second meta-analysis of 108 studies in 10,632 teams found cultural diversity leads to process losses through task conflict.[30] Diversity presents a challenge to the team leader in that there is a greater need to manage conflict. But it appears to be worth the effort since process gains are realized through increased creativity and satisfaction in diverse teams. Effective team leaders credit diversity for being a key reason for team creative outputs that directly impacts organizational success.[31]

 Critical Thinking Questions: How can a team leader ensure that diversity does not result in conflict that negatively affects performance? Describe specifically what a team leader can do to manage diverse viewpoint during a team discussion.

COHESION

Learning Objective 9.5: Demonstrate how to assess the cohesion of your team.

Cohesion is defined as "the resultant of all the forces acting on the members to remain part of the group."[32] These forces depend on the attractiveness or unattractiveness of the prestige of the group, the group members, and/or the group's activities. The mutual attraction of the member to the group is the most important determinant of cohesion.[33] When cohesion is strong, the group is motivated to perform and is better able to coordinate activities for success. In cohesive teams, there is a sense of "we-ness" since team members tend to use *we* rather than *I* to describe the team and its activities.[34] Meta-analytic studies have found that team cohesion and team performance are positively and significantly related.[35,36] For example, one review reports the average cohesive team performed 18% higher than the average noncohesive team.[37]

You may be working in a team for a project for your OB course (or another course). The extent to which your team is cohesive can be assessed by asking the following questions:[38]

- How well do members of your group get along with each other?
- How well do members of your group stick together (i.e., remain close to each other)?
- Would you socialize with the members of your group outside of class?
- How well do members of your group help each other on the project?
- Would you want to remain a member of this group for future projects or in future courses?

 Critical Thinking Questions: Explain why cohesion in teams may not always be a good thing. Discuss the downside of a team being too cohesive.

Coaching for Cohesion

A review of the relationship between cohesiveness and team performance concluded that in 83% of the studies, team cohesiveness was significantly and positively related to team performance.[39] Research on sports psychology has examined the relationship between coaching style and team cohesion. When coaches exhibit training, being democratic, supporting, and giving feedback, team cohesion is higher.[40] An in-depth interview study of male and female athletes in college sports plus a case study of a Division I college football team was conducted to determine the effects of coaching styles on team cohesion.[41] This study found that using abusive language, treating the relationship as a superior or subordinate one, being unfair, lacking communication, and ridiculing players all related to lower team cohesion. Motivational coaching (being inspirational, having a personal relationship with athletes, showing support, and having dedication) was related to higher team cohesion. The case study of the football team indicated that players felt that bragging about the abilities of their teammates, talking about the quality of their opponent, giving motivational speeches, and conducting a team prayer increased feelings of team cohesion. Interestingly, teasing and sarcasm by the coach was acceptable to the team members and they saw this as part of the game, and it made them feel closer to both their teammates and the coach. While teasing may be "out of bounds" for a manager, this research on coaching shows that being inspirational and developing personal relationships will enhance your team's cohesion.

Discussion Questions:

1. To what extent can these findings for sports teams be applied to teams at work? What are the limitations of using sports examples?

2. In these studies, training, being democratic, showing support, and giving feedback were important in developing team cohesion. Which do you think is most important and why?

Sources: Jowett, S., & Chaundy, V. (2004). An investigation into the impact of coach leadership and coach–athlete relationship on group cohesion. *Group Dynamics: Theory, Research and Practice, 8*(4), 302–331; Widmeyer, W. N., Carron, A. V., & Brawley, L. R. (1993). Group cohesion in sport and exercise. *Handbook of Research on Sport Psychology*, 672–692; Turman, P. D. (2003). Coaches and cohesion: The impact of coaching techniques on team cohesion in the small group sport setting. *Journal of Sport Behavior, 26*(1), 86–104.

TEAM NORMS

Learning Objective 9.6: Explain how team norms influence team behaviors.

In addition to cohesion, **team norms** also have a powerful effect on team member attitudes and behaviors. Norms are defined as informal and interpersonal rules that team members are expected to follow.[42] These standards may be explicit and formally stated by the leader or members of the team. But norms may also be implicit. They are not written down, and communication of the norms to team members depends on the ability of the leader (or team members) to effectively convey the expected behaviors. Norms have a powerful influence on team behavior, and they are often difficult to change. For example, at golf courses, it is expected that you wear a collared shirt. While this isn't written down anywhere and golf courses do not post dress codes, you will notice that most people wear a collared shirt on the

**Implicit Norms**

course. This is an example of an implicit norm. If you show up at a golf course in a T-shirt, members may look at you as not understanding the norms of playing on the course (if you didn't know this, remember that you learned it here!) Implicit norms are tricky in that they are difficult to detect, and it is easy to misinterpret them. One way to make norms explicit is by developing a team charter.

The Team Charter

One of the best ways that a leader can make norms explicit and clearly communicate them to team members is by engaging the team to develop a team charter, as mentioned earlier in this chapter. In creating a team charter, not only is the team purpose clarified but the expectations for behavior are set forth (e.g., required attendance at meetings). Norms provide an important regulatory function in teams. Once they are developed through a charter and agreed upon, misunderstandings should be fewer and a team member violating a norm (e.g., missing meetings) can be reminded of the group's commitment to attendance. Some groups even apply sanctions to the violation of norms such as fines or social ostracism. However, sanctioning systems are ineffective if they are not applied consistently. In other words, it is important to keep in mind principles of organizational justice as described in Chapter 7 if sanctions are applied.

The influences of having a team charter and performance strategies of 32 teams of MBA students was studied using a business strategy simulation.[43] Taking the time to develop a high-quality team charter and performance strategies paid off in terms of more effective team performance over time. Teams that had quality charters and strategies outperformed teams with poor quality charters and strategies. Charters are an important tool the leader can use to get their team off to a good start by developing a sense of purpose and performance strategies. Toolkit Activity 9.1 contains specific guidelines for developing a team charter.

Team Metrics

In addition to the team charter, it is also important to have measures (or metrics) to assess how a team is performing over time and to provide feedback to team members. There are three types of metrics for teamwork:

1. **Task metrics.** These are the "what" of teamwork. They relate to the actual work the team is performing. For example, task metrics might be goals for quantity and/or quality and deadlines for the project completion. It is important to set 30-day targets as mini-goals toward task completion so team members have a sense of forward momentum.
2. **Process metrics.** These are the "how" of teamwork. These metrics are assessment of how the teamwork is operating. For example, process metrics might be assessments of team communication or who is participating. Teams often focus on task goals to the exclusion of process goals, but they are important because the process affects task performance.
3. **Individual development metrics.** These metrics relate to how much individuals are developing new skills and learning through teamwork. For example, individual development metrics might be how well one team member is developing leadership abilities from working with the

team. Individual development is important to track, since the hallmark of a high-performance team is when team members genuinely care about the development of their teammates.[44]

Critical Thinking Question: Provide additional examples of task, process, and individual development metrics. Provide an example of an organization-level metric related to teamwork.

Strong team norms give rise to shared understandings within teams, known as **team mental models (TMMs).** These models and why they are important for team process and performance will be discussed next.

TEAM MENTAL MODELS

Learning Objective 9.7: Explain why team-shared mental models are important.

TMMs "are team members' shared, organized understanding and mental representation of knowledge about key elements of the team's relevant environment" (p. 897).[45] TMMs are related to effective team processes and performance[46] because they serve a number of functions, including (1) allowing team members to interpret information similarly, (2) sharing expectations concerning the future, and (3) developing similar reasoning as to why something happens.[47] Teams with highly developed TMMs are fundamentally "on the same page" with respect to sharing a common view of what is occurring in the team. This makes decision making more efficient and enhances team performance.[48] A summary of how TMMs affect performance and other team outcomes is shown in Figure 9.3. The shared similarity of TMMs translates demographic factors, skills, and training into shared norms, effective team processes, and higher performance. A meta-analysis of 65 studies of TMMs and performance found that teams with shared mental models interacted more frequently, were more motivated, had higher job satisfaction, and were rated as more productive by others.[49]

TMMs affect team processes, including how decisions are made and who makes them. Shared understandings emerge in TMMs determine how much participation by members is allowed, for example. The next sections discuss participation and team decision-making options available to team leaders.

PARTICIPATION IN TEAM DECISIONS

Learning Objective 9.8: Compare the leader options for participative decision making using the normative model.

Leadership research has long recognized that leaders have options in making decisions ranging from making the decision themselves or **delegating** the decision to a team.[50] Table 9.1 shows the **normative decision-making model,** which shows that team decisions fall on a continuum

Figure 9.3 Team Mental Models and Outcomes

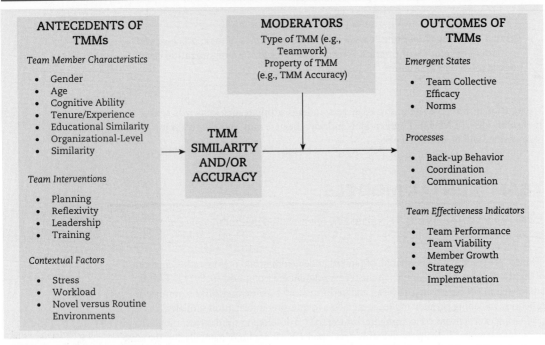

ANTECEDENTS OF TMMs

Team Member Characteristics

- Gender
- Age
- Cognitive Ability
- Tenure/Experience
- Educational Similarity
- Organizational-Level
- Similarity

Team Interventions

- Planning
- Reflexivity
- Leadership
- Training

Contextual Factors

- Stress
- Workload
- Novel versus Routine Environments

MODERATORS

Type of TMM (e.g., Teamwork)
Property of TMM (e.g., TMM Accuracy)

TMM SIMILARITY AND/OR ACCURACY

OUTCOMES OF TMMs

Emergent States

- Team Collective Efficacy
- Norms

Processes

- Back-up Behavior
- Coordination
- Communication

Team Effectiveness Indicators

- Team Performance
- Team Viability
- Member Growth
- Strategy Implementation

Source: Mohammed, S., Ferzandi, L., & Hamilton, K. (2010). Metaphor no more: A 15-year review of the team mental model construct. *Journal of Management, 36*(4), 876–910. p. 892.

ranging from leaders making the decision themselves to delegating the decision to the team.[51] Between these two points, there are **consultative** modes of decision making. The manager can consult followers one-on-one or as a group. They also have the option of serving as the **facilitator** of a group decision. Involving the right people in group decision making has been shown to result in higher quality decisions and more support for decision implementation.[52,53] However, key elements of the situation are important to consider when applying the normative decision-making model of participation. These factors include the following:[54]

1. How significant is the decision?
2. How likely is it that your team members will disagree?
3. Do you (or your team) have the knowledge necessary to make the decision?
4. Do you need commitment from your team?
5. How likely is it that you will have commitment from your team?
6. Is there a time constraint?
7. Is team interaction difficult or impossible?
8. Do your team members function effectively as a team?
9. Is development of your team members important?
10. Do members of your team agree with your goals (and those of the organization)?

Table 9.1	The Normative Decision-Making Model			
Decide	**Consult (Individually)**	**Consult (Group)**	**Facilitate**	**Delegate**
You make the decision alone and either announce or "sell" it to the group. You may use your expertise in collecting information— from the group or others—that you deem relevant to the problem.	You present the problem to group members individually, get their suggestions, and then make the decision.	You present the problem to group members in a meeting, get their suggestions, and then make the decision.	You present the problem to the group in a meeting. You act as facilitator, defining the problem to be solved and the boundaries within which the decision must be made. Your objective is to get concurrence on a decision. Above all, you take care to ensure that your ideas are not given any greater weight than those of others simply because of your position.	You permit the group to make the decision within prescribed limits. The group undertakes the identification and diagnosis of the problem, developing alternative procedures for solving it and deciding on one or more alternative solutions. While you play no direct role in the group's deliberations unless explicitly asked, your role is an important one behind the scenes, providing needed resources and encouragement.

Source: Vroom, V. H. (2003). Educating managers for decision making and leadership. *Management Decision, 41*(10), 968–978.

Techniques for Brainstorming

Employees value being able to participate in group decisions, and research has shown involving them in decisions increases their satisfaction and the chances of success.[55,56] Results from a study of over 400 decisions that had been made by managers in medium to large organizations found that over half of the decisions failed (they were either never implemented or fell apart within 2 years).[57] While some decisions failed due to technical issues such as the problem being defined wrong, the best predictors of success were the involvement and participation of key stakeholders. Specifically, decisions that used participation to foster implementation succeeded more than 80% of the time.

Involving followers in decisions is one important aspect of team decision making. OB research has also investigated the effectiveness of decision-making processes. These techniques are essential for a leader to learn since decision quality may be affected by how the decision is made by the team. The next sections will discuss **brainstorming**, **consensus**, multivoting, **nominal group technique (NGT)**, and stepladder.

TEAM DECISION-MAKING METHODS

Learning Objective 9.9: Explain five team decision-making methods.

Brainstorming

Brainstorming is one of the most common forms of team decision making.[58] Brainstorming should be used when the team needs to produce a creative solution. It enhances the creative process because **idea generation** is separated from **idea evaluation.** Members are trained not to critique ideas but just to write them down as the group generates solutions to a problem. Ideas are typically written on flip chart paper or a whiteboard so that everyone can see them. The team meets in a separate session to evaluate the ideas generated and decide on a course of action. IDEO is a successful product design company, and their rules for brainstorming are shown in the boxed insert.

Consensus

Consensus decision making is another technique that is commonly used in organizations. In many cases, consensus is preferable to voting (although voting is more common). Voting creates winners and losers and may result in a lack of commitment to implement the decision. In a consensus decision-making process, everyone can say they have been heard and will support the final decision. The following steps are suggested for reaching consensus:[59]

BEST PRACTICES

IDEO's Rules for Brainstorming

1. **Defer judgment.** Creative spaces don't judge. They let the ideas flow so that people can build on each other and foster great ideas. You never know where a good idea is going to come from. The key is to make everyone feel like they can say the idea on their mind and allow others to build on it.

2. **Encourage wild ideas.** Wild ideas can often give rise to creative leaps. In thinking about ideas that are wacky or out there, we tend to think about what we really want without the constraints of technology or materials. We can then take those magical possibilities and perhaps invent new technologies to deliver them.

3. **Build on the ideas of others.** Being positive and building on the ideas of others take some skill. In conversation, we try to use *and* instead of *but…*

4. **Stay focused on the topic.** We try to keep the discussion on target; otherwise, you can diverge beyond the scope of what we're trying to design for.

5. **Have one conversation at a time.** There are lots of conversations happening at once, which is great! Always think about the topic and how the ideas could apply.

6. **Be visual.** In live brainstorms, we use colored markers to write on Post-it notes that are put on a wall. Nothing gets an idea across faster than drawing it. It doesn't matter how terrible of a sketcher you are! It's all about the idea behind your sketch. You could also try your hand at sketching it out or mocking it up on the computer. We love visual ideas as the images make them memorable. Does someone else's idea excite you? Maybe make them an image to go with their idea.

7. **Go for quantity.** Aim for as many new ideas as possible. In a good session, up to 100 ideas are generated in 60 minutes. Crank the ideas out quickly.

Discussion Questions:

1. Provide an example of how a team leader can train team members to defer judgment.
2. What do you think a team leader should do after brainstorming? In other words, how should the final decision be made?

Source: OpenIDEO. (2011). 7 tips on better brainstorming. http://www.openideo.com/blog/seven-tips-on-better-brainstorming.

1. **Introduction.** It typically takes fewer than 5 minutes and covers the following:

   - Why are we talking about this? Why does it matter?
   - History of the issue (including results of any previous meetings on it).
   - Goal for this item at this particular meeting (a report, decision, to gather input, etc.).

   At the end of the initial presentation, others who have factual knowledge of the issue are sometimes invited to add in further bits about the issue—as long as it doesn't go on for too long.

2. **Clarifying questions.** These are simple questions just to make sure everyone in the room fully understands what has been presented or proposed.

3. **Discussion.** This is the exploratory phase, where people are invited to ask further questions, show the full diversity of perspectives, raise challenges and concerns, and so on. Agreements and disagreements on general direction are noted and the reasons for them examined—not just what the positions are but why and any underlying value conflicts they represent.

4. **Establish basic direction.** What is the sense of the meeting, in terms of basic direction on this issue? Here we seek general or philosophical agreement—an agreement in principle.

5. **Synthesize or modify proposal (as needed).** Integrate what's been shared, and make it as specific as needed, recognizing that some details will always be left to implementation. Again, notice agreements and disagreements (this time on the specifics of the proposal), and work with the underlying reasons, then generate ideas for addressing and resolving concerns, emerging with a proposal that has substantial group support. Periodically the facilitator may ask, "Are there any remaining unresolved concerns?"

6. **Call for consensus.** The facilitator clearly restates the proposal and then asks people to indicate where they are.

7. **Record.** The note taker reads back the decision to the group. In addition, they record any implementation information needed (tasks, who's responsible, timelines, etc.).

At the point that the facilitator calls for consensus (Step 6), participants typically have the following options:

> **Agreement:** "I support this proposal and am willing to abide by and help implement it."
>
> **Stand Aside:** "I have major concerns with the proposal and agree to stand aside and let the group proceed with it." The choice to stand aside may be based on (but is not limited to) any of the following:

- Disagreement with the proposal or the process used to reach the decision
- Personal values or principles
- Personal impact or need—for example, "I can't afford this" or "I'd have to leave the group."

If someone stands aside, their name and reason are traditionally recorded in the minutes. That person is relieved of lead implementation responsibilities yet is still bound to follow the decision.

> **Blocking:** "I believe this proposal would be majorly detrimental to our group, because either it goes against our fundamental principles or it would lead to a disastrous outcome." Note that none of the following are appropriate reasons to block:

- To get your way or because you prefer a different proposal, or no proposal
- Because you'd have to leave the group if the proposal passed
- Tradition: Because things have always been done a certain way
- Because the proposed action doesn't fit your personal needs (or finances)
- To fulfill your personal moral values or how you want to live

In order to function and prevent tyranny of the minority, consensus-based groups rely on having a robust response to inappropriate blocks. The form of this response varies but usually includes both procedural and cultural elements.

> **Abstain:** "I choose not to participate in the making of this decision." It is typically used because a participant feels uninformed or not ready to participate.

Some groups include other options, such as consent with reservations: "I support the basic thrust of this proposal and have one or more minor unresolved concerns."

Consensus is one of the most commonly used and effective decision-making processes in organizations. The previously given guidelines should be followed in situations in which the support of all members of a team is needed for effective implementation of the decision.

 Critical Thinking Question: Explain why following the consensus guidelines will result in more support for the implementation of a decision rather than simply voting on it.

Multivoting

In practice, it is often required that votes be taken. Given that voting has a number of disadvantages including dissatisfaction with decisions and lack of commitment, the leader should know that multivoting is another decision-making option. The steps for multivoting follow.[60] As with other team decision-making techniques, you need a flip chart or whiteboard, marking pens, plus 5 to 10 slips of paper for each individual, and a pen or pencil for each individual.

1. **Display the list of options.** Combine duplicate items. Organize large numbers of ideas, and eliminate duplication and overlap. List reduction may also be useful.
2. **Number (or letter) all items.**

3. **Decide how many items must be on the final reduced list.** Decide also how many choices each member will vote for. Usually, five choices are allowed. The longer the original list, the more votes will be allowed—up to 10.

4. **Working individually, each member selects the five items (or whatever number of choices is allowed) he or she thinks most important.** Then each member ranks the choices in order of priority, with the first choice ranking highest. For example, if each member has five votes, the top choice would be ranked five, the next choice four, and so on. Each choice is written on a separate paper, with the ranking underlined in the lower right corner.

5. **Tally votes.** Collect the papers, shuffle them, and then record the votes on a flip chart or whiteboard. The easiest way to record votes is for the note-taker to write all the individual rankings next to each choice. For each item, the rankings are totaled next to the individual rankings.

6. **If a decision is clear, stop here. Otherwise, continue with a brief discussion of the vote.** The purpose of the discussion is to look at dramatic voting differences, such as an item that received both 5 and 1 ratings, and avoid errors from incorrect information or understandings about the item. The discussion should not pressure anyone to change his or her vote. Also, if a team member or members feel strongly that an option should be considered, the team can put it back in the voting process.

7. **Repeat the voting process in Steps 4 and 5.** If greater decision-making accuracy is required, this voting may be done by weighting the relative importance of each choice on a scale of 1 to 10, with 10 being most important. As can be seen from this process, multivoting allows for multiple rounds and discussion as the list gets reduced. It allows team members to have more of a voice in the final decision through a series of votes rather than just one.

 Critical Thinking Questions: What are the advantages and disadvantages of multivoting? Would you consider using this technique? Why or why not?

Nominal Group Technique

The NGT is a more structured process that may be effective if there are status differences in the team or if the team has one or more dominating participants. The group meets face-to-face, but the discussion is more restricted than in brainstorming or consensus decision making. This process reduces status differentials since participants write their ideas on index cards, and they are collected by a facilitator. This process is particularly effective when the team has a dominating participant who shuts down the team discussion with criticism. Research has indicated that NGT works better than brainstorming.[61] NGT is often used by senior management teams as a preparation tool for productive strategy meetings. The steps for the NGT follow:[62]

1. Each team member independently writes their ideas on the problem on 3x5 cards or slips of paper.
2. Each member presents one idea to the team. The cards are collected by the facilitator who can either read them or redistribute them randomly to the team members who then read the ideas on the card. This way, no one is identified with a particular idea.
3. The discussion continues until all ideas are heard and recorded.
4. The team discusses the ideas and asks questions to clarify them.
5. Each team member then silently ranks the ideas independently. The idea with the highest total ranking is the final decision.

Stepladder

The stepladder technique is a newer technique and may also be an effective way to combat the challenge of dominating participants in the team. It has five basic steps:

1. **Present the task.** Before getting together as a group, present the task or problem to all members. Give everyone sufficient time to think about what needs to be done and to form their own opinions on how to best accomplish the task or solve the problem.
2. **Two-member discussion.** Form a core group of two members. Have them discuss the problem.
3. **Add one member.** Add a third group member to the core group. The third member presents ideas to the first two members *before* hearing the ideas that have already been discussed. After all three members have laid out their solutions and ideas, they discuss their options together.
4. **Repeat, adding one member at a time.** Repeat the same process by adding a fourth member and so on to the group. Allow time for discussion after each additional member has presented his or her ideas.
5. **Final decision.** Reach a final decision only after all members have been brought in and presented their ideas.[63]

An experiment was conducted to see if the stepladder technique resulted in higher-quality decisions compared to consensus decision making.[64] Stepladder groups produced significantly higher-quality decisions than did conventional groups in which all members worked on the problem at the same time. Stepladder group decisions surpassed the quality of their best individual members' decisions 56% of the time. In contrast, conventional group decisions surpassed the quality of their best members' decisions only 13% of the time. The stepladder technique is suggested as a way to prevent teams from making decision errors such as **groupthink.** Groupthink and other team challenges will be discussed in the following sections.

TEAM CHALLENGES

Despite the best efforts to form an effective team by using a charter and establishing norms that result in cohesion, teams still encounter challenges. In fact, cohesion may work against the team and result in what is known as groupthink. Groupthink and other challenges to established teams are discussed in the following sections.

Groupthink

Groupthink is a team decision-making challenge that arises due to a high degree of cohesiveness and group norms that result in conformity.[65] Groupthink is defined as the conformity-seeking tendency of the group, which results in compromised decision making. Due to group pressure, the team does not survey all alternatives and expressions of views that go against the majority of team member are suppressed. Team members apply direct pressure on dissenters and urge them to go along with the majority. The symptoms of groupthink are as follows:

1. **Group rationalization.** The team members generate explanations that support their preferred course of action.
2. **Direct pressure.** Those who speak out against the group decision are pressured into conformity.
3. **Suppression.** Members with differing views don't share them with the group for fear of ostracism and/or ridicule.
4. **Illusion of unanimity.** The team members believe that they are in agreement. But in fact, they are not. Dissenting views have been suppressed. Not speaking is interpreted as support for the team decision.

Groupthink occurs most often in highly cohesive groups and when the group is confident about their course of action early in the process.[66] The initial research on groupthink involved case studies of public policy decision such as the Bay of Pigs Invasion of Cuba and the attack on Pearl Harbor.[67] Experimental research has partially supported Janiss' theory.[68] For example, an experiment tested groupthink and found partial support for the theory in that direct pressure from leaders increased the symptoms of groupthink.[69] Teams with directive leaders proposed and discussed fewer alternatives than groups with leaders who encouraged member participation. These teams were also willing to comply with the leaders' proposed solutions when the leaders stated their preferences early in the group discussion. The *Challenger* space shuttle disaster case has been interpreted using groupthink.[70] In this scenario, the decision by NASA to launch the space shuttle when temperatures were too low for O-rings to function properly resulted in the death of six astronauts and a civilian teacher. The analysis concludes that directive leadership and time pressure contributed to the impaired decision-making process of NASA engineers.

To minimize groupthink, the leader can avoid being too directive and encourage everyone to participate fully in team discussions. They could also employ the NGT or stepladder technique instead of consensus decision making to provide more structure and avoid conformity. The leader can assign a member of the team to play the devil's advocate, which is a role that challenges team assumptions and decisions throughout the process.

Critical Thinking Questions: Why is directive leadership the strongest antecedent to groupthink? What else can leaders do to prevent putting undue pressure on a group to conform to their decision preferences?

Most students recognize groupthink symptoms since they have probably occurred in student project teams. Think about a time when you felt like disagreeing with your team but stayed silent because the team was cohesive or you didn't want to create conflict. You

Social Loafing

may have been a victim of groupthink. A second group challenge that is common in student project teams is **social loafing.** You will recognize this one if you have ever been in a team where you (or a subgroup of team members) did all the work but others got the credit but didn't contribute.

Social Loafing

Social loafing is defined as the reduction in motivation and effort when individuals work collectively compared with when they work individually or coactively (i.e., they work with others but do not combine inputs into a group product).[71] Social loafing occurs more often in larger teams where individuals can hide in the team.[72] When there is skill redundancy, some team members may feel that their contributions are not valued. If others are slacking, then team members may stop contributing. Team members may not see the goal as valuable or agree with it, so they don't contribute. There are individual differences as well: Research has shown men are more likely to social loaf than women, and those from individualistic cultures are more likely to loaf.[73] Leaders can prevent social loafing by doing the following:

1. Keep teams small (four to six members)
2. Set meaningful team goals
3. Set clear roles for team members
3. Eliminate redundancy
4. Select members with high motivation and affinity for teamwork
5. Provide feedback and coaching to members who social loaf

Virtual Teams

Today, more work is being conducted through the Internet, in virtual teams. Virtual teams are defined as "functioning teams that rely on technology-mediated communication while crossing several different boundaries."[74] Such teams rely on technology to communicate, and this has significantly changed how teamwork is conducted. It has been suggested that virtual teams have more challenges in developing the needed TMMs needed to be effective.[75] In many cases, virtual team members are geographically dispersed and may even be working in different countries and time zones. A comparison of computer-mediated teams to face-to-face teams in a longitudinal study found the relationship between technology and performance depended on experience with the technology.[76] The results also suggested the newness of the medium to team members and not the newness of the group led to poorer task performance for computer groups. A review of studies on computer-mediated groups reported computer-based groups generated more ideas but had more limited interactions and took longer to complete their work compared with teams that met face-to-face.[77] Virtual teams may have less social support and direct interaction among team members, which is needed to build trust.[78] A meta-analysis of more than 5,000 teams found virtual teams share less information.[79] Also, virtual work and the use of e-mail in combination may change the distribution of information within an organization, and change knowledge flows.[80]

A study of student teams was conducted in which the leaders of virtual teams were compared with those in face-to-face teams.[81] Researchers found that leader behaviors focusing on the task and monitoring of performance significantly impacted the performance of virtual teams. Leaders can enhance the effectiveness of virtual teams by establishing trust, carefully monitoring e-mail, attending to team progress, and by sharing the team's work with others.[82] Advanced information technology (IT) will have a significant impact on leadership in organizations in the future, and leaders must be aware of the impact for leading virtual teams.[83] Additional guidelines for leading virtual teams are shown in Table 9.2.

Table 9.2 Practices of Effective Virtual Team Leaders	
Leadership Practices of Virtual Team Leaders	**How Do Virtual Team Leaders Do It?**
1 Establish and Maintain Trust Through the Use of Communication Technology	• Focusing the norms on how information is communicated • Revisiting and adjusting the communication norms as the team evolves ("virtual get-togethers") • Making progress explicit through use of team virtual workspace • Equal "suffering" when setting up meetings across different time zones
2 Ensure Diversity in the Team Is Understood, Appreciated, and Leveraged	• Prominent team expertise directory and skills matrix in the virtual workspace • Virtual sub-teaming to pair diverse members and rotate sub-team members • Allowing diverse opinions to be expressed through use of asynchronous electronic means (e g., electronic discussion threads)
3 Manage Virtual Work-Cycle and Meetings	• All idea divergence between meetings (asynchronous idea generation) and idea convergence and conflict resolution during virtual meetings (synchronous idea convergence) • Use the start of virtual meeting (each time) for social relationship building • During meeting—ensure through "check-ins" that everyone is engaged and heard from • End of meeting—ensure that the minutes and future work plan is posted to team repository
4 Monitor Team Progress Through the Use of Technology	• Closely scrutinize asynchronous (electronic threaded discussion and document postings in the knowledge repository) and synchronous (virtual meeting participation and instant messaging) communication patterns • Make progress explicit through balanced scorecard measurements posted in the team's virtual workspace
5 Enhance External Visibility of the Team and Its Members	• Frequent report-outs to a virtual steering committee (comprised of local bosses of team members)
6 Ensure Individuals Benefit From Participating in Virtual Teams	• Virtual reward ceremonies • Individual recognition at the start of each virtual meeting • Making each team member's "real location" boss aware of the member's contribution

Critical Thinking Question: Provide an example of a type of work that cannot be done by a virtual team. Why do you think this would be the case?

One of the advantages of virtual teams is that team members can be geographically dispersed. Members can contribute to teamwork from anywhere in a country or the world. In many cases, virtual teams are comprised of members from different cultures. Cultural differences affect teams (you will learn more about the effects of cultural values in Chapter 12). The challenge of multicultural team participation is addressed next.

Multicultural Teams

Not all team processes translate cross-culturally. One study surveyed members of 461 SMWTs in four countries: the United States, Finland, Belgium, and the Philippines.[84] Resistance to SMWTs was affected by cultural values of collectivism and power distance. Collectiveness is group orientation and power distance is respect for authority. Also, the degree of determinism (i.e., the belief that "people should not try to change the paths their lives are destined to take") affected reactions to the implementation of SMWTs. Employees in the Philippines were significantly more likely to reject self-management compared to employees in the United States. Caution should be exercised when implementing SMWTs and other forms of participation in countries with high power distance. Individuals in high power distance cultures respect authority and expect the leader to have all the answers. They may be confused by a leader who asks for their input and make the attribution that the leader is not competent to make the decision alone. Similar reactions to the offer of participation might be found in Russia and Mexico.[85,86] Participation in countries with high power distance may not be appropriate, and managers should check cultural assumptions before offering participation to multicultural teams.

Throughout this chapter, a clear theme is that the leader can set up groups for success by directing the group toward a meaningful goal, selecting the right decision-making tools, and preventing groupthink. In the concluding section of this chapter, the importance of team leadership is discussed further.

LEADERSHIP IMPLICATIONS: EMPOWERING THE TEAM

Research has shown that team leaders engage in certain behaviors that enhance team performance. A team leader who creates the right climate for a team increases empowerment.[87] **Leadership climate** is effective when a team leader gives their team many responsibilities, asks the team for advice when making decisions, is not too controlling, allows the team to set its own goals, stays out of the way when the team works on its performance problems, tells the team to expect a lot from itself, and trusts the team. A study of 62 teams in a Fortune 500 company found leadership climate is related to team performance through team empowerment.[88] More empowered teams are more productive and proactive than less empowered teams and have higher levels of customer service, job satisfaction, and commitment. Empowerment is also related to lower employee cynicism and "time theft" (spending time on non-work-related activities during working hours).[89] A meta-analysis of relationships between leader behaviors and team performance found task-focused behaviors are moderately related to perceived team effectiveness and team productivity. However, person-focused behaviors are more related to perceived team effectiveness, team productivity, and team learning than task-focused behaviors. Examining specific leader behaviors, empowerment behaviors accounted for nearly 30% of the variance in team learning.[90] Empowerment seems to be a critical aspect of the development of highly effective teams. Team members need to feel that they have the power to make significant decisions about their work.

In some cases, empowerment takes the form of the team being self-managed. SMWTs are teams that are empowered to lead themselves without a formal assigned leader. In a SMWT, decisions regarding the specific ways that tasks are performed are left up to the members of the team.[91] These teams are now common at the workplace, and they have been related to higher job satisfaction and commitment.[92] SMWTs are in place in 79% of Fortune 1000 companies and in 81% of manufacturing companies.[93] The role of the leader in a SMWT is to relate (build trust), scout (seek information and diagnose problems), persuade (gain external support and influence the team), and empower (delegate and coach). The research evidence on SMWTs reports mixed results, however. While members report that they are more satisfied, team performance may be more difficult to attain without a leader. For example, SMWT members don't manage conflict well, and this may result in an erosion of trust.[94] A study of SMWTs that compared them to traditional teams found that claims of the effectiveness of self-management may have been inflated; SMWTs did not perform better than traditional teams.[95] In sum, it appears that leadership matters for team performance. However, it is important that the leader create the right leadership climate for the team and empower the team to act.

 Critical Thinking Questions: Explain why the existence of SMWTs that also have a team leader poses a paradox for the leader. If a team is self-managed, what is the leader's role?

KEY TERMS

additive task, 225

adjourning, 226

brainstorming, 237

cohesion, 230

collective effect, 225

consensus, 237

consultative, 236

delegating, 235

facilitator, 236

forming, 226

groupthink, 242

idea evaluation, 238

idea generation, 238

leadership climate, 246

nominal group technique (NGT), 237

normative decision-making model, 235

norming, 226

performing, 226

punctuated equilibrium, 227

self-managed work team (SMWT), 225

social loafing, 244

storming, 226

synergy, 226

team affect, 230

team charter, 227

team mental models (TMMs), 235

team norms, 233

team performance curve, 226

team viability, 230

work teams, 224

SUGGESTIONS FOR FURTHER READING

Gostick, A., & Elton, C. (2010). *The orange revolution: How one great team can transform an entire organization*. New York, NY: Free Press.

Katzenbach, J. R., & Smith, D. K. (1993). *The wisdom of teams: Creating the high-performance organization*. New York, NY: Harper Business.

Senge, P. M. (1990). *The fifth discipline: The art and practice of the learning organization*. New York, NY: Currency Doubleday.

TOOLKIT ACTIVITY 9.1

The Team Charter

Getting Started: Developing Ground Rules

Anyone who plays sports has to learn the rules. Anyone who learns to play an instrument has to learn the techniques. The rules of "how we do things here" (the etiquette of the situation, the appropriate behaviors) are the ground rules.

Teams often begin making assumptions about ground rules. Members believe that everyone knows how it should be and how everyone should behave. When someone else's behavior fails to conform to one's own expectations, people tend to be surprised. Even more importantly, because the rules are not clear and because there has been no discussion as to how problems will be managed, unnecessary conflict follows. This assignment serves the following objectives:

- Gives you the opportunity to get to know your team members
- Provides a short but *important* task so that the team can learn to function quickly without a large portion of your grade resting on the initial outcome
- Enables the team to develop and understand the rules of conduct expected of each team member

Your team will be required to submit a team charter. The following points that must be included in your charter are listed next, with some examples of the kinds of questions that might be addressed. However, use these as starting points; be sure to address any other important issues that come up in your discussions.

Attendance

How often should we meet?
How long should our meetings be?
When is it okay to miss a meeting?

Lateness

Since team meetings should start on time, how do we deal with lateness?
What does "on time" mean?

Interruptions

How do we deal with interruptions?
What is allowed? Phone calls? Messages?

Food, Coffee, or Smoking Breaks

Do we have food or coffee?
Who cleans up?
How many breaks should we have?
How much socializing is permissible?

Participation

What do we mean by participation?
How do we encourage participation?
Are there group norms that we can establish to encourage participation?

Goals

What are the team's goals and objectives?
What is the team's mission?
How will the team keep members motivated?
How will the team reward itself (and individual members) for a job well done?

Norms

What behaviors are permissible?
How do we deal with inappropriate humor?
How do we deal with people who dominate, resist, are too quiet, are too noisy, etc.?
How will we monitor our progress?
What important roles need to be assumed by team members during the semester? How will these roles be assigned?

Decision Making

How do we make decisions?
What decisions must be agreed to by all?
What does consensus mean?

Conflict

How will the team encourage positive (creative) conflict and discourage negative (dysfunctional) conflict?
How can the team encourage and manage differences of opinion and different perspectives?

TOOLKIT

Sanction Issues (What Will the Team Do With Deviates?)

How will the team deal with members who violate the agreed-upon norms of the team? For example, how will social loafing or inadequate participation be dealt with?

Firing Team Members

What are the specific rules or criteria for firing a team member? (You must give two written notices to the person and a copy to the professor prior to dismissal.)

Team Member Strengths and Weaknesses

Each team member should be identified (name, phone number, e-mail) along with an assessment of his or her strengths and his or her areas for improvement.

Other

Are there other issues that have a positive or negative impact on the team?

The Next Step: A Name and a Logo

After your team has prepared its team charter, create a name for your team and design a logo. The name and logo should be meaningful to the team, reflecting an attribute that the team members believe is important (humor is allowed and encouraged, but both the team logo and name should be meaningful). The name is limited to one or two words. Write a brief explanation of your name and logo choice. Give a copy to your instructor (along with your team charter). Your team charter should also include the following:

- A cover page with the following printed on it: the team name; team logo; team member names; and course name, number, and section
- A page with team member names, phone numbers, and e-mail addresses
- Team charter rules and expectations
- A brief explanation of your team name and logo choice

Source: Adapted from: Cox, P. L., & Bobrowski, P. E. (2000). The team charter assignment: Improving the effectiveness of classroom teams. *Journal of Behavioral and Applied Management, 1*(1), 92–103.

TOOLKIT ACTIVITY 9.2

The Marshmallow Challenge (Team Exercise)

The Marshmallow Challenge has been tested worldwide consultant Tom Wujec. Wujec has run the challenge with different categories of teams such as CEO teams, teams of architects, teams of engineers, teams of business students, and teams of kindergarten children.

First, form teams of four people. You need a measuring tape and watch. Run the challenge with your group, and then watch the debriefing video provided at the web link below.

The goals and rules of the Marshmallow Challenge follow.

1. **Build the tallest freestanding structure:** The winning team is the one that has the tallest structure measured from the tabletop surface to the top of the marshmallow. That means the structure cannot be suspended from a higher structure, like a chair, ceiling, or chandelier.

2. **The entire marshmallow must be on top:** The entire marshmallow needs to be on the top of the structure. Cutting or eating part of the marshmallow disqualifies the team.
3. **Use as much or as little of the kit:** The team can use as many or as few of the 20 spaghetti sticks, as much or as little of the string or tape. The team cannot use the paper bag that the materials are in as part of their structure.
4. **Break up the spaghetti, string, or tape:** Teams are free to break the spaghetti, cut up the tape and string to create new structures.
5. **Observe the time limit:** You have 18 minutes to build your structure.

Source: www.marshmallowchallenge.com

TOOLKIT ACTIVITY 9.3

How to Run an Effective Meeting (Checklist)

Before the meeting:

- ☐ Set goals for the meeting, and prepare an agenda.
- ☐ Prioritize issues to be discussed, including carryover issues from previous meetings.
- ☐ Consult with team members to finalize the agenda.
- ☐ Research information necessary for making important decisions (or delegate this).
- ☐ Arrange logistics: date, time, place, catering. Select a comfortable and convenient meeting place.
- ☐ Send out announcements and reminders for the meeting, including the meeting agenda.
- ☐ Arrange for AV equipment, flip charts, markers, and other supplies.
- ☐ Arrive early to set up, and check for adequate lighting, ventilation, heating, or air-conditioning.
- ☐ Arrange seating, and post directional signs if needed.
- ☐ Prepare name tags or tent cards if needed.

During the meeting:

- ☐ Greet people as they arrive individually.
- ☐ Announce the nearest restrooms.
- ☐ Have the agenda at each person's place or projected on screen.
- ☐ Set a welcoming tone: introductions (you may want to include an icebreaker exercise if time permits).
- ☐ Review minutes from the previous meeting if appropriate.
- ☐ Provide background information, and review the meeting goals.
- ☐ Be courteous, respectful, and inclusive during the discussions.
- ☐ Start and finish the meeting on time.

Bring closure:

- ☐ Make decisions.
- ☐ Prepare action plans and follow up.
- ☐ Summarize main points and what was accomplished during the meeting.
- ☐ Schedule the next meeting (if needed).

After the meeting:

- ☐ E-mail participants, and thank them for their contributions.
- ☐ Distribute minutes of the meeting and action plans.
- ☐ Include a reminder about the next meeting.

Texting All Teams: Amazon Enters the Cell Phone Market

Cell phones are nothing new. But imagine if you got to help develop the new phone from Amazon. Would it slide open to have double touch screens so you can do two things at once? Would it allow you to video call several of your friends at once? Would you be able to use your phone as a USB drive and let it attach to computers or projectors for presentations? Or would you design it to fit the business niche, with advanced teleconferencing abilities so that you could deliver a presentation and run a meeting all through your phone from anywhere?

Lab126 is Amazon's private Skunk Works that employs over 1,600 people. The lab spent the past 5 years developing Amazon's new smartphone called the Fire Phone. It includes sensors that allow phone users to operate the phone and play games without having to touch the screen. The phone also has infrared cameras that allow images to move with the user and show images in 3-D.

Development of the Fire Phone began in 2009 and was hindered by technical and organizational challenges. Employees were tasked with the mission of creating a phone that would be different and better for Amazon's most engaged customers. To do so, teams were created and put in charge of finding the right cameras, how to stabilize the 3-D effect, how to use camera tracking for scrolling and interacting with the menus, how to enhance the integration with the Amazon App Store and Prime, and how to make customers aware of the new features. Leadership on the project changed several times, with CEO Jeff Bezos even stepping in to lead the project. The teams themselves had to deal with conflicts among one another, balancing the desires of management, the drive to make something cool, and the budgetary and technological requirements.

Discussion Questions

1. In designing the Fire Phone, Amazon employees were tasked with being very creative. What do you think the different feature teams did to come up with creative ideas for the phone? How do you think Amazon evaluated the team's success?
2. With such a creative team, it's likely you'll come up with a number of ideas. How would the team decide what would be the best features to include? What factors do you think will be the biggest in making the decision? When should you call in a leader or supervisor?
3. How could leadership changes hinder the team's relationships and effectiveness? Which do you think would have the most impact: the leader's attitude, the leader's personality, or the leader's style?
4. You've come up with what you think is a great idea for the phone, and your teammates, who you have developed a very good relationship with, like it as well. How can you be sure that it is a good idea and not a by-product of the groupthink effect?

Source: Developed from Stone, B. (2014, June 17). Inside the secretive R & D lab behind the Amazon Fire Phone. *Businessweek.* Retrieved from http://www.businessweek.com/articles/2014-06-17/inside-the-secretive-r-and-d-lab-behind-the-amazon-phone#r=nav-f-story; Pierce, D. (2014, June 18). The Amazon smartphone is here: Meet the Fire Phone: A $199 phone with 3D cameras and all the Amazon services in the world. Retrieved from http://www.theverge .com/2014/6/18/5819516/meet-the-fire-phone

Teamwork Orientation

This self-assessment exercise identifies your propensity toward working in teams. The goal is for you to learn about yourself. There are no right or wrong answers, and this is not a test. You don't have to share your results with others unless you wish to do so.

Instructions: Circle the response that best describes your behavior.

As an example, the answer to a statement could look like this:

I enjoy communicating in teams.

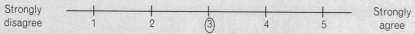

Strongly disagree — 1 — 2 — ③ — 4 — 5 — Strongly agree

This response indicates that you neither agree nor disagree with the statement.

1. The basic idea of the team concept is good.

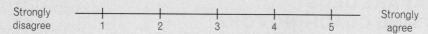

Strongly disagree — 1 — 2 — 3 — 4 — 5 — Strongly agree

2. Teams are essential for effective organizational functioning.

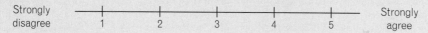

Strongly disagree — 1 — 2 — 3 — 4 — 5 — Strongly agree

3. I feel positive about working in a team.

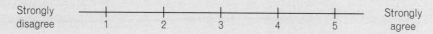

Strongly disagree — 1 — 2 — 3 — 4 — 5 — Strongly agree

4. Teams are good for organizations.

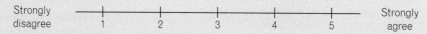

Strongly disagree — 1 — 2 — 3 — 4 — 5 — Strongly agree

5. The team concept helps organizations.

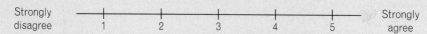

Strongly disagree — 1 — 2 — 3 — 4 — 5 — Strongly agree

Scoring: Add your responses to determine your total for team orientation. Higher scores suggest a higher propensity for teamwork. In general, scores from 5 to 12 indicate a lower interest in being on a team and scores above 13 indicate a higher interest in being on a team.

Source: Adapted from Scandura, T. A. (1995). *Management practices survey.* University of Miami, Coral Gables, FL.

10

MANAGING CONFLICT AND NEGOTIATION

WHAT ARE CEOS GETTING COACHING FOR?

A recent poll conducted by Stanford University and the Miles Group asked CEOs two questions: What skills are you working on? What skills do you think you need more development for? They also asked their boards of directors what skills CEOs need development in. The results are shown in the upcoming graph. Conflict management skills were the most mentioned skill that CEOs believed they needed development in (42.9% reported needing to develop this skill). What is also interesting about these poll results is that CEOs also reported that they were working on skills related to conflict management such as listening (32.1%) and persuasion (14.3%). Overall, many of the skills the CEOs were working on were organizational behavior (OB)-related and the one that they were receiving the most coaching for is leadership—specifically sharing leadership and delegating (37.2%). Despite getting coaching for sharing leadership, the CEOs (35.7%) still reported that they needed even more development in this area. Their boards agreed with 22% reporting that their CEO needed shared leadership skills. From the board's point of view, the ability to mentor followers and develop talent was the most often mentioned skill (24.4%). The results of this poll underscore the importance of interpersonal skills and the ability to manage **conflict** was the number one skill needing development:

> Conflict management is critical in the CEO role—just about anything that gets to the CEO's desk has an element of pleasing someone and making someone else unhappy. When the CEO avoids conflict, it can shut down the whole organization: Decisions are not made and problems fester, creating a domino effect of unproductive behaviors down the ladder. A CEO who can manage and channel conflict in a constructive way can get to the root of issues, apply rigor to the team's thinking, and, ultimately drive the best outcomes. So cultivating this skill can be a powerful tool to help the entire organization.[1]

This chapter will review the research on conflict management in organizations. The relationship between conflict and performance will be emphasized, with coverage of both interpersonal two-party and team conflict.

Learning Objectives

After studying this chapter, you should be able to do the following:

10.1: Describe the causes of conflict in organizations and devise solutions for them.

10.2: Compare and contrast the five conflict resolution styles.

10.3: Explain how team conflict affects team performance.

10.4: Explain how third-party interventions can reduce conflict.

10.5: Provide an example of how managing conflict differs across cultures.

10.6: Describe the negotiation process, and explain the difference between integrative and distributive bargaining.

10.7: Illustrate how perspective taking enhances negotiation by providing an example.

Get the edge on your studies at edge.sagepub.com/scandura
- Take the chapter quiz
- Review key terms with eFlashcards
- Explore multimedia resources, SAGE readings, and more!

⑤SAGE edge™

Critical Thinking Questions: Do you agree that conflict resolution is the most important skill that leaders need? Which other skills do you think are most important?

Interpersonal
Conflict

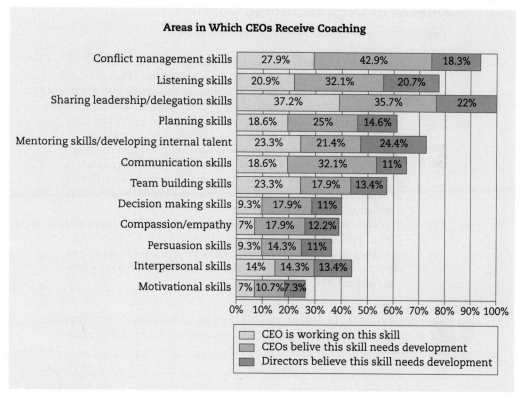

Areas in Which CEOs Receive Coaching

Skill	CEO is working on this skill	CEOs believe this skill needs development	Directors believe this skill needs development
Conflict management skills	27.9%	42.9%	18.3%
Listening skills	20.9%	32.1%	20.7%
Sharing leadership/delegation skills	37.2%	35.7%	22%
Planning skills	18.6%	25%	14.6%
Mentoring skills/developing internal talent	23.3%	21.4%	24.4%
Communication skills	18.6%	32.1%	11%
Team building skills	23.3%	17.9%	13.4%
Decision making skills	9.3%	17.9%	11%
Compassion/empathy	7%	17.9%	12.2%
Persuasion skills	9.3%	14.3%	11%
Interpersonal skills	14%	14.3%	13.4%
Motivational skills	7%	10.7%	7.3%

☐ CEO is working on this skill
◩ CEOs belive this skill needs development
◼ Directors believe this skill needs development

Source: Gavett, G. (2013). Research: What CEOs really want from coaching. (retrieved on December 23, 2013 from: http://blogs.hbr.org/2013/08/research-ceos-and-the-coaching/).

WHAT IS CONFLICT?

Learning Objective 10.1: Describe the causes of conflict in organizations and devise solutions for them.

Conflict is defined as "the process that begins when one party perceives that the other has negatively affected, or is about to negatively affect, something that he or she cares about" (p. 653).[2] Note that conflict is a perception, and as discussed in Chapter 5, perceptions don't always line up with reality. However, they do influence behavior and they can be changed, which is essential for leaders to keep in mind as they approach conflict resolution in organizations. Managing conflict is a skill that managers at all levels need, not just CEOs. This suggests that managing conflict is an important aspect of a leader's job and that most leaders are not well equipped to deal with it. In this chapter, we will review the evidence-based research on conflict and discuss how it can be effectively managed. First, it is important to understand what causes conflict in the first place (so that some conflict might be avoided).

Causes of Organizational Conflict

There are three general sources of organizational conflict):[3]

1. **Substantive conflict.** This occurs because people have different opinions on important issues in the organization that affect them. For example, there may be differences of opinion about which advertising campaign would best promote a new product. Such conflict can result in better decisions because both sides have to defend their position.
2. **Affective conflict.** This is conflict that engenders strong emotions such as anger or disgust. This may be due to personality differences or arguments. For example, two individuals in the organization escalate an argument to the level of shouting (it happens). This form of conflict may be highly disruptive to both parties and may even create stress for other members of the work group.
3. **Process conflict.** At times, people disagree on what course of action to pursue or the best way to operate even after a decision has been made. For example, team members may disagree on what aspects of a project should be assigned to specific individuals. This type of conflict reduces team performance.

 Critical Thinking Questions: How do the three forms of conflict relate to one another? For example, how might affective conflict affect process conflict?

An organizational development (OD) company provides some specific examples of where conflict in organizations may originate and recommend solutions a leader may follow to resolve each type:[4]

1. Personalities

   - Organizational strife is sometimes traced to personalities (as we learned in Chapter 3). This is one person differing with another based on how he or she feels about that person.
   - Solution: Train everyone to recognize the personality types along with their inherent strengths and weaknesses so that they understand one another. For example, the Big Five personality assessment (included in this textbook in Self-Assessment 3.1 for Chapter 3) can be given to team members. Based on the results, team members can discuss their personality differences and how they affect team interactions (extraverts may be dominating the team meetings, for example).

2. Sensitivity/hurt

Dealing with
Differences

- This occurs when a person, because of low self-esteem, insecurity, or other factors in his or her personal life, sometimes feels attacked by perceived criticism.
- Solution: Adopt the belief that even negative behaviors may have a positive intention. Use active listening, and ask questions to understand the root cause of the problem.

3. Differences in perception and values

- Most conflict results from the varying ways people view the world. These incongruent views are traceable to differences in personality, culture, race, experience, education, occupation, and socioeconomic class, as examples.
- Solution: A leader must set and communicate the values for the organization.

4. Differences over facts

- A fact is a piece of data that can be quantified or an event that can be documented. Arguments over facts typically need not last very long since they are verifiable. But a statement like "It is a fact that you are insensitive to my feelings" is neither documentable nor quantifiable is actually a difference in perception.
- Solution: Have a neutral third party or expert arbitrate the dispute (third-party interventions will be discussed later in this chapter).

5. Differences over goals and priorities

- This is a disagreement over strategy. For example, this may be an argument about whether a bank should focus more resources on international banking or on community banking. Another example would be whether or not to increase the amount of advanced professional training given to employees.
- Solution: A leader must set, communicate, and enforce the goals and values for the organization.

6. Differences over methods

- Two sides may have similar goals but disagree on how to achieve them. For example, a manager and their direct reports may not agree on how a training program should be conducted.
- Solution: Try perspective taking (see Case Study 10.1). Read the case study and practice perspective taking on a controversial issue where people have different points of view. Another alternative is to have a neutral third party or expert arbitrate the dispute.

7. Competition for scarce resources

- This occurs when there are limited resources that must be allocated in the organization. For example, two managers might argue over who has the greater need for an assistant, whose budget should be increased more, or how to allocate recently purchased computers.

- Solution: Upper-level management must set and communicate the values hierarchy for the organization. Resources can then be allocated based upon alignment with the organization's priorities.

8. Competition for supremacy

   - This occurs when one person seeks to outdo or outshine another person. You might see it when two employees compete for a promotion or for power. Depending on personalities, this type of conflict can be visible or very subtle.
   - Solution: A leader must set and communicate the values for the organization and emphasize that everyone's contribution matters.

9. Misunderstanding

   - The majority of what looks like interpersonal conflict is actually a communication breakdown. Communication, if not attended to, is as likely to fail as to succeed. And when it does, a listener's incorrect inferences about a speaker's intent often create interpersonal conflict. Communication will be discussed in more detail in Chapter 11.
   - Solution: Ask this question—"What else could this mean?"— before assuming a negative intent of the other person.

10. Unfulfilled expectations

    - Many of the causes listed previously can be linked to one person not fulfilling the expectations of another. Unfulfilled expectations are often the cause of firings and other forms of relational breakdown. Expectations go unfulfilled because they may be unreasonable, inappropriate, too numerous, or unstated.
    - Solution: Use active listening and questioning techniques to set and clarify expectations on a regular basis (not only during the performance appraisal process).

 Critical Thinking Question: How would you resolve a conflict between two of your direct reports who both want an office with a window when there is only one such office available?

As these examples illustrate, the leader can take actions that affect whether conflict is dysfunctional or may become productive. It is also clear from the solutions suggested that conflict may result in either higher or lower performance in organizations. The next section discusses whether conflict can be good for an organization.

Is Conflict Always Bad?

OB research has recognized that there are some situations where conflict may have a positive effect on performance.[5] There is a difference between unproductive (dysfunctional) organizational conflict and functional (productive) conflict. Conflict may be productive if it aligns with the goals of the organization and improves performance.[6] Dysfunctional conflict can harm relationships between leaders and followers and among teammates and ultimately harms performance.[7] A useful way to think about the relationship between conflict and performance is shown in Figure 10.1. As shown in the figure, on the left-hand side, if conflict is too low, there may be apathy and a lack of constructive discussion regarding important issues that need to be addressed. People may even be avoiding conflict, which is dysfunctional. As the level of conflict increases, performance increases as long as the conflict is aligned with the goals of the organization and does not become personal.

 Conflict and Creativity

Productive (functional) conflict enhances organizational performance.[8] However, at a point, too much conflict may become unproductive or even dysfunctional, particularly if it brings affective conflict in which individuals become frustrated or angry. Performance may begin to suffer as the level of conflict becomes too much and begins to disrupt the work process. For example, people may become so involved with the conflict that they spend time complaining to one another rather than on work that needs to be performed. Thus, it is important to keep in mind that how conflict is managed by the leader plays a pivotal role in channeling conflict toward the organization's goals and ensuring that unproductive conflict is resolved before it harms performance. This approach focuses on **task conflict**, but this is only one form of conflict—**relationship conflict** exists in organizations as well, and research has shown that they may affect performance differently.

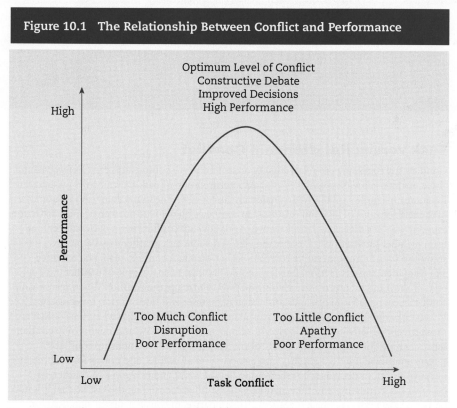

Figure 10.1 The Relationship Between Conflict and Performance

Optimum Level of Conflict
Constructive Debate
Improved Decisions
High Performance

High

Performance

Too Much Conflict
Disruption
Poor Performance

Too Little Conflict
Apathy
Poor Performance

Low

Low   Task Conflict   High

Source: Adapted from: Duarte, M., & Davies, G. (2003). Testing the conflict–performance assumption in business-to-business relationships. *Industrial Marketing Management*, 32(2), 91–99.

Planned Conflict: The Devil Made Me Do It!

Planned, or programmed, conflict is the process of raising differences of opinions regardless of the preferred course of action of the decision makers. Devil's advocacy is a technique in which one member is assigned to be play a role of the devil's advocate and critically evaluate the leader's (or a team's) decision. This is one of the recommended strategies for preventing groupthink (refer to Chapter 9). The devil's advocate method is the application of critical thinking to decisions to uncover assumptions and provide a reality check. Devil's advocacy leads to higher-quality recommendations and assumptions compared to consensus decision making (Schweiger, Sandberg, & Ragan, 1986).[9] Appropriate application of the devil's advocate method may increase the creativity of decisions and avoid errors. The steps for the devil's advocacy approach are as follows:

1. Propose a course of action.
2. Assign a devil's advocate to critique the proposal.
3. Present the critique to the decision maker(s).
4. Gather additional information if the critique reveals it is needed.
5. Make a decision to adopt, modify, or end the proposed course of action.
6. Monitor the implementation of the decision.

Discussion Questions:

1. Explain why assigning a devil's advocate during a decision-making meeting reduces groupthink.
2. Give an example of a decision you have been involved in that might have benefited from the assignment of a devil's advocate using the previously given steps.

Sources: Cosier, R. A., & Schwenk, C. R. (1990). Agreement and thinking alike: Ingredients for improper decisions. *Academy of Management Executive,* 4(1), 72–73; Schweiger, D. M., Sandberg, W. R., & Ragan, J. R. (1987). Group approaches for improving strategic decision making: A comparative analysis of dialectical inquiry, devil's advocacy, and consensus. *Academy of Management Journal, 29*(1), 51–71.

Task Versus Relationship Conflict

Conflict may focus on task-related issues or around relationship issues.[10,11] Disagreements about resource allocation, policies, or even interpretation of data are known as task conflict. Relationship conflict involves personality clashes or differences in values.[12] A meta-analysis of the relationships of task and relationship conflict with team performance and satisfaction found strong negative associations between relationship conflict, team performance, and team member satisfaction.[13] Despite the idea that some task conflict may be positive, this study also found strong negative correlations between task conflict, team performance, and team member satisfaction. Leaders should first diagnose the type of conflict (task or relationship) and then provide coaching on how to manage the conflict. When relationship conflicts occur, performance and satisfaction may suffer and intervention is necessary. When task conflicts emerge, team performance may benefit but only when the conflict is managed constructively by the leader. It is important to keep task and relationship conflict separate. Emotions play an important role in linking task and relationship conflict.[14] Group emotional intelligence (EI), good working relationships, and norms for suppressing negative emotions decrease the relationship between task and relationship conflict. In other words, regulating emotions may keep the conflict focused on the task so that it is not perceived as a personal attack on others. To summarize, in considering the potential for conflict to be productive, active conflict management by the leader to develop a climate of openness and trust is essential or conflict may harm performance. In addition, regulating emotions also helps focus the conflict on the task and not personal relationships.

 Critical Thinking Questions: What can a leader do specifically to keep followers focused on the task? How can a leader develop trust with followers so that conflict management is effective?

As this section has suggested, conflict at work may become personal. It may even escalate to more intense levels. The next section discusses workplace aggression and violence and how leaders should address it.

Workplace Aggression and Violence

Workplace incivility appears to be on the rise (refer to the boxed insert). In some cases, incivility may escalate to aggression or even workplace violence.[15] The U.S. Department of Labor reports that every year, 2 million people in the United States are victims of nonfatal violence at the workplace.[16] They cite data from the U.S. Department of Justice, which found violence to be a leading cause of fatal injuries at work with about 1,000 workplace homicides per year. This violence occurs in a variety of situations, including robberies and other crimes, actions by dissatisfied clients or customers, and acts perpetrated by disgruntled coworkers or coworkers who have been fired.

It is difficult to profile the type of employee who may commit workplace violence, but a combination of personal and workplace factors must be considered. For example, alcohol use or a history of aggression may combine with perceived organizational injustice to evoke a violent response.[17] The term *going postal* denotes the situation in which organizational members suddenly become extremely violent, derived after several incidents in the U.S. Postal Service in the late 1980s involving workplace homicides. Another incident reported in the media was a Connecticut Lottery Corporation accountant who searched for and then killed the corporation's president and three of his supervisors before killing himself.[18] Despite such media accounts of workplace violence, most aggression experienced by employees emanates from unhappy clients or customers.[19] The statistics on workplace aggression and violence are sobering, and it is important that leaders recognize it early and ensure that referrals are made to get employees the help they need (Chapter 13 will cover more ways that leaders can help employees cope with work pressures).

An important way that a leader can avoid escalation of conflict into workplace incivility or aggression is to engage in effective conflict resolution. The following sections will discuss different conflict-handling styles. It is important for a leader to recognize his or her own predisposition toward conflict as a first step to becoming effective at resolving conflicts at work.

From the previously given discussion of workplace aggression, it is clear that leaders need to take an active role in resolving workplace conflicts before they escalate. A

Is the Workplace Becoming More Uncivilized? Send in Miss Manners!

Workplace incivility is "low intensity deviant behavior with ambiguous intent to harm the target, in violation of workplace norms for mutual respect. Uncivil behaviors are characteristically rude and discourteous, displaying a lack of regard for others."[20] Results of public polls suggest that incivility at work is increasing with four out of five employees viewing disrespect and a lack of courtesy as a serious problem.[21] Nearly three out of five believe that the problem of workforce incivility is getting worse. One study found 71% of employees surveyed reported experiencing incivility at work at least once in the prior 5 years.[22] Another study of 603 nurses found 33% had experienced verbal abuse in the previous 5 days.[23] The rise of incivility may be due to the increasing rates of change; people don't have the time to be "nice" anymore. Another explanation is generational differences; the "me generation" is focused more on their own concerns and lacks respect for others.[24] Workplace incivility has been linked to outcomes for individuals and the organization. For example, a study conducted in a large public-sector organization found workplace incivility is related to sexual harassment and that both were detrimental to female employees'

well-being.[25] When employees experience incivility, they respond in various ways, including losing work time to avoid the uncivil person, decreasing their effort, thinking about quitting, and leaving the job to avoid the instigator.[26] Workplace incivility predicts burnout, which, in turn, predicts employees' intentions to quit.[27] In response to this growing concern, organizations are beginning to set zero-tolerance expectations for rude and disrespectful behaviors at work.[28] Others are even implementing training in proper etiquette for managers.[29] Workplace incivility needs to be addressed to reduce the personal and professional impact on employees and leaders need to take a proactive role to prevent it.

Discussion Questions:

1. Provide an example of an incident that you have experienced that was rude and discourteous, displaying a lack of regard for others. This can be an example you or another person at work or school experienced.

2. How did the experience of incivility (previously described) make you feel? What did you do about it?

Sources: Andersson, L. M., & Pearson, C. M. (1999). Tit-for-tat? The spiraling effect of incivility in the workplace. *Academy of Management Review, 24*(3), 452–471; Cortina, L. M., Johnson, P. R., & Indvik, J. (2001). Rudeness at work: Impulse over restraint. *Public Personnel Management, 30,* 457–465; Coutu, D. L. (2003, September). In praise of boundaries: A conversation with Miss Manners. *Harvard Business Review,* 41–45; Graydon, J., Kasta, W., & Khan, P. (1994, November–December). Verbal and physical abuse of nurses. *Canadian Journal of Nursing Administration,* 70–89; Magley, V. J., Williams, J. H., & Langhout, R. D. (2001). Incivility in the workplace: Incidence and impact. *Journal of Occupational Health Psychology, 6,* 64–80; Pearson, C., Andersson, L., & Porath, C. (2000, Fall). Assessing and attacking workplace incivility. *Organizational Dynamics,* 123–137; Taylor, S. G., Bedeian, A. G., Cole, M. S., & Zhang, Z. (in press). Developing and testing a dynamic model of workplace incivility change. *Journal of Management.* doi:0149206314535432.

leader should be able to adapt to situations and adjust their conflict resolution style as needed. However, most people have a dominant style that they use, particularly when they are under stress. It's important to know what your tendencies are toward avoiding conflict. Complete Self-Assessment 10.1 to learn what your conflict resolution style is so that you are aware of how you approach conflict. Complete the assessment before you read further.

CONFLICT RESOLUTION STYLES

Learning Objective 10.2: Compare and contrast the five conflict resolution styles.

Conflict resolution can be seen as two dimensions in a space that reflect possible outcomes for handling interpersonal conflict.[30,31] First, a person involved in a conflict is concerned with the satisfaction of their *own* concerns in a dispute. Second, the person may or may not also be concerned with the satisfaction of the *other party's* concerns. This may be represented by two dimensions, thus combining concern for self and others. This conceptualization was refined,[32] and a measure of conflict-handling styles called the Rahim Organizational Conflict Inventory (ROCI-II) was developed.[33] This framework is shown in Figure 10.2, depicting "concern for self" on the horizontal axis from high to low and "concern for others" on the vertical axis from low to high. By combining these two concerns, different approaches toward resolving conflicts result: integrating, obliging, dominating, avoiding, and compromising.

Figure 10.2   Two-Dimensional Model of the Styles of Handling Interpersonal Conflict

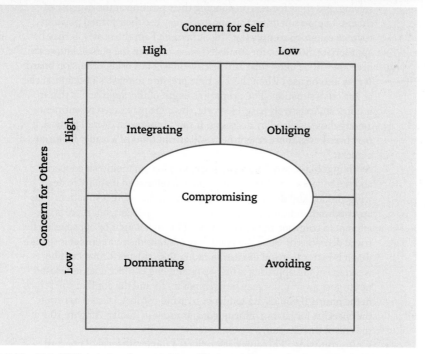

Source: Rahim, M. A. (1985). A strategy for managing conflict in complex organizations. *Human Relations, 38*(1), 81–89. p. 84.

These five conflict-handling styles are:[34,35]

Interdependence

- **Integrating.** Both parties confront the issue directly and discuss alternative courses of action. The strength of this approach is that it should provide a mutual benefits (win-win) solution and results in the conflict being resolved for the long term. The major drawback to this approach is that it is time consuming. This approach is the most appropriate for complex problems, strategic planning, and innovation.
- **Obliging.** In this approach, Figure 10.2 indicates that a person's concern for themselves is low but their concern for others is high. A person with a predisposition toward obliging "gives in" to the demands of others and may neglect his own concerns. It might be the best approach if the person is not sure they are right about a preferred course of action or it is politically best because the matter is so important to the other party. If used as a strategy, the person should consider requesting a reciprocated exchange in the future because they gave in the first time. It is not the best for complex problems and may result in a short-term solution. If it becomes a pattern, the obliging person may become resentful over time. The weakness of this strategy is that it is temporary, but its strength is that it will resolve the problem rather quickly.
- **Dominating.** In this approach, the individual is high with respect to his or her own concerns but low with respect to the concerns of others. People adopting this approach take a win-lose approach to problem solving, and their focus is on winning their position at the expense of others. The person using this approach may use their formal position to force others to comply (i.e., "do it because I am the boss"). It may be appropriate, however, for small decisions, or when the person knows the decision will be unpopular and discussion will not bring others on board. It may also be used when there is time pressure to make a decision, such as in a crisis situation. The primary strength of this approach is that it is quick and relatively easy. However, this style may breed resentment among those affected by decisions. If this becomes an overall pattern, it may breed even more resentment and attributions of a leader being an autocrat.
- **Avoiding.** In the avoiding style, a person is low on their own concerns and the concerns of others. This approach reflects an inability to deal with conflict, and the person withdraws from the conflict situation. This approach sidesteps the issues, which may be important, but there is no attempt to confront and resolve them. This style might be appropriate for trivial decisions or when the possibility of unproductive conflict is so high that it is better to avoid discussion rather than risk performance. The weakness of this approach is that by pretending conflict does not exist it rarely goes away and it may be a temporary fix and the conflict will return in the future. If you have a tendency to avoid conflict, be sure to review the checklist for having difficult conversations in Toolkit Activity 10.1 at the end of this chapter.
- **Compromising.** This approach reflects a moderate level of concern for the self and for others. It is a give-and-take approach to conflict in which concessions are made in exchange for getting some aspects of the

desired outcome. It is appropriate when parties have strongly opposing views and there is little hope of an integrative solution. It may also be the only possible approach when both parties have equivalent influence in the organization (e.g., two equally powerful vice presidents competing for resources). However, this approach may result in suboptimal or even strange solutions, which try to include disparate views. The main strength is that everyone gets something in a compromise; however, it is important to keep in mind that no one is completely satisfied with the outcome. For this reason, it can be unproductive and worse that even the dominating or obliging styles. Also, with compromise, there is not creative problem solving or an attempt to come up with a win-win solution as in the integrating style.

Critical Thinking Questions: Is one style better overall than the others for resolving conflict? Or does it depend on the situation like situational leadership? If you think it depends, what are the situational factors that should be considered?

While some early research suggested that the integrative style is best, later research suggests that the right conflict resolution style may depend upon the situation.[36,37] It is important to first correctly diagnose the conflict situation before selecting an intervention strategy. Generally, integrating is best for complex and strategic decisions, with compromise as a second option. The other styles may be effective to resolve smaller problems that occur on a day-to-day basis in the organization.[38] Table 10.1 lists the five conflict-handling styles and when they are appropriate or inappropriate.

This chapter has focused on interpersonal conflict to this point—conflict between two parties and strategies for conflict resolution. Toolkit Activity 10.1 offers a checklist for "difficult conversations," which is helpful in preparing for a one-on-one discussion with a person you have a conflict with. Conflict may also occur in teams; this situation may be among the most challenging for a leader to work through. Consider student teams that you have worked on during your undergraduate or graduate experience. Did they all run smoothly and free of conflict? If they did, you may consider yourself to be very lucky. Most students report that they have experienced dysfunctional and unproductive conflict that caused stress and perhaps even resulted in getting lower grades on team projects. Leaders in organizations have similar challenges with team conflict. Fortunately, the study of conflict at the team level has emerged as an important area of OB research that offers guidance for reducing team conflict.

TEAM CONFLICT AND PERFORMANCE

Learning Objective 10.3: Explain how team conflict affects team performance.

Conflict within teams produces stress and arguments that distract the team from working on the task and thus harms performance.[39] All types of conflict (task, relationship, and process) are detrimental to member satisfaction.[40,41] However, moderate levels of task conflict actually improve team performance because this stimulates information exchange

Table 10.1 Conflict-Handling Strategies and Situations Where They Are Appropriate or Inappropriate

Conflict Style	Situations Where Appropriate	Situations Where Inappropriate
Integrating	1. Issues are complex. 2. Synthesis of ideas is needed to come up with better solutions. 3. Commitment is needed from other parties for successful implementation. 4. Time is available for problem solving. 5. One party alone cannot solve the problem 6. Resources possessed by different parties are needed to solve their common problems.	1. The task or problem is simple. 2. Immediate decision is required. 3. Other parties are unconcerned about outcome. 4. Other parties do not have problem-solving skills.
Obliging	1. You believe that you may be wrong. 2. The issue is more important to the other party. 3. You are willing to give up something in exchange for something from the other party in the future. 4. You are dealing from a position of weakness. 5. Preserving a relationship is important.	1. The issue is important to you. 2. You believe that you are right. 3. The other party is wrong or unethical.
Dominating	1. The issue is trivial. 2. A speedy decision is needed. 3. An unpopular course of action is implemented. 4. It is necessary to overcome assertive subordinates. 5. An unfavorable decision by the other party may be costly to you. 6. Subordinates lack expertise to make technical decisions. 7. The issue is important to you.	1. The issue is complex. 2. The issue is not important to you. 3. Both parties are equally powerful. 4. The decision does not have to be made quickly. 5. Subordinates possess a high degree of competence.
Avoiding	1. The issue is trivial. 2. Potential dysfunctional effect of confronting the other party outweighs benefits of resolution. 3. A cooling off period is needed.	1. The issue is important to you. 2. It is your responsibility to make a decision. 3. Parties are unwilling to defer; the issue must be resolved. 4. Prompt attention is needed.
Compromising	1. Goals of parties are mutually exclusive. 2. Parties are equally powerful. 3. Consensus cannot be reached. 4. Integrating or dominating style is not successful. 5. A temporary solution to a complex problem is needed.	1. One party is more powerful. 2. The problem is complex enough, needing problem-solving approach.

Source: Rahim, M. A. (2002). Toward a theory of managing organizational conflict. *International Journal of Conflict Resolution, 13*(3), 206–235.

among team members. Task conflict and differences of opinion may improve decision quality by forcing members to see other viewpoints and think creatively.[42,43,44] Effective teamwork results in higher performance when conflict exists. For example, a study of 57 self-managed work teams (SMWTs; discussed in Chapter 9) found teams that improve or maintain top performance over time engage in three conflict resolution strategies:

Team Conflict and Performance

1. They focus on the content of interactions rather than delivery style.
2. They explicitly discuss reasons behind any decisions in distributing work assignments.
3. They assign work to members who have the relevant task expertise rather than assigning by other common means such as volunteering, default, or convenience.[45]

High-performing teams are more proactive in anticipating the need to resolve their conflicts and search for strategies that apply to all team members. Thus, the relationship between conflict and performance may depend upon how the team resolves conflict.

A meta-analysis found that the conflict to performance relationship in teams is more complex than previously assumed.[46] Task conflict and performance are more positively related when the association between task and relationship conflict is relatively weak. Also, the relationship of conflict to performance is stronger for top management teams rather than non-top management teams. Finally, when performance is measured by financial performance or decision quality rather than overall performance, there was a stronger effect of team conflict on performance. This meta-analysis provides support for the inverted-U relationship shown in Figure 10.1 at the team level.

The relationship of team conflict to performance appears to hold in other cultures. A test of the inverted-U relationship was conducted in two separate studies of work teams in Taiwan and Indonesia.[47] This study found the relationship between task conflict and team effectiveness outcomes varies as a function of the level of relationship conflict in the team. For team performance, the curvilinear relationship (inverted U) holds when relationship conflict is low but that task conflict is negatively related to performance when relationship conflict is high as shown in Figure 10.3. The authors concluded the following: "Team members who have high relationship conflict and interpersonal tensions are more likely to bicker so intensely that the slightest task conflict is associated with performance declines."[48] Therefore, both task and relationship conflict matter in terms of understanding the impact of conflict on team performance.

Critical Thinking Questions: How would you address one essential team member who continually interrupts others, creating conflict within the team, which harms the team's productivity? Would your approach be different if this team member were from another culture (Taiwan, for example)?

Despite attempts by leaders to facilitate conflict resolution, at times, conflict can continue for a long period of time and become complicated. There are situations where a third party must be called in to help resolve the conflict. This is sometimes done to avoid costly litigation. There are a number of options for resolving conflict using a third party. The next section discusses these options.

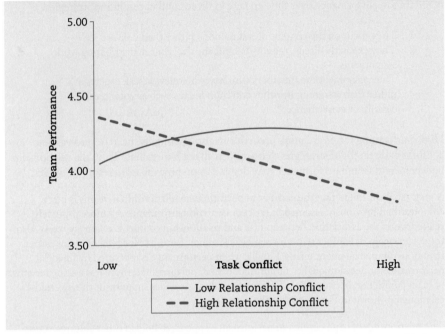

Figure 10.3 The Interaction of Task Conflict and Relationship Conflict in Predicting Team Performance

Source: Shaw, J. D., Zhu, J., Duffy, M. K., Scott, K. L., Shih, H. A., & Susanto, E. (2011). A contingency model of conflict and team effectiveness. *Journal of Applied Psychology, 96*(2), 391–400. p. 397.

THIRD-PARTY INTERVENTIONS

Learning Objective 10.4: Explain how third-party interventions can reduce conflict.

Facilitation is when a leader intervenes to resolve a conflict. Leaders should ask the following questions when they are attempting to resolve a conflict:[49]

1. Is intervention necessary or appropriate?
2. If so, what type of intervention is most appropriate?
3. Is the leader the appropriate person to intervene?
4. If not, should the services of an independent resource person be provided? If so, how might the leader make use of the resource person?

If the answer to the third question above is no, then the leader needs to consider other options to resolve the conflict by bringing in an independent resource person. These options are known as **alternative dispute resolution,** which are methods to resolve conflict that both parties agree to without involving litigation. There are a variety of techniques available, which range from the leader bringing in a third party to restore damaged relationships to legally binding arbitration.[50] The most commonly used alternative dispute resolution approaches used by organizations follow. For example, your university may have an **ombudsperson,** who works for the university but hears grievances from students on an informal basis and attempts to resolve them. Your university may also have an honor code council, which is an example of a **peer review** process (or dispute resolution panel) for resolving cases of alleged cheating by students. In organizations, a leader may call in a neutral third party (e.g., another manager) to attempt to resolve the conflict (known as **conciliation**).

Sometimes the conflict has become so complex that a more formalized dispute resolution method is needed. For example, mediation is when a third-party neutral person is called in to resolve the conflict. Mediators are formally trained to perform this role; typically they are outside of the organization in which the conflict has occurred. The mediator does not make a decision; their role is to help the parties reach an acceptable solution. In arbitration, both parties agree in advance to accept the decision, and it is made by a neutral third party. The decision of the arbitrator is legally binding on the parties. Mediation and arbitration are the most expensive, and thus, many organizations have ombudspersons or peer review available if the leader cannot resolve the conflict through facilitation or conciliation.

Critical Thinking Question: In the United States, employers have a legal right to require mandatory arbitration if their employees have a grievance. Do you agree or disagree? Explain your position.

RESOLVING CONFLICT ACROSS CULTURES

Learning Objective 10.5: Provide an example of how managing conflict differs across cultures.

Addressing conflict when working with a person from another culture requires knowledge of cultural differences (you will learn more about national culture values in Chapter 12). Research has shown that conflict resolution styles may differ by culture.[51] One study examined conflict resolution styles of MBA students from highly ranked programs in the United States, China, the Philippines, and India.[52] The study found that Chinese students are more likely to report an avoiding style, whereas the U.S. students were more likely to report a competing style. This is explained by the Chinese being more likely to value harmony over discord. In contrast, managers in the United States are more competitive and individualistic. Similar findings have been reported for U.S. students compared with Mexican students.[53]

Well-managed conflict contributes significantly to successful leadership in China.[54] Given China's emergence as a world market leader, they place an emphasis on openness and collaboration, which is consistent with their cultural values for group harmony. Another study compared conflict resolution styles for North American, Arab, and Russian negotiators.[55] This research found that North Americans tended to rely more on facts and logic. Arabs, in contrast, used emotional appeals to persuade others and made concessions during the bargaining process. Russians made few concessions and based their persuasion on

Tips for Negotiation

ideal principles. Research conducted on 409 expatriates suggests the following guidelines for resolving cross-cultural conflict (ranked in order of importance):[56]

1. Be a good listener.
2. Be sensitive to the needs of others.
3. (tied with the #2 skill) Be cooperative, rather than overly competitive.
4. Advocate inclusive (participative) leadership.
5. Compromise rather than dominate.
6. Build rapport through conversations.
7. Be compassionate and understanding.
8. Avoid conflict by emphasizing harmony.
9. Nurture others (develop and mentor).

Critical Thinking Question: How would you address conflict due to cultural differences in a team you lead that has members who are from China, Venezuela, and the United States?

The key takeaway from the research on cross-cultural conflict resolution is that the leader needs to consider the impact that national culture values may have on a person's perception of conflict and how to resolve it. In general, people from the United States tend to adopt a more competitive (or dominating) style.

One of the most common conflict-laden situations a leader encounters involves negotiation. Whether negotiating a deal with a supplier or a pay raise with a follower, negotiation is one of the key applications of conflict resolution techniques learned in this chapter. Conflict resolution styles, for example, may influence how a leader enters into a bargaining situation. For example, if a leader has a dominating style, they are only concerned about their own outcomes. With this style, it may be impossible to develop a win-win bargaining solution. The negotiation process is described in the following sections.

NEGOTIATION

Learning Objective 10.6: Describe the negotiation process, and explain the difference between integrative and distributive bargaining.

The steps involved in an ideal negotiation situation are shown in Figure 10.4. As shown in the figure, preparation for the negotiation is the first step. A leader needs to do their homework so they have all of the facts and possible options researched prior to negotiation. Next, the process of building the relationship follows. Not all negotiations start out discussing business. Often, there is an exchange of personal greetings prior to the actual bargaining process. This is an area to pay attention to in cross-cultural negotiations. For example, Arabs may prefer to get to know the negotiating partner better prior to negotiation. Next, the process of gathering and using information follows. For example, in a real estate negotiation, the seller's agent often has conducted a market analysis of the value of the property so that the buyer gets the property at a fair price. This information is shared with the seller, particularly if the price the seller wants is significantly above the market. The next step is the bidding process—offers

Figure 10.4 Steps in the Negotiation Process

Phase 1	Phase 2	Phase 3	Phase 4	Phase 5	Phase 6	Phase 7
Preparation →	Relationship building →	Information gathering →	Information using →	Bidding →	Closing the deal →	Implementing the agreement

Source: Thompson, L. (2012). *The mind and the heart of the negotiator* (5th ed.). Upper Saddle River, NJ: Prentice Hall.

and counteroffers are extended until a mutually agreeable solution is attained. Finally, the implementation of the decision involves the execution of the contract. In a purchasing situation, this would be the transfer of money and goods and/or services.

 Negotiation

There are two general types of negotiation—distributive and integrative—and these will be discussed next. Generally, distributive bargaining is hardball whereas integrative bargaining takes a softer approach to the deal. A meta-analysis of 34 studies analyzed the impact of hard and soft bargaining strategies on economic and emotional negotiation in distributive negotiations.[57] Hard bargaining led to higher economic outcomes, but soft bargaining led to higher emotional outcomes such as satisfaction and relationship development. Your approach to negotiation on these dimensions may determine how successful you are at getting the best deal. However, it is important to keep in mind what your goals are: getting the best deal, preserving the quality of the relationship, or both.

Distributive Bargaining

The distinction to remember about distributive bargaining is that the negotiator approaches the process as a "zero-sum" game. In other words, one person gains at the expense of the other. The negotiation views the possible outcome as a **fixed pie,** meaning that there is a limited amount of goods to be divided up and the goal is to get the largest share. Each negotiator has a goal, or target point, of what they want to get from the bargaining process. They may also have a **best alternative to a negotiated agreement (BATNA)** if they have prepared properly. This concept was put forth in the best-selling book *Getting to Yes: How to Get What You Want Without Giving In.*[58] The BATNA is an alternative that negotiators will accept if the negotiation reaches an impasse and they can't get their ideal outcome. If neither the preferred alternative nor the BATNA is accepted, then there is no deal. The strategies the negotiator uses in distributive bargaining involve making the first offer to anchor the bargaining process since people focus on the first information they see (recall the "primacy" effect discussed in Chapter 5).[59] Another tactic that research has shown to be effective is to use a deadline to put pressure on the person you are bargaining with to make a decision faster.[60] For example, an employer may make a job offer and request that the applicant respond within 1 week (known as an "exploding offer").

Integrative Bargaining

Integrative bargaining differs from distributive bargaining in one significant way: The parties do not see the process as a zero-sum game, and they believe that an agreement can be reached that satisfies all concerns.[61] Thus, they view the possible outcome space as an **expanding pie** in which a "win-win" solution can be reached. In general, integrative bargaining is preferable,

Make Conflict Productive

particularly when the parties value having a long-term relationship. No one walks away from the negotiation as a loser, so there are no hard feelings. Negotiators are more likely to want to bargain with one another again after an integrative bargain is reached—even the losing party.[62] For integrative bargaining to work, individuals need to be willing to share information (this is more difficult to achieve than it may seem because people tend to want to hide information on their goals and acceptable outcomes during negotiation). Another successful tactic is to put more issues out for discussion during a negotiation.[63] This is known as "sweetening the deal" with added incentives and different features. For example, when negotiating for a new car, dealers will often throw in extras such as an upgraded stereo system or sunroof to get the buyer focused on features other than the price of the car. To be effective in integrative bargaining, negotiators also need to get past the fixed position of one another and discuss what their real interests are.[64] This gets to what people really value since money has symbolic meaning in some cases (recall the discussion of the meaning of money from Chapter 8). For example, a person who is presenting their product on *Shark Tank*, a popular TV show where entrepreneurs pitch their products and services to investors, might really want to maintain control over their invention rather than make more money. Thus, they might accept an offer of less money but more control over their business in the long run. By focusing on interests, the investor might get a higher percentage of the profit by letting the inventor control their business. Finally, integrative bargaining requires creativity and the ability to think of novel solutions that can address the concerns of both parties.[65] A review of research on negotiation found that the principles put forth in Fisher and Ury's *Getting to Yes* have generally been supported by research evidence.[66] This book is recommended reading for all leaders, and the reference is provided in Suggestions for Further Reading at the end of this chapter.

Successful conflict resolution and negotiation requires the leader to be able to empathize with another person and view the situation as they do. Empathy is part of being emotionally intelligent (discussed in Chapter 3). Research has indicated that some individuals have a greater ability to engage in seeing another person's point of view than others. The concluding section discusses perspective taking and how it plays a key role in conflict resolution and negotiation.

LEADERSHIP IMPLICATIONS: PERSPECTIVE TAKING

Learning Objective 10.7: Illustrate how perspective taking enhances negotiation by providing an example.

Having EI and empathy may be a critical skill for resolving conflict and effective negotiation. To do this, a person needs to be able to see the situation from the other party's point of view. This is called **perspective taking,** which is defined as the ability to see things from another person's perspective that holds a view that conflicts with your own. There are two reasons why perspective taking helps resolve conflict.[67] First, when people engage in active perspective taking, they are more likely to empathize with the other person. Second, the expression of perspective taking relates to positive attributions about another person's behavior, such as recognizing the effects of external circumstances on what they do. Case Study 10.1 is a case study of a real situation that created a great deal of controversy. This is a good chance to practice your perspective-taking skills after you read the case study to see if you can see a situation from another point of view using empathy.

In this chapter, essential research evidence on identifying and resolving conflict was reviewed. Five conflict resolution styles were described with an emphasis on the leader being able to adapt the style used to the situation. In general, the integrating style is best for complex problems. The role of conflict at the team level was discussed, noting the importance of identifying task and relationship conflict so that a leader can manage the conflict appropriately. Workplace incivility extends to the classroom. Research has examined student perceptions of incivility of professors. Students' perceptions of incivility fall into two areas: a professor's competence and interest as well as respect for the individualism of students.[68] This chapter also covered conflict resolution in the context of negotiations and compared distributive bargaining with integrative bargaining. Toolkit Activity 10.2 offers an opportunity to practice win-win negotiating skills to negotiate a better salary. The chapter ends with the leadership implication of perspective taking where you see things from another person's point of view. Perspective taking is essential for both conflict resolution and negotiation.

$SAGE edge™

edge.sagepub.com/scandura

Want a better grade? Go to **edge.sagepub.com/scandura** for the tools you need to sharpen your study skills.

KEY TERMS

alternative dispute resolution, 268
best alternative to a negotiated agreement (BATNA), 271

conciliation, 269
conflict, 254
expanding pie, 271
facilitation, 268
fixed pie, 271

ombudsperson, 269
peer review, 269
perspective taking, 272
relationship conflict, 259
task conflict, 259

SUGGESTIONS FOR FURTHER READING

Brinkman, R., & Kirschner, R. (2012). *Dealing with people you can't stand: How to bring out the best in people at their worst.* New York, NY: McGraw-Hill.

Fisher, R., & Ury, W. (1981). *Getting to yes: Negotiating agreement without giving in.* Boston, MA: Houghton Mifflin.

Rahim, M. A. (2002). *Managing conflict in organizations* (3rd ed.). Westport, CT: Quorum Books.

Stone, D., Patton, B., & Heen, S. (1999). *Difficult conversations: How to discuss what matters most.* New York, NY: Penguin.

TOOLKIT ACTIVITY 10.1

Checklist for Difficult Conversations

☐ Before you jump into a difficult conversation, spend some private time to identify the difficulty and acknowledge different points of view.

- How do you see the situation?
- What assumptions are you making? What stories are you telling yourself?
- How might the other person perceive the same situation?
- What emotions is this problem stirring up for you?
- What is the impact of this situation on you, and what hypothesis do you have about the other person's intention?

☐ Be certain this is a conversation that is worth having.

- What is your purpose in addressing this issue or having this conversation?
- What will likely happen if you ignore this problem? How will you feel?
- How is this problem affecting the productivity and morale of your unit?

☐ Invite the other person to talk with you. Emphasize your interest in working well together and hearing their point of view. A couple of sentences you might consider using are as follows: "I would like to understand where you are coming from on ..." or "Can you say a little more about how you see things about ...?"

☐ Start the conversation by "seeking first to understand." Ask the other person an open-ended question that will get him or her to describe how he or she sees the situation. Do your very best listening. Listen with empathy. Acknowledge the other person's feelings and point of view. Paraphrase to see if you got it right.

☐ Share your own point of view, your intentions, and your feelings. Use I statements. Describe how you believe you got to where you are, including how you contributed to the problem. Take responsibility for your part.

☐ Talk about the future and what can happen differently so you don't end up in the same place. Offer what you plan to do differently. Ask the person what suggestions they have to resolve the situation. Suggest what you think the other person could do.

☐ Thank the other person for talking with you. Offer why it was important to resolve this conflict.

Source: Stone, D., Patton, B., & Heen, S. (1999). *Difficult conversations: How to discuss what matters most.* New York, NY: Penguin.

TOOLKIT ACTIVITY 10.2

Salary Negotiation

For this role-play exercise, you will find another classmate to negotiate with. Choose one of the roles (but don't look at the role of your negotiating partner, and don't show him or her the role you have been assigned).

Role of Pat (Boss)

You are the brand manager of a division of an organization that makes a variety of household products. You are in charge of a major brand of laundry detergent located in a downtown area in the Midwest. You have been having some trouble finding the right candidate for your open position in marketing research. While the job has been advertised, you have been taking on this responsibility in addition to your own job duties, so you are motivated to fill the position.

You are seriously considering the application of Terry, who is about to graduate with an MBA from a good school in Florida. You were impressed with Terry's assertiveness in pursuing the opportunity, and the interviews went well. Terry lacks specific marketing research experience but he has a great personality that you feel will be a good fit with others in your division. You are concerned that Terry may not want to relocate from great weather in South Florida to dreary winter weather in the Midwest, but you are ready to make the job offer.

Your company does not pay high salaries but has a generous bonus plan that could be up to 10% of the base salary. Typically, someone with Terry's lack of experience would start between $80,000 to $85,000, and you are prepared to make an offer in this range. You have been working for the company for 3 years, and you make $115,000. You may also offer relocation expenses up to $5,000.

You have another alternative candidate who did not interview as well but has an MBA from Wharton and has done an internship in marketing research at a competitor. This applicant is asking for $105,000 to start, and you don't like his attitude about insisting on this salary level. You wonder if his personality will be a good fit with your team.

You need to meet with Terry and make a decision whether to make the offer and the terms.

Role of Terry (Applicant)

You are graduating from a good business school in South Florida with an MBA in management in late May. You took a variety of management electives (leadership and teams) and enjoyed them, but you also enjoyed your introduction to a marketing course where you did a marketing research project on preferences for soft drinks. Your fiancée lives in the Midwest and does not want to relocate too far from where the family lives. You have found what you think is a perfect job in marketing research as an entry-level position with great management potential for the future. The job is a large metropolitan area that is listed in the top 10 in terms of quality of life due to major sports, a lively music scene, and fabulous restaurants. Based on your experience leading teams, you know this is the right job to really show your managerial skills.

You had two interviews that went well, and you liked Pat, who would be your boss. You feel that you would enjoy working with Pat and the division team members (some of whom you met during the interviews). You are sure that you made a positive impression on Pat although you lack specific experience in marketing research. You are good at statistics and feel that you can apply them in a marketing research position. You are expecting an offer from Pat in your next meeting, but you feel that you will have to negotiate for a good package.

You have done research at the career center at your school, and you know that this company has rather strict salary ranges for entry-level positions. You learned that starting salaries for management majors start at $80,000, but the average salaries for recent MBA graduates is around $100,000. You also learned that the company is doing well financially, and they can afford to pay well. You think you are above average in your leadership potential, and your friends are telling you not to accept an offer less than $100,000.

You have gotten a quote from a moving company from South Florida to the midwestern city where the company is located, and moving your furniture and car would cost around $9,000. You are hoping that the company can pay you in advance for the moving expenses.

You have another job offer with a small consulting firm in the Midwest. The offer is good at $100,000, including the bonus and stock options. You are certain that the potential for upward mobility would not be as good as it would be with a larger consumer products company. Also, the location is not as desirable as the consumer products company because it is a small city with limited quality of life opportunities.

Salary Negotiation Exercise Summary

Names: _____ (Pat: Boss)

_____ (Terry: Candidate)

Did you reach an agreement? ____ Yes ____ No

If not, why not? _____

_____

If so, what was the final agreement?

Salary _____

Benefits _____

Other _____

How satisfied are you with the agreement you made?

Pat:

| 1 | 2 | 3 | 4 | 5 | 6 | 7 | 8 | 9 | 10 |

Not at all Satisfied   Somewhat Satisfied   Very Satisfied

Terry:

| 1 | 2 | 3 | 4 | 5 | 6 | 7 | 8 | 9 | 10 |

Not at all Satisfied   Somewhat Satisfied   Very Satisfied

TOOLKIT ACTIVITY 10.3

Negotiation Style Assessment

Negotiating Partner's Name: _____

Your Name: _____

Instructions: Please rate your negotiating partner on the following aspects of performance in the negotiation you just completed. Do not be overly harsh or overly lenient.

1. My negotiating partner understood my interests.

Unacceptable	Poor	Acceptable	Very good	Exceptional
1	2	3	4	5

2. My negotiating partner saw things from my perspective.

Unacceptable	Poor	Acceptable	Very good	Exceptional
1	2	3	4	5

3. My negotiating partner adapted to my negotiating style.

Unacceptable	Poor	Acceptable	Very good	Exceptional
1	2	3	4	5

4. My negotiating partner was trustworthy.

Unacceptable	Poor	Acceptable	Very good	Exceptional
1	2	3	4	5

5. My negotiating partner managed the negotiation process well.

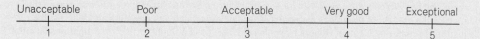

Unacceptable	Poor	Acceptable	Very good	Exceptional
1	2	3	4	5

6. My negotiating partner recognized opportunities for win-win outcomes.

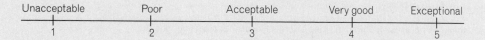

Unacceptable	Poor	Acceptable	Very good	Exceptional
1	2	3	4	5

Total: Add the responses for questions 1 through 6: _____ (scores range from 6 to 30). In general, a low score for integrative (win-win) bargaining style is between 6 and 19 and a high score for integrative bargaining style is above 19.

CASE STUDY 10.1

Perspective Taking: Captain Owen Honors

Naval captain Owen Honors was fired for the production of video skits with offensive content using navy equipment starring his crew members during 2006 and 2007. The following case study illustrates how different parties can view the same events differently leading to conflict:

On January 1, 2011, Norfolk's newspaper the *Virginian-Pilot* greeted the new year with a story of videos produced, written, and featuring naval captain Owen Honors, at the time commander of the USS *Enterprise*. Four days later, Captain Honors, 49, had been relieved of his command and essentially put on desk duty pending further investigation. The cited reason was this: "profound lack of good judgment and professionalism."

The *Virginian-Pilot* article reports that anonymous men and women, who served on the ship at the time the videos were created and aired, complained immediately to no avail. In fact, Captain Honors stated this in the introduction of his "last video": "Over the years I've gotten several complaints about inappropriate material during these videos, never to me personally but, gutlessly, through other channels." He then suggests the following: "This evening, all of you bleeding hearts... why don't just go ahead and hug yourself for the next 20 minutes or so, because there's a really good chance you're gonna be offended."

Although it appears that Captain Honors' supervisors learned of the videos at the time, Captain Honors was not reprimanded—other than told to cease production of them—and was ultimately promoted to commander of the USS *Enterprise* in May of 2010. It is important to note that it is not public knowledge as to who knew about the videos prior to the *Virginian-Pilot* article.

As a result of the videos surfacing, the Navy stripped Captain Honors of command of the USS *Enterprise*. However, the "firing" of Captain Owen Honors has not quieted the public debate over the videos or the naval response.

To do nothing is to condone. By not acting at the time, the navy essentially condoned the videos and Captain Honors' making of them. Perhaps the current navy leadership's response is one impacted by public relations; perhaps the existence of the videos had been the secret of a select few who protected Captain Honors from being penalized in the past. Whatever the impetus for the action taken, at this point the navy has made a public decision not to condone the videos or the behavior.

The public debate, however, exemplifies what so often happens in a conflict: Each side demands that the other side admit defeat and agree that the other side is right. Regardless of an individual's perspective—one of support for Captain Honors, one of agreement with the navy's decision, seeing nothing objectionable in the videos, or finding the videos offensive—the discourse is one of proving the other side wrong. Once this happens, the conflict grows and the discussion becomes polarized with each side refusing to consider how the other opinion is not wrong, just different.

As this scenario illustrates, the same events may be viewed and interpreted differently by different individuals who deeply care about an issue. Some support Captain Honors because he was attempting to entertain his crew members, and the videos had been shown for some time airing on the closed circuit televisions on the ship. Others view the content of the videos as repulsive sexual harassment and gay slurs and feel that the navy was justified in removing Captain Honors from his post. This case brought forth strong emotions on either side, indicating that people really care about the outcome or the issues that surfaced from the production of the videos.

Discussion Questions

1. Do you think the navy was justified in firing Captain Honors? Explain your position.
2. How open are you to another point of view on this case?
3. Take the opposite position to your point of view, and write a paragraph explaining the other point of view. For example, if you think the navy was wrong to fire Captain Honors, then write a statement that supports firing him.
4. Think about the other alternatives to conflict—compromise and collaboration—that don't involve one side losing and the other winning. In situations like the one in the case, is it possible for both sides to come to a compromise or collaboration? Why or why not? How might the number of parties play a role in the type of solution generated?

Source: Johnston, E. (2011). Workplace conflict case study: The navy & Capt. Owen Honors. Retrieved on December 13, 2012, from http://cfrmediation.com/workplace-conflict-case-study-the-navy-capt-owen-honors.

SELF-ASSESSMENT 10.1

Conflict Resolution Styles

This self-assessment exercise identifies your conflict resolution styles. There are no right or wrong answers, and this is not a test. The purpose of this assessment is for you to learn about yourself. You don't have to share your results with other classmates unless you wish to do so.

Part I. Taking the Assessment

Purpose:

1. To identify your conflict style
2. To examine how your conflict style varies in different contexts or relationships

Directions:

1. Think of two different situations (A and B) where you have a conflict, a disagreement, an argument, or a disappointment with someone, such as a roommate or a work associate. Write the name of the person for each situation that follows.
2. According to the following scale, fill in your scores for Person A and Person B. For each question, you will have two scores. For example, on question 1, the scoring might look like this: 1. 2 | 5 (see the example below).

Directions for taking the conflict scale: Please respond to the following 25 items. Be honest. There are no right or wrong answers!

You will be presented with some questions representing your approach to conflict.

As an example, the answers to situations could look like this:

Person A: __Miriam__ (write first name) Person B __Jose__ (write first name)

I try to resolve conflict constructively.

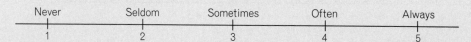

Person A __2__ | Person B __5__

This response indicates that you seldom try to resolve conflict with Miriam/constructively but you always try to resolve conflict with Jose constructively.

Person A: _____ (write first name)   Person B _____ (write first name)

1. I avoid being put on the spot. I keep conflicts to myself.

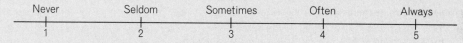

Person A _____ | Person B _____

2. I use my influence to get my ideas accepted.

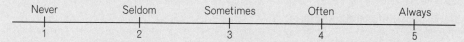

Person A _____ | Person B _____

3. I usually try to "split the difference" in order to resolve an issue.

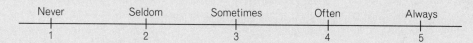

Person A _____ | Person B _____

4. I generally try to satisfy the other's needs.

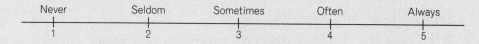

Person A _____ | Person B _____

5. I try to investigate an issue to find a solution acceptable to both of us.

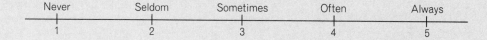

TOOLKIT

Person A _____ | Person B _____

6. I usually avoid open discussion of my differences with the other.

Never	Seldom	Sometimes	Often	Always
1	2	3	4	5

Person A _____ | Person B _____

7. I use my authority to make a decision in my favor.

Never	Seldom	Sometimes	Often	Always
1	2	3	4	5

Person A _____ | Person B _____

8. I try to find a middle course to resolve an impasse.

Never	Seldom	Sometimes	Often	Always
1	2	3	4	5

Person A _____ | Person B _____

9. I usually accommodate the other's wishes.

Never	Seldom	Sometimes	Often	Always
1	2	3	4	5

Person A _____ | Person B _____

10. I try to integrate my ideas with the other's to come up with a decision jointly.

Never	Seldom	Sometimes	Often	Always
1	2	3	4	5

Person A _____ | Person B_____

11. I try to stay away from disagreement with the other.

Never	Seldom	Sometimes	Often	Always
1	2	3	4	5

Person A _____ | Person B _____

12. I use my expertise to make a decision that favors me.

Never	Seldom	Sometimes	Often	Always
1	2	3	4	5

Person A _____ | Person B _____

13. I propose a middle ground for breaking deadlocks.

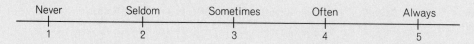

| Never | Seldom | Sometimes | Often | Always |
| 1 | 2 | 3 | 4 | 5 |

Person A _____ | Person B _____

14. I give in to the other's wishes.

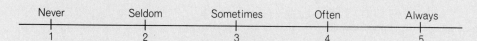

| Never | Seldom | Sometimes | Often | Always |
| 1 | 2 | 3 | 4 | 5 |

Person A _____ | Person B _____

15. I try to work with the other to find solutions that satisfy both of our expectations.

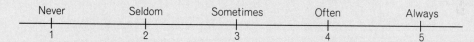

| Never | Seldom | Sometimes | Often | Always |
| 1 | 2 | 3 | 4 | 5 |

Person A _____ | Person B _____

16. I try to keep my disagreement to myself in order to avoid hard feelings.

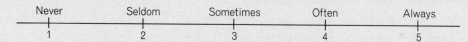

| Never | Seldom | Sometimes | Often | Always |
| 1 | 2 | 3 | 4 | 5 |

Person A _____ | Person B _____

17. I generally pursue my side of an issue.

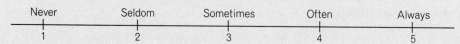

| Never | Seldom | Sometimes | Often | Always |
| 1 | 2 | 3 | 4 | 5 |

Person A _____ | Person B _____

18. I negotiate with the other to reach a compromise.

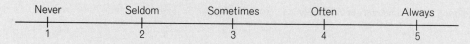

| Never | Seldom | Sometimes | Often | Always |
| 1 | 2 | 3 | 4 | 5 |

Person A _____ | Person B _____

19. I often go with the other's suggestions.

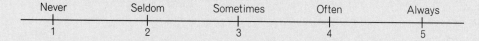

| Never | Seldom | Sometimes | Often | Always |
| 1 | 2 | 3 | 4 | 5 |

Person A _____ | Person B _____

20. I exchange accurate information with the other so we can solve a problem together.

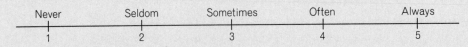

| Never | Seldom | Sometimes | Often | Always |
| 1 | 2 | 3 | 4 | 5 |

Person A _____ | Person B _____

21. I try to avoid unpleasant exchanges with the other.

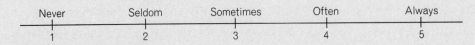

| Never | Seldom | Sometimes | Often | Always |
| 1 | 2 | 3 | 4 | 5 |

Person A _____ | Person B _____

22. I sometimes use my power to win.

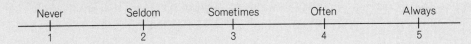

| Never | Seldom | Sometimes | Often | Always |
| 1 | 2 | 3 | 4 | 5 |

Person A _____ | Person B _____

23. I use give-and-take so that a compromise can be made.

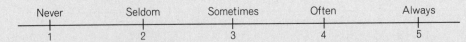

| Never | Seldom | Sometimes | Often | Always |
| 1 | 2 | 3 | 4 | 5 |

Person A _____ | Person B _____

24. I try to satisfy the other's expectations.

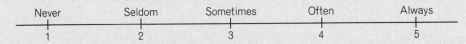

| Never | Seldom | Sometimes | Often | Always |
| 1 | 2 | 3 | 4 | 5 |

Person A _____ | Person B _____

25. I try to bring all our concerns out in the open so that the issues can be resolved.

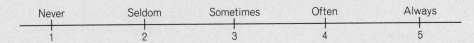

| Never | Seldom | Sometimes | Often | Always |
| 1 | 2 | 3 | 4 | 5 |

Person A _____ | Person B _____

TOOLKIT

Part II. Scoring Instructions

Add up your scores on the following questions:

A|B	A|B	A|B	A|B	A|B
1. __|__	2. __|__	3. __|__	4. __|__	5. __|__
6. __|__	7. __|__	8. __|__	9. __|__	10. __|__
11. __|__	12. __|__	13. __|__	14. __|__	15. __|__
16. __|__	17. __|__	18. __|__	19. __|__	20. __|__
21. __|__	22. __|__	23. __|__	24. __|__	25. __|__
__|__	__|__	__|__	__|__	__|__
A | B	A | B	A | B	A | B	A | B
Avoiding Totals	Dominating Totals	Compromising Totals	Obliging Totals	Integrating Totals
A__ | B__	A__ | B__	A__ | B__	A__ | B__	A__ | B__

Scoring Interpretation

This questionnaire is designed to identify your conflict style and examine how it varies in different relationships. By comparing your total scores for the different styles, you can discover which conflict style you rely most heavily upon and which style you use least. Furthermore, by comparing your scores for Person A and Person B, you can determine how your style varies or stays the same in different relationships. Your scores on this questionnaire are indicative of how you responded to a particular conflict at a specific time and therefore might change if you selected a different conflict or a different relationship. The conflict style questionnaire is not a personality test that labels or categorizes you; rather, it attempts to give you a sense of your more dominant and less dominant conflict styles.

Scores from 21 to 25 are representative of a very strong style.

Scores from 15 to 20 are representative of a strong style.

Scores from 11 to 15 are representative of an average style.

Scores from 5 to 10 are representative of a weak style.

Source: Adapted from Rahim, M. A., & Magner, N. R. (1995). Confirmatory factor analysis of the styles of handling interpersonal conflict: First-Order factor model and its invariance across groups. In W. Wilmot & J. Hocker (2011), Interpersonal conflict (pp. 146–148). Washington, DC: American Psychological Association. (Reprinted from Journal of Applied Psychology, 80[1], 122–132.)

TOOLKIT

11

ORGANIZATIONAL COMMUNICATION

"THIN SLICING" A CONVERSATION

Can the first few minutes of communication define the course of the conversation and the benefits or costs derived from it? These first few minutes are referred to as "thin slices" of behavior. Thin slices were studied by having college students evaluate 30-second video clips of instructors teaching a class.[1] These quick evaluations significantly predicted teacher ratings at the end of the semester. Research on thin slicing has shown that early interactions (minutes) predict conviction of criminals and divorce (in some cases, months or years in the future).[2] This fascinating line of research has revealed the surprising finding that observation of a thin slice of behavior (minutes or even seconds) predicts important outcomes such as professional competence as rated by a person conducting an employment interview. Early cues are often based on both verbal and nonverbal behaviors in communication.

An experimental study examined whether conversational dynamics early in negotiation predict the attractiveness of an employment package.[3] Researchers examined four types of initial communication: activity level, conversational engagement, emphasis, and vocal mirroring. Activity level refers to how much time a person is speaking during the conversation. Conversational engagement is how much influence one person has on the turn-taking process of speaking. Emphasis is the variation in the person's tone, stress, and rhythm. Finally, vocal mirroring is copying of the others' behaviors (e.g., body movements, facial expressions, or speech). The results of this experiment showed that 30% of the variation in negotiators' success was due to these four conversational behaviors *during the first five minutes* of negotiation interactions that lasted up to 45 minutes. Negotiators that had high activity, engagement, emphasis, and mirroring during the first five minutes received better employment deals (salary, vacation days, job assignment, company car, signing bonus, moving expense reimbursement, and a preferable insurance provider). While you might find this amazing, your communication in the first few minutes of a meeting may determine the benefits you derive from it. This research highlights the importance of communicating effectively at work. In this chapter, research on organizational communication will be discussed—and this knowledge is essential for leaders.

Learning Objectives

After studying this chapter, you should be able to do the following:

11.1: Describe the communication process, and discuss sources of noise in the process.

11.2: Provide an example of how communication apprehension affects the communication process.

11.3: Compare and contrast different forms of communication networks.

11.4: Discuss the advantages and disadvantages of electronic communication.

11.5: Provide an example of how to communicate effectively across cultures.

11.6: Discuss the significance of the percentages of verbal and nonverbal face-to-face communication.

11.7: Explain why employees remain silent or withhold information and how to address this.

Get the edge on your studies at
edge.sagepub.com/scandura

- Take the chapter quiz
- Review key terms with eFlashcards
- Explore multimedia resources, SAGE readings, and more!

⑤SAGE edge™

WHAT IS ORGANIZATIONAL COMMUNICATION?

Learning Objective 11.1: Describe the communication process, and discuss sources of noise in the process.

Organizational communication is "the process by which individuals stimulate meaning in the minds of other individuals by means of verbal or nonverbal messages in the context of a formal organization."[4] As indicated in the research discussed in the previous section on thin slicing, communication is important for negotiating the best deals. Also, positive organizational communication relates to both job performance and satisfaction.[5,6,7] One of the earliest statements regarding the importance of organizational communication is found in *The Functions of the Executive*: "The first function of the executive is to develop and maintain a system of communication."[8] Organizational communication is a specialized field today and emerged as a scientific discipline by the 1960s.[9] Organizational communication has been referred to as "the social glue that ties organizations together."[10] Entire books have been written on organizational communication (see the Suggestions for Further Reading at the end of this chapter). However, the purpose of this chapter is to provide you with the essential knowledge of communication needed to lead effectively.

The Communication Process

The Shannon–Weaver model of communication is essential to understanding the two-party communication process.[11] The key elements of the communication process are shown in Figure 11.1. These are described in the following sections.

Figure 11.1 The Communication Process

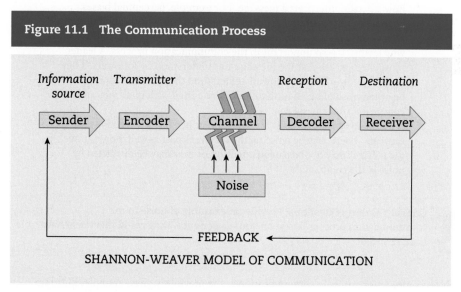

SHANNON-WEAVER MODEL OF COMMUNICATION

Source: Weaver, W. (1949). Recent contributions to the mathematical theory of communication. *The mathematical theory of communication, 1*, 1–12.

1. **The sender.** This is the source transmission who selects a desired message out of a set of possible messages. The selected message may consist of written or spoken words, pictures, music, or combinations of these. The message may also contain nonverbal behaviors such as gestures. For example, a leader prepares a speech for her employees consisting of a written outline and a PowerPoint presentation that contains graphs and pictures.

2. **Encoding.** This is the transformation of the message into the signal, which is sent over the communication channel from the transmitter to the receiver. For example, if a leader makes a speech to employees, the leader is the encoder.

3. **The channel.** The channel is the medium that transmits the message. In the previously given example, the channels are the leader's voice and the projector that shows slides that accompany the speech. The choice of communication channel (or medium) is influenced by institutional conditions (e.g., incentives, trust, and physical proximity) and situational conditions (e.g., urgency, task) and by the routine use of the media over time.[12] Research has indicated that the choice of communication medium (e.g., e-mail versus face-to-face) affects both attitudes and behaviors of the receiver.[13]

4. **Decoding.** The receiver then decodes the message sent through the selected channel or channels by translating what is seen and heard into an understanding of the message. This is not a perfect process since there is **noise** in the communication process that affects the decoding process. Noise is any communication barrier that may affect how a person interprets a message. For example, perceptual biases, language choice, cultural differences, and the room being too hot may affect how a person decodes a message and result in errors. This is why feedback is so important in the communication process. A leader must check to see that the message was understood by followers. They need to know whether followers understood the speech. This might be accomplished by inviting followers to e-mail with questions and comments after the speech.

5. **The receiver.** The receiver is the person or persons who receive the message. There may be noise on the receiver's part as well. For example, the receiver may not be paying attention or they may be distracted by noise in the room.

 Critical Thinking Questions: Provide an example of noise in the communication process based on your experience. How could this noise have been reduced?

Noise represents barriers to communication as the previously given examples illustrate. There are other examples of barriers to communicating effectively in organizations, and these are discussed next.

BARRIERS TO EFFECTIVE COMMUNICATION

Learning Objective 11.2: Provide an example of how communication apprehension affects the communication process.

Communication Apprehension

Tips for Communication

Some people are uncomfortable communicating with others, and it seems clear that this imposes a significant barrier to their success as a leader. Communication researchers define **communication apprehension (CA)** as "an individual's level of fear or anxiety with either real or anticipated communication with another person or persons."[14] CA may affect communication between two parties, team participation, or giving presentations. A meta-analysis of 36 studies on CA found that it is negatively related to both the quality and quantity of communication behavior.[15] CA may affect numerous aspects of behavior in organizations. For example, people with high CA may seek jobs with lower communication requirements and would seek less advice or assistance from their managers.[16] A study of CA and leadership abilities of 263 students found CA was detrimental to performance although these students had high intellectual ability (their GPA was not a factor).[17] The research showed CA was negatively associated with students' perceptions of their adaptability, appreciation for a multicultural world, and willingness to take on leadership roles. The authors recommend self-awareness (being aware that you are high in CA) and assertiveness training to overcome this communication barrier. Leaders should be aware that some followers may have CA and attempt to draw them out in one-on-one conversations before asking them to speak in a team meeting or make a presentation.

Language

Words may have different meanings to different people even if they are communicating in the same language. Slang, or colloquial terms, are used in organizations and can be bewildering to new employees or those outside of the organization. For example, a new employee may be told by her boss to "scale" her ideas for a new product implementation. What does it mean to scale something in business? Josh Lawry, general manager at 2nd Watch, a premier cloud partner for Amazon Web Services (AWS), noted that the word *scale* is often used in business and can have different meanings depending on the context.[18] Some common examples include the following: "Are we operating the business at scale?" (allocating and optimizing resources to drive the greatest results) or "Are we taking advantage of the scale of our business?" (another way to say size) or "Can the product scale up or scale down depending on demand?" (increasing or decreasing capacity). This example shows that beyond vocabulary, it is important to understand the context of business jargon and multiple meanings for the same phrase.

Critical Thinking Questions: Provide an example of jargon or slang used in an organization that could be misinterpreted by a new employee. Then, provide an alternative way of stating this concept so that it is more easily understood.

Due to noise and communication barriers, it is important for the receiver of a communication to provide feedback to the sender to ensure that the communicated message was understood correctly. This can be accomplished through **active listening**.

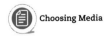
Choosing Media

Active Listening

In his impactful psychology book *A Way of Being*, Carl Rogers described "active listening" as the way of listening that is "a creative, active, sensitive, accurate, empathic, nonjudgmental listening."[19] Experimental research has shown study participants who receive active listening responses feel they are understood better than participants who receive either advice or a simple acknowledgment. This research also found participants with active listening responses were more satisfied with their conversations. Active listening has three components:

1. It demonstrates moderate to high nonverbal involvement.
2. It reflects the speaker's message using verbal paraphrasing.
3. It may include asking questions that encourage speakers to elaborate on his or her experiences.[20]

Leaders must become active listeners to be more effective since listening allows them to verify their communications clarify messages and encourage more two-way communication with followers.[21] Kevin Sharer, the former CEO of biotechnology giant Amgen, stated the following:

> As you become a senior leader, it's a lot less about convincing people and more about benefiting from complex information and getting the best out of the people you work with. Listening for comprehension helps you get that information, of course, but it's more than that: it's also the greatest sign of respect you can give someone.[22]

Active listening is also a powerful tool used by effective salespeople—they do more listening than talking to their potential customers.[23] Guidelines for active listening are provided in Table 11.1.

Toolkit Activity 11.1 at the end of this chapter is an active listening exercise that you can use to practice active listening and receive feedback on your listening accuracy. The exercise involves a dyadic (or two-party) conversation. However, in organizations, it is important to recognize that communication often occurs through networks that flow in all directions (upward communication, downward communication, and lateral communication).

Critical Thinking Questions: Why do you think that people in organizations have a difficult time listening? What can organizations do increase the degree to which their leaders listen to their followers?

COMMUNICATION NETWORKS

Learning Objective 11.3: Compare and contrast different forms of communication networks.

Communication flows through relatively reliable patterns in organizations. Figure 11.2 depicts some of common communication networks. First, the Wheel network indicates all

Table 11.1 Guidelines for Active Listening in Organizations

1. Listen for Total Meaning

Any message a person tries to get across usually has two components: the content of the message and the feeling or attitude underlying this content. Both are important; both give the message meaning. It is this total meaning of the message that we try to understand.

2. Respond to Feelings

In some instances, the content is far less important than the feeling that underlies it. To catch the full flavor or meaning of the message, one must respond particularly to the feeling component. Each time, the listener must try to remain sensitive to the total meaning the message has to the speaker. What is he trying to tell me? What does this mean to him? How does he see this situation?

3. Note All Cues

Not all communication is verbal. The speaker's words alone don't tell us everything he is communicating. And, hence, truly sensitive listening requires that we become aware of several kinds of communication besides verbal. The way in which a speaker hesitates in his speech can tell us much about his feelings—so, too, can the inflection of his voice. He may stress certain points loudly and clearly and may mumble others. We should also note such things as the person's facial expressions, body posture, hand movements, eye movements, and breathing. All of these help to convey his total message.

Source: Adapted from Rogers, C. R., & Farson, F. E. (1987). In R. G. Newman, M. A. Danzinger, & M. Cohen (Eds.), *Communicating in business today.* Washington, DC: Heath & Company.

Figure 11.2 Communication Networks

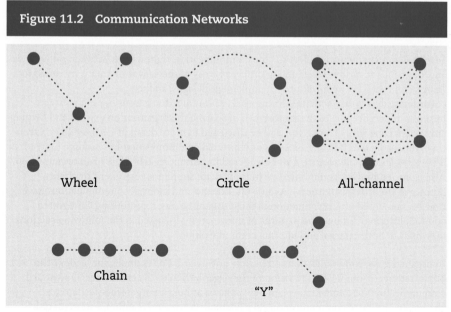

Wheel Circle All-channel

Chain "Y"

Source: Adapted from Leavitt, Harold J. (1951) Some effects of certain communication patterns on group performance. *Journal of Abnormal and Social Psychology, 46.*

communication flows through one person who is most likely the group leader. This is the most centralized communication network shown. The next one is the **Circle** communication network in which each person can communicate with two others located adjacent to them. The **All Channel (or Star)** pattern is more decentralized and allows a free flow of information among all group members. The **Chain** gives a flow of information among members although the people are at the end of the chain. Finally, the **Y-Pattern** is slightly less centralized than the all channel network since two persons are closer to the center of the network.

Critical Thinking Question: Which communication network is the most effective in terms of an organization's ability to innovate? Why?

Communication Flows in Organizations

Organizational communication may be external or internal. **External communication** refers to information that is shared with the public through marketing and public relations efforts.[24] These communication flows are important because leaders must create a positive impression with various stakeholders such as customers, shareholders, the government, and the general public. For example, when a flight from Fort Lauderdale, Florida, to Newark, New Jersey, left travelers stranded on the tarmac at the wrong airport for more than 7 hours in November 2011, Rob Maruster, JetBlue's CEO at the time, made an apology in a video message posted on blog.jetblue.com. More than 100 passengers on Saturday's flight were left on board the plane without food, water, or functioning bathrooms, causing a public relations nightmare for the airline. JetBlue has had difficulty shaking this image; Forbes named JetBlue one of the "worst airlines." JetBlue's troubles continue to be profiled in the media. In June 2014, a woman's young daughter urinated in her seat during a flight delay of a flight from New York to Boston. Flight attendants refused to let the child go to the restroom during the delay on the tarmac. JetBlue publicly apologized—again.[25]

Internal communication refers to "the communication transactions between individuals and/or groups at various levels and in different areas of specialization that is intended to design and redesign organizations, to implement designs, and to co-ordinate day-to-day activities."[26] Internal communication is considered a strategic business imperative due to the importance of sharing the organization's vision and helping employees cope with change (this will be discussed in more detail in Chapter 15).[27] Over time, the distinction between external and internal communication has become blurred. This is because employees are now considered important stakeholders of an organization. Also, some employees communicate externally with suppliers, customers, or clients (known as **boundary spanners**). As a result, external and internal communications have now become fused into one function in most organizations, representing "integrated communications."[28] Thus, the patterns of information discussed in the following sections may refer to both external and internal communication.

In organizations, communications often flow downward. For example, the leader of an organization communicates the vision of the organization to the employees. Downward communication is essential to explain new policies or help an organization adapt to change. In a study of communications in a hospital, downward communication on task and administrative matters was related to performance of nurses, but the relationship was influenced by the tasks performed, the organization's context, and individual differences.[29] In other words, the organizational culture or follower personalities may play a role in how communications are *interpreted*.

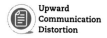 **Upward Communication Distortion**

In addition to downward communication from leaders at the top of the organization and bosses, communication may be lateral or flow sideways in the organization. Lateral communication takes place among peers or members of the same team or work group. This form of communication may either support or challenge the information received in downward communication. For example, a leader may communicate that all employees must be on time for work, but the members of a work group may challenge this by communicating an informal norm that it is acceptable to be late. Lateral communications may also reflect conflicts among team members that negatively impact satisfaction and performance. On the positive side, effective lateral communication in support of the organization's goals can enhance adaptability and effectiveness since peers may be more available to provide information quickly than superiors.

Upward communication refers to the process by which employees communicate with others who are higher in the organizational hierarchy.[30] Upward communication provides essential feedback to leaders regarding whether messages to employees have been understood. Upward communication is also important to assess the morale of employees and learn of their progress on goals. In some instances, a follower will offer an idea for improving something by communicating it to a person higher in the organization. Employees are closer to the work and the customers and also learn more about what might be improved. It is important for leaders to encourage upward communication from their followers.

An experimental study found that followers' reputations and perceptions of their competence were affected by whether they communicated in a way that indicated the importance of their idea to the organization's goals. Also, the study found that supervisors were more likely to grant requests if the follower was not seen as aggressive or self-promoting in making it.[31] Thus, upward communication, if done effectively, may enhance a person's reputation in the organization.

Upward communication from subordinate to superior relates to (a) information about the subordinate himself, (b) information about coworkers and their problems, (c) information about organizational practices and policies, and (d) information about what needs to be done and how to do it.[32] This information is clearly essential for the leader to know; thus, accuracy is important. However, upward communication is more likely to be distorted than other directions of communication.[33] Ensuring truthful upward communication is recognized as a serious problem.[34,35] The accuracy of upward communication is improved if the followers trust their boss, believe the boss has influence over their career, and have high mobility aspirations.[36,37] Upward communication is essential for leaders to implement change for the following reasons:

- The promotion of shared leadership and an enhanced willingness by managers to act on employee suggestions
- A greater tendency by employees to report positive changes in their managers' behavior
- Actual rather than perceived improvements in management behavior following feedback

Informal
Channels of
Communication

- A reduced gap between managers' self-ratings and those of their subordinates
- The creation of improved forums for obtaining information, garnering suggestions, defusing conflict, and facilitating the expression of discontent
- An enhancement of organizational learning
- Better decision quality (currently, it is estimated that about half of decisions in organizations fail—largely because of insufficient participation)
- Enhanced participation[38]

Critical Thinking Questions: Why do you think followers distort information when they communicate with those higher in the organization? What can be done to address this concern?

The Grapevine

Much communication in organizations happens through the informal network known as the **grapevine**. The term *grapevine* is believed to have originated during the Civil War when messages were transmitted through telegraph lines strung from tree to tree resembling grapevines.[39] Information transmitted through grapevines is often rumor and gossip, but it is still an important source of information that leaders need to tap into. For example, a survey of 419 managers found 89% of those surveyed believed that the grapevine carried rumors that reflected a lack of trust in organizational leaders and their policies.[40]

Rumors that flow through the organizational grapevine can be destructive.[41] They "can drain productivity, reduce profits, create stress in the workplace, or sully a company's image. Some rumors tear at a company's credibility, with both personnel and customers. In other instances, rumors have catapulted firms into financial disaster."[42] Leaders should be aware that the grapevine may even lead to litigation if rumors and gossip contain defamation, fraud or misrepresentations, invasion of privacy, harassment, or discrimination as well as cause emotional distress for an employee. In such cases, leaders are expected to take reasonable action to squelch the rumor mill.[43]

Despite the evidence that the grapevine is often negative, some research has shown benefits. One study found that gossip is a powerful tool to control behavior in groups. Gossip kept group members in line by discouraging social loafing (refer back to Chapter 9 for a refresher on this team challenge).[44] Thus, while most see gossip as a negative force, it may have benefits. Another benefit is information about working for an organization transmitted through the grapevine influences whether job applicants view employment opportunities as attractive and want to apply to work for a particular organization.[45]

Common internal corporate rumors include those connected with organizational change, such as layoffs, reorganizations, mergers, and changes in management.[46] The grapevine allows employees to vent during organizational change. In a study of a hospital undergoing change, there were more negative rumors than positive rumors in the grapevine. Also, employees exposed to negative rumors reported more stress.[47] Leaders should not ignore the grapevine; it can be an important part of the socialization of employees.[48] In sum, the grapevine is an important source of information in organizations that leaders need to monitor since it has been shown to have both negative and positive effects.

Communication Networks and Ethics

The Enron Corporation was the seventh-largest business organization by 2001 and employed over 21,000 people in 40 countries with gross revenues of over $100 billion. Enron was "an exceedingly successful global financial powerhouse from very simple beginnings."[49] By the end of 2001, the organization was suddenly insolvent and filed for bankruptcy after the company admitted to inflating reports of earnings. Following investigations, the Federal Energy Regulatory Commission (FERC) conducted investigations and released the e-mail records of 158 employees from the company over a period of 3.5 years to help the public understand what happened in what is now considered "one of the United States' most disastrous business failures."[50]

The e-mail communications analyzed by researchers found Enron executives' communication networks "lit up" with activity. As interpersonal communication became more intense and spread through the networks, formal chains of command previously in place were ignored. Executives deferred to others in the e-mails, resulting in "groupthink" (explained in Chapter 9). For example, peers of equal rank deferred to their peers to preserve their status by protecting themselves from being seen as "overstepping one's place."[51]

Could anything have been done to prevent the Enron meltdown? Executives failed to (a) communicate appropriate values to create a moral climate, (b) maintain adequate communication to be informed regarding organizational operations, and (c) maintain openness to signs of problems.[52] The lessons from Enron seem clear: Leaders must communicate their expectations for integrity for their followers as well as their peers.

Discussion Questions:

1. Explain how the grapevine had both negative and positive effects in this case.
2. Discuss this case in terms of the characteristics of groupthink from Chapter 9 (group rationalization, direct pressure, suppression, and illusion of unanimity). What role do you think communication plays in the emergence of groupthink?

Sources: Diesner, J., Frantz, T. L., & Carley, K. M. (2005). Communication networks from the Enron email corpus "It's always about the people. Enron is no different." *Computational & Mathematical Organization Theory, 11*(3), 201–228; Fragale, A. R., Sumanth, J. J., Tiedens, L. Z., & Northcraft, G. B. (2012). Appeasing equals: Lateral deference in organizational communication. *Administrative Science Quarterly, 57*(3), 373–406; O'Connor, M. A. (2002). Enron board: The perils of groupthink. *University of Cincinnati Law Review, 71,* 1233–1471; Seeger, M. W., & Ulmer, R. R. (2003). Explaining Enron communication and responsible leadership. *Management Communication Quarterly, 17*(1), 58–84.

The Research in Action box on Enron indicates that much communication in organizations is through electronic means. What is also clear is that organizations have the right to monitor the communications of their employees and most employees feel that this is acceptable as long as long as they are notified in advance.[53] So a leader must be careful regarding what is transmitted in e-mails. The next section discusses the emerging importance of understanding the implications of electronic communication in its various forms including e-mail, texting, social media, and videoconferencing.

 Critical Thinking Question: Do you agree that organizations have the right to monitor employee e-mails and other forms of electronic communication? Why or why not?

ELECTRONIC COMMUNICATION

Learning Objective 11.4: Discuss the advantages and disadvantages of electronic communication.

E-Mail

E-Mail

E-mail has become a primary mode for communicating in organizations. Even employees who work in offices next to one another often communicate by e-mail rather than face-to-face! A study of face-to-face and e-mail communication in a Fortune 500 office equipment firm employing over 100,000 people employed interviews, questionnaires, and actual e-mails. Researchers found that more information is conveyed in e-mail than other communication mediums: People paid less attention to social cues that suppress information and were more uninhibited in e-mails.[54] Due to this inhibition, harassment may be more likely to occur through e-mail compared to face-to-face interactions. In some cases, this harassment includes comments that are sexual in nature.[55] Organizations should have formal policies for harassment that include "**e-harassment**."[56]

Leaders should avoid e-harassment. However, some e-mail offenses are more subtle. The Internet has evolved over time, and there are now rules for how to be polite in e-mail. This is termed **netiquette** (e-mail etiquette). Whether you are communicating with a prospective employer or to others you work with, it is sound advice to show good manners. Without knowing netiquette, you might annoy or even offend someone unintentionally. These rules developed as norms (unwritten rules) over time so everyone may not be aware of them (refer to Chapter 9 for a discussion of the powerful impact of norms). According to one communication expert, "netiquette rules are based on common sense and respect, but since email is so quick, we often forget that we are still using a form of written communication."[57] Ten rules for netiquette are shown in Table 11.2. You should be familiar with these rules to avoid social blunders in email communication.

Research on e-mail usage and performance is mixed. The amount of e-mail sent and received is positively related to job performance.[58] Yet, some research suggests checking e-mail frequently may result in interruptions that affect the flow of work.[59] Frequently checking e-mail has been related to information overload and stress.[60,61] High levels of e-mail use in the workplace relate to avoidant decisional styles such as procrastination.[62] A study of knowledge workers found employees adapt to e-mail interruptions through new work strategies as they negotiate the constant connectivity of communication media. For example, employees find ways to leverage the importance of e-mail for environmental monitoring by setting aside uninterrupted work time by shutting off e-mail alerts.[63]

The lack of visual cues may lead to difficulty interpreting the meaning of e-mail communication. Miscommunications of emotion occur in e-mail messages more than face-to-face communications, and this affects both the relationships and the information conveyed. These miscommunications affect both satisfaction and performance.[64]

Text Messages

With the ubiquitous use of smartphones and other mobile devices, employees can now check e-mail and send text messages more frequently than ever—even during evenings

Table 11.2 Netiquette Rules

1. Imagine your message on a billboard. Anything you send can be forwarded, saved and printed by people it was never intended for. Never send anything that will reflect badly on you or anyone else.

2. Remember that company emails are company property. Emails sent from your workplace can be monitored by people besides the sender and reader, and are technically company property.

3. Avoid offensive comments. Anything obscene, libelous, offensive or racist does not belong in a company email, even as a joke.

4. Keep your message cool. Email messages can easily be misinterpreted because we don't have the tone of voice or body language to gives us further cues. Using multiple explanation points, emoticons, and words in all capital letters can be interpreted as emotional language.

5. Be careful about forwarding messages. If you aren't sure if the original sender would want to forward the message, don't do it.

6. Don't expect an answer right away. Email messages may be delivered quickly, but your recipient may not read it right away.

7. Don't sacrifice accuracy for efficiency. Don't send sloppy, unedited email. Experts say that for every grammar mistake in an email, there's an average of three spelling mistakes. While the odd spelling mistake is overlooked, when your readers have to break communication to decipher a word or message, at best, you'll look sloppy, if not illiterate. At worst, they may stop reading.

8. Include the message thread. Keep the original message for a record of your conversation. However, when sending a new message to the same person, start a new thread with a new subject line.

9. Don't type in all CAPS. It's perceived as YELLING. However, don't write with only small letters, as this is perceived as your being lazy, because it makes it more difficult for people to read.

10. Write clear, organized messages, with a subject line that gives enough information for the reader to file it and find it later.

Source: Goldman, L. (2007). Netiquette rules—10 best rules for email etiquette. Retrieved on February 22, 2014, from http://ezinearticles.com/?Netiquette-Rules---10-Best-Rules-for-Email-Etiquette&id=785177.

and weekends. Text messages are far more likely to be sent from handheld mobile devices than from desktop or laptop computers. The Cellular Telecommunications & Internet Association (CTIA) reports that, as of December 2012, there were 171.3 billion text messages that were sent in the United States (includes Puerto Rico, the Territories, and Guam) every month.[65] For business communications, it is important to follow the rules of grammar and capitalization and avoid abbreviations (*brb* for "be right back," for example). Due to their brevity, text messages will probably never replace e-mail as the primary mode for electronic business communications. Also, there are concerns about the privacy of text messages. Finally, general business expectations are that sending text messages at work is not a good use of time or is undesirable behavior.[66] However, a recent study conducted found that the use of smartphones during working hours to take short breaks increased employee well-being. The authors believe that the use of smartphones may have benefits, but too much time using social media may harm productivity.[67]

Voice Mail

When smartphones are used seems to be an important consideration. An interview study conducted found mobile text and e-mail usage patterns "are dangerous, distracting, anti-social and . . . infringe on work-life boundaries."[68] This research also found that many employees check e-mail during their commutes to and from work.

 Critical Thinking Question: List the advantages and disadvantages of being able to access work e-mail from a mobile device.

Social Networking

You are probably familiar with social networking sites such as Facebook, Twitter, LinkedIn, and Instagram. As discussed earlier in this chapter, being central to a communication network may result in more power. But social networking has caveats. It is important to keep in mind that if your social media site such as Facebook is public, your current or prospective employers might check it. It's best to assume that what you post may become public, so discretion matters. For example, employees have been fired for writing about their employer in inappropriate ways in blogs (web logs).[69] The First Amendment does not protect employees by giving them the right to say whatever they want about their job or employer, and many employers now have specific blogging policies, including Cisco, IBM, Intel, and Microsoft.[70]

On the other hand, blogs have become popular as a way for leaders to promote their organization. Twitter is a microblog that limits messages to 140 characters called "tweets." A social media strategist noted that "smart brands use Twitter in meaningful ways, and most of them use their brand name as a way to make sure customers can find and recognize them."[71] She cited Chevrolet, Wachovia, The Home Depot, Zappos.com, and the Red Cross as some of the most successful Twitter brands.

 Critical Thinking Question: Discuss the advantages and disadvantages of using social media to promote an organization's public image.

Another challenge for organizations due to the use of the Internet at work is **cyberslacking**. Research has documented an increase in the use the Internet for personal use during working hours. This may include using social media, shopping, looking at pornography, and looking for another job while at work: "When employees use workplace PCs for personal reasons, the immediate effect is a loss of productivity . . . . Time is an asset and a misuse of that asset is just as wrong as the misuse of any other asset" (p. 56).[72] One study found that 60% of companies surveyed had disciplined employees for inappropriate use of the Internet during work.[73]

Despite the rise of e-mail as the main communication mode for organizations, there still appears to be a need for face-to-face contact. Being able to see another person is important since face-to-face contact is much richer due to the ability to read nonverbal messages that accompany the words. Thus, videoconferencing is now an important communication mode for organizations.

Videoconferencing

Conference Calls

Videoconferencing (or conducting virtual meetings) has long been an important communication mode at the workplace. Virtual meetings may be through the telephone only (a conference call) or they may be face-to-face. Skype has made it possible to speak to one or more persons face-to-face nearly everywhere in the world. Videoconferencing is advantageous because you are able to discern emotions through the tone of voice and/or facial expressions. Most large organizations depend on videoconferencing to coordinate work among employees who are not colocated. Accenture, a technology consulting firm, installed 35 videoconferencing rooms at its offices around the world. In 1 month alone, its consultants used virtual meetings to avoid 240 international trips and 120 domestic flights for an annual saving of millions of dollars and countless hours of tiring travel for its workers.[74] Thus, there are cost savings plus reductions in employee travel stress that result from the use of videoconferencing. Videoconferencing has not replaced face-to-face meetings at companies such as IBM, but rather, it has reduced the number of travel days. For example, Darryl Draper, the national manager of customer service training for Subaru of America, used to travel 4 days a week for 9 months of the year. Now, much of her training is done online.[75]

Today, for most organizations, having a social media plan is an essential business strategy.[76] The landscape for social media in business is a new one, but it is clear that on both a personal and business level, social media will significantly impact organizational behavior (OB) in the years ahead. The use of the Internet at work has brought both opportunities for organizations and new challenges. Some challenges stem from the nature of the communication process itself and apply to both electronic and face-to-face communication.

The use of e-mail and videoconferencing has made it possible to communicate with employees and customers anywhere in the world. For example, many videoconference calls take place in globally distributed teams, where employees from a number of different countries participate. Thus, cross-cultural communication is now more important than ever, and this applies to electronic as well as face-to-face interactions.

CROSS-CULTURAL COMMUNICATION

Learning Objective 11.5: Provide an example of how to communicate effectively across cultures.

An executive from India referred to women in the organization as "females," and U.S. women in the organization thought this was an odd way to refer to them and were offended. As this example illustrates, the ability to communicate effectively with those from other cultures is now an essential leadership skill.[77] There is a difference between cross-cultural and intercultural communication. Cross-cultural communication compares one culture to another, and intercultural communication focuses on the behavior of two individuals' communication patterns.[78] For example, a cross-cultural communication study of 124 managers from the United States and Russia found cultural values of power distance and collectivism affected communication competence

Cross-Cultural
Miscommunication

and performance in teams.[79] An example of an intercultural study examined business meetings between British and Chinese managers and found mismatches in expectations regarding silence during meetings resulted in feelings of "uncomfortable silence."[80] Another example of miscommunication due to literal translation in intercultural communication follows:

> In translating an English financial report, a translator from Xian, by taking the surface value of words, translated terms like red gold, green sheet, and white goods as chijin (gold in red color), ludan (paper in green color), and baihuo (goods in white color) literally so that the clients had no idea what the expressions referred to.[81]

Bilingualism has been shown to improve communication efficiency—especially when both parties are at least partially fluent with respect to the language of the person they are working with.[82]

Differences in language are only part of the challenge of communication with a person from another culture. It has been noted that "language-related inefficiencies take numerous forms: loss of information, added work, loss of learning opportunities, and disruption of the collaborative process".[83] Misunderstandings often occur to cultural value differences. For example, perceptions of time, individualism, risk, relationship orientation, and power distance may affect intercultural communications.[84, 85] The next chapter will discuss cultural values in more detail (Chapter 12).

There are eight levels of differences on which cross-cultural communication can falter: when to talk; what to say; pacing and pausing; listenership; intonation; prosody; formality; indirectness; and cohesion and coherence.[86] There are several ways to address such cross-cultural communication challenges. For example, emotional intelligence (EI; discussed in Chapter 3) has been positively associated with communication competence.[87] Preparation for cross-cultural communication challenges and active listening also improves communication with persons from a culture other than one's own.[88] Finally, training in cross-cultural communication is also effective.[89,90]

Another important aspect of cross-cultural communication is nonverbal communication. Gestures may not mean the same thing in different cultures. For example, in the United States, not making eye contact may be associated with not telling the truth. However, in certain Arabic cultures, it may be viewed as rude and intrusive to look into another person's eyes. Another example is how close you should be to a person. In Japan, people are comfortable at about 30.2 inches apart in Venezuela, it is 32.2 inches; and in the United States, it is 35.4.[91] For example, someone from Venezuela could make someone from the United States very uncomfortable by unknowingly invading their space. As these examples illustrate, knowledge of the meaning of nonverbal communication is essential in preparing for an expatriate assignment or interaction with persons from cultures other than your own (expatriation will be discussed in more detail in the next chapter).

You Just Don't Understand: Women and Men in Conversation

Women and men communicate differently at the workplace.[92] This is in part due to fundamental differences in why men and women communicate in the first place. Most men see themselves as individuals in a hierarchically structured world where they are trying to get ahead. In contrast, most women see themselves as bringing closeness, confirmation, and support to the world. Hence, when women display *connection*, which they think is positive (i.e., thanking their boss for being a mentor), a male mentor might interpret this as *lack of independence* or insecurity. When presented with a problem, men often respond with "I'll fix it for you." Men see themselves as problem solvers and focus on solutions. Women are more likely to show empathy when a problem is brought to their attention: "I support you and want you to know you're not alone." Thus, in leadership positions, a man might interpret a women showing empathy and listening as not being an active problem solver.

Other differences in communication styles at work have been found.[93] For example, women apologize more often. Also, women tend to have a more indirect communication style compared to men. Another example is that men and women have different views about giving praise. Many women believe that if their boss does not praise them, their work is not acceptable. Women appear to need more feedback (men believe that if their boss says nothing, then everything is fine).

Leaders must remember that understanding gender differences in communication is a two-way street. Leaders need to understand that men and women have different communication styles. The need for feedback or showing empathy is not a sign of weakness. In fact, women may be well-suited for organizations interested in a more emotionally intelligent workplace.

Discussion Questions:

1. Explain how you could use active listening (discussed earlier in this chapter) to more effectively communicate with someone of the opposite gender.
2. This research is based upon generalizations, and leaders must be careful not to stereotype employees. Give an example of a man who exhibits a more female pattern of indirect communication. Give an example of a woman who exhibits a direct communication style (these examples can be from your experience or from leaders in the media).

Sources: Tannen, D. (1990). *You just don't understand: Women and men in conversation.* New York, NY: William Morrow; Tannen, D. (1994). *Talking from 9 to 5: How women's and men's conversational styles affect who gets heard, who gets credit, and what gets done at work.* New York, NY: Simon & Schuster.

Nonverbal communication is important for all forms of face-to-face and telephone conversation. Even on the telephone, nonverbal communication, such as a sigh or grunt, will be interpreted by the receiver and may change the intended meaning of the message. Next, we will discuss the evidence on nonverbal communication in organizations.

 Visual Aids and Job Performance

NONVERBAL COMMUNICATION

Learning Objective 11.6: Discuss the significance of the percentages of verbal and nonverbal face-to-face communication.

 Body Language

As shown in Figure 11.3, when it comes to face-to-face communication, approximately 7% of a person's understanding of others is attributed to words, whereas 38% is attributed to verbal tone and 55% is attributed to facial expressions.[94] The meaning of a message can even be negated by a facial expression or a person rolling their eyes. For example, if a person says, "I love my accounting class" and rolls their eyes, it means the opposite of what they are saying. If a verbal message contradicts a verbal message, the nonverbal message will carry the meaning. On the other hand, nonverbal messages can reinforce a verbal message. For example, a leader can raise their voice slightly while speaking to emphasize a point they are making to the team. Nonverbal communication includes facial expressions, posture, gestures, and tone of voice. Leaders are observed constantly, and every action is analyzed by others.[95] So, it's important to pay attention to nonverbal as well as verbal communication. Think of it this way: "Leaders are never *not* communicating. As a result, increasing their awareness of nonverbal communication may be a key factor in improving their communication skills and ultimately helping them to become better leaders."[96]

Figure 11.3   Elements of Face-to-Face Communication

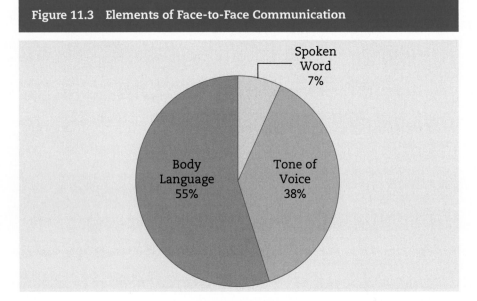

Sources: Ambler, G. (2013). When it comes to leadership everything communicates. Retrieved on March 1, 2014, from http://www.georgeambler.com/when-it-comes-to-leadership-everything-communicates; Mehrabian, A. (1981). *Silent messages* (2nd ed.). Belmont, CA: Wadsworth.

To this point, we have been discussing processes of communication where information is shared between and/or among employees in organizations. However, what happens when there is no communication? In other words, what are the consequences when employees remain silent? The next section summarizes the evidence on organizational silence and its implications for leadership.

SILENCE

Learning Objective 11.7: Explain why employees remain silent or withhold information and how to address this.

Employee silence is the intentional withholding of meaningful information from management, which includes asking questions expressing concerns and offering suggestions.[97] Climates of organizational silence emerge due to organizational structures or policies, managerial practices, and degree of demographic dissimilarity between employees and top managers.[98] A sample of 461 MBAs and managers were asked if they had intentionally remained silent about an issue at work, and 95% stated that they had.[99] The types of incidents reported in the study are shown in Table 11.3. The most common type of silence incident was unfair treatment (21%). Given recent attention to ethics at the workplace, it is disturbing that the second most common silence incident was someone else behaving unethically (17.6%). Concerns about a coworker's competence or performance (16.8%) and operational process concerns and/or ideas for improvement (13.3%) were other areas where employees withheld information.

Withholding information by remaining silent is a barrier to organizational change and compromises the ability to hear different points of view on important organizational matters.[100] Organizational silence can have detrimental effects on decision making by blocking alternative views, negative feedback, and accurate information.[101] Managerial secrecy combined with employee silence may combine to enable corruption.[102] Remaining silent has negative consequences for employees as well. Research has shown silence is negatively related to job satisfaction and organizational commitment.[103] In sum, organizational silence has numerous negative outcomes for both employees and the organization.

Can leaders take actions to reduce silence? Research on employee voice suggests formalized employee involvement and a participative climate both encourage employees to provide opinions, which reduce organizational silence.[104, 105] For example, a study of police officers found building trust with higher-level managers and building communication bridges

Table 11.3 Types of Incidents to Which Respondents Reported Remaining Silent

Experienced unfair treatment	21%
Someone else behaving unethically	17.6%
Concerns about a coworker's competence or performance	16.8%
Operational process concern and/or idea for improvement	13.3%
Disagreement or concerns with company policies or decisions	6.5%
Personal performance issue	6.2%
Concerns about supervisor or management competence	6.0%
Someone else being treated unfairly	3.5%
Personal career issue or concern	1.9%
Unclear	7.2%

Note: A total of 1,240 incidents where employees reported they remained silent. Unclear responses could not be categorized.

Source: Brinsfield, C. T. (2013). Employee silence motives: Investigation of dimensionality and development of measures. *Journal of Organizational Behavior, 34*(5), 671–697. p. 675.

reduced officer silence.[106] Also, ethical leadership supports employees and encourages them be more confident to speak up in a constructive way.[107]

 Critical Thinking Question: What are the potential costs of organizational silence? Give an example where an employee withholding information damages the performance of an organization.

As the preceding discussion indicates, leaders have an influence on the degree to which employees voice their concerns and suggestions up the organizational hierarchy. There are additional ways that theories of communication inform leadership, and the next section addresses the power of framing, which is essential for leaders in communication with followers and others.

LEADERSHIP IMPLICATIONS: THE MANAGEMENT OF MEANING

In an influential *Harvard Business Review* article, Deborah Tannen stated, "Talk is the lifeblood of managerial work."[108] Without a doubt, spoken communication (i.e., face-to-face, phone, or videoconferencing) is a powerful way to influence others as a leader. But we also learned in this chapter that "talk" does not only mean verbal face-to-face conversation but may also mean electronic communication and the powerful influence of nonverbal behavior. The knowledge and skills discussed in this chapter are essential for a leader to be effective. This is because leaders manage meaning for their followers. Leaders create a frame of reference for employees particularly during times of organizational change.[109] Regardless of the communication channel chosen (i.e., verbal, nonverbal, face-to-face, one-on-one, or formal presentations), leaders interpret what is happening in the organization and what it means for employees. Leaders, thus, frame organizational events. Framing is managing meaning by using talk to get followers to act.[110] To do so, leaders may use metaphors, jargon, and stories in their communications. We are all familiar with "spin" during political campaigns. This is also employed by leaders to reframe a negative event that has occurred.[111]

The relationship with the boss also matters; research has shown that effective communication from leaders relates to follower satisfaction and motivation.[112] The quality of leader–member exchange (LMX; discussed in Chapter 2) strongly influences subordinates' satisfaction with personal feedback and supervisory communication. Good relationships with followers also positively influence team and organizational communication. One study concludes "the quality of LMX has a 'spillover' or 'ripple' effect on perceptions of communication satisfaction in other forms of communication interaction."[113] Thus, the context of a positive working relationship affects perceptions of communication in general in an organization.

In sum, leaders influence followers through effective communication that helps them make sense of organizational events. They also use effective communication to give followers a sense of meaning in their work, which motivates them. Communication is fundamental to leadership since leaders are constantly communicating at all organizational levels and to their constituents outside of the organization.

⑤SAGE edge™

edge.sagepub.com/scandura

Want a better grade? Go to **edge.sagepub.com/scandura** for the tools you need to sharpen your study skills.

KEY TERMS

active listening, 287
All Channel (or Star)
   network, 290
boundary spanners, 290
Chain network, 290
Circle network, 290
communication
   apprehension (CA), 287
cyberslacking, 296

downward
   communication, 288
e-harassment, 294
external
   communication, 290
framing, 302
grapevine, 292
intercultural
   communication, 297
internal communication, 290

lateral
   communication, 288
netiquette, 294
noise, 286
Shannon–Weaver
   model of
   communication, 285
upward communication, 288
Wheel network, 288
Y-Pattern network, 290

SUGGESTIONS FOR FURTHER READING

Burgess, C., & Burgess, M. (2014). *The social employee: Success lessons from IBM, AT&T, Dell and Cisco on building a social culture.* New York, NY: McGraw-Hill.

Cotton, G. (2013). *Say anything to anyone, anywhere: 5 keys to successful cross-cultural communication.* New York, NY: John Wiley.

Fairhurst, G. T. (2010). *The power of framing: Creating the language of leadership.* New York, NY: John Wiley.

Richmond, V. P., McCroskey, J. C., & McCroskey, L. L. (2005). *Organizational communication for survival: Making work, work.* New York, NY: Allyn & Bacon.

Tannen, D. (1994). *Talking from 9 to 5: How women's and men's conversational styles affect who gets heard, who gets credit, and what gets done at work.* New York, NY: Simon & Schuster.

TOOLKIT ACTIVITY 11.1

Active Listening Exercise

Asking about what causes negative emotions can provide much information about someone's values, beliefs, and needs. By asking questions, we increase our understanding. Increased understanding leads to compassion, empathy, and a sense of connection with others.

In this exercise, you will partner with another classmate. Ask them to tell you about a setback in their life that they felt strongly about. Listen for feelings, values, and beliefs. Make notes using the form in this activity.

Focus on the feelings and the causes of them, not the details of the story. Try to get to the underlying thoughts below the emotions. While listening, remember not to give advice or try to solve the person's problems.

> How did this person feel (name at least five feelings)?
> What does this person value?
> What needs were not met?
> What are some of the person's beliefs?

After you have noted the person's values, needs, and beliefs, share them with the person. Ask the person to circle on a scale from 1 to 10 how accurate you were in identifying them using the following scale.

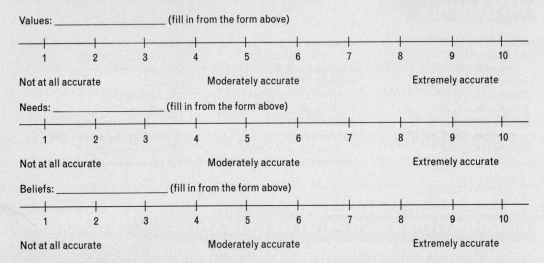

Values: _____ (fill in from the form above)

| 1 | 2 | 3 | 4 | 5 | 6 | 7 | 8 | 9 | 10 |

Not at all accurate   Moderately accurate   Extremely accurate

Needs: _____ (fill in from the form above)

| 1 | 2 | 3 | 4 | 5 | 6 | 7 | 8 | 9 | 10 |

Not at all accurate   Moderately accurate   Extremely accurate

Beliefs: _____ (fill in from the form above)

| 1 | 2 | 3 | 4 | 5 | 6 | 7 | 8 | 9 | 10 |

Not at all accurate   Moderately accurate   Extremely accurate

If time permits, switch roles and let the other person practice active listening.

Discussion Questions

1. Did you feel an increased level of empathy with the person as you were listening to them describe their experience? In other words, could you put yourself "in their shoes" and see the situation the way they did?
2. Was it difficult just to listen and not try to give advice? Why or why not?
3. How accurate were you in identifying the person's values, needs, and beliefs? Were you surprised at your feedback?
4. If you were the person describing the setback in your life, how did it feel to be listened to?
5. If you were the person describing the setback, what did the listener do that helped you continue speaking? Provide them with this feedback.

CASE STUDY 11.1

Communication: What Message Is Yahoo Really Relaying?

In the late 1990s, almost every browser had Yahoo as its home page, and Yahoo was a market leader. But by the early 2000s, Yahoo lost its leadership position in content aggregation, web searches, and ad placement. In the early days of the Internet, Yahoo was a popular search engine, news site, and social forum that received decent revenues from online display advertising. While it did each of these acceptably, competitors entered the market and developed greater competencies and have now taken over. Google now leads the search engine industry, while Facebook cornered the social networking market. Currently, Yahoo has no technology advantage, no product advantage, and no market advantage. While the company is hanging in there, revenues are flat and there is no clear strategic direction forward.

Yahoo's board has been aware of these problems and has been trying to find the right CEO to turn things around. In 2012, Marissa Mayer was selected as the CEO of Yahoo in hopes that the former Google executive could bring new life to the struggling company. This is the fourth CEO within a year, and the company is in dire need of a new strategy and visionary leadership. During her first year, she reduced costs, got all employees new smartphones to be better in touch with what customers are using, and started pushing the app development market. However, there is still much to do to make Yahoo competitive again.

Mayer's bet is that employees will be inspired by "spontaneous interactions" to create new products and services that will enhance Yahoo's bottom line. She's had some success resulting from such interactions before. The new mobile app called Yahoo Weather came to be when someone from the Weather team and someone from the Flickr team encountered one another serendipitously on the Yahoo campus. After sharing projects, new ideas started flowing and led to the creation of the app. To inspire and capture more of these ideas, Mayer rolled out a policy that eliminated telecommuting at Yahoo. In the memo sent to all its employees, Yahoo executives wrote the following:

> To become the absolute best place to work, communication and collaboration will be important, so we need to be working side-by-side. That is why it is critical that we are all present in our offices. Speed and quality are often sacrificed when we work from home. We need to be one Yahoo, and that starts with physically being together.

Thousands of Yahoo's employees telecommute at least once a week. Telecommuting allows employees greater flexibility in doing their jobs; managing their personal lives; and facilitating meetings between employees, customers, or suppliers. Previously, Yahoo used teleconferencing and videoconferencing to allow telecommuters to be part of meetings, and other work could be completed via e-mail, over the phone, or by using the company's virtual private network. The removal of the policy is leaving a number of its employees with families in a lurch and may force some employees to leave Yahoo. Further, telecommuting can reduce costs, as companies need less office space and less technology as well as spend less on electricity and employee benefits.

With the new policy, all employees will be forced to complete the normal 9 to 5 at the offices, though they are allowed to telecommute on weekends and after hours. Will the time in the office be as productive as Mayer hopes, or will the policy lead to different kinds of inefficiency? Only time will tell.

Discussion Questions

1. The memo stated this: "Speed and quality are often sacrificed when we work from home." How might Yahoo executives have come to this conclusion?
2. What type of message did such a decision send to Yahoo employees? To the rest of the world? How might the medium (an internal memo) have affected the employees' interpretation? What would have been a better way to communicate this change to employees?
3. How do you think this policy change affected employee attitudes and employee motivation? Do you think that this change positively or negatively affect communication within the organization in the short and long term? How could the situation influence organizational effectiveness?
4. Do you think that Yahoo really needed to remove telecommuting to enhance communication and collaboration? To enhance speed and quality? What else could Mayer and Yahoo managers done to motivate employees to be more accurate, swifter, more creative, more talkative, and more collaborative?
5. It seems that Mayer is counting on her employees to come up with the answer that will revitalize the company. What kinds of communication channels will be required? What changes do you think should be made to Yahoo's other policies and culture in order to facilitate the needed communication for new ideas?

Sources: Essig, T. (2013, February 28). Bodies matter: The inconvenient truth in Marissa Mayer banning telecommuting at Yahoo. *Forbes.* Retrieved from http://www.forbes.com/sites/toddessig/2013/02/28/bodies-matter-the-inconvenient-truth-in-marissa-mayer-banning-telecommuting-at-yahoo; Guynn, J. (2013, February 26). Yahoo CEO Marissa Mayer causes uproar with telecommuting ban. *Los Angeles Times.* Retrieved from http://articles.latimes.com/2013/feb/26/business/la-fi-yahoo-telecommuting-20130226; Johnson, D. (2013, August 9). In defense of Yahoo's telecommuting ban. Retrieved from http://www.cbsnews.com/news/in-defense-of-yahoos-telecommuting-ban; Null, C. (2013, May 13). Why Yahoo's telecommuting ban is still bad for business. *PCWorld.* Retrieved from http://www.pcworld.com/article/2038639/why-yahoos-telecommuting-ban-is-still-bad-for-business.html

SELF-ASSESSMENT 11.1

Quality of Communication Experience

This self-assessment exercise provides feedback on how you feel about communication with another person. There are no right or wrong answers, and this is not a test. You don't have to share your results with others unless you wish to do so.

Part I. Taking the Assessment

You will be presented with some questions representing how you feel about your communication with another person.

As an example, the answer to a question could look like this:

I liked communicating with this person.

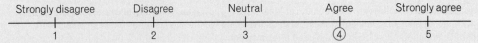

This response indicates that you agree that you liked communicating with this person.

Circle the response that indicates your agreement with each of the following statements.

1. I understood what the other side was saying.

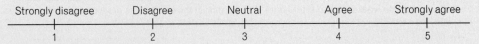

2. I understood what was important to the other side.

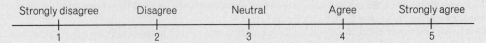

3. We clarified the meaning if there was a confusion of the messages exchanged.

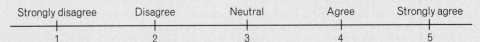

4. I think the other side understood me clearly.

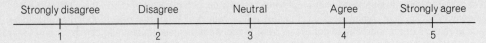

5. The messages exchanged were easy to understand.

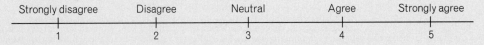

6. The other side responded to my questions and requests quickly during the interaction.

Strongly disagree	Disagree	Neutral	Agree	Strongly agree
1	2	3	4	5

7. The conversation ran smoothly without any uncomfortable silent moments, or I did not notice any uncomfortable silent moments.

Strongly disagree	Disagree	Neutral	Agree	Strongly agree
1	2	3	4	5

8. I was willing to listen to the other side's perspectives.

Strongly disagree	Disagree	Neutral	Agree	Strongly agree
1	2	3	4	5

9. When the other side raised questions or concerns, I tried to address them immediately.

Strongly disagree	Disagree	Neutral	Agree	Strongly agree
1	2	3	4	5

10. One or both of us kept silent from time to time (reversed).

Strongly disagree	Disagree	Neutral	Agree	Strongly agree
1	2	3	4	5

11. I was nervous talking to the other side (reversed).

Strongly disagree	Disagree	Neutral	Agree	Strongly agree
1	2	3	4	5

12. I felt the other side trusted me.

Strongly disagree	Disagree	Neutral	Agree	Strongly agree
1	2	3	4	5

13. I felt the other side was trustworthy.

Strongly disagree	Disagree	Neutral	Agree	Strongly agree
1	2	3	4	5

14. I felt comfortable interacting with the other side.

Strongly disagree	Disagree	Neutral	Agree	Strongly agree
1	2	3	4	5

15. The other side seemed comfortable talking with me.

Strongly disagree	Disagree	Neutral	Agree	Strongly agree
1	2	3	4	5

Part II. Scoring Instructions

First, reverse score items 10 and 11: 5=1; 1=5; 4=2; 2=4; 3=3.

Then, add the numbers you circled in each of the columns to derive your scores for the quality of communication experience.

Clarity	Responsiveness	Comfort
1. _____	6. _____	11. _____
2. _____	7. _____	12. _____
3. _____	8. _____	13. _____
4. _____	9. _____	14. _____
5. _____	10. _____	15. _____
Totals	_____	_____

Interpretation

Clarity—the degree of comprehension of the meaning being communicated. Meaning encompasses not only factual information but also ideas, emotions, and values conveyed through symbols and actions. Scores can range from 5 to 25. In general scores from 5 to 14 are lower and scores above 15 are higher.

Responsiveness—refers to the other party's overtures fulfilled expectations regarding how they react to you. Scores can range from 5 to 25. In general scores from 5 to 14 are lower and scores above 15 are higher.

Comfort—experienced by communicators, it reflects the affective aspect of communication, and it is the ease and pleasantness felt when interacting with the other person. Scores can range from 5 to 25. In general scores from 5 to 14 are lower and scores above 15 are higher.

Source: Liu, L.A., Chua, C. H., & Stahl, G. (2010) Quality of communication experience: Definition, measurement, and implications for intercultural negotiations. Journal of Applied Psychology, 95(3), 469–487.

12

CROSS-CULTURAL DIFFERENCES AND ADJUSTMENTS

GLOBAL DIVERSITY: A KEY WORKFORCE TREND

In today's multinational context, leaders regularly interact with those whose assumptions about work behavior differ from their own. Global diversity is identified as a key workforce trend in a *2013 Human Capital Trends* report:

> In the midst of ongoing global expansion and a worldwide shortage of critical talent, companies are stepping up efforts—at very different speeds and levels of investment—to recruit and retain a workforce diverse in both demographics and ideas.[1]

Being effective in cross-cultural interactions is now a necessary leadership skill. Research has shown that unsuccessful cross-cultural interactions lead to "failed integration that can seriously affect the realization of desired organizational outcomes such as successful technology transfer, knowledge-sharing, and the general realization of global growth."[2] This chapter covers research and practical applications of national culture, cross-cultural organizational behavior (OB), and the process of cross-cultural adjustment. The ability to lead across cultures is now essential for becoming an effective leader.

Culture is so ubiquitous that we rarely think about it until we travel to another country. Then it becomes obvious that our own culture influences the way we think because we are struck by the fact that people from other cultures dress, think, and behave differently than we do. Some characterize the French as rude for their abrupt attitudes toward Americans who are loud in restaurants. However, another explanation is that the physical space in many older French restaurants is smaller and customers are closer to one another. Many French people are brought up to be quiet in public spaces because they want to focus on the conversations of the person they are with and not everyone else in the restaurant. This preference is passed down from their grandparents and parents, and they don't question why it is not appropriate to be boisterous in places for intimate dining.

Learning Objectives

After studying this chapter, you should be able to do the following:

12.1: Explain why culture is important for understanding organizational behavior (OB).

12.2: Compare and contrast high-context and low-context cultures.

12.3: Provide examples of cultures that scored high and low on each of Hofstede's dimension of national culture.

12.4: Discuss the key findings from the Global Leadership and Organizational Behavior Effectiveness (GLOBE) project international study of leadership effectiveness.

12.5: Provide an example of a tight culture based on cultural tightness–looseness research.

12.6: Discuss the importance of developing global leaders and the impact this has on an organization.

12.7: Devise a plan for coping with the symptoms of culture shock.

12.8: Explain the steps for an expatriate to take when adjusting to a cross-cultural assignment.

Get the edge on your studies at **edge.sagepub.com/scandura**
- Take the chapter quiz
- Review key terms with eFlashcards
- Explore multimedia resources, SAGE readings, and more!

$SAGE edge™

Global Diversity

Fortunately, there has been a lot of research on cultural values and how they make their mark on the work environment. There are frameworks that guide the adjustment process, including adjustment for leaders on expatriate assignments. This topic is important to being an effective leader both at home as well as abroad given the changing landscape of business. Multinational corporations are common, and many products are built either partly or entirely with contributions from other countries. Products and services are marketed abroad. The best-selling book *The World Is Flat* describes a new world where organizations are becoming global villages with contributors from anywhere in the world due to advances in technology and the Internet.[3] For example, many organizations employ workers in other countries to staff call centers. Your lab results may be read by a technician in Australia and sent back to your doctor while she is sleeping in the United States, and they will be waiting for her electronically at 6:00 a.m. As discussed in Chapter 11, multinational corporations require work to be geographically dispersed, and team members communicate with one another only through e-mail or teleconference meetings. With these global changes in work, the effective leader will be equipped with a sound understanding of culture, cultural differences, and how to adjust quickly when other cultural values are encountered. Leading across cultures has become an essential skill set in today's working world.

WHAT IS CULTURE?

Learning Objective 12.1: Explain why culture is important for understanding organizational behavior (OB).

Before defining culture, it should be noted that the culture of an organization is also important to understand and will be covered in Chapter 14 of this textbook. National culture is an elusive concept in terms of definition. Definitions typically employed in OB have their roots in sociology or anthropology. Sociologists define *culture* as follows:

- It is shared by almost all members of a social group.
- Older members of the group pass it on to younger members.
- It shapes behavior or structures one's perception of the world (such as morals, laws, and customs).[4]

A straightforward definition of culture is that it is the unstated standard operating procedures or ways of doing things.[5] As this definition implies, culture is comprised of things that we can see (e.g., the clothing a person wears or the objects they display in their home) and things we cannot see (e.g., how they define morality and what they value).

A useful way to think about culture is the analogy of an iceberg (see Figure 12.1).[6] As shown in the figure, at the observable level, we can see dress, home or office décor, language, and even customs that are followed (what holidays are celebrated, as an example). However, under the surface, there are expectations of acceptable behavior, such as whether or not you should enter another's personal space. So what we can observe is only the tip of the iceberg, and leaders may make errors if they only rely upon what can be seen. These unobservable aspects' attributes of culture are often so deeply rooted in a person's world view that they are not questioned by them. For example, some people have little respect for authority and even lampoon political leaders, whereas other cultures have such a high respect for authority that they don't question those in power. From the previously given examples, it is clear that cultural values affect OB. A leader can't assume that what works in their native culture will work everywhere in the world. And only viewing the tip of the iceberg can be treacherous when dealing with people of different cultural backgrounds. As with the iceberg, a leader may get into difficulties by not being able to see what is underneath the surface. Fortunately, today we have sonar and GPS to locate and estimate the size of what's underneath the surface of the ocean. Like sonar, there is research in OB that helps us to understand what's underneath the culture iceberg. This chapter will provide evidence-based guidelines that are essential to a leader being effective in today's international context.

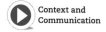 Context and Communication

 Critical Thinking Question: Give an example of an assumption about another culture that may influence your working relationship with a person from that culture.

HIGH-CONTEXT VERSUS LOW-CONTEXT CULTURES

Learning Objective 12.2: Compare and contrast high-context and low-context cultures.

High-context cultures rely heavily on situational cues for meaning when perceiving and communicating with others. For example, in a high-context culture, a person may

---

Figure 12.1 The Culture Iceberg: Observable and Unobservable Aspects of Culture

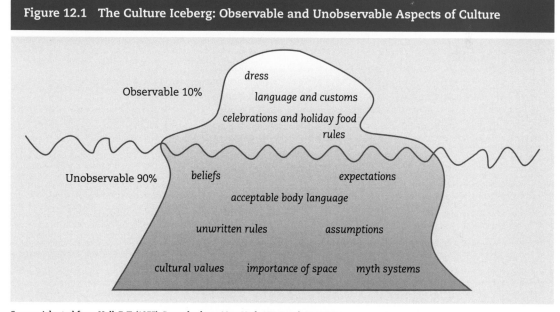

Observable 10%
dress
language and customs
celebrations and holiday food
rules

Unobservable 90%
beliefs   expectations
acceptable body language
unwritten rules   assumptions
cultural values   importance of space   myth systems

Source: Adapted from Hall, E. T. (1977). *Beyond culture.* New York, NY: Random House.

need to get to know a negotiating partner as a person before proceeding to business. In **low-context cultures,** written and spoken words carry the burden of shared meanings. So when negotiating with a person from a low-context culture, you can expect that the person will want to see a written formal agreement early in the process as a reference. From these examples, it is clear that employees bring their national culture values with them to work every day and that understanding them is essential to succeed as a leader. Examples showing the range from high- and low-context cultures (from low to high) are shown in Figure 12.2.[7,8]

The situation with Brian and Chan described in Case Study 12.1 at the end of this chapter can be understood by considering that China is a high-context culture (Chan took extra meaning from Brian's words because he is from a culture that relies on situations to determine meaning). However, Brian is from a relatively low-context culture (the United States) in which his words were not meant to be a personal attack on Chan but rather about the work. A common phrase we hear in the United States is "it's not personal, it's just business." To an employee from a high-context culture, this might not make sense since they look to situations including those at the workplace to understand whether they are a worthy person.

One of the most often-quoted definitions of *culture* is "the collective mental programming of the mind which distinguishes the members of one human group from

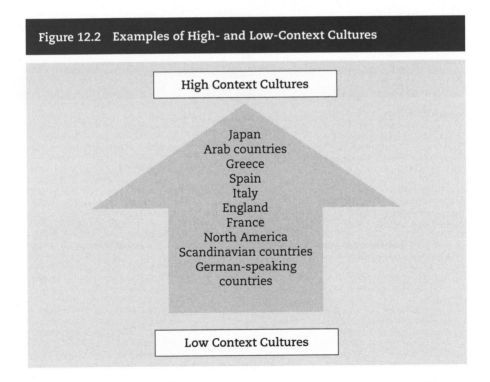

Figure 12.2 Examples of High- and Low-Context Cultures

High Context Cultures

Japan
Arab countries
Greece
Spain
Italy
England
France
North America
Scandinavian countries
German-speaking
countries

Low Context Cultures

"I'm Lovin' It"—But What Is It I Love?

A fascinating analysis of websites conducted from high-context and low-context cultures demonstrated that high-context cultures place a strong emphasis on relationships in advertising.[9] People in high-context cultures derive meaning from the social environment. Advertisements in high-context cultures showed families having happy interactions. In low-context cultures, however, the emphasis in advertising tends to be on the individual. People from low-context cultures tend to take things literally and have more social distance from others. For example, an ad with the same slogan, "I'm lovin' it," had different images in Switzerland (a young woman relaxing and listening to headphones) compared with an ad from India (which showed a man with a shopping cart running in a supermarket with a small boy in the seat of the cart). Thus, "loving it" in a low-context culture means blocking out the outside world, whereas "loving it" in a

high-context culture involves public spaces and close family relationships. Recall that high-context culture reflects the degree to which people see themselves as embedded and connected, so the advertising in high-context cultures shows people in relationships and groups rather than separate and alone.

Discussion Questions:

1. Provide another example from your experience or advertising of a (a) high-context and (b) a low-context communication.
2. Describe how team members from a high-context culture (Japan) would interact with members from a low-context culture (Germany). How can these cultural differences be addressed?
3. Provide an example of how a low-context culture would approach a business negotiation.

Source: Würtz, E. (2005). A cross-cultural analysis of websites from high-context cultures and low-context cultures. *Journal of Computer-Mediated Communication*, 11(1), article 13. Retrieved from http://jcmc.indian .edu/vol11/issue1/wuertz.html.

another . . . the interactive aggregate of common characteristics that influence a human group's response to its environment."[10] This definition has become famous among managers, and its author is one of the most-cited researchers in the social sciences. In addition to offering a definition of culture, Hofstede articulated four cultural values that have received much research attention. In 1988, a fifth cultural value, time orientation (called Confucian Dynamism), was added.[11] These cultural values remain the most well-known framework for understanding cross-cultural differences in a variety of disciplines including management. Next, we will review them and the research on these cultural values, which has had a large impact on how we view the effects on national culture in organizations.

HOFSTEDE'S CULTURAL VALUES

Learning Objective 12.3: Provide examples of cultures that scored high and low on each of Hofstede's dimension of national culture.

Hofstede's Cultural Dimensions

The five cultural values articulated by Hofstede and his colleagues follow, and their definitions are summarized in Table 12.1. Brief definitions and examples of countries with the United States as the referent culture for comparison purposes are provided next.

Power distance—deference to authority (e.g., the United States is low, China is high)

Collectivism–individualism—group orientation (e.g., the United States is low, Russia is high)

Uncertainty avoidance—risk aversion (e.g., the United States is low, France is high)

Relationship orientation (masculinity–femininity)—a focus on people over material things (e.g., the United States is low and the Netherlands is high on femininity/relationship orientation)

Confucian dynamism (long-term orientation)—a focus on the future rather than the past and present[12] (e.g., the United States is low, Japan is high)

Hofstede collected surveys from employees all over the world—initially from 40 countries.[13] His research was later expanded to 62 countries (116,000 managers and employees working for the large multinational company IBM were surveyed twice).[14] Hofstede found cultural values remained relatively stable over time. With this large database, he was able to create cultural clusters of countries. For example, Venezuela, Peru, Mexico, and Argentina are high power distance and collectivist cultures.[15] In contrast, the United States, Great Britain, Canada, and Australia are relatively lower on power distance and higher on individualism. Spain, France, Belgium, and Italy are higher on power distance but also relatively more individualistic cultures.

There has been a great deal of research interest in OB on the dimensions of national culture and collectivism in particular.[16,17] For example, being a loyal team member is expected to be more important in collectivist cultures compared to individualist cultures.[18,19] Research has linked collectivism to positive team outcomes.[20,21,22] The high level of individualism in the United States may help explain why teams have been more challenging to implement in the United States compared with some Asian cultures such as Japan. In individualistic cultures, employees' personal relationships with supervisors are important since they view the relationship as being tied to advancement and monetary rewards.[23] A recent meta-analysis showed that cooperation and performance was higher in collectivistic cultures compared to individualistic cultures.[24]

Power distance has been linked to leadership and team behavior. For example, for individuals with high power distance, high-quality relationships with their boss may not be expected, and they don't attempt to manage their boss because they tend to have unquestioning deference to authority.[25] In contrast, for employees with low power distance, relative position and status in the organizations are likely to be overlooked, and they may see themselves as equal to their supervisors.[26]

Hofstede's research has had a large effect on both research and practice in management. This framework has been instrumental in the overseas implementation of many business systems, including compensation, budget control, entrepreneurial behavior, training design, conflict resolution, work group dynamics, innovation, and leadership.[27,28]

Table 12.1 Hofstede's Cultural Values

Low Score on Cultural Value	High Score on Cultural Value
Individualism: Social organization is loose, and people care for themselves and their immediate family.	**Collectivism:** Social organization is tight, and people are loyal to their in-group and/or organization.
Low Power Distance: People prefer that power be equally distributed in an egalitarian way.	**High Power Distance:** People accept power differences and respect authority.
Low Uncertainty Avoidance: People tolerate uncertainty and ambiguity. They are willing to take risks.	**High Uncertainty Avoidance:** People feel threatened by uncertainty and ambiguity. They are risk averse and create rules to create stability.
Masculinity: People value assertiveness and strive to acquire money and things.	**Femininity:** People value caring for one another and the quality of life.
Short-term oriented: People value the past and present, expecting short-term gain.	**Long-term oriented:** People plan for the future, persist, and value being thrifty.

Sources: Hofstede, G. (1980). *Culture's consequences: International differences in work-related values.* Beverly Hills, CA: SAGE; Hofstede, G. (1991). *Culture's consequences: International differences in work-related values* (2nd ed.). Newbury Park, CA: SAGE; Hofstede, G., & Bond, M. H. (1988). The Confucius connection: From cultural roots to economic growth. *Organizational Dynamics, 16*(4), 5–21.

Critical Thinking Question: Do you think that cultures around the world are becoming more "westernized" (in other words, like the United States)? Why or why not?

Criticisms and Usefulness of Hofstede's Research

Despite the high level of research interest and management application of these cultural values, the Hofstede model has been criticized for relevancy (i.e., the values and measures were developed in 1980). Other criticisms are that it is not possible to characterize all people in one culture the same way. Also, the use of nations for the study is a limitation of the research (i.e., the United States and Canada are similar). The Hofstede studies also lacked attention to political influences on the data collected in the 1980s and the use of only one company (IBM) for the original research. Some scholars believe that culture is complex and cannot be captured in only four or five dimensions.[29] Hofstede's measures and statistical analyses have been criticized for their lack of validity and rigor.[30] One review points out some strengths of Hofstede's work: The study was published when there was little work on culture and spurred a great deal of research interest, his approach was systematic and rigorous for the time, and other studies have generally confirmed the initial results.

A meta-analysis of research covering 30 years on the Hofstede cultural values analyzed 598 studies (and over 200,000 employees and managers). Hofstede's original four cultural

GLOBE Studies

value dimensions and work outcomes were equally important. All five cultural values were significantly and positively related to organizational commitment, identification, citizenship behavior, team-related attitudes, and feedback seeking. However, personality and demographics were better predictors of performance, absenteeism, and turnover than cultural values.[31]

The work of Hall and Hofstede laid the foundations for research on cross-cultural OB. Another large-scale study of cultural differences specifically focused on leadership. The **Global Leadership and Organizational Behavior Effectiveness (GLOBE)** project at Wharton sought to understand differences in leader behaviors and relationships with relevant organizational outcomes worldwide. We will review this study next.

GLOBE STUDIES OF CROSS-CULTURAL LEADERSHIP

Learning Objective 12.4: Discuss the key findings from the Global Leadership and Organizational Behavior Effectiveness (GLOBE) project international study of leadership effectiveness.

The GLOBE project described and predicted the relationship of specific cultural variables to leadership and organizational processes and their effectiveness. The GLOBE researchers refined and extended the Hofstede cultural value framework. GLOBE involved 170 social scientists and management scholars from 61 cultures throughout the world to collect, analyze, and interpret data collected from employees and managers. This research identified nine cultural concepts that were shown to be relevant to perceptions of leadership. As with Hofstede, this research identified power distance and uncertainty avoidance as cultural values. Collectivism was split into two dimensions—loyalty to the group and loyalty to institutions (such as the organization you work for). In addition, the GLOBE project identified humane orientation, assertiveness, gender egalitarianism, and future orientation, which is similar to Confucian Dynamism and performance orientation. The nine GLOBE cultural dimension definitions and sample questionnaire items are shown in Table 12.2.

Table 12.2 GLOBE Cultural Dimensions and Sample Questionnaire Items

Culture Construct Definitions	Sample Questionnaire Item
Power distance: The degree to which members of a collective expect power to be distributed equally.	Followers are expected to obey their leaders without question.
Uncertainty avoidance: The extent to which a society, organization, or group relies on societal norms, rules and procedures to alleviate unpredictability of future events.	Most people lead highly structured lives with few unexpected events.
Humane orientation: The degree to which a collective encourages and rewards individuals for being fair, altruistic, generous, caring and kind to others.	People are generally very tolerant of mistakes. Aging parents generally live at home with their children.

Culture Construct Definitions	Sample Questionnaire Item
Institutional collectivism: The degree to which organizational and societal institutional practices encourage and reward collective distribution of resources and collective action.	Leaders encourage group loyalty even if individual goals suffer.
In group collectivism: The degree to which individuals express pride, loyalty and cohesiveness in their organizations or families.	Aging parents generally live at home with their children.
Assertiveness: The degree to which individuals are assertive, dominant and demanding in their relationships with others.	People are generally dominant.
Gender egalitarianism: The degree to which a collective minimized gender inequality.	Boys are encouraged more than girls to attain a higher education. (reverse-scored).
Future orientation: The extent to which a collective encourages future-oriented behaviors such as delaying gratification, planning and investing in the future.	More people live for the present than for the future. (reverse-scored).
Performance orientation: The degree to which a collective encourages and rewards group members for performance improvement and excellence.	Students are encouraged to strive for continuously improved performance.

Source: Adapted from House, R., Javidan, M., Hanges, P., & Dorfman, P. (2002). Understanding cultures and implicit leadership theories across the globe: An introduction to project GLOBE. *Journal of World Business, 37*(1), 3–10.

Based upon the GLOBE research and the 61 countries included in the study, cultures appear to vary on the nine dimensions. High- and low-scoring country examples are shown for each of the dimensions.

Cultural Dimension	Highest	Lowest
Power distance	Argentina, Spain, Russia	Denmark, Israel, Costa Rica
Uncertainty avoidance	Switzerland, Denmark, Austria	Russia, Hungary, Venezuela
Humane orientation	Philippines, Ireland, Egypt	Spain, France, Singapore
Institutional collectivism	Sweden, South Korean, Japan	Greece, Argentina, Italy
In-Group collectivism	Iran, India, China	Finland, Netherlands, Sweden
Assertiveness	Germany (former East), Spain	New Zealand, Japan, Kuwait, United States
Gender egalitarianism	Hungary, Poland, Sweden	Morocco, India, China
Future orientation	Canada, Singapore, Denmark	Russia, Argentina, Italy
Performance orientation	Hong Kong, Taiwan, United States	Argentina, Greece, Venezuela

Cultural
Perceptions

In addition to refining cultural values, the GLOBE research team also examined the question of whether or not there were any leadership behaviors that appeared to be acceptable across cultures. Their analysis found that there are certain culturally endorsed attributes of leadership, which may be universal. This is known as the **culturally endorsed implicit leadership theory (CLT),** which identified the following leadership behaviors that were perceived as effective across cultures.

1. **Charismatic/value-based**—the ability to inspire and motivate others to high performance
2. **Team-Oriented**—effective team building and implementing a common goal
3. **Participative**—involving others in decisions and implementations
4. **Humane-Oriented**—being supportive and showing consideration, compassion, and generosity
5. **Autonomous**—independent and individualistic leadership
6. **Self-protective**—ensuring safety and security of individuals including face-saving

Thus, GLOBE research found that employees may have some similar conceptions of leadership based on implicit assumptions regarding what constitutes effective leadership. These belief systems affect the way that a person responds to directives from a leader. GLOBE uncovered some important underlying perceptions regarding what is deemed effective in terms of leadership and offers some practical advice for leaders operating abroad.[32] There appear to be some cultural "universals" according to GLOBE: having integrity, having vision, being inspirational, and building teams. Also, there are universal attributes of ineffective leadership: being a loner, being irritable, and being autocratic. Other attributes may depend on the culture: individualism, being conscious of status, and risk taking.

Critical Thinking Questions: What are the advantages of knowing cultural values that generalize across cultures? Is it more useful to learn about cultural values that are unique to a culture? Why or why not?

CULTURAL TIGHTNESS–LOOSENESS

Learning Objective 12.5: Provide an example of a tight culture based on cultural tightness–looseness research.

Cultural tightness–looseness is described as the strength of social norms and the level of sanctioning within societies.[33] **Tightness** is associated with order and efficiency, conformity, and low rates of change. In contrast, **looseness** is associated with social disorganization, deviance, innovation, and openness to change. Tightness–looseness is reflected by the clarity and pervasiveness of norms within societies and the degree of tolerance for deviation from these norms. The theory of tightness–looseness is intended to be complementary to the Hofstede values framework. The first factor delineating tight and loose societies is the level of accountability in organizations and the extent to which individuals have a sense of accountability. A large-scale study assessed cultural tightness–looseness in 33 cultures with the following survey questions (respondents were asked to agree or disagree with the questions on a 6-point scale):

Interviews with Global Leaders

1. There are many social norms that people are supposed to abide by in this country.
2. In this country, there are very clear expectations for how people should act in most situations.
3. People agree upon what behaviors are appropriate versus inappropriate in most situations in this country.
4. People in this country have a great deal of freedom in deciding how they want to behave in most situations (reverse-scored; higher scores indicate more cultural tightness).
5. In this country, if someone acts in an inappropriate way, others will strongly disapprove.
6. People in this country almost always comply with social norms.[34]

This research found the 33 cultures studied varied with respect to tightness–looseness. Tight cultures had more social controls and were more likely to be autocratic. They were also more likely to have more rules and laws, for example. Examples of tight cultures are India, Malaysia, and Pakistan. Examples of relatively loose cultures are Hungary, Israel, and the Ukraine. The United States had a score of 5.1, which was a bit below the overall average score of 6.5 across all respondents from all cultures. So the United States can be seen as somewhat loose.

Cultural tightness is likely a response to ecological and historical threats such as population density, conflict, natural disasters, and disease (as examples). Also, governments, the media, education, laws, and religion shape cultural tightness. These aspects relate to the structure of norms and tolerance for deviation from them, and this affects the degree of structure in everyday situations, including OB. Researchers conclude that "understanding tight and loose cultures is critical for fostering cross-cultural coordination in a world of increasing global interdependence."[35] Research on cultural tightness–looseness is relatively new, but this approach shows a great deal of promise for enhancing our understanding of cross-cultural OB.

Following this foundation in cultural value differences, we next turn to the development of global leaders. Experts have concluded that most of today's managers lack the global leadership skills needed to be effective in the multinational business context.[36] One study estimated that 85% of Fortune 500 companies have a shortage of global managers.[37] The critical skills needed for effective global leadership and how they can be developed will be discussed in the following sections.

DEVELOPING GLOBAL LEADERS

Learning Objective 12.6: Discuss the importance of developing global leaders and the impact this has on an organization.

In a recent interview, Carlos Ghosn, the chairman and CEO of the Renault-Nissan alliance, was asked about the importance of cross-cultural management education for managers. Here was his reply:

More and more, managers are dealing with different cultures. Companies are going global, and teams are spread across the globe. If you're head of engineering, you have to deal with divisions in Vietnam, India, China or Russia, and you have to work across cultures. You have to know how to motivate people who speak different languages, who have different cultural contexts, who have different sensitivities and habits. You have to get prepared to deal with teams who are multicultural, to work with people who do not all think the same way as you do.[38]

Ghosn's view is shared by other top executives who view the ability to influence people from other cultures as the most important skill required for their own success.[39] **Global mind-set** has been defined as a set of individual attributes that enhance a manager's ability to influence others who are different from them.[40]

The global mind-set is developed through three interrelated skills: **cultural intelligence (CQ)**, **cultural retooling**, and integrative acculturation (becoming bicultural). The next sections elaborate on these leadership skills; all of them are needed to develop effective working relationships with others that result from a mutual adjustment process resulting in a third culture.

The Third Culture

The **third culture** has been defined as "the construction of a mutually beneficial interactive environment in which individuals from two different cultures can function in a way beneficial to all involved."[41] The third culture consists of shared frameworks, value systems, and communication patterns that emerge when people from different cultures interact. This is an important concept because it is through a mutual adjustment process over time that a third culture emerges, which has features of both so that both parties can be comfortable interacting. While this is a two-person example, third (or hybrid) cultures have also been shown to be important for team harmony and performance.[42] The process of the development of the third culture is shown in Figure 12.3. As shown in this figure, third cultures emerge over four phases as follows:

- **Phase 1.** Initial contact may result in the person withdrawing from the other person (or culture). For example, an expatriate travels to the city of Al Ain in the United Arab Emirates (UAE) from Argentina to develop a contract for oil exports. The expatriate insists that business colleagues taste wine brought as a gift from Argentina. The Arab executives are uncomfortable and limit their interactions after this exchange.
- **Phase 2.** The parties evaluate the need for continued interaction. As the discussions continue, the UAE representatives realize that a business between Argentina may open additional markets in Latin America, and the executive from Argentina has valuable contacts. The parties have options at this point. They may choose to rely on their own cultural values and not adapt. At this point, the interaction might end so the risk of staying with one's own values must be evaluated. For extended interactions, however, the parties begin a natural process of mutual adjustment. The need for ongoing and mutually beneficial interactions supports the cultural adjustment process.

- **Phase 3.** The dependence of the parties on one another is clear by this point. Norms for interaction have evolved to the point where they feel "natural" to both parties. Positive outcomes reinforce the motivations for continued adjustment, and a third culture emerges that accommodates both parties' cultures. Following the previously given example, the attractiveness of the Latin American market for oil exports motivates the UAE executives to explain why their religious and cultural beliefs don't allow them to drink alcohol. Both parties become accustomed to cultural differences in cultural values and a balanced approach emerges.
- **Phase 4.** Interdependence results in more nuanced development and maintenance of the third culture. There is a continued process of open communication, and the process becomes dependent on trust. In the previously given example, the executive from Argentina contacts the home office and requests that alternative gifts of leather binders be sent

Figure 12.3   Model of Third-Culture Building

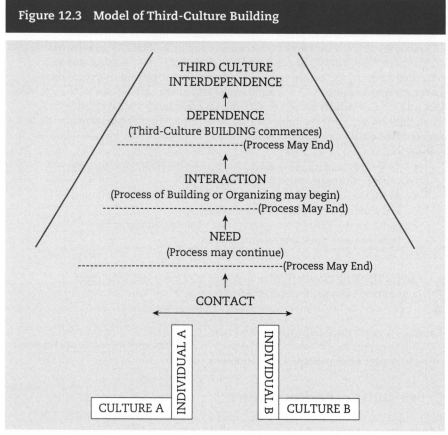

Source: Casrnir, F. L. (1999). Foundations for the study of intercultural communication based on a third-culture building model. *International Journal of Intercultural Relations, 23*(1), 91–116.

immediately. This example illustrates that there is a type of intelligence that emanates from an interest in learning about other cultures and a willingness to make adjustments. The next section discusses research on Cultural Intelligence, CQ.

Cultural Intelligence

CQ has been defined as an individual's capabilities to function and manage effectively in culturally diverse settings.[43] Like emotional intelligence (EI; as discussed in Chapter 3), CQ can be cultivated by first assessing one's strengths and weaknesses in CQ, undergoing training in cross-cultural interactions, and then applying CQ learning to real life cross-cultural situations to build confidence.[44] To assess your CQ, complete Self-Assessment 12.1 in the Toolkit at the end of this chapter. CQ is composed of four dimensions: metacognitive, cognitive, motivational, and behavioral, as shown in Figure 12.4. **Metacognitive CQ** refers to the cognitive processing necessary to recognize and understand expectations appropriate for different cultural situations. **Cognitive CQ** refers to self-awareness and the ability to detect cultural patterns. **Motivational CQ** refers to persistence and goal setting for cross-cultural interactions. **Behavioral CQ** is the ability to adjust to others' cultural practices.

The cognitive aspect of CQ predicts cultural judgment whereas motivational CQ predicts cultural adaptation. Both cognitive and behavioral CQ predicts task performance.[45] But can CQ be acquired through training? Two multination studies compared students' CQ before taking cross-cultural management courses to their scores afterward. Student CQ was significantly higher after taking courses that included CQ, with stronger effects found for cognitive CQ than motivational or behavioral. Thus, there is some indication that CQ can be learned.[46] CQ training should include assessment and training on all facets of CQ:

- **Cognitive (and metacognitive)**—acquiring information on the new culture and engaging in self-reflection
- **Motivational**—developing culture-specific confidence (self-efficacy) and setting goals for cross-cultural adjustment
- **Behavioral**—includes role-plays to model and practice effective behaviors with those from another culture.[47]

 Critical Thinking Question: What aspect of CQ do you feel is the most important for a leader to develop? Why?

Thus, CQ involves the ability to learn about other cultures and develop the confidence and skills to engage in new behaviors. Adaptation is a key aspect of success in working with others to achieve a third culture both one-on-one and in teams.

Cross-Cultural Adjustment

With respect to cross-cultural adjustment, four acculturation strategies are possible: **assimilation, separation, marginalization,** and **integration.**[48,49] Assimilation involves relinquishing cultural heritage and adopting the beliefs and behaviors of the new

Figure 12.4 Dimensions of Cultural Intelligence

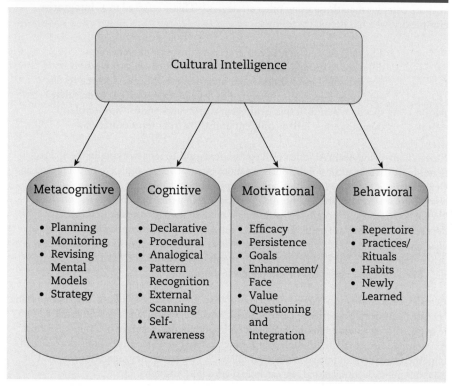

Sources: Adapted from Earley, P. C., & Ang, S. A. (2003). *Cultural intelligence: Individual interactions across cultures.* Stanford, CA: Stanford University Press; Eisenberg, J., Lee, H., Bruck, F., Brenner, B., Claes, M, Mironski, J., & Bell, R. (2013). Can business schools make students culturally competent? Effects of cross-cultural management courses on cultural intelligence. *Academy of Management Learning & Education,* 12(4), 603–621.

culture. For example, a Chinese person adopts an English name to better fit in with U.S. coworkers. Separation involves maintaining only the heritage culture without intergroup relations. For example, a Russian scientist avoids contact with coworkers by eating lunch at his desk. Marginalization involves rejecting both the old and new culture. For example, a Filipino expatriate working in Saudi Arabia does not celebrate Christmas or Ramadan. Integration (or biculturalism) involves maintaining one's cultural heritage and adopting a new cultural identity; the identities remain independent of one another. For example, a Cuban immigrant to the United States speaks Spanish at home with her family but speaks English at work.

We have learned a lot about how people adjust to different cultures from the study of bicultural individuals. Biculturals are defined as "people who have internalized more than one cultural profile."[50] These individuals are therefore comfortable operating in two different cultures, and they have been found to have more cross-cultural adaptive skills compared to monoculturals (those comfortable with only one culture).

Acculturation Strategies

Integrative Acculturation: Biculturals

Biculturals have higher metacognitive CQ skills and have been shown by research to be more complex than those using other strategies.[51] This is referred to as **integrative complexity,** which is defined as follows:

> The degree to which a person accepts the reasonableness of different cultural perspectives on how to live, both at the micro interpersonal level and at more macro organizational-societal levels and, consequently, is motivated to develop integrative schemas that specify when to activate different worldviews and/or how to blend them together into a coherent holistic mental representation.[52]

Research involving Asian American college students and Israelis working in the United States found that bicultural individuals are more integratively complex in both cultural and work situations compared to assimilated or separated individuals. Integrative complexity was assessed by asking study participants to write answers to questions like "What does it mean to you to be bicultural?" and then trained raters scored them for the degree to which they were able to recognize causality, see issues from different points of view, and show value trade-offs. This research also showed that pressure to acculturate drives individuals toward more integrative complexity.[53] Hence, integrative complexity might be developed rather than a completely in-born trait.

Research on acculturation suggests that is possible to adjust to a new culture. This is important because many people experience **culture shock**, which is stressful and uncomfortable when a new culture is experienced for the first time. It's important to remember that this is a normal reaction, and you can work through your feelings of stress in stages. In addition, as a leader, it's important to understand that some of your followers may be recent immigrants who may be experiencing such conflicts and you can help them adjust through CQ.

CULTURE SHOCK

Learning Objective 12.7: Devise a plan for coping with the symptoms of culture shock.

Culture shock has become a common term, and most people are now familiar with the concept. The term was coined by an anthropologist who defined *culture shock* as the distress experienced by a traveler from the loss of familiar patterns of social interaction.[54] He described several "symptoms" of culture shock, including the following:

1. Stress due to the effort required to make necessary adjustments
2. Having a sense of loss from missing family and friends—"homesickness"
3. Wanting to avoid interactions with persons from the host culture
4. Feeling helpless and wanting to depend on those from one's home country
5. Having a fear of being robbed or injured, or becoming ill
6. Being angry at delays and inconveniences experienced
7. Feeling incompetent from not being able to cope with the new environment.

Culture shock is a series of phases a person goes through—particularly expatriates on assignment. First, the expatriate is excited and finds the new culture to be "exotic." Then, he begins to feel it is "wicked and silly." Finally, he sees it as "dissimilar and diverse."[55] The process of culture shock from pre-departure to reentry is shown in Figure 12.5. As this figure illustrates, the impact of cultural transitions on well-being follows a W-shaped curve. During the pre-departure phase, there is a sense of excitement and anticipation of experiencing a new adventure in another culture. On arrival, there is typically a sense of confusion due to jet lag and getting accommodated to one's surroundings. As noted previously, most expatriates experience a honeymoon period followed by a plunge when they begin to encounter difficulties in understanding cultural practices and values. Over time, reconciliation occurs, and the expatriate begins to adjust and accommodate to the new environment. Nearing the time he will return home, there is a similar excitement as that of pre-departure where the expatriate puts things in order in the host country and makes preparations to return to his home country.

 Culture Shock

Figure 12.5 Stages of Culture Shock

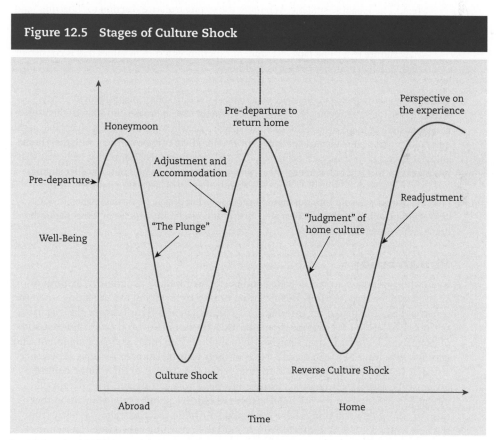

Source: Gaw, K. F. (2000). Reverse culture shock in students returning from overseas. *International Journal of Intercultural Relations*, 24(1), 83–104; Oberg, K. (1960). Culture shock adjustment to new cultural environments. *Practical Anthropology*, 7, 177–182.

Critical Thinking Question: Give an example of when you found something troubling about a different culture. What did you do?

Cultural Retooling

The psychological process of adaptation to another culture is called cultural retooling.[56] Using longitudinal data from foreign-born master's degree students in the United States, researchers found that during cultural retooling individuals experience internal conflicts. This conflict can be related to either values or disruptions in routines. Cultural retooling follows three distinct phases:

> **Phase 1. Deep conflict**—feeling illegitimate and awkward (e.g., A Japanese student does not feel comfortable talking about her strengths at networking events.)
> **Phase 2. Ambivalence**—adjusting and not feeling as negative about the behavior (e.g., The Japanese student overcomes the strong negative reaction to "boasting" and begins to imitate others at networking events.)
> **Phase 3. Authenticity**—naturally engaging in the new behavior consistent with the new culture (e.g., The Japanese student experiences a shift in values that is consistent with talking about her strengths to others.)

Not all of the participants in the study experienced the third phase of authenticity. They adapted using different strategies. Some took an integrative approach and allowed themselves to change (telling themselves it was okay to behave a certain way because it is acceptable in the new culture and personalizing experiences by making them more congruent with their home culture). Using an instrumental approach, those finding themselves in conflict recognize that it is necessary to adapt by switching their culture's behavior for a new one. Another strategy was to suppress their conflict by telling themselves they were just acting out a role. This research provides insight into the thought processes that people go through when making cross-cultural adjustments. The next adjustment discussed is the process of returning to the home culture after an assignment.

Repatriation

Even when an expatriate has adjusted and performed well on assignment, he must also be prepared for **repatriation**. Repatriation, or reentry, refers to the transition when the expatriate has completed the international assignment and returns home.[57] Expatriates are at risk of leaving the organization after they return. It has been estimated that 10% of expatriates leave their firm shortly after completing an international assignment, and another 14% leave between 2 and 3 years of their return.[58] Expatriates may experience a similar sequence of culture shock feelings when they return to their home culture. Successful expatriates become accustomed to their host culture and are tolerant of unfamiliar situations and work habits. **Reverse culture shock** is the realization that time has moved on and things have not stood still while the expatriate was away from the home office.[59, 60] Things have changed, and the returning expatriate experiences confusion and disappointment that may lead to a temporary state of depression and a sense of loss. Upon return to the home country, they may even look judgmentally upon their home culture as they realize some of the negative aspects of their own national culture. Successful expatriates become accustomed to their host culture and are tolerant of unfamiliar situations and work habits. They may be disappointed in the reactions of coworkers and superiors upon their return—as noted previously. Also, they feel that their work abroad is not understood or appreciated and expected rewards and promotions may not follow.[61] Other employees who stayed home may have been promoted, and the expatriate was "out of sight, out of mind" in the eyes of their supervisor. Finally, there is a readjustment phase (whether they expatriate leaves the job or not) in which there is resolution of the reentry culture shock and the expatriate puts the experience into perspective.

As shown in Figure 12.5, the expatriate can expect a series of "culture bumps" and research suggests the following steps to cope with them:

1. Pinpoint the specific time when you felt different or uncomfortable.
2. Define the situation.
3. List the behaviors of the other person(s).
4. List your own behavior.
5. List your feelings in the situation.
6. List the behaviors you expect from people in your own culture in that same situation.
7. Reflect on the underlying value in your culture that prompts that behavior expectation.[62]

Communication and validation are important to successful repatriation.[63,64] Communication is how much information the expatriate has regarding what is happening at home while on assignment. With higher levels of communication, those who return are more proactive, effective, and satisfied with their jobs after they return.[65] Fortunately, today we have Skype and Google hangouts (virtual face-to-face chat rooms), which allow expatriates to have face-to-face contact with their families and colleagues while on assignment. If the family is living abroad with the expatriate, the spouse has a significant influence on the expatriate adjustment process.[66] Culture shock may be more difficult for the spouse who may feel isolated while the expatriate has peers at work to interact with.[67] Validation refers to the amount of recognition the expatriate gets for success on the international assignment. This may, include a promotion—those who are promoted after an expatriate assignment adjust better than those who are not.[68]

It is important to keep this in mind and anticipate the "highs" and "lows" that will likely be experienced while on an expatriate assignment. Being able to work through culture shock is critical for expatriates since many organizations now expect significant international experience as a prerequisite to promotion to the highest rank. It has been reported that "companies like GE, Citigroup, Shell, Siemens, and Nokia are using international assignments of high potential employees as the means to develop their managers' global leadership mindset and competencies."[69] International assignments are the most effective source for developing global leaders.[70] So if you have aspirations to be an executive-level leader, it is important for you to understand the process of expatriate cross-cultural adjustment and be ready for the adjustment process of culture shock. Fortunately, OB researchers have been studying this process for a number of years.

CROSS-CULTURAL ADJUSTMENT FOR EXPATRIATES

Learning Objective 12.8: Explain the steps for an expatriate to take when adjusting to a cross-cultural assignment.

Jack Welch stated that the CEOs of the future will be able to adjust to other cultures:

> The Jack Welch of the future cannot be like me. I spent my entire career in the U.S. The next head of General Electric will be somebody who spent time in Bombay, in Hong Kong, in Buenos Aires. We have to send our best and brightest overseas and make sure they have the training that will allow them to be the global leaders who will make GE flourish in the future.[71]

Welch was right. His successor, Jeffrey Immelt held a series of leadership positions with GE that included marketing and global product development, and Vice President of Worldwide Marketing and Product Management for GE Appliances. Despite the prevalence and importance of expatriates on international assignments, poor cross-cultural adjustment often results in dissatisfaction and lower performance.[72,73] This can be costly for organizations that make a significant investment in training, relocating, and compensating expatriates. Some estimate the failure rate (leaving an assignment early) to be between 8% and 12%.[74,75,76] Recently, a study of global leadership trends was released by the consulting firm Right Management, which found that managers still fail in overseas assignments. A survey of 202 CEOs and senior human resource management professionals was conducted and found that just 58% of overseas assignments were considered to be successful, and there was little difference based upon the region.[77] With respect to the costs, for the United States, expatriate failure costs have been estimated to be about $1 million per failure,[78,79] and the total economic impact of failure ranges between $2 billion and $2.5 billion.[80,81] There are psychological effects on expatriates and decreased productivity that are not accounted for in these estimates.[82]

A study of the adjustment experiences of 213 expatriates from three U.S.-based Fortune 500 companies found perceived support from the organization influenced their adjustment.[83] Expatriates' adjustment was, in turn, related to their performance as rated by their supervisors. Surface-level cultural differences (e.g., food, housing, and climate) were most strongly related to general adjustment. However, deep-level cultural differences (e.g., values and assumptions) affected work and interaction adjustment, and expatriates who reported self-transcendence had an easier time adjusting to their expatriate assignment. Self-transcendence includes universalism (understanding, appreciation, tolerance, and protection for the welfare of all people and for nature) and benevolence (preservation and enhancement of the welfare of people with whom one is in frequent personal contact).[84]

Critical Thinking Questions: Have you been on a study abroad experience (or an expatriate assignment)? Describe your process of cultural adjustment. If you have not been on a study abroad experience (or expatriate assignment), explain why.

Expatriate managers need to realize that they don't have to go it alone. Adjustments in personal interactions with people from a host culture were a significant predictor of

Increasing Cultural Agility

Many organizations like Coca-Cola and Gillette International rotate executives on international assignments to develop managers' cultural agility according to Laura Curnett Santana from the Center for Creative Leadership. Cultural agility is a person's flexibility with respect to adjusting to another culture. Santana suggests five tactics to increase your cultural agility and improve your effectiveness as a leader:[85]

1. **Switch your frame of reference.** Set aside your own beliefs, listen, and watch. For example, keep an open mind about the foods and customs of another culture you encounter.
2. **Be curious.** Ask nonjudgmental questions. For example, ask a person from China why they are reluctant to speak in class.
3. **Look for commonalities.** Ask what seems familiar, and find value in this situation. For example, ask a person from another culture what they want for their children and grandchildren. By asking this question, you may find that most cultures want their children to have good health, happiness, and prosperity.
4. **Reflect and learn.** Process your experiences, and reflect on what is familiar and what is new. For example, try to understand why you might be fearful of people from the Middle East.
5. **Champion others.** Let others know when you discover the expertise of others or learn that someone is doing something valuable. For example, when a person makes an adjustment to your culture, be sure to provide them with positive feedback by telling them you appreciate the gesture.

Discussion Questions:

1. Which of the five tactics for cultural agility do you feel is most important and why?
2. Provide an example of a time when you were uncomfortable with something you experienced with a person from another culture. Reflect on this experience. What did you learn from this?.

Source: Santana, L. (2010). Five ways to boost your cross-cultural agility. *Forbes*. Retrieved on August 1, 2013, from www.forbes.com/2010/09/29/cross-cultural-agility-globalization-leadership-managing-ccl.html. Visit ccl.org for more information.

expatriate retention in a study of 321 U.S. expatriates assigned to the Pacific Rim or Western Europe.[86] Also, having a mentor provides both career and social support that are essential.[87] Mentors are key resources before, during, and after international assignments and are often indispensable for facilitating promotions after the assignment ends. Expatriates must think in terms of having a network of mentors who can provide support for adaptation in terms of host country culture, task assistance, and office culture (these may or may not be the same mentor and can be supervisors, peers, or someone outside of the organization).[88] Finally, training in cross-cultural interactions, culture, and language has been shown to improve adjustment for expatriates.[89]

LEADERSHIP IMPLICATIONS: "EXPLAIN BEFORE BLAME"

The effective leader must keep the phrase "explain before blame" in mind when interacting with people from other cultures—employees, supervisors, peers, customers, and negotiating partners. Culture, like personality, is something that is relatively stable, and the leader's best tools are to understand it and learn to develop mutually adjusted relationships with those from different cultures. The tips for cultural agility should be helpful in explain before blame. It is important to keep an open mind and be curious about other cultures. It's fine to politely ask questions about other cultural values and practices. Try to focus on what you have in common. For example, the GLOBE research reviewed in this chapter indicated that there are some cultural universals that define effective leadership. Focus on what you have learned from cross-cultural interactions and support others by providing positive feedback.

In summary, the skills needed for successful interactions with another culture are CQ, cultural retooling, and an integrative approach to acculturation. It is also important to anticipate and develop a plan to cope with culture shock if you embark on an expatriate assignment. These guidelines are also helpful for the reentry process for those returning from an international assignment. This chapter has hopefully increased your awareness of the effects of culture on OB. The effective leader must be able to suspend judgment (explain before blame) and use their CQ to effectively adjust to those from other cultures whether assigned in the United States or abroad. By now, you realize that in today's global environment, cross-cultural differences affect every aspect of OB. Throughout this textbook, we have referenced research on how culture affects leader effectiveness with respect to perceptions, motivation, negotiation, teams, and more.

KEY TERMS

assimilation, 322
behavioral CQ, 322
cognitive CQ, 322
cultural intelligence (CQ), 320
cultural retooling, 320
cultural tightness–looseness, 318
culturally endorsed implicit leadership theory (CLT), 318

cultural looseness, 318
cultural tightness, 318
culture shock, 324
Global Leadership and Organizational Behavior Effectiveness (GLOBE) project, 316
global mind-set, 320
high-context cultures, 311
integration, 322

integrative complexity, 324
low-context cultures, 312
marginalization, 322
metacognitive CQ, 322
motivational CQ, 322
repatriation, 326
reverse culture shock, 326
separation, 322
third culture, 320

SUGGESTIONS FOR FURTHER READING

Deloitte Consulting. (2013). Resetting horizons. Human capital trends report. Retrieved on August 1, 2013, from http://www.deloitte.com/view/en_US/us/Services/consulting/human-capital/human-capital-trends/index.htm

Earley, P. C., & Ang, S. A. (2003). *Cultural intelligence: Individual interactions across cultures*. Stanford, CA: Stanford University Press.

Friedman, T. L. (2006). *The world is flat: A brief history of the twenty-first century*. New York, NY: Macmillan.

House, R. J., Dorfman, P. W., Javidan, M., Hanges, P. J., & Sully de Luque, M. (2013). *Strategic leadership across cultures: GLOBE Study of CEO leadership behavior and effectiveness in 24 countries*. Thousand Oaks, CA: Sage.

Jeannet, J. (2000). *Managing with a global mindset*. New York, NY: Financial Times Press.

TOOLKIT ACTIVITY 12.1

Journey to Sharahad

Background

This exercise simulates an intercultural exchange between Americans and a fictional culture. Participants role-playing either culture can learn from the experience. The task is simple, but the cultural barriers are considerable.

The briefing sheets for the roles are on the following pages. It is important that you do not read the briefing sheet for the other culture or the discussion questions following the briefing sheets. First, the Sharahadans and Americans will go to separate rooms to discuss how to role play their cultures (10 minutes).

You will join a small group of 4 or 5 (more than one group can participate at once). Each group should have 2 "Americans" and 2-3 "Sharahadans." You will discuss the situation for 15-20 minutes and then return to the classroom for debriefing.

Situation: the Americans have proposed a business meeting in order to gather information on Mizar Marketing. The questions relate to what kind of performance the Sharahadans can promise the Americans as their distributors. If the information is favorable, they will propose a profitable deal for both sides.

Sharahadan Briefing Sheet

You are representatives of Mizar Marketing, Inc., a computer distributorship in the country of Sharahad. Mizar has been very successful marketing and distributing computers in this region for the last 12 years. Your company has witnessed steady double-digit growth every year it has been in business. You attribute this to your astute customer service skills and your ability to literally speak the language of all of your customers. Your company currently distributes 100,000 units a year (and earns a commission of 15% on each unit sold). You anticipate continued growth—but then, who can predict the future?

An American computer company has contacted Mizar and requested a meeting. You assume that this meeting is some kind of exploratory visit to see if Mizar can serve as the American company's distributor. You are looking forward to meeting the American representatives, even though you don't know much about American culture (although you do speak English).

Sharahadan culture exhibits very different communication patterns and values. Sharahadans pride themselves on their ability to speak expressively and to interact with others in a close personal manner. This involves using

intense eye contact and standing very close to the person to whom they are speaking (6-12" distance is quite common). Sharahadans like to **establish personal relationships before conducting business** and prefer to discuss personal matters first. Sharahadans are also likely **to discuss multiple topics simultaneously**, switching back and forth to keep the conversion animated, and always interjecting personal matters into the business at hand. **Sharahadans do not speculate on future events.** Any kind of prediction or claim about what will done in the future is foreign to Sharahadan ways. **Sharahadans are also very humble**, and never brag about their achievements (bragging is considered taboo), preferring instead to use such phrases as "I have been fortunate" or "God willing" to refer to past successes or future goals. Last, Sharahadans **often imply real meanings nonverbally, usually through their degree of enthusiasm**. For example, louder vocalizations, closer proximity, and physical contact (such as a hand on another person's shoulder) always accompany positive messages (such as agreement or when giving genuine compliments).

Mizar has two major competitors in the region: Altair Computers and Vega International. Both Altair and Vega sell fewer computers than your company does and have been in business for less time. They each sell about 50,000 units a year, and currently experience a 5% annual growth rate. However, you would consider it rude to point out their deficiencies so bluntly, preferring instead to let your judgement show in your lack of enthusiasm when you praise them.

Whatever behavior your American guests display, you will always treat them with respect and communicate with them for at least 15-20 minutes—even if they violate your cultural norms.

American Briefing Sheet

You and another business associate are sales representatives from an American computer company. You have been chosen to travel far away to the country of Sharahad. Your company has learned that Mizar Marketing, Inc. in Sharahad can distribute your computers in this region of the world for a much cheaper price than your current distributor, Altair Computers. You have come to meet with the company's representatives. **Your goal is to close a deal with them, asking them to sell 10,000 units a year of which their commission will be 15%.** Your current distributor in this region (Altair Computers) can currently sell only 5,000 of your computers (at a commission rate of 25%). Any deal that increases your sales volume and reduces the current commission rate would be considered an improvement and should be accepted.

You did not want to come on this trip. You know very little about the Sharahadan culture. You have heard rumors that the Sharahadans are pushy and loud, have difficulty giving straight answers, and do not take business very seriously. You arrived on a flight late last night, and had a rough night of sleep at the hotel. You have seen little of the country yet. This meeting is your first real experience with the host culture. Fortunately, you know that the representatives at the meeting will speak English, although from your earlier communications, you get the impression that they are not well versed in American cultural norms.

Your plan is to start the meeting by getting right down to business and exploring whether Mizar can meet your needs. **Before you can propose any deals, however, you need to confirm the following about Mizar Marketing**: (1) Are they growing and do they have a plan for continued expansion? (2) Can they sell additional 10,000 units a year? (3) Are they committed to high standards of customer satisfaction? If the answers to these questions are unclear or unsatisfactory, there is little point in proposing a deal.

Because you cannot afford to alienate Altair (in case this deal doesn't go through), you would prefer not to mention who your current distributor is.

As you and your partner walk into Mizar's corporate headquarters, you are amazed at the surroundings: ornate Sharahadan office suites and conference rooms furnished with both traditional and modern fixtures. After making your introductions to the people in the outer offices you are shown into a modest looking room. There, the representatives of Mizar await you. You approach them — ready to act in your most professional manner—and ready to close the deal in 15–20 minutes . . .

Source: Journey to Sharahad. Phil Darg. 1999, all rights reserved. Distributed by globalEDGE.

Discussion Questions

1. Did you come to an agreement? What was the agreement? If not, why not?
2. [For the Americans:] What kinds of cultural differences did you notice in your discussion with the Sharahadans?
3. [For the Sharahadans:] What things did your American guests do that you found confusing or frustrating?
4. What are the real world implications of an exercise such as this one?

CASE STUDY 12.1

"A Person Needs Face Like a Tree Needs Bark"

American Brian Cook meets with his Chinese change manager Chan Ling and his team at the Beijing office of a European corporation to discuss last month's delay in the change deadlines. He questions Chan Ling repeatedly about his team's underperformance. Brian openly states he believes the team is not pushing hard enough and that there is a lack of commitment. He stresses than Ling is accountable for the results of the team and that he should have informed him about the issues. Ling nods silently and peers out the window. He picks up his papers, walks through the door without further discussion, and never returns (actual example with fictitious names).

Chan Ling has lost face. The directness of Brian's questioning was interpreted by Chan as personal insult. He saw Brian as rude, and their working relationship ended abruptly based on this incident. Chan also terminated his employment with the company at a time when he was really needed. What happened?

In China, as in other cultures around the world, "face" is more important than anything else. Face is related to the Western concept of dignity, but it goes much deeper than that. There is a Chinese proverb that reads *Ren yao lian, shu yao pi* ("A person needs face, like a tree needs bark"). Losing face has serious consequences for people from such cultures since there is a profound emotion of shame associated with losing face, and this may reflect on the person, their families, or even their entire community. Chan felt a deep sense of embarrassment from Brian's assertive questioning style, which is commonly accepted in the United States and many other Western cultures. What Brian didn't realize is that this is not acceptable in all cultures; thus, his leadership effectiveness was compromised.

Source: Boot, A., & Siebelink, H. (2013). Cross-cultural leadership: How to avoid making people lose face. Retrieved on July 21, 2013, from www.leadershipwatch-aadboot.com/2013/07/14/cross-cultural-leadership-how-to-avoid-making-people-lose-face. Reprinted with permission.

Discussion Questions

1. How could Brian have prepared more effectively for his international assignment (refer to the guidelines for culture shock and cultural agility)?
2. What cultural values (Hofstede; GLOBE) help explain Chan's reaction? What are the differences between the United States and China?
3. What should Brian do now? Develop a plan for addressing the situation.

SELF-ASSESSMENT 12.1

What Is Your Cultural Intelligence?

This self-assessment exercise identifies your approach to interacting with people from different cultures. There are no "right or wrong" answers, and this is not a test. You don't have to share your results with others unless you wish to do so.

Part I. Taking the Assessment

You will be presented with some questions representing different situations involving cross-cultural interaction. Answer each question using the scale below each question.

As an example, the answer to a situation could look like this:

I like to try foods from international restaurants.

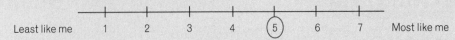

Least like me   1   2   3   4   ⑤   6   7   Most like me

1. I am conscious of the cultural knowledge I use when interacting with people with different cultural backgrounds.

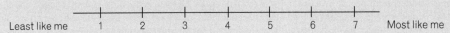

Least like me   1   2   3   4   5   6   7   Most like me

2. I know the legal and economic systems of other cultures.

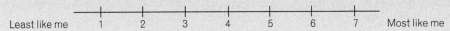

Least like me   1   2   3   4   5   6   7   Most like me

3. I enjoy interacting with people from different cultures.

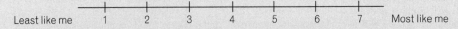

Least like me   1   2   3   4   5   6   7   Most like me

4. I change my verbal behavior (e.g., accent, tone) when a cross-cultural interaction requires it.

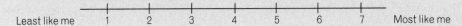

Least like me   1   2   3   4   5   6   7   Most like me

5. I adjust my cultural knowledge as I interact with people from a culture that is unfamiliar to me.

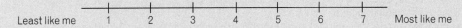

Least like me   1   2   3   4   5   6   7   Most like me

6. I know the rules (e.g., vocabulary, grammar) of other languages.

Least like me   1   2   3   4   5   6   7   Most like me

7. I am confident that I can socialize with locals in a culture that is unfamiliar to me.

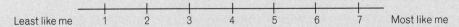

Least like me   1   2   3   4   5   6   7   Most like me

8. I use pause and slience differently to suit different cross-cultural situations.

Least like me   1   2   3   4   5   6   7   Most like me

9. I am conscious of the cultural knowledge I apply to cross-cultural interactions.

Least like me   1   2   3   4   5   6   7   Most like me

10. I know the cultural values and religious beliefs of other cultures.

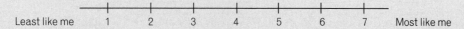

Least like me   1   2   3   4   5   6   7   Most like me

11. I am sure I can deal with the stresses of adjusting to a culture that is new to me.

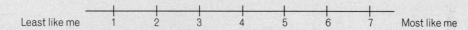

Least like me   1   2   3   4   5   6   7   Most like me

12. I vary the rate of my speaking when a cross-cultural situation requires it.

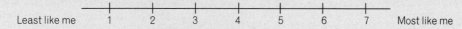

Least like me   1   2   3   4   5   6   7   Most like me

13. I check the accuracy of my cultural knowledge as I interact with people from different cultures.

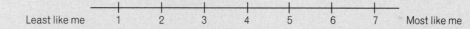

Least like me   1   2   3   4   5   6   7   Most like me

14. I know the marriage systems of other cultures.

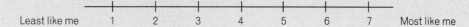

Least like me   1   2   3   4   5   6   7   Most like me

15. I enjoy living in cultures that are unfamiliar to me.

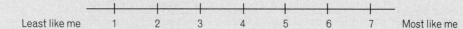

Least like me   1   2   3   4   5   6   7   Most like me

16. I change my nonverbal behavior when a cross-cultural situation requires it.

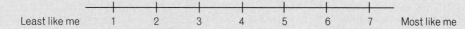

Least like me   1   2   3   4   5   6   7   Most like me

17. I know the arts and crafts of other cultures.

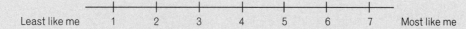

Least like me   1   2   3   4   5   6   7   Most like me

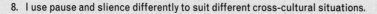

TOOLKIT

18. I am confident that I can get accustomed to the shopping conditions in a different culture.

Least like me   1   2   3   4   5   6   7   Most like me

19. I alter my facial expressions when a cross-cultural interaction requires it.

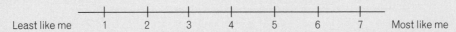

Least like me   1   2   3   4   5   6   7   Most like me

20. I know the rules of expressing nonverbal behaviors in other cultures.

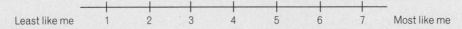

Least like me   1   2   3   4   5   6   7   Most like me

Part II. Scoring Instructions

In Step I, you rated yourself on 20 questions. Add the numbers you circled in each of the columns to derive your score for the four aspects of cultural intelligence (CQ). These dimensions have been shown through research to be related to cross-cultural adjustment and leader effectiveness and are described in the section on CQ in this chapter.

Metacognitive	Cognitive	Motivational	Behavioral
1. _____	2. _____	3. _____	4. _____
5. _____	6. _____	7. _____	8. _____
9. _____	10. _____	11. _____	12. _____
13. _____	14. _____	15. _____	16. _____
17. _____	18. _____	19. _____	20. _____
Total _____	_____	_____	_____

Sources: Eisenberg, J., Lee, H. J., Brueck, F., Brenner, B., Claes, M. T., Mironski, J., & Bell, R. (2013). Can business schools make students culturally competent? Effects of cross-cultural management courses on cultural intelligence. *Academy of Management Learning and Education, 12*(4), 603–621. DOI: 10.5465/amle.2012.0022.

SECTION V

CREATING CHANGE

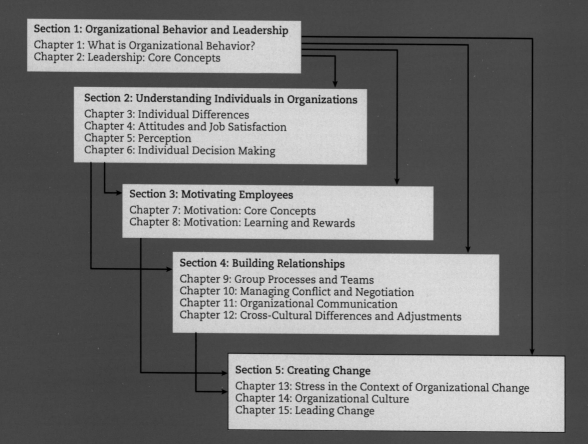

Section 1: Organizational Behavior and Leadership

Chapter 1: What is Organizational Behavior?
Chapter 2: Leadership: Core Concepts

Section 2: Understanding Individuals in Organizations

Chapter 3: Individual Differences
Chapter 4: Attitudes and Job Satisfaction
Chapter 5: Perception
Chapter 6: Individual Decision Making

Section 3: Motivating Employees

Chapter 7: Motivation: Core Concepts
Chapter 8: Motivation: Learning and Rewards

Section 4: Building Relationships

Chapter 9: Group Processes and Teams
Chapter 10: Managing Conflict and Negotiation
Chapter 11: Organizational Communication
Chapter 12: Cross-Cultural Differences and Adjustments

Section 5: Creating Change

Chapter 13: Stress in the Context of Organizational Change
Chapter 14: Organizational Culture
Chapter 15: Leading Change

13

STRESS IN THE CONTEXT OF ORGANIZATIONAL CHANGE

"ROAD WARRIORS"

Research has examined the impact of business travel on executive stress. A *Wall Street Journal* article described the travel demands of Michael Bonsignore, the CEO of Honeywell, describing sleep deprivation, delays, disruption to regular eating habits, and constant time pressure as he travelled over 200,000 miles a year.[1] Executive travel is necessary in today's global environment with the need to coordinate multinationals and make global deals. While e-mail and videoconferencing has somewhat reduced the need to travel (see Chapter 11), the article concludes with "the need to go out and develop key relationships has increased markedly, and many feel this cannot be accomplished via the telephone or through other electronic means."[2] It can be expected that business travel will remain a fact of life for many leaders, resulting in travel stress.

Travel, including business travel, can be exciting, but research has identified sources of stress related to business travel at three points: pre-trip stress, trip stress, and post-trip stress.[3] Pre-trip stressors involve planning, trying to accomplish tasks at work before leaving, and taking care of issues for the home and family. Travel itself can be very stressful and includes trip stress such as having flight delays or cancellations, losing luggage, and clearing security and customs. Travel disrupts diet, exercise, and sleeping patterns, particularly the international travel that is so often needed in today's global business arena. As discussed in Chapter 12, adjusting to the host country and culture shock are sources of stress as well. After the trip, post-trip stress sets in due to readjustment to the job and family life. Often, a returning executive has a full calendar of people needing urgent meetings after returning to the office.

Organizations have responded to travel stress in a number of ways, including travel and jet lag training, and maintaining contact with executives while they travel.[4] The availability of the Internet on long flights has helped executives to stay in contact with their work and family. The executive also needs to take care of themselves by maintaining a healthy diet and exercising. Some have found that music or meditation helps relieve travel stress. Planning ahead and careful packing can alleviate travel stress by ensuring that the business traveler has access to necessities while traveling. Try to avoid checking luggage, if possible, and pack your carry-on with a change of clothing, toiletries, and healthy snacks.

Learning Objectives

After studying this chapter, you should be able to do the following:

13.1: Define *stress,* and discuss the estimated costs to business.

13.2: Explain how stress affects performance, attitudes, and turnover.

13.3: Provide an example of the relationship between organizational change and stress.

13.4: Identify the stressors that come from the work environment.

13.5: Compare and contrast the three types of strain that may occur.

13.6: Discuss the prevalence of work stress on a global scale.

13.7: Develop a plan for coping with stress during change.

13.8: Recommend organizational interventions and policies that help employees cope with stress.

Get the edge on your studies at edge.sagepub.com/scandura
- Take the chapter quiz
- Review key terms with eFlashcards
- Explore multimedia resources, SAGE readings, and more!

$SAGE edge™

Being a high-ranking executive involves a great deal of business travel, and it is perhaps not surprising that it is listed as one of the most stressful occupations (see Table 13.1). However, perhaps even more stressful occupations are those that are dangerous, such as serving in the military or being a firefighter or an airline pilot (both occupations have a great deal of responsibility of the lives of others). Some jobs are considered "dirty jobs" since they have unpleasant working conditions (e.g., doing construction work during humid summer months). In other cases, the job entails dealing with rude customers. If you are looking for a job that is one of the least stressful, consider the jobs similar to those in the left-hand column.

 Stress

Table 13.1 Least Stressful and Most Stressful Jobs in the United States

Least Stressful	Most Stressful
1. Audiologist	1. Enlisted Military Personnel
2. Hair Stylist	2. Military General
3. Jeweler	3. Firefighter
4. University Professor	4. Airline Pilot
5. Seamstress/Tailor	5. Event Coordinator
6. Dietician	6. Public Relations Executive
7. Medical Records Technician	7. Senior Corporate Executive
8. Librarian	8. Newspaper Reporter
9. Multimedia Artist	9. Police Officer
10. Drill Press Operator	10. Taxi Driver

Source: Giang, V. (2014). The 10 most stressful jobs of 2014. Retrieved on March 3, 2014, from http://www.businessinsider.com/most-stressful-jobs-2014-1.

WHAT IS STRESS?

Learning Objective 13.1: Define *stress*, and discuss the estimated costs to business.

This chapter reviews the fundamental definitions and research on stress at work. Then, stress in the context of organizational change will be discussed since this is a major source of work-related stress that is on the rise.

We all think we know what stress is and that we know how to cope. Take the following stress fact or fiction quiz to see how much you know about stress:

True or False?

1. People who feel stress are nervous to start with.
2. You always know when you are under stress.
3. Prolonged physical exercise will weaken your resistance to stress.
4. Stress is always bad.
5. Stress can cause unpleasant problems, but at least it can't kill you.
6. Stress can be controlled with medication.
7. Work-related stress can be left at the office and not brought home.
8. Stress is only in the mind; it's not physical.
9. Stress can be eliminated.
10. There's nothing you can do about stress without making drastic changes in your lifestyle.

The correct answer for all ten questions is *false*. If you answered *true* to even one, you're a victim of a stress myth.[5]

Person–Environment Fit

This chapter will present research evidence and dispel some of the stress myths. There are both individual and organizational contributors to the experience of work stress. The focus of the chapter will be on individual stress and how to cope with it. However, a link will be made between the impacts of organizational change on how individuals experience stress.

A useful explanation of the link between the organizational situation and an individual's response is the degree of congruence between the person and the work situation, called **person–environment (P–E) fit**. P-E fit theory defines stress as a perceived dynamic state involving uncertainty about something important.[6] More specifically, stress is "a discrepancy between an employee's perceived state and desired state, provided that the presence of this discrepancy is considered important to the employee."[7] In other words, stress is the difference between the demands (or **stressors**) placed on a person and their ability to cope with the demands and reach their goals.

Psychological job strain is defined as the combination of greater psychological job demands and lower **job control**.[8] This results in **organizational stress,** which has been shown to have serious consequences to employees in terms of their well-being and health. In addition, stress costs organizations billions of dollars each year:

> Nearly half of all workers suffer from moderate to severe stress while on the job, according to a recent survey. And 66 percent of employees report that they have difficulty focusing on tasks at work because of stress. Stress has been called the "health epidemic of the 21st century" by the World Health Organization and is estimated to cost American businesses up to $300 billion a year.[9]

One study of more than 46,000 U.S. employees found health care costs were 46% higher for workers who experienced high stress.[10] Also, it is estimated that half of the days employees are absent from work are due to stress.[11] The estimates for the cost of stress also include lower productivity due to **job burnout** as well as workplace accidents. Job burnout "is a prolonged response to chronic stressors on the job."[12] Symptoms of burnout are exhaustion, cynicism, detachment from work, and feelings of ineffectiveness or failure.[13] Burnout is a serious problem for many employees and affects their attitudes motivation and job performance. Toolkit Activity 13.1 at the end of this chapter contains a list of the warning signs of burnout to aid in the recognition of this serious condition in yourself and others.

 Burnout

 Critical Thinking Questions: How would you know if a coworker is experiencing burnout from work? What would you do about it?

STRESS AND ORGANIZATIONAL PERFORMANCE

Learning Objective 13.2: Explain how stress affects performance, attitudes, and turnover.

A survey of 1,950 adults found most are living with stress that is higher than what they believe to be healthy and that they are not having much success at managing or reducing their stress. Specific survey results included the following: [14]

- Forty-two percent of adults report that their stress level has increased, and 36% say their stress level has stayed the same over the past 5 years (see Figure 13.1).
- Sixty-one percent of adults say that managing stress is extremely or very important, but only 35% report they are doing a very good or excellent job at this.
- Forty-four percent of adults say they are not doing enough (or are not sure) to manage their stress, but 19% say they never engage in stress management activities.
- Money (71%), work (69%), and the economy (59%) continue to be the most commonly reported sources of stress.

These survey results show that work is one of the primary sources of stress in people's lives. But can stress have a positive side? Next, research on the negative and possible positive impacts of stress will be discussed.

Stress can be performance enhancing or disruptive. A study of executive stress found that the experience of challenging or rewarding job experiences related differently to outcomes than stress from associated with hindering or constraining job experiences. There are two general types of stress: **challenge-related stress** and **hindrance-related stress.** Challenge-related stress may be positive, or what is known as **eustress**, or "good stress" from the Greek root *eu* for "good."[15] Hindrance-related stress is excessive or undesirable constraints that interfere with an individual's ability to achieve goals, creating "negative stress."[16]

Figure 13.1   Unhealthy Levels of Stress

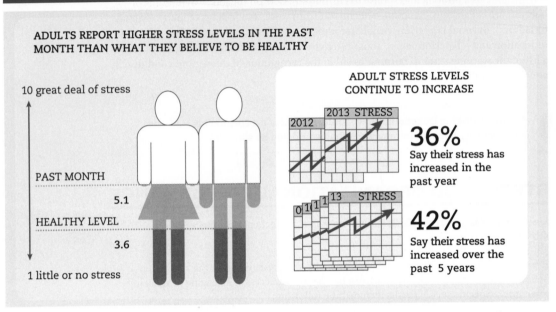

ADULTS REPORT HIGHER STRESS LEVELS IN THE PAST MONTH THAN WHAT THEY BELIEVE TO BE HEALTHY

10 great deal of stress

PAST MONTH

5.1

HEALTHY LEVEL

3.6

1 little or no stress

ADULT STRESS LEVELS CONTINUE TO INCREASE

2012   2013 STRESS

36%
Say their stress has increased in the past year

0 1 1 13   STRESS

42%
Say their stress has increased over the past 5 years

Source: Stress in America. (2013). American Psychological Association. Retrieved on March 3, 2014, from http://www.stressinamerica.org.

 Consequences of Stress

Some executives actually thrive on the good stress, and there may be an optimum level of stress for performance for some individuals, known as the Yerkes–Dodson law.[17, 18] This law states that performance increases with increasing stress to an optimum point, but then the stress becomes too much and performance declines. The Yerkes–Dodson law suggests that the relationship between pressure and performance looks like an inverted U, as shown in Figure 13.2. Increased arousal can help improve performance but only to a certain point. At the point when arousal becomes excessive, performance diminishes. Psychologists Robert Yerkes and John Dillingham Dodson discovered that mild electrical shocks could be used to motivate rats to complete a maze, but when the electrical shocks became too strong, the rats would scurry around in random directions to escape. Increasing stress and arousal helps focus attention on tasks but only up to a certain point. For example, when you are studying for an exam, an optimal level of stress can help you concentrate and remember the correct answers while taking the exam. However, too much stress ("test anxiety") impairs your ability to focus and you start missing answers.

These forms of stress are not limited to executives, however. Both forms of stress relate to psychological strain, but one study found that hindrance-related stress is more related to lessened loyalty and intentions to quit.[19] Hindrance-related stress also negatively affects learning. However, a challenging learning environment increases learning.[20] A meta-analysis of 183 independent samples found support for the negative relationship of hindrance stress to job satisfaction and organizational commitment and positive relationships with turnover

Figure 13.2   The Inverted-U Relationship Between Pressure and
Performance

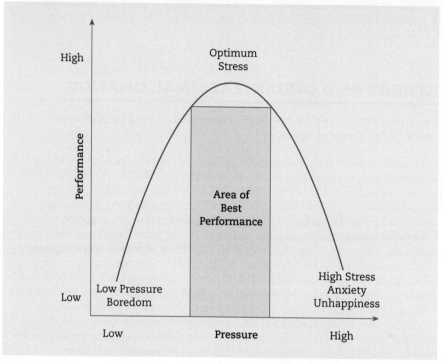

Source: Diamond, D. M., Campbell, A. M., Park, C. R., Halonen, J., & Zoladz, P. R. (2007). The temporal dynamics
model of emotional memory processing: a synthesis on the neurobiological basis of stress-induced amnesia,
flashbulb and traumatic memories, and the Yerkes-Dodson law. *Neural Plasticity,* 1–33. p. 3.

intentions, turnover, and withdrawal behaviors (absenteeism and turnover).[21] Challenge
stressors had the opposite effect on these outcomes.

Stress negatively impacts job performance and attitudes. Stress relates to lower job
satisfaction, organizational commitment, and job involvement as well as higher frustration
(these are psychological outcomes). Second, stress is related to more use of health care,
sick days, and workers' compensation claims (physical outcomes). Third, stress is related
to lower job performance, more counterproductive behavior, and accidents (behavioral
outcomes).[22]

The previous sections provide the essential understanding of how stress relates to work
outcomes. Stress has been increasing due to organizational change, which brings both
challenges and hindrances for employees due to more uncertainty at work. Uncertainty
creates strain, and it is not surprising that employees experience heightened levels of stress
during organizational change. As noted earlier, the theme of this chapter is the link between

Stress During Change

organizational change and individual stress responses. Next, the research on organizational change as a source of stress will be discussed.

Critical Thinking Question: Research suggests that stress is not necessarily always negative. Give an example of when stress can be a positive force in organizations.

STRESS AND ORGANIZATIONAL CHANGE

Learning Objective 13.3: Provide an example of the relationship between organizational change and stress.

Stress has been rising at the workplace due to organizational change. Change increases uncertainty and disrupts employees' regular work routines.[23] Employee resistance to organizational change is one of the most common sources of work stress.[24] The new organizational reality is one of competition with mergers, acquisitions, downsizings, and restructurings. These forces have increased psychological strain from work.[25] Uncertainty during organizational change may be related to layoffs, pay cuts, fewer promotion opportunities, and changes to the culture of the organization (the importance of organizational culture will be discussed in Chapter 14).[26] **Change uncertainty** may be due to strategic, structural, and job-related factors.[27] The uncertainty about outcomes and the perceived importance of these outcomes combine to produce this type of stress.[28] For example, a hospital was studied as it underwent a major divisional consolidation. Employees were surveyed before and after the change was implemented; results showed stress was related to job dissatisfaction, intent to quit, and work-related irritation after the consolidation.[29] However, organizational commitment reduced the stress effect.

Organizations are stressed due to environmental pressures to compete or even stay out of bankruptcy in some cases. This stress translates into stress experienced by individuals as organizations try to adapt to the demands of their environment. Organizational change affects all aspects of work design due to increases in shift work, night and weekend work, increases in overtime work, demands of employees being asked to work faster, and not having enough time to finish their work.[30] The intensification of work (fast pace and constant change) over the past three decades has also resulted in strained relationships with customers, coworkers, and supervisors.[31] It has been noted that "change is difficult for an institution and for its employees. There is uncertainty about the future, about what the organization will 'look like,' and how the employees feel they will fit into the new structure" (p. 16).[32] A study followed the level of perceived stress over time and found that stress increased during the 2008–2009 economic recession, particularly for college-educated, White men, aged 45 to 64 years who were employed full-time.[33] This may be due to threat of job loss, actual job loss, and/or the loss of retirement funds during the recession.

Both organizations and individuals can take actions to alleviate the stress due to change.[34] One study of a consolidation of human resource functions across divisions of an Australian public service organization found organizations can manage the frequency of change and the planning involved in change.[35] An important finding of this study was that supportive leadership made a difference in the reports of stress during the change. Employees also need to develop coping mechanisms to deal with the stress of organizational change. Table 13.2 has tips for coping with stress due to change. For example, try to become accustomed to change and increase pace of work to keep up with changes.

Identifying Stressors

While change uncertainty is a major source of stress, it is not the only one. As noted previously, organizational change brings additional strains to roles and responsibilities. So in addition to uncertainty, change may bring about role conflicts and overload. Next, other sources of work-related stress, which often stem from organizational change, are discussed next.

SOURCES OF WORK-RELATED STRESS

Learning Objective 13.4: Identify the stressors that come from the work environment.

Stressors are situations and events that result in an employee experiencing strain.[36] The following stressors found at work are physical, task-related, role, social, work schedule-related, career-related, traumatic events, and stressful change processes.[37] For example, some work has physical demands such as the repetitive nature of factory work or transcription for a court reporter. Work schedule stress may be due to having to work the night shift in a hospital. Career-related stress may emanate from anxiety over whether or not a promotion will be earned. Some of these stressors come from roles that employees must play in the organization (e.g., playing the devil's advocate role in a highly contentious group—devil's advocate was discussed in Chapter 9).

Role Stress

As we learned in Chapter 9, roles are the behaviors that are expected of a person in a particular organizational context. People learn their roles in organizations and "act" them out daily. Roles can be a source of stress in a number of ways because they place demands on a person to fulfill expectations. **Role ambiguity** occurs where there is a lack of specificity or predictability about what a person's role is.[38] In short, the person does not know what is expected, which may be due to not understanding what a boss requires, for example. **Role conflict** occurs when there are incompatible demands regarding what a person's role is.[39] For example, a person's boss may want an employee to work late, but their coworkers want them to leave when they do so they don't look bad (intersender role conflict). Role conflict may also happen when organizational requirements conflict with personal values (person–role conflict). Interrole conflict occurs when a person holds multiple roles at the same time and feels torn by the demands of different role senders. For example, a student wants to please the professor by studying for a midterm exam but friends want to go out to dinner with them the night before the exam.

Role overload is a third form of role-related stress and it is caused by too much work, time pressure, and deadlines that a person feels unable to meet.[40] Role overload may be quantitative (the number of demands) or qualitative, which refers to an employee not having the qualifications to perform their work role.[41]

Table 13.2   Surviving the Stress of Organizational Change

1. **Don't count on anyone else coming along to relieve your stress.**

   Put *yourself* in charge of managing the pressure. There's a good chance you're the only one in your work situation who will, or even *can*, do much to lighten your psychological load.

2. **The organization is going to change—it must—if it is to survive and prosper.**

   Rather than banging your head against the wall of hard reality and bruising your spirit, invest your energy in making quick adjustments. Turn when the organization turns. Practice instant alignment. Your own decisions may do more to determine your stress level than anything the organization decides to do.

3. **Accept fate, and move on.**

   Don't yield to the seductive pull of self-pity, at least for any extended period of time. Acting like a victim threatens your future. You're better off if you appear resilient and remain productive. Just stand proud, pick up the pieces, and start putting your career back together.

4. **Study the situation intently.**

   Figure out how the game has changed, how priorities have been reordered. Decide which aspects of your job you should focus on to leverage up your effectiveness the most.

5. **Don't fall into the trap of believing there's such a thing as a low-stress organization that's on track to survive.**

   In fact, just the opposite is true. You serve your best interests by aligning with an outfit that's got the guts to endure the pains of change and by avoiding those organizations destined to go belly-up because of their desire for short-term comfort.

6. **Ask yourself if the struggle makes sense.**

   Are you really in a position to control the situation, or will you just get emotionally tired trying? Sometimes the most mature, most dignified, and most sensible move is to nobly accept what we can't change.

7. **Keep in step with the organization's intended rate of change.**

   March to the cadence that's being called by the people in charge instead of allowing yourself to take whatever amount of time you want or feel you need. Don't lag behind—there's little chance a lull will come along and give you a chance to play catch-up.

8. **Reengineer your job.**

   Eliminate unnecessary steps, get rid of busywork, and unload activities that don't contribute enough to the organization's current goals. Focus your efforts on doing the right things, and ditch those duties that don't count much, even if you can do them magnificently right.

9. **Speed up.**

   Cover more ground. Put your faith in action—in mobility—and maximize your personal productivity.

10. **Now's the time for some serious mind control.**

    Instead of worrying about bad things that might happen, get busy trying to create the kind of future you want. The best insurance policy for tomorrow is to make the most productive use of today.

11. **Remember the advice of Jonathan Kozol—"Pick battles big enough to matter, small enough to win."**

12. **Fall in love with your job, and keep the romance alive.**

Don't let the stress of change drive a wedge between you and your work. Sure, your employer will benefit if you are committed, but not as much as you will. High job commitment is a gift you should give to yourself.

13. **Stretch yourself today so you'll be in better shape tomorrow.**

Reach for new assignments that broaden your experience base. Remember that one of the best techniques for stress prevention is to keep updating your skills so you're highly employable.

14. **Develop a greater tolerance for constant changes in the game plan. For mid-course corrections. For raw surprise.**

Allow a little more confusion in your life. Be willing to feel your way along, to wing it. Think of your job as having movable walls—flex to fit the immediate demands of the situation instead of struggling to make the job adapt to you.

15. **Be careful in what you use as evidence to evaluate how much the organization cares about people.**

High stress and heavy pressure may provide the best proof that management's heart is in the right place. All things considered, trying to keep you comfortable could be the most cold-blooded management move of all.

Source: Pritchett, P., & Pound, R. (1995). *A survival guide to the stress of organizational change.* Used with full permission of PRITCHETT, LP. All rights are reserved. For more information, see www.pritchettnet.com and www.mergerintegration.com.

Reconciling conflicts between work and family roles (known as **work–life balance**) is a specific form of interrole conflict that has received a great deal of research. Work–life balance is when demands of participation in work are incompatible with demands of participation in family life. This conflict can have an important effect on the quality of both work and family life.[42] Research has indicated that conflicts between work and family roles negatively affect employee well-being.[43,44] It is not uncommon for employees to carry stress home with them from the workplace (known as the **crossover stress effect**) and this affects family interactions. A study of 142 police couples found that police officers who were experiencing stress were more likely to display anger, spend time away from the family, be uninvolved in family matters, and have unsatisfactory marriages.[45] Other research on working couples found burnout in one partner affects the other.[46] There is also **family-to-work conflict,** which is another form of the crossover effect. This occurs when family problems cross over to work, and research has found this affects job performance, psychological distress, alcohol abuse, and physical health.[47]

A study of graduates in the early years of their career concluded that although graduates seek work–life balance, their concern for career success draws them into a situation where they work increasingly long hours and experience an increasingly unsatisfactory relationship between home and work.[48] This underscores the importance of organizational policy and practice to help employees manage the relationship between work and family. There are a number of sources of stress that come from outside the workplace, and Toolkit Activity 13.2 is an assessment where you can determine how much stress comes from events in your life.

Critical Thinking Questions: Which of the role-related stress sources do you think creates the most strain? Why?

In addition to role stress, some stress emanates from the culture of the organization and/or the behavior of supervisors. The next sections will discuss toxic organizational cultures and **abusive supervision** as sources of stress.

"Toxic" Workplaces

Employees lower in the hierarchy of bureaucratic organizations experience more frustration and anger compared to managers. A study found that employees who had jobs at lower levels in an organization's hierarchy felt more powerless and had less control over their work. They also report more emotional distress, medication use, cardiovascular disturbance, gastrointestinal disturbance, and allergy respiratory disturbance.[49] A study of engineers found frustration was associated with anger reactions, latent hostility, job dissatisfaction, and work-related anxiety.[50] Toxic workplaces may be exacerbated by change situations. Political behavior may increase during times of organizational turmoil and this represents an additional source of stress.

In many situations, it is necessary to engage in organizational politics to survive or advance in the organization. Highly political organizations reward employees who engage in hardball influence tactics, take credit for the work of others, join powerful coalitions, and have connections to high-ranking supporters in the organization.[51] This may place strain on employees who feel they must engage in these behaviors. Organizational politics are a hindrance stressor, and research has shown significant relationships between perceptions of organizational politics and psychological strain. For example, a study of Israeli employees found job distress was an immediate response to organizational politics. Also, organizational politics resulted in aggressive behavior by employees.[52] A meta-analysis found turnover intentions, job dissatisfaction, lower commitment, and lower job performance are all affected by perceptions of politics. Also, the strain from politics at work reduces organizational citizenship behaviors (OCBs) toward individuals and organizations.[53]

Abusive Supervision

In Chapter 9, it was noted that the workplace is becoming less civilized, and incidences of harassment and bullying at work are rising. Having a "bad boss" may be a source of stress for employees. Supervisors have a lot of power over followers and control their work experiences to a great extent. Some supervisors engage in hostile behavior known as abusive supervision.[54] Supervisors may ridicule, spread rumors, take credit for work done by followers, give the "silent treatment," and/or withhold information.[55] Research has shown that such supervisory abuse is related to psychological distress, anxiety, and emotional exhaustion.[56] Research has also shown that abusive supervision may even evoke a "paranoid" reaction from followers that is characterized as hypervigilance, rumination, and sinister attributions about others.[57] Employees may be affected even when they are not the target of workplace abuse. For example, one study found that employees who watched supervisors abuse customers were more likely to have intentions to leave their jobs.[58]

Are Ethical Dilemmas a Source of Stress?

A study of top real estate agents examined stress reactions to violations of codes of ethics. The researchers used a creative approach using voice analysis. Respondents were tape-recorded, and then responses to questions about ethics violations were analyzed for stress in the voice. They found 20% of the respondents exhibited stress when asked questions regarding ethics.[59] **Ethics-induced stress** is the result of pressure, workload, and an emphasis on merit for advancement in the organization and "may occur when an individual's ethical outlook or standards differ significantly from the prevailing ethical ethos, environment, or standards of members of the organization in which she or he is employed."[60] It is stressful for employees when they are asked to do something they consider to be unethical. A study of 304 customer service representatives found that ethics-induced stress is related to burnout and fatigue. Representatives were asked about how much stress was due to "having to sometimes stretch the truth in dealing with customers" and "having to lie a little bit to satisfy customer objections."[61]

A nationwide study of 229 oncology nurses found 80% of the nurses reported high ethics stress (an average of 6 or higher on a scale from 1 to 10). The top three ethics stressors were pain management and cost containment as well as making decisions in the best interest of the patient.[62]

Pressures to violate ethical standards are a very real source of stress for employees. Having a job that requires a person to do something that is at odds with their values creates psychological strain and burnout. Ethics-induced stress is yet another reason why organizations should adopt a proactive stance on ethics.

Discussion Questions:

1. Describe a situation at school or work where you felt pressure from others to do something unethical. How did you feel in this situation?
2. What can leaders do to be proactive about ethics to help employees avoid the experience of ethics-related stress?

Sources: Allmon, D. E., & Grant, J. (1990). Real estate sales agents and the code of ethics: A voice stress analysis. *Journal of Business Ethics, 9*(10), 807–812; Bischoff, S. J., DeTienne, K. B., & Quick, B. (1998). Effects of ethics stress on employee burnout and fatigue: An empirical investigation. *Journal of Health and Human Services Administration, 21*(4), 512–532; Menzel, D. C. (1996). Ethics stress in public organizations. *Public Productivity & Management Review, 20,* 70–83; Raines, M. L. (2000). Ethical decision making in nurses: Relationships among moral reasoning, coping style, and ethics stress. *JONA'S Healthcare Law, Ethics and Regulation, 2*(1), 29–41.

Poor supervision is a root cause of stress at the workplace.[63] This occurs for two primary reasons: Abusive supervisors place additional job demands on employees, and they don't provide support to help employees cope. To address the problem of abusive supervision, organizations are encouraged to set up confidential (or even anonymous) reporting "hotlines" so that supervisory abuse can be reported.[64] Also, training that focuses on appropriate supervisory behaviors may alleviate stress and improve employee well-being.[65]

Critical Thinking Questions: Have you ever experienced (or observed) a situation of abusive supervision? What did you do about it? If you did nothing, what would you do differently?

Abusive supervision is a serious concern in organizations. But supervisors are not the only sources of stress due to work relationships. A review of the literature on "coworkers behaving badly" found that **deviant behavior** of coworkers violates organizational norms may include "aggression, bullying, harassment, incivility and social undermining."[66] The literature on deviant behavior in organizations has documented negative impacts of deviance on attitudes, emotions, and performance. Deviant, dysfunctional, and counterproductive behavior of a coworker affects others in three ways. First, there are **direct effects** where the employee is the target of a coworker's deviant act. Second, there are **indirect effects,** or vicarious impact, in which an employee is affected by learning of another coworker's deviant behaviors. Third, there can also be **ambient impact** in which collective deviant behavior creates a hostile working environment. Coworker deviant behavior is considered a workplace demand and creates stress for the target. Being mistreated by one's coworkers creates emotional strain, which leads to lower morale and turnover.[67]

STRESS EPISODE

Learning Objective 13.5: Compare and contrast the three types of strain that may occur.

The stress response "is the generalized, patterned, unconscious mobilization of the body's natural energy resources when confronted with a demand or stressor" (p. 3).[68] The nervous and hormonal systems of an individual are activated producing adrenaline, and this may result in an elevated heart rate, perspiration, and tightening of the muscles. This is known as the **fight-or-flight response,** which is the result of human evolution in which the response was needed to attack predators or run away from them.

Strains resulting from the stressors reviewed in the previous section trigger a stress episode as depicted in Figure 13.3. Responses may be physiological, psychological, and/or behavioral.[69] These strains are listed next with examples found in research on stress at the workplace (however, one stressful event may trigger one, two, or all three of the following strains for an employee).

1. **Physiological**—high blood pressure, coronary heart disease, high cholesterol, stomach ulcers, compromised immune system
2. **Psychological**—anxiety, burnout, emotional exhaustion, fatigue, hostility, irritation, tension, lower self-confidence, and self-esteem
3. **Behavioral**—accidents and errors, alcohol use, caffeine intake, drug use, smoking, workplace deviance (e.g., doing inferior work on purpose, stealing, damaging property)

As we learned in Chapter 3, personality factors may influence or moderate the degree to which a given individual experiences stress. The **Type A** behavior pattern was discussed as a personality characteristic that may negatively affect your health. Research has found additional personality factors including the need for control[70] and hardiness.[71]

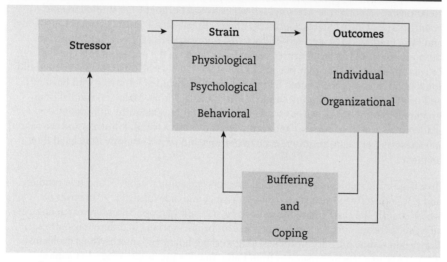

Figure 13.3 Stress Episode

Source: Viswesvaran, C., Sanchez, J. I., & Fisher, J. (1999). The role of social support in the process of work stress: A meta-analysis. *Journal of Vocational Behavior, 54*(2), 314–334.

Hardiness refers to the ability to "bounce back" after experiencing a stressful event. Being optimistic has also been related to the ability to cope with stress.[72] People who are more pessimistic (i.e., "the glass is half empty") have a higher risk for depression, more health problems, and lower levels of achievement.[73] Optimism may be learned and this may affect a person's ability to cope with stress. And optimism may vary by culture. One study found mainland Chinese to be less optimistic than North Americans.[74]

There may be cultural differences in stress and coping, and research has been conducted in other countries. It is clear that the problem of workplace stress is now a global phenomenon, and the next section discusses international and cross-cultural research on stress.

STRESS IS A GLOBAL CONCERN

Learning Objective 13.6: Discuss the prevalence of work stress on a global scale.

The prevalence of work stress has been documented in numerous countries, including the United Kingdom,[75] Germany,[76] Sicily,[77] Saudi Arabia,[78] and China[79] to name a few. Stress has been related to outcomes of lower satisfaction and increased turnover intentions in other cultures as well. For example, a study of public sector employees working in Botswana found stress related to turnover.[80] This has raised the question of whether the

Coping

stressor-strain model reported in much of the literature is universal, prompting cross-cultural comparisons.

Relationships among role stressors, self-efficacy, and burnout were studied in nine countries (i.e., United States, Germany, France, Brazil, Israel, Japan, China, Hong Kong, and Fiji). Findings indicated self-efficacy had a universally negative association with burnout across all regions. Further, self-efficacy reduced the impact of role conflict and/or role ambiguity on burnout in eight of the nine cultures (the relationship did not hold for role ambiguity in the United States).[81] The relationship of job stress with burnout and turnover intentions among employees in Canada, China, Malaysia, and Pakistan examined four job stressors (i.e., work overload, conflict, ambiguity, and resource inadequacy) as well as burnout and turnover motivation. Overall job stress and the four job stressors were significantly related to burnout and turnover motivation in all four countries. [82]

Two large-scale studies of cross-cultural stressors and cultural values found role conflict and role ambiguity to be related to power distance and individualism.[83,84] In terms of which country may experience the most stress, a review of cross-cultural research on stress suggests there are different sources of stress for people working in different countries.[85] For example, time pressure, deadlines, long working hours, and interpersonal problems are a source of stress for executives from Latin America and South Africa. In China and the United States, the most frequently reported stressors were poor working conditions, equipment failure, lack of training, difficulties with teamwork, and lack of structure. In the United States, the lack of adequate control was reported more frequently than in other countries. While cross-cultural research on stress is relatively new, evidence suggests that stress occurs worldwide.

There may be differences in how people cope with stress that depend on culture, however. For example, Indian and U.S. employees in similar jobs tend to use different coping strategies to deal with work-related strain. Indians preferred to talk with family members and close friends about their frustrations. U.S. employees engage in more action-oriented coping mechanisms to deal with the source of the stress.[86] This may be the result of having more job "decision" latitude, which is "the working individual's potential control over job-related decision making" (p. 697).[87] For example, problem-focused coping and job latitude reduced stress in a study of the United States, New Zealand, Germany, Spain, South Africa, and Japan.[88] The next section reviews coping mechanisms for job stress in more detail.

COPING

Learning Objective 13.7: Develop a plan for coping with stress during change.

Coping is defined as "constantly changing cognitive and behavioral efforts to manage specific external and/or internal demands that are appraised as taxing or exceeding the resources of the person."[89] There are two types of coping: **behavioral methods** (problem-solving behaviors) and **cognitive methods** (managing thoughts and emotions).[90] Examples of behavioral (or active) coping strategies are keeping a positive outlook, working harder, and seeking advice and help.[91] Examples of cognitive methods include reordering life priorities and convincing oneself that work isn't all that important. Men and women may cope differently. A meta-analysis found that women are more likely than men to engage in most forms of coping strategies. In particular, the strongest effects showed that women were more likely to use strategies that involved verbal expressions by seeking emotional support. For example, they were more likely than men to ruminate about problems and use positive self-talk.[92] As shown in Figure 13.4, there are a number of specific ways that both male and female employees can cope with work stress.

An employee's ability to cope with stress relates to their well-being and job performance. For example, research has shown that active coping with organizational change has significant effects on extrinsic (higher salary, rank, and performance as well as lower career plateauing) and intrinsic career outcomes for employees (organizational commitment, job satisfaction).[93] Emotional strategies help as well. The ability to detach from work during off-job time is an important factor that helps to protect employee well-being and work engagement.[94] As Figure 13.4 suggests, one coping strategy is to ask for assistance or support when experiencing stress. The next section discusses research on the buffering effects of **social support** from others.

Figure 13.4 Coping Strategies

	Problem-Focused	Emotion-Focused
Behavioral Methods	Working harder Seeking assistance Acquiring more resources	Engaging in non-work activities Seeking support Venting anger
Cognitive Methods	Planning and organizing Focusing on job duties Take one step at a time	Tell yourself you always come through Escape and detachment Convince yourself work doesn't matter

Source: Adapted from Latack, J.C., & Havlovic, S. J. (1992). Coping with job stress: A conceptual evaluation framework for coping measures. *Journal of Organizational Behavior*, 13(5), 479–508.

Critical Thinking Questions: Which coping strategies in Figure 13.4 work best for you and why? Are there any that don't work? Explain why. Develop a plan for coping with change that you are experiencing (or may experience in the future).

Social Support

Social support is the help that people receive when they experience job demands. Support during a stress episode is beneficial. This is called the **"buffering effect"** because help from others serves as a buffer from stress and strain.[95] Social support is a resource for coping with stress that comes from others—family, friends, coworkers, and supervisors. Social support may be emotional or **instrumental**.[96] Based on a longitudinal study of blue-collar workers, the buffering effect of social support on work hours, employee health, and well-being is a function of the pattern of exchange relations between an employee and his or her close support providers (friends and family).[97] Social support aids in stress management for the following reasons:[98]

- By building up the person's sense of identity and belonging
- By improving self-image
- By enhancing the sense of control and mastery over the stressful situation

A meta-analysis found social support is negatively related to both stressors and strains.[99] Social support may help prevent a stress episode as well as alleviate the stress when it occurs. Leaders may play a key role is providing both instrumental and social support for employees experiencing stress.

Given the high costs of stress, organizations have developed interventions and policies to help their employees cope with stress. In many of these interventions, the emphasis is on prevention and these strategies will be reviewed next.

PREVENTIVE STRESS MANAGEMENT IN ORGANIZATIONS

Learning Objective 13.8: Recommend organizational interventions and policies that help employees cope with stress.

Given the rising costs of workplace stress, organizations have been addressing stress through a variety of policy changes and interventions. **Preventive stress management** is a set of methods that promote health at the workplace and avoid distress.[100] While organizations assume that employees will take some individual responsibility for preventing stress, it is a clear trend that organizations are being more proactive regarding stress management. Many organizations have **wellness programs** that offer workshops on time management, weight loss, alcohol and/or drug abuse, smoking cessation, and exercise. Reviews of the research on these organizational interventions have shown that they minimally impact employee well-being and performance.[101] Yet, a more recent meta-analytic study of 36 wellness programs found they are effective in helping employees cope with workplace stress.[102]

Does Time Management Work?

There have been a number of popular books written about time management over the years. For example, *How to Get Control of Your Time and Your Life* has sold millions of copies and is considered a classic.[103] But is this supported by research evidence? Research shows that there are four aspects of time management: (1) setting goals and priorities (e.g., "I break down tasks"), (2) mechanics of planning and scheduling (e.g., "I write reminder notes"), (3) perceived control of time (e.g., "I am overwhelmed by tasks"—reversed), and (4) having a preference for disorganization (e.g., "I have a messy workspace"—reversed).[104]

The most predictive time management factor was the perceived control of time. The 165 students who completed a time management survey reported higher GPAs, work and life satisfaction, and lower stress (less role ambiguity, less role overload, and reported fewer job-related health issues such as headaches and insomnia) when they felt that had more control over their time. A study of 353 government employees found that engaging in time management behaviors reduced tension and increased job satisfaction but did not relate to job performance.

Also, employees that had attended time management training (a half-day seminar) did not report any significant differences in stress, satisfaction, or performance.[105]

Time management may alleviate stress while you are a student and also on the job. Also, job and life satisfaction may be enhanced. However, the link to job performance is less clear. Time management training may not have the impact that much of the popular press claims. Following the general guidelines suggested by this research may be just as beneficial as training: Set goals and priorities, schedule tasks well, and stay organized.

Discussion Questions:

1. One factor is the degree to which a person's work area is organized—that is, not messy. Is your work area organized? Do you think it makes a difference in your stress and performance?
2. Why do you think that time management is not related clearly to productivity (recall the discussion of eustress and the inverted-U relationship between pressure and performance discussed earlier in this chapter)?

Sources: Macan, T. H. (1994). Time management: Test of a process model. *Journal of Applied Psychology, 79*(3), 381; Macan, T. H., Shahani, C., Dipboye, R. L., & Phillips, A. P. (1990). College students' time management: Correlations with academic performance and stress. *Journal of Educational Psychology, 82*(4), 760.

Employee Assistance Programs

When an employee exhibits a clear stress reaction that is affecting his relationships with coworkers and performance, a referral may be made for counseling through an **employee assistance program (EAP).** These programs have become common in most large organizations. Although these counseling programs may be in-house, they are usually delivered through an outside agency. The employer typically offers the services of the EAP as an employee benefit. EAPs may provide counseling, information, and referrals appropriate for treatment and support services. Most universities offer free counseling services for students who may be experiencing stress in coping with the demands of school and/or work and family.

Work Redesign

Work redesign was discussed in Chapter 7 as a way to increase the intrinsic motivation and performance of employees. The design of jobs may also lessen the experience of work stress. In a study conducted in Sweden, work was redesigned to improve the quality of work life and this intervention alleviated work stress.[106] Another study found that when workers are able to create their own job designs to solve problems in their work, they experience less fatigue.[107] Employees felt they had more job control, which is the authority to make decisions about their job on a day-to-day basis. The study also measured negative affectivity (being pessimistic) and cognitive failure, and the results are shown in Figure 13.5. This study also found asking for social support and executing job control to solve problems encourages further job redesign. Thus, work redesign appears to reduce stress—particularly when followers are empowered to make changes to their work to solve the problems they face.

Figure 13.5 The Relationship Between Job Control, Fatigue, Negative Affectivity, and Cognitive Failure

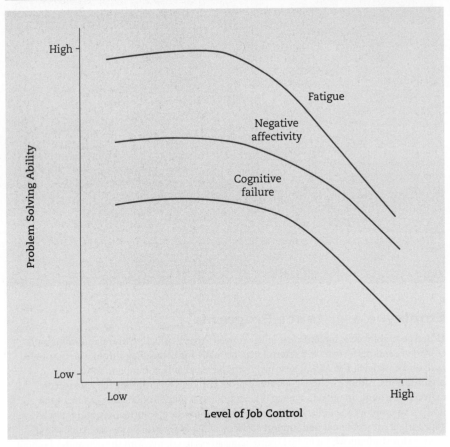

Source: Daniels, K., Beesley, N., Wimalasiri, V., & Cheyne, A. (2013). Problem solving and well-being exploring the instrumental role of job control and social support. *Journal of Management, 39*(4), 1016–1043. p. 1033.

RESEARCH IN ACTION

Can Coping Increase Stress?

A recent development in research on coping is the conservation of resources (COR) theory. People conserve their cognitive (thoughts) and emotional resources at work so that they can cope better.[108] Having to deal with stressors depletes such resources leading to even more burnout and even depression. In a sense, coping becomes a stressor itself, and people try to cope in ways that conserve their physical, cognitive, and emotional resources to the fullest extent they possibly can. For this reason, people are more likely to change their thoughts and emotions rather than actively cope by solving the problem actively. For example, if a person has a conflict with a coworker that is causing them stress, they may dismiss the coworker as a jerk and not confront them directly about the behavior that is causing stress. By avoiding confrontation, emotional resources are conserved. This explains why stressors in the workplace are often not addressed actively and a person may endure the stress for a long time and not do anything to change it. There is a growing body of evidence that coping itself may be a source of workplace stress and that people carefully choose their coping mechanisms to conserve their emotional resources.[109,110]

Discussion Questions:

1. Provide an example of using an emotion-focused strategy to reduce stress. Why is this less emotional effort than a problem-focused strategy (refer to Figure 13.4)?
2. Explain why the source of social support (people at work compared with family and friends) makes a difference in the COR and stress.

Sources: Halbesleben, J. R. B. (2006). Sources of social support and burnout: A meta-analytic test of the conservation of resources model. *Journal of Applied Psychology, 91*(5), 1134–1145; Hobfoll, S. E. (1989). Conservation of resources: A new attempt at conceptualizing stress. *American Psychologist, 44*(3), 513–524; Ito, J. K., & Brotheridge, C. M. (2003). Resources, coping strategies, and emotional exhaustion: A conservation of resources perspective. *Journal of Vocational Behavior, 63*(3), 490–509.

Critical Thinking Questions: As this section indicates, organizations spend a lot of money helping employees cope with stress through prevention and wellness programs. Should they? In other words, do you think that employees should take responsibility for their own coping?

LEADERSHIP IMPLICATIONS: HELPING EMPLOYEES COPE

Workplace stress is a "leadership challenge" and "the challenge for leaders is to create organizational cultures and work environments in which people may produce, serve, grow and be valued."[111] This chapter has reviewed various personality and organizational factors that may create anxiety for employees. Organizational change is stressful for everyone. First, leaders need to develop plans for coping with stress themselves so that they are able to provide support to their followers. As noted previously, supervisors can provide social support for employees undergoing stress by active listening (refer back to Chapter 11). A supervisor may also make appropriate referrals to an EAP or wellness program. Also, having a high-quality relationship with a boss who provides social support prevents burnout.[112] Leaders can provide emotional support by listening but can also help their followers actively problem solve to address the workplace stressors. Leaders should use both emotion-focused and problem-focused strategies with their followers to help them cope with change.

Ensuring the well-being of employees is essential to current thinking on positive organizational behavior (POB). During times of organizational change, it is important to ensure the well-being of followers. This requires the ability to show compassion for others at work. Compassion from a leader is noticing, feeling, and understanding the suffering of a follower. Based upon this understanding, the leader takes action to alleviate the person's suffering.[113] Thus, a leader should view followers as "whole people" who bring their emotions to the workplace with them, and assist with work–life balance concerns. Finally, leaders should promote compassionate organizational practices such as the prevention interventions discussed in this chapter.

$SAGE edge™

edge.sagepub.com/scandura

Want a better grade? Go to **edge.sagepub.com/scandura** for the tools you need to sharpen your study skills.

KEY TERMS

abusive supervision, 348

ambient impact, 350

behavioral methods, 352

buffering effect, 354

challenge-related stress and eustress, 341

change uncertainty, 344

cognitive methods, 352

crossover stress effect, 347

deviant behavior, 350

direct effects, 350

employee assistance program (EAP), 355

ethics-induced stress, 349

family-to-work conflict, 347

fight-or-flight response, 350

hindrance-related stress, 341

indirect effects, 350

instrumental support, 354

job burnout, 341

job control, 340

organizational stress, 340

person–environment (P–E) fit, 340

preventive stress management, 354

role ambiguity, 345

role conflict, 345

role overload, 345

social support, 353

stressors, 340

Type A, 350

wellness programs, 354

work–life balance, 347

SUGGESTIONS FOR FURTHER READING

Bhagat, R. S., Segovis, J. C., & Nelson, T. A. (2012). *Work stress and coping in the era of globalization.* New York, NY: Routledge.

Biron, C., Karankika-Murray, M., & Cooper, C. L. (2012). *Improving organizational interventions for stress and well-being.* New York, NY: Routledge.

Charlesworth, E. A., & Nathan, R. G. (2004). *Stress management: A comprehensive guide to wellness.* New York, NY: Random House.

Lakein, A. (1973). *How to get control of your time and your life.* New York, NY: Signet.

Pritchett, P., Pound, R., & Pritchett, P. (1995). *A survival guide to the stress of organizational change.* New York, NY: Pritchett & Associates.

TOOLKIT ACTIVITY 13.1

Warning Signs of Burnout

Pay attention to your coworkers and/or classmates. If you see them exhibiting the following symptoms, they may be on the path to burnout. What can you do to help them?

Physical signs and symptoms of burnout

- Feeling tired and drained most of the time
- Lowered immunity, feeling sick a lot

- Frequent headaches, back pain, muscle aches
- Change in appetite or sleep habits

Emotional signs and symptoms of burnout

- Sense of failure and self-doubt
- Feeling helpless, trapped, and defeated
- Loss of motivation
- Increasingly cynical and negative outlook

- Detachment, feeling alone in the world

- Decreased satisfaction and sense of accomplishment

Behavioral signs and symptoms of burnout

- Withdrawing from responsibilities
- Isolating yourself from others
- Procrastinating, taking longer to get things done

- Using food, drugs, or alcohol to cope
- Taking out your frustrations on others
- Skipping work or coming in late and leaving early

Source: "Preventing Burnout." ©Helpguide.org. Retrieved on March 26, 2014 from http://www.helpguide.org/mental/burnout_signs_symptoms.htm.

TOOLKIT ACTIVITY 13.2

Stressful Life Events

Listed here are many of the events in life that have been found to produce individual stress reactions. The numerical value represents the degree of disruption that event causes in the average person's life. Some studies have found that people experiencing serious illnesses also had high scores on the life event scale. Generally, the higher your score, the greater the probability you will experience a major health change in the near future. Since individuals differ in their abilities to handle stress, this score should be taken as a rough guide only.

For each of the events you have experienced during the past 12 months, transfer the value to the second column. Add all of your entries in the second column to obtain your total stress score.

Events:	Stress value	Enter "stress value" if this event applies to me.
1. My spouse/partner died.	100	
2. I got a divorce.	73	
3. I separated from my spouse/partner.	65	
4. I spent time in jail.	63	
5. A close family member died.	63	
6. I had a major illness or injury.	58	
7. I got married.	50	
8. I was fired at work.	47	
9. I had a marital reconciliation.	45	
10. I retired.	45	
11. I became pregnant.	40	
12. My family gained a new member.	39	
13. I changed to a different occupation.	36	
14. My son or daughter left home.	29	
15. I had trouble with my in-laws.	29	
16. I had an outstanding personal achievement.	28	
17. I started or finished high school or college.	26	
18. I had a change in my living conditions.	25	
19. I had trouble with my boss.	25	
20. My working hours or conditions changed.	20	
21. I had a change in my residence.	20	

Events:	Stress value	Enter "stress value" if this event applies to me.
22. I changed schools.	20	
23. My social activities changed.	18	
24. My sleeping habits changed.	16	
25. My eating habits changed.	15	
26. I took a vacation.	13	
27. I celebrated the holidays.	12	
28. I had minor violations of the law (traffic or parking tickets, etc.).	11	

MY TOTAL SCORE: _____

Scoring:

0–150: Low stress

151–300: Moderate stress

301+ : High or extreme stress

Source: Adapted from Holmes, T. H., & Rahe, R. H. (1967). The social readjustment rating scale. *Journal of Psychosomatic Research, 11*, 213–218.

CASE STUDY 13.1

The Price of Entrepreneurship

All jobs have stress, risk, and drama associated with them. Television programs from the past decade (*Deadliest Catch, Ax Men, Does Someone Have to Go?, Kitchen Nightmares,* and *Restaurant: Impossible,* to name a few) have captured a number of different challenges employees and business owners face on a daily basis. Business owners have more stress and anxiety than other employees since they have the double-edged sword of having to deal with stress and having to help their employees cope with stress. Read the following situation(s), and think about how you would handle the pressure.

Situation 1: You and a friend from college own a restaurant. You started this business thinking that your management skills and your friend's culinary skills and experience would generate great success. The first year things went pretty well, and while you weren't raking in money, you made enough to generally cover expenses. This year, however, things have changed, and the restaurant is now losing $1,000 a week. You realize this is a problem as you don't have a large cash reserve since most of you and your partner's money went into starting the restaurant. As you are struggling to pay your suppliers, employees, and other creditors, it's taking a toll on the relationship with your business partner as you are starting to argue more about money and strategy. Further, you and your spouse just learned that you two will be having a baby. To make matters even worse, you passed a sign on the way to work announcing that a new restaurant is opening up a few blocks away. Sadly, you can't call Gordon Ramsay, as he's no longer filming *Kitchen Nightmares,* and Robert Irvine is busy on other projects at the moment.

Situation 2: You run a management consulting firm that focuses on helping clients boost their output. For the past 10 years, things have been going well. You've developed a sound list of clients who engage in repeat business, and you and your staff are typically able to generate 10 to 20 new client projects a year. However, last year the world entered into another global financial crisis, and for the past 9 months, you've not gotten any new business. You've let go half of your staff, and to keep things afloat, you've exhausted your personal savings and assets—including your car and jewelry.

Situation 3: Last year, you started up an engineering technology firm. You've been in contract negotiations with a large oil manufacturing firm that is considering becoming a strategic investor. You're hoping that they sign the 400-page contract you sent them last month and deposit the million dollars due upon signing to your corporate account soon, but there has been no indication from the oil company whether or not they will sign. At present, you have exactly $7.85 in the bank. You are 60 days late on your car payment and 90 days behind on the mortgage. The IRS had filed a lien against you. Your home phone, cell phone, and cable TV have all been turned off. In less than a week, the natural gas company is scheduled to suspend service to your house, and then there would be no heat or way to prepare food.

Discussion Questions

1. In these scenarios, both personal as well as business life are creating stress. How can the situation in your personal life make the stress in your business better or worse?
2. For each of these scenarios, you're definitely suffering a lot of stress. How might stress affect your attitude? What should you do to avoid creating a toxic work environment?
3. In some of these situations, the employees know things are bad and are likely feeling stressed and worried. What can you do to help employees cope with the situation? How can you keep your best employees committed and not jump ship to other, more stable firms?
4. With all this stress, how might you motivate yourself to keep going? How would you balance the need to cope from problems with the responsibility of giving it your all to keep your business going?
5. Sometimes businesses fail. According to the Small Business Administration, more businesses close each month than open, and more than half of all new start-up businesses won't last 5 years (www .SBA.gov). If your business were to fail, what would you do to cope with the stress and emotional turbulence from its closing? How could you turn such a negative experience into something positive?

Source: Bruder, J. (2013, September). The psychological price of entrepreneurship. *INC Magazine.*

SELF-ASSESSMENT 13.1

Perceived Stress Scale

This self-assessment exercise indicates how much stress you are experiencing. There is no "one best" answer to these questions and the goal is for you to learn about yourself. There are no right or wrong answers and this is not a test. You don't have to share your results with classmates unless you wish to do so.

Part I. Taking the Assessment

You will be presented with some questions representing different situations. Circle the response that indicates how often you experience the situation.

As an example, the answer to a situation could look like this:

In the last month, how often have you ...

Felt as though there were not enough hours in the day?

Never   Almost never   Sometimes   (Fairly often)   Very often

This response indicates that you feel like there were not enough hours in the day often in the last month.

In the last month, how often have you . . .

1. Felt confident about your ability to handle your personal problems?

    Never   Almost never   Sometimes   Fairly often   Very often

2. Felt that you were on top of things?

    Never   Almost never   Sometimes   Fairly often   Very often

3. Been able to control irritations in your life?

    Never   Almost never   Sometimes   Fairly often   Very often

4. Felt that things were going your way?

    Never   Almost never   Sometimes   Fairly often   Very often

5. Felt nervous and stressed?

    Never   Almost never   Sometimes   Fairly often   Very often

6. Been angered because of things that were outside your control?

    Never   Almost never   Sometimes   Fairly often   Very often

7. Been upset because of something that happened unexpectedly?

    Never   Almost never   Sometimes   Fairly often   Very often

8. Felt difficulties were piling up so high that you could not overcome them?

    Never   Almost never   Sometimes   Fairly often   Very often

9. Found that you could not cope with all the things that you had to do?

    Never   Almost never   Sometimes   Fairly often   Very often

10. Felt that you were unable to control the important things in your life?

    Never   Almost never   Sometimes   Fairly often   Very often

Part II. Scoring the Assessment

For each of the questions, write down your score based on the following scale:

Questions 1 through 4:		Questions 5 through 10:	
Never	= 5	Never	=1
Almost never	= 4	Almost never	= 2
Sometimes	= 3	Sometimes	= 3
Fairly often	= 2	Fairly often	= 4
Very often	= 1	Very often	= 5

Question Score

1.   _____
2.   _____
3.   _____
4.   _____
5.   _____
6.   _____
7.   _____
8.   _____
9.   _____
10.   _____

Total: _____

Total Score: _____

37–50: indicates a high level of stress

24–36: indicates a moderate level of stress

10–23: indicates a low level of stress

Source: Cohen, S., & Williamson, G. (1988). Perceived stress in a probability sample of the United States. In S. Spacapan & S. Oskamp (Eds.), *The social psychology of health: Claremont symposium on applied social psychology*. Newbury Park, CA: Sage.

14

ORGANIZATIONAL CULTURE

WHEN ELEPHANTS LEARN TO DANCE

In 1990, IBM had its most profitable year ever. By 1993, the computer industry had changed so rapidly that the company was losing almost $16 billion, and IBM was about to file for bankruptcy. The company was a victim of its own lumbering size and an insular corporate culture that resulted in decision makers ignoring the rise of the personal computer market. In 1993, Louis V. Gerstner became the chairman and CEO of the distressed company. In his book *Who Says Elephants Can't Dance?* Gerstner describes the turnaround he led from 1993 to 2002.[1]

When Gerstner started as CEO, industry analysts were calling upon the board to break IBM up into smaller companies to save it. Gerstner addressed IBM's severe financial crisis in the early 1990s and managed to keep the company solvent. In his own opinion, Gerstner's decision to keep the company together and "teach the elephant to dance" was the most important decision he ever made. Changing the culture of the organization was one of Gerstner's primary targets. IBM was hierarchical and traditional. Managers tended to overanalyze data and use data selectively to support their arguments. Gerstner empowered people to act and focused employees on bringing value to the customer in the marketplace. He believed that culture isn't just one aspect of the game; it *is* the game. Gerstner's most important and proudest accomplishment was to institute a culture that brought IBM closer to its customers by inspiring employees to drive toward customer-defined success. The "new IBM" and its culture with a strong customer focus resulted in a company that was on the brink of financial disaster to one that thrived.

Learning Objectives

After studying this chapter, you should be able to do the following:

14.1: Define *organizational culture,* and describe the seven characteristics.

14.2: Explain the relationship between national culture and organizational culture.

14.3: Demonstrate understanding of the two characteristics of strong cultures by providing examples.

14.4: Explain how employees learn organizational culture through the socialization process.

14.5: Discuss four ways that employees learn organizational culture.

14.6: Compare and contrast *organizational culture* and *climate*.

Get the edge on your studies at edge.sagepub.com/scandura
- Take the chapter quiz
- Review key terms with eFlashcards
- Explore multimedia resources, SAGE readings, and more!

⑤SAGE edge™

WHAT IS ORGANIZATIONAL CULTURE?

Learning Objective 14.1: Define *organizational culture*, and describe the seven characteristics.

Organizational Culture

Organizational culture is "the pattern of basic assumptions, that a given group has invented, discovered, or developed in learning to cope with its problems of external adaptation and internal integration, and that have worked well enough to be considered valid, and, therefore, to be taught to new members as the correct way to perceive, think, and feel in relation to those problems."[2] This definition is rather complex; however, culture can be thought of as a set of shared meanings that people in organizations have with respect to how to adapt to the environments and procedures to cope with change. There are three levels of culture, as shown in Figure 14.1:

1. **Artifacts and creations**—for example, the architecture of the buildings, the office decoration including artwork, and the way that people dress reflect the organization's culture. This can also include organization charts and new employee orientation materials.

2. **Values**—the reasons people give for their behavior. These values can be stated (or **espoused**), or they may be unconscious and people act them out (**enacted**). For example, a person may state that they believe in treating customers with respect (an espoused value). Treating customers nicely is an example of an enacted value.

3. **Assumptions**—underlie values and are often unconscious to people in organizations because they don't question them. For example, an assumption might be the view of the organization's relationship to the environment (some view the environment as something to be exploited for financial gain, while others may view the environment as something that must be protected). Another example is the nature of human nature (some may view employees as fundamentally lazy, and others may view employees as hard working and well-intentioned). Schein maintained that to really understand an organization's culture, a person must go beyond what they can see and hear (artifacts and creations) and gain a deeper awareness of values first and then assumptions. What we can observe is an expression of values that are typically rooted in fundamental assumptions.

Critical Thinking Questions: Provide an example of an artifact found in an organization. Trace it to the underlying values and assumptions it represents.

Seven Characteristics of Culture

A research study compared the organizational cultures of 15 organizations in four industries in the service sector (public accounting, consulting, the U.S. Postal Service, and transportation of household goods). Cultural values differed across these sectors and were

Figure 14.1   Schein's Levels of Culture

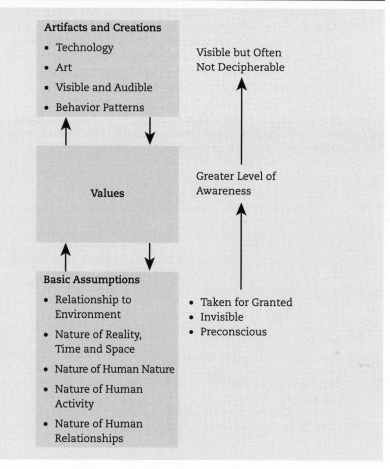

Artifacts and Creations
- Technology
- Art
- Visible and Audible
- Behavior Patterns

Visible but Often
Not Decipherable

Values

Greater Level of
Awareness

Basic Assumptions
- Relationship to Environment
- Nature of Reality, Time and Space
- Nature of Human Nature
- Nature of Human Activity
- Nature of Human Relationships

- Taken for Granted
- Invisible
- Preconscious

Source: Schein, E. H. (1984). Coming to a new awareness of organizational culture. *Sloan Management Review,* 25(2), 3–16. p. 4.

related to the levels of industry technology and growth. The seven characteristics and examples from this research follow.[3]

1. **Innovation and risk taking.** Most cultures in the service industries studied were average on this dimension with transportation showing the highest score.
2. **Attention to detail.** Consulting and accounting firms were highest on this dimension.
3. **Outcome orientation.** All companies studied in the service industry were high on this dimension.

4. **People orientation.** All companies studied in the four industries were average on this dimension.
5. **Team orientation.** All companies studied were average, but consulting firms were slightly higher on working in teams as part of their culture.
6. **Aggressiveness (easygoingness reversed).** All industries were average; however, consulting firms were less easygoing than other companies.
7. **Stability.** Most industries were average on stability; however, the U.S. Postal Service was higher than other organizations on the need for stability as part of the organization's culture.

Is Your Culture in Trouble?

Management consultant Randy Pennington has worked with corporations like Procter & Gamble and Marriott in numerous industry sectors for over 20 years. In his book *Results Rule! Build a Culture That Blows the Competition Away*, he provided the following list of things to look for in an organization culture that limits results:[4]

- **High turnover and low morale.** Good employees decide to pursue other opportunities. Individuals remaining with the organization become demoralized and lethargic in the performance of their duties.
- **Ongoing inconsistency.** Everyone has an off-day occasionally. Performance that continually gyrates all over the map is a reflection on the culture. Consistency is one mark of a *Results Rule!* organization.
- **Lack of focus on the external environment.** Cultures in distress look internally at all the things that are going wrong. *Results Rule!* cultures focus on serving the customer. They compete against others in the marketplace rather than against themselves.
- **Short-term thinking.** Survival in today's competitive marketplace requires constant attention to results. That, however, should not be an excuse for short-term thinking. *Results Rule!* cultures refuse to sacrifice

long-term viability for short-term success. They look for both.
- **Rise of destructive subcultures.** Pride in one's team is admirable. Allowing team pride to deteriorate into impenetrable organizational silos is a sure sign of a fractured culture.
- **Undermining the success of others.** Disagreements that turn into vendettas and information purposely withheld are the symptoms of a culture where *team* is considered a four-letter word.
- **Increased cynicism.** Cultures that are in trouble look at all change—good or bad— through cynical eyes that assume the worst possible outcome.

Results Rule! cultures take a critical look at opportunities to improve and embrace those that offer a satisfactory return on investment (ROI) and energy.

Discussion Questions:

1. Which of the previously given challenges indicating a troubled culture are most important in your opinion? Explain why.
2. How can short-term and long-term thinking be accomplished at the same time? What specifically can a leader do to keep employees focused on both?
3. What can leaders do to address the problem of cynicism of employees during times of change?

Source: Pennington, R. (2006). *Results rule! Build a culture that blows the competition away.* New York, NY: John Wiley.

NATIONAL CULTURE
AND ORGANIZATIONAL CULTURE

Learning Objective 14.2: Explain the relationship between national culture and organizational culture.

In Chapter 12, the role of national culture values and their influence on organizational behavior (OB) was discussed. Since the term *culture* is used for both national and organizational cultures, this may be a source of confusion. Results of the Global Leadership and Organizational Behavior Effectiveness (GLOBE) studies of leadership (discussed in Chapter 12) across cultures suggest that national culture has a strong influence on organizational culture.[5] A study of 10 European cultures found national culture values (power distance and collectivism) influence the development of organizational culture. However, the values of the founders of companies and key leaders also have an influence on organizational culture.[6] National culture constrains organizational culture but only partially.[7]

A large-scale research program learned that four organizational culture values appear to be important in most cultures: **adaptability, involvement, mission,** and **consistency.** Adaptability is the ability to transfer the demands of the market into organizational actions. Involvement is building human capability, ownership, and responsibility. Mission is defining the meaningful long-term direction for the organization. Consistency is defining values and subsystems that are the basis of a strong culture. This model of organizational culture is shown in Figure 14.2.[8]

Figure 14.2   The Denison Model of Organizational Culture

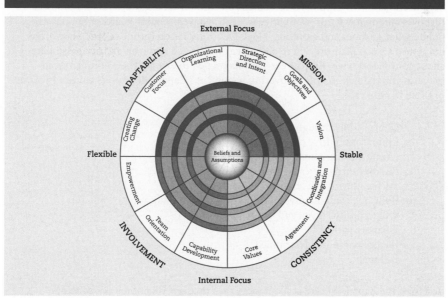

Source: Denison, D. R., Haaland, S., & Goelzer, P. (2004). Corporate culture and organizational effectiveness: Is Asia different from the rest of the world? *Organizational Dynamics,* 33(1), 98–109. p. 101.

Understanding
Strong Cultures

Mission and consistency are most related to profitability. Adaptability and mission are the best predictors of sales growth. Adaptability and involvement best predict innovation.[9] These organizational culture values appear relevant to all cultures; however, they are expressed differently in each culture.[10] For example, a study involving surveys from 179 foreign-owned firms operating in Russia and case studies found that all four values matter, but adaptability was most important for Russian organizations.[11] While what constitutes a strong culture may vary, research suggests that having a strong organizational culture makes a difference in terms of organizational effectiveness in all cultural contexts.

STRONG ORGANIZATIONAL CULTURES

Learning Objective 14.3: Demonstrate understanding of the two characteristics of strong cultures by providing examples.

Strong cultures are based on two characteristics, high levels of agreement among employees about what they value and high intensity toward these values. If both are high, a strong culture exists. Some organizations are characterized by high levels of intensity but low agreement. In this case, employees and/or groups are at war with one another over what is important for the organization to value.[12] For example, salespeople focus on customer-driven product features while accountants focus on cost containment. Thus, while both groups intensely value what they do, they disagree on priorities.

Strong organizational cultures are critical to bottom-line performance in large organizations).[13,14,15] Employee agreement on cultural values is also related to lower turnover among newly hired employees.[16,17] You have probably heard of Zappos, the online seller of shoes and clothing. The CEO, Tony Hsieh (pronounced "Shay"), has developed a strong culture where employees very much agree on and are passionate about customer service. Employees are encouraged to express their uniqueness in executing on the mission of "delivering happiness." Zappos defines its culture in terms of these 10 core values:

1. Deliver wow through service.
2. Embrace and drive change.
3. Create fun and a little weirdness.
4. Be adventurous, creative, and open-minded.
5. Pursue growth and learning.
6. Build open and honest relationships with communication.
7. Build a positive team and family spirit.
8. Do more with less.
9. Be passionate and determined.
10. Be humble.

To Hsieh, the Zappos culture is about more than money: "It's not me saying to our employees, this is where our culture is. It's more about giving employees the permission and encouraging them to just be themselves."[18]

Critical Thinking Questions: What role do you think the fact that Tony Hsieh founded Zappos plays in his ability to influence the culture? Would this be more difficult in an older organization? Explain.

In addition to understanding the strong overall culture in an organization such as aggressiveness, it is also important to know that organizations have subcultures. For example, the marketing department of an organization may have a risk-taking orientation whereas the accounting department may not because they value stability. This is because a strong culture of stability may inhibit the marketing department's ability to be flexible. Organizations can increase flexibility without losing their strong overall culture by encouraging subcultures.[19] In this way, organizations reap the benefits of a strong culture while remaining responsive to change. For example, Procter & Gamble has a strong culture of attention to detail and outcome orientation, but their research departments encourage innovation and trial-and-error experimentation.

Organizational Subcultures

Three general subcultures exist in most organizations. **Operators** are the line managers and employees who are involved in making products, delivering services, and interacting with customers directly. The operators value teamwork and desire engagement with the work they do. **Engineers** represent the second type of organizational subculture, and this group focuses on designing systems to support the work of operations such as employees who design a manufacturing facility. This may also include employees who design and implement information technology (IT) systems, financial analysis systems, and marketing research. The third group, **executives,** have worked their way up organizational career ladders and are financially responsible to their board of directors and shareholders. This group often has to "make the tough financial decisions based on imperfect information."[20] Executives manage large numbers of people and divisions and rely on policies and reward systems to maintain control. They may lose touch with their customers and employees at lower levels in the organizational hierarchy.

In recent years, however, executive teams have become more enlightened regarding the importance of having a positive organizational culture that values employees. They also have found ways to stay in closer touch with their customers. For example, Amazon CEO Jeff Bezos has a public e-mail address, jeff@amazon.com. He reads many customer complaints and forwards them to the relevant employee at Amazon, with a one-character addition: a question mark.[21]

Critical Thinking Questions: Provide examples of how executives can stay in touch with their customers. How can executives promote an organizational culture that values employees?

As the previous discussion suggests, organizational culture has a significant impact on employee attitudes and behavior. It is important for a leader to understand the forces that shape organizational culture. The next sections discuss how employees learn organizational culture. First, the process of socialization is discussed, followed by ways that employees learn culture through stories, **rituals,** symbols, and language.

SOCIALIZATION

Learning Objective 14.4: Explain how employees learn organizational culture through the socialization process.

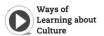
Ways of Learning about Culture

Organizational socialization is defined as the process an organization utilizes to ensure that new members acquire necessary attitudes, behaviors, knowledge, and skills to become productive organizational members.[22] When a new hire joins a company, the first six months on the job is characterized as a series of reality "shocks" as they are exposed to the unwritten rules defining the organizational culture in the organization.[23] For example, the job may be considered an 8-hour workday, but the new hire notices that everyone works at least 10 hours a day. The process of socialization follows the following steps: organizational anticipatory socialization, organizational entry and assimilation, and **metamorphosis**.[24] This process is diagrammed in Figure 14.3, and these steps are discussed in the following sections.

Anticipatory Socialization

Organizational **anticipatory socialization** is the process an individual goes through as they attempt to find an organization to join. Organizational anticipatory socialization has two basic processes: recruiting and selection.[25] For example, as a student nears graduation, they visit the placement center at the university to learn about job opportunities and meet

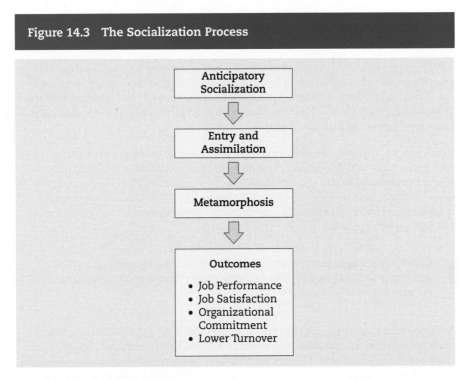

Figure 14.3   The Socialization Process

Anticipatory Socialization

⬇

Entry and Assimilation

⬇

Metamorphosis

⬇

Outcomes

- Job Performance
- Job Satisfaction
- Organizational Commitment
- Lower Turnover

Source: Jablin, F. M. (1987). Organizational entry, assimilation, and exit. In: L. L. Putnam, K. H. Roberts, & L. W. Porter (eds), *Handbook of organizational communication: An interdisciplinary perspective* (pp. 679–740). Beverly Hills, CA: Sage.

recruiters. The student then determines which jobs are the best fit to their college major, skills, and the type of organization they want to work for. For example, the student may want to work for a large organization as opposed to a small one. During the organizational anticipatory socialization stage, both the applicant and the organization are looking for evidence of a good person–organization fit. The recruitment process may involve psychological testing and interviews to determine how well a person will fit with the culture. HR expert Andrew Greenberg suggests asking the interview questions in Table 14.1 to assess an employee's fit with organizational culture.

Organizational Entry and Assimilation

The **preentry** step occurs from the time someone is offered the job to when they actually start working. There are three important issues that arise during the preentry stage. First, the types of messages a new employee receives from the organization prior to starting work could include realistic job previews in which the members of the organization attempt to clarify what the job will be like. These might be different than what was discussed in the hiring process and may be either positive or negative surprises. Second, new employees are typically concerned about how they are seen by existing organizational members and engage in impression management (discussed in Chapter 2)—the process (either conscious or unconscious) where an individual deliberately attempts to influence the perceptions and opinions of others. For example, the new hire might mention the rankings of their university to enhance the perceptions of their qualifications for the job. Third, current organizational members form perceptions of the new hire and consider how well they will fit in. These perceptions may result in unrealistic expectations so it's important to seek feedback in a new job to correct misconceptions.

Next, the entry phase occurs, which happens when the new member starts work. The new member begins to assimilate within the organizational culture. During the entry period, new employees begin to understand the organization's culture and work expectations.

Table 14.1 Interview Questions to Determine an Employee's Fit With a Strong Culture

Question	Purpose
1. If you could be doing anything, what would you do?	This question assesses passions and interests for culture fit.
2. What are your top three values?	This question helps you figure out if the candidate's values match those for the position, department, or team.
3. Have the candidate read the company's mission and value statements and discuss how they fit with their personal values.	This question reveals how closely a candidate's personal values align with the company's values.
4. If hired, what would you accomplish in your first week on the job?	This question shows a candidate's expectations and organizational skills.

Source: Greenberg, A. (2014). Start asking unique interview questions. Retrieved on December 28, 2014, from http://www.recruitingdivision.com/start-asking-unique-interview-questions-2.

This may include a formal orientation program to help the new employee learn the rules and expectations of the organization—the explicit dictates that govern employee behavior within the organization. For example, an orientation program may include a session on the ethical code of the organization. **Onboarding** is the process of welcoming and orienting new organizational members to facilitate their adjustment to the organization, its culture, and its practices. It refers to the process of facilitating new members' adjustment to the organization and its culture.[26] In addition to orientation and training, the organization may assign a formal mentor or "buddy" during this phase to help the new employee learn the norms of the organization. As discussed in Chapter 9, the informal expectations about how new employees should behave within the organization are "unwritten rules" that govern how new employees should act. For example, employees may be expected to eat lunch at their desk while working, but this is not specifically written down anywhere.

Metamorphosis

The final stage of organizational entry and assimilation is the metamorphosis stage. During this stage, a person transforms from a new employee to an established contributor who is valued and trusted by other members of the organization. Metamorphosis completes the socialization process—the new employee is comfortable with the organization, their boss, and their work group. They have internalized the organizational culture and understand their job, as well as the rules, procedures, and norms. Expectations are clear regarding what good performance means in the organization. Successful metamorphosis positively affects job performance, job satisfaction, and commitment to the organization. Also, there is a lower chance that the person will look for another job or quit.[27] Most often, this transition occurs over a long time period. However, the process may start over again (preentry through and assimilation to metamorphosis) if a person gets a promotion to a new role in the organization.

 Critical Thinking Questions: How can you make your socialization process smoother when you enter into a new organization? What can you do now to prepare for the preentry and entry phases?

As discussed previously, one of the important parts of the socialization process is a new employee learning the organizational culture. Culture is learned through a number of mechanisms including stories, rituals, symbols, and language. These are discussed in the following sections.

HOW EMPLOYEES LEARN CULTURE

Learning Objective 14.5: Discuss four ways that employees learn organizational culture.

Stories

Storytelling is now recognized as an important way to understand how employees make sense of what happens at work.[28] Storytelling is the sharing of knowledge and experiences through narrative and anecdotes to communicate lessons, complex ideas, concepts, and causal connections.[29] People try to understand complex events in ways that are integrated and make sense in the order they occurred. Stories are important because they aid comprehension and suggest a causal order for events. They convey shared meanings and values representing the organizational culture and guide behavior.[30] For example, stories told by charitable organizations are typically designed to evoke a series of emotions.[31] First, the potential donor feels negative emotions when they hear a story told about animals that are in need of rescue. Next, a story is told about animals being helped by the generosity of others, evoking a positive emotion and desire to help.

Interpreting Organizational Culture

An example of an organizational story that is told at McDonald's about its founder Ray Kroc follows:

> When Ray Kroc was running McDonald's from its Oakbrook, Illinois headquarters, he often drove by Chicago area McDonald's restaurants. Usually he asked his driver to stop so he could check things out. One sunny July afternoon, they were about to pass a McDonald's; Kroc told the driver, "We need to stop at this one." As they pulled into a parking space, he noticed that the flowering bushes were littered with shake cups, colorful Happy Meal boxes, messy napkins and other trash. Inside, Kroc asked for the manager. Only the assistant manager was there, so Kroc called the manager and waited for the anxious man to rush in after a speedy drive from his nearby home. "What can I do for you, sir?" the manager asked Kroc. Kroc led him to the parking lot, "Look. We don't want trash around our sites." So all three—driver, manager, and Ray Kroc—worked together to pick the trash out of the bushes. You'd better believe there was never again any trash in the parking lot of that location![32]

Critical Thinking Questions: What have you learned about the organizational culture of McDonald's from this story? What did you learn about Kroc's leadership style?

Rituals

Rituals are defined as "a form of social action in which a group's values and identity are publicly demonstrated or enacted in a stylized manner, within the context of a specific occasion or event."[33] An example of a ritual is a graduation ceremony at a university. Rituals reinforce the cultural values of the organization by providing a tangible way for employees to see the values espoused. For example, the Grammy Awards are a ritual that reinforces cultural values of the National Academy of Recording Arts and Sciences through performances, emotionally charged awards, legitimacy of artists, and creating links among the members.[34] Many organizations hold similar ceremonies and corporate dinners where top employees are rewarded for their contributions.

Symbols

Symbols represent the sharing of knowledge through access and exposure to images, diagrams, or objects, which represent or illustrate a culture value or an idea. Examples include a map of a city, the alien emoji, or a corporate logo.[35] Organizations make use of symbols in a variety of ways. Material symbols are office size and whether or not the office has a window.[36] For example, the C-suite offices may be located on the top floor of the building to reinforce the idea that these individuals have attained the highest level in the organization. Symbols include how a leader is expected to dress at work.[37] For example, while it may not be written down as a policy, new managers may be expected to wear navy blue or gray suits.

Language

As discussed in Chapter 11, organizations may have specific language, jargon, or acronyms that can be confusing to a new employee. These terms and usage may be unique to the organization and represent the organizational culture and how it is transmitted to newcomers. The language used to refer to employees reflects underlying values. For example, some organizations have stopped using the term *employees* in favor of *team members*. Another example is the manner in which employees at Disneyland are trained to refer to customers as "guests." Rides are referred to as "attractions." Disneyland is divided into "backstage," "on-stage," and "staging" regions.[38] The language used by Disneyland employees demonstrates is core values of valuing guests and providing a "magical experience" for them as part of its strong organizational culture.

 Critical Thinking Questions: Provide an example of storytelling, a ritual, a symbol, or language that you encountered when you learned an organizational culture based on your experience (this can be from your experience in a fraternity/sorority, sports team, or at work). Explain how this helped you understand what the expected behaviors were in the organization.

Organizational culture influences employee behaviors as the previously given examples demonstrate. Organizational culture creates organizational climates. These concepts are related but not exactly the same. For example, understanding organizational culture relies primarily on qualitative methods such as case studies. On the other hand, research on **organizational climate** relies more on quantitative research and surveys that measure employee perceptions.[39] The distinction between culture and climate continues in the following section.

ORGANIZATIONAL CLIMATE

Learning Objective 14.6: Compare and contrast *organizational culture* and *climate*.

Organizational climate has been defined as "shared perceptions of the way things are around here."[40] Organizational climate is the level of agreement in perceptions about the organization and work environment among employees. While the analysis of culture relies on understanding of an organization's fundamental assumptions as discussed in the previous section, climate research is concerned with representing employees' shared perceptions of values in a static way as states that they experience at a point in time. Another key distinction between culture and climate is that culture is viewed as evolving over time and is studied from a sociology or anthropology viewpoint. Climate can be altered through management interventions.[41] In sum, the difference between culture and climate is that culture is an *evolved context* and climate is a *situation* that employees are in.[42]

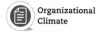

Organizational Climate

Culture and climate aren't the same, but they are not completely different either. Culture results in climate by reinforcing the shared perceptions employees have about what is valued. The **climcult** perspective suggests that culture and climate work together to influence how people experience their work environment.[43] Climcult borrows from the research on climate and culture and has the following elements:

- A global climate or culture for well-being
- Strategy focused on policies, practices, procedures, and behaviors expected and rewarded
- Processes focused on policies, practices, procedures, and behaviors that are expected and rewarded
- Socialization practices through which values and beliefs for strategy and processes are transmitted
- Myths and stories used for transmitting those same beliefs and values[44]

The climcult perspective suggests combining survey measures of climate and culture to gain a more complete view of how people describe their organization's values and their work experiences.[45] For example, a measure of the climate for quality would have measures of how followers view their leaders support for quality initiatives (climate). Culture items would be added to reflect how the leaders tells stories about things that went wrong when quality standards were not adhered to (culture). Climate focuses on perceptions, and culture focuses on the underlying assumptions and values. Both are important to understand the influence of organizational culture on employee behavior.

How Leaders Influence Climate

The ability of leaders to influence climate matters. A meta-analysis of 51 studies with 70 samples found climate affects individual-level outcomes through its impact on underlying cognitive and affective states. Three aspects of climate (affective, cognitive, and instrumental) significantly and positively impact job performance, psychological well-being, and withdrawal (e.g., turnover intentions) through their impact on organizational commitment and job satisfaction.[46] Table 14.2 shows the dimensions of organizational culture. Culture significantly impacts on the dependent variables studied in OB (refer back to Chapter 1 for a list of these variables). Also, research on climate summarizes much of what we have learned in this textbook regarding how attitudes of employees toward their work relate to work outcomes.

There are a number of facets of climate that have been studied including service, justice, safety, diversity, and innovation.[47,48,49,50,51] As discussed in Chapter 13, some organizational climates are "toxic," and abusive supervision occurs in such climates. Toolkit Activity 14.1 is an exercise in which you will compare two different organizations in terms of their service climate. Another specific type of organizational climate that has been studied is **ethical climate,** and the next section describes this line of research.

Table 14.2 Dimensions of Organizational Climate

Affective facet—people involvement; interpersonal or social relations

- Participation: Perceived influence in a process of joint decision making; participation in setting goals and policies
- Warmth: Perceived feelings of good fellowship in workgroup; prevalence of friendly, informal social groups; perceived helpfulness of supervisors and coworkers; emphasis on mutual support
- Social rewards: Praise from others used to reward work, rewards based on effort and time spent on work; formal recognition and awards based on ability and effort
- Cooperation: Perceived helpfulness of supervisors and coworkers; emphasis on mutual support

Cognitive facet—psychological involvement; self-knowledge and development

- Growth: Perceived emphasis on personal growth and development on job; emphasis on skill improvement
- Innovation: Perceived emphasis on innovation and creativity in work
- Autonomy: Perceived freedom to be own boss; plan and control over work
- Intrinsic rewards: Formal recognition and awards based on ability and effort

Instrumental facet—task involvement and processes

- Hierarchy: Perceived emphasis on going through channels; locus of authority in supervisory personnel
- Structure: Perception of formality and constraint in the organization; orderly environment; emphasis on rules, regulations, and procedures
- Extrinsic rewards: Extrinsic rewards of pay, assignments, advancement based on ability and time spent on work
- Achievement: Perception of challenge, demand for work, and continuous improvement of performance

Source: Ostroff, C. (1993). The effects of climate and personal influences on individual behavior and attitudes in organizations. *Organizational Behavior and Human Decision Processes, 56*(1), 56–90.

Ethical Climate

In Chapter 2, you learned that ethical leadership has emerged as an important new direction in OB research. Leaders influence an organization's ethical climate and employee attitudes. Leader moral development (i.e., the capacity for ethical reasoning) influences ethical climate, employee job satisfaction, and turnover intentions. This effect is stronger for younger organizations.[52] Research suggests the following five aspects of ethical climates:[53]

1. **Caring.** "Our major concern is always what is best for the other person."
2. **Law and Code.** "People are expected to comply with the law and professional standards over and above other considerations."
3. **Rules.** "Everyone is expected to stick by company rules and procedures."
4. **Instrumental.** "In this company, people are mostly out for themselves."
5. **Independence.** "Each person in this company decides for themselves what is right and wrong."

A survey of 872 employees of four firms found that organizations have distinct types of ethical climates, and the ethical climate is shaped by norms, bureaucracy, and the history of the organization.[54] Another study of 1,525 employees and their supervisors in 300 units in different organizations found that ethical climate made a difference in terms of the effects of ethical leadership and employee misconduct. Employees responded more to their leaders' ethical behaviors when the climate supported ethics.[55] A meta-analysis of 42 studies of ethical climate found caring climates were related to job satisfaction and organizational commitment, whereas instrumental climates were negatively related to these outcomes.[56] Thus, ethical climates matter and leaders should develop the moral climate of the organization in addition to behaving ethically.

Diversity Climate and Intentions to Quit

Diversity climate has been defined as "employees' shared perceptions of the policies, practices, and procedures that implicitly and explicitly communicate the extent to which fostering and maintaining diversity and eliminating discrimination is a priority in the organization."[57] The influence of diversity climate on turnover intentions was studied in a sample of managerial employees in a national retail organization.[58] Positive diversity climates were associated most negatively with turnover intentions among Blacks, followed in order of strength by Hispanics and then Whites. Organizational commitment (loyalty to the organization, as discussed in Chapter 4) alleviated the effect of race and diversity climate perceptions on turnover intentions. In other words, if managers are loyal to the organization, they are less likely to quit even if the diversity climate is poor. Results from a sample of 5,370 managers found the effect of a pro-diversity climate was strongest among Blacks. Contrary to the hypotheses, however, White men and women exhibited slightly stronger effects than Hispanic personnel.

These results suggest that a pro-diversity climate is not implemented at the expense of White employees. In fact, White men and women were also more likely to indicate lower intentions to quit when they perceived support for diversity. Although the strength of association varied by race, the total effect of diversity climate on turnover intentions was negative across all racial groups. Also, organizational commitment may reduce the effects of diversity climate on turnover intentions.

Discussion Questions:

1. Explain why organizational commitment (loyalty, as discussed in Chapter 4) reduced the effects of a lesser diversity climate on intentions to quit.

2. Were you surprised by the study's findings? Why do you think White managers were also positively affected by pro-diversity climates in their organizations?

3. This study was conducted using a sample of managers in retail organizations. How might the results be the same or different in a manufacturing organization, a hospital, or a university? Explain your answers.

RESEARCH IN ACTION

Sources: Gelfand, M. J., Nishii, L. H., Raver, J., & Schneider, B. (2005). Discrimination in organizations: An organizational level systems perspective. In R. Dipboye & A. Colella (Eds.), *Discrimination at work: The psychological and organizational bases* (pp. 89–116). Mahwah, NJ: Lawrence Erlbaum; McKay, P. F., Avery, D. R., Tonidandel, S., Morris, M. A., Hernandez, M., & Hebl, M. R. (2007). Racial differences in employee retention: Are diversity climate perceptions the key? *Personnel Psychology, 60*(1), 35–62.

Changing Organizational Culture

LEADERSHIP IMPLICATIONS: CHANGING ORGANIZATIONAL CULTURE

This chapter reviewed the research on organizational culture and discussed its relationship to national culture. The benefits of a strong organizational culture in terms of financial performance and employee attitudes were explained. The ways that organizational culture develops include stories, rituals, symbols, and language. Leaders need to understand how cultures develop because research has suggested that leaders can influence culture.

There are three key managerial tools for leveraging culture for performance:[59]

Tool #1: Recruiting and Selecting People for Culture Fit

Selection is the process of choosing new members of the organization. This requires planning for what the organization will need to reward in the future in terms of knowledge, skills, and abilities of employees. Selection is linked to organizational culture because organizations strive to hire people who fit the culture. For example, Whole Foods Market tries to recruit employees who believe in environmental conservation.[60] In some cases, skills may be traded off for an applicant who fits the culture because skills are easier to learn than values.

Tool #2: Managing Culture Through Socialization and Training

As discussed earlier in this chapter, socialization is the process by which an individual learns the norms of the group and organization. The new employee learns the values, expectations, and what behaviors are needed to succeed in the organization. Two key aspects of effective socialization are ensuring that employees acquire cultural knowledge and that they bond with one another. During the socialization process, a new employee is exposed to stories, rituals, symbols, and language that transmit the organizational culture. Most organizations have an orientation program for onboarding new employees and regular training programs that reinforce the organization's cultural values.

Tool #3: Managing Culture Through the Reward System

As discussed in Chapter 8, the reward system is one of the most important ways that leaders can influence employee behavior and performance. Rewards need to be clearly aligned with the organization's culture. Through rewards, employee behaviors that are consistent with the culture are reinforced. For example, rewards are combined with rituals when an organization has a celebration that recognizes top sales performers for the year.

The previously given tools for changing organizational culture are important for the leader to know. Culture is one aspect of OB that changes, but it is not the only one. Organizations today are undergoing rapid and frequent change. Leading organizational change will be discussed in the next chapter.

$SAGE edge™

Want a better grade? Go to **edge.sagepub.com/scandura** for the tools you need to sharpen your study skills.

KEY TERMS

adaptability, 369
anticipatory
    socialization, 372
climcult, 377
consistency, 369
enacted values, 366
engineers, 371
espoused values, 366

ethical climate, 377
executives, 371
involvement, 369
metamorphosis, 372
mission, 369
onboarding, 374
operators, 371

organizational
    climate, 376
organizational
    culture, 366
preentry, 373
rituals, 371

SUGGESTIONS FOR FURTHER READING

Gerstner, L. V. (2003). *Who says elephants can't dance? Leading a great enterprise through dramatic change.* New York, NY: Harper Paperbacks.

Pennington, R. (2006). *Results rule! Build a culture that blows the competition away.* New York, NY: John Wiley.

Hsieh, T. (2010). *Delivering happiness: A path to profits, passion, and purpose.* New York, NY: Hachette Books.

TOOLKIT ACTIVITY 14.1

Comparing Organizational Cultures: IDEO and Amazon

IDEO and Amazon are both successful companies. Use the templates on the next pages to compare and contrast their organizational cultures. The information can be searched on the Internet using Google or some other search engine. Try to find the most specific information you can. For example, for artifacts, don't just state "open plan offices." Describe what the offices look like and what is in them.

	IDEO	AMAZON
Size		
Strategic Focus (cost minimization, innovation/creativity)		

(Continued)

(Continued)

	IDEO	AMAZON
Structural Design (simple, bureaucracy, matrix, boundary-less) Structural Elements: • Specialization • Departmentalization • Chain of command • Span of control • Centralization • Formalization		
Organizational Culture • Artifacts • Values • Assumptions		
Role of the Leader in Shaping Culture? • How is "good performance" defined? • Recruitment/Selection • Training/Development • Rewarding/$$		
Role of the Leader in Shaping Culture?		
Impact: Employee Satisfaction & Turnover		
Impact: Organization Performance		

Source: Developed by Marie Dasborough, University of Miami. Used with permission.

CASE STUDY 14.1

Culture Clash at B-MED

B-MED is a medical equipment distributor that sells and services medical equipment in the Caribbean and Latin American region for General Electric (GE) Healthcare, Medtronic Corporation, Steris Corporation, and AGFA Healthcare. B-MED was founded in 1984 by Bob Samuels and was run as a small family-owned business with fewer than 10 employees for 25 years. B-MED sold small medical equipment such as EKG machines, patient monitors, anesthesia machines, and defibrillators. Since there were only a few products in these lines, B-MED only needed a small staff that consisted of three salespersons, five administrative persons, and two engineers. The staff was mostly composed of Samuels' family members or friends of the family.

The company was a traditional vertical organization, where Samuels made all decisions. Since B-MED had strong financial performance, Samuels rewarded hard work with bonuses and commissions and verbally reprimanded those who did not do as he asked. Employees were generally driven by extrinsic motivation and fear of punishment. They lacked intrinsic motivation and a sense of responsibility and accomplishment. Their input and suggestions were not valued by Samuels. However, the relatively small size of the company meant that B-MED's employees accepted the status quo and performed well enough to generate sufficient revenue to sustain B-MED's profitability.

During the second quarter of 2010, everything changed for B-MED. Samuels received a call from the vice president of GE Healthcare, informing Samuels that B-MED has been chosen to take on the full line of equipment GE Healthcare offered. B-MED would take over the distribution rights from another company (MM Healthcare) because they were no longer meeting GE performance goals. Samuels jumped at the opportunity without considering the large investment in capital, personnel, and equipment required to successfully handle the entire GE line. After the call, Samuels informed his son Craig of the good news. While Craig was excited, he also knew that his father's management style would have to change. He told his father, "This could make us really rich, or really poor." Samuels didn't understand—the potential profits blinded him from seeing the challenges of expanding the company.

The new line of GE equipment included MRI scanners, CT scanners, X-ray machines, nuclear medicine machines, and ultrasound equipment. B-MED had to acquire a large install base consisting of hundreds of pieces of equipment. This new equipment carried service contracts, requiring B-MED to support a broader range of services to their customers. To meet this demand, B-MED started a new company in Trinidad (CASI) and hired 12 new engineers to service existing customers. The majority of these engineers came from MM Healthcare.

MM Healthcare was managed and organized much differently than B-MED. MM Healthcare had a modern structure that was flat with few middle managers. This gave the employees of MM Healthcare a sense of ownership and had enhanced the company's culture by capitalizing on employees feeling empowered and in control. When MM Healthcare's employees were hired by B-MED, they were extremely grateful to have their jobs back, but these feelings of satisfaction quickly dissipated. The CASI employees found themselves in a traditional organization, where their voices were not heard and their opinions did not matter. Further, B-MED's management did not have the proper tools, safety equipment, or safety procedures in place. The new employees began to complain and voice their opinions to B-MED's existing employees. This caused tension between the two groups since B-MED's employees were loyal to Samuels.

To add to the tension, B-MED grew rapidly. In addition to the new engineers, they hired additional sales staff and administrative staff. B-MED was now a company of more than 50 employees located in Trinidad and Miami. The original staff at B-MED began to blame the staff in Trinidad for all of the problems B-MED was facing. The staff in Trinidad blamed Samuels' bureaucratic style of management and his lack of commitment to his employees. The tension between the two groups had a direct effect on the performance of employees. The high level of tension created stress among the employees, creating a toxic workplace.

Samuels ignored stress levels in the company, low job satisfaction, and the lack of intrinsic motivation. The turnover rate of employees increased at an alarming rate, and the company's bottom line suffered substantially. Samuels was no longer able to meet commissions and bonuses that were promised, which removed his ability to extrinsically motivate his employees through compensation. Samuels could only motivate employees through coercive power (threats and punishment). Needless to say, B-MED found itself in a very bad financial state, with unmotivated employees and unhappy customers.

Discussion Questions

1. Compare and contrast the cultures of B-MED and MM Healthcare, using the seven characteristics of culture discussed in this chapter.
2. Explain why existing B-MED employees were willing to work for Samuels without any issues, yet the employees from MM Healthcare had issues.
3. Being that the two sets of employees came from different regions (i.e., Miami and Trinidad), explain the role of national culture in understanding the organizational culture issues in this case. What could have been done to ensure that both cultures (social and institutional) would mesh together?
4. What can be done to address the organizational culture clash in B-MED and restore profitability?

SELF-ASSESSMENT 14.1

Comparing Service Climates

This assessment identifies an organization's service climate. Visit a local restaurant or retail establishment, and rate their service climate by observing employees or asking employees these seven questions. Then visit another establishment of the same type (i.e., restaurant or retail), and perform the same rating. How do the service climates compare? You don't have to share your results with others unless you wish to do so. We will discuss the interpretations of this assessment in class.

Part I. Performing the Assessments

Instructions: Circle the response that best describes what employees experience in the organization.

As an example, the answer to a statement could look like this:

The business keeps customers informed of changes that affect them.

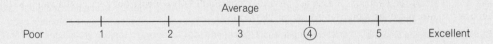

1. How would you rate the job knowledge and skills of employees in this business to deliver superior quality work and service?

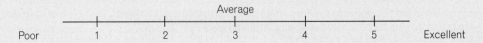

2. How would you rate efforts to measure and track the quality of the work and service in the business?

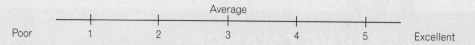

Poor   1   2   Average 3   4   5   Excellent

3. How would you rate the recognition and rewards employees receive for the delivery of superior work and service?

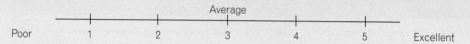

Poor   1   2   Average 3   4   5   Excellent

4. How would you rate the overall quality of service provided by the business?

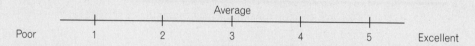

Poor   1   2   Average 3   4   5   Excellent

5. How would you rate the leadership shown by management in the business in supporting the service quality effort?

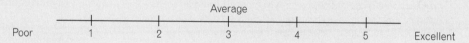

Poor   1   2   Average 3   4   5   Excellent

6. How would you rate the effectiveness of communication efforts to both employees and customers?

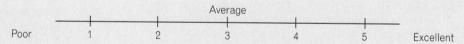

Poor   1   2   Average 3   4   5   Excellent

7. How would you rate the tools, technology, and other resources provided to employees to support the delivery of superior quality work and service?

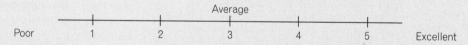

Poor   1   2   Average 3   4   5   Excellent

Part II. Scoring Instructions

Add up the scores for the items for each business you rated. Scores range from 7 (low service climate) to 35 (high service climate). Write the scores for the two businesses here:

Business A Service Climate   Business B Service Climate

_____   _____

Discussion Question

Explain why you think the service climates were the same or different in the two businesses you observed.

Source: Adapted from Schneider, B., White, S. S., & Paul, M. C. (1998). Linking service climate and customer perceptions of service quality: Test of a causal model. *Journal of Applied Psychology, 83*(2), 150–163.

15

LEADING CHANGE

HELPING EMPLOYEES EMBRACE CHANGE

A recent study was conducted by consulting firm McKinsey & Company to examine organizational behavior (OB) (people and processes), and how it relates to financial success from changes such as mergers and cost reduction strategies. The company studied change initiatives started by top management at 40 organizations, including banks, hospitals, and manufacturers. These change programs had specific financial targets that were expected to have a large economic impact on the organization. Some organizations (58%) failed to meet the financial goals of their organizational change initiative. The remaining 42% of these companies met their financial goals (or exceeded them—in some cases by as much as 200 to 300%). The companies with the lowest returns had poor change management practices and companies that gained big returns had strong ones.[1] These change practices are shown for three levels of management. While senior managers play a key role in articulating the need for change and leading the change process, this study also shows that managers play an important leadership role by providing feedback, skills, tools, and motivation for their followers to succeed.

As the McKinsey study indicates, effective leadership of organizational change can have significant bottom-line impact for organizations. Most organizations today are undergoing changes. Figure 15.1 shows key cultural shifts that have taken place in the evolution of work. For example, organizational hierarchies have been replaced with flatter organizational structures. In the past, employees worked 9:00 a.m. to 5:00 p.m. in offices, but there has been a shift toward flexible working hours and working from anywhere through mobile technology. Instead of information being held by the top executive team, information is shared with employees throughout organizations. Hand-held mobile devices have become the primary means of communication in organizations. Leadership styles have shifted from command and control to inspirational. These changes are powerful forces that affect organizations and leaders must help employees cope with them. The next section will review some of the major forces that are drivers of organizational change.

Factors for Successful Change

Senior managers	
Commitment	Put initiative at top of agenda
Communication	Relate single, clear, compelling story–no mixed messages
Financial incentives	Reward senior managers if initiative is successful
Nonfinancial incentives	Provide recognition for strong performance
Leadership	Identify owner/champion
Stretch targets	Upload goals with mantralike consistency; team "lives or dies" by the numbers
Middle managers	
Decision authority	Exercise consistent control over defined set of tasks
Skills in managing people	Provide feedback to employees on status of initiative
Skills in managing projects	Achieve measurable milestones in timely manner
Frontline staff	
Skills	Consider training key aspect of initiative
Tools	Make technology and techniques available to employees
Motivation	Clearly reward excellent performance to improve morale

Source: LaClair, J. A., & Rao, R. P. (2002). Helping employees embrace change. *The McKinsey Quarterly, 4*, 17–20.

FORCES DRIVING ORGANIZATIONAL CHANGE

Learning Objective 15.1: Describe the forces driving organizational change.

There are numerous forces for change in organizations. Some examples are provided in Table 15.1 For example, Chapter 3 discussed the impact of **workforce diversity** due to gender, race/ethnicity, and generations at work. Changes in the workforce as well as cultural differences (Chapter 12) will continue to be a force for organizational change. The economy represents a significant source for change. For example, economic recessions result in major changes such as downsizing and restructuring. Technology changes are rapid, and organizations must keep up with these advances. As discussed in Chapter 11 of this book, technology advances have resulted in changes in how people communicate inside and outside of the organization. Globalization represents a significant source of change for organizations with the rise of the multinational corporation. Increased globalization of markets has also given rise to competition from abroad in addition to competing with firms within a given country. As consumers, we enjoy a broader array of product options, lower prices, and increased attention to customer service. However, intense competition may lead to industry shakeouts, and we have seen some giants faltering such as AOL who didn't see Google's competitive threat until it was too late.

Figure 15.1   The Evolution of Work

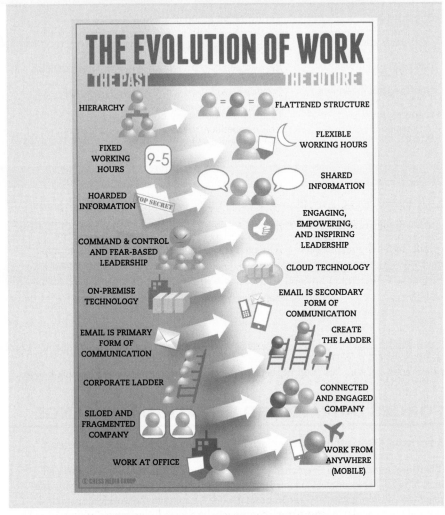

Source: Retrieved on April 2, 2014 from: http://www.forbes.com/sites/jacobmorgan/2013/09/10/the-evolution-of-work/. Courtesy of Jacob Morgan, Principal and co-founder of Chess Media Group, Best-selling author, most recently The Future of Work (2013).

PLANNED ORGANIZATIONAL CHANGE

Learning Objective 15.2: Explain why planned organizational change is necessary.

The forces for organizational change have resulted in the need for organizations to be **proactive** rather than **reactive** in reading the environment they operate in. The idea of

Table 15.1 Forces Driving Organizational Change

Force for Change	Examples
Workforce diversity	Sex, race/ethnicity, cultural differences, age/generation
The economy	Recession, government policy, rising health care costs
Technology	Mobile devices, social media, Internet security, robotics
Globalization	Multinational corporations, political instability, fair trade, sustainability, outsourcing, emerging markets
Competition	Global competition, mergers and acquisitions, customer standards, time to market

being proactive when it comes to change is not new and dates to the classic management book *Overcoming Organizational Defenses*.[2] Yet, most organizations still are in reactive mode (i.e., "putting out fires") when it comes to change. Change may also be incremental (e.g., adding blue dots to a detergent) or radical (e.g., a major restructuring).[3,4] Putting these concepts together (reactive/proactive and incremental/radical) results in a useful framework for classifying the types of organizational change (see Figure 15.2). As shown in the figure, the most intense form of change is proactive and radical, and it is often when an organization engages in planned organizational change using OD interventions.

Figure 15.2 Types of Planned Organizational Change

	Reactive	Proactive
Incremental	**Put out small fires!** Solve problems on a day-to-day basis. Quick fixes to short-term concerns.	**Tweaking.** Anticipate and plan. Improve current ways of doing things. Fine tune. Guided evolution.
Radical	**Stop the bleeding!** Crisis management. Industry shakeups, economic turmoil, financial shocks.	**Transformation.** Do things fundamentally differently. Change basic assumptions. Revolution.

Engaging an Older Workforce

A workforce shift to be aware of is that people are living longer and staying in the workforce longer. The following best practices for adapting the organization for an aging workforce are suggested:[5]

1. **Flexible, half-time retirement.** Retirees can work part-time while drawing part of their retirement funds so they earn a full salary and keep their benefits.
2. **Prioritizing older workers' skills in hiring and promotions.** The organization puts more emphasis on "loyalty, track records, competence, and common sense," which are valuable to organizations. A study from the Sloan Center on Aging and Work found that older workers have more respect, maturity, and networking skills.
3. **Creating new positions or adapting old ones.** This practice is retraining workers for jobs that better suit their skill sets. For example, a retail store might retrain a cashier to be a customer service representative to move them to a job with less physical demands. Older workers

may be better suited for project management, community relations, and mentoring new employees as additional examples.
4. **Changing workplace ergonomics.** Organizations can adapt the work environment to better suit older workers. For example, BMW has made "inexpensive tweaks" to workplace ergonomics, such as easier to read computer screens, and has seen productivity increase by 7% and the assembly line defect rate drop to zero.

Discussion Questions:

1. Explain what role seniority should play in the determination of promotions. Discuss the pros and cons of basing promotions on seniority.
2. Explain why older workers may be more respectful when dealing with customers. Consider the role of maturity in your answer.
3. Provide an example of how an existing job could be modified to better suit the skill set of an older worker.

Source: Adapted from North, M., & Hershfield, H. (2014). Four ways to adapt to an aging workforce. Retrieved on April 8, 2014, from http://blogs.hbr.org/2014/04/four-ways-to-adapt-to-an-aging-workforce.

ORGANIZATIONAL SUBSYTEMS INVOLVED IN PLANNED CHANGE

Learning Objective 15.3: Compare and contrast the four subsystems involved in planned organizational change.

Planned organizational change involves four organizational subsystems:

1. **Formal organization.** This provides the coordination and control necessary for organized activity; examples are formal structures and reward systems.
2. **Social factors.** These factors include individual differences, team interactions, and the organizational culture.

3. **Technology.** This is how raw materials and inputs transform into outputs, such as work flow design and job design.
4. **Physical setting.** These are the characteristics of the physical space and how it is arranged.[6]

An example of culture change implementation that is proactive and radical is the cultural change at Yum! Brands, Inc.[7] Yum! Brands (Pizza Hut, Taco Bell, and KFC) was able to create a new culture after the restaurants were spun off from PepsiCo Inc. All three companies had strong founders and changing and integrating the three cultures was a challenging task for the new vice chair, David Novak. Pizza Hut, Taco Bell, and KFC had been successful under the marketing and finance-driven culture of Pepsi, but they still had very different traditions and underlying assumptions about what success means. The actions that Yum! took to create a new culture were as follows:

1. Starting with a set of shared values to define a culture across the three brands
2. Founding the new company in a way that that embodied the new culture
3. Using new titles to signal intentions and signify new cultural meanings
4. Creating a coaching management system to maximize restaurant performance
5. Developing a recognition culture to reinforce the new culture's values
6. Realigning reward systems to validate and "walk the talk" on values
7. Measuring the effectiveness and commitment of senior managers to the values

Critical Thinking Questions: Evaluate how well Yum! Brands addressed four subsystems (formal organization, social factors, technology, physical setting). Did they need to address all of them? Why or why not?

ORGANIZATIONAL DEVELOPMENT

Learning Objective 15.4: Provide an example of an organizational development (OD) intervention.

Organizational development (OD) is a collection of social psychology methods employed to improve organizational effectiveness and employee well-being. OD reflects the insight that "there is nothing so practical as a good theory."[8] OB is an applied science, and theories of OB are applied in organizational settings through OD interventions. Also, the researchers of the Hawthorne studies (described in Chapter 1 of this book) found paying attention to workers increased productivity. Thus, OB can be considered to be the theory and research that underlies the practical application of OD interventions in the workplace. There is a difference between *theories of change* and *theories of changing*.[9] Theories of change try to answer the question of how and why change occurs (e.g., the impact of the Affordable Care Act on employee benefit plans). Theories of change focus on how to implement successful organizational change (e.g., enhancing the ethical climate). Academics tend to write about theories of change, and management

Employee Intentions and Change

practitioners tend to write about theories of changing.[10] This chapter focuses on theories of changing with an emphasis on the leader's role in creating and sustaining organizational change. Organizational leaders and consultants have experimented with a variety of organizational change interventions. Specific examples of OD interventions follow.

Examples of Organizational Development Interventions

Survey feedback is one of the most commonly employed OD techniques. Throughout this textbook, you have taken a number of self-assessments at the end of the chapters that are the types of surveys that employees take (e.g., refer back to Table 4.1 in Chapter 4 for an example of a measure of job satisfaction). Data are collected from employees regarding their attitudes toward work, and their confidentiality is assured. This data is then analyzed and reported back to the organization as group averages. For example, a survey report might state that 55% of the employees surveyed indicate that they don't trust the top management team of the organization. This report becomes a starting point for further OD efforts, which may result in task forces to address the concerns identified in the survey. Most large organizations today conduct attitude surveys of their employees—typically on an annual basis. Participation in surveys should be organization-wide to ensure that the survey results accurately reflect employee attitudes.[11] Surveys are a key tool for understanding important organizational issues.

Workout was pioneered at General Electric (GE) and provided a method for employees to get new ideas heard by top management without having to go through hierarchical levels of bureaucracy. Other organizations have adopted this OD intervention.[12] Workout has several steps:[13]

1. The manager introduces a problem to a team of employees who have relevant expertise.
2. The manager leaves, and the employees work together for about 2 days on the problem.
3. The manager returns, and the employees report their proposals to solve the problem.
4. On the spot, the manager must accept the proposals, decline them, or ask for more information.

If more information is requested, a process to make a final decision must be articulated.

Sometimes a leader needs an outside point of view on an organizational issue and hires a consultant with OD expertise who assists in a helping mode.[14] This process is called **process consultation** and may focus on such matters as interpersonal relationships and communication. The consultant does not offer a solution to the problem but rather guides the leader to solve it through coaching. In this process, the leader develops their own skills in understanding and addressing the problem but may call upon the consultant later if needed for further coaching.

As you learned in Chapter 9, teams (when people work well together) can result in high levels of performance and learning for employees. Organizations are increasingly relying on teams to work on complex tasks and generate new ideas. Thus, **team building** has emerged as an important OD intervention. Team building employs group activities that involve a great deal of interaction among team members to increase trust.[15] A meta-analysis showed that OD interventions do affect satisfaction and attitudes with team building being one of the more effective interventions.[16] Despite the popularity of team building, research has not shown strong relationships to team performance. A meta-analysis of team building interventions and performance found no overall effect. However, examination of the specific aspects of team building showed that interventions emphasizing role clarification were more likely to increase performance, and the effects of team building decreased as a function of the size of the team.[17] Team building seems to affect attitudes more than performance. Also, focusing on what roles members are playing in a team (e.g., leading, analyzing, presenting, supporting, and recording) within a small team is recommended for improved performance.

Appreciative inquiry (AI) is a recently developed OD intervention that is an example of action research (described in the appendix of this textbook). AI is consistent with emerging ideas from positive psychology and OB.[18,19] The basic assumption is that people move in the direction that they visualize for the future. Participants begin the AI process by reflecting on a peak experience and then engage conversation about it with others in a group setting. Questions are asked regarding why the moment was positive. Examples of topics in AI are learning, leadership, communication, or work relationships as examples.[20] Individual reflections on the peak experience are then linked to develop a shared meaning for the group. AI is a process where the group learns what it has done well and focuses on strengths.[21,22] An example of AI applied to your learning experiences in your OB course is provided in Toolkit Activity 15.1. While AI has generated a lot of interest by practitioners, empirical support has been mixed.[23]

Planned organizational change can have a number of targets including structure, technology, processes, teams, and people.[24] More recently, **sustainability** has become a target of OD interventions with an emphasis on preserving the environment.[25] For example, most organizations now participate in recycling programs, and many adopt fair-trade practices in importing goods from other countries. Such initiatives require changes to the fundamental assumptions regarding the organization's culture as discussed in Chapter 14.

 Critical Thinking Questions: Which OD intervention(s) would you rely on for implementing a change in your organization's (or university's) approach to environmental conservation? Why?

RESISTANCE TO CHANGE

Learning Objective 15.5: Discuss the reasons why people resist organizational change.

When faced with an organizational change, employee reactions vary from **resistance**, **compliance**, or **commitment to change**. Resistance means that the employees fight the

Why People Resist Change

change and try to undermine it.[26] In compliance, they simply go along with the change but secretly hope that it is a program that will come to an end soon. Commitment to change is the most desirable reaction in which the employees support change and help the organization implement it.[27] Since resistance is the most difficult reaction for the leader to deal with, this section will focus on understanding and overcoming resistance to change.

Research on resistance to change dates back to a classic study of participative decision making conducted with a strong research design.[28] Employees were transferred to new jobs in which they encountered significant changes to their work. Interviews revealed employees resisted changes in their work methods due to resentment, frustration, and a loss of hope of regaining their formal levels of proficiency. A second experiment was then conducted in which the control group was transferred to new jobs, but they were allowed to participate in the changes through chosen representatives; this group recovered rapidly and reached a higher level of productivity compared to the group that was not allowed to participate in the change. This study shows that OD can impact resistance to change through an intervention that increased employee participation in the process. Lack of participation and input to the change is one reason employees resist change. There are a number of others that include both personal reasons and organizational reasons.[29,30,31] Personal reasons include habit, security, economic, and fear of the unknown. Organizational reasons for resistance are structural inertia (the structure is too rigid to support the change), group inertia, threats to expertise, and threats to established power relationships.

How to Overcome Resistance to Change

The introduction to this chapter showed results from a McKinsey survey on how organizations help employees embrace change. A classic *Harvard Business Review* article offers the following additional guidelines to help overcome resistance to change:[32]

1. **Being educated and communicating** reduces misinformation about the change and helps convince employees that change is needed.
2. **Participating matters**, as demonstrated by the participative decision making study described in the previous section. People are more likely to accept changes that they help design.
3. **Building support and commitment** reduces resistance because employees have the support through counseling or sabbaticals to ease the strain. Commitment to the organization also increases commitment to change.
4. **Developing positive relationships** through trust in management increases commitment to organizational change. Research has shown that high-quality leader–member exchange (LMX) relationships reduce resistance.[33,34] Leaders provide explanations to followers that help them cope with change and commit to it.[35]
5. **Implementing changes fairly** improves the chances that employees will accept change. As reviewed in Chapter 7, organizational justice is a major concern of most employees, and it becomes even more important during change.
6. **Selecting people who accept change** supports changes since research shows that people have personality traits that enable them to be more flexible when it comes to coping with change.[36]

Ethical Leadership During Organizational Change

Research indicates that leaders play an important role during change by supporting the change and taking part in its implementation.[37] It has been argued that transformational leadership that is faked is not true transformational leadership. Leaders who lead transformation efforts exhibit leadership that depends upon "(1) the moral character of the leaders and their concerns for self and others; (2) the ethical values embedded in the leaders' vision, articulation, and program, which followers can embrace or reject; and (3) the morality of the processes of social ethical choices and action in which the leaders and followers engage and collectively pursue."[38] Thus, ethical behavior is an essential underpinning of transformational leadership. But does such ethical conduct by leaders make a difference in satisfaction and performance during organizational change?

A survey of 199 employees and their supervisors found ethical leadership matters in the context of organizational change.[39] Technology changes were the change that was most frequently listed as having the most impact, followed by downsizing, and then restructuring. Other changes reported were relocations, mergers, process changes, and people-centered changes. These changes have a significant impact on employees' regular work routines and cause stress as discussed in Chapter 13. If an employee senses that their leader is behaving unethically, this may exacerbate the stress and result in lower performance. Followers need to be able to trust the integrity of their leaders during change. In addition, the degree to which employees felt that they were involved in the organization's change process made a difference as well. For example, having leaders discuss changes with employees results in higher job satisfaction, performance, and organizational citizenship behavior (OCB) during organizational change.

Discussion Questions:

1. Do you agree or disagree with the statement that transformational leadership cannot be faked? Explain your position.
2. Explain why perceptions of leaders behaving unethically creates stress during organizational change. Consider the role of change uncertainty.
3. In addition to discussing changes with employees, describe some other actions that leaders can take to improve employee adjustment to organizational change.

Sources: Bass, B. M., & Steidlmeier, P. (1999). Ethics, character, and authentic transformational leadership behavior. *The Leadership Quarterly, 10*(2), 181–217; Sharif, M. M., & Scandura, T. A. (2014). Do perceptions of ethical conduct matter during organizational change? Ethical leadership and employee involvement. *Journal of Business Ethics, 124*(2), 185–196; Whelen-Berry, K. S., Gordon, J. R., & Hinings, C. R. (2003). Strengthening organizational change processes: Recommendations and implications from a multi-level analysis. *Journal of Applied Behavioral Science, 39*(2), 186–207.

The article also includes these tactics, but they may backfire and should only be used as last resorts:

7. **Manipulation and cooptation tactics are sometimes used in organizational transitions because they are relatively less expensive than the tactics listed previously.** Manipulation occurs when change agents use underhanded techniques such as the selective sharing of information and careful staging of events. Cooptation is basically "buying" the support of those who are needed. For example, members of a task force for change would be paid a bonus for serving on the task force.

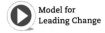

8. **Coercion should be used rarely, if at all, as discussed in the leadership chapter of this book (Chapter 2).** Direct threats of loss of status, pay, or other things that employees care about may gain short-term compliance, but these tactics will rarely gain commitment to the change.

As the previous section indicates, real leadership is necessary to effectively implement organizational change. The most effective tactics for overcoming resistance and gaining support are communication and building relationships and support for the change. The next section discusses the models for leading change that have been shown to produce the best results.

Critical Thinking Question: Provide an example of manipulation, co-optation, or coercion during change. Evaluate the effectiveness of this tactic.

LEADING CHANGE

Learning Objective 15.6: Compare and contrast the models for leading organizational change (i.e., Lewin, Kotter).

After the issue of resistance to change is anticipated, analyzed, and addressed, the next step in changing organizations is to implement the change process through effective leadership. Next, the models of leading others through change will be discussed.

Lewin's Three-Step Model

The three-step model is the starting point for understanding the fundamental process of leading change. As shown in Figure 15.3, there are three steps in the change process: unfreezing, changing, and refreezing. First, unfreezing challenges the status quo by shaking up assumptions; next, changing represents movement toward a new desired state. Finally refreezing the changes by reinforcing and restructuring is the third phase to make the changes permanent. Think about an ice pack that you use when you have a sports injury. When you take it out of the freezer, it is hard and can't be changed much. As you use it, it becomes soft and malleable (this is the changing phase). After 20 minutes, you put it back in the freezer, and it becomes solid again. Change is like this: When people and systems are in the frozen stage, you can't change them. You have to literally "heat things up" to soften the attitudes and assumptions about change so that the system is malleable like a defrosted ice pack. Once you have the changes you want in place, you reinforce the new behaviors with rewards or change the structure to support the change (refreezing).

Employees will tend toward the status quo or equilibrium, so there needs to be constant attention to refreezing the new system and behaviors after a change is implemented. For example, an organization that wants to implement teams must first challenge the old assumptions regarding working alone and getting rewarded for individual effort. A new organizational chart is presented to employees, showing teams the new way that work will

Figure 15.3 Lewin's Three-Step Model of Organizational Change

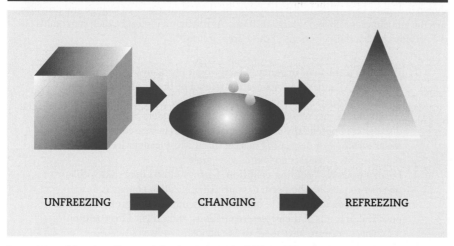

UNFREEZING ➡ CHANGING ➡ REFREEZING

Source: Adapted from http://www.mindtools.com/pages/article/newPPM_94.htm.

be organized. Some employees may resist the team concept and even leave the organization as the change is implemented. There may be storms and team conflict (things are heating up). Once there are successful teams in place, then the new approach can be refrozen by offering team rewards and reinforcing the new organizational chart.

As this example illustrates, the Lewin model is still relevant today. A review of research evidence on organizational change over the past several decades concluded that "rather than being outdated or redundant, Lewin's approach is still relevant to the modern world."[40] Lewin's approach is based upon field theory and the analysis of forces for and against organizational change. This approach will be discussed next.

Force Field Analysis

To implement organizational change using the three-step model, a **force field analysis** of the forces for and against an organizational change should be conducted.[41] The steps in force field analysis follow:

1. Define the problem (current state) and the target situation (target state).
2. List forces working for and against the desired changes.
3. Rate the strength of each force.
4. Draw a diagram (the length of line denotes strength of the force).
5. Indicate how important each force is.
6. List how to strengthen each important supporting force.
7. List how to weaken each important resisting force.
8. Identify resources needed to support forces for change, and reduce forces against change.
9. Make an action plan: timing, milestones, and responsibilities.

Kotter's Eight-Step Model

Another important model for leading change is the Kotter eight-step model, which is shown in Figure 15.4. This model elaborates on the Lewin model of change and provides specific guidelines for changing organizations. As the figure indicates, each step builds on the previous one, and descriptions of these steps follow.[42]

1. **Establish a sense of urgency.** Change typically begins with leaders noticing challenges the organization faces. The threat of losing ground in some way sparks these people into action, and they, in turn, try to communicate that sense of urgency to others. Leaders begin a frank discussion of potentially unpleasant facts such as increased competition, lower earnings, or decreasing market share. Most leaders are convinced that business as usual is no longer acceptable.
2. **Form a powerful guiding coalition.** Change efforts may start with just one or two people who begin to convince others that change is needed. In this step, an initial core of believers is assembled (this group should be powerful in terms of their roles, reputations, and skills). This coalition for change needs to have three to five people.
3. **Create a vision.** A compelling "picture" of the future must be created. This vision motivates people and keeps the change processes aligned.

Figure 15.4   Kotter's Eight-Step Model for Leading Change

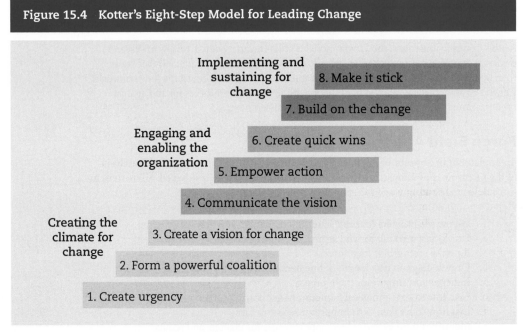

Source: Kotter, J. P. (1995). Leading change: Why transformation efforts fail. *Harvard Business Review, 73*(2), 59–67. Reprinted with permission from Harvard Business Review.

This vision needs to be communicated to employees clearly and effectively in 5 minutes or less.

4. **Communicate the vision.** Regardless of how much communication leaders think is needed, they should multiply that by 10. Every possible communication channel should be utilized including the CEO's speech, meetings, newsletters, e-mail, and face-to-face conversation as examples. Employees will be looking to see that the leaders in the organization are behaving consistently with the vision.

5. **Empower others to act on the vision.** Employees should be allowed to participate in making changes in their areas. This may require restructuring work and allowing key people the time to focus on the change effort. Also, this involves providing the money and support needed to bring about change.

6. **Plan for and create short-term wins.** Change takes time, and change efforts sometimes lose momentum as frustrations set in with employees. Plan and execute celebrations of short-term successes to reinforce people's efforts and maintain their commitment and motivation. This provides proof to employees that their efforts are working.

7. **Consolidate improvements and sustain the momentum for change.** A change process can take 5 to 10 years—as force field analysis shows, the forces against change such as resistance may result in regression to the prior ways of doing things. Leaders should resist the temptation to declare the change a success too soon. Leaders must enter the process believing that their efforts will take years.

8. **Institutionalize the new approaches.** A leader will know that the change is frozen in place when followers believe that it is "the way we do things around here." Employees understand that their efforts have led to a different outcome for the organization. The organization's leaders serve as role models for the new ways.

The Kotter model has shown to be a useful road map for guiding organizational change. Research has also shown that there are other elements that help ensure successful organizational change. In the next section, the research evidence on change implementation is reviewed, and it generally supports what Kotter envisioned in the eight-step model.

 Critical Thinking Question: Show how the Kotter model relates to the Lewin three-step model. In other words, which steps in the Kotter model represent unfreezing, changing, and refreezing?

EFFECTIVE CHANGE IMPLEMENTATION

Learning Objective 15.7: Discuss the role of executive leadership in implementing successful organizational change.

Research has shown that executive leadership—**top management support**—is important during organizational change.[43] A meta-analysis found little or no commitment to change from employees when top management support for change was low.[44] This is important because employee attitudes have also been shown to influence the success of organizational change.[45] One key attitude is commitment to change.[46]

Organizational **restructuring and downsizing** is one of the most challenging types of organizational change. Yet, economic realities often require such radical organizational change for the organization to survive. These changes often result in layoffs that damage the morale of those who remain in the organization. A study of an organization undergoing a downsizing found that communication and fostering **innovation** helped maintain employee morale.[47] Bob Sutton's article "How to Be a Good Boss in a Bad Economy" suggests that during a downturn you need to rethink your leadership role in terms of focusing on "predictability, understanding, control and compassion."[48]

 Critical Thinking Question: What specific actions can a leader take to maintain the morale of the survivors of layoffs through showing compassion?

Innovation has become a requirement in many industries. In a recent *Harvard Business Review* article, the Innovator's DNA is described. Innovators ask "Why?" "Why not?" and "What if?"[49] Owens Corning recently transformed its managers into innovators through setting new expectations, training, and support. Owens Corning implemented game-changing innovations in all of its businesses and improved both market share and pricing. They enhanced existing products through innovation and launched new products in the alternative energy, transportation, and communications markets. The result was that new products started since 2010 accounted for $853 million in sales in the first half of 2013—more than 30% of total company sales.[50] As the Owens Corning example indicates, change may lead to enhanced organizational performance, and the research evidence supports this for both domestic and multinational firms.[51,52]

LEADERSHIP IMPLICATIONS: CREATING LEARNING ORGANIZATIONS

By creating what is known as a **learning organization,** leaders can facilitate organizational change by having a workplace that is flexible and innovative.[53,54] Peter Senge's influential book *The Fifth Discipline* describes learning organizations as follows:

> Learning organizations are where people continually expand their capacity to create the results they truly desire, where new and expansive patterns of thinking are nurtured, where collective aspiration is set free, and where people are continually learning to see the whole together.[55]

The five leadership learning disciplines in learning organizations are shown in Figure 15.5:

1. **Personal mastery**—competence plus the discipline of continually clarifying and deepening our personal vision, of focusing our energies, of developing patience, and of seeing reality objectively.

Figure 15.5   The Learning Organization

Organizational
Learning

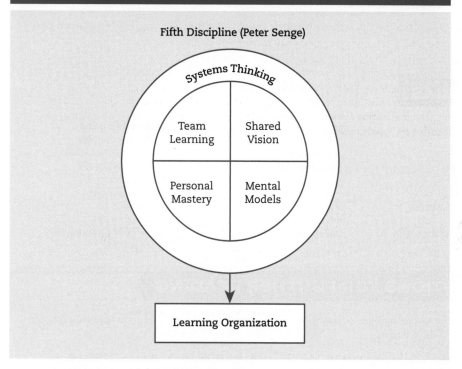

Fifth Discipline (Peter Senge)

Systems Thinking

| Team Learning | Shared Vision |
| Personal Mastery | Mental Models |

Learning Organization

Source: Retrieved on March 31, 2014, from http://www.comindwork.com/weekly/2012-04-16/productivity/
fifth-discipline-by-peter-senge-is-systems-thinking.

2. **Mental models**—deeply ingrained assumptions, generalizations, or even pictures and images that influence how we understand the world and how we take action.

3. **Building shared vision**—the sharing of a long-term view of the future, which is uplifting, and encourages experimentation and innovation.

4. **Team learning**—aligning and developing teams to generate results they want. People on the team act and learn together. They grow rapidly from team interactions.

5. **Systems thinking**—learning from experience, understanding cause and effect. This component integrates all of the others and is the fifth discipline.

You may have noticed that Senge's model incorporates much of the thinking on organizational change covered in this chapter. It includes a shared vision of the the future as described in the Lewin and Kotter change process models. It also reflects a focus on teams and systems thinking and is thus an excellent summary for this chapter on leading change. By creating a learning organization, leaders prepare employees to be ready for the challenge of change.

⑤SAGE edge™

edge.sagepub.com/scandura

Want a better grade? Go to **edge.sagepub.com/scandura** for the tools you need to sharpen your study skills.

KEY TERMS

appreciative inquiry (AI), 393
changing, 396
commitment to change, 393
compliance, 393
force field analysis, 397
innovation, 400
learning organization, 400

organizational development (OD), 391
proactive, 388
process consultation, 392
reactive, 388
refreezing, 396
resistance, 393

restructuring and downsizing, 400
survey feedback, 392
sustainability, 393
team building, 393
top management support, 399
unfreezing, 396
workforce diversity, 387
workout, 392

SUGGESTIONS FOR FURTHER READING

Argyris, C. (1990). *Overcoming organizational defenses.* Boston, MA: Allyn & Bacon.

Bennis, W. G. (1966). *Changing organizations.* New York, NY: McGraw-Hill.

Burke, W. W. (2010). *Organization change: Theory and practice.* Thousand Oaks, CA: Sage.

Kanter, R. M. (1984). *Change masters.* New York, NY: Simon & Schuster.

Senge, P., Kleiner, A., Roberts, C., Ross, R., Roth, G., & Smith, B. (1999). *The dance of change: The challenges of sustaining momentum in learning organizations.* New York, NY: Doubleday.

TOOLKIT ACTIVITY 15.1

Appreciative Inquiry

Think back on this course and the learning experiences that you participated in. Choose one that you think was a great learning experience. After completing this form, form a small group with other students and discuss your experiences. Develop some suggestions for your professor to implement in future classes.

1. What happened that made it a great learning experience?
2. Describe the experience.
3. What did you learn?
4. What three wishes do you have that would make learning always like this?

Source: Adapted from Conklin, T. A., & Hartman, N. S. (2013). Appreciative inquiry and autonomy-supportive classes in business education: A semi longitudinal study of AI in the classroom. *Journal of Experiential Education, 37*(3), 285–309. doi: 10.1177/1053825913514732

CASE STUDY 15.1

Alighting Innovation in the Utility Industry

There are 3,200 utilities that make up the U.S. electrical grid that sell $400 billion worth of electricity per year. However, that's slowly changing. Companies such as Comcast, NineStar Connect, and Vivint have started selling their customers electricity along with their services. Comcast offers its XFINITY customers in Pennsylvania the opportunity to purchase electricity as well as phone, Internet, and TV services. NineStar Connect offers electricity, phone, broadband and home security to customers in central Indiana. Vivint, an alarm system company on the East Coast, installs solar panels on alarm clients' homes for free and then requires the homeowner to purchase the electricity that is generated. Any excess is sold to the local power company. Google, while it has not formally entered the market, has its own wholesale power license and has purchased Nest, which makes a "learning thermostat." Industry experts speculate that it will only be a matter of time before Google formally enters the market.

With this influx of new competitors, utilities will have to start learning to compete. Michael Peevey, the president of the California Public Utilities Commission, states that these days utilities "hold their own fate in their hands. They can do nothing but complain or moan about technological change or they can try to adapt."[56]

Utilities lose revenues when businesses and residential customers switch to solar and wind power and lose additional money from having to buy any excess electricity generated. Utilities have to maintain the power transmission lines across the grid. Customers often are assessed fees in their bills that help cover line maintenance, but those who are selling back power don't pay these fees while still using the power lines.

Further, utility companies face a number of regulations and are limited in their actions. For instance, utilities in Louisiana, Idaho, and California want to impose fees or taxes on solar users but have been rejected by regulators. It is unlikely that U.S. regulators will ever completely do away with electric companies as there will always be a need to have a secure supply of power. Thus, these companies will always have to incur the expense of maintaining the power lines with a dwindling customer base.

Additionally, most utility companies are behind the times on technology. While there are smart meters, most utilities have a limited presence in customer homes with programmable thermostats. They could have a greater presence if they were to invest in developing better in-home energy management tools (like the thermostats offered by Nest). Nor have many utilities looked into apps for phones or tablets that can help consumers manage their electricity use.

Finally, the utilities themselves have been getting in the way of their own success. Over a decade ago, Peevey recommended to the California utilities to enter the solar power business. He suggested they put solar panels on people's homes and then build the cost of installation into the rate base. The CEOs of the utility companies balked at Peevey's calls for change. Most CEOs replied back to his innovative ideas: "It's not our culture." This is true, as most electric companies didn't have a need to innovate its production processes or products for decades.

Anthony Earley Jr., CEO of Pacific Gas and Electric Company, realizes the seriousness of the threat these problems pose. He knows that his company needs to change, but where should his company start?

Discussion Questions

1. What changes will the company need to make? In what areas should the company start making changes?
2. Looking at the change models presented in the text, how might you unroll the changes you came up with? How can leaders help or hinder change?
3. How can planning for organizational change help the company adapt? Think of several specific functional areas or processes that can be used to help facilitate this planned change.

4. What can you do to help overcome employees' resistance to change both before the changes are implemented as well as during the change process? Is it simply behaviors that will need to change, or will attitudes need to change as well?

Sources: Martin, C., Chediak, M., & Wells, K. (2013, August 22). Why the U.S. power grid's days are numbered. *Businessweek.* Retrieved from http://www.businessweek.com/articles/2013-08-22/homegrown-green-energy-is-making-power-utilities-irrelevant#p; Smith, S. J. (2014, May 28). Barclays warns that U.S. electric utilities are under solar threat. The Works. Retrieved from http://nextcity.org/daily/entry/barclays-downgrade-us-electric-utility-sector-solar-threat; Goossens, E., Chediak, M., & Polson, J. (2014, May 29). Technarians at the gate: How Google could become your next power company. Bloomberg. Retrieved from http://www.bloomberg.com/news/2014-05-29/tv-web-phone-electricity-a-new-threat-to-utilities.html.

SELF-ASSESSMENT 15.1

Leading Through Change Assessment

This self-assessment exercise identifies your approach(es) to leading through change. There is no "one best" approach—all have strengths and weaknesses. There are no "right or wrong" answers, and this is not a test. You don't have to share your results with others unless you wish to do so. We will discuss the interpretations of this assessment together during the seminar.

Part I. Taking the Assessment

You will be presented with some questions representing different approaches to leading through change. If you don't currently have direct reports ("followers"), answer the questions with respect to how you approach others (for example, your peers) during change.

As an example, the answer to a situation could look like this:

I encourage my followers to participate in decisions affecting them.

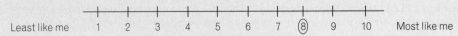

Least like me   1   2   3   4   5   6   7   (8)   9   10   Most like me

1. I assign tasks to followers to implement change.

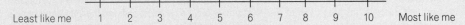

Least like me   1   2   3   4   5   6   7   8   9   10   Most like me

2. I try to keep the morale of my followers high during change.

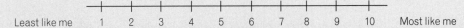

Least like me   1   2   3   4   5   6   7   8   9   10   Most like me

3. I set ground rules and leave it up to my followers to change.

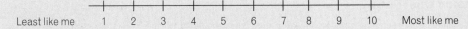

Least like me   1   2   3   4   5   6   7   8   9   10   Most like me

4. I use logic to convince my followers to change.

Least like me   1   2   3   4   5   6   7   8   9   10   Most like me

5. I expect my followers to be committed to the goals of change.

Least like me   1   2   3   4   5   6   7   8   9   10   Most like me

6. I believe that change is best implemented when few people are involved.

Least like me   1   2   3   4   5   6   7   8   9   10   Most like me

7. I try to emphasize that followers will be satisfied with the benefits of change.

Least like me   1   2   3   4   5   6   7   8   9   10   Most like me

8. I leave decisions on change and its implementation to my followers.

Least like me   1   2   3   4   5   6   7   8   9   10   Most like me

9. I explain the reasons for the change to my followers.

Least like me   1   2   3   4   5   6   7   8   9   10   Most like me

10. I communicate clear goals for change.

Least like me   1   2   3   4   5   6   7   8   9   10   Most like me

11. I demonstrate my expertise with respect to change to my followers.

Least like me   1   2   3   4   5   6   7   8   9   10   Most like me

12. I rely on good working relationships to get things done during change.

Least like me   1   2   3   4   5   6   7   8   9   10   Most like me

13. My followers decide what changes are needed.

Least like me   1   2   3   4   5   6   7   8   9   10   Most like me

14. I present the need for change logically to my followers.

Least like me   1   2   3   4   5   6   7   8   9   10   Most like me

15. I emphasize the rewards from commitment to change.

Least like me   1   2   3   4   5   6   7   8   9   10   Most like me

16. I ask my followers to complete tasks efficiently during change.

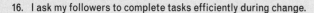

Least like me   1   2   3   4   5   6   7   8   9   10   Most like me

17. I explain how change will improve morale.

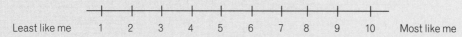

Least like me   1   2   3   4   5   6   7   8   9   10   Most like me

18. I allow my followers to follow their own course of action with respect to change.

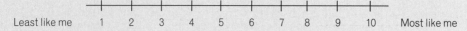

Least like me   1   2   3   4   5   6   7   8   9   10   Most like me

19. I prefer to implement change slowly to allow followers to adjust to it.

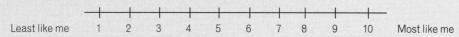

Least like me   1   2   3   4   5   6   7   8   9   10   Most like me

20. I show followers how the goals of change positively impact our organization's performance.

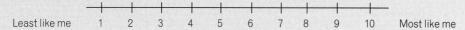

Least like me   1   2   3   4   5   6   7   8   9   10   Most like me

Part II. Preliminary Scoring Instructions

In Part I, you rated yourself on 20 questions. Copy the numbers you circled in each of the columns to derive your score for the approaches to leading through change. During class, we will discuss each approach and its strengths and weaknesses, as well as discuss how you can be more effective in leading change. (If you have been given a peer form for others to rate you, score it as well and bring it with you.)

Approach A	Approach B	Approach C	Approach D	Approach E
1. _____	2. _____	3. _____	4. _____	5. _____
6. _____	7. _____	8. _____	9. _____	10. _____
11. _____	12. _____	13. _____	14. _____	15. _____
16. _____	17. _____	18. _____	19. _____	20. _____
Total _____	_____	_____	_____	_____

Now, enter your scores in high to low order in Column 2 of the following table. On the first line of Column 3, enter your difference score, which is obtained by subtracting Line 2 of Column 2 from Line 1 of Column 2. Then take the difference for your second and third choices and record it on the second line of Column 3. Continue taking differences between each of your scores and recording them. The difference between scores indicates the likelihood that a person will shift styles: a low score (1–5) suggests switching; a high score (over 5) suggests resistance to shifting. We will discuss why it is important to be able to shift your style.

Your Choice	Leading Through Change Approach (LETTER)	Score (High to Low) (Column 2)	Differences Between Scores (Column 3)
1st primary	_____	_____	_____
2nd backup	_____	_____	_____
3rd backup	_____	_____	_____
4th backup	_____	_____	_____
5th backup	_____	_____	_____

Brief explanations of the five approaches to leading through change follow.

Directive controlling (A). The leader using this approach has maximum concern for efficient accomplishment of operational goals and little concern about whether followers are committed to change. This leader views followers as parts of a machine that must implement change. He or she believes that people must be directed and monitored because they don't have the willingness or ability to change. This leader relies on his or her own expertise. Maintaining control over the situation is important to this leader.

Relationship focused (B). The leader following this approach focuses on the followers' satisfaction and commitment to the change. The operational goals and outcomes from the change are not as important as the morale during change. Decisions about change are delegated to followers who are encouraged to design their own change process. Relationship development is important to this leader.

Status quo (C). This leader's approach to change shows little concern for either operational goals or people. The leader does not want to be involved in change and is "waiting it out" until the change passes and new directives are given from his or her superiors. This leader sees change as disruptive and would rather have a stable environment. Security is important to this leader.

Rational–incremental (D). This leader balances concerns for operational goals with people. This rational leader makes trade-offs between the organizations goals for change and followers' concerns about it. This leader views moderate change as the best course of action (i.e., evolution rather than revolution) and is concerned that changing systems too quickly will be disruptive and harm productivity. This leader will implement change in small increments to allow people to adjust slowly to change. Explaining the reasons for change to followers is important to this leader.

Goal setting (E). This leader using this approach focuses on communication specific, measurable, actionable, relevant, and time-based (SMART) goals. He or she follows up to ensure that goals are met by followers. This leader also wants personal commitment from followers to the goals of change and his or her vision for the future. He or she makes the link between goal commitment, attainment, and organizational rewards. He or she tries to show how followers' actions impact the bottom-line performance of the organization. Goal acceptance is important to this leader.

You may have found that you use different approaches to change. In fact, most people have more than one approach to change, and this may depend upon the situation. The purpose of this assessment is to make you aware of different approaches to leading others during change and give you feedback on preferred approaches. The differences calculated in the assessment indicate how flexible you may be in changing your style (small differences between scores indicates a tendency to switch your approach if needed whereas large differences suggest that you rely heavily on one approach). You may want to work on adding another approach (your second highest score would be a good place to start).

This assessment may be used as a point of departure for further reflection and observation concerning the way you attempt to lead people through change. To obtain a better understanding of your change style, ask your followers, supervisor, and peers how they view you in terms of these five approaches.

APPENDIX

RESEARCH DESIGNS USED IN ORGANIZATIONAL BEHAVIOR

Organizational behavior (OB) researchers make choices regarding the type of study they will conduct. For example, a study of leader behavior and engagement could be conducted by collecting surveys from a sample of workers in an organization. All research designs have strengths and weaknesses. Therefore, you need to be aware of them so that you may critically evaluate research. The following types of research may be conducted in organizational settings.[1]

QUALITATIVE AND QUANTITATIVE RESEARCH

Qualitative research typically involves interviewing people in organizations and gathering detailed information through transcriptions of the interviews (data may also be gathered through observations or company documents). **Quantitative research** designs involve collecting data through organizational surveys containing measures of OB concepts. An example of a job satisfaction survey measure is found in Table 1.2 in Chapter 1.

EXPERIMENTAL AND QUASI-EXPERIMENTAL STUDIES

Inferences of what causes what in organization can be found in **experimental** studies, and they are the best way to determine what causes behavior in organizations.[2] Much is known about behavior in small groups, for example, from rigorous studies conducted with student samples in very controlled settings (laboratory experiments). In such studies, there is a control group (a group that receives attention but not the study focus) to guard against the Hawthorne effect we learned about earlier; you might get results due to the researchers paying attention to the subjects in the study. For example, the effects of creativity training on the creative output of engineers were studied in a quasi-experiment.[3] The engineers were randomly assigned to the two groups (experimental and control), and the level of divergent thinking was measured before and after creativity training was conducted. By controlling for alternative explanations with the control group, researchers could be reasonably certain that the increase in divergent thinking was due to the creativity training. The result of this study was an evaluation of how effective the creativity training was in changing the creative behavior of the engineers who were trained.

CORRELATIONAL FIELD STUDY

This study is based on survey data collected in organizational settings. The **correlational field study** is the most common research design employed. Data are gathered by having organizational members complete survey forms, and then data are analyzed using statistical methods. It is desirable in a correlational field study to have data from multiple sources (from employees and their immediate supervisors, for example) to increase the value of the research to the organization. For example, a correlational field study may include measures of leader behavior rated by employees and ratings of performance provided by their supervisors and/or from company records.

CASE STUDY

There are short case studies at the end of each chapter of this textbook. A **case study** is a description of a situation in an organization. The goal is to describe the situation in great detail, paying particular attention to the context. Due to the specificity of the case to a particular organization, it may not apply to other situations. Also, case studies cannot explain what causes behavior, and this is one of the biggest limitations of this research.

ACTION RESEARCH

Action research is the process of problem specification and then interventions (i.e., actions) until the researcher understands how the intervention is affecting the organization. Multiple cycles of interventions are conducted, and the next stage of diagnosis may result in the intervention changing on the next cycle. This requires a large commitment from the organization being studied due to the time invested and the potential disruption of organizational processes. Action research is valuable but is not as common as other types of OB research.

MIXED METHODS RESEARCH

As noted earlier, there is a distinction between qualitative and quantitative research. However, some OB researchers combine both qualitative (e.g., interviews) and quantitative (e.g., surveys) in a single study that is called **mixed methods research**.[4] In doing so, they attempt to understand something that occurs in an organizational setting in depth by balancing the strengths and weaknesses of different research designs. For example, to understand the perceptions of the fairness of a new compensation plan, the researchers would first conduct interviews with 20 employees to understand the employees' feelings regarding fair pay. Based on these interviews, a survey would then be constructed and administered to a random sample of 300 employees to see how well the initial interviews with 20 employees' feelings about the pay plan represent all employees.

META-ANALYSIS

Meta-analysis is a quantitative approach to literature review on a topic.[5] A meta-analysis allows the researcher to combine numerous studies conducted over a period of time to gain an overall summary of an area such as goal setting. The researchers gather a large pool of studies and look for overall trends. The studies in the pool have been conducted by different researchers in different organizations. This increases the confidence that the findings of the meta-analysis will generalize to new situations. Meta-analysis summarizes an entire field of study in an efficient way for students and researchers interested in a topic. In a sense, a meta-analysis can be thought of as a "study of studies," and this book will often rely on them to provide you with an overview of a research area in OB.

In choosing a research design, OB researchers must make trade-offs. For example, the laboratory experiment provides the most rigorous test of hypotheses, but it often lacks the realism of organizational settings. Case studies, on the other hand, provide an in-depth qualitative understanding of challenges managers face in the real world but lack the statistical rigor to be generalized to other organizations; however, they cannot be used to test hypotheses. The strengths and weaknesses of the various research designs discussed in this section are summarized in Table 1A.

Table 1A Strengths and Weaknesses of Different Research Designs

Research Design	Strengths	Weaknesses
Experimental	Can draw conclusions about causality; can maximize study control in the laboratory	May not accurately reflect organizational context; many studies use student subjects
Quasi-experimental	Can simulate benefits of experiments in a real-world setting	More difficult to justify causality than in true (laboratory) experiment
Correlational field study	Expedient way to examine hypothesized relationships in a real-world setting	Less control than experiment; difficult to rule out alternative explanations for findings
Case study	Provides in-depth understanding of real organizational problems	Difficult to generalize findings to other organizations; can't be used to test hypotheses
Action research	Real managers investigate important problems they face	Often not rigorous; generally not accepted by the research community
Mixed methods	Takes advantage of the strengths of qualitative and quantitative research	Difficult and time consuming to implement; costly, careful planning and design choices are required
Meta-analysis	Summarizes a large body of research of time and draws generalizable conclusions	There may be a bias because most studies published show significance; must find unpublished research

Critical Thinking Questions: If you were going to study how to improve employee productivity, which research method would you use? Why?

KEY TERMS

action research, 461
case study, 461
correlational field
study, 461

experimental, 460
meta-analysis, 462
mixed methods
research, 461

qualitative research, 460
quantitative research, 460

A-B-C analysis: systematic planning in OB mod, examining antecedents, behaviors, and consequences

absenteeism: regularly staying away from work or school without good reason

abusive supervision: hostile behavior toward followers that may include ridiculing, spreading rumors, taking credit for work done by followers, giving the "silent treatment," and/or withholding information

active: doing something about job dissatisfaction

active listening: way of listening that is "a creative, active, sensitive, accurate, empathic, nonjudgmental listening"[1]

adaptability: the ability to transfer the demands of the market into organizational actions

additive task: a performance goal that can be met by adding up individual contributions

adjourning: the team finalizes its work and disbands

affect: one's attitude comprised of both emotions and moods

affective commitment: employee's emotional attachment to an organization

affective: the emotional part of an attitude

aggregating: adding up individual responses to create a group-level measure

agreeableness: a characteristic in which one is affable, tolerant, sensitive, trusting, kind, and warm

All Channel (or Star) network: more decentralized and allows a free flow of information among all group members

alternative dispute resolution: methods to resolve conflict that both parties agree to without involving litigation

ambient impact: collective deviant behavior that creates a hostile working environment

anticipatory socialization: the process an individual goes through as they attempt to find an organization to join

appreciative inquiry (AI): an OD intervention in which people reflect on peak experiences and visualize the future

apprising: persuading the target of influence that complying with the influencer will advance his career

assimilation: relinquishing cultural heritage and adopting the beliefs and behaviors of the new culture

attributions: a person's attempt to assign a cause to a behavior or event they observe

authentic leadership: knowing oneself and behaving in a way that is consistent with what is intuitively right; this includes the fours dimensions of self-awareness, relational transparency, internalized moral perspectives, and balanced processing.

autonomy: ability to work alone without supervision

availability bias: readily available information that comes to a person's mind affects a decision

behavioral: an intention to act based upon the cognitions and affect experienced

behavioral CQ: the ability to adjust to others' cultural practices

behavioral methods: problem-solving behaviors

behaviorally anchored rating scales (BARS): a vertical scale presented with specific examples of performance

belief updating: initial information affects the conclusion one draws, and this conclusion then impacts later judgments

best alternative to a negotiated agreement (BATNA): an alternative that negotiators will accept if the negotiation reaches an impasse and they can't get their ideal outcome

boomers: born between 1946 and 1964; called this due to the baby boom that occurred after World War II

boundary spanners: individuals in an organization who link the organization's internal networks and/or external constituents together

bounded ethicality: an unconscious psychological process that hinders the quality of decision making

bounded rationality: when decision makers have limits on their ability to assimilate large amounts of information

brainstorming: generating a large quantity of ideas in a face-to-face team meeting

broaden-and-build model: a process by which emotions serve to both broaden employee experiences and then allow them to build better functioning organizations

buffering effect: support during a stress episode that prevents stress

calculus-based trust (CBT): a form of trust based upon keeping records of what another person does for you and what you do for them

career indecision: "the difficulties preventing individuals from making a career decision"[2]

central tendency error: giving ratings that center in the middle of a scale

Chain network: gives a flow of information among members although the people are at the end of the chain

challenge-related stress and eustress: good stress

change uncertainty: uncertainty due to strategic, structural, and/or job-related change

changing: represents movement toward a new desired state

Circle network: each person can communicate with two others located adjacent to them

climcult: culture and climate work together to influence how people experience their work environment

coalition: seek the aid or support others

coding: linking the information you need to remember to something familiar and easily retrievable

cognitive: a statement of belief about something

cognitive CQ: refers to self-awareness and the ability to detect cultural patterns

cognitive dissonance: incompatibility between two or more attitudes or between attitudes and behavior

cognitive evaluation theory: another term for self-determination theory

cognitive methods: managing thoughts and emotions

cohesion: team spirit experienced in high-performing teams

collaboration: offer to provide assistance or resources to the person being asked to do something

collective effect: a work project that reflects the contributions of everyone on the team

combining tasks: creating natural work units by putting tasks together to create a more challenging and complex work assignment

commitment to change: employees support change and help the organization implement it

communication apprehension (CA): "an individual's level of fear or anxiety with either real or anticipated communication with another person or persons"[3]

compassion : noticing, feeling, and understanding the suffering of a follower

competence: "a cluster of related knowledge, skills and attitudes that affects a major part of one's job (a role or responsibility), that correlates with performance on the job, that can be measured against well-accepted standards, and that can be improved via training and development"[4]

compliance: employees simply go along with the change but secretly hope that it is a program that will come to an end soon

conciliation: calling in a neutral third party to attempt to resolve the conflict

conflict: "the process that begins when one party perceives that the other has negatively affected, or is about to negatively affect, something that he or she cares about"[5]

conscientiousness: being organized, systematic, punctual, achievement oriented, and dependable

consensus: discussing ideas and deferring a final decision until everyone can say they have been heard and will support the final decision

consistency: defining values and subsystems that are the basis of a strong culture

constructive: a positive response to job dissatsifaction

consultation: invites the person to be involved with a proposed idea and may be used in any direction as well

consultative: asking for input from team members one-on-one or as a group and then making the final decision

continuance commitment: degree to which an employee is aware of the costs of leaving the organization

contrast effect: evaluation of a characteristic of an object or person affected by comparisons with other objects or people ranking higher or lower on the characteristic

core self-evaluation: "fundamental premises that individuals hold about themselves and their functioning in the world"[6]

counterdependent: employees who resent authority and being told what to do

creativity: "production of a novel and appropriate response, product, or solution to an open-ended task"[7]

critical thinking: the objective analysis and evaluation of an issue in order to form a judgment

crossover stress effect: a phenomenon that occurs when employees carry stress home with them from the workplace, which affects family interactions

cultural intelligence (CQ): an individual's capabilities to function and manage effectively in culturally diverse settings

cultural looseness: associated with social disorganization, deviance, innovation, and openness to change

culturally endorsed implicit leadership theory (CLT): a theory that identifies leadership behaviors perceived as effective and ineffective across cultures

cultural retooling: the psychological process of adaptation to another culture

cultural tightness: associated with order and efficiency, conformity, and low rates of change

cultural tightness–looseness: the strength of social norms and the level of sanctioning within societies

culture shock: the distress experienced by a traveler from the loss of familiar patterns of social interaction

cyberslacking: using the Internet for personal reasons during working hours

360 degree performance appraisal: the input from a number of these sources is included to provide a more comprehensive view of an employee's performance

deep-level diversity: "differences among members' attitudes, beliefs, and values"[8]

delegating: allowing a team (or individual) to make a final decision

destructive: a negative response to job dissatisfaction

deviant behavior: "aggression, bullying, harassment, incivility and social undermining"[9]

direct effects: an employee is the target of a coworker's deviant act

distributive justice: perceived fairness of how rewards are distributed

disturbance handler: one who resolves conflict and chooses strategic alternatives

downward communication: the process by which employees communicate with others who are lower in the organizational hierarchy

e-harassment: e-mail or other electronic communication directed at a specific person that causes substantial emotional distress and serves no legitimate purpose

elaborative interrogation: people are asked to generate their own explanations of factual statements presented to them

emotional contagion: the negative mood of one employee spreads to others in their group

emotional intelligence (EI): "ability to monitor one's own and others' feelings and emotions, to discriminate among them and to use this information to guide one's thinking and actions"[10]

emotional labor: the effort required to effectively manage emotions to be successful on the job

emotions: brief but intense feelings triggered by specific events that disrupt a person's thinking

employability: "an attribution employers make about the probability that job candidates will make positive contributions to their organizations"[11]

employee assistance program (EAP): programs "designed to help employees deal with problems that seriously affect job performance"[12]

employee engagement: "the investments of an individual's complete self into a role"[13]

employee: engagement a relatively enduring state of mind referring to the simultaneous investment of personal energies in the experience or performance of work

enacted values: values that are acted out

engineers: this group focuses on designing systems to support the work of operations such as employees who design a manufacturing facility

entrepreneur: one who looks for new ideas and opportunities

equity theory: a theory that looks at how people compare their inputs to their outcomes

escalation of commitment: when individuals continue a failing course of action after receiving feedback that shows it isn't working

espoused values: values that are stated

ethical climate: the moral atmosphere of the work environment and the level of ethics practiced within a an organization

ethical leadership: leadership that promotes honesty, and acts based on moral values and beliefs

ethics-induced stress: result of pressure, workload, and an emphasis on merit for advancement in the organization

executives: employees who have worked their way up organizational career ladders and are financially responsible to their board of directors and shareholders

expanding pie: enlarging the pool of resources so that a negotiation can end in a "win-win" agreement where both feel that they got the best possible outcome

external attribution: people believe that a person's behavior is due to situational factors

external communication: information that is shared with the public through marketing and public relations efforts

extraversion: a trait of a person who is outgoing, talkative, and sociable as well as enjoys social situations

extrinsic: motivation based on rewards from the organization's compensation system, such as pay and bonuses

"extrinsics in service of intrinsics": refers to how extrinsic rewards may support an employee's sense of competence if they don't undermine autonomy

extrinsic motivation: involves the performance → outcome instrumentality between the task and a tangible reward

facilitation: when a leader intervenes to resolve a conflict

facilitator: one who helps the team make a decision by asking questions and reflecting statements, but not influencing the final decision

family-to-work conflict: family problems cross over to work

feedback seeking: an individual's general level of proactive activity with respect to obtaining feedback from the work environment

feedback: knowledge of results of a person's efforts

fight-or-flight response: the result of human evolution in which the response was needed to attack predators or run away from them

fixed pie: only a limited amount of goods are divided and the goal is to get the largest share

fixed: a specified amount of time or number of responses

flow: when a person experiences a challenging opportunity aligned with their skills

force field analysis: analyzing the forces for and against a change

forming: the first stage of team development when the team members meet for the first time

framing: managing meaning by using talk to get followers to act by using metaphors, jargon, and stories in their communications

framing: whether questions are presented as gains or losses

fundamental attribution error: tendency to attribute other people's behavior to internal factors such as character traits or abilities, but when explaining one's own behavior, people tend to attribute the cause to the situation

gain-sharing plans: compensation is tied to unit-level performance, where revenue increases (or cost savings) are shared with employees

Galatea effect: when an individual sets high expectations for himself or herself and then performs to these expectations

generation Xers, or gen Xers: born between 1965 and 1980; sometimes referred to as the "baby busters" or "latchkey kids"

Global Leadership and Organizational Behavior Effectiveness (GLOBE) project: a large-scale research program that sought to understand differences in leader behaviors and relationships with relevant organizational outcomes worldwide

global mind-set: a set of individual attributes that enhance a manager's ability to influence others who are different from them

Golem effect: when an individual sets low expectations for himself or herself and then performs to these expectations

grapevine: the circulation of unofficial information in an organization

groupthink: the conformity-seeking tendency of a group

growth need strength: refers to a person's need to learn new things, grow, and develop from working

halo error: occurs when the rater's overall positive impression or evaluation strongly influences ratings of specific attributes

Hawthorne effect: positive responses in attitudes and performance when researchers pay attention to a particular group of workers

heuristic: decision rules

high-context cultures: cultures that rely heavily on situational cues for meaning when perceiving and communicating with others

hindrance-related stress: excessive or undesirable constraints that interfere with an individual's ability to achieve goals, creating "negative stress"

hindsight bias, or I-knew-it-all-along effect: the tendency for individuals with outcome knowledge (hindsight) to claim they would have estimated a probability of occurrence for the reported outcome that is higher than they would have estimated in foresight (without the outcome information)

horizontal: adding different tasks at the same level

horns error: occurs when the rater's overall negative impression or evaluation strongly influences ratings of specific attributes

humble leadership: a style of leadership where leaders tend to view themselves more objectively, others more appreciatively, and new information or ideas more openly

hygienes: things like supervision, pay, company policies, and the working conditions

idea evaluation: discussing the strengths and weaknesses of ideas

idea generation: creating new ideas

identification-based trust (IBT): form of trust characterized by the leader and follower sharing the same goals and objectives

imaging: linking verbal information to visual images

implicit leadership schemas: traits and characteristics a person thinks are linked to being a leader

impression management: set of behaviors that people use to protect their self-image or change the way they are seen by others (or both)

indirect effects: an employee is affected by learning of another coworker's deviant behaviors

individual rights: rights that protect an individual within an organization and guide ethical decision making

industry level: the aggregate of productive enterprises in a particular field, often named after its principal product or service (for example, the health care industry)

influence: the exercise of power to change the behavior, attitudes, and/or values of an individual or group

informational justice: refers to the perceived fairness of the communications made by leaders during a process

in-group members: group members who perform to the specifications in their job descriptions and go above and beyond and take on extra work

innovation: the generation, acceptance, and implementation of new ideas, processes, products, or services

inspirational appeals: an appeal made to followers' values and ideals or to seeks to arouse the target

person's emotions to gain commitment for a request or proposal

Instrumental support: focuses on problem solving during a stress episode

integration: maintaining one's cultural heritage and adopting a new cultural identity

integrative complexity: "the degree to which a person accepts the reasonableness of different cultural perspectives on how to live, both at the micro interpersonal level and at more macro organizational-societal levels and, consequently, is motivated to develop integrative schemas that specify when to activate different worldviews and/or how to blend them together into a coherent holistic mental representation"[14]

intercultural communication: focuses on the behavior of two individuals' communication patterns

interdependent: employees who depend on one another to get things done in the group and organization

internal attribution: people infer that an event or a person's behavior is due to his or her own character traits or abilities

internal communication: "the communications transactions between individuals and/or groups at various levels and in different areas of specialization that is intended to design and redesign organizations, to implement designs, and to co-ordinate day-to-day activities"[15]

interpersonal justice: refers to how employees are treated by their leaders including respect and propriety

interval: provision of reinforcement based on time

intrinsic: motivation related to the value of the work itself

intrinsic motivation: when someone works on a task because they find it interesting and gain satisfaction from the task itself

involvement: building human capability, ownership, and responsibility

job burnout: "a prolonged response to chronic stressors on the job"[16]

job control: "the degree to which an individual perceives that s/he can control where, when, and how s/he works"[17]

job crafting: extent to which individuals can demonstrate initiative in designing their own work

job enrichment: redesigning jobs so that they are more challenging to the employee and have less repetitive work

job involvement: how much an employee identifies with his or her job and views his or her performance at work as an essential part of his or her self-esteem

job rotation: involves cross-training or allowing workers to do different jobs

job satisfaction: how content an individual is with his or her job, whether or not they like the job or aspects of it, such as the nature of work or supervision.

just world hypothesis: need to believe that the world is fair and that people get what they deserve

justice: emphasizes fair treatment and the right to pursue happiness

knowledge-based trust (KBT): trust grounded in experience of how predictable the other person is

lateral communication: the process by which employees communicate with others at the same level in the organizational hierarchy

law of effect: past actions that led to positive outcomes tend to be repeated, whereas past actions that led to negative outcomes will diminish

law of reciprocity: universal belief that if someone does something for you, they should be paid back

leader -member exchange (LMX): the quality of the working relationship that is developed with each follower

leadership climate: effective behaviors, attitudes, and environmental conditions created by a leader that enhance team performance and increase empowerment

learning organization: an organization skilled at creating, acquiring, interpreting, transferring, retaining knowledge, and at purposefully modifying its behavior to reflect new knowledge and insights

low-context cultures: cultures in which written and spoken words carry the burden of shared meanings

management by objectives (MBO): a performance appraisal program where leaders meet with their direct reports and set specific performance objectives jointly

marginalization: rejecting both the old and new culture

mentoring: intense developmental relationship whereby advice, counseling, and developmental opportunities are provided to a protégé by a mentor, which, in turn, shapes the protégé's career experiences

metacognitive CQ: the cognitive processing necessary to recognize and understand expectations appropriate for different cultural situations

metamorphosis: a person transforms from a new employee to an established contributor who is valued and trusted by other members of the organization

millennials: born between 1981 and 1999; look for flexibility and choice

Minnesota twin family study: conducted from 1979 to 1999, which followed identical and fraternal twins who were separated at an early age

mission: defining the meaningful, long-term direction for the organization

moods: general feeling states that are not related to something that happens to a person but are not intense enough to interrupt regular thought patterns or work

moral outrage: severe reaction to perceived injustice

motivational CQ: refers to persistence and goal setting for cross-cultural interactions

motivation–work cycle match: understanding that innovation occurs in phases and intrinsic motivation may be more important during the idea generation phase

motivator–hygiene theory: another term for the Herzberg two-factor theory

motivators: factors that satisfy workers when they think about their job, such as advancement, recognition, and achievement

negotiator: one who protects the interests of the business by interacting within teams, departments, and the organization

netiquette: e-mail etiquette

neuroticism: represents a tendency to be anxious or moody

noise: any communication barrier that may affect how a person interprets a message

nominal group technique (NGT): group meets face-to-face but discussion is more restricted than in brainstorming or consensus decision making

normative commitment: moral obligation to stay with the organization—because it is the right thing to do

normative decision-making model: shows that team decisions fall on a continuum ranging from leaders making the decision themselves to delegating the decision to the team

norming: a stage of team development where members of the team form a cohesive unit and close relationships among team members develop

observational learning: learning from watching others

ombudsperson: a person who hears grievances on an informal basis and attempts to resolve them

onboarding: the process of welcoming and orienting new organizational members to facilitate their adjustment to the organization, its culture, and its practices

openness: a person's willingness to embrace new ideas and new situations

operant conditioning: a theory that proposes that behavior is a function of consequences

operators: the line managers and employees who are involved in making products, delivering services, and interacting with customers directly

organizational behavior (OB): the study of individuals and their attitudes and behaviors at work

organizational behavior modification (OB mod): programs that apply reinforcement theory in organizations

organizational climate: level of agreement in perceptions about the organization and work environment among employees

organizational commitment: an employee's desire to remain a member of an organization

organizational culture: "the pattern of basic assumptions, that a given group has invented, discovered, or developed in learning to cope with its problems of external adaptation and internal integration, and that have worked well enough to be considered valid, and, therefore, to be taught to new members as the correct way to perceive, think, and feel in relation to those problems"[18]

organizational development (OD): a collection of social psychology methods employed to improve organizational effectiveness and employee well-being

organizational justice: overall perception of what is fair in an organization

organizational level: an entire entity structured and managed to pursue collective goals with a structure that determines relationships between the different activities and the members

organizational neuroscience: examines the potential of brain science to enhance prediction of OB

organizational stress: negative environmental factors or stressors associated with a particular job

out-group members: group members who perform to the specifications in their job descriptions but don't go above and beyond and don't take on extra work

overconfidence bias: hubris, or inflated confidence in how accurate a person's knowledge or estimates are

overdependent: employees who are compliant and give in all of the time

overpayment inequity: the perception that a person's outcomes are greater than they deserve compared to another person's outcomes, given their inputs

passive: not responding to job dissatisfaction

pay dispersion: how pay rates differ across individuals

pay inequity: perceived unfairness of how pay is distributed

peer review: a panel of a grievant's peers that hears the concern and attempts to resolve it

perceived organizational support (POS): "employees pay attention to whether the organization values their contributions and cares about their well-being"[19]

perception: process through which people organize and interpret sensory information to give meaning to their world

perceptions of organizational politics: a person's perception of others' behavior strategically designed to maximize short-term or long-term self-interest

performing: the team meets its goals and completes tasks

personal appeals: asking someone to carry out a request or support a proposal out of friendship or asking for a personal favor before saying what it is

personal power: influence over others, the source of which resides in the person instead of being vested by the position he or she holds

personality: "regularities in feeling, thought and action that are characteristic of an individual"[20]

person–environment (P–E) fit: the degree of congruence between the person and the work situation

perspective taking: the ability to see things from another person's perspective that holds a view that conflicts with your own

political skill: ability to effectively understand others at work and to use such knowledge to influence others to act in ways that enhance one's personal and/or organizational objectives

position power: authority and influence bestowed by a position or office on whoever is occupying it

positive and negative affect: positive and negative feelings

power: the potential of one person (or group) to influence another person or group

preentry: occurs from the time someone is offered the job to when they actually start working

pre-trip stress: involves planning, trying to accomplish tasks at work before leaving, and taking care of issues for the home and family

preventive stress management: a set of methods that promote health at the workplace and avoid distress

primacy effect: perseverance of beliefs based upon what is observed first

proactive: actively attempting to make alterations to the work place and its practices

proactive influence tactics: positive and negative ways of influencing others

procedural justice: perception of how fair the process was in making decisions that affect employees

process consultation: a consultant with OD expertise assists in a helping mode

profit-sharing plans: employee bonuses are based upon reaching a financial target such as return on assets or net income

prosocial motivation: new concept of motivation that assesses the degree to which employees behave in a way that benefits society as a whole

prosocial motivation: the desire to have a positive impact on other people or groups

prospect theory: a perspective that highlights the importance of uncertainty and risk to the decision-making process

psychological capital (PsyCap): the value of individual differences, including efficacy, optimism, hope, and resiliency

psychological empowerment: "intrinsic task motivation manifested in a set of four cognitions reflecting an individual's orientation to his or her work role: competence, impact, meaning, and self-determination"[21]

punctuated equilibrium: transition between an early phase of inactivity followed by a second phase of significant acceleration toward task completion

Pygmalion effect: perceptions of performance expectations play a significant role in improving performance

ratio: provision of reinforcement is based on the number of responses (attempts)

rational persuasion: use of logic and facts, a tactic commonly employed by leaders

reactive: when an organization makes changes in its practices after some threat or opportunity has already occurred

recency effect: when people remember the most recently presented items or experiences

refreezing: reinforcing and restructuring the changes

rehearsal: repetition of information

reinforcement theory: another term for operant conditioning

reinforcers: something that increases or decreases behavior

relationship conflict: personality clashes or differences in values

repatriation: the transition when the expatriate has completed the international assignment and returns home

resistance: employees fight the change and try to undermine it

resource allocator: one who decides how to prioritize the direction of resources

restructuring and downsizing: reorganization that includes laying off employees

reverse culture shock: the distress experienced by an expatriate when they assimilate to a foreign culture and have trouble adjusting to their native culture when they return home

rituals: "a form of social action in which a group's values and identity are publicly demonstrated or enacted in a stylized manner, within the context of a specific occasion or event"[22]

role ambiguity: a lack of specificity or predictability about what a person's role is

role conflict: occurs when there are incompatible demands regarding what a person's role is

role overload: role-related stress caused by too much work, time pressure, and deadlines

satisfice: making a decision that is satisfactory but perhaps not optimal

schedules of reinforcement: various ways in which reinforcers can be administered

self-actualization: the drive to meet our fullest capacity (e.g., growth and feeling fulfilled as a person)

self-determination: a person's needs for autonomy and competence

self-efficacy: an individual's belief in his or her capacity to execute the behaviors necessary to produce specific performance levels

self-managed work team (SMWT): a team where there is typically no designated leader

self-serving bias: when a person attributes successes to internal factors and failures to situational factors

sense of meaning: how much work goals align with an employee's personal standards (i.e., how well the work "fits" the employee's values)

separation: maintaining only the heritage culture without intergroup relations

servant leadership: going beyond one's self-interest to help followers grow and to promote their well-being

Shannon–Weaver model of communication: framework describing the communication process including the sender, encoding, channel, noise, receiver, and decoding of a message

social identity: a way to explain how people view their own place in society through membership in various groups

social learning theory: extends operant conditioning to consider the fact that people can learn from watching other people succeed or fail

social loafing: the reduction in motivation and effort when individuals work collectively compared with when they work individually or coactively

social pressure: influence from peers that may strengthen the relationship of an attitude toward behavior

social support: help that people receive when they experience job demands

solution implementation: creating options in the form of actions that get results and gain acceptance

state-like characteristics: characteristics that are relatively changeable and can be developed through awareness and/or training

stereotypes: judging a person based on their membership in a group

stock options: a variation of profit sharing where employees are given stock options as part of their compensation package

storming: a stage of team development where conflicts emerge regarding the goals and contributions of team members; and there may be challenges to the leader

stressors: demands

sunk costs fallacy: a person has already invested in this course of action and does not recognize what they invested initially is sunk (or gone)

surface-level diversity: "differences among group members in overt, biological characteristics that are typically reflected in physical features"[23]

survey feedback: data are collected from employees regarding their attitudes toward work, reports are created, and shared with the organization

sustainability: values, governance, transparency, and ethics, as well as such goals as diversity, social responsibility, supporting human and employee rights, protecting the environment, and contributing to the community

synergy: the team can produce something beyond the sum of individual member contributions

task conflict: disagreements about resource allocation, policies, or even interpretation of data

team affect: team atmosphere

team building: group activities that involve a great deal of interaction among team members to increase trust

team charter: a document developed by a team that clarifies team direction and establishes ground rules

team mental models (TMMs): shared understandings within teams

team norms: informal and interpersonal rules that team members are expected to follow

team performance curve: recognizes that team performance over the course of the life of the team is not always linear and performance does not always increase over time

team viability: collective sense of belonging similar to team cohesion

third culture: "the construction of a mutually beneficial interactive environment in which individuals from two different cultures can function in a way beneficial to all involved"[24]

three "lines" of power: lines of supply, information, and support

top management support: executive-level managers review plans, follow up on results, and facilitate change efforts

traditionalists: born between 1900 and 1945 and are retiring or passed on

trait-like: personality characteristics that are relatively stable over time

transactional leadership: leadership behaviors that motivate followers through rewards and corrective actions

transformational leadership: leadership behaviors that mobilize extra effort from followers through emphasis on change through articulating a new vision for the organization

turnover intentions: employees' thoughts about quitting their jobs

turnover: the rate at which employees leave a workforce and are replaced

two-factor theory: relates lower- and higher-order needs and relates them to job satisfaction

Type A behavior: a behavior pattern characterized by hostility, time urgency, impatience, and a competitive drive

Type B behavior: a behavior pattern characterized by a relaxed demeanor, steady work habits, a non-competitive nature, and a desire to be liked by others

Type C behavior: a behavior pattern characterized by predictability, loyalty, patience, thoughtfulness, an attention to detail, and seriousness.

Type D behavior: a behavior pattern characterized by an aversion to leading, punctuality, contentment, and giving support to others

underpayment inequity: the perception that a person's outcomes are not fair compared to another person's outcomes, given their inputs

unfreezing: challenges to the status quo through shaking up assumptions

upward communication: the process by which employees communicate with others who are higher in the organizational hierarchy

utilitarianism: consideration of decisions that do the most good for the most people

valences (Vs): the value an individual places on the rewards of an outcome (positive or negative)

variable: the timing of reinforcement varies

vertical: adding decision-making responsibility

wellness programs: workplace interventions that include time management, weight loss, alcohol and/or drug abuse, smoking cessation, and exercise

Wheel network: all communication flows through one person who is most likely the group leader

wicked organizational problems: complex and changing decision scenarios

work redesign: load jobs with more of the core characteristics that have been shown to motivate

work team: a small number of people with complementary skills who are committed to a common purpose, performance goals, and approach for which they hold themselves mutually accountable

workforce diversity: sex, race/ethnicity, cultural differences, and age/generation as examples

work–life balance: when demands of participation in work are incompatible with demands of participation in family life

workout: a method for generating new ideas using employee participation and empowerment

Y-Pattern network: slightly less centralized than the all channel network since two persons are closer to the center of the network

zone of indifference: the range in which attempts to influence a person will be perceived as legitimate and will be acted on without a great deal of thought

NOTES

Chapter 1

1. Egan, T. (2013, June 20). Checking out. *New York Times Opinionator.*
2. Taylor, F. W. (1911). *The principles of scientific management.* New York, NY: Harper.
3. Mayo, E. (1949). *Hawthorne and the Western Electric Company, The social problems of an industrial civilization.* New York, NY: Routledge.
4. Baron, J. N. (2013). Empathy wages? Gratitude and gift exchange in employment relationships. *Research in Organizational Behavior, 33,* 113–134.
5. Briner, R. B., Denyer, D., & Rousseau, D. M. (2009). Evidence-based management: Construct cleanup time? *Academy of Management Perspectives, 4,* 19–32.
6. Pfeffer, J., & Sutton, R. (2006, January). Evidence-based management. *Harvard Business Review,* 1–16.
7. Sutton, R. (2006). Breakthrough business ideas? Retrieved from http://bobsutton.typepad.com/my_weblog/2006/07/breakthrough_bu.html
8. Surowiecki, J. (2004). *The wisdom of crowds.* New York, NY: Random House.
9. "Cocaine" drink is illegal too, FDA says. (2007). *Los Angeles Times.* Retrieved from http://articles.latimes.com/print/2007/apr/12/business/fi-cocaine12
10. Price, L. (2012). Former Circuit City chief tells all. *Richmond Business Sense.* Retrieved from http://www.richmondbizsense.com/2012/10/18/former-circuit-city-chief-tells-all
11. Glaser, E. M. (1941). *An experiment in the development of critical thinking.* New York, NY: Teachers College, Columbia University.
12. Kurland, D. (2000). Critical thinking skills. Retrieved from www.criticalreading.com
13. Paul, R., & Elder, L. (2008). *The miniature guide to critical thinking concepts and tools.* Dillon Beach, CA: Foundation for Critical Thinking Press.
14. Mitroff, I. (1998). *Smart thinking for crazy times: The art of solving the right problems.* San Francisco, CA: Berrett-Koehler Publishers.
15. Organ, D. W. (1988). *Organizational citizenship behavior: The good soldier syndrome.* (pp. 1–43). Lexington, MA: Lexington Books.
16. Williams, L. J., & Anderson, S. E. (1991). Job satisfaction and organizational commitment as predictors of organizational citizenship and in-role behaviors. *Journal of Management, 17,* 601–617.
17. Podsakoff, N. P., Whiting, S. W., Podsakoff, P. M., & Blume, B. D. (2009). Individual- and organizational-level consequences of organizational citizenship behaviors: A meta-analysis. *Journal of Applied Psychology, 94,* 122–141.
18. Hoppock, R. (1935). *Job satisfaction.* New York, NY: Harper.
19. Macey, W., & Schneider, B. (2008). The meaning of employee engagement. *Industrial and Organizational Psychology, 1,* 3–30.
20. Christian, M. S., Garza, A. S., & Slaughter, J. D. (2011). Work engagement: A quantitative review and test of its relations with task and contextual performance. *Personnel Psychology, 64,* 89–136.
21. Deci, E. L., Koestner, R., & Ryan, R. M. (1999). A meta-analytic review of experiments examining the effects of extrinsic rewards on intrinsic motivation. *Psychological Bulletin, 125,* 627–668.
22. Grant, A. (2008). Does intrinsic motivation fuel the prosocial fire? Motivational synergy in predicting persistence, performance and productivity. *Journal of Applied Psychology, 93,* 48–58.
23. Hom, P. W., Caranikas-Walker, F., Prussia, G. E., & Griffeth, R. W. (1992). A meta-analytical structural equations analysis of a model of employee turnover. *Journal of Applied Psychology, 77,* 890–909.
24. Waldman, D. A., & Yammarino, F. J. (1999). CEO charismatic leadership: Levels-of-management and levels-of-analysis effects. *Academy of Management Review, 24,* 266–285.

Chapter 2

1. Edelman, R. (2013). *2013 trust barometer Executive summary.* Retrieved from http://www.edelman.com/insights/intellectual-property/2015-edelman-trust-barometer/trust-and-innovation-edelman-trust-barometer/global-results
2. Northouse, P. G. (2013). *Leadership: Theory and practice* (6th ed.). Thousand Oaks, CA: Sage.
3. Yukl, G. (2013). *Leadership in organizations* (8th ed.). Boston, MA: Pearson.
4. Bennis, W. (1989). *On becoming a leader.* New York, NY: Basic Books.
5. Zaleznik, A. (2004, January). Managers and leaders—Are they different? *Harvard Business Review: Best of HBR,* 74–81.
6. Hersey, P., & Blanchard, K. H. (1988). *Management of organizational behavior: Utilizing human resources.* Englewood Cliffs, NJ: Prentice Hall.
7. Bass, B. M. (1985). *Leadership and performance beyond expectations.* New York, NY: Free Press.
8. Bass, B. M., & Avolio, B. J. (1990). *Transformational leadership development: Manual for the multifactor leadership questionnaire.* Palo Alto, CA: Consulting Psychologists Press.
9. Avolio, B. J. (2011). *Full range leadership development* (2nd ed.). Thousand Oaks, CA: Sage.
10. Ibid., p. 65.
11. Lowe, K., Kroeck, K. G., & Sivasubramaniam, N. (1996). Effectiveness correlates of transformational and transactional leadership: A meta-analytic review. *The Leadership Quarterly, 7,* 385–425.
12. Bono, J. E., & Judge, T. A. (2004). Personality and transformational and transactional leadership: A meta-analysis. *Journal of Applied Psychology, 89*(5), 901–910.
13. Scandura, T. A., Graen, G. B., & Novak, M. A. (1986). When managers decide not to decide autocratically: An investigation of leader-member exchange and decision influence in managerial dyads. *Journal of Applied Psychology, 71,* 484–491.
14. Erdogan, B., & Bauer, T. N. (2010). Differentiated leader–member exchanges: The buffering role of justice climate. *Journal of Applied Psychology, 95*(6), 1104–1120.
15. Henderson, D. J., Liden, R. C., Glibkowski, B. C., & Chaudhry, A. (2009). LMX differentiation: A multilevel review and examination of its antecedents and outcomes. *The Leadership Quarterly, 20*(4), 517–534.
16. Johnson, J., Truxillo, D. M., Erdogan, B., Bauer, T. N., & Hammer, L. (2009). Perceptions of overall fairness: Are effects on job performance moderated by leader-member exchange? *Human Performance, 22*(5), 432–449.
17. Scandura, T. A. (1999). Rethinking leader-member exchange: An organizational justice perspective. *The Leadership Quarterly, 10,* 25–40.

18. Graen, G. B., & Scandura, T. A. (1987). Toward a psychology of dyadic organizing. In B. Staw & L. L. Cummings, *Research in organizational behavior* (Vol. 9, pp. 175–208). Greenwich, CT: JAI Press.

19. Bauer, T. N., & Green, S. G. (1996). Development of leader-member exchange: A longitudinal test. *Academy of Management Journal, 39*(6), 1538–1567.

20. Gabarro, J., & Kotter, J. (2005). Managing your boss. *Harvard Business Review: Best of HBR*, 90–99.

21. Kelley, J. (2013). How to manage your boss. American Management Association. Retrieved on November 23, 2013, from www.Amanet.org/training/articles/printverson/how-to-manage-Your-Boss.aspx

22. Graen, G. B., Cashman, J., Ginsburgh, S., & Schiemann, W. (1977). Effects of linking-pin quality upon the quality of working life of lower participants: A longitudinal investigation of the managerial understructure. *Administrative Science Quarterly, 22*(3), 491–504.

23. Eby, L. T. (1997). Alternative forms of mentoring in changing organizational environments: A conceptual extension of the mentoring literature. *Journal of Vocational Behavior, 51*(1), 125–144.

24. Scandura, T. A., & Schriesheim, C. A. (1994). Leader-member exchange and supervisor career mentoring as complementary constructs in leadership research. *Academy of Management Journal, 37*(6), 1588–1602.

25. Kram, K. E. (1988). *Mentoring at work: Developmental relationships in organizational life*. Lanham, MD: University Press of America.

26. Allen, T. D., Eby, L., Poteet, M., Lentz, E., & Lima, L. (2004). Career benefits associated with mentoring for protégés: A meta-analysis. *Journal of Applied Psychology, 89*, 127–136.

27. Higgins, M. C., & Kram, K. E. (2001). Reconceptualizing mentoring at work: A developmental network perspective. *Academy of Management Review, 26*(2), 264.

28. Green, S. G., & Bauer, T. N. (1995). Supervisory mentoring by advisers— relationships with doctoral-student potential, productivity, and commitment. *Personnel Psychology, 48*(3), 537–561.

29. Mayer, R. C., Davis, J. H., & Schoorman, F. D. (1995). An integrative model of organizational trust. *Academy of Management Review, 20*, 709–734.

30. Colquitt, J., Scott, B. A., & LePine, J. A. (2007). Trust, trustworthiness, and trust propensity: A meta-analytic test of their unique relationships with risk taking and job performance. *Journal of Applied Psychology, 92*, 909–927.

31. Rousseau, D. M., Sitkin, S. B., Burt, R. S., & Camerer, C. (1998). Not so different after all: A cross-discipline view of trust. *Academy of Management Review, 23*(3), 393–404.

32. Dirks, K. T., & Ferrin, D. L. (2002). Trust in leadership: Meta-analytic findings and implications for research and practice. *Journal of Applied Psychology, 87*(4), 611–628.

33. Shapiro, D., Sheppard, B. H., & Cheraskin, L. (1992). Business on a handshake. *Negotiation Journal, 8*(4), 365–377.

34. Lewicki, R. J., & Bunker, B. B. (1996). Developing and maintaining trust in work relationships. In R. M. Kramer & T. R. Tyler (Eds.), *Trust in organizations: Frontiers of theory and research* (pp. 114–139). Thousand Oaks, CA: Sage.

35. Scandura, T. A., & Pellegrini, E. K. (2008). Trust and leader-member exchange: A closer look at relational vulnerability. *Journal of Leadership and Organization Studies, 15*(2), 100–101.

36. Kim, P. H., Dirks, K. T., & Cooper, C. D. (2009). The repair of trust: A dynamic bilateral perspective and multilevel conceptualization. *Academy of Management Review, 34*(3), 401–422.

37. Kim, P. H., Ferrin, D. L., Cooper, C. D., & Dirks, K. T. (2004). Removing the shadow of suspicion: The effects of apology versus denial for repairing competence-versus integrity-based trust violations. *Journal of Applied Psychology, 89*(1), 104–118.

38. Ferrin, D. L., Kim, P. H., Cooper, C. D., & Dirks, K. T. (2007). Silence speaks volumes: The effectiveness of reticence in comparison to apology and denial for responding to integrity-and competence-based trust violations. *Journal of Applied Psychology, 92*(4), 893–908.

39. Kim, P. H., Dirks, K. T., Cooper, C. D., & Ferrin, D. L. (2006). When more blame is better than less: The implications of internal vs. external attributions for the repair of trust after a competence-vs. integrity-based trust violation. *Organizational Behavior and Human Decision Processes, 99*(1), 49–65.

40. Shapiro, D. L. (1991). The effects of explanations on negative reactions to deceit. *Administrative Science Quarterly, 36*(4), 614–630.

41. Bottom, W. P., Gibson, K., Daniels, S. W., & Murnighan, J. K. (2002). When talk is not cheap: Substantive penance and expressions of intent in rebuilding cooperation. *Organization Science, 13*(5), 497–513.

42. Gibson, K. Bottom, W., & Murnighan, J. K. (1999). Once bitten: Defection and cooperation in a cooperative enterprise. *Business Ethics Quarterly, 9*(1), 69–85.

43. Schweitzer, M. E., Hershey, J. C., & Bradlow, E. T. (2006). Promises and lies: Restoring violated trust. *Organizational Behavior and Human Decision Processes, 101*(1), 1–19.

44. Dirks, K. T., Kim, P. H., Ferrin, D. L., & Cooper. C. D. (2011). Understanding the effects of substantive responses on trust following a transgression. *Organizational Behavior and Human Decision Processes, 114*(2), 87–103.

45. Hill, L. (1994). Power dynamics in organizations. *Harvard Business School Note, 9*, 1–13.

46. French, J. R. P., & Raven, B. (1960). The bases of social power. In D. Cartwright & A. Zander (Eds.), *Group Dynamics* (2nd ed., pp. 607–623). New York, NY: Harper and Row.

47. Yukl, G. (2013). *Leadership in organizations* (8th ed.). Boston, MA: Pearson.

48. Barnard, C. (1938). *Functions of the executive*. Cambridge, MA: Harvard University Press.

49. Kanter, R. M. (1979). Power failure in management circuits. *Harvard Business Review, 57*(4), 65–75.

50. Kipnis, D., Schmidt, S. M., & Wilkinson, I. (1980). Intraorganizational influence tactics: Explorations in getting one's way. *Journal of Applied Psychology, 65*(4), 440–452.

51. Yukl, G. (2013). *Leadership in organizations* (8th ed.). New York, NY: Pearson.

52. Cohen, A. R., & Bradford, D. L. (2005). *Influence without authority* (2nd ed.). New York, NY: Wiley.

53. Gouldner, A. W. (1960). The norm of reciprocity: A preliminary statement. *American Sociological Review, 25*(2), 161–178.

54. Kacmar, K. M., Bozeman, D. P., Carlson, D. P., & Anthony, W. P. (1999). An examination of the perceptions of organizational politics model: Replication and extension. *Human Relations, 52*(3), 383–416.

55. Ahearn, K. K., Ferris, G. R., Hochwarter, W. A., Douglas, C., & Ammeter, A. P. (2004). Leader political skill and team performance. *Journal of Management*, *30*(3), 309–327.

56. Brown, M. E., & Treviño, L. K. (2006). Ethical leadership: A review and future directions. *The Leadership Quarterly*, *17*(6), 595–616.

57. Mayer, D. M., Aquino, K., Greenbaum, R., & Kuenzi, M. (2012). Who displays ethical leadership, and why does it matter? An examination of antecedents and consequences of ethical leadership. *Academy of Management Journal*, *55*(1), 151–171.

58. Mayer, D. M., Kuenzi, M., Greenbaum, R., Bardes, M., & Salvador, R. (2009). How low does ethical leadership flow? Test of a trickle-down model. *Organizational Behavior and Human Decision Processes*, *108*(1), 1–13.

59. Russell, R .F., & Stone, A. G. (2002). A review of servant leadership attributes: Developing a practical model. *Leadership & Organization Development Journal*, *23*(3), 145–157.

60. George, B., Sims, P., & McLean, A. (2007). Discovering your authentic leadership. *Harvard Business Review*, 129–138.

61. Walumbwa, F., Avolio, B., Gardner, W., Wernsing, T., & Peterson, S. (2008). Authentic leadership: Development and validation of a theory-based measure. *Journal of Management*, *34*(1), 89–126.

62. Kidder, R. M. (2003). *How good people make tough choices: Resolving the dilemmas of ethical living*. New York, NY: HarperCollins.

63. Greenleaf, R. K. (1977). *Servant leadership* (Vol. 7). New York, NY: Paulist Press.

64. Barbuto, J. E., & Wheeler, J. W. (2006). Scale development and construct clarification of servant leadership. *Group & Organization Management*, *31*(3), 300–326.

65. Liden, R. C., Wayne, S. J., Zhao, H., & Henderson, D. (2008). Servant leadership: Development of a multidimensional measures and multilevel assessment. *The Leadership Quarterly*, *19*(2), 161–177.

66. Liden, R. C., Wayne, S. J., Liao, C., & Meuser, J. D. (2014). Servant leadership and serving culture: Influence on individual and unit performance. *Academy of Management Journal*, *37*(5), 1434–1452.

67. Hu, J., & Liden, R. C. (2011). Antecedents of team potency and team effectiveness: An examination of goal and process clarity and servant leadership. *Journal of Applied Psychology*, *96*, 851–862.

68. Owens, B. P., & Hekman, D. R. (2012). Modeling how to grow: An inductive examination of humble leader behaviors, contingencies, and outcomes. *Academy of Management Journal*, *55*(4), 787–818.

69. George, B. Sims, P., McLean, A., & Mayer, D. (2007, February). Discovering your authentic leadership. *Harvard Business Review*, 129–138.

70. Neider, L. L., & Schriesheim, C. A. (2011). The authentic leadership inventory (ALI): development and empirical tests. *The Leadership Quarterly*, *22*(6), 1146–1164.

Chapter 3

1. Markowitz, E. (2013). Lesson from Zynga: Not all founders make good public company CEOs. Retrieved on July 18, 2013, from http://www.inc.com/eric-markowitz/zynga-mark-pincus-not-all-founders-are-good-ceos.html

2. Wasserman, N. N. (2003). Founder-CEO succession and the paradox of entrepreneurial success. *Organization Science*, *14*(2), 149–172.

3. http://www.nytimes.com/2015/04/09/technology/mark-pincus-zyngas-founder-returns-as-ceo.html?_r=0

4. Snyder, M., & Cantor, N. (1998). Understanding personality and social behavior: A functionalist strategy. In D. T. Gilbert, S. T. Fiske, & G. Lindzey (Eds.), *The handbook of social psychology* (4th ed., pp. 635–679). New York, NY: McGraw-Hill.

5. Waller, N. G., Kojetin, B. A., Bouchard, T. J., Lykken, D. T., & Tellegen, A. (1990). Genetic and environmental influences on religious interests, attitudes, and values: A study of twins reared apart and together. *Psychological Science*, *1*(2), 138–142.

6. Lykken, D. T., Bouchard, T. J., McGue, M., & Tellegen, A. (1993). Heritability of interests: A twin study. *Journal of Applied Psychology*, *78*(4), 649–661.

7. Keller, L. M., Bouchard, T. J., Arvey, R. D., Segal, N. L., & Dawis, R. V. (1992). Work values: Genetic and environmental influences. *Journal of Applied Psychology*, *77*(1), 79–88.

8. Murray, J. B. (1990). Review of the Myers-Briggs Type Indicator. *Perceptual and Motor Skills*, *70*, 1187–1202.

9. Myers, I. B. (with Myers, P. B.). (1995). *Gifts differing*. Mountain View, CA: Consulting Psychologists Press.

10. Pittenger, D. J. (2005). Cautionary comments regarding the Myers-Briggs Type Indicator. *Consulting Psychology Journal: Practice and Research*, *57*(3), 210–221.

11. Arnau, R. C., Green, B. A., Rosen, D. H., Gleaves, D. H., & Melancon, J. G. (2003). Are Jungian preferences really categorical? An empirical investigation using taxometric analysis. *Personality and Individual Differences*, *34*(2), 233–251.

12. Myers, P. B., & Myers, K. D. (1998). *Introduction to type* (6th ed.). Mountain View, CA: Consulting Psychologists Press.

13. Barrick, M. R., & Mount, M. K. (1990). Another look at the validity of personality: A dimensional perspective. Presented at the annual meetings of the Society for Industrial and Organizational Psychology, Miami Beach, FL.

14. Barrick, M. R., Mount, M. K., & Judge, T. A. (2001). The FFM personality dimensions and job performance: Meta-analysis of meta-analyses. *International Journal of Selection and Assessment*, *9*(1–2), 9–30.

15. Judge, T. A., Higgins, C. A., Thoresen, C. J., & Barrick, M. R. (1999). The big five personality traits, general mental ability, and career success across the life span. *Personnel Psychology*, *52*(3), 621–652.

16. Barrick, M. R., & Mount, M. K. (1993). Autonomy as a moderator of the relationships between the Big Five personality dimensions and job performance. *Journal of Applied Psychology*, *78*(1), 111–118.

17. LePine, J. A., Colquitt, J. A., & Erez, A. (2000). Adaptability to changing task contexts: Effects of general cognitive ability, conscientiousness, and openness to experience. *Personnel Psychology*, *53*(3), 563–595.

18. Friedman, M., & Rosenman, R. H. (1974). *Type A behavior and your heart*. New York, NY: Knopf.

19. McLeod, S. A. (2011). *Type A personality: Simply psychology*. Retrieved on July 13, 2013, from http://www.simplypyschology.org/personality-a.html

20. Booth-Kewley, S., & Friedman. H. S. (1987). Psychological predictors of heart disease: A quantitative review. *Psychological Bulletin*, *101*(3), 343–362.

21. Riggio, R. E. (2012). Are you a Type A or B personality? Cutting edge leadership. *Psychology Today*. Retrieved from www.psychologytoday.com/blog/cutting-edge-leadership/201206/are-you-type-or-type-or-b-personality

22. Miller, R., & Krauskopf, C. J. (1999). The personality assessment system as a conceptual framework for the Type A coronary-prone behavior pattern. *The Best of Personality Assessment System Journals,* 121–132.

23. Pederson, S. S., Van Domburg, R. Theuns, D. A. M. J., Jordaens, L., & Erman, R. A. M. (2004). Type D personality is associated with increased anxiety and depressive symptoms in patients with an implantable cardioverter defibrillator and their partners. *Psychosomatic Medicine, 66,* 714–719.

24. Arvey, R. D., Rotundo, M., Johnson, W., Zhang, Z., & McGue, M. (2006). The determinants of leadership role occupancy: Genetic and personality factors. *The Leadership Quarterly, 17*(1), 1–20.

25. Howell, J., & Frost, P. (1989). A laboratory study of charismatic leadership. *Organizational Behavior and Human Decision Processes, 43*(2), 243–269.

26. Judge, T. A., & Long, D. M. (2012). Individual differences in leadership. In D. V. Day & J. Antonakis (Eds.), *The nature of leadership* (pp. 179–217). Thousand Oaks, CA: Sage.

27. Pederson, S. S., & Denollet, J. (2003). Is Type D personality here to stay? Emerging evidence across cardiovascular disease patient groups. *Current Cardiology Reviews, 2*(3), 205–213.

28. Friedman, H. S., Hall, J. A., & Harris, M. J. (1985). Type A behavior, nonverbal expressive style, and health. *Journal of Personality and Social Psychology, 48*(5), 1299–1315.

29. Kobasa, S. C. (1979). Stressful life events, personality, and health: An inquiry into hardiness. *Journal of Personality and Social Psychology, 37*(1), 1–11.

30. Kobasa, S. C, Maddi, S. R., & Kahn, S. (1982). Hardiness and health: A prospective study. *Journal of Personality and Social Psychology, 42*(1), 168–177.

31. Uchino, B. N., Cacioppo, J. T., & Kiecolt-Glaser, J. K. (1996). The relationship between social support and physiological processes: A review with emphasis on underlying mechanisms and implications for health. *Psychological Bulletin, 119*(3), 488–531.

32. Luthans, F., Avey, J. B., Avolio, B. J., Norman, S. M., & Combs, G. M. (2006). Psychological capital development: Toward a micro-intervention. *Journal of Organizational Behavior, 27*(3), 387–393.

33. Luthans, F., Avolio, B. J., Avey, J. B., & Norman, S. M. (2007). Positive psychological capital: Measurement and relationships with performance and satisfaction. *Personnel Psychology, 60*(3), 541–572.

34. Ibid.

35. Luthans, F., Avey, J. B., Avolio, B. J., Norman, S. M., & Combs, G. M. (2006). Psychological capital development: Toward a micro-intervention. *Journal of Organizational Behavior, 27*(3), 387–393.

36. Luthans, F., & Youssef, C. M. (2004). Investing in people for competitive advantage. *Organizational Dynamics, 33*(2), 143–160.

37. Avey, J., Wernsing, T. S., & Luthans, F. (2008). Can positive employees help positive organizational change? Impact of psychological capital and emotions on relevant attitudes and behaviors. *Journal of Applied Behavioral Science, 44*(1), 48–70.

38. Fredrickson, B. L. (2000). Why positive emotions matter in organizations: Lessons from the broaden-and-build model. *The Psychologist-Manager Journal, 4*(2), 131–142.

39. Barsade, S. G. (2002). The ripple effect: Emotional contagion and its influence on group behavior. *Administrative Science Quarterly, 47*(4), 644–675.

40. Fredrickson (2000).

41. Lazarus, R. S. (1991). *Emotion and adaptation.* New York, NY: Oxford University Press.

42. Tangney, J. P. (1995). Shame and guilt in interpersonal relationships. In J. P. Tangney & K. W. Fisher (Eds.), *Self-conscious emotions: The psychology of shame, guilt, embarrassment, and pride* (pp. 114–139). New York, NY: Guilford.

43. Brief, A. P., & Weiss, H. M. (2002). Organizational behavior: Affect in the workplace. *Annual Review of Psychology, 53*(1), 379–307.

44. Lyubomirsky, S., King, L., & Diener, E. (2005). The benefits of frequent positive affect: Does happiness leader to success? *Psychological Bulletin, 131*(6), 803–855.

45. Staw, B. M., Sutton, R. I., & Pelled, L. H. (1994). Employee positive emotion and favorable outcomes in the workplace. *Organization Science, 5*(1), 51–71.

46. Wright, T. A., & Staw, B. M. (1999). Affect and favorable work outcomes: Two longitudinal tests of the happy-productive worker thesis. *Journal of Organizational Behavior, 20*(1), 1–23.

47. Rothbard, N. P., & Wilks, S. L. (2011). Waking up on the right or wrong side of the bed: Start-of-workday mood, work events, employee affect, and performance. *Academy of Management Journal, 54*(5), 959–980.

48. George, J. M. (1990). Personality, affect, and behavior in groups. *Journal of Applied Psychology, 75*(2), 107–116.

49. Goleman, D. (1995). *Emotional intelligence: Why it can matter more than IQ.* New York, NY: Bantam Books.

50. Salovey, P., & Mayer, J. D. (1990). Emotional intelligence. *Imagination, Cognition, and Personality, 9*(3), 185–211.

51. Law, K. S., Wong, C. S., & Song, L. J. (2004). The construct and criterion validity of emotional intelligence and its potential utility for management studies. *Journal of Applied Psychology, 89*(3), 483–496.

52. Ibid.

53. Côté, S., & Miners, C. T. (2006). Emotional intelligence, cognitive intelligence, and job performance. *Administrative Science Quarterly, 51*(1), 1–28.

54. Bar-On, R., Handley, R., & Fund, S. (2005). The impact of emotional intelligence on performance. In V. Druskat, F. Salas, & G. Mount (Eds.), *Linking emotional intelligence and performance at work: Current research evidence* (pp. 3–20). Malwah, NJ: Lawrence Erlbaum.

55. Cavallo, K., & Brienza, D. (2004). *Emotional competence and leadership excellence at Johnson & Johnson: The emotional intelligence and leadership study.* New Brunswick, NJ: Consortium for Research on Emotional Intelligence in Organizations (Rutgers University).

56. Farh, C. I., Seo, M., & Tesluk, P. E. (2012). Emotional Intelligence, teamwork effectiveness, and job performance: The moderating role of job context. *Journal of Applied Psychology, 97*(4), 890–900.

57. Kirk, B. A., Schutte, N. S., & Hine, D. W. (2011). The effect of an expressive writing intervention for employees on emotional self-efficacy, emotional intelligence, affect, and workplace incivility. *Journal of Applied Social Psychology, 41*(1), 179–195.

58. Slaski, M., & Cartwright, S. (2003). Emotional intelligence training and its implications for stress, health, and performance. *Stress and Health, 19*(4), 233–239.

59. Schutte, N. S., Malouff, J. M., & Thorsteinsson, E. B. (2013). Increasing emotional intelligence through training: Current status and future directions. *International Journal of Emotional Education, 5*(1), 56–72.

60. Goleman, D., Boyatzis, R., & McKee, A. (2013). *Primal leadership: Unleashing the power of emotional intelligence.* Cambridge MA: Harvard Business School Press.

61. Davies, M., Stankov, L., & Roberts, R. D. (1998). Emotional intelligence: In search of an elusive construct. *Journal of Personality and Social Psychology, 75*(4), 989–1015.

62. Landy, F. J. (2005). Some historical and scientific issues related to research on emotional intelligence. *Journal of Organizational Behavior, 26*(4), 411–424.

63. Locke, E. A. (2005). Why emotional intelligence is an invalid concept. *Journal of Organizational Behavior, 26*(4), 425–431.

64. Zeidner, M., Matthews, G., & Roberts, R. D. (2004). Emotional intelligence in the workplace: A critical review. *Applied Psychology: An International Journal, 53*(3), 371–399.

65. Van Rooy, D. L., & Viswesvaran, C. (2004). Emotional intelligence: A meta-analytic investigation of predictive validity and nomological net. *Journal of Vocational Behavior, 65*(1), 71–95.

66. Cooper, R. K. (1997). Applying emotional intelligence in the workplace. *Training and Development, 51*(12), 31–33.

67. Cherniss, C. (1999). *The business case for emotional intelligence.* The consortium for research on emotional intelligence in organizations. Retrieved on July 15, 2013, from http://www.eiconsortium.org

68. Ashkanasy, N. M., & Daus, C. S. (2002). Emotion in the workplace: The new challenge for managers. *Academy of Management Executive, 16*(1), 76–86.

69. Hochschild, A. R. (1983). *The managed heart: Commercialization of human feeling.* Berkeley: University of California Press.

70. Rafaeli, A. (1989). When cashiers meet customers: An analysis of the role of supermarket cashiers. *Academy of Management Journal, 32*(2), 245–273.

71. Brotheridge, C., & Grandey, A. A. (2002). Emotional labor and burnout: Comparing two perspectives of "people work." *Journal of Vocational Behavior, 60*(1), 17–39.

72. Grandey, A. A. (2003). When "the show must go on": Surface acting and deep acting as determinants of emotional exhaustion and peer-rated service delivery.

73. Barsade, S. G. (2002). The ripple effect: Emotional contagion and its influence on group behavior. *Administrative Science Quarterly, 47*(4), 644–675.

74. Pugh, D. (2001). Service with a smile: Emotional contagion in service encounters. *Academy of Management Journal, 44*(5), 1018–1027.

75. Barger, P. B., & Grandey, A. A. (2006). Service with a smile and encounter satisfaction: Emotional contagion and appraisal mechanisms. *Academy of Management Journal, 49*(6), 1229–1238.

76. Askanasy & Daus (2002).

77. Becker, W. J., Cropanzano, R., & Sanfey, A. G. (2011). Organizational neuroscience: Taking organizational theory inside the neural black box. *Journal of Management, 37*(4), 933–961.

78. Antonakis, J. (2011). Predictors of leadership: The usual suspects and the suspect traits. In A. Bryman, D. Collinson, K. Grint, B. Jackson, & M. Uhl-Bien (Eds.), *SAGE handbook of leadership* (pp. 269–285). Thousand Oaks, CA: Sage.

79. Lindebaum, D. (2013). Ethics and the neuroscientific study of leadership: A synthesis and rejoinder to Ashkanasy, Cropanzano and Becker, and McLagan. *Journal of Management Inquiry, 22*(3), 317–323.

80. Fairholm, G. W. (1994). Leading diverse followers. *Journal of Leadership Studies, 1,* 82–93.

81. Harrison, D. A., Price, K. H., & Bell, M. P. (1998). Beyond relational demography: Time and the effects of surface-and deep-level diversity on work group cohesion. *Academy of Management Journal, 41*(1), 96–107.

82. Ibid.

83. Meister, J. (2013). The boomer-millennial workplace clash: Is it real? *Forbes.* Retrieved on July 10, 2013, from www .forbes.cm/sites/jeannemeister/2013/2013/ 06/04/the-boomer-millennial-workplace-clash-is-it-real

84. Page, S. E. (2007). Making the difference: Applying a logic of diversity. *Academy of Management Perspectives, 21*(4), 6–20.

85. Stein, J. (2013, May). The me me me generation: Millennials are lazy, entitled narcissists who still live with their parents. Why they'll save us all. *Time,* pp. 28–34.

86. Joplin, J. R. W., & Daus, C. S. (1997). Challenges of leading a diverse workforce.

88. Gilbert, J. A., & Ivancevich, J. (2000). Valuing diversity: A tale of two organizations. *Academy of Management Executive, 14*(1), 93–105.

89. Brown, K. W., & Ryan, R. M. (2003). The benefits of being present: Mindfulness and its role in psychological well-being. *Journal of Personality and Social Psychology, 84*(4), 822–848.

90. Riddle, D. (2012). Three keys to mindful coaching. *Forbes.* Retrieved on July 16, 2013, from www.forbes.com/sites/ ccl/2012/01/23/three-keys-to-mindful-leadership-coaching

91. Ibid.

92. Jha, A., Krompinger, J., & Baime, M. J. (2007). Mindfulness training modifies subsystems of attention. *Cognitive, Affective, & Behavioral Neuroscience, 7*(2), 109–119.

93. Cox, T. H., & Blake, S. (1991). Managing cultural diversity: Implications for organizational competitiveness. *Academy of Management Executive, 5*(3), 45–56.

94. Dezso, C. L., & Ross, D. G. (2012). Does female representation in top management improve firm performance? A panel data investigation. *Strategic Management Journal, 33*(9),1072–1089.

95. Ibid.

Chapter 4

1. Thurstone, L. L. (1928). Attitudes can be measured. *American Journal of Sociology, 33*(4), 529–554.

2. Allport, G. (1935). Attitudes. In C. Murchison (Ed.), *A handbook of social psychology* (pp. 789–844). Worcester, MA: Clark University Press.

3. Eagly, A. H., & Chaiken, S. (1993). *The psychology of attitudes.* New York, NY: Harcourt Brace Jovanovich College Publishers.

4. Rosenberg, M. J., & Hovland, C. I. (1960). Cognitive, affective and behavioral components of attitudes. In M. J. Rosenberg & C. I. Hovland (Eds.), *Attitude organization and change: An analysis of consistency among attitude components.* New Haven, CT: Yale University Press.

5. Breckler, S. J. (1984). Empirical validation of affect, behavior, and cognition as distinct components of an attitude, *Journal of Personality and Social Psychology, 47*(6), 1191–1205.

Academy of Management Journal, 46(1), 86–96.

Academy of Management Executive, 11(3), 32–45.

6. Crites, Jr., S. L., Fabrigar, L. R., & Petty, R. E. (1994). Measuring the affective and cognitive properties of attitudes: Conceptual and methodological issues. *Personality and Social Psychology Bulletin, 20*(6), 619–663.

7. Bagozzi, R. (1992). The self-regulation of attitudes, intentions, and behavior. *Social psychology quarterly, 55*(2), 178–204.

8. Festinger, L. (1957). *A theory of cognitive dissonance*. Stanford, CA: Stanford University Press.

9. Harrison, D. A., Newman, D. A., & Roth, P. L. (2006). How important are job attitudes: Meta-analytic comparisons of integrative behavioral outcomes and time sequences. *Academy of Management Journal, 49*(2), 305–325.

10. Riketta, M. (2008). The causal relation between job attitudes and performance: A meta-analysis of panel studies. *Journal of Applied Psychology, 93*(2), 472–481.

11. Ajzen, I., & Fishbein, M. (1977). Attitude-behavior relations: A theoretical analysis and review of empirical research. *Psychological Bulletin, 84*(5), 888–918.

12. Glasman, L. R., & Albarracin, D. (2006). Forming attitudes that predict future behavior: A meta-analysis of the attitude-behavior relation. *Psychological Bulletin, 132*(5), 778–822.

13. Locke, E. A. (1976). The nature and causes of job satisfaction. In M. D. Dunnette (Ed.), *Handbook of industrial and organizational psychology* (pp. 1297–1349). Chicago, IL: Rand McNally.

14. Smith, P. C. (1992). In pursuit of happiness: Why study general job satisfaction? In C. J. Cranny, P. C. Smith, & E. F. Stone (Eds.), *Job satisfaction: How people feel about their jobs and how it affects their performance* (pp. 5–20). New York, NY: Lexington Books.

15. Wright, T. A. (2003). Positive organizational behavior: An idea whose time has truly come. *Journal of Organizational Behavior, 24*(4), 437–442.

16. Andreassi, J. K., Lawter, L., Brockerhoff, M., & Rutigliano, P. (2012). Job satisfaction determinants: A study across 48 nations. *Business Faculty Publications*, Paper 220. Retrieved on April 24, 2014, from http://digitalcommons.sacredheart.edu/wcob_fac/220

17. Van Ryzin, G. G. (2014). The curious case of the post 9-11 boost in government job satisfaction. *American Review of Public Administration, 44*(1), 59–74.

18. Judge, T. A., Thoresen, J. E., Bono, J. E., & Patton, G. K. (2001). The job satisfaction-job performance relationship: A qualitative and quantitative review. *Psychological Bulletin, 127*(3), 376–407.

19. Smith, P. C., Kendall, L. M., & Hulin, C. L. (1985). *The job descriptive index*. Bowling Green, OH: Department of Psychology, Bowling Green State University.

20. Ironson, G. H., Smith, P. C., Brannick, M. T., Gibson, W. M., & Paul, K. B. (1989). Construction of a job in general scale: A comparison of global, composite, and specific measures. *Journal of Applied Psychology, 74*(2), 193–200.

21. Russell, S. S., Spitzmuller, C., Lin, L. F., Stanton, J. M, Smith, P. C., & Ironson, G. H. (2004). Shorter can also be better: The abridged job in general scale. *Educational and Psychological Measurement, 64*(5), 878–893.

22. Judge, Thoresen, et al. (2001).

23. Rusbult, C. E., Farrell, D., Rogers, G., & Mainous III, A. G. (1988). Impact of exchange variables on exit, voice, loyalty, and neglect: An integrative model of responses to declining job satisfaction. *Academy of Management Journal, 31*(3), 599–627.

24. Wanberg, C. R., Zhu, J., & Van Hooft, E. A. J. (2010). The job search grind: Perceived progress, self-reactions, and self-regulation of search effort. *Academy of Management Journal, 53*(4), 788–807.

25. Judge, T. A., Erez, A., & Bono, J. E. (1998). The power of being positive: The relation between positive self-concept and job performance. *Human Performance, 11*(2–3), 167–187.

26. Wanberg, C. R., Glomb, T., Song, Z., & Sorenson, S. (2005). Job-search persistence during unemployment: A ten wave longitudinal study. *Journal of Applied Psychology, 90*(3), 411–430.

27. Judge, T. A., & Bono, J. E. (2001). Relationship of core self-evaluations traits—self-esteem, generalized self-efficacy, locus of control, and emotional stability—with job satisfaction and job performance: A meta-analysis. *Journal of Applied Psychology, 86*(1), 80–92.

28. Cooper-Hakim, A., & Viswesvaran, C. (2005). The construct of work commitment: Testing an integrative framework. *Psychological Bulletin, 131*(2), 241–259.

29. Mathieu, J. E., & Zajac, D. M. (1990). A review and meta-analysis of the antecedents, correlates, and consequences of organizational commitment. *Psychological Bulletin, 108*(2), 171–194.

30. Meyer, J. P., Stanley, D. J., Herscovitch, L., & Topolnytsky, L. (2002). Affective, continuance, and normative commitment to the organization: A meta-analysis of antecedents, correlates, and consequences. *Journal of Vocational Behavior, 61*(1), 20–52.

31. Klein, H. J., Becker, T. E., & Meyer, J. P. (2009). *Commitment in organizations: Accumulated wisdom and new directions*. New York, NY: Routledge/Psychology Press.

32. Meyer, J. P., & Allen, N. J. (1997). *Commitment in the workplace: Theory, research, and application*. Thousand Oaks, CA: Sage.

33. Meyer, J. P., & Allen, N. J. (1991). A three-component conceptualization of organizational commitment. *Human Resource Management Review, 1*(1), 61–89.

34. Blau, G. J., & Boal, K. B. (1989). Using organizational commitment and job involvement interactively to predict turnover. *Journal of Management, 15*(1), 115–127.

35. Diefendorff, J. M., Brown, D. J., Kamin, A. M., & Lord, R. G. (2002). Examining the roles of job involvement and work centrality in predicting organizational citizenship behaviors and job performance. *Journal of Organizational Behavior, 23*(1), 93–108.

36. Blau, G. J., & Boal, K. B. (1987). Conceptualizing how job involvement and organizational commitment affect turnover and absenteeism. *Academy of Management Review, 12*(2), 288–300.

37. Rich, B. L., Lepine, J. A., & Crawford, E. R. (2010). Job engagement: Antecedents and effects on job performance. *Academy of Management Journal, 53*(3), 617–635.

38. Harter, J. K., Schmidt, F. L., & Hayes, T. L. (2002). Business-unit-level relationships between employee satisfaction, employee engagement, and business outcomes: A meta-analysis. *Journal of Applied Psychology, 87*(2), 268–279.

39. Gallup. (2013). State of the American workforce: Employee engagement insights for U.S. business leaders. Retrieved on January 8, 2014, from http://www.gallup.com/strategicconsulting/163007/state-american-workplace.aspx). p. 12.

40. Rhoades, L., & Eisenberger, R. (2002). Perceived organizational support: A review of the literature. *Journal of Applied Psychology, 87*(4), 698–714.

41. Schaufeli, W. B., & Bakker, A. B. (2004). Job demands, job resources, and their relationship with burnout and engagement: A multi-sample study. *Journal of Organizational Behavior*, 25(3), 293–315.

42. Bakker, A. B., Hakanen, J. J., Demerouti, E., & Xanthopoulou, D. (2007). Job resources boost work engagement, particularly when job demands are high. *Journal of Educational Psychology*, 99(2), 274–284.

43. Eisenberger, R., Huntington, R., Hutchison, S., & Sowa, D. (1986). Perceived organizational support. *Journal of Applied Psychology*, 71(3), 500–507.

44. Shore, L. M., & Shore, T. H. (1995). Perceived organizational support and organizational justice. In R. S. Cropanzano & K. M. Kacmar (Eds.), *Organizational politics, justice, and support: Managing the social climate of the workplace* (pp. 149–164). Westport, CT: Quorum.

45. Rhoades, L., Eisenberger, R., & Armeli, S. (2001). Affective commitment to the organization: The contribution of perceived organizational support. *Journal of Applied Psychology*, 86(5), 825–836.

46. Eisenberger, R., Stinglhamber, F., Vandenberghe, C., Sucharski, I., & Rhoades, L. (2002). Perceived supervisor support: Contributions to perceived organizational support and employee retention. *Journal of Applied Psychology*, 87(3), 565–573.

47. Eder, P., & Eisenerger, R. (2008). Perceived organizational support: Reducing the negative influence of coworker withdrawal behavior. *Journal of Management*, 34(1), 55–68.

48. Riggle, R. J., Edmondson, D. R., & Hansen, J. D. (2009). A meta-analysis of the relationship between perceived organizational support and job outcomes: 20 years of research. *Journal of Business Research*, 62(10), 1027–1030.

49. Spreitzer, G. M. (1995). Psychological empowerment in the workplace: Dimensions, measurement, and validation. *Academy of Management Journal*, 38(4), 1442–1465.

50. Ibid.

51. Joo, B.-K., & Shim, J. H. (2010). Psychological empowerment and organizational commitment: The moderating effect of organizational learning culture. *Human Resource Development International*, 13(4), 425–441.

52. Spreitzer, G. M. (1996). Social structural characteristics of psychological empowerment. *The Academy of Management Journal*, 39(2), 483–504.

53. Spreitzer, G. M., Kizilos, M. A., & Nason, S. W. (1997). A dimensional analysis of the relationship between psychological empowerment and effectiveness, satisfaction, and strain. *Journal of Management*, 23(5), 679–704.

54. Avolio, B. J. (1999). *Full leadership development: Building the vital forces in organizations*. Thousand Oaks, CA: Sage.

55. Avolio, B. J., Zhu, W., Koh, W., & Bhatia, P. (2004). Transformational leadership and organizational commitment: Mediating role of psychological empowerment and moderating role of structural distance. *Journal of Organizational Behavior*, 2(8), 951–968.

56. Shamir, B., Zakay, E., Breinin, E., & Popper, M. (1998). Correlates of charismatic leader behavior in military units: subordinates' attitudes, unit characteristics and superiors' appraisal of leader performance. *Academy of Management Journal*, 41(4), 387–409.

57. Dulebohn, J. H., Bommer, W. H., Liden, R. C., Brouer, R. L., & Ferris, G. R. (2012). A meta-analysis of antecedents and consequences of leader-member exchange: Integrating the past with an eye toward the future. *Journal of Management*, 38(6), 1715–1759.

58. Bono, J. E., & Judge, T. A. (2003). Self-concordance at work: Toward understanding the motivational effects of transformational leaders. *Academy of Management Journal*, 46(5), 554–571.

59. Piccolo, R. F., & Colquitt, J. A. (2006). Transformational leadership and job behaviors: The mediating role of core job characteristics. *Academy of Management Journal*, 49(2), 327–340.

60. Rosso, B. D., Dekas, K. H., & Wrzesniewski, A. (2012). On the meaning of work: A theoretical integration and review. *Research in Organizational Behavior*, 30, 91–127. p. 101.

61. Steger, M. F., Dik, B. J., & Duffy, R. D. (2012). Measuring meaningful work: The work and meaning inventory (WAMI). *Journal of Career Assessment*, 20(3), 1–16.

62. Ibid.

63. KPMG's 2011 U.S. Hospital Nursing Labor Costs Survey. (2011). Retrieved from: http://www.natho.org/pdfs/KPMG_2011_Nursing_LaborCostStudy.pdf

64. Kovner, C. T., Brewer, C. S., Fairchild, S., Poormina, S., Kim, H., & Djukic, M. (2007). Newly licensed RN's characteristics, work attitudes, and intentions to work. *American Journal of Nursing*, 107(9), 58–70.

65. KPMG's 2011 US Hospital Nursing Labor Costs Survey. (2011).

66. Jones, C. B. (2008). Revisiting nurse turnover costs: Adjusting for inflation. *Journal of Nursing Administration*, 38(1), 11–18.

Chapter 5

1. Kahneman, D., Krueger, A. B., Schkade, D., Schwarz, N., & Stone, A. A. (2006). Would you be happier if you were richer? A focusing illusion. *Science*, 30(312), 1908–1910.

2. Nisbett, R. E., & Ross, L. (1980). *Human inference: Strategies and shortcomings of social judgment*. Englewood Cliffs, NJ: Prentice Hall.

3. Luchins, A. S. (1942). Mechanization in problem solving: The effect of Einstellung. *Psychological Monographs*, 54(6), 1–95.

4. Allport, G. W. (1979). *The nature of prejudice*. Cambridge, MA: Addison-Wesley.

5. Asch, S. E. (1946). Forming impressions of personality. *Journal of Abnormal and Social Psychology*, 41(3), 258–290.

6. Nisbett, R. E., & Wilson, T. D. (1977). Telling more than we can know: Verbal reports on mental processes. *Psychological Review*, 84(3), 231–259.

7. Dennis, M. J., & Ahn, W. K. (2001). Primacy in causal strength judgments: The effect of initial evidence for generative versus inhibitory relationships. *Memory & Cognition*, 29(1), 152–164.

8. Willis, J., & Todorov, A. (2006). First impressions making up your mind after a 100-ms exposure to a face. *Psychological Science*, 17(7), 592–598.

9. Tetlock, P. (1983). Accountability and the perseverance of first impressions. *Social Psychology Quarterly*, 46(4), 285–292.

10. Murdock, B. B. (1962). The serial position effect of free recall. *Journal of Experimental Psychology*, 64(5), 482–488.

11. Greene, R. L. (1986). Sources of recency effects in free recall. *Psychological Bulletin*, 99(2), 221–228.

12. Highouse, S., & Gallo, A. (1997). Order effects in personnel decision making. *Human Performance*, 10(1), 31–46.

13. Atkinson, R. C., & Shiffrin, R. M. (1971). The control processes of short-term memory. Technical Report 173, Psychology Series. Stanford, CA: Institute for Mathematical Studies in the Social Sciences. Retrieved on September 8, 2013, from www.suppesscorpus.stanford.edu/techreports/IMMS_173.pdf

14. Ibid.

15. Tversky, A., & Kahneman, D. (1973). Availability: A heuristic for judging frequency and probability. *Cognitive Psychology, 5*(2), 207–232.

16. Ibid.

17. Levy, B. (2002). *Remember every name, every time: Corporate America's memory master reveals his secrets.* New York, NY: Fireside Books.

18. Schwartz, N., Bless, H., Strack, F., Klumpp, G., Rittenauer-Schatka, H., & Simons, A. (1991). Ease of retrieval as information: Another look at the availability heuristic. *Journal of Personality and Social Psychology, 61*(2), 195–202.

19. Anderson, C. A. (1982). Inoculation and counterexplanation: Debiasing techniques in the perseverance of social theories. *Social Cognition, 1*(2), 126–139.

20. Slusher, M. P., & Anderson, C. A. (1996). Using causal persuasive arguments to change beliefs and teach new information: The mediating role of explanation availability and evaluation bias in the acceptance of knowledge. *Journal of Educational Psychology, 88*(1), 110–122.

21. Pressley, M., Symons, S., McDaniel, M. A., Snyder, B. L., & Turnure, J. E. (1988). Elaborative interrogation facilitates acquisition of confusing facts. *Journal of Educational Psychology, 80*(3), 268–278.

22. Goodstadt, B., & Kipnis, D. (1970). Situational influences on the use of power. *Journal of Applied Psychology, 54*(3), 201–207.

23. Kipnis, D., & Vanderveer, R. (1971). Ingratiation and the use of power. *Journal of Personality and Social Psychology, 17*(3), 280–286.

24. Ivancevich, J. M. (1983). Contrast effects in performance evaluation and reward practices. *Academy of Management Journal, 26*(3), 465–476.

25. Latham, G. P., Wexley, K. N., & Pursell, E. D. (1975). Training managers to minimize rating errors in the observation of behavior. *Journal of Applied Psychology, 60*(5), 550–555.

26. Chapman, D. S., & Zweig, D. I. (2005). Developing a nomological network for interview structure: Antecedents and consequences of the structured selection interview. *Personnel Psychology, 58*(3), 673–702.

27. Rosenzweig, P. (2007). *The halo effect.* New York, NY: Free Press.

28. Thorndike, E. L. (1920). A constant error in psychological ratings. *Journal of Applied Psychology, 4*(1), 25–29.

29. Balzer, W. K., & Sulsky, L. M. (1992). Halo and performance appraisal research: A critical examination. *Journal of Applied Psychology, 77*(6), 975–985.

30. Saal, F. E., Downey, R. G., & Lahey, M. A. (1980). Rating the ratings: Assessing the psychometric quality of rating data. *Psychological Bulletin, 88*(2), 413–428.

31. Cooper, W. H. (1981). Ubiquitous halo. *Psychological Bulletin, 90*(2), 218–244.

32. Viswesvaran, C., Schmidt, F. L., & Ones, D. S. (2005). Is there a general factor in ratings of job performance? A meta-analytic framework for disentangling substantive and error influences. *Journal of Applied Psychology, 90*(1), 108–131.

33. Heider, F. (1958). *The psychology of interpersonal relations.* Hillsdale, NJ: Lawrence Erlbaum.

34. Martinko, M. J., Harvey, P., & Douglas, S. C. (2007). The role, function, and contribution of attribution theory to leadership: A review. *The Leadership Quarterly, 18*(6), 561–585.

35. Ross, L. (1977). The intuitive psychologist and his shortcomings: Distortions in the attribution process. In L. Berkowitz (Ed.), *Advances in experimental social psychology* (Vol. 10, pp. 173–220). New York, NY: Academic Press.

36. Martinko, M. J., & Gardner, W. L. (1987). The leader member attribution process. *Academy of Management Review, 12*(2), 235–249.

37. Martinko, M. J., Douglas, S. C., & Harvey, P. (2006). Attribution theory in industrial and organizational psychology: A review. *International Review of Industrial and Organizational Psychology, 21*, 127–187.

38. Eberly, M. B., Holley, E. C., Johnson, M. D., & Mitchell, T. R. (2011). Beyond internal and external: A dyadic theory of relational attributions. *Academy of Management Review, 36*(4), 731–753.

39. Meindl, J. R., Ehrlich, S. B., & Dukerich, J. M. (1985). The romance of leadership. *Administrative Science Quarterly, 30*(1), 78–102.

40. Rosenthal, R., & Jacobson, L. (1968). *Pygmalion in the classroom: Teacher expectation and pupils' intellectual development.* New York, NY: Holt, Rinehart and Winston.

41. Riggio, R. E. (2009). Pygmalion leadership: The power of positive expectations. *Psychology Today.* Retrieved from http://www.psychologytoday.com/blog/cutting-edge-leadership/200904/pygmalion-leadership-the-power-positive-expectations

42. Eden, D. (1993). Leadership and expectations: Pygmalion effects and other self-fulfilling prophecies in organizations. *The Leadership Quarterly, 3*(4), 271–305.

43. Bezuijen, X. M., van den Berg, P. T., van Dam, K., & Thierry, H. (2009). Pygmalion and employee learning: The role of leader behaviors. *Journal of Management, 35*(5), 248–267.

44. Eden, D., & Shani, A. B. (1982). Pygmalion goes to boot camp: Expectancy, leadership, and trainee performance. *Journal of Applied Psychology, 67*(2) 194–199.

45. McNatt, D. B. (2000). Ancient Pygmalion joins contemporary management: A meta-analysis of the result. *Journal of Applied Psychology, 85*(2), 314–322.

46. Davidson, O. B., & Eden, D. (2000). Remedial self-fulfilling prophecy: Two field experiments to prevent Golem effects among disadvantaged women. *Journal of Applied Psychology, 85*(3), 386–398.

47. Nanatovich, G., & Eden, D. (2008). Pygmalion effects among outreach supervisors and tutors: Extending sex generalizability. *Journal of Applied Psychology, 93*(6), 1382–1389.

48. Rosenthal, R. (1973). The mediation of Pygmalion effects: A four factor "theory." *Papua New Guinea Journal of Education, 9*, 1–12.

49. McNatt, D. B., & Judge, T. A. (2004). Boundary conditions of the Galatea Effect: A field experiment and constructive replication. *Academy of Management Journal, 47*(4), 550–565.

50. Manzoni, J. F., & Barsoux, J. L. (1997). The set-up-to-fail syndrome. *Harvard Business Review, 76*(2), 101–113.

51. Davidson & Eden (2000).

52. Oz, S., & Eden, D. (1994). Restraining the Golem: Boosting performance by changing the interpretation of low scores. *Journal of Applied Psychology, 79*(5), 744–754.

53. Fugate, M., Kinicki, A. J., & Ashforth, B. E. (2004). Employability: A psycho-social construct, its dimensions, and applications. *Journal of Vocational Behavior, 65*(1), 14–38.

54. Hogan, R., Chamorro-Premuzic, T., & Kaiser, R. B. (2013). Employability and career success: Bridging the gap between theory and reality. *Industrial and Organizational Psychology*, 6(1), 3–16. p. 11.

55. Fugate, M., & Kinicki, A. J. (2008). A dispositional approach to employability: Development of a measure and test of implications for employee reactions to organizational change. *Journal of Occupational and Organizational Psychology*, 81(3), 503–527.

56. Ghumann, S., & Ryan, A. M. (2013). Not welcome here: Discrimination towards women who wear the Muslim headscarf. *Human Relations*, 66(5), 671–698.

57. King, E. B., & Ahmad, A. S. (2010). An experimental field study of discrimination against Muslim job applicants. *Personnel Psychology*, 63(4), 881–906.

58. Hilton, J. L., & Von Hippel, W. (1996). Stereotypes. *Annual Review of Psychology*, 47(1), 237–271.

59. Schlenker, B. R. (1980). *Impression management: The self-concept, social identity, and interpersonal relations* (pp. 21–43). Monterey, CA: Brooks/Cole Publishing Company.

60. Wayne, S. J., & Liden, R. C. (1995). Effects of impression management on performance ratings: A longitudinal study. *Academy of Management Journal*, 38(1), 232–260.

61. Bolino, M. C., Kacmar, K. M, Turnley, W. H., & Gilstrap, J. B. (2008). A multi-level review of impression management motives and behaviors. *Journal of Management*, 34(6), 1080–1109.

62. Ibid.

63. Wayne, S. J., & Ferris, G. (1990). Influence tactics, affect, and exchange quality in supervisor-subordinate interactions: a laboratory experiment and field study. *Journal of Applied Psychology*, 75(5), 487–499.

64. Yukl, G. (2013). *Leadership in organizations* (8th ed.) Boston, MA: Pearson.

65. Carney, D. R., Cuddy, A. J. C., & Yap, A. J. (2010). Power posing: Brief nonverbal displays affect neuroendocrine levels and risk tolerance. *Psychological Science*, 21(10), 1363–1368.

66. Rosenberg, R. S. (2011). The superheros: Inside the mind of batman and other larger-than-life-heroes. *Psychology Today*. Retrieved on September 15, 2013, from www.psychologytoday.com/blog/the-superheroes/201107/superherostance

67. Murphy, K. (2013). The right stance can be reassuring. *New York Times*. Retrieved on September 15, 2013, from www.nytimes.com/2013/05/05/fashion/the-right-stance-can-be-reassuring-studied.html?ref=fashion&_r=1&&

68. Hogg, M. A. (2001). A social identity theory of leadership. *Personality and Social Psychology Review*, 5(3), 184–200.

69. Tajfel, H. (1972). Social categorization. English manuscript of 'La catégorisation sociale.' In S. Moscovici (Ed.), *Introduction à la Psychologie Sociale* (Vol. 1, pp. 272–302). Paris: Larousse. p. 292.

70. Hogg, M. A., Terry, D. J., & White, K. M. (1995). A tale of two theories: A critical comparison of identity theory with social identity theory. *Social Psychology Quarterly*, 58(4), 255–269.

71. Hogg (2001).

72. Ashforth, B. E., & Mael, F. (1989). Social identity theory and the organization. *Academy of Management Review*, 14(1), 20–39.

73. Phillips, J. S., & Lord, R. G. (1981). Causal attributions and perceptions of leadership. *Organizational Behavior and Human Performance*, 28(2), 143–163.

74. Lord, R. G., Foti, R. J., & Phillips, J. S. (1982). A theory of leadership categorization. In J. G. Hunt, U. Sekaran, & C. Schriesheim (Eds.), *Leadership: Beyond establishment views* (pp. 104–121). Carbondale: Southern Illinois University Press.

75. Phillips, J. S., & Lord, R. G. (1982). Schematic information processing and perceptions of leadership in problem-solving groups. *Journal of Applied Psychology*, 67(4), 486–492.

76. Lord, R. G. (1985). An information processing approach to social perceptions, leadership perceptions and behavioral measurement in organizational settings. In B. M. Staw & L. L. Cummings (Eds.), *Research in organizational behavior* (Vol. 7, pp. 85–128). Greenwich, CT: JAI Press.

77. Engle, E. M., & Lord, R. G. (1997). Implicit theories, self-schemas, and leader-member exchange. *Academy of Management Journal*, 40(4), 988–1010.

Chapter 6

1. Harnish, V. (2012). *The greatest business decisions of all time: How Apple, Ford, IBM, Zappos, and others made radical choices that changed the course of business*. New York, NY: Fortune.

2. Dean, J. W., & Sharfman, M. P. (1996). Does decision process matter? A study of strategic decision-making effectiveness. *Academy of Management Journal*, 39(2), 368–396.

3. Mintzberg, H. (1975, July–August). The manager's job: folklore and fact. *Harvard Business Review*, 49–61.

4. Mintzberg, H. (1988). *Mintzberg on management: Inside our strange world of organizations*. New York, NY: Free Press.

5. Tasler, N. (2013). *Why quitters win*. Henderson, NV: Motivational Press. Retrieved from http://www.nicktasler.com/author

6. Potworowski, G. (2010). Varieties of indecisive experience: Explaining the tendency to not make timely and stable decisions. Unpublished doctoral dissertation, University of Michigan, Ann Arbor.

7. Bacanli, F. (2006). Personality characteristics as predictors of personal indecisiveness. *Journal of Career Development*, 32(4), 320–332.

8. Gati, I., Gadassi, R., Saka, N., Hadadi, Y., Ansenberg, N., Friedmann, R., & Asulin-Peretz, L. (2010). Emotional and personality-related aspects of career decision-making difficulties: Facets of career indecisiveness. *Journal of Career Assessment*, 19(1), 3–20. p. 3

9. Germeijs, V., & De Boeck, P. (2002). A measurement scale for indecisiveness and its relationship to career indecision and other types of indecision. *European Journal of Psychological Assessment*, 18(2), 113–122.

10. Shafir, E., & LeBoeuf, R. A. (2002). Rationality. *Annual Review of Psychology*, 53(1), 491–495.

11. Simon, H. A. (1986). Rationality in psychology and economics. *Journal of Business*, S209–S224.

12. Nutt, P. (1984). Types of organizational decision processes. *Administrative Science Quarterly*, 29(3), 414–450.

13. Mitroff, I. (1998). *Smart thinking for crazy times: The art of solving the right problems*. San Francisco, CA: Berrett-Koehler.

14. Russo, J. E., Carlson, K. A., & Meloy, M. G. (2006). Choosing an inferior alternative. *Psychological Science*, 17(10), 899–904.

15. Thompson, L., & Hrebec, D. (1986). Lose-lose agreements in interdependent decision making. *Psychological Bulletin*, 120(3), 396–409.

16. Simon, H. A. (1977). *The new science of management decisions* (2nd ed.). Englewood Cliffs, NJ: Prentice Hall.

17. Augier, M. (2001). Simon says: Bounded rationality matters. *Journal of Management Inquiry, 10*(3), 268–275.

18. Plous, S. (1993). *The psychology of judgment and decision making*. New York, NY: McGraw-Hill.

19. March, J. G. (1978). Bounded rationality and the psychology of choice. *The Bell Journal of Economics, 9*(2), 587–608.

20. Kahneman, D., & Tversky, A. (1979). Prospect theory: An analysis of decision under risk. *Econometrica, 47*(2), 263–291.

21. Jarrehult, B. (2013). The importance of stupid, irrational decisions. *Innovation Management*. Retrieved on September 23, 2013, from www.innovationmanagement. se/2013/09/06/the-importance-of-stupid-irrational-decisions p. 3

22. Taleb, N. N. (2010). *The black swan: The impact of the highly improbable fragility*. New York, NY: Random House.

23. Joslyn, S., & LeClerc, J. (2013). Decisions with uncertainty: The glass half full. *Current Directions in Psychological Science, 22*(4), 308–315. p. 314

24. Stanovich, K. E., & West, R. F. (2000). Individual differences in reasoning: Implications for the rationality debate? *Behavioral & Brain Sciences, 23*(5), 645–665.

25. Gladwell, M. (2007). *Blink: The power of thinking without thinking*. New York, NY: Little, Brown.

26. Hogarth, R. M. (2010). Intuition: A challenge for psychological research on decision making. *Psychological Inquiry, 21*(4), 338–353. p. 339

27. Dane, E., & Pratt, M. (2007). Exploring intuition and its role in managerial decision making. *Academy of Management Review, 32*(1), 33–54. p. 36

28. Simon, H. A. (1987). Making management decisions: The role of intuition and emotion. *Academy of Management Executive, 1*(1), 57–64. p. 63

29. Zhao, S. (2009). The nature and value of common sense to decision making. *Management Decision, 47*(3), 441–453.

30. Hayashi, A. (2001, February). When to trust your gut. *Harvard Business Review*, 59–65.

31. Burke, L. A., & Miller, M. K. (1999). Taking the mystery out of intuitive decision making. *Academy of Management Executive, 13*(4), 91–99. p. 95

32. Sinclair, M., Ashkanasy, N., & Chattopadhyay, P. (2010). Affective antecedents of affective decision making. *Journal of Management & Organization, 16*(3), 382–398.

33. Graham, T., & Ickes, W. (1997). When women's intuition isn't greater than men's. In W. Ickes (Ed.), *Empathic accuracy* (pp. 117–143). New York, NY: Guilford Press.

34. Maio, G. R., & Esses, V. M. (2001). The need for affect: Individual differences in the motivation to approach or avoid emotions. *Journal of Personality, 69*(4), 583–615.

35. Andrade, E. B., & Ariely, D. (2009). The enduring impact of transient emotions on decision making. *Organizational Behavior and Human Decision Processes, 109*(1), 1–8.

36. Hogarth (2010).

37. Shah, A. J., & Oppenheimer, D. (2008). Hueristics made easy: An effort reduction framework. *Psychological Bulletin, 134*(2), 207–222.

38. Kruglanski, A. W., & Gigerenzer, G. (2011). Intuitive and deliberate judgments are based on common principles. *Psychological Review, 118*(1), 97–109.

39. Harnish, V. (2012). *The greatest business decisions of all time: How Apple, Ford, IBM, Zappos, and others made radical choices that changed the course of business*. New York, NY: Fortune.

40. Wood, G. (1978). The knew-it-all-along effect. *Journal of Experimental Psychology, Human Perception and Performance, 4*(2), 345–353.

41. Hawkins, S. A., & Hastie, R. (1990). Hindsight: Biased judgments of past events after the outcomes are known. *Psychological Bulletin, 107*(3), 311–327. p. 311.

42. Guilbault, R. L., Bryant, F. B., Brockway, J. H., & Posavac, E. J. (2004). A meta-analysis of research on hindsight bias. *Basic and Applied Social Psychology, 26*, 103–117.

43. Burdeau, C., & Mohr, H. (2010, May 1). BP didn't plan for major oil spill. *Businessweek*. Retrieved on October 25, 2013, from http://www.businessweek.com/ ap/financialnews/D9FDULS81.htm

44. Russo, J. E., & Schoemaker, P. J. (1992). Managing overconfidence. *Sloan Management Review, 33*(2), 7–17.

45. Shipman, A. S., Byrne, C. L., & Mumford, M. D. (2010). Leader vision formation and forecasting: The effects of forecasting extent, resources, and timeframe. *The Leadership Quarterly, 21*(3), 439–456.

46. Fast, N. J., Sivanathan, N., Mayer, N. D., & Galinsky, A. D. (2012). Power and overconfident decision making. *Organizational Behavior and Human Decision Processes, 117*(2), 249–260.

47. Camerer, C. F., & Johnson, E. J. (1997). The process-performance paradox in expert judgment: How can experts know so much and predict so badly? In W. M. Goldstein & R. M. Hogarth (Eds.), *Research on judgment and decision making: Currents, connections, and controversies* (pp. 342–364). Cambridge, UK: Cambridge University Press.

48. McKenzie, C. R. M., Liersch, M. J., & Yaniv, I. (2008). Overconfidence in interval estimates: What does expertise buy you? *Organizational Behavior and Human Decision Processes, 107*(2), 179–191.

49. Fast et al. (2012).

50. Staw, B. M. (1981). The escalation of commitment to a course of action. *Academy of Management Review, 6*(4), 577–587.

51. Staw, B. M. (1976). Knee-deep in the big muddy: A study of escalating commitment to a chosen course of action. *Organizational Behavior and Human Performance, 16*(1), 27–44.

52. Brockner, J. (1992). The escalation of commitment to a failing course of action: Toward theoretical progress. *Academy of Management Review, 17*(1), 39–61.

53. Montealegre, R., & Keil, M. (2000). Deescalating information technology projects: Lessons from the Denver International Airport. *MIS Quarterly, 24*(3), 417–447.

54. Arkes, H. R., & Blumer, C. (1985). The psychology of sunk costs. *Organizational Behavior and Human Decision Processes, 35*(1), 124–140.

55. Moon, H. (2001). Looking forward and looking back: Integrating complete and sunk-cost effects within an escalation-of-commitment progress decision. *Journal of Applied Psychology, 86*(1), 104–113.

56. Khanin, D., & Mahto, R. V. (2013). Do venture capitalists have a continuation bias? *Journal of Entrepreneurship, 22*(2), 203–222.

57. Schoorman, F. D. (1988). Escalation bias in performance appraisals: An unintended consequence of supervisor participation in hiring decisions. *Journal of Applied Psychology, 73*(1), 58–62.

58. Staw, B. M., Barsade, S. G., & Koput, D. W. (1997). Escalation at the credit window: A longitudinal study of bank executives' recognition and write-off of problem loans. *Journal of Applied Psychology, 82*(1), 130–142.

59. Beshears, J., & Milkman, K. L. (2011). Do sell-side stock analysts exhibit escalation of commitment? *Journal of Economic Behavior & Organization, 77*(3), 304–317.

60. Wong, K. F. E., & Kwong, J. Y. Y. (2007). The role of anticipated regret in escalation of commitment. *Journal of Applied Psychology, 9*(2), 545–554.

61. Grant, A. (2013). How to escape from bad decisions. *Psychology Today*. Retrieved on October 25, 2013, from www.psychologytoday.com/blog/give-and-take/201307/how-to-escape-bad-decisions

62. Gino, F. (2013). *Sidetracked: Why our decisions get derailed, and how we can stick to the plan.* Boston, MA: Harvard University Press.

63. Cavanagh, G., Moberg, D., & Valasquez, M. (1981). The ethics of organizational politics. *Academy of Management Review, 6*(3), 363–374.

64. Fritzsche, D. J., & Becker, H. (1984). Linking management behavior to ethical philosophy: An empirical investigation. *Academy of Management Journal, 27*(1), 166–175.

65. Stead, W. E., Worrell, D. L., & Stead, J. G. (1990). An integrative model for understanding and managing ethical behavior in business organizations. *Journal of Business Ethics, 9*(3), 233–242.

66. Chugh, D., Bazerman, M. H., & Banaji, M. R. (2005). Bounded ethicality as a psychological barrier to recognizing conflicts of interest. In *National Science Foundation/Carnegie Bosch Institute Conference on Conflicts of Interest, Tepper School of Business*. Pittsburgh, PA: Carnegie Mellon University. Portions of this research were presented at the aforementioned conference. Cambridge: Cambridge University Press.

67. Shalvi, S., Dana, J., Handgraaf, M. J., & De Dreu, C. K. (2011). Justified ethicality: Observing desired counterfactuals modifies ethical perceptions and behavior. *Organizational Behavior and Human Decision Processes, 115*(2), 181–190.

68. Franken, R. E. (1994). *Human motivation* (3rd ed.). Belmont, CA: Brooks/Cole Publishing.

69. Kabanoff, B., & Rossiter, J. R. (1994). Recent developments in applied creativity. In C. L. Cooper & L. T. Robertson (Eds.), *International review of industrial and organizational psychology* (Vol. 9, pp. 283–324). New York, NY: John Wiley.

70. Amabile, T. M. (2012). Componential theory of creativity. Working Paper #12-096. Cambridge, MA: Harvard Business School. Retrieved from http://www.hbs.edu/faculty/Publication%20Files/12-096.pdf

71. Tierney, P., Farmer, S. M., & Graen, G. B. (1999). An examination of leadership and employee creativity: The relevance of traits and relationships. *Personnel Psychology, 52*(3), 591–620.

72. George, J. M., & Zhou, J. (2001). When openness to experience and conscientiousness are related to creative behavior: An interactional approach. *Journal of Applied Psychology, 86*(3), 513–524.

73. Kuncel, N. R., Hezlett, S. A., & Ones, D. S. (2004). Academic performance, career potential, creativity, and job performance: Can one construct predict them all? *Journal of Personality and Social Psychology, 86*(1), 148–161.

74. Csikszentmihalyi, M. (1975). *Beyond boredom and anxiety.* San Francisco, CA: Jossey-Bass.

75. Csikszentmihalyi, M., & LeFevre, J. (1989). Optimal experience in work and leisure. *Journal of Personality and Social Psychology, 56*(5), 815–822.

76. Ibid.

77. Amabile, T. M. (1998). How to kill creativity. *Harvard Business Review, 76*(5), 76–87.

78. Basadur, M. (2004). Leading others to think innovatively together: Creative leadership. *The Leadership Quarterly, 15*(1), 103–121.

79. Burkus, D. (2013). *The myths of creativity: The truth about how innovative companies and people generate great ideas.* San Francisco, CA: Jossey-Bass.

80. Amabile (1998).

81. Chiu, C.-Y., & Hong, Y. (2005). Cultural competence: Dynamic processes. In A. Elliot & C. S. Dweck (Eds.), *Handbook of motivation and competence* (pp. 489–505). New York, NY: Guilford Press.

82. Basadur (2004).

83. Basadur, M. S., Graen, G. B., & Green, S. G. (1982). Training in creative problem solving: Effects on ideation and problem finding in an applied research organization. *Organizational Behavior and Human Performance, 30*, 41–70.

84. Basadur, M. S., Runco, M. A., & Vega, L. A. (2000). Understanding how creative thinking skills, attitudes and behaviors work together: A causal process model. *Journal of Creative Behavior, 34*(2), 77–100.

85. Basadur, M. S. (1995). *The power of innovation.* London, UK: Pitman Professional.

86. Tierney, P., Farmer, S. M., & Graen, G. B. (1999). An examination of leadership and employee creativity: The relevance of traits and relationships. *Personnel Psychology, 52*(3), 591–620.

87. Ibid.

88. Volmer, J., Spurk, D., & Niessen, C. (2012). Leader–member exchange, job autonomy, and creative work involvement. *The Leadership Quarterly, 23*(3), 456–465.

89. Shalley, C. E., Zhou, J., & Oldham, G. R. (2004). The effects of personal and contextual characteristics on creativity: Where should we go from here? *Journal of Management, 30*(6), 933–958.

Chapter 7

1. Duckworth, A. L., Peterson, C., Matthews, M. D., & Kelly, D. R. (2007). Grit: Perseverance and passion for long-term goals. *Journal of Personality and Social Psychology, 92*(6), 1087–1101. p. 1087.

2. Packard, E. (2007). Grit: It's what separates the best from the merely good. *American Psychological Association: In Brief.* Retrieved from http://www.apa.org/monitor/nov07/grit.aspx

3. Judge, T. A., & Ilies, R. (2002). Relationship of personality to performance motivation: A meta-analytic review. *Journal of Applied Psychology, 87*(4), 797–807.

4. Steers, R., Mowday, R., & Shapiro, D. (2004). The future of work motivation theory. *Academy of Management Review, 29*(3), 379–387. p. 379.

5. Kanfer, R. (1990). Motivation theory and industrial and organizational psychology. In M. D. Dunnette (Ed.), *Handbook of industrial and organizational psychology* (Vol. 1, 2nd ed., pp. 75–170). Palo Alto, CA: Consulting Psychologists Press.

6. Maslow, A. (1954). *Motivation and personality.* New York, NY: Harper & Row.

7. Wahba, M. A., & Bridwell, L. G. (1976). Maslow reconsidered: A review of research on the need hierarchy theory. *Organizational Behavior and Human Performance, 15*(2), 212–240.

8. McClelland, D. C. (1961). *The achieving society.* New York, NY: Van Nostrand Reinhold.

9. Miner, J. B., Smith, N. R., & Bracker, J. S. (1994). Role of entrepreneurial task motivation in the growth of technologically innovative firms:

Interpretations from follow-up data. *Journal of Applied Psychology, 79*(4), 627–630.

10. Herzberg, F., Mausner, B., & Snyderman, B. (1959). *The motivation to work.* New York, NY: John Wiley.

11. House, R. J., & Wigdor, L. A. (1967). Herzberg's dual-factor theory of job satisfaction and motivations: A review of the evidence and criticism. *Personnel Psychology, 20*(4), 369–389.

12. Herzberg et al. (1959).

13. Locke, E. A. (1968). Toward a theory of task motivation and incentives. *Organizational Behavior and Human Performance, 3*(2), 157–189.

14. Locke, E. A., & Latham, G. P. (2002). Building a practically useful theory of goal setting and task motivation: A 35-year odyssey. *American Psychologist, 57*(9), 705–717.

15. Tubbs, M. E. (1986). Goal setting: A meta-analytic examination of the empirical evidence. *Journal of Applied Psychology, 71*(3), 474–483.

16. Carroll, S. J., & Tosi, H. L. (1973). *Management by objectives.* New York, NY: Macmillan.

17. Wofford, J. C., Goodwin, V. L., & Premack, S. (1992). Meta-analysis of the antecedents of personal goal level and of the antecedents and consequences of goal commitment. *Journal of Management, 18*(3), 595–615.

18. Latham, G. P., Erez, M., & Locke, E. A. (1988). Resolving scientific disputes by the joint design of crucial experiments by the antagonists: Application to the Erez–Latham dispute regarding participation in goal setting. *Journal of Applied Psychology, 73*(4), 753.

19. Shaw, K. N. (2004). Changing the goal-setting process at Microsoft. *Academy of Management Executive, 18*(4), 139–142.

20. Shaw (2004).

21. Tubbs (1986).

22. Ivancevich, J. M., & McMahon, J. T. (1982). The effects of goal setting, external feedback and self-generated feedback on outcomes variables: A field experiment. *Academy of Management Journal, 25*(2), 359–372.

23. Ordonez, L. D., Schweitzer, M. E., Galinsky, A. D., & Bazerman, M. (2009). Goals gone wild: The systemic side effects of overprescribing goal setting. *Academy of Management Perspectives, 23*(1), 6–16.

24. Locke, E. A., & Latham, G. P. (2009). Has goal setting gone wild, or have its attackers abandoned good scholarship? *Academy of Management Perspectives, 23*(1), 17–23.

25. Hackman, J. R., & Oldham, G. R. (1976). Motivation through the design of work: Test of a theory. *Organizational Behavior and Human Performance, 16*(2), 250–279.

26. Bond, F. W., Flaxman, P. E., & Bunce, D. (2008). The influence of psychological flexibility on work redesign: Mediated moderation of a work reorganization intervention. *Journal of Applied Psychology, 93*(3), 645.

27. Hackman, J. R., & Oldham, G. R. (1980). *Work redesign.* Reading, MA: Addison-Wesley.

28. Hackman, J. R., & Suttle, J. L. (Eds.). (1977). *Improving life at work.* Glenview, IL: Scott Foresman.

29. Erskine, L. & Howell, J. (2010). Spar Applied Systems: Anna's challenge. Ivey Management Services. In W. G. Rowe & L. Guerrero (Eds.), *Cases in leadership* (3rd ed.), Thousand Oaks, CA: Sage. (Original work published 1997)

30. Grant, A. M. (2007). Relational job design and the motivation to make a prosocial difference. *Academy of Management Review, 32*(2), 393–417.

31. Grant (2007, p. 65).

32. Grant, A. M. (2008). The significance of task significance: Job performance effects, relational mechanisms, and boundary conditions. *Journal of Applied Psychology, 93*(1), 108–124.

33. Grant, A. M., & Parker, S. K. (2009). Redesigning work design theories: The rise of relational and proactive perspectives. *Academy of Management Annals, 3*(1), 317–375.

34. Humphrey, S. E., Nahrgang, J. D., & Morgeson, F. P. (2007). Integrating motivational, social, and contextual work design features: A meta-analytic summary and theoretical extension of the work design literature. *Journal of Applied Psychology, 92*(5), 1332–1356.

35. Campion, M. A., & McClelland, C. L. (1993). Follow-up and extension of the interdisciplinary costs and benefits of enlarged jobs. *Journal of Applied Psychology, 78*(3), 339–351.

36. Fried, Y., & Ferris, G. R. (1987). The validity of the job characteristics model: A review and meta-analysis. *Personnel Psychology, 40*(2), 287–322.

37. Griffin, R. W. (1983). Objective and social sources of information in task redesign: A field experiment. *Administrative Science Quarterly, 28*(2), 184–200.

38. Orpen, C. (1979). The effects of job enrichment on employee satisfaction, motivation, involvement, and performance: A field experiment. *Human Relations, 32*(3), 189–217.

39. Pritchard, R. D. Harrell, M. M., Diaz-Grandos, D., & Guzman, M. J. (2008). The productivity measurement and enhancement system: A meta-analysis. *Journal of Applied Psychology, 93*(3), 540–567.

40. Subramony, M. (2009). A meta-analytic investigation of the relationship between HRM bundles and firm performance. *Human Resource Management, 48*(5), 745–768.

41. Wrzesniewski, A., & Dutton, J. E. (2001). Crafting a job: Revisioning employees as active crafters of their work. *Academy of Management Review, 26*, 179–201. p. 180.

42. Ibid.

43. Oldham, G. R., & Hackman, J. R. (2010). Not what it was and not what it will be: The future of job design research. *Journal of Organizational Behavior, 31*(2-3), 463–479. p. 470.

44. Lind, E. A., & Tyler, T. R. (1988). *The social psychology of procedural justice.* New York, NY: Springer.

45. Adams, J. S. (1965). Inequity in social exchange. In L. Berkowitz (Ed.), *Advances in experimental social psychology* (Vol. 2, pp. 267–299). New York, NY: Academic Press.

46. Ambrose, M. L., & Kulik, C. T. (1999). Old friends, new faces: Motivation in the 1990s. *Journal of Management, 25*, 231–292.

47. Greenberg, J. (1990). Employee theft as a reaction to underpayment inequity: The hidden cost of pay cuts. *Journal of Applied Psychology, 75*, 561–568.

48. Blakely, G. L., Andrews, M. C., & Moorman, R. H. (2005). The moderating effects of equity sensitivity on the relationship between organizational justice and organizational citizenship behaviors. *Journal of Business & Psychology, 20*(2), 259–273.

49. Moorman, R. H. (1991). Relationship between organizational justice and organizational citizenship behaviors: Do fairness perceptions influence employee citizenship? *Journal of Applied Psychology, 76*, 845–855.

50. Greenberg, J. (1987). A taxonomy of organizational justice theories. *Academy of Management Review, 12*(1), 9–22

51. Cropanzano, R., Bowen, D. E., & Gilliland, S. W. (2007). The management of organizational justice. *Academy of Management Perspectives*, 34–48. p. 34.

52. Bies, R. J. (1987). The predicament of injustice: The management of moral outrage. *Research in Organizational Behavior*, 9, 289–319.

53. Ambrose, M. L., Seabright, M. A., & Schminke, M. (2002). Sabotage in the workplace: The role of organizational justice. *Organizational Behavior and Human Decision Processes*, 89(1), 947–965.

54. Tyler, T. R., & Caine, A. (1981). The role of distributive and procedural fairness in the endorsement of formal leaders. *Journal of Personality and Social Psychology*, 41(4), 643–655.

55. Colquitt, J. A. (2001). On the dimensionality of organizational justice: A construct validation of a measure. *Journal of Applied Psychology*, 86(3), 386–400.

56. Adams (1965).

57. Leventhal, G. S. (1980). What should be done with equity theory? New approaches to the study of fairness in social relationships. In K. Gergen, M. Greenberg, & R. Willis (Eds.), *Social exchange: Advances in theory and research* (pp. 27–55). New York, NY: Plenum Press.

58. Thibaut, J., & Walker, L. (1975). *Procedural justice: A psychological analysis*. Hillsdale, NJ: Lawrence Erlbaum.

59. Colquitt (2001).

60. Cohen-Charash, Y., & Spector, P. (2001). The role of justice in organizations: A meta-analysis. *Organizational Behavior and Human Decision Processes*, 86(2), 278–321.

61. Huseman, R. C., Hatfield, J. D., & Miles, E. W. (1987). A new perspective on equity theory: The equity sensitivity construct. *Academy of Management Review*, 12(2), 222–234.

62. Miles, E. W., Hatfield, J. D., & Huseman, R. C. (1994). Equity sensitivity and outcome importance. *Journal of Organizational Behavior*, 15(7), 585–596.

63. Bing, M. N., & Burroughs, S. M. (2001). The predictive and interactive effects of equity sensitivity in teamwork-oriented organizations. *Journal of Organizational Behavior*, 22(3), 271–290.

64. Blakely et al. (2005).

65. Shore, T. H. (2004). Equity sensitivity theory: Do we all want more than we deserve? *Journal of Managerial Psychology*, 19(7), 722–772.

66. Bies, R. J., & Moag, J. S. (1986). Interactional justice: Communication criteria of fairness. *Research on negotiation in organizations*, 1(1), 43–55.

67. Colquitt (2001).

68. Bies & Moag (1986).

69. Bies, R. J., & Shapiro, D. L. (1988). Voice and justification: Their influence on procedural fairness judgments. *Academy of Management Journal*, 31(3), 676–685.

70. Scandura, T. A. (1999). Rethinking leader-member exchange: An organizational justice perspective. *The Leadership Quarterly*, 10(1), 25–40.

71. Erdogan, B., & Bauer, T. N. (2010). Differentiated leader-member exchanges: The buffering role of justice climate. *Journal of Applied Psychology*, 95(6), 1104–1120.

72. Li, N., Liang, J., & Crant, J. M. (2010). The role of proactive personality in job satisfaction and organizational citizenship behavior: A relational perspective. *Journal of Applied Psychology*, 95(2), 395–404.

73. Cooper, C. D., & Scandura, T. A. (2012). Was I unfair? Antecedents and consequences of managerial perspective taking in a predicament of injustice. In C. A. Schriesheim & L. L. Neider (Eds.), *Research in management: Perspectives on trust and justice* (Vol. 9). Greenwich, CT: Information Age Publishing.

74. Porter, L. W., & Lawler III, E. E. (1968). *Managerial attitudes and performance*. Homewood, IL: Irwin.

75. Ambrose, M. L., & Kulik, C. T. (1999). Old friends, new faces: Motivation in the 1990s. *Journal of Management*, 25(3), 231–292. p. 240.

76. Vroom, V. H. (1964). *Work and motivation*. New York, NY: John Wiley.

77. Dewhurst, M. (2009). Motivating people: Getting beyond money [Commentary.] *McKinsey Quarterly*. Retrieved on January 2, 2014, from http://www.mckinsey.com/insights/organization/motivating_people_getting_beyond_money

78. Ibid.

79. Mitchell, T. R. (1974). Expectancy models of job satisfaction, occupational preference and effort: A theoretical, methodological, and empirical appraisal. *Psychological Bulletin*, 81(12), 1053–1077.

80. Van Eerde, W., & Thierry, H. (1996). Vroom's expectancy models and work-related criteria: A meta-analysis. *Journal of Applied Psychology*, 81(5), 575–586.

81. Bandura, A. (1994). *Self-efficacy*. New York, NY: John Wiley.

82. Bono, J. E., & Judge, T. A. (2003). Self-concordance at work: Toward understanding the motivational effects of transformational leaders. *Academy of Management Journal*, 46(5), 554–571.

83. House, R. J. (1971). A path-goal theory of leadership effectiveness. *Administrative Science Quarterly*, 16(3), 321–328.

84. House, R. J., & Mitchell, T. R. (1974). Path-goal theory of leadership. *Journal of Contemporary Business*, 3(4), 81–97.

85. Wofford, J. C., & Liska, L. Z. (1993). Path-goal theories of leadership: A meta-analysis. *Journal of Management*, 19(4), 857–876.

86. Schriesheim, C. A., & Neider, L. L. (1996). Path-goal leadership theory: The long and winding road. *The Leadership Quarterly*, 7(3), 317–321.

Chapter 8

1. Kube, S., Maréchal, M. A., & Puppe, C. (2012). The currency of reciprocity: Gift-exchange in the workplace. *American Economic Review*, 102(4), 1644–1662.

2. Tang, T. L. P. (1992). The meaning of money revisited. *Journal of Organizational Behavior*, 13(2), 197–202.

3. Thorndike, E. L. (1911). *Animal intelligence*. New York, NY: Macmillan.

4. Skinner, B. F. (1971). *Contingencies of reinforcement*. East Norwalk, CT: Appleton-Century-Crofts.

5. Latham, G. P., & Huber, V. L. (1991). Schedules of reinforcement: Lessons from the past and issues for the future. *Journal of Organizational Behavior Management*, 12(1), 125–149.

6. Pinder, C. (2008). *Work motivation in organizational behavior*. New York, NY: Psychology Press.

7. Komacki, J. L., Coombs, T., & Schepman, S. (1996). Motivational implications of reinforcement theory. In R. M. Steers, L. W. Porter, & G. Bigley (Eds.), *Motivation and work behavior* (6th ed., pp. 87–107). New York, NY: McGraw-Hill.

8. Welsh, D. H. B., Luthans, F., & Sommer, S. M. (1993). Organizational behavior modification goes to Russia: Replicating an experimental analysis across cultures and tasks. *Journal of Organizational Behavior Management*, 13(2), 15–35.

9. Stajkovic, A. D., & Luthans, F. (1997). A meta-analysis of the effects of

organizational behavior modification on task performance, 1975–95. *Academy of Management Journal, 40*(5), 1122–1149.

10. Locke, E. A. (1980). Latham vs. Komaki: A tale of two paradigms. *Journal of Applied Psychology, 65*(1), 16–23.

11. Bandura, A. (1977). *Social learning theory.* Upper Saddle River, NJ: Prentice Hall.

12. Porter, L. W., & Lawler, E. E. III. (1968). *Managerial attitudes and performance.* Homewood, IL: Irwin-Dorsey.

13. Vroom, V. H. (1964). *Work and motivation.* New York, NY: John Wiley.

14. Porter & Lawler (1968).

15. Barbuto, Jr., J. E., & Scholl, R. W. (1998). Motivation sources inventory: Development and validation of new scales to measure an integrative taxonomy of motivation. *Psychological Reports, 82*(3), 1011–1022.

16. Ibid.

17. Deci, E. L. (1972). Intrinsic motivation, extrinsic reinforcement, and inequity. *Journal of Personality and Social Psychology, 22*(1), 113–120.

18. Deci, E. L., Connell, J. P., & Ryan, R. M. (1989). Self-determination in a work organization. *Journal of Applied Psychology, 74*(4), 580–590.

19. Deci, E. L., Koestner, R., & Ryan, R. M. (1999). A meta-analytic review of experiments examining the effects of extrinsic rewards on intrinsic motivation. *Psychological Bulletin, 125*(6), 627–668.

20. Deci, E. L., & Ryan, R. M. (1985). *Intrinsic motivation and self-determination in human behavior.* New York, NY: Plenum.

21. Koestner, R., Ryan, R. M., Bernieri, F., & Holt, K. (1984). Setting limits on children's behavior: The differential effects of controlling versus informational styles on intrinsic motivation and creativity. *Journal of Personality, 52*(3), 233–248.

22. Deci et al. (1989).

23. Amabile, T. M. (1993). Motivational synergy: Toward new conceptualizations of intrinsic and extrinsic motivation in the workplace. *Human Resource Management Review, 3*(3), 185–201.

24. Leong, K. C. (2013). Google reveals its 9 principles of innovation. *Fast Company: How to be a success at everything.* Retrieved on December 1, 2013, from http://www.fastcompany.com/3021956/how-to-be-a-success-at-everything/googles-nine-principles-of-innovation

25. Gilson, L. L., & Madjar, N. (2011). Radical and incremental creativity:

Antecedents and processes. *Psychology of Aesthetics, Creativity and the Arts, 5*, 21–28.

26. Aguinis, H., Joo, H., & Gottfredson, R. K. (2013). What monetary rewards can and cannot do: How to show employees the money. *Business Horizons, 56*(2), 241–259.

27. Brown, M. P., Sturman, M. C., & Simmering, M. J. (2003). Compensation policy and organizational performance: The efficiency, operational, and financial implications of pay levels and pay structure. *Academy of Management Journal, 46*(6), 752–762.

28. Kerr, S. (2009). *Reward systems: Does yours measure up?* Cambridge, MA: Harvard Business School Press.

29. Aguinis et al. (2013).

30. Ibid.

31. Rynes, S. L., Gerhart, B., & Park, L. (2005). Personnel psychology: Performance evaluation and pay for performance. *Annual Review of Psychology, 56*, 571–600.

32. Viwesvaran, C., & Ones, D. (2000). Perspectives on models of job performance. *International Journal of Selection and Assessment, 8*(4), 216–226. p. 224.

33. Cascio, W. F., & Aguinis, H. (2010). *Applied psychology in human resource management* (7th ed.). Upper Saddle River, NJ: Prentice Hall.

34. Heidemeier, H., & Moser, K. (2009). Self-other agreement in job performance ratings: A meta-analytic test of a process model. *Journal of Applied Psychology, 94*(2), 353–370.

35. Atwater, L. E., Brett, J. F., & Charles, A. C. (2007). Multisource feedback: Lessons learned and implications for practice. *Human Resource Management, 46*(2), 285–307.

36. Brett, J. F., & Atwater, L. E. (2001). 360° feedback: Accuracy, reactions, and perceptions of usefulness. *Journal of Applied Psychology, 86*(5), 930–942.

37. Fedor, D. B., Bettenhausen, K. L., & Davis, W. (1999). Peer reviews: Employees' dual roles as raters and recipients. *Group and Organization Management, 24*(1), 92–120.

38. Ng, K., Koh, C., Ang, S., Kennedy, J. C., & Chan, K. (2011). Rating leniency and halo in multisource feedback ratings: Testing cultural assumptions of power distance and individualism-collectivism. *Journal of Applied Psychology, 96*(5), 1033–1044.

39. Caruso, J. (2011). Case study: Starwood Hotels takes 360-degree feedback to a new level. Retrieved from http://web.viapeople.com/viaPeople-blog/bid/65018/Case-Study-Starwood-Hotels-Takes-360-Degree-Feedback-to-a-New-Level

40. Locher, A. H., & Teel, K. S. (1988, September). Appraisal trends. *Personnel Journal,* 139–145.

41. Kerr (2009).

42. McGregor, J. (2013). For whom the bell curve tolls. *The Washington Post.* Retrieved on November 20, 2013, from http://www.washingtonpost.com/blogs/on-leadership/wp/2013/11/20/for-whom-the-bell-curve=tolls

43. Mount, M. K., & Scullen, S. E. (2001). Multisource feedback ratings: What do they really measure? In M. London (Ed.), *How people evaluate others in organizations* (pp. 155–176). Mahwah, NJ: Lawrence Erlbaum.

44. Murphy, K. R., & Balzer, W. K. (1989). Rater errors and rating accuracy. *Journal of Applied Psychology, 74*(4), 619–624.

45. Ng et al. (2011).

46. Rynes et al. (2005).

47. Kerr (2009).

48. Ramirez, J. C. (2013). Rethinking the review: After 50 years of debate, has the time come to chuck the performance review? Retrieved on November 20, 2013, from www.hronline.com/HRE/view/story.jhtml?id=534355695&

49. McGregor (2013).

50. Ramirez (2013).

51. Morris, D. (2013). Forget reviews, let's look forward. Executive Perspectives. Retrieved on November 20, 2013, from http://blogs.adobe.com/conversations/tag/donna-morris

52. Bersin, J. (2013). Is it time to scrap performance appraisals? *Forbes.* Retrieved on December 2, 2013, from http://www.forbes.com/sites/joshbersin/2013/05/06/time-to-scrap-performance-appraisals

53. Boswell, W. R., & Boudreau, J. W. (2002). Separating the developmental and evaluative performance appraisal uses. *Journal of Business Psychology, 16*(3), 391–412.

54. Culbertson, S. S., Henning, J. B., & Payne, S. C. (2013). Performance appraisal satisfaction. *Journal of Personnel Psychology, 12*(4), 189–195.

55. Deming, W. E. (1986). *Out of the crisis.* Cambridge, MA: MIT Center for Advanced Engineering Study.

56. Pfeffer, J. (1998). Six dangerous myths about pay. *Harvard Business Review, 76*(3), 108–120.

57. Cable, D. M., & Judge T. A. (1994). Pay preferences and job search decisions: A person-organization fit perspective. *Personnel Psychology, 47*(2), 317–348.

58. Trevor, C. O., Gerhart B., & Boudreau, J. W. (1997). Voluntary turnover and job performance: Curvilinearity and the moderating influences of salary growth and promotions. *Journal of Applied Psychology, 82*(1), 44–61.

59. Rynes et al. (2005).

60. Ashford, S. J., & Cummings, L. L. (1983). Feedback as an individual resource: Personal strategies of creating information. *Organizational Behavior and Human Performance, 32*(3), 370–398.

61. Ashford, S. J., Blatt, R., & Vandewalle, D. (2003). Reflections on the looking glass: A review of research on feedback-seeking behavior in organizations. *Journal of Management, 29*(6), 773–779.

Chapter 9

1. Gostick, A., & Elton, C. (2010). *The orange revolution: How one great team can transform an entire organization.* New York, NY: Free Press.

2. Katzenbach, J. R., & Smith, D. K. (1993). *The wisdom of teams: Creating the high-performance organization.* New York, NY: Harper Business. p. 45.

3. Ibid.

4. Ibid.

5. Weldon, E., & Weingart, L. R. (1993). Group goals and group performance. *British Journal of Social Psychology, 32*(4), 307–334.

6. DeShon, R. P., Kozlowski, S. W., Schmidt, A. M., Milner, K. R., & Wiechmann, D. (2004). A multiple-goal, multilevel model of feedback effects on the regulation of individual and team performance. *Journal of Applied Psychology, 89*(6), 1035–1056.

7. Tuckman, B. (1965). Developmental sequence in small groups. *Psychological Bulletin, 63*, 384–399.

8. Tuckman, B., & Jensen, M. (1977). Stages of small group development. *Group and Organizational Studies, 2*, 419–427.

9. Gersick, C. J. G. (1988). Time and transition in work teams: Toward a new model of group development. *Academy of Management Journal, 31*(1), 9–41.

10. Seers, A., & Woodruff, S. (1997). Temporal pacing in task forces: Group development or deadline pressure? *Journal of Management, 23*(2), 169–187.

11. Katzenbach & Smith (1993).

12. McGrath, J. E. (1984). *Groups: Interaction and performance* (Vol. 14). Englewood Cliffs, NJ: Prentice Hall.

13. Barrick, M. R., Stewart, G. L., Neubert, M. J., & Mount, M. K. (1998). Relating member ability and personality to work-team processes and team effectiveness. *Journal of Applied Psychology, 83*(3), 377–391.

14. Edmondson, A. (1999). Psychological safety and learning behavior in work teams. *Administrative Science Quarterly, 44*(2), 350–383.

15. Marks, M. A., Sabella, M. J., Burke, C. S., & Zaccaro, S. J. (2002). The impact of cross-training on team effectiveness. *Journal of Applied Psychology, 87*(1), 3–13.

16. Hackman, J. R. (1987). The design of work teams. In J. W. Lorsch (Ed), *Handbook of organizational behavior* (pp. 315–342). Englewood Cliffs, NJ: Prentice Hall.

17. Cohen, S. G., & Bailey, D. E. (1997). What makes teams work: Group effectiveness research from the shop floor to the executive suite. *Journal of Management, 23*(3), 239–290.

18. LePine, J. A., Piccolo, R. F., Jackson, C. L., Mathieu, J. E., & Saul, J. R. (2008). A meta-analysis of teamwork processes: tests of a multidimensional model and relationships with team effectiveness criteria. *Personnel Psychology, 61*(2), 273–307.

19. Mathieu, J., Maynard, M. T., Rapp, T., & Gilson, L. (2008). Team effectiveness 1997–2007: A review of recent advancements and a glimpse into the future. *Journal of Management, 34*(3), 410–476.

20. Senge, P. M. (1990). *The fifth discipline: The art and practice of the learning organization.* New York, NY: Currency Doubleday.

21. Argote, L., Gruenfeld, D., & Naquin, C. (2001). Group learning in organizations. In M. E. Turner (Ed.), *Groups at work: Theory and research* (pp. 369–409). Mahwah, NJ: Lawrence Erlbaum.

22. Edmondson (1999).

23. Kostopoulos, K. C., Spanos, Y. E., & Prastacos, G. P. (2013). Structure and function of team learning emergence: A multilevel empirical validation. *Journal of Management, 39*(6), 1430–1461.

24. Kurtzberg, T. R., & Amabile, T. M. (2001). From Guilford to creative synergy: Opening the black box of team level creativity. *Creativity Research Journal, 13*(4), 285–294.

25. Gilson, L. L., & Shalley, C. E. (2004). A little creativity goes a long way: An examination of teams' engagement in creative processes. *Journal of Management, 30*(4), 453–470.

26. Gilson, L. L. (2001). *Diversity, dissimilarity and creativity: Does group composition or being different enhance or hinder creative performance.* Washington, DC: Academy of Management Meetings.

27. Gilson & Shalley (2004).

28. Cox, T., & Blake, S. (1991). Managing cultural diversity: Implications for organizational competitiveness. *Academy of Management Executive, 5*(3), 45–56.

29. Horwitz, S. K., & Horwitz, I. B. (2007). The effects of team diversity on team outcomes: A meta-analytic review of team demography. *Journal of Management, 33*(6), 987–1015.

30. Stahl, G. K., Maznevski, M. L., Voigt, A., & Jonsen, K. (2009). Unraveling the effects of cultural diversity in teams: A meta-analysis of research on multicultural work groups. *Journal of International Business Studies, 41*(4), 690–709.

31. Egan, T. M. (2005). Creativity in the context of team diversity: Team leader perspectives. *Advances in Developing Human Resources, 7*(2), 207–225.

32. Festinger, L. (1950). Informal social communication. *Psychological Review, 57*, 271–282. p. 274.

33. Evans, C. R., & Jarvis, P. A. (1980). Group cohesion: A review and re-evaluation. *Small Group Behavior, 11*, 359–370.

34. Cartwright, D. (1968). The nature of group cohesiveness. In D. Cartwright & A. Zander (Eds.), *Group dynamics: Research and theory* (3rd ed., pp. 91–109). New York, NY: Harper & Row.

35. Neal, D. J., Cohen, R. R., Burke, M. J., & McLendon, C. L. (2003). Cohesion and performance in groups: A metaanalytic clarification of construct relations. *Journal of Applied Psychology, 88*(6), 989–1004.

36. Gully, S. M., Devine, D. J., & Whitney, D. J. (1995). A meta-analysis of cohesion and performance: Effects of level of analysis and task interdependence. *Small Group Research, 26*(4), 497–520.

37. Evans, C. R., & Dion, K. L. (1991). Group cohesion and performance: A meta-analysis. *Small Group Research, 22*(2), 175–186.

38. Lee, C., & Fahr, J.-L. (2004). Joint effects of group efficacy and gender diversity on group cohesion and performance. *Applied Psychology: An International Review, 53*(1), 136–154.

39. Widmeyer, W. N., Carron, A. V., & Brawley, L. R. (1993). Group cohesion in sport and exercise. *Handbook of Research on Sport Psychology*, 672–692.

40. Jowett, S., & Chaundy, V. (2004). An investigation into the impact of coach leadership and coach-athlete relationship on group cohesion. *Group dynamics: Theory, research and practice, 8*(4), 302–331.

41. Turman, P. D. (2003). Coaches and cohesion: The impact of coaching techniques on team cohesion in the small group sport setting. *Journal of Sport Behavior, 26*(1), 86–104.

42. Hogg, M. A., & Reid, S. A. (2006). Social identity, self-categorization, and the communication of group norms. *Communication Theory, 16*(1), 7–30.

43. Mathieu, J. E., & Rapp, T. L. (2009). Laying the foundation for successful team performance trajectories: The roles of team charters and performance strategies. *Journal of Applied Psychology, 94*(1), 90–103.

44. Katzenbach & Smith (1993).

45. Mohammed, S., Ferzandi, L., & Hamilton, K. (2010). Metaphor no more: A 15-year review of the team mental model construct. *Journal of Management, 36*(4), 876–910.

46. Klimoski, R., & Mohammed, S. (1994). Team mental model: Construct or metaphor? *Journal of Management, 20*(2), 403–437.

47. Rouse, W. B., Cannon-Bowers, J. A., & Salas, E. (1992). The role of mental models in team performance in complex systems. *IEEE Transactions on Systems, Man, & Cybernetics, 22*, 1296–1308.

48. Mohammed et al. (2010).

49. DeChurch, L. A., & Mesmer-Magnus, J. R. (2010). The cognitive underpinnings of effective teamwork: A meta-analysis. *Journal of Applied Psychology, 95*(1), 32–53.

50. Vroom, V. H., & Yetton, P. W. (1973). *Leadership and decision making*. Pittsburgh, PA: University of Pittsburgh Press.

51. Vroom, V. H. (2003). Educating managers for decision making and leadership. *Management Decision, 41*(10), 968–978.

52. Scully, J. A., Kirkpatrick, S. A., & Locke, E. A. (1995). Locus of knowledge as a determinant of the effects of participation on performance, affect, and perceptions. *Organizational Behavior and Human Decision Processes, 61*(3), 276–288.

53. Vroom, V. H., & Jago, A. G. (1988). *The new leadership: Managing participation in organizations*. Englewood Cliffs, NJ: Prentice Hall.

54. Vroom (2003).

55. Miller, K. I., & Monge, P. R. (1986). Participation, satisfaction, and productivity: A meta-analytic review. *Academy of Management Journal, 29*(4), 727–753.

56. Wagner, J. A. (1994). Participation's effects on performance and satisfaction: A reconsideration of research evidence. *Academy of Management Review, 19*(2), 312–330.

57. Nutt, P. C. (2002). *Why decisions fail: Avoiding the blunders and traps that lead to debacles*. Williston, VT: Berrett-Koehler.

58. Osborn, A. F. (1979). *Applied imagination: Principles and procedures of creative thinking* (3rd ed.). New York, NY: Scribner's.

59. Bressen, T. (2012). Consensus decision-making: What, why, how. In J. Orsi & J. Kassan (Eds.), *Practicing law in the sharing economy: Helping people build cooperatives, social enterprise, and local sustainable economies*. Chicago, IL: ABA Books.

60. Tague, N. R. (2004). *The quality toolbox* (2nd ed.). Milwaukee, WI: ASQ Quality Press.

61. Faure, C. (2004). Beyond brainstorming: Effects of different group procedures on selection of ideas and satisfaction with the process. *The Journal of Creative Behavior, 38*(1), 13–34.

62. Delbecq, A. L., Van de Ven, A. H., & Gustafson, D. H. (1975). *Group techniques for program planning: A guide to nominal group and Delphi processes*. Glenview, IL: Scott, Foresman.

63. The stepladder technique: Making better group decisions. (n.d.). Retrieved from http://www.mindtools.com/pages/article/newTED_89.htm#sthash.c6PFOpJh.dpuf

64. Rogelberg, S. G., Barnes-Farrell, J. L., & Lowe, C. A. (1992). The stepladder technique: An alternative group structure facilitating effective group decision making. *Journal of Applied Psychology, 77*(5), 730–737.

65. Janis, I. L. (1972). *Victims of groupthink: A psychological study of foreign-policy decisions and fiascoes*. Boston, MA: Houghton-Mifflin.

66. Goncalo, J. A., Polman, E., & Maslach, C. (2010). Can confidence come too soon? Collective efficacy, conflict and group performance over time. *Organizational Behavior and Human Decision Processes, 113*(1), 13–24.

67. Janis (1972).

68. Esser, J. K. (1998). Alive and well after 25 years: A review of groupthink research. *Organizational Behavior and Human Decision Processes, 73*(2), 116–141.

69. Leana, C. R. (1985). A partial test of Janis' groupthink model: Effects of group cohesiveness and leader behavior on defective decision making. *Journal of Management, 11*(1), 5–18.

70. Moorhead, G., Ference, R., & Neck, C. P. (1991). Group decision fiascoes continue: Space shuttle *Challenger* and a revised groupthink framework. *Human Relations, 44*(6), 539–550.

71. Comer, D. R. (1995). A model of social loafing in real work groups. *Human Relations, 48*(6), 647–667.

72. Liden, R. C., Wayne, S. J., Jaworski, R. A., & Bennett, N. (2004). Social loafing: A field investigation. *Journal of Management, 30*(2), 285–304.

73. Karau, S. J., & Williams, K. D. (1993). Social loafing: A meta-analytic review and theoretical integration. *Journal of Personality and Social Psychology, 65*(4), 681.

74. Martins, L. L., Gilson, L. L., & Maynard, M. T. (2004). Virtual teams: What do we know and where do we go from here? *Journal of Management, 30*(6), 805–835. p. 807.

75. Maynard, M. T., & Gilson, L. L. (2014). The role of shared mental model development in understanding virtual team effectiveness. *Group & Organization Management, 39*(1), 3–32.

76. Hollingshead, A. B., McGrath, J. E., & O'Connor, K. M. (1993). Group task performance and communication technology a longitudinal study of computer-mediated versus face-to-face work groups. *Small Group Research, 24*(3), 307–333.

77. Hollingshead, A. B., & McGrath, J. E. (1995). Computer-assisted groups: A critical review of the empirical research. In R. A. Guzzo & E. Salas (Eds.), *Team effectiveness and decision making in organizations* (pp. 46–78). San Francisco, CA: Jossey-Bass.

78. Wilson, J. M., Straus, S. G., & McEvily, B. (2006). All in due time: The development of trust in computer-mediated and face-to-face teams. *Organizational Behavior and Human Decision Processes, 99*(1), 16–33.

79. Mesmer-Magnus, J. R., & DeChurch, L. A. (2009). Information sharing and team performance: A meta-analysis. *Journal of Applied Psychology, 94*(2), 535–546.

80. Griffith, T. L., Sawyer, J. E., & Neale, M. A. (2003). Virtualness and knowledge in teams: Managing the love triangle of organizations, individuals, and information technology. *MIS Quarterly, 27*(2), 265–287.

81. Carte, T. A., Chidambaram, L., & Becker, A. (2006). Emergent leadership in self-managed virtual teams. *Group Decision and Negotiation, 15*(4), 323–343.

82. Malhotra, A., Majchrzak, A., & Rosen, B. (2007). Leading virtual teams. *Academy of Management Perspectives, 21*(1), 60–70.

83. Avolio, B. J., Kahai, S., & Dodge, G. E. (2001). E-leadership: Implications for theory, research, and practice. *The Leadership Quarterly, 11*(4), 615–668.

84. Kirkman, B. L., & Shapiro, D. L. (2001). The impact of cultural values on job satisfaction and organizational commitment in self-managing work teams: The mediating role of employee resistance. *Academy of Management Journal, 44*(3), 557–569.

85. Elenkov, D. S. (1998). Can American management concepts work in Russia? *California Management Review, 40*(4), 133–156.

86. Nicholls, C. E., Lane, H. W., & Brechu, M. B. (1999). Taking self-managed teams to Mexico. *Academy of Management Executive, 13*(3), 15–25.

87. Kirkman, B. L., & Rosen, B. (1999). Beyond self-management: Antecedents and consequences of team empowerment. *Academy of Management Journal, 42*(1), 58–74.

88. Chen, G., Kirkman, B. L., Kanfer, R., Allen, D., & Rosen, B. (2007). A multilevel study of leadership, empowerment, and performance in teams. *Journal of Applied Psychology, 92*(2), 331–346.

89. Lorinkova, N. M., & Perry, S. J. (in press). When is empowerment effective? The role of leader-leader exchange in empowering leadership, cynicism, and time theft. *Journal of Management.* doi:0149206314560411

90. Burke, C. S., Stagl, K. C., Klein, C., Goodwin, G. F., Salas, E., & Halpin, S. M. (2006). What type of leadership behaviors are functional in teams? A meta-analysis. *Leadership Quarterly, 17*(3), 288–307.

91. Erez, A., Lepine, J. A., & Elms, H. (2002). Effects of rotated leadership and peer evaluation on the functioning and effectiveness of self-managed teams: A quasi-experiment. *Personnel Psychology, 55*(4), 929–948.

92. Cordery, J. L., Mueller, W. S., & Smith, L. M. (1991). Attitudinal and behavioral effects of autonomous group working: A longitudinal field study. *Academy of Management Journal, 34*(2), 464–476.

93. Druskat, V. U., & Wheeler, J. V. (2003). Managing from the boundary: The effective leadership of self-managing work teams. *Academy of Management Journal, 46*(4), 435–457.

94. Langfred, C. W. (2007). The downside of self-management: A longitudinal study of the effects of conflict on trust, autonomy, and task interdependence in self-managing teams. *Academy of Management Journal, 50*(4), 885–900.

95. DeVaro, J. (2008). The effects of self-managed and closely managed teams on labor productivity and product quality: An empirical analysis of a cross-section of establishments. *Industrial Relations: A Journal of Economy and Society, 47*(4), 659–697.

Chapter 10

1. Gavett, G. (2013). Research: What CEOs really want from coaching. Retrieved on December 23, 2013, from http://blogs .hbr.org/2013/08/research-ceos-and-the-coaching

2. Thomas, K. W. (1992). Conflict and negotiation processes in organizations. In M. D. Dunnette & L. M. Hough (Eds.), *Handbook of industrial and organizational psychology* (2nd ed., Vol. 3, pp. 651–717). Palo Alto, CA: Consulting Psychologists Press.

3. Dirks, K. T., & McLean Parks, J. (2003). Conflicting stories: The state of the science of conflict. In J. Greenberg (Ed.), *Organizational behavior: The state of the science* (2nd ed., pp. 283–324). Mahwah, NJ: Lawrence Erlbaum.

4. Maximum Advantage. (2013). Ten causes of interpersonal conflict. Retrieved on December 12, 2013, from http://www .maximumadvantage.com/ten-causes-of-conflict.html

5. Tjosvold, D. (2006). Defining conflict and making choices about its management: Lighting the dark side of organizational life. *International Journal of Conflict Resolution, 17*(2), 87–95.

6. Robbins, S. P. (1978). "Conflict management" and "conflict resolution are not synonymous terms. *California Management Review, 21*(2), 67–75.

7. Jehn, K. A., & Mannix, E. A. (2001). The dynamic nature of conflict: A longitudinal study of intragroup conflict and group performance. *Academy of Management Journal, 44*(2), 238–251.

8. Amason, A. C. (1996). Distinguishing the effects of functional and dysfunctional conflict on strategic decision making: Resolving a paradox for top management teams. *Academy of Management Journal, 39*(1), 123–148.

9. Schweiger, D. M., Sandberg, W. R., & Ragan, J. R. (1987). Group approaches for improving strategic decision making: A comparative analysis of dialectical inquiry, devil's advocacy, and consensus. *Academy of Management Journal, 29*(1), 51–71.

10. Jehn, K. A. (1995). A multimethod examination of the benefits and detriments of intragroup conflict. *Administrative Science Quarterly, 40*(2), 256–282.

11. Jehn, K. A. (1997). A qualitative analysis of conflict types and dimensions in organizational groups. *Administrative Science Quarterly, 42*(3), 530–557.

12. De Dreu, C. K. W., & Van de Vliert, E. (Eds.). (1997). *Using conflict in organizations.* Thousand Oaks, CA: Sage.

13. De Dreu, C. K. W., & Weingart, L. R. (2003). Task versus relationship conflict, team performance, and team member satisfaction: A meta-analysis. *Journal of Applied Psychology, 88*(4), 741–749.

14. Yang, J., & Mossholder, K. W. (2004). Decoupling task and relationship conflict: The role of intragroup emotional processing. *Journal of Organizational Behavior, 25*(5), 589–605.

15. Barling, J., Dupré, K. E., & Kelloway, E. K. (2009). Predicting workplace aggression and violence. *Annual Review of Psychology, 60*, 671–692.

16. U.S. Department of Labor. (2014). DOL Workplace Violence Program. Retrieved on September 2, 2014, from http:// www.dol.gov/oasam/hrc/policies/dol-workplace-violence-program.htm

17. Barling, J. (1996). The prediction, experience, and consequences of workplace violence. In G. R. VandenBos & E. Q. Bulatao (Eds.), *Violence on the job: Identifying risks and developing solutions*

(pp. 29–49). Washington, DC: American Psychological Association.

18. Springer J. (1998, March 7). Worker kills 4 at lottery headquarters. *Hartford Courant.* Retrieved from http://www.pulitzer.org/archives/6203

19. Barling, Dupré, & Kelloway (2009).

20. Andersson, L. M., & Pearson, C. M. (1999). Tit-for-tat? The spiraling effect of incivility in the workplace. *Academy of Management Review, 24*(3), 452–471. p. 457.

21. Pearson, C., Andersson, L., & Porath, C. (2000, Fall). Assessing and attacking workplace incivility. *Organizational Dynamics,* 123–137.

22. Johnson, P. R., & Indvik, J. (2001). Rudeness at work: Impulse over restraint. *Public Personnel Management, 30*(4), 457–465.

23. Graydon, J., Kasta, W., & Khan, P. (1994, November–December). Verbal and physical abuse of nurses. *Canadian Journal of Nursing Administration,* 70–89.

24. Andersson & Pearson (1999).

25. Lim, S., & Cortina, L. M. (2005). Interpersonal mistreatment in the workplace: the interface and impact of general incivility and sexual harassment. *Journal of Applied Psychology, 90*(3), 483–496.

26. Cortina, Johnson, & Indvik (2001).

27. Taylor, S. G., Bedeian, A. G., Cole, M. S., & Zhang, Z. (in press). Developing and testing a dynamic model of workplace incivility change. *Journal of Management.* doi:0149206314535432

28. Pearson, C. M., & Porath, C. L. (2005). On the nature, consequences and remedies of workplace incivility: No time for "nice"? Think again. *The Academy of Management Executive, 19*(1), 7–18.

29. Coutu, D. L. (2003, September). In praise of boundaries: A conversation with Miss Manners. *Harvard Business Review,* 41–45.

30. Kilmann, R. H., & Thomas, K. W. (1977). Developing a forced-choice measure of conflict-handling behavior: The "MODE" instrument. *Educational and Psychological Measurement, 37*(2), 309–325.

31. Thomas, K. W. (1992). Conflict and negotiation processes in organizations. In M. D. Dunnette & L. M. Hough (Eds.), *Handbook of industrial and organizational psychology* (2nd ed., Vol. 3, pp. 651–717). Palo Alto, CA: Consulting Psychologists Press.

32. Rahim, M. A. (1985). A strategy for managing conflict in complex organizations. *Human Relations, 38*(1), 81–89.

33. Rahim, A., & Magner, N. (1995). Confirmatory factor analysis of the styles of handling interpersonal conflict: first-order factor model and its invariance across groups. *Journal of Applied Psychology, 80*(1), 122–132.

34. Ibid.

35. Rahim, M. A. (2002). Toward a theory of managing organizational conflict. *International Journal of Conflict Resolution, 13*(3), 206–235.

36. Blake, R. R., & Mouton, J. S. (1964). *The managerial grid.* Houston, TX: Gulf Publishing.

37. Rahim, M. A., & Bonoma, R. V. (1979). Managing organizational conflict: A model for diagnosis and intervention. *Psychological Reports, 44,* 1323–1344.

38. Rahim (2002).

39. Hackman, J. R., & C. G. Morris. (1975). Group tasks, group interaction process, and group performance effectiveness: A review and proposed integration. In L. Berkowitz (Ed.), *Advances in experimental social psychology* (pp. 45–99). San Diego, CA: Academic Press.

40. Jehn (1995).

41. Jehn (1997).

42. Amason (1996).

43. Hollenbeck, J. R., Ilgen, D. R., Sego, D. J., Hedlund, J., Major, D. A., & Phillips, J. (1995). Multilevel theory of team decision making: Decision performance in teams incorporating distributed expertise. *Journal of Applied Psychology, 80*(2), 292–316.

44. Schwenk, C. (1990). Conflict in organizational decision making: An exploratory study. *Management Science, 36*(4), 436–449.

45. Behfar, K. J., Peterson, R. S., Mannix, E. A., & Trochim, W. M. K. (2008). The critical role of conflict resolution in teams: A close look at the links between conflict type, conflict management strategies, and team outcomes. *Journal of Applied Psychology, 93*(2), 170–188. p. 170.

46. De Wit, F. R. C., Greer, L. L., & Jehn, K. A. (2012). The paradox of intragroup conflict: A meta-analysis. *Journal of Applied Psychology, 97*(2), 360–390.

47. Shaw, J. D., Zhu, J., Duffy, M. K., Scott, K. L., Shih, H. A., & Susanto, E. (2011). A contingency model of conflict and team effectiveness. *Journal of Applied Psychology, 96*(2), 391–400.

48. Shaw et al. (2011, p. 398).

49. Nugent, P. S., & Broedling, L. A. (2002). Managing conflict: Third-party interventions for managers. *Academy of Management Executive, 16*(1), 139–154.

50. U.S. Office of Personnel Management. (2012). ADR methods and techniques. *Alternative dispute resolution: A resources guide* (pp. I-1 to I-6).

51. Gelfand, M. J., Higgins, M., Nishii, L. H., Raver, A., Dominguez, A., Murakami, F., . . . Toyama, M. (2002). Culture and egocentric perceptions of fairness in conflict and negotiation. *Journal of Applied Psychology, 87*(5), 833–845.

52. Morris, M. W., Williams, K. Y., Leung, K., Larrick, R., Mendoza, M. T., Bhatnagar, D., . . . Hu, J.-C. (1998). Conflict management style: Accounting for cross-national differences. *Journal of International Business Studies, 29*(4), 729–747.

53. Gabrielidis, C., Stephan, W. G., Ybarra, O., Dos Santos Pearson, V. M., & Villareal, L. (1997). Preferred styles of conflict resolution: Mexico and the U.S. *Journal of Cross-Cultural Psychology, 28*(6), 661–677.

54. Tjosvold, D., Hui, C., & Law, K. S. (2001). Constructive conflict in China: Cooperative conflict as a bridge between East and West. *Journal of World Business, 36*(2), 166–183.

55. Glenn, J., Witmeyer, D., & Stevenson, K. A. (1977). Cultural styles of persuasion. *Journal of Intercultural Relations, 1*(3), 52–66.

56. Tung, R. L. (1998). American expatriates abroad: From neophytes to cosmopolitans. *Journal of World Business, 33*(2), 125–144.

57. Hüffmeier, J., Freund, P. A., Zerres, A., Backhaus, K., & Hertel, G. (2011). Being tough or being nice? A meta-analysis on the impact of hard-softline strategies in distributive negotiations. *Journal of Management, 40*(3), 866–892.

58. Fisher, R., & Ury, W. (1981). *Getting to yes: Negotiating agreement without giving in.* Boston, MA: Houghton Mifflin.

59. Magee, J. C., Galinsky, A. D., & Gruenfeld, D. H. (2007). Power, propensity to negotiate, and moving first in competitive interactions. *Personality and Social Psychology Bulletin, 33*(2), 200–212.

60. Moore, D. A. (2004). Myopic prediction, self-destructive secrecy and the unexpected benefits of revealing final deadlines in negotiation. *Organizational Behavior and Human Decision Processes, 94*(2), 125–139.

61. Fisher & Ury (1981).

62. Curhan, J. R., Elfenbein, H. A., & Xu, H. (2006). What do people value when

they negotiate? Mapping the domain of subjective value in negotiation. *Journal of Personality and Social Psychology*, *91*(3), 493–512.

63. Naquin, C. E. (2003). The agony of opportunity in negotiation: Number of negotiable issues, counterfactual thinking, and feelings of satisfaction. *Organizational Behavior and Human Decision Processes*, *91*(1), 97–107.

64. Ten Velden, F. S., Beersma, B., & De Dreu, C. K. W. (2010). It takes two to tango: The effect of dyads' epistemic motivation composition in negotiation. *Personality and Social Psychology Bulletin*, *36*(11), 1454–1466.

65. De Dreu, C. K.W., Weingart, L. R., & Kwon, S. (2000). Influence of social motives on integrative negotiation: A meta-analytic review and test of two theories. *Journal of Personality and Social Psychology*, *78*(5), 889–905.

66. Thompson, L., & Leonardelli, G. J. (2004). The big bang: The evolution of negotiation research. *Academy o/ Management Executive*, *18*(3), 113–117.

67. Parker, S. K., & Axtell, C. M. (2001). Seeing another viewpoint: Antecedents and outcomes of employee perspective taking. *Academy of Management Journal*, *44*(6), 1085–1100.

68. Stork, E., & Hartley, N. T. (2011). Classroom incivilities: Students' perceptions about professors' behaviors. *Contemporary Issues in Education Research (CIER)*, *2*(4), 13–24.

Chapter 11

1. Ambady, N., & Rosenthal, R. (1993). Half a minute: Predicting teacher evaluations from thin slices of nonverbal behavior and physical attractiveness. *Journal of Personality and Social Psychology*, *64*(3), 431–441.

2. Ambady, N., & Rosenthal, R. (1992). Thin slices of expressive behavior as predictors of interpersonal consequences: A meta-analysis. *Psychological Bulletin*, *111*(2), 256–274.

3. Curhan, J. R., & Pentland, A. (2007). Thin slices of negotiation: predicting outcomes from conversational dynamics within the first 5 minutes. *Journal of Applied Psychology*, *92*(3), 802–811.

4. Richmond, V. P., McCroskey, J. C., & McCroskey, L. L. (2005). *Organizational communication for survival: Making work, work*. New York, NY: Allyn & Bacon. p. 20.

5. O'Reilly, C. A. (1980). Individuals and information overload in organizations: Is more necessarily better? *Academy of Management Journal*, *23*(4), 684–696.

6. Pincus, J. D. (1986). Communication satisfaction, job satisfaction, and job performance. *Human Communication Research*, *12*(3), 395–419.

7. Pincus, J. D., Knipp, J. E., & Rayfield, R. E. (1990). Internal communication and job satisfaction revisited: The impact of organizational trust and influence on commercial bank supervisors. *Journal of Public Relations Research*, *2*(1–4), 173–191.

8. Barnard, C. I. (1938). *The functions of the executive*. Cambridge, MA: Harvard University Press. p. 236.

9. Redding, W. C. (1985). Stumbling toward identity: The emergence of organizational communication as a field of study. In R. D. McPhee & P. K. Tompkins (Eds.), *Organizational communication: Traditional themes and new directions* (pp. 15–54). Beverly Hills, CA: Sage.

10. Blair, R., Roberts, K. H., & McKechnie, P. (1985). Vertical and network communication in organizations: The present and the future. *Organizational communication: Traditional themes and new directions* (pp. 55–77). Beverly Hills, CA: Sage. p. 55.

11. Weaver, W. (1949). Recent contributions to the mathematical theory of communication. *The Mathematical Theory of Communication*, *1*, 1–12.

12. Watson-Manheim, M. B., & Bélanger, F. (2007). Communication media repertoires: Dealing with the multiplicity of media choices. *MIS Quarterly*, *31*(2), 267–293.

13. Treviño, L. K., Webster, J., & Stein, E. W. (2000). Making connections: Complementary influences on communication media choices, attitudes, and use. *Organization Science*, *11*(2), 163–182.

14. McCroskey, J. C. (1977). Oral communication apprehension: A summary of recent theory and research. *Human Communication Research*, *4*(1), 78–96. p. 78.

15. Allen, M. T., & Bourhis, J. (1996). The relationship of communication apprehension to communication behavior: A meta-analysis. *Communication Quarterly*, *44*, 214–225.

16. Pate, L. E., & Merker, G. E. (1978). Communication apprehension: Implications for management and organizational behavior. *Journal of Management*, *4*(2), 107–119.

17. Blume, B. D., Baldwin, T. T., & Ryan, K. C. (2013). Communication Apprehension: A barrier to students' leadership, adaptability, and multicultural appreciation. *Academy of Management Learning & Education*, *12*(2), 158–172.

18. Lawry, J. (2012). What does scale mean in business? Retrieved on February 25, 2014, from http://joshlowryblog.com/2012/03/15/what-does-scale-mean-in-business

19. Rogers, C. R. (1980). *A way of being*. Boston, MA: Houghton Mifflin.

20. Weger, Jr., H., Castle Bell, G., Minei, E. M., & Robinson, M. C. (2014). The relative effectiveness of active listening in initial interactions. *International Journal of Listening*, *28*(1), 13–31.

21. Knippen, J. T., & Green, T. B. (1994). How the manager can use active listening. *Public Personnel Management*, *23*(2), 357–359.

22. Fleming, T. (2012). Why I'm a listener: Amgen CEO Kevin Sharer. Retrieved on April 7, 2014, from http://www.mckinsey.com/insights/leading_in_the_21st_century/why_im_a_listener_amgen_ceo_kevin_sharer

23. Brooks, B. (2003). The power of active listening. *American Salesman*, *48*(6), 12–14.

24. Van Riel, C. B. M. (1995). *Principles of corporate communication*. Upper Saddle River, NJ: Prentice Hall.

25. Burton, P. (2014). Mom: Flight attendant refused bathroom access, 3-year old forced to urinate in seat. Retrieved on September 5, 2014, from http://boston.cbslocal.com/2014/06/13/mom-flight-attendant-refused-bathroom-access-3-year-old-forced-to-urinate-in-seat

26. Frank, A., & Brownell, J. (1989), *Organizational communication and behavior: Communicating to improve performance*. Orlando, FL: Holt, Rinehart and Winston. pp. 5–6.

27. Dolphin, R. A. (2005). Internal communications: Today's strategic imperative. *Journal of Marketing Communications*, *11*(3), 171–190.

28. Miller, D. A., & Rose, P. B. (1994). Integrated communications: A look at

reality instead of theory. *Public Relations Quarterly, 39,* 13–16.

29. Anderson, J., & Level, D. A. (1980). The impact of certain types of downward communication on job performance. *Journal of Business Communication, 17*(4), 51–59.

30. Waldron, V. R. (1999). Communication practices of followers, members, and protégés: The case of upward influence tactics. *Communication Yearbook, 22,* 251–300.

31. Foste, E. A., & Botero, I. C. (2012). Personal reputation effects of upward communication on impressions about new employees. *Management Communication Quarterly, 26*(1), 48–73.

32. Jablin, F. M. (1979). Superior–subordinate communication: The state of the art. *Psychological Bulletin, 86*(6), 1201–1222.

33. Gaines, J. H. (1980). Upward communication in industry: An experiment. *Human Relations, 33*(12), 929–942.

34. Chow, C., Hwang, R., & Liao, W. (2000). Motivating truthful upward communication of private information: an experimental study of mechanisms from theory and practice. *Abacus, 36,* 160–179.

35. Tourish, D., & Robson, P. (2006). Sensemaking and the distortion of critical upward communication in organizations. *Journal of Management Studies, 43*(4), 711–730.

36. Read, W. (1962). Upward communication in industrial hierarchies. *Human Relations, 15,* 3–16.

37. Roberts, K. H., & O'Reilly, C. A. (1974). Failures in upward communication in organizations: Three possible culprits. *Academy of Management Journal, 17*(2), 205–215.

38. Tourish, D. (2005). Critical upward communication: Ten commandments for improving strategy and decision making. *Long Range Planning, 38*(5), 485–503. p. 488.

39. Crampton, S. M., Hodge, J. W., & Mishra, J. M. (1998). The informal communication network: Factors influencing grapevine activity. *Public Personnel Management, 27*(4), 569–584.

40. Ibid.

41. Baker, J. S., & Jones, M. A. (1996). The poison grapevine: How destructive are gossip and rumor in the workplace. *Human Resource Development Quarterly, 7*(1), 75–86.

42. DiFonzo, N., Bordia, P., & Rosnow, R. L. (1994). Reining in rumors. *Organizational Dynamics, 23*(1), 47–62. p. 47.

43. Zachary, M. K. (1996). The office grapevine: A legal noose. *Getting results... For the hands-on manager: Plant edition, 41*(8), 6–7.

44. Beersma, B., & Van Kleef, G. A. (2011). How the grapevine keeps you in line: Gossip increases contributions to the group. *Social Psychological and Personality Science, 2*(6), 642–649.

45. Van Hoye, G., & Lievens, F. (2009). Tapping the grapevine: A closer look at word-of-mouth as a recruitment source. *Journal of Applied Psychology, 94*(2), 341–352.

46. DiFonzo, N., & Bordia, P. (2002). Rumors and stable-cause attribution in prediction and behavior. *Organizational Behavior and Human Decision Processes, 88*(2), 785–800.

47. Bordia, P., Jones, E., Gallois, C., Callan, V. J., & DiFonzo, N. (2006). Management are aliens! Rumors and stress during organizational change. *Group & Organization Management, 31*(5), 601–621.

48. Nicoll, D. C. (1994). Acknowledge and use your grapevine. *Management Decision, 32*(6), 25–30.

49. Diesner, J., Frantz, T. L., & Carley, K. M. (2005). Communication networks from the Enron email corpus: "It's always about the people. Enron is no different." *Computational & Mathematical Organization Theory, 11*(3), 201–228. p. 201.

50. O'Connor, M. A. (2002). Enron board: The perils of Groupthink. *University of Cincinnati Law Review, 71,* 1233–1471. p. 1233.

51. Fragale, A. R., Sumanth, J. J., Tiedens, L. Z., & Northcraft, G. B. (2012). Appeasing equals: Lateral deference in organizational communication. *Administrative Science Quarterly, 57*(3), 373–406. p. 373.

52. Seeger, M. W., & Ulmer, R. R. (2003). Explaining Enron communication and responsible leadership. *Management Communication Quarterly, 17*(1), 58–84.

53. Hoffman, W. M., Hartman, L. P., & Rowe, M. (2003). You've got mail . . . and the boss knows: A survey by the Center for Business Ethics of companies' email and Internet monitoring. *Business and Society Review, 108*(3), 285–307.

54. Sproull, L., & Kiesler, S. (1986). Reducing social context cues: Electronic mail in organizational communication. *Management Science, 32*(11), 1492–1512.

55. Whitty, M. T., & Carr, A. N. (2006). New rules in the workplace: Applying object-relations theory to explain problem Internet and email behaviour in the workplace. *Computers in Human Behavior, 22*(2), 235–250.

56. Borstorff, P., Graham, G., & Marker, M. (2006). E-harassment: employee perceptions of E-technology as a source of harassment. *Journal of Applied Management and Entrepreneurship, 11*(3), 51–67.

57. Goldman, L. (2007). Netiquette rules—10 best rules for email etiquette. Retrieved on February 22, 2014, from http://ezinearticles.com/?Netiquette-Rules—10-Best-Rules-for-Email-Etiquette&id=785177

58. Mano, R. S., & Mesch, G. S. (2010). E-mail characteristics, work performance and distress. *Computers in Human Behavior, 26*(1), 61–69.

59. Jackson, J., Dawson, R., & Wilson, D. (2003a). Reducing the effect of e-mail interruptions on employees. *International Journal of Information Management, 23*(1), 55–65.

60. 3/M. (2003b). Understanding e-mail interaction increases organizational productivity. *Communications of the ACM, 48*(6), 80–84.

61. Szóstek, A. M. (2011). "Dealing with my emails": Latent user needs in email management. *Computers in Human Behavior, 27*(2), 723–729.

62. Phillips, J. G., & Reddie, L. (2007). Decisional style and self-reported email use in the workplace. *Computers in Human Behavior, 23*(5), 2414–2428.

63. Wajcman, J., & Rose, E. (2011). Constant connectivity: Rethinking interruptions at work. *Organization Studies, 32*(7), 941–961.

64. Byron, K. (2008). Carrying too heavy a load? The communication and miscommunication of emotion by Email. *Academy of Management Review, 33*(2), 309–327.

65. Cellular Telecommunications & Internet Association. (2014). Wireless quick facts. R on February 21, 2014, from http://www.ctia.org/your-wireless-life/how-wireless-works/wireless-quick-facts

66. Herbsleb, J. D., Atkins, D. L., Boyer, D. G., Handel, M., & Finholt, T. A. (2002). Introducing instant messaging and chat in the workplace. *Proceedings of the SIGCHI conference on Human factors in computing systems, 4*(1), 171–178.

67. Kim, S., & Niu, Q. (2014). Smartphone: It can do more than you think. Presented at the annual meeting of the Society for Industrial & Organizational Psychology, Honolulu, HI.

68. Middleton, C. A., & Cukier, W. (2006). Is mobile email functional or dysfunctional? Two perspectives on mobile email usage. *European Journal of Information Systems, 15*(3), 252–260. p. 252.

69. Crawford, K. (2005). Have a blog, lose your job? *CNN/Money*, 15.

70. Black, T. (2010). How to handle employee blogging. Retrieved on February 21, 2014, from http://www.inc.com/guides/2010/04/employee-blogging-policy.html

71. Van Grove, J. (2009). 40 of the best twitter brands and the people behind them. Retrieved on February 21, 2014, from http://mashable.com/2009/01/21/best-twitter-brands

72. Johnson, P. R., & Indvik, J. (2004). The organizational benefits of reducing cyberslacking in the workplace. *Journal of Organizational Culture, Communications, and Conflict, 8*(2), 55–62. p. 56.

73. Greenfield, D. & Davis, R. (2002). Lost in cyberspace: the Web @work. *CyberPsychology & Behavior, 5*(4), 347–353.

74. Lohr, S. (2008). As travel costs rise, more meetings go virtual. *New York Times.* Retrieved on February 21, 2014, from http://www.nytimes.com/2008/07/22/technology/22meet.html?_r=0&pagewanted=print

75. Ibid.

76. Burgess, C., & Burgess, M. (2014). *The social employee: Success lessons from IBM, AT&T, Dell and Cisco on building a social culture.* New York, NY: McGraw-Hill.

77. Macnamara, J. R. (2004). The crucial role of research in multicultural and cross-cultural communication. *Journal of Communication Management, 8*(3), 322–334.

78. Levine, T. R., Park, H. S., & Kim, R. K. (2007). Some conceptual and theoretical challenges for cross-cultural communication research in the 21st century. *Journal of Intercultural Communication Research, 36*(3), 205–221.

79. Matveev, A. V., & Nelson, P. E. (2004). Cross cultural communication competence and multicultural team performance perceptions of American and Russian managers. *International Journal of Cross Cultural Management, 4*(2), 253–270.

80. Spencer-Oatey, H., & Xing, J. (2003). Managing rapport in intercultural business interactions: A comparison of two Chinese-British welcome meetings. *Journal of Intercultural Studies, 24*(1), 33–46.

81. Lohr, S. (2008). As travel costs rise, more meetings go virtual. *New York Times.* Retrieved on February 21, 2014, from http://www.nytimes.com/2008/07/22/technology/22meet.html?_r=0&pagewanted=print

82. Burgess & Burgess (2014).

83. Levine, T. R., Park, H. S., & Kim, R. K. (2007). Some conceptual and theoretical challenges for cross-cultural communication research in the 21st century. *Journal of Intercultural Communication Research, 36*(3), 205–221.

84. Gudykunst, W. B., Matsumoto, Y., Ting-Toomey, S., Nishida, T., Kim, K., & Heyman, S. (1996). The influence of cultural individualism-collectivism, self construals, and individual values on communication styles across cultures. *Human Communication Research, 22*(4), 510–543.

85. Zhang, T., & Zhou, H. (2008). The significance of cross-cultural communication in international business negotiation. *International Journal of Business and Management, 3*(2), 103–109.

86. Tannen, D. T. (1984). The pragmatics of cross-cultural communication. *Applied Linguistics, 5*(3), 189–195.

87. Washington, M. C., Okoro, E. A., & Okoro, S. U. (2013). Emotional intelligence and cross-cultural communication competence: An analysis of group dynamics and interpersonal relationships in a diverse classroom. *Journal of International Education Research, 9*(3), 241–246.

88. Huang, L. (2010). Cross-cultural communication in business negotiations. *International Journal of Economics & Finance, 2*(2), 196–199.

89. Littrell, L. N., & Salas, E. (2005). A review of cross-cultural training: Best practices, guidelines, and research needs. *Human Resource Development Review, 4*(3), 305–334.

90. Nixon, J. C., & Dawson, G. A. (2002). Reason for cross-cultural communication training. *Corporate Communications: An International Journal, 7*(3), 184–191.

91. Sussman, N., & Rosenfeld, H. (1982). Influence of culture, language and sex on conversational distance. *Journal of Personality and Social Psychology, 42*(1), 67–74.

92. Tannen, D. (1990). *You just don't understand: Women and men in conversation.* New York, NY: William Morrow.

93. Tannen (1994).

94. Mehrabian, A. (1981). *Silent messages* (2nd ed.). Belmont, CA: Wadsworth.

95. Ambler, G. (2013). When it comes to leadership everything communicates. Retrieved on March 1, 2014, from http://www.georgeambler.com/when-it-comes-to-leadership-everything-communicates

96. Gentry, W. A., & Kuhnert, K. W. (2007). Sending signals: Nonverbal communication can speak volumes. *Leadership in Action, 27*(5), 3–7. p. 4.

97. Tangirala, S., & Ramanujam, R. (2008). Employee silence on critical work issues: The cross level effects of procedural justice climate. *Personnel Psychology, 61*(1), 37–68.

98. Park, C., & Keil, M. (2009). Organizational silence and whistle-blowing on IT projects: An integrated model. *Decision Sciences, 40*(4), 901–918.

99. Brinsfield, C. T. (2013). Employee silence motives: investigation of dimensionality and development of measures. *Journal of Organizational Behavior, 34*(5), 671–697.

100. Morrison, E. W., & Milliken, F. J. (2000). Organizational silence: A barrier to change and development in a pluralistic world. *Academy of Management Review, 25*(4), 706–725.

101. Bies, R. J., & Tripp, T. M. (1999). Two faces of the powerless: Coping with tyranny. In R. M. Kramer & M. A. Neale (Eds.), *Power and influence in organizations* (pp. 203–219). Thousand Oaks, CA: Sage.

102. De Maria, W. (2006). Brother secret, sister silence: Sibling conspiracies against managerial integrity. *Journal of Business Ethics, 65*(3), 219–234.

103. Nikolaou, I., Vakola, M., & Bourantas, D. (2011). The role of silence on

employees' attitudes "the day after" a merger. *Personnel Review, 40*(6), 723–741.

104. Huang, X., Vliert, E. V. D., & Vegt, G. V. D. (2005). Breaking the silence culture: Stimulation of participation and employee opinion withholding cross-nationally. *Management and Organization Review, 1*(3), 459–482.

105. Van Dyne, L. V., Ang, S., & Botero, I. C. (2003). Conceptualizing employee silence and employee voice as multidimensional constructs. *Journal of Management Studies, 40*(6), 1359–1392.

106. Karaca, H. (2013). An exploratory study on the impact of organizational silence in hierarchical organizations: Turkish national police case. *European Scientific Journal, 9*(23), 38–50.

107. Zehir, C., & Erdogan, E. (2011). The association between organizational silence and ethical leadership through employee performance. *Procedia-Social and Behavioral Sciences, 24*, 1389–1404.

108. Tannen, D. (1995). The power of talk: Who gets heard and why. *Harvard Business Review, 73*(5), 138–148. p. 148.

109. Smircich, L., & Morgan, G. (1982). Leadership: The management of meaning. *Journal of Applied Behavioral Science, 18*(3), 257–273.

110. Fairhurst, G. T. (2010). *The power of framing: Creating the language of leadership.* New York, NY: John Wiley.

111. 3/M. (1993). Echoes of the vision when the rest of the organization talks total quality. *Management Communication Quarterly, 6*(4), 331–371.

112. Richmond, V. P., & McCroskey, J. C. (2000). The impact of supervisor and subordinate immediacy on relational and organizational outcomes. *Communications Monographs, 67*(1), 85–95.

113. Mueller, B. H., & Lee, J. (2002). Leader-member exchange and organizational communication satisfaction in multiple contexts. *Journal of Business Communication, 39*(2), 220–244. p. 235.

Chapter 12

1. Deloitte Consulting. (2013). Resetting horizons: Human capital trends report. Retrieved on August 1, 2013, from http://www.deloitte.com/view/en_US/us/Services/consulting/human-capital/human-capital-trends/index.htm p. 3.

2. Brannen, M. Y., & Peterson, M. F. (2009). Merging without alienating: Interventions promoting cross-cultural organizational integration and their limitations. *Journal of International Business Studies, 40*(3), 468–489. p. 468.

3. Friedman, T. L. (2006). *The world is flat: A brief history of the twenty-first century.* New York, NY: Macmillan.

4. Adler, N. J. (1997). *International dimensions of organizational behavior* (3rd ed.). Cincinnati, OH: South-Western. p. 19.

5. Gelfand, M. J., Erez, M., & Aycan, Z. (2007). Cross-cultural organizational behavior. *Annual Review of Psychology, 58*, 479–514.

6. Hall, E. T. (1977). *Beyond culture.* New York, NY: Random House.

7. Hall, E. T. (2000). Context and meaning. *Intercultural communication: A Reader, 9*, 34–43.

8. Hall, E. T., & Hall, M. R. (1990). *Understanding cultural differences.* Boston: MA: Intercultural Press.

9. Würtz, E. (2005). A cross-cultural analysis of websites from high-context cultures and low-context cultures. *Journal of Computer-Mediated Communication, 11*(1), article 13. Retrieved from http://jcmc.indiana.edu/vol11/issue1/wuertz.html

10. Hofstede, G. (1980). *Culture's consequences: International differences in work-related values.* Beverly Hills, CA: Sage. p. 25.

11. Hofstede, G., & Bond, M. H. (1988). The Confucius connection: From cultural roots to economic growth. *Organizational Dynamics, 16*(4), 5–21.

12. Ibid.

13. Hofstede (1980).

14. 3/M. (1991). *Culture's consequences: International differences in work-related values* (2nd ed.). Newbury Park, CA: Sage.

15. 3/M (1980).

16. Gelfand et al. (2007).

17. Oyserman, D., Coon, H. M., & Kemmelmeier, M. (2002). Rethinking individualism and collectivism: Evaluation of theoretical assumptions and meta-analyses. *Psychological Bulletin, 128*(1), 3–72.

18. Markus, H. R., & Kitayama, S. (1991). Culture and the self: Implications for cognition, emotion, and motivation. *Psychological Review, 98*(2), 224–253.

19. Triandis, H. C. (1995). *Individualism and collectivism.* Boulder, CO: Westview Press.

20. Eby, L. T., & Dobbins, G. H. (1997). Collectivistic orientation in teams: an individual and group-level analysis. *Journal of Organizational Behavior, 18*(3), 275–295.

21. Erez, M., & Somech, A. (1996). Is group productivity loss the rule or the exception? Effects of culture and group-based motivation. *Academy of Management Journal, 39*(6), 1513–1537.

22. Gibson, C. B. (1999). Do they do what they believe they can? Group efficacy and group effectiveness across tasks and cultures. *Academy of Management Journal, 42*(2), 138–152.

23. Triandis, H. C., & Gelfand, M. J. (1998). Converging measurement of horizontal and vertical individualism and collectivism. *Journal of Personality and Social Psychology, 74*(1), 118–128.

24. Marcus, J., & Le, H. (2013). Interactive effects of levels of individualism-collectivism on cooperation: A meta-analysis. *Journal of Organizational Behavior, 34*(6), 813–834.

25. Chen, Y., Friedman, R., Yu, E., Fang, W., & Lu, X. (2009). Supervisor–subordinate guanxi: Developing a three dimensional model and scale. *Management and Organization Review, 5*(3), 375–399.

26. Fischer, R., & Mansell, A. (2009). Commitment across cultures: A meta-analytical approach. *Journal of International Business Studies, 40*(8), 1339–1358.

27. Michael, J. (1997). A conceptual framework for aligning managerial behaviors with cultural work values. *International Journal of Commerce and Management, 7*(3), 81–101.

28. Smith, P. (1998). *The new American cultural sociology.* New York, NY: Cambridge University Press.

29. Jones, M. (2007, June 24–26). Hofstede—Culturally questionable? Presented at the *Oxford Business & Economics Conference,* Oxford, UK.

30. Dorfman, P. W., & Howell, J. P. (1988). Dimensions of national culture and effective leadership patterns: Hofstede revisited. *Advances in International Comparative Management, 3*, 127–150.

31. Taras, V., Kirkman, B. L., & Steel, P. (2010). Examining the impact of culture's consequences: A three-decade, multilevel, meta-analytic review of Hofstede's cultural value dimensions. *Journal of Applied Psychology, 95*(3), 405–439.

32. Javidan, M., Dorfman, P. W., Sully de Luque, M., & House, R. J. (2006). In the eye of the beholder: Leadership lessons from project GLOBE. *Academy of Management Perspectives, 20*(1), 67–90.

33. Gelfand, M. J., Nishii, L. H., & Raver, J. L. (2006). On the nature and importance of cultural tightness-looseness. *Journal of Applied Psychology, 91*(6), 1225–1244.

34. Gelfand, M. J., Raver, J. L., Nishii, L., Leslie, L. M., Lun, J., Lim, B. C., . . . &

Yamaguchi, S. (2011). Differences between tight and loose cultures: A 33-nation study. *Science, 332*, 1100–1104.

35. Ibid. p. 1104.

36. Hollenbeck, G. P., & McCall, M. W. (2003). Competence, not competencies: Making global executive development work. In W. Mobley & P. Dorfman (Eds.), *Advances in global leadership* (Vol. 3). Oxford, UK: JAI Press.

37. Gregersen, H. B., Morrison, A., & Black, J. S. (1998). Developing leaders for the global frontier. *Sloan Management Review, 40*, 21–32.

38. Stahl, G., & Brannen, M. Y. (2013). Building cross-cultural leadership competence: An interview with Carlos Ghosn. *Academy of Management Learning & Education, 12*(3), 494–502. p. 495.

39. Smith, A., Caver, K., Saslow, S., & Thomas, N. (2009). *Developing the global executive: Challenges and opportunities in a changing world*. Pittsburgh, PA: Development Dimensions International, Inc.

40. Beechler, S., & Javidan, M. (2007). Leading with a global mindset. In M. Javidan, R. M. Steers, & M. A. Hitt (Eds.), *The global mindset (advances in international management)* (Vol. 19, pp. 131–169). New York, NY: Emerald Group Publishing.

41. Casrnir, F. L. (1999). Foundations for the study of intercultural communication based on a third-culture building model. *International Journal of Intercultural Relations, 23*(1), 91–116. p. 92.

42. Earley, P. C., & Mossakowski, E. (2004, October). Cultural intelligence. *Harvard Business Review*, 139–146.

43. Earley, P. C., & Ang, S. A. (2003). *Cultural intelligence: Individual interactions across cultures*. Stanford, CA: Stanford University Press.

44. Earley & Mossakowski (2004).

45. Ang, S., Van Dyne, L., Kohl, C., Ng, K. Y., Templer, K. J., Tayl, C., & Chandrasekar, N. A. (2007). Cultural intelligence: Its measurement and effects on cultural judgment and decision making, cultural adaptation and task performance. *Management and Organization Review, 3*(3), 335–371.

46. Eisenberg, J., Lee, H., Bruck, F., Brenner, B., Claes, M., Mironski, J., & Bell, R. (2013). Can business schools make students culturally competent? Effects of cross-cultural management courses on cultural intelligence. *Academy of Management Learning & Education, 12*(4), 603–621.

47. Earley, P. C., & Peterson, R. S. (2004). The elusive cultural chameleon: Cultural intelligence as a new approach to training for the global manager. *Academy of Management Learning & Education, 3*(1), 100–115.

48. Berry, J. W. (1980). Acculturation as varieties of adaptation. In A.M. Padilla (Ed.), *Acculturation theory, models and some new findings* (pp. 9–25). Boulder, CO: Westview.

49. Bourhis, R. Y., Moise, L. C., Perreault, S., & Senecal, S. (1997). Towards an interactive acculturation model: A social psychological approach. *International Journal of Psychology, 32*(6), 369–386.

50. Thomas, D. C., Brannen, M. Y., & Garcia, D. (2010). Bicultural individuals and intercultural effectiveness. *European Journal of Cross-Cultural Competence and Management, 1*, 315–333. p. 315.

51. Ibid.

52. Tadmor, C. T., & Tetlock, P. E. (2006). Biculturalism: A model of the effects of second-culture exposure on acculturation and integrative complexity. *Journal of Cross-Cultural Psychology, 37*(2), 173–190. p. 174.

53. Tadmor, C. T., Tetlock, P. E., & Peng, K. (2009). Acculturation strategies and integrative complexity the cognitive implications of biculturalism. *Journal of Cross-Cultural Psychology, 40*(1), 105–139.

54. Oberg, K. (1960). Culture shock adjustment to new cultural environments. *Practical Anthropology, 7*, 177–182.

55. Young, R. (2011). Cross-cultural skills: Essential for expatriate success. *The Chronicle of Higher Education*. Retrieved on July 30, 2013, from http://chronical.com/article/Cross-Cultural-Skills/128782/)

56. Molinsky, A. (2013). The psychological processes of cultural retooling. *Academy of Management Journal, 56*(3), 683–710.

57. Adler, N. J. (1981). Re-entry: Managing cross-cultural transitions. *Group & Organization Studies, 6*(3), 341–356.

58. Dolins, I. L. (1999). 1998 global relocation survey: Current trends regarding expatriate activity. *Employment Relations Today, 25*(4), 1–11.

59. Gaw, K. F. (2000). Reverse culture shock in students returning from overseas. *International Journal of Intercultural Relations, 24*(1), 83–104.

60. Hsiaoying, T. (1995). Sojourner adjustment: The case of foreigners in Japan. *Journal of Cross-Cultural Psychology, 26*(5), 523–536.

61. Feldman, D. C., & Tompson, H. B. (1992). Entry shock, culture shock:

Socializing the new breed of global managers. *Human Resource Management, 31*(4), 345–362.

62. Archer, C. M. (1986). Culture bump and beyond. In J. M. Valdes (Ed.), *Culture bound: Bridging the cultural gap in language teaching*. Cambridge, UK: Cambridge University Press.

63. Black, J. S., & Gregersen, H. B. (1992). When Yankee comes home: Factors related to expatriate and spouse repatriation adjustment. *Journal of International Business Studies, 22*(4), 671–695.

64. Black, J. S., Gregersen, H. B., & Mendenhall, M. E. (1992). *Global assignments: Successfully expatriating and repatriating international managers*. San Francisco, CA: Jossey-Bass.

65. Gregersen, H. B., & Black, J. S. (1990). A multifaceted approach to expatriate retention in international assignments. *Group & Organization Management, 15*(4), 461–485.

66. Black, J. S., & Stephens, G. K. (1989). The influence of the spouses on American expatriate adjustment in overseas assignments. *Journal of Management, 15*(4), 529–544.

67. Adler, N. J. (2008). *International dimensions of organizational behavior* (5th ed.). Mason, OH: Thomson.

68. Gregersen, H. B., & Black, J. S. (1992). Antecedents to commitment to a parent company and a foreign operation. *Academy of Management Journal, 35*(1), 65–90.

69. Javidan et al. (2006).

70. Conner, J. (2000, Summer–Fall). Developing the global leaders of tomorrow. *Human Resource Management, 39*(2&3), 146–157.

71. Black, J. S., Gregersen, H. B., Mendenhall, M., & Stroh, L. K. (1999). *Globalizing people through international assignments*. New York, NY: Addison-Wesley. p. 1.

72. Kraimer, M. L., Wayne, S. J., & Jaworski, R. A. (2001). Sources of support and expatriate performance: The mediating role of expatriate adjustment. *Personnel Psychology, 54*(1), 71–99.

73. Shaffer, M. A., & Harrison, D. A. (1998). Expatriates' psychological withdrawal from international assignments: Work, nonwork, and family influences. *Personnel Psychology, 51*(1), 87–118.

74. Harzing, A. W. K. (1995). The persistent myth of high expatriate failure rates. *International Journal of Human Resource Management, 6*(2), 457–474.

75. Forster, N. (1997). The persistent myth of high expatriate failure rates: A

reappraisal. *International Journal of Human Resource Management, 8*(4), 414–433.

76. Daniels, J. D., & Insch, G. (1998). Why are early departure rates from foreign assignments lower than historically reported? *Multinational Business Review, 6*(1), 13–23.

77. Right Management. (2013). Many managers found to fail in overseas assignments. Retrieved on September 10, 2013, from www.right.com/news-and-events/press-releases/2013-press-releases/item25142.aspx

78. Torbiörn, I. (1994). Operative and strategic use of expatriates in new organizations and market structures. *International Studies of Management & Organization, 24*(3), 5–17.

79. Shannonhouse, R. (1996). Overseas-assignment failures. *USA Today/International Edition*, p. 8.

80. Harrison, J. (1994). Developing successful expatriate managers: A framework for the structural design and strategic alignment of cross-cultural training programs. *Human Resource Planning, 17*, 17–35.

81. Kotabe, M., & Helsen, K. (1998). *Global marketing management* (2nd ed.). New York, NY: John Wiley.

82. Forster (1997).

83. Kraimer et al. (2001).

84. Van Vianen, A. E., De Pater, I. E., Kristof-Brown, A. L., & Johnson, E. C. (2004). Fitting in: Surface-and deep-level cultural differences and expatriates' adjustment. *Academy of Management Journal, 47*(5), 697–709.

85. Santana, L. (2010). Five ways to boost your cross-cultural agility. *Forbes*. Retrieved on August 1, 2013, from www.forbes.com/2010/09/29/cross-cultural-agility-globalization-leadership-managing-ccl.html

86. Gregersen & Black (1990).

87. Feldman, D. C., & Thomas, D. C. (1992). Career issues facing expatriate managers. *Journal of International Business Studies, 23*(2), 271–294.

88. Mezias, J. M., & Scandura, T. A. (2005). A needs-driven approach to expatriate adjustment and career development: A multiple mentoring perspective. *Journal of International Business Studies, 36*(5), 519–538.

89. Black, J. S., & Mendenhall, M. (1990). Cross-cultural training effectiveness: A review and theoretical framework for future research. *Academy of Management Review, 15*(1), 113–136.

Chapter 13

1. Gostick, A., & Elton, C. (2010). *The orange revolution: How one great team can transform an entire organization*. New York, NY: Free Press.

2. Katzenbach, J. R., & Smith, D. K. (1993). *The wisdom of teams: Creating the high-performance organization*. New York, NY: Harper Business. p. 45.

3. Ibid.

4. Ibid.

5. Weldon, E., & Weingart, L. R. (1993). Group goals and group performance. *British Journal of Social Psychology, 32*(4), 307–334.

6. DeShon, R. P., Kozlowski, S. W., Schmidt, A. M., Milner, K. R., & Wiechmann, D. (2004). A multiple-goal, multilevel model of feedback effects on the regulation of individual and team performance. *Journal of Applied Psychology, 89*(6), 1035–1056.

7. Tuckman, B. (1965). Developmental sequence in small groups. *Psychological Bulletin, 63*, 384–399.

8. Tuckman, B., & Jensen, M. (1977). Stages of small group development. *Group and Organizational Studies, 2*, 419–427.

9. Gersick, C. J. G. (1988). Time and transition in work teams: Toward a new model of group development. *Academy of Management Journal, 31*(1), 9–41.

10. Seers, A., & Woodruff, S. (1997). Temporal pacing in task forces: Group development or deadline pressure? *Journal of Management, 23*(2), 169–187.

11. Katzenbach & Smith (1993).

12. McGrath, J. E. (1984). *Groups: Interaction and performance* (Vol. 14). Englewood Cliffs, NJ: Prentice Hall.

13. Barrick, M. R., Stewart, G. L., Neubert, M. J., & Mount, M. K. (1998). Relating member ability and personality to work-team processes and team effectiveness. *Journal of Applied Psychology, 83*(3), 377–391.

14. Edmondson, A. (1999). Psychological safety and learning behavior in work teams. *Administrative Science Quarterly, 44*(2), 350–383.

15. Marks, M. A., Sabella, M. J., Burke, C. S., & Zaccaro, S. J. (2002). The impact of cross-training on team effectiveness. *Journal of Applied Psychology, 87*(1), 3–13.

16. Hackman, J. R. (1987). The design of work teams. In J. W. Lorsch (Ed), *Handbook of organizational behavior* (pp. 315–342). Englewood Cliffs, NJ: Prentice Hall.

17. Cohen, S. G., & Bailey, D. E. (1997). What makes teams work: Group effectiveness research from the shop floor to the executive suite. *Journal of Management, 23*(3), 239–290.

18. LePine, J. A., Piccolo, R. F., Jackson, C. L., Mathieu, J. E., & Saul, J. R. (2008). A meta-analysis of teamwork processes: tests of a multidimensional model and relationships with team effectiveness criteria. *Personnel Psychology, 61*(2), 273–307.

19. Mathieu, J., Maynard, M. T., Rapp, T., & Gilson, L. (2008). Team effectiveness 1997–2007: A review of recent advancements and a glimpse into the future. *Journal of Management, 34*(3), 410–476.

20. Senge, P. M. (1990). *The fifth discipline: The art and practice of the learning organization*. New York, NY: Currency Doubleday.

21. Argote, L., Gruenfeld, D., & Naquin, C. (2001). Group learning in organizations. In M. E. Turner (Ed.), *Groups at work: Theory and research* (pp. 369–409). Mahwah, NJ: Lawrence Erlbaum.

22. Edmondson (1999).

23. Kostopoulos, K. C., Spanos, Y. E., & Prastacos, G. P. (2013). Structure and function of team learning emergence: A multilevel empirical validation. *Journal of Management, 39*(6), 1430–1461.

24. Kurtzberg, T. R., & Amabile, T. M. (2001). From Guilford to creative synergy: Opening the black box of team level creativity. *Creativity Research Journal, 13*(4), 285–294.

25. Gilson, L. L., & Shalley, C. E. (2004). A little creativity goes a long way: An examination of teams-engagement in creative processes. *Journal of Management, 30*(4), 453–470.

26. Gilson, L. L. (2001). *Diversity, dissimilarity and creativity: Does group composition or being different enhance or hinder creative performance*. Washington, DC: Academy of Management Meetings.

27. Gilson & Shalley (2004).

28. Cox, T., & Blake, S. (1991). Managing cultural diversity: Implications for organizational competitiveness. *Academy of Management Executive, 5*(3), 45–56.

29. Horwitz, S. K., & Horwitz, I. B. (2007). The effects of team diversity on team outcomes: A meta-analytic

review of team demography. *Journal of Management, 33*(6), 987–1015.

30. Stahl, G. K., Maznevski, M. L., Voigt, A., & Jonsen, K. (2009). Unraveling the effects of cultural diversity in teams: A meta-analysis of research on multicultural work groups. *Journal of International Business Studies, 41*(4), 690–709.

31. Egan, T. M. (2005). Creativity in the context of team diversity: Team leader perspectives. *Advances in Developing Human Resources, 7*(2), 207–225.

32. Festinger, L. (1950). Informal social communication. *Psychological Review, 57*, 271–282. p. 274.

33. Evans, C. R., & Jarvis, P. A. (1980). Group cohesion: A review and re-evaluation. *Small Group Behavior, 11*, 359–370.

34. Cartwright, D. (1968). The nature of group cohesiveness. In D. Cartwright & A. Zander (Eds.), *Group dynamics: Research and theory* (3rd ed., pp. 91–109). New York, NY: Harper & Row.

35. Neal, D. J., Cohen, R. R., Burke, M. J., & McLendon, C. L. (2003). Cohesion and performance in groups: A metaanalytic clarification of construct relations. *Journal of Applied Psychology, 88*(6), 989–1004.

36. Gully, S. M., Devine, D. J., & Whitney, D. J. (1995). A meta-analysis of cohesion and performance: Effects of level of analysis and task interdependence. *Small Group Research, 26*(4), 497–520.

37. Evans, C. R., & Dion, K. L. (1991). Group cohesion and performance: A meta-analysis. *Small Group Research, 22*(2), 175–186.

38. Lee, C., & Fahr, J.-L. (2004). Joint effects of group efficacy and gender diversity on group cohesion and performance. *Applied Psychology: An International Review, 53*(1), 136–154.

39. Widmeyer, W. N., Carron, A. V., & Brawley, L. R. (1993). Group cohesion in sport and exercise. *Handbook of Research on Sport Psychology*, 672–692.

40. Jowett, S., & Chaundy, V. (2004). An investigation into the impact of coach leadership and coach-athlete relationship on group cohesion. *Group dynamics: Theory, research and practice, 8*(4), 302–331.

41. Turman, P. D. (2003). Coaches and cohesion: The impact of coaching techniques on team cohesion in the small group sport setting. *Journal of Sport Behavior, 26*(1), 86–104.

42. Hogg, M. A., & Reid, S. A. (2006). Social identity, self-categorization, and the communication of group norms. *Communication Theory, 16*(1), 7–30.

43. Mathieu, J. E., & Rapp, T. L. (2009). Laying the foundation for successful team performance trajectories: The roles of team charters and performance strategies. *Journal of Applied Psychology, 94*(1), 90–103.

44. Katzenbach & Smith (1993).

45. Mohammed, S., Ferzandi, L., & Hamilton, K. (2010). Metaphor no more: A 15-year review of the team mental model construct. *Journal of Management, 36*(4), 876–910.

46. Klimoski, R., & Mohammed, S. (1994). Team mental model: Construct or metaphor? *Journal of Management, 20*(2), 403–437.

47. Rouse, W. B., Cannon-Bowers, J. A., & Salas, E. (1992). The role of mental models in team performance in complex systems. *IEEE Transactions on Systems, Man, & Cybernetics, 22*, 1296–1308.

48. Mohammed et al. (2010).

49. DeChurch, L. A., & Mesmer-Magnus, J. R. (2010). The cognitive underpinnings of effective teamwork: A meta-analysis. *Journal of Applied Psychology, 95*(1), 32–53.

50. Vroom, V. H., & Yetton, P. W. (1973). *Leadership and decision making.* Pittsburgh, PA: University of Pittsburgh Press.

51. Vroom, V. H. (2003). Educating managers for decision making and leadership. *Management Decision, 41*(10), 968–978.

52. Scully, J. A., Kirkpatrick, S. A., & Locke, E. A. (1995). Locus of knowledge as a determinant of the effects of participation on performance, affect, and perceptions. *Organizational Behavior and Human Decision Processes, 61*(3), 276–288.

53. Vroom, V. H., & Jago, A. G. (1988). *The new leadership: Managing participation in organizations.* Englewood Cliffs, NJ: Prentice Hall.

54. Vroom (2003).

55. Miller, K. I., & Monge, P. R. (1986). Participation, satisfaction, and productivity: A meta-analytic review. *Academy of Management Journal, 29*(4), 727–753.

56. Wagner, J. A. (1994). Participation's effects on performance and satisfaction: A reconsideration of research evidence. *Academy of Management Review, 19*(2), 312–330.

57. Nutt, P. C. (2002). *Why decisions fail: Avoiding the blunders and traps that lead to debacles.* Williston, VT: Berrett-Koehler.

58. Osborn, A. F. (1979). *Applied imagination: Principles and procedures of creative thinking* (3rd ed.). New York, NY: Scribner's.

59. Rogelberg, S. G., Barnes-Farrell, J. L., & Lowe, C. A. (1992). The stepladder technique: An alternative group structure facilitating effective group decision making. *Journal of Applied Psychology, 77*(5), 730–737.

60. Janis, I. L. (1972). *Victims of groupthink: A psychological study of foreign-policy decisions and fiascoes.* Boston, MA: Houghton-Mifflin.

61. Goncalo, J. A., Polman, E., & Maslach, C. (2010). Can confidence come too soon? Collective efficacy, conflict and group performance over time. *Organizational Behavior and Human Decision Processes, 113*(1), 13–24.

62. Janis (1972).

63. Bressen, T. (2012). Consensus decision-making: What, why, how. In J. Orsi & J. Kassan (Eds.), *Practicing law in the sharing economy: Helping people build cooperatives, social enterprise, and local sustainable economies.* Chicago, IL: ABA Books.

64. Tague, N. R. (2004). *The quality toolbox* (2nd ed.). Milwaukee, WI: ASQ Quality Press.

65. Faure, C. (2004). Beyond brainstorming: Effects of different group procedures on selection of ideas and satisfaction with the process. *The Journal of Creative Behavior, 38*(1), 13–34.

66. Delbecq, A. L., Van de Ven, A. H., & Gustafson, D. H. (1975). *Group techniques for program planning: A guide to nominal group and Delphi processes.* Glenview, IL: Scott, Foresman.

67. The stepladder technique: Making better group decisions. (n.d.). Retrieved from http://www.mindtools.com/pages/article/newTED_89.htm#sthash.c6PFOpJh.dpuf

68. Esser, J. K. (1998). Alive and well after 25 years: A review of groupthink research. *Organizational Behavior and Human Decision Processes, 73*(2), 116–141.

69. Leana, C. R. (1985). A partial test of Janis' groupthink model: Effects of group cohesiveness and leader behavior on defective decision making. *Journal of Management, 11*(1), 5–18.

70. Moorhead, G., Ference, R., & Neck, C. P. (1991). Group decision fiascoes continue: Space shuttle *Challenger* and a revised groupthink framework. *Human Relations, 44*(6), 539–550.

71. Comer, D. R. (1995). A model of social loafing in real work groups. *Human Relations, 48*(6), 647–667.

72. Liden, R. C., Wayne, S. J., Jaworski, R. A., & Bennett, N. (2004). Social loafing: A field investigation. *Journal of Management, 30*(2), 285–304.

73. Karau, S. J., & Williams, K. D. (1993). Social loafing: A meta-analytic review and theoretical integration. *Journal of Personality and Social Psychology, 65*(4), 681.

74. Martins, L. L., Gilson, L. L., & Maynard, M. T. (2004). Virtual teams: What do we know and where do we go from here? *Journal of Management, 30*(6), 805–835. p. 807.

75. Maynard, M. T., & Gilson, L. L. (2014). The role of shared mental model development in understanding virtual team effectiveness. *Group & Organization Management, 39*(1), 3–32.

76. Hollingshead, A. B., McGrath, J. E., & O'Connor, K. M. (1993). Group task performance and communication technology a longitudinal study of computer-mediated versus face-to-face work groups. *Small Group Research, 24*(3), 307–333.

77. Hollingshead, A. B., & McGrath, J. E. (1995). Computer-assisted groups: A critical review of the empirical research. In R. A. Guzzo & E. Salas (Eds.), *Team effectiveness and decision making in organizations* (pp. 46–78). San Francisco, CA: Jossey-Bass.

78. Wilson, J. M., Straus, S. G., & McEvily, B. (2006). All in due time: The development of trust in computer-mediated and face-to-face teams. *Organizational Behavior and Human Decision Processes, 99*(1), 16–33.

79. Mesmer-Magnus, J. R., & DeChurch, L. A. (2009). Information sharing and team performance: A meta-analysis. *Journal of Applied Psychology, 94*(2), 535–546.

80. Griffith, T. L., Sawyer, J. E., & Neale, M. A. (2003). Virtualness and knowledge in teams: Managing the love triangle of organizations, individuals, and information technology. *MIS Quarterly, 27*(2), 265–287.

81. Carte, T. A., Chidambaram, L., & Becker, A. (2006). Emergent leadership in self-managed virtual teams. *Group Decision and Negotiation, 15*(4), 323–343.

82. Malhotra, A., Majchrzak, A., & Rosen, B. (2007). Leading virtual teams. *Academy of Management Perspectives, 21*(1), 60–70.

83. Avolio, B. J., Kahai, S., & Dodge, G. E. (2001). E-leadership: Implications for theory, research, and practice. *The Leadership Quarterly, 11*(4), 615–668.

84. Kirkman, B. L., & Shapiro, D. L. (2001). The impact of cultural values on job satisfaction and organizational commitment in self-managing work teams: The mediating role of employee resistance. *Academy of Management Journal, 44*(3), 557–569.

85. Elenkov, D. S. (1998). Can American management concepts work in Russia? *California Management Review, 40*(4), 133–156.

86. Nicholls, C. E., Lane, H. W., & Brechu, M. B. (1999). Taking self-managed teams to Mexico. *Academy of Management Executive, 13*(3), 15–25.

87. Kirkman, B. L., & Rosen, B. (1999). Beyond self-management: Antecedents and consequences of team empowerment. *Academy of Management Journal, 42*(1), 58–74.

88. Chen, G., Kirkman, B. L., Kanfer, R., Allen, D., & Rosen, B. (2007). A multilevel study of leadership, empowerment, and performance in teams. *Journal of Applied Psychology, 92*(2), 331–346.

89. Lorinkova, N. M., & Perry, S. J. (in press). When is empowerment effective? The role of leader-leader exchange in empowering leadership, cynicism, and time theft. *Journal of Management.* doi:0149206314560411

90. Burke, C. S., Stagl, K. C., Klein, C., Goodwin, G. F., Salas, E., & Halpin, S. M. (2006). What type of leadership behaviors are functional in teams? A meta-analysis. *Leadership Quarterly, 17*(3), 288–307.

91. Erez, A., Lepine, J. A., & Elms, H. (2002). Effects of rotated leadership and peer evaluation on the functioning and effectiveness of self-managed teams: A quasi-experiment. *Personnel Psychology, 55*(4), 929–948.

92. Cordery, J. L., Mueller, W. S., & Smith, L. M. (1991). Attitudinal and behavioral effects of autonomous group working: A longitudinal field study. *Academy of Management Journal, 34*(2), 464–476.

93. Druskat, V. U., & Wheeler, J. V. (2003). Managing from the boundary: The effective leadership of self-managing work teams. *Academy of Management Journal, 46*(4), 435–457.

94. Langfred, C. W. (2007). The downside of self-management: A longitudinal study of the effects of conflict on trust, autonomy, and task interdependence in self-managing teams. *Academy of Management Journal, 50*(4), 885–900.

95. DeVaro, J. (2008). The effects of self-managed and closely managed teams on labor productivity and product quality: An empirical analysis of a cross-section of establishments. *Industrial Relations: A Journal of Economy and Society, 47*(4), 659–697.

96. Beehr, T. A., & McGrath, J. E. (1992). Social support, occupational stress and anxiety. *Anxiety, Stress, and Coping, 5*(1), 7–19.

97. Nahum-Shani, I., & Bamberger, P. A. (2011). Explaining the variable effects of social support on work-based stressor–strain relations: The role of perceived pattern of support exchange. *Organizational Behavior and Human Decision Processes, 114*(1), 49–63.

98. Thoits, P. A. (1995). Stress, coping and social support processes: Where are we? What next? *Journal of Health and Social Behavior, 35*, 53–79.

99. Viswesvaran, C., Sanchez, J. I., & Fisher, J. (1999). The role of social support in the process of work stress: A meta-analysis. *Journal of Vocational Behavior, 54*(2), 314–334.

100. Quick, J. C., Quick, J. D., Nelson, D. L., & Hurrell, Jr., J. J. (1997). *Preventive stress management in organizations.* Washington, DC: APA Books.

101. Briner, R. B., & Reynolds, S. (1999). The costs, benefits, and limitations of organizational level stress interventions. *Journal of Organizational Behavior, 20*(5), 647–664.

102. Richardson, K. M., & Rothstein, H. R. (2008). Effects of occupational stress management intervention programs: A meta-analysis. *Journal of Occupational Health Psychology, 13*(1), 69–93.

103. Lakein, A. (1973). *How to get control of your time and your life.* New York, NY: Signet.

104. Macan, T. H., Shahani, C., Dipboye, R. L., & Phillips, A. P. (1990). College students' time management: Correlations with academic performance and stress. *Journal of Educational Psychology, 82*(4), 760.

105. Macan, T. H. (1994). Time management: Test of a process model. *Journal of Applied Psychology, 79*(3), 381.

106. Theorell, T. (1999). How to deal with stress in organizations? A health perspective on theory and

practice. *Scandinavian Journal of Work, Environment & Health, 25*(6), 616–624.

107. Daniels, K., Beesley, N., Wimalasiri, V., & Cheyne, A. (2013). Problem solving and well-being exploring the instrumental role of job control and social support. *Journal of Management, 39*(4), 1016–1043.

108. Hobfoll, S. E. (1989). Conservation of resources: A new attempt at conceptualizing stress. *American Psychologist, 44*(3), 513–524.

109. Halbesleben, J. R. B. (2006). Sources of social support and burnout: A meta-analytic test of the conservation of resources model. *Journal of Applied Psychology, 91*(5), 1134–1145.

110. Ito, J. K., & Brotheridge, C. M. (2003). Resources, coping strategies, and emotional exhaustion: A conservation of resources perspective. *Journal of Vocational Behavior, 63*(3), 490–509.

111. Quick, J. C., Quick, J. D., Nelson, D. L., & Hurrell, Jr., J. J. (1997). *Preventive stress management in organizations.* Washington, DC: APA Books. pp. 12–13.

112. Thomas, C. H., & Lankau, M. J. (2009). Preventing burnout: The effects of LMX and mentoring on socialization, role stress, and burnout. *Human Resource Management, 48*(3), 417–432.

113. Dutton, J. E., Workman, K. M., & Hardin, A. E. (2014). Compassion at work. *Annual Review of Organizational Psychology and Organizational Behavior, 1,* 277–304.

Chapter 14

1. Gerstner, L. V. (2003). *Who says elephants can't dance? Leading a great enterprise through dramatic change.* New York, NY: Harper Paperbacks.

2. Schein, E. H. (1984). Coming to a new awareness of organizational culture. *Sloan Management Review, 25*(2), 3–16. p. 3.

3. Chatman, J. A., & Jehn, K. A. (1994). Assessing the relationship between industry characteristics and organizational culture: How different can you be? *Academy of Management Journal, 37*(3), 522–553.

4. Pennington, R. (2006). *Results rule! Build a culture that blows the competition away.* New York, NY: John Wiley.

5. House, R. J., Hanges, P. J., Javidan, M., Dorfman, P. W., & Gupta, V. (Eds.). (2004). *Culture, leadership, and organizations: The GLOBE study of 62 societies.* Thousand Oaks, CA: Sage.

6. Van Muijen, J. J., & Koopman, P. L. (1994). The influence of national culture on organizational culture: A comparative study between 10 countries. *European Journal of Work and Organizational Psychology, 4*(4), 367–380.

7. Gerhart, B. (2009). How much does national culture constrain organizational culture? *Management and Organization Review, 5*(2), 241–259.

8. Denison, D. R., Haaland, S., & Goelzer, P. (2004). Corporate culture and organizational effectiveness: Is Asia different from the rest of the world? *Organizational Dynamics, 33*(1), 98–109.

9. Denison, D. R., & Mishra, A. K. (1995). Toward a theory of organizational culture and effectiveness. *Organization Science, 6*(2), 204–223.

10. Denison et al. (2004).

11. Fey, C. F., & Denison, D. R. (2003). Organizational culture and effectiveness: can American theory be applied in Russia? *Organization Science, 14*(6), 686–706.

12. O'Reilly, C. (1989). Corporations, culture, and commitment: Motivation and social control in organizations. *California Management Review, 31*(4), 9–25.

13. Barney, J. B. (1986). Organizational culture: Can it be a source of sustained competitive advantage? *Academy of Management Review, 11*(3), 656–665.

14. Gordon, G. G., & DiTomaso, N. (1992). Predicting corporate performance from organizational culture. *Journal of Management Studies, 29*(6), 783–798.

15. Sørensen, J. B. (2002). The strength of corporate culture and the reliability of firm performance. *Administrative Science Quarterly, 47*(1), 70–91.

16. O'Reilly, C. A., Chatman, J. A., & Caldwell, D. F. (1991). People and organizational culture: A profile comparison approach to assessing person-organization fit. *Academy of Management Journal, 34*(3), 487–516.

17. Vandenberghe, C. (1999). Organizational culture, person-culture fit, and turnover: A replication in the health care industry. *Journal of Organizational Behavior, 20*(2), 175–184.

18. Rosenbaum, S. (2010). The happiness culture: Zappos isn't a company, it's a mission. Retrieved from http://www.fastcompany.com/1657030/happiness-culture-zappos-isnt-company-its-mission

19. Boisnier, A., & Chatman, J. (2003). Cultures and subcultures in dynamic organizations. In E. Mannix & R. Petersen (Eds.), *The dynamic organization* (pp. 87–114). Mahwah, NJ: Lawrence Erlbaum.

20. Schein, E. H. (1996). Culture: The missing concept in organization studies. *Administrative Science Quarterly, 41*(2), 229–240. p. 237.

21. Stone, B. (2013). The secrets of Bezos: How Amazon became the everything store. *Business Week.* Retrieved on April 9, 2014, from http://www.businessweek.com/articles/2013-10-10/jeff-bezos-and-the-age-of-amazon-excerpt-from-the-everything-store-by-brad-stone

22. Wanberg, C. R. (2012). Facilitating organizational socialization: An introduction. In C. R. Wanberg (Ed.), *The Oxford handbook of organizational socialization* (pp. 17–21). New York, NY: Oxford University Press.

23. Schein, E. H. (2003). Organizational socialization and the profession of management. In L. W. Porter, H. L. Angle, & R. W. Allen (Eds.), *Organizational influence processes* (pp. 283–294). New York, NY: M. E. Sharpe.

24. Jablin, F. M. (1987). Organizational entry, assimilation, and exit. In L. L. Putnam, K. H. Roberts, & L. W. Porter (Eds.), *Handbook of organizational communication: An interdisciplinary perspective* (pp. 679–740). Newbury Park, CA: Sage.

25. Kramer, M. W. (2010). *Organizational socialization: Joining and leaving organizations.* Malden, MA: Polity.

26. Bauer, T. N., & Erdogan, B. (2011). Organizational socialization: The effective onboarding of new employees. In S. Zedeck (Ed.), *APA handbook of industrial and organizational psychology, Vol. 3: Maintaining, expanding, and contracting the organization. APA Handbooks in Psychology* (pp. 51–64). Washington, DC: American Psychological Association.

27. Bauer, T. N., Bodner, T., Erdogan, B., Truxillo, D. M., & Tucker, J. S. (2007). Newcomer adjustment during organizational socialization: A meta-analytic review of antecedents, outcomes, and methods. *Journal of Applied Psychology, 92*(3), 707–721.

28. Boje, D. M. (1995). Stories of the storytelling organization: A postmodern analysis of Disney as "Tamara-Land." *Academy of Management Journal, 38*(4), 997–1035.

29. Sole, D., & Wilson, D. G. (2002). Storytelling in organizations: The power and traps of using stories to share knowledge in organizations. LILA, Harvard, Graduate School of Education Retrieved on December 31, 2014, from http://www.providersedge.com/docs/km_articles/Storytelling_in_Organizations.pdf

30. Weick, K. (1995). *Sensemaking in organizations*. Thousand Oaks, CA: Sage.

31. Merchant, A., Ford, J. B., & Sargeant, A. (2010). Charitable organizations' storytelling influence on donors' emotions and intentions. *Journal of Business Research*, 63(7), 754–762.

32. Morgan, S., & Dennehy, R. F. (1995). Organizational storytelling: Telling tales in the business classroom. *Developments in Business Simulation & Experiential Exercises*, 22, 160–165.

33. Islam, G., & Zyphur, M. J. (2009). Rituals in organizations: A review and expansion of current theory. *Group & Organization Management*, 34(1), 114–139. p. 116.

34. Anand, N., & Watson, M. R. (2004). Tournament rituals in the evolution of fields: The case of the Grammy Awards. *Academy of Management Journal*, 47(1), 59–80.

35. Sole & Wilson (2002).

36. Rafaeli, A., & Pratt, M. G. (Eds.). (2013). *Artifacts and organizations: Beyond mere symbolism*. New York, NY: Psychology Press.

37. Rafaeli, A., & Pratt, M. G. (1993). Tailored meanings: On the meaning and impact of organizational dress. *Academy of Management Review*, 18(1), 32–55.

38. Van Maanen, J. (1996). The smile factory: Work at Disneyland. In P. J. Frost, L. F. Moore, M. R. Louis, & C. C. Lundberg, *Reframing organizational culture* (pp. 58–76). Newbury Park, CA: Sage.

39. Denison, D. R. (1996). What is the difference between organizational culture and organizational climate? A native's point of view on a decade of paradigm wars. *Academy of Management Review*, 21(3), 619–654.

40. Reichers, A. E., & Schneider, B. (1990). Climate and culture: An evolution of constructs. *Organizational Climate and Culture*, 1, 5–39. p. 22.

41. Denison (1996).

42. Ostroff, C., Kinicki, A. J., & Tamkins, M. M. (2003). *Organizational culture and climate*. New York, NY: John Wiley.

43. Schneider, B., Ehrhart, M. G., & Macey, W. H. (2013). Organizational climate and culture. *Annual Review of Psychology*, 64, 361–388.

44. Schneider, B., Ehrhart, M. G., & Macey, W. H. (2011). Organizational climate research: Achievements and the road ahead. In N. M. Ashkanasy, C. P. M. Wilderom, & M. F. Peterson (Eds.), *The handbook of organizational culture and climate* (2nd ed., pp. 29–49). Thousand Oaks, CA: Sage. p. 42.

45. Ibid.

46. Carr, J. Z., Schmidt, A. M., Ford, J. K., & DeShon, R. P. (2003). Climate perceptions matter: A meta-analytic path analysis relating molar climate, cognitive and affective states, and individual level work outcomes. *Journal of Applied Psychology*, 88(4), 605.

47. Ehrhart, K. H., Witt, L. A., Schneider, B., & Perry, S. J. (2011). Service employees give as they get: Internal service as a moderator of the service climate–service outcomes link. *Journal of Applied Psychology*, 96(2), 423–431.

48. Gonzalez-Roma, V., Peiro, J. M., & Tordera, N. (2002). An examination of the antecedents and moderator influences of climate strength. *Journal of Applied Psychology*, 87(3), 465–473.

49. Naumann, S. E., & Bennett, N. (2000). A case for procedural justice climate: Development and test of a multilevel model. *Academy of Management Journal*, 43(5), 881–889.

50. Pugh, S. D., Dietz, J., Brief, A. P., & Wiley, J. W. (2008). Looking inside and out: The impact of employee and community demographic composition on organizational diversity climate. *Journal of Applied Psychology*, 93(6), 1422–1428.

51. Wallace, J. C., Popp, E., & Mondore, S. (2006). Safety climate as a mediator between foundation climates and occupational accidents: A group-level investigation. *Journal of Applied Psychology*, 91(3), 681–688.

52. Schminke, M., Ambrose, M. L., & Neubaum, D. O. (2005). The effect of leader moral development on ethical climate and employee attitudes. *Organizational Behavior and Human Decision Processes*, 97(2), 135–151.

53. Victor, B., & Cullen, J. B. (1988). The organizational bases of ethical work climates. *Administrative Science Quarterly*, 33(1), 101–125.

54. Ibid.

55. Mayer, D. M., Kuenzi, M., & Greenbaum, R. L. (2010). Examining the link between ethical leadership and employee misconduct: The mediating role of ethical climate. *Journal of Business Ethics*, 95(1), 7–16.

56. Martin, K. D., & Cullen, J. B. (2006). Continuities and extensions of ethical climate theory: A meta-analytic review. *Journal of Business Ethics*, 69(2), 175–194.

57. Gelfand, M. J., Nishii, L. H., Raver, J., & Schneider, B. (2005). Discrimination in organizations: An organizational level systems perspective. In R. Dipboye & A. Colella (Eds.), *Discrimination at work: The psychological and organizational bases* (pp. 89–116). Mahwah, NJ: Lawrence Erlbaum. p. 104.

58. McKay, P. F., Avery, D. R., Tonidandel, S., Morris, M. A., Hernandez, M., & Hebl, M. R. (2007). Racial differences in employee retention: Are diversity climate perceptions the key? *Personnel Psychology*, 60(1), 35–62.

59. Chatman, J. A., & Cha, S. E. (2003). Leading by leveraging culture. *California Management Review*, 45(4), 20–34.

60. Margolis, S. (2010). *Building a culture of distinction*. New York, NY: Workplace Culture Institute.

Chapter 15

1. LaClair, J. A., & Rao, R. P. (2002). Helping employees embrace change. *The McKinsey Quarterly*, 4, 17–20.

2. Argyris, C. (1990). *Overcoming organizational defenses*. Boston, MA: Allyn & Bacon.

3. Oswick, C., Grant, D., Michelson, G., & Wailes, N. (2005). Looking forwards: Discursive directions in organizational change. *Journal of Organizational Change Management*, 18(4), 383–390.

4. Weick, K. E., & Quinn, R. E. (1999). Organizational change and development. *Annual Review of Psychology*, 50(1), 361–386.

5. North, M., & Hershfield, H. (2014). Four ways to adapt to an aging workforce. Retrieved on April 8, 2014, from http://blogs.hbr.org/2014/04/four-ways-to-adapt-to-an-aging-workforce

6. Robertson, P. J., Roberts, D. R., & Porras, J. I. (1993). Dynamics of planned organizational change: Assessing empirical support for a theoretical model. *Academy of Management Journal*, 36(3), 619–634.

7. Mike, B., & Slocum, J. W. (2003). Slice of reality-changing culture at Pizza Hut and Yum! Brands, Inc. *Organizational Dynamics*, 32(4), 319–330.

8. Lewin, K. (1951). *Field theory in social science*. New York, NY: Harper & Row. p. 169.

9. Bennis, W. G. (1966). *Changing organizations*. New York, NY: McGraw-Hill.

10. Austin, J. R., & Bartunek, J. M. (2006). Theories and practices of organizational development. In J. Gallos (Ed.), *Organization development* (pp. 89–128). San Francisco, CA: Jossey-Bass.

11. Edwards, J. E., & Thomas, M. D. (1993). The organizational survey process: General steps and practical considerations. *American Behavioral Scientist, 36*(4), 419–442.

12. Austin & Bartunek (2006).

13. Bunker, B. B., & Alban, B. T. (1997). *Large group interventions*. San Francisco, CA: Jossey-Bass.

14. Schein, E. H. (1990). A general philosophy of helping: Process consultation. *Sloan Management Review, 31*(3), 57–64.

15. Dyer Jr., W. G., Dyer, J. H., & Dyer, W. G. (2013). *Team building: Proven strategies for improving team performance*. New York, NY: John Wiley.

16. Neuman, G. A., Edwards, J. E., & Raju, N. S. (1989). Organizational development interventions: A meta-analysis of their effects on satisfaction and other attitudes. *Personnel Psychology, 42*(3), 461–489.

17. Salas, E., Rozell, D., Mullen, B., & Driskell, J. E. (1999). The effect of team building on performance: An integration. *Small Group Research, 30*(3), 309–329.

18. Cooperrider, D. L., & Srivastva, S. (1987). Appreciative inquiry in organizational life. *Research in Organizational Change and Development, 1*(1), 129–169.

19. Luthans, F., & Church, A. H. (2002). Positive organizational behavior: Developing and managing psychological strengths. *Academy of Management Executive, 16*(1), 57–75.

20. Conklin, T. A., & Hartman, N. S. (2014). Appreciative inquiry and autonomy-supportive classes in business education: A semi longitudinal study of AI in the classroom. *Journal of Experiential Education, 37*(3), 285–309.

21. Bushe, G. R. (1999). Advances in appreciative inquiry as an organization development intervention. *Organization Development Journal, 17*(2), 61–68.

22. Bushe, G. R., & Coetzer, G. (1995). Appreciative inquiry as a team-development intervention: A controlled experiment. *Journal of Applied Behavioral Science, 31*(1), 13–30.

23. Bushe, G. R., & Kassam, A. F. (2005). When is appreciative inquiry transformational? A meta-case analysis. *The Journal of Applied Behavioral Science, 41*(2), 161–181.

24. Beer, M., Eisenstat, R. A., & Spector, B. (1993). Why change programs don't produce change. In C. Mabey & B. Mayon-White (Eds.), *Managing change*. London, UK: P.C.P.

25. Benn, S., Dunphy, D., & Griffiths, A. (2014). *Organizational change for corporate sustainability* (3rd ed.). New York, NY: Routledge.

26. Lines, R. (2004). Influence of participation in strategic change: Resistance, organizational commitment and change goal achievement. *Journal of Change Management, 4*(3), 193–215.

27. Herscovitch, L., & Meyer, J. P. (2002). Commitment to organizational change: Extension of a three-component model. *Journal of Applied Psychology, 87*(3), 474–487.

28. Coch, L., & French, J. R. (1948). Overcoming resistance to change. *Human Relations, 1*(4), 512–532.

29. Burke, W. W. (2010). *Organization change: Theory and practice*. Thousand Oaks, CA: Sage.

30. Katz, D., & Kahn, R. L. (1978). *The social psychology of organizations* (2nd ed.). New York, NY: John Wiley.

31. Nadler, D. A. (1987). The effective management of organizational change. *Handbook of organizational behavior* (pp. 358–369). Englewood Cliffs, NJ: Prentice Hall.

32. Kotter, J. P., & Schlesinger, L. A. (1978). Choosing strategies for change. *Harvard Business Review, 57*(2), 106–114.

33. Furst, S. A., & Cable, D. M. (2008). Employee resistance to organizational change: Managerial influence tactics and leader-member exchange. *Journal of Applied Psychology, 93*(2), 453–462.

34. Tierney, P. (1999). Work relations as a precursor to a psychological climate for change: The role of work group supervisors and peers. *Journal of Organizational Change Management, 12*(2), 120–134.

35. Rousseau, D. M., & Tijoriwala, S. A. (1999). What's a good reason to change? Motivated reasoning and social accounts in promoting organizational change. *Journal of Applied Psychology, 84*(4), 514–528.

36. Oreg, S. (2006). Personality, context, and resistance to organizational change. *European Journal of Work and Organizational Psychology, 15*(1), 73–101.

37. Whelen-Berry, K. S., Gordon, J. R., & Hinings, C. R. (2003). Strengthening organizational change processes: Recommendations and implications from a multi-level analysis. *Journal of Applied Behavioral Science, 39*(2), 186–207.

38. Bass, B. M., & Steidlmeier, P. (1999). Ethics, character, and authentic transformational leadership behavior. *The Leadership Quarterly, 10*(2), 181–217. p. 181.

39. Sharif, M. M., & Scandura, T. A. (2014). Do perceptions of ethical conduct matter during organizational change? Ethical leadership and employee involvement. *Journal of Business Ethics, 124*(2), 185–196.

40. Burnes, B. (2004). Kurt Lewin and the planned approach to change: A re-appraisal. *Journal of Management Studies, 41*(6), 977–1002. p. 977.

41. Lewin (1951).

42. Kotter, J. P. (1995). Leading change: Why transformation efforts fail. *Harvard Business Review, 73*(2), 59–67.

43. Nadler, D. A., & Tushman, M. L. (1990). Beyond the charismatic leader: Leadership and organizational change. *California Management Review, 32*(2), 77–97.

44. Rodgers, R., Hunter, J. E., & Rogers, D. L. (1993). Influence of top management commitment on management program success. *Journal of Applied Psychology, 78*(1), 151–155.

45. Neuman, G. A., Edwards, J. E., & Raju, N. S. (1989). Organizational development interventions: A meta-analysis of their effects on satisfaction and other attitudes. *Personnel Psychology, 42*(3), 461–489.

46. Herscovitch, L., & Meyer, J. P. (2002). Commitment to organizational change: Extension of a three-component model. *Journal of Applied Psychology, 87*(3), 474–487.

47. Mishra, A. K., Mishra, K. E., & Spreitzer, G. M. (2009). Downsizing the company without downsizing morale. *MIT Sloan Management Review, 50*(3), 39–44.

48. Sutton, R. I. (2009, June). How to be a good boss in a bad economy. *Harvard Business Review*, pp. 42–50. p. 44.

49. Dyer, J., Gregersen, H., & Christensen, C. (2013). *The Innovator's DNA: Mastering the five skills of disruptive innovators*. Cambridge, MA: Harvard Business Press.

50. Paxton, R. (2014). How Owens Corning trains managers for innovation. Retrieved

on April 2, 2014, from http://www
.shrm.org/Publications/hrmagazine/
EditorialContent/2014/Pages/0214-
Owens-Corning-innovation.aspx

51. Burke, W. W., &
Litwin, G. H. (1992). A causal model of
organizational performance and change.
Journal of Management, 18(3), 523–545.

52. Lau, C. M., & Ngo, H. Y. (2001).
Organization development and
firm performance: A comparison of
multinational and local firms. *Journal of
International Business Studies, 32*(1), 95–114.

53. Miller, D. (1996). A preliminary typology
of organizational learning: Synthesizing
the literature. *Journal of Management, 22*(3),
485–505.

54. Vera, D., & Crossan, M. (2004). Strategic
leadership and organizational learning.
Academy of Management Review, 29(2),
222–240.

55. Senge, P. M. (1990). *The fifth discipline.*
New York, NY: Doubleday. p. 3.

56. http://www.bloomberg.com/bw/
articles/2013-08-22/homegrown-green-
energy-is-making-power-utilities-
irrelevant#p3

Appendix

1. Tharenou, P., Donohue, R., & Cooper, B.
(2007). *Management research methods.*
Cambridge, UK: Cambridge University
Press.

2. Cook, T. D., & Campbell, D. T. (1979).
*Quasi-experimentation: Design and analysis
issues for field settings.* Boston, MA:
Houghton Mifflin.

3. Basadur, M., Graen, G. B., & Scandura,
T. A. (1986). Training effects on attitudes
toward divergent thinking among
manufacturing engineers. *Journal of Applied
Psychology, 71*(4), 612–617.

4. Creswell, J. (2003). *Research design:
Qualitative, quantitative, and mixed methods
approaches* (2nd ed.). Thousand Oaks,
CA: Sage.

5. Glass, G. V., McGaw, B., & Smith, M.
L. (1981). *Meta-analysis in social research.*
Beverly Hills, CA: SAGE.

Glossary

1. McCroskey, J. C. (1977). Oral
communication apprehension: A summary
of recent theory and research. *Human
Communication Research, 4*(1), 78–96.

2. Gati, I., Gadassi, R., Saka, N., Hadadi,
Y., Ansenberg, N., Friedmann, R., &
Asulin-Peretz, L. (2010). Emotional and
personality-related aspects of career
decision-making difficulties: Facets of
career indecisiveness. *Journal of Career
Assessment, 19*(1), 3.

3. McCroskey, J. C. (1977). Oral
communication apprehension: A summary
of recent theory and research. *Human
Communication Research, 4*(1), 78–96.

4. Parry, S. B. (1996). The quest for
competences: Competency studies can
help you make HR decision, but the
results are only as good as the study.
Training, 33, 50.

5. Thomas, K. W. (1992). Conflict and
negotiation processes in organizations. In
M. D. Dunnette & L. M. Hough (Eds.),
*Handbook of industrial and organizational
psychology* (2nd ed., Vol. 3, pp. 651–717).
Palo Alto, CA: Consulting Psychologists
Press.

6. Judge, T. A., Erez, A., & Bono, J. E. (1998).
The power of being positive: The relation
between positive self-concept and job
performance. *Human Performance, 11*(2–3),
167–187.

7. Amabile, T. M. (2012). Componential
theory of creativity. Working Paper #12-
096. Cambridge, MA: Harvard Business
School. Retrieved from http://www.hbs.
edu/faculty/Publication%20Files/12-096.
pdf

8. Harrison, D. A., Price, K. H., & Bell, M.
P. (1998). Beyond relational demography:
Time and the effects of surface-and
deep-level diversity on work group
cohesion. *Academy of Management
Journal, 41*(1), 96–107.

9. Robinson, S. L., Wang, W., & Kiewitz,
C. (2014). Coworkers behaving badly:
The impact of coworker deviant behavior
upon individual employees. *Annual
Review of Organizational Psychology and
Organizational Behavior, 1*, 123–143.

10. Salovey, P., & Mayer, J. D. (1989).
Emotional intelligence. *Imagination,
Cognition and Personality, 9*(3), 185–211.

11. Hogan, R., Chamorro-Premuzic, T.,
& Kaiser, R. B. (2013). Employability
and career success: Bridging the gap
between theory and reality. *Industrial and
Organizational Psychology, 6*(1), 3–16.

12. Colantonio, A. (1989). Assessing the
effects of employee assistance programs:
a review of employee assistance program
evaluations. *The Yale Journal of Biology and
Medicine, 62*(1), 13.

13. Rich, B. L., Lepine, J. A., & Crawford, E.
R. (2010). Job engagement: Antecedents
and effects on job performance. *Academy
of Management Journal, 53*(3), 617–635.

14. Tadmor, C. T., & Tetlock, P. E. (2006).
Biculturalism: A model of the effects
of second-culture exposure on
acculturation and integrative
complexity. *Journal of Cross-Cultural
Psychology, 37*(2), 173–190.

15. Frank, A., & Brownell, J. (1989),
*Organizational communication and behavior:
Communicating to improve performance.*
Orlando, FL: Holt, Rinehart and Winston.
pp. 5–6.

16. Maslach, C. (1998). *A multidimensional
theory of burnout.* In C. L. Cooper (Ed.),
Theories of organizational stress. Oxford,
UK: Oxford University Press. p. 68.

17. Kossek, E. E., Lautsch, B. A., & Eaton,
S. C. (2006). Telecommuting, control,
and boundary management: Correlates
of policy use and practice, job control,
and work–family effectiveness. *Journal of
Vocational Behavior, 68*(2), 350.

18. Schein, E. H. (1984). Coming to a new
awareness of organizational culture. *Sloan
Management Review, 25*(2), 3–16.

19. Eisenberger, R., Huntington, R.,
Hutchison, S., & Sowa, D. (1986).
Perceived organizational support. *Journal
of Applied Psychology, 71*(3), 500–507.

20. Snyder, M., & Cantor, N. (1998).
Understanding personality and social
behavior: A functionalist strategy. In
D. T. Gilbert, S. T. Fiske, & G. Lindzey
(Eds.), *The handbook of social psychology*
(4th ed., pp. 635–679). New York, NY:
McGraw-Hill.

21. Spreitzer, G. M. (1995). Psychological
empowerment in the workplace:
Dimensions, measurement, and validation.
Academy of Management Journal, 38(4),
1442–1465.

22. Islam, G., & Zyphur, M. J. (2009). Rituals
in organizations A review and expansion
of current theory. *Group & Organization
Management, 34*(1), 114–139.

23. Harrison, D. A., Price, K. H., & Bell, M.
P. (1998). Beyond relational demography:
Time and the effects of surface-and
deep-level diversity on work group
cohesion. *Academy of Management
Journal, 41*(1), 96–107.

24. Casrnir, F. L. (1999). Foundations for the
study of intercultural communication
based on a third-culture building model.
*International Journal of Intercultural
Relations, 23*(1), 91–116.

INDEX

Avery, D. R., 379
Avey, J. B., 62
Avolio, B. J., 48, 62

B-MED, 383–384
Bailey, D. E., 230
Balu, G. J., 97
Bandura, A., 201
Bardford, D. L., 44
Barnard, C., 41
Barrick, M. R., 59
Basadur, M. S., 156, 157, 158
Basking, K., 214
Bass, B. M., 395
Bay of Pigs invasion, 243
Bedeian, A. G., 262
Beesley, N., 356
Behavior modification. *See*
  Organizational behavior
  modification (OB mod)
Behavior to modify, 200
Behavioral component of attitude,
  88, 88 (figure), 89
Behavioral coping methods,
  352–353, 353 (figure)
Behavioral CQ, 322, 323 (figure)
Behavioral stress responses,
  350, 351 (figure)
Behaviorally anchored rating
  scales (BARS), 208
Behaviors category, 229, 230
Belief updating, 112
Bell, R., 323, 336
Benevolents, 180
Bennis, W. G., 25
Berkowitz, L., 178
Bersin, J., 210
Best alternative to a negotiated
  agreement (BATNA), 271
Bezos, J., 371
Bias. *See* Decision bias/traps
Biculturals, 324
Bidding in negotiation, 270–271,
  271 (figure)
Big Five personality characteristics,
  59–60, 59 (table), 61, 62
Big Five Personality Test, 82–83
Bing, M. N., 180
Bischoff, S. J., 349
Black, J. S., 34
Black swan event, 142
Blakely, G. L., 180
Blatt, R., 212
Blogs, 296
Boal, K. B., 97
Bobrowski, P. E., 250

Body language, 125–126
Boer, P., 221
Bolino, M. C., 125, 136
Bond, M. H., 315
Bonn, C. J., 106
Boomers, 71, 72 (table)
Boot, A., 333
Born leaders, 61
Boundary spanners, 290
Bounded ethnicality, 152–153
Bounded rationality, 140, 141, 153
Brain function:
  attitudes and, 69
  intuition and, 144
  leadership research and, 69
  mirror neurons, role modeling
    and, 69
  neuroscience, ethics issues
    with, 70
  See also Neuroscience
Brainstorming, 237–238
Brawley, L. R., 233
Brenner, B., 323, 336
Briggs, K., 58
British Petroleum (BP), 149, 150
Broaden-and-build model, 64
Brotheridge, C. M., 357
Bruck, F., 323
Bruder, J., 362
Buffering effect, 354
Building the relationship in
  negotiation, 270, 271 (figure)
Bunker, B. B., 36, 37
Burkus, D., 155
Burnout, 68, 262
  See also Job burnout; Stress
Burroughs, S. M., 180

Calculus-based trust (CBT), 35,
  36 (figure)
Campbell, A. M., 343
Career indecision, 139
Career mentoring, 33–34
Carley, K. M., 293
Carney, D. R., 125
Carron, A. V., 233
Case studies:
  change leadership, 403–404
  cross-cultural differences, 333
  IBM diversity management,
    80–81
  individual decision making,
    161–162
  job satisfaction, 103–104
  leadership practices, 51–52
  motivation, 190

organizational behavior, 20–21
organizational communication,
  304–305
organizational culture clash,
  383–384
pay inequity, 205, 219
perception, 129–130
perspective taking, 277–278
work teams, 252
Case study research, 410, 411 (table)
Casrnir, F. L., 321
The Cellular Telecommunications
  & Internet Association
  (CTIA), 295
Center for Creative Leadership, 77
Central tendency error, 209
Chain communication network,
  289 (figure), 290
Challenge-related stress, 341, 343
Challenger space shuttle disaster, 243
Chamorro-Premuzic, T., 124
Change leadership, 344–345, 386
  aging workforce, best practices
    for, 390
  bottom-line impact of, 386
  case study for, 403–404
  changing phase and, 396,
    397 (figure)
  commitment to change and, 393,
    394, 399–400
  competition need and, 387,
    389 (table)
  compliance and, 393, 394
  culture change implementation
    and, 391
  directive controlling approach
    and, 407
  downsizing and, 400
  drivers of organizational change
    and, 387, 389 (table)
  economic necessity and, 387,
    389 (table)
  effective change implementation
    and, 399–400
  ethical leadership practices
    and, 395
  evolution of work and, 386,
    388 (figure)
  force field analysis and, 397
  frontline staff and, 387
  globalization pressures and, 387,
    389 (table)
  goal-setting approach and, 408
  incremental change and, 389,
    389 (figure)
  innovation and, 400, 403–404

conflict-handling styles, applications of, 265, 266 (table)

conflict-performance relationship and, 258–259, 259 (figure), 265, 267, 268 (figure)

conflict resolution styles and, 263–265, 263 (figure)

conflict resolution styles assessment and, 278–283

cross-cultural conflict resolution and, 269–270

difficult conversations checklist, 274

dominating resolution style and, 263 (figure), 264, 266 (table)

facilitator role and, 268

high-performing teams and, 267

integrating resolution style and, 263 (figure), 264, 266 (table)

leadership role in, 261–262

mediator role and, 269

obliging resolution style and, 263(figure), 264, 266 (table)

ombudsperson role and, 269

peer review resolution process and, 269

perspective taking and, 277–278

self-assessment for, 278–283

team-level conflict and, 265, 267, 268 (figure)

third-party interventions and, 268–269

toolkit activities for, 274–277

See also Conflict; Negotiation

Confucian dynamism, 313, 314, 315 (table), 316

Conklin, T. A., 402

Conscientiousness, 59, 59 (table), 83

Consensus guidelines, 238–240, 243

Consent with reservations, 240

Consequences of behavior, 200

Conservation of resources (COR) theory, 357

Consistency cultural value, 369–370, 369 (figure)

Constructive response to dissatisfaction, 93 (figure), 94

Consultation, 42 (table), 43

Consultative decision mode, 236

Contingencies of reinforcement, 196, 197 (figure)

Contingent reward, 26, 27 (figure)

Continuance commitment, 96

Continuous reinforcement, 196, 198

Contrast effect, 115–116

Control need, 351

Coping, 351

action-oriented coping mechanisms and, 352

behavioral coping methods and, 352–353, 353 (figure)

buffering effect and, 354

cognitive coping methods and, 352, 353, 353 (figure)

conservation of resources theory and, 357

emotion-focused coping and, 353, 353 (figure)

emotional social support and, 354

employee well-being/job performance and, 353

gender differences in, 353

instrumental social support and, 354

leadership challenge of, 357–358

problem-focused coping and, 352, 353 (figure)

self-talk strategy and, 353

social support and, 353, 354, 356

stress inducement and, 357

See also Preventive stress management; Strain; Stress

Core self-evaluation assessment, 94–95, 104–106

Corporate citizens, 96, 97 (figure)

Correlational field study, 410, 411 (table)

Correspondence. *See* Attitude-behavior correspondence

Cortina, L. M., 262

Cosier, R. A., 260

Counterdependence, 33

Coutu, D. L., 262

Cox, P. L., 250

Creative thinking, 153

creative leadership model and, 156–157, 158 (figure)

creative problem-solving and, 153–154, 160–161

creativity, definition of, 153

flow, emotional states and, 154

myths of creativity and, 154, 155 (table)

personality traits and, 153–154

problem finding activity and, 157, 158 (figure)

problem solving activity and, 157, 158 (figure)

self-assessment of, 162–165

solution implementation activity and, 157, 158 (figure)

three-component model of creativity and, 154, 157 (figure)

See also Critical thinking; Individual decision making

Creativity, 153

creative thinking skills and, 154, 157 (figure)

definition of, 153

expertise and, 154, 157 (figure)

goal-setting and, 173

leadership support of, 158–159

motivation and, 154, 157 (figure)

multicultural experiences and, 156

myths of, 154, 155 (table)

team creativity and, 231–232

three-component model of, 154, 157 (figure)

See also Creative thinking

Critical thinking, 3

behaviors in, 9 (table)

definition of, 8

diverse/inclusive work environment, development of, 75

evidence-based management and, 8

guidelines for, 8, 9 (table)

plan implementation, employee buy-in and, 10

questioning strategy and, 8, 10

skills in, 9 (table)

See also Creative thinking

Cross-cultural communication, 297–299

Cross-cultural differences, 309–310

assertiveness and, 317 (tables)

assimilation and, 322–323

case study for, 333

collectivism/individualism orientations and, 314, 315 (table), 352

communication, repatriation success and, 327

Confucian dynamism and, 313, 314, 315 (table), 316

cross-cultural adjustment, acculturation strategies and, 322–323

cross-cultural leadership, GLOBE studies of, 316–318, 316–317 (tables)

leader moral development and, 378

organizational change implementation and, 395

servant leadership and, 35, 46–47, 48 (table)

trickle-down effect and, 45

utilitarianism and, 152

See also Fairness; Individual decision making; Leadership

Ethical organizational climate, 377, 378–379

Ethics-induced stress, 349

Eustress, 341

Evidence-based management (EBM), 4, 6

authentic innovation and, 6

breakthrough studies/ideas and, 6

collective brilliance, development/utilization of, 6–7

critical thinking process and, 8–10, 9 (table)

Delphi decision-making method and, 6, 7

drawbacks/virtues, highlighting of, 7

ideologies/theories, neutral stance toward, 8

information, sources of, 6, 8

questioning strategy and, 8, 10

standards of application for, 6–8

success/failure stories, sound practices illustration and, 7–8

See also Leadership; Organizational behavior (OB); Scientific method

Exchange, 42 (table), 43

Excuses, 38

Executives, 371

Expanding pie outcome, 271

Expatriate cross-cultural adjustment, 326–329

Expectancy theory, 182, 184–185, 184 (figure)

Experimental studies, 409, 411 (table)

Expert power, 39, 40, 41 (figure)

Expertise, 154, 157 (figure)

Explanations, 37

Explicit team standards, 233

External attribution, 117, 119 (figure), 120

External communication flow, 290

Extraversion, 59, 59 (table), 83

Extrinsic motivation, 12, 202–205

See also Rewards

Extrinsics in service of intrinsics, 204

FACE (focus/ask/comment/employ) memory method, 114

Facebook, 296

Facet job satisfaction measures, 91–92

Facilitator role, 236, 267, 268

Fairness, 177

benevolents and, 180

distributive justice and, 177–179

empathy and, 182

entitleds and, 180

equity sensitives and, 180

equity sensitivity, fairness concerns and, 180

equity theory and, 177–179, 178 (figure)

leader effectiveness and, 181

leader fairness, reputation for, 181–182

moral outrage and, 179

organizational citizenship behaviors and, 182

organizational justice and, 176, 179–181, 181 (figure)

overpayment inequity and, 180

perception of fairness, motivation and, 179

underpayment inequity and, 180

See also Ethical leadership; Fairness norms; Motivation

Fairness norms, 29, 29 (figure), 99

Family-to-work conflict, 347

Farrell, D., 93

Farson, F. E., 289

Feedback, 34

behavior modification process and, 200

feedback channels, development of, 176

higher performance levels and, 173

job characteristics model and, 174, 175 (figure)

performance appraisals and, 210–211

performance management process and, 206

rewards as, 204

survey feedback technique and, 392

See also Punishment; Reinforcement theory; Rewards

Feedback seeking, 211–212, 212 (figure)

Ferrin, D. L., 35

Ferzandi, L., 236

Fight-or-flight response, 350

Filipczak, B., 72

Finholt, T. A., 83, 192

First Amendment rights, 296

Fisher, J., 351

Fixed-interval reinforcement, 197, 198 (figure)

Fixed pie outcome, 271

Fixed-ratio reinforcement, 197–198, 198 (figure)

Flow, 154

Fluency heuristic, 147, 148 (table)

Force field analysis, 397

Forecasting. *See* Prediction

Forming phase, 226–229, 228 (figure)

Fragale, A. R., 293

Framing in decision making, 142–143, 143 (table)

Framing messages, 302

Frantz, T. L., 293

French, J. R. P., 39, 41

Friedman, M., 60

Fugate, M., 134

Full-range leadership development model, 26–28, 27 (figure), 50–51

Fundamental attribution error, 117–118

Gain-sharing plans, 209

Galatea effect, 121, 188

Galinsky, A. D., 156

Gardner, W., 48

Gavett, G., 255

Gaw, K. F., 325

Gelfand, M. J., 379

Gender egalitarianism, 317 (tables)

General Electric Company, 209, 328, 392

Generation Xers (Gen Xers), 71–72, 72 (table), 74

Gerstner, L. V., 365

Ghosn, C., 319, 320

Ghumann, S., 123

Giang, V., 339

Gigerenzer, G., 148

Gilstrap, J. B., 125

Gino, F., 152

Gladwell, M., 144, 145

service climates comparison and, 384–385

socialization process and, 372–374, 372 (figure), 373 (table), 380

stability orientation and, 368, 371

storytelling and, 371, 374–375, 380

strong organizational cultures and, 370–371, 373 (table)

subcultures and, 371

symbols and, 371, 375–376, 380

team orientation and, 368

toolkit activity for, 381–382

training process and, 380

troubled culture, signs of, 368

values and, 366, 367 (figure), 369–370, 369 (figure)

See also Organizational climate

Organizational development (OD), 391

appreciative inquiry intervention and, 393

interventions for, 392–393

process consultation method and, 392

survey feedback technique and, 392

sustainability goal and, 393

team building intervention and, 392–393

theories of change and, 391–392

theories of changing and, 392

workout intervention and, 392

See also Change leadership

Organizational justice, 176, 179

components of, 179–180, 181 (figure)

distributive justice and, 177–179

informational justice and, 180

interactional/interpersonal justice and, 180

moral outrage and, 179

performance management process and, 206

procedural justice and, 179

sabotage, unfairness perceptions and, 179

See also Fairness; Justice; Motivation

Organizational-level analysis, 14, 15 (table)

Organizational neuroscience, 69, 70

Organizational politics, 44–45, 348

Organizational reasons for resistance, 394

Organizational stress, 340

Ostroff, C., 378

Out-group members, 28–29, 29 (figure), 182

Output dimension, 229

Overconfidence bias, 149–150

Overdependence, 33

Overpayment inequity, 180

Owens Corning, 400

Park, C. R., 343

Partial reinforcement, 196, 197–198, 198 (figure)

Participative leadership, 185

Passive response to dissatisfaction, 92, 93 (figure)

Path-goal theory (PGT), 185, 186 (figure)

achievement-oriented leadership and, 185

directive leadership and, 185

follower ability, adjusted expectations and, 186

formal authority systems and, 186

job design and, 186

motivating leadership behaviors and, 185, 187

participative leadership and, 185

specific situations, leader adaptation to, 185–186

supportive leadership and, 185, 186

work group norms and, 186

See also Motivation

Patton, B., 274

Paul, M. C., 385

Pay dispersion, 205

Pay for performance incentive systems, 205

Pay inequity, 205, 219

Pearl Harbor attack, 243

Pearson, C. M., 262

Peer pressure, 3

Peer review conflict resolution, 269

Pennington, R., 368

Perceived organizational support (POS), 97, 98, 99

Perception, 109, 110–111, 110–111 (figures)

attribution bias, avoidance of, 118

attribution theory and, 117–120, 126–127

attributions and, 110, 117

availability bias and, 113–115

belief updating and, 112

body language and, 125–126

case study for, 129–130

coding technique and, 113

contrast effects and, 115–116

Ebbinghaus illusion and, 115, 116 (figure)

elaborative interrogation and, 115

employability perceptions and, 122–124, 124 (figure), 130–134

fairness perceptions, motivation and, 179

fairness, perceptions of, 182

Glaltea effect and, 121

Golem effect and, 121–122

halo error and, 116–117

imaging technique and, 113

implicit leadership schemas and, 126–127

impression management strategies and, 124–126, 125 (table), 134–136

leader-member exchange quality and, 29, 30–31 (table)

name recall, techniques for, 114

organizational politics, perceptions of, 44–45

perceptual errors and, 111–112

Pygmalion effect and, 120, 121–122, 128–129

recency effect and, 112–113

rehearsal/repetition of information and, 113

romance of leadership perspective and, 120

self-assessments for, 130–138

self-fulfilling prophecy and, 121

social identity and, 126

stereotypes and, 112, 123

toolkit activity for, 128–129

Perceptual errors, 111–112

Performance appraisals, 213–214

behaviorally anchored rating scales and, 208

central tendency error and, 209

challenging issues with, 209–211

check-in conversations and, 210

compensation packages and, 209

cultural values, influence of, 209

evaluator-coach dual role and, 209–210

feedback opportunity of, 206, 210–211

forced-ranking method and, 209

individual benefits of, 207

lenient ratings and, 209

normal ranking distribution
and, 210
organizational benefits of,
207–208, 209
performance ratings, sources
of, 207
results-based rewards and,
209, 210
teamwork, discouragement
of, 211
360 degree performance appraisal
and, 207–208
See also Job performance;
Learning; Performance
management; Rewards
Performance category, 229, 230
Performance management, 205–207
behaviorally anchored rating
scales and, 208
forced-ranking method and,
209, 210
goal setting and, 206
methods of, 208–209
organizational justice and, 206
pay equity and, 206
performance management
role-play and, 214–219
performance ratings, sources
of, 207
successful implementation, example
of, 207–208
360 degree performance appraisal
and, 207–208
See also Learning; Motivation;
Performance appraisals;
Rewards
Performing phase, 226–229,
228 (figure)
Persistence, 169
Person-environment (P-E) fit,
340–341
Personal appeals, 42 (table), 43
Personal leadership development
plan, 18–20
Personal power, 39
Personal reasons for resistance, 394
Personality, 57
affective events theory and, 68,
69 (figure)
agreeableness and, 59,
59 (table), 83
Big Five personality
characteristics and, 59–60,
59 (table), 61, 62
Big Five Personality Test and,
82–83

born leaders and, 61
conscientiousness and, 59,
59 (table), 83
creativity and, 153–154
emotional stability and, 60
extraversion and, 59, 59 (table), 83
health status, personality traits
and, 60–62, 62 (figure)
heredity, role of, 57
hiring decisions and, 60
indecisiveness and, 138
neuroticism and, 59, 59 (table), 83
openness and, 59, 59 (table), 60, 83
organizational change,
adjustment to, 60
state-like characteristics and, 62
trait-like characteristics and, 62
Type A behaviors and, 60, 61,
62 (figure), 84–85
Type B behaviors and, 60, 61,
62 (figure), 84–85
Type C behaviors and, 60, 61,
62 (figure)
Type D behaviors and, 60–61,
62 (figure)
See also Affect; Diversity;
Emotions; Individual
differences; Moods; Myers-
Briggs Type Indicator
(MBTI); Psychological
capital (PsyCap)
Perspective taking:
case study of, 277–278
negotiation skill and, 272
Persuasion:
rational persuasion and, 45
See also Influence; Power
Peterson, S., 48
Physiological need, 169
Physiological stress responses, 350,
351 (figure)
Piccolo, R. F., 93
Pierce, D., 252
Pincus, M., 56
Pink, D. H., 203
Podsakoff, N. P., 93
Political skill, 44
definition of, 45
perceptions of organizational
politics and, 44–45, 348
political acumen assessment and,
52–54
Polson, J., 404
Porath, C., 262
Porter, L. W., 372
Position power, 39

Positive affect, 65
Positive organizational behavior
(POB), 358
Positive reinforcement,
196, 197 (figure)
Post-trip stress, 338
Potential teams, 229
Pound, R., 347
Power, 38
bases of, 39–40, 41 (figure)
coercive power and, 39, 40,
41 (figure)
commitment to, 39, 40,
41 (figure)
compliance and, 39, 41 (figure)
definition of, 38
expert power and, 39, 40,
41 (figure)
influence attempts, possible
outcomes of, 39–40,
41 (figure)
information, access to, 40
legitimate power and, 39, 40,
41 (figure)
material support and, 40
organizational networks, position
within, 33
organizational sources of,
40–41
perceptions of organizational
politics and, 44–45
personal power and, 39
political skill and, 44, 45
position power and, 39
referent power and, 39, 40,
41 (figure)
resistance to, 39, 41 (figure)
reward power and, 39, 40,
41 (figure)
supported risk-taking
and, 40
three lines of power and, 42
zone of indifference and,
40, 41 (figure)
See also Ethical leadership;
Influence; Leadership
Power distance, 314,
315–317 (tables), 352
Power need (nPow), 170
PRACH (primacy/recency/
availability/contrast/halo)
biases, 112
primacy effect and, 112
recency effect and, 112–113
See also Perception
Pre-trip stress, 338

Type C behavior pattern, 60, 61, 62 (figure)
Type D behavior pattern, 60–61, 62 (figure)

Ulmer, R. R., 293
Uncertainty avoidance, 314, 315–317 (tables)
Underpayment inequity, 180
Unfreezing phase, 396, 397 (figure)
Unobservable aspects of culture, 310–311, 311 (figure)
Unproductive conflict, 258, 259
Upward communication flow, 288, 291–292
Upward exchange process, 32–33, 34
Utilitarianism, 152
Utility industry innovation, 403–404

Valences, 184, 186 (figure)
Validation, 327
Van de Ven, A. H., 7
Van Ryzin, G. G., 91
Vandewalle, D., 212
Variable-interval reinforcement, 197, 198 (figure)
Variable/random reinforcement, 196, 198 (figure)
Variable-ratio reinforcement, 198, 198 (figure)
Vertical job loading, 174, 175
Videoconferencing, 297
Violence, 261
Virtual meetings, 297
Virtual teams, 244–246, 245 (table)
Visweswaran, C., 351
Voice, 301
Von Hippel, W., 123
Vroom, V. H., 184, 237

Walumbwa, F., 48
Weaver, W., 285
Welch, J., 209, 328
Wellness programs, 354
Wells, K., 404
Wernsing, T., 48
Western Electric Company, 3
Wheel communication network, 288, 289 (figure), 290
Whelen-Berry, K. S., 395
White, S. S., 385
Whole Foods Market, 380
Wicked organizational problems, 147
Widmeyer, W. N., 233
Wilks, S. L., 65

Williams, J. H., 262
Williamson, G., 364
Wilmot, W., 283
Wimalasiri, V., 356
Wood, G., 188
Work as Meaning Inventory, 100, 101 (table)
Work groups, 225–226
Work-life balance, 347
Work redesign, 174
    autonomy/discretion and, 176
    client relationships, establishment of, 175–176
    feedback channels, development of, 176
    growth need strength and, 174
    horizontal job loading and, 174, 175
    job crafting and, 176, 177 (table)
    job enrichment strategies and, 174
    job rotation and, 174–175
    stress prevention and, 356, 356 (figure)
    vertical job loading and, 174, 175
    See also Job characteristics theory (JCT); Job crafting; Job satisfaction; Motivation
Work teams, 224
    additive task and, 225
    attitudes category and, 229, 230
    behaviors category, 229, 230
    brainstorming and, 237–238
    case study for, 252
    challenges in, 242–246
    cohesion of, 230, 232–233
    collective effect and, 225
    conflict within, 229–230, 265, 267, 268 (figure)
    consensus guidelines and, 238–240, 243
    consultative decision mode and, 236
    decision process methods and, 237–242
    delegated decision making and, 235
    effective meeting checklist and, 251
    effective teams, model of, 229–232, 230 (figure)
    emotional intelligence and, 66
    empowerment of, 246–247
    executive teams and, 371
    explicit team standards and, 233
    facilitator role and, 236

feedback opportunities and, 226, 234
five-stage development model and, 226–228, 228 (figure)
groupthink and, 243–244
high-performance teams and, 229
idea generation/evaluation and, 238
implicit team standards and, 233
individual development metrics and, 234–235
input-process-output model and, 229
leadership climate and, 246–247
Marshmallow Challenge team exercise and, 250–251
multicultural teams and, 246
multivoting process and, 240–241
nominal group technique and, 241–242
normative decision-making model, 235–237, 237 (table)
participatory decision process and, 235–237
performance appraisals and, 211
performance category and, 229
performance metrics and, 234–235
potential teams and, 229
process metrics and, 234
pseudo teams and, 229
punctuated equilibrium process and, 227–228
real teams and, 229
self-assessment for, 25–253
self-managed work teams and, 226, 246, 247, 267
SMART goals and, 226
social loafing and, 244
stepladder technique and, 242, 243
synergy and, 226
task metrics and, 234
team affect and, 230
team building intervention and, 392–393
team charter, 227, 234, 248–250
team creativity and, 231–232
team, definitions of, 225
team development process and, 226–229
team learning and, 230–231, 401
team mental models and, 235, 236 (figure), 244
team norms and, 227, 233–235
team performance curve and, 228–229, 228 (figure)